UNION PACIFIC

THE REBIRTH 1894–1969

Other books by the author

THE GREAT RICHMOND TERMINAL

EDWARD PORTER ALEXANDER

A HISTORY OF THE LOUISVILLE & NASHVILLE RAILROAD

PRISONERS OF PROGRESS: AMERICAN INDUSTRIAL CITIES 1850–1920
with Harvey A. Kantor

THE LIFE AND LEGEND OF JAY GOULD

UNION PACIFIC:
THE BIRTH OF A RAILROAD 1862–1893

E. H. Harriman

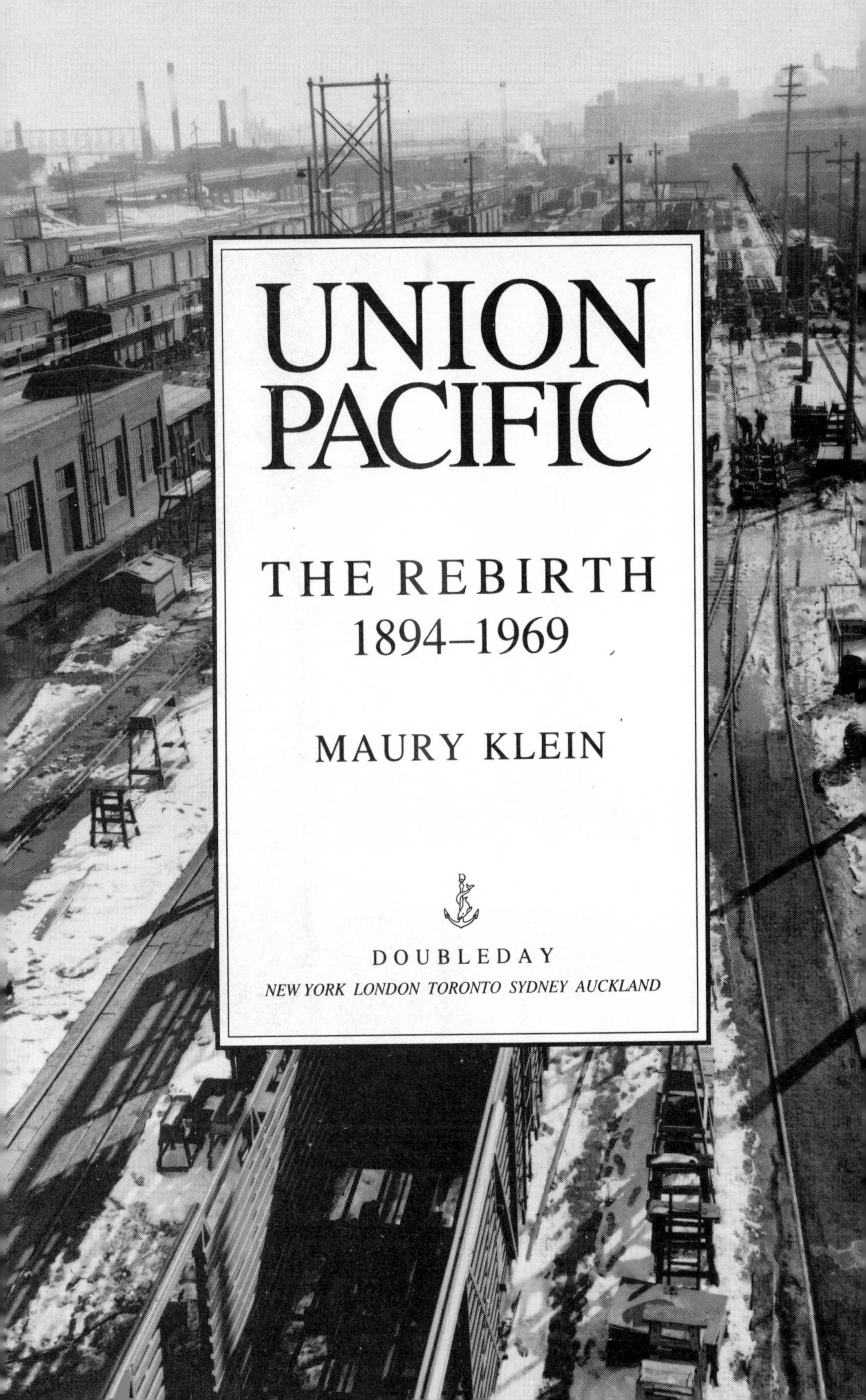

UNION PACIFIC

THE REBIRTH 1894–1969

MAURY KLEIN

DOUBLEDAY
NEW YORK LONDON TORONTO SYDNEY AUCKLAND

All photographs contained herein, except those so noted, are the property of the Union Pacific Railroad Museum.

PUBLISHED BY DOUBLEDAY
a division of Bantam Doubleday Dell Publishing Group, Inc.
666 5th Avenue, New York, New York 10103

DOUBLEDAY and the portrayal of an anchor with a dolphin are trademarks of Doubleday, a division of Bantam Doubleday Dell Publishing Group, Inc.

Design by Richard Oriolo

Library of Congress Cataloging-in-Publication Data

Klein, Maury, 1939–
Union Pacific.
Includes bibliographies and indexes.
Contents: v. 1. Birth of a railroad, 1862–1893—
v. 2. The rebirth, 1894–1969.
1. Union Pacific Railroad Company. I. Title.
TF25.U5K53 1987 385′.065′78 86-16732
ISBN 0-385-17728-3 (v. 1)
ISBN 0-385-17735-6 (v. 2)

Printed in the United States of America

January 1990

FIRST EDITION

For my wife,
DIANA
And my father,
HARRY KLEIN (1903–1988)
Who both believed against all odds

CONTENTS

Part III
THE NEW RAILROAD
1940–1969

RAILROAD SHORT TITLES

Alton	Chicago & Alton
Atchison	Atchison, Topeka & Santa Fe
Burlington	Chicago, Burlington & Quincy
Frisco	St. Louis & San Francisco
Gulf	Union Pacific, Denver & Gulf
Katy	Missouri, Kansas & Texas
Milwaukee	Chicago, Milwaukee & St. Paul
Northwestern	Chicago & Northwestern
Rio Grande	Denver & Rio Grande
Rio Grande Western	Denver & Rio Grande Western
Rock Island	Chicago, Rock Island & Pacific
Southern	Colorado & Southern

ACKNOWLEDGMENTS

The research and writing of this volume was funded by the Union Pacific Corporation, which provided not only generous support but also free access to company files (except for certain records involved in pending litigation) and complete editorial freedom. The views and interpretations expressed in this volume, therefore, are mine and in no way represent those of the corporation.

The support of the Union Pacific Corporation went far beyond its financial commitment. Without exception its officers and employees have cheerfully heeded my requests for material or information and done whatever they can to expedite my work. Their cooperation helped transform a large and complex task into a labor of love, and their interest in the project has given me a host of new associations for which I shall always be grateful. To a large extent they are responsible for the virtues of this book and I for whatever errors and weaknesses remain.

While it is impossible to name every person who rendered assistance, a few merit special attention. In the corporate office in New York (now Bethlehem, Pennsylvania), Marvin H. Zim was the indispensable man handling my every need with dispatch and understanding. James P. Coughlin, the office manager (now retired), was invaluable for his knowledge of the old records and for his willingness to search out the answers to particular inquiries. I am also grateful to Irene J. Colgan, Nancy R. Connors, and Harvey Turner.

At the Union Pacific System's offices in Omaha, Joe McCartney, the director of public relations, smoothed the path for my work and encouraged it in every way. Donald D. Snoddy, curator of the Union Pacific Museum, was always there when needed and always willing to handle any problem I threw at him. Among other things he called my attention to several key sources for this project, such as the E. J. Connors papers. Ken Longe, Thomas E. LaHood, Eileen M. Wirth, and William R. Ulrich field a variety of requests for information. Michael P. Flanagan of the law department helped with materials in his area.

In St. Louis Tim Hogan, Wally Fussner, and Robert L. Sponsler answered my requests with their usual dispatch and good cheer. Former general solicitor Randall B. Kester provided me with useful information in Portland. Jim Ady in Salt Lake City made available to me certain old records in his possession.

I am especially grateful to the individuals, most of them former Union Pacific officers and employees, who submitted to lengthy interviews for this project: Frank Acord; Edd H. Bailey; Frank E. Barnett; D. O. Churchill; James H. Evans; William Foral; William J. Fox; Elbridge T. Gerry; W. Averell Harriman; Stanley J. How; Earl O. Joest; C. Otis Jett; Ralph Judson; Edgar A. Klippel, Jr.; Jervis Langdon, Jr.; Robert A. Lovett; Francis Melia; Charles J. Meyer; Thomas E. Murray; George Proudfit; E. L. Prouty; E. C. Schafer; and Reginald M. Sutton.

A host of librarians and archivists extended to me their usual courtesy, enthusiasm, and expertise. Mary Chatfield, librarian at the Baker Library, Harvard Graduate School of Business Administration, provided helpful advice on a variety of topics and free access to crucial resources for the project. Florence Lathrop of Baker's Corporate Records section handled numerous requests and inquiries with her usual aplomb. At the Hagley Library in Wilmington, Delaware, where the last chapters of this volume were written, Elizabeth Gray Kogen, Diane Partnoy, Heddy Richter, Juliet Patrick, Michael Nash, and Chris Baer all helped make my work there a pleasure.

W. Thomas White of the James J. Hill Reference Library in St. Paul, John Aubrey of the Newberry Library in Chicago, Mary Ann Jensen and Andy Thomson of the Firestone Library at Princeton University, Andrea Paul of the Nebraska State Museum and Archives, Bernard J. Crystal of the Butler Library at Columbia University, Richard Crawford of the National Archives, and Margaret N. Haines of the Oregon Historical Society were uniformly helpful. At home Mimi Keefe and the staff of the University of Rhode Island library did everything possible to expedite my work. In particular I wish to thank Vicki Burnett, Lucille W. Cameron, Martha Hills, Sylvia C. Krausse, Judith MacDonald, and Marie Rudd.

A number of people deserve special mention for their contributions to this project. Martha A. Parker, my research assistant, devoted long hours to a difficult task without complaint. Joan Flinspach, formerly of the General Grenville M. Dodge House, provided helpful information about the general and his house. William J. Rich III helped make available to me the materials at Arden Farms, where George Paffenbarger provided free access, office support, and helpful advice. Frank Allston of IC Industries generously allowed me to examine some early minute books and records of the Illinois Central. Rita Naikelis spent long and frustrating hours getting the maps for this volume just as I wanted them.

A number of colleagues offered freely of their advice and materials on particular subjects, among them William D. Burt, Don L. Hofsommer, Priscilla Long, Albro Martin, Lloyd J. Mercer, and Glenn Porter. Mrs. Robert Knutson graciously provided information and materials on her grandfather, Carl R. Gray. Frank A. Vanderlip, Jr., helped me understand his banker father. Harold W. Kuebler, my editor at Doubleday, rode herd on the manuscript with good cheer and encouragement.

Finally, I wish to acknowledge the two individuals whose indirect support was essential to this project. My wife, Diana C. Klein, bore the burdens of a long and difficult project with patience and understanding. John C. Kenefick, the former chairman of the Union Pacific System, has been the mainspring of this project from its inception and has eagerly awaited the appearance of this volume. I hope he will not be disappointed in the result.

INTRODUCTION

Any historian of American business or railroads knows that precious little has been written on the carriers and their fate in the twentieth century. This is not surprising. The nineteenth century was the golden age for American railroads. It has the most stirring sagas, the cleanest story lines, the happiest endings, and the most colorful cast of characters. Life got more complicated after 1900 for everyone, including the railroads. The sagas moved indoors, the story lines got more involved, the characters more drab, and the endings anything but happy in most cases.

This was in fact true of American business in general, but the railroads occupied a unique role in the American economy and American life. In the nineteenth century they were the pioneers in big business, the conquerers of the West, the network of steel that held an expanding industrial system together. They were at the forefront of everything from finance to technology, and a man could have no prouder job than one with the railroad.

By 1920 this was no longer the case. The railroads were still important, but no longer the leading edge of progress. They had not shrunk in importance; rather the nation and its economy had grown with incredible speed. New technologies rose to challenge their supremacy in transport, reducing the once mighty iron horse to simply one more steed in the stable. With the hubris of all who occupy the center stage of history, the railroads let time pass them by until they became emblems of a bygone age.

The railroads did much to fashion this image of themselves. Like most maturing enterprises they allowed success to make them complacent, conservative, obstinate. While the world around them changed rapidly, they stood stolidly in the shackles of tradition, clinging to the old ways as if sheer repetition could somehow restore the golden age. But industries cannot reclaim their past any more than men can regain their youth.

The history of railroads in the twentieth century, then, has been one of constant, grudging adjustment to new conditions that threatened not merely their supremacy but their very existence. In its own way this story is fully as fascinating and important as the earlier saga because it allows us to glimpse the larger life cycle of a key industry rather than just its youthful triumphs. The bloom of innocence has long since faded from American industry in this, the second century of its life. We need to know far more about its patterns of growth and decay, strength and weakness, death and transfiguration.

The railroads offer exceptional insights into these patterns because they set the precedents followed by so many other industries. For example, they furnished the model for federal regulation of business in the twentieth century, and for collective bargaining at the national level. Neither model turned out very well, but their influence ran wide and deep beyond the rail industry.

Writing about railroads in the modern era presents some novel problems. Because so much of their activity transfers to the national level, the story of a single road cannot be understood outside this larger context. Then there is the problem of competition. In the nineteenth century railroads competed mostly with each other; after 1920 they faced stiff challenges from new modes of transport. To grasp the role of railroads, therefore, one must know something of cars, trucks, buses, airplanes, barges, and pipelines. Throughout I have tried to give the reader enough context to understand why railroads behaved the way they did in the face of these new external forces.

Volume II of this history has posed a very different challenge than did Volume I. Since the earlier story of the Union Pacific had been told many times by many people, the task there was to sweep away the myths, half-truths, and inaccuracies that had distorted it for generations. For the modern era the task is to tell a tale that has not yet been told, and to tell it honestly and well.

The biography of every firm is both unique in its own right and grist for the larger patterns of business history. While the history of the railroad industry may be more than the sum of its parts, it is inexplicable without the insights furnished by the story of individual roads. We still need good case studies, but a corporate history is useless to anyone unless it tells the whole story, warts and all. Otherwise, it is no more believable than a commercial or a campaign biography.

The Union Pacific, like all firms, has had its share of warts as well as triumphs, and I have treated them with candor. It is a cliché of life that people learn from their mistakes, and this holds true for corporations as well. The ultimate fate of a company often depends on how well it handles weakness and adversity. In business as in medicine, pathology offers a far surer and swifter road to cure than denial.

MAURY KLEIN
Narragansett, R.I.

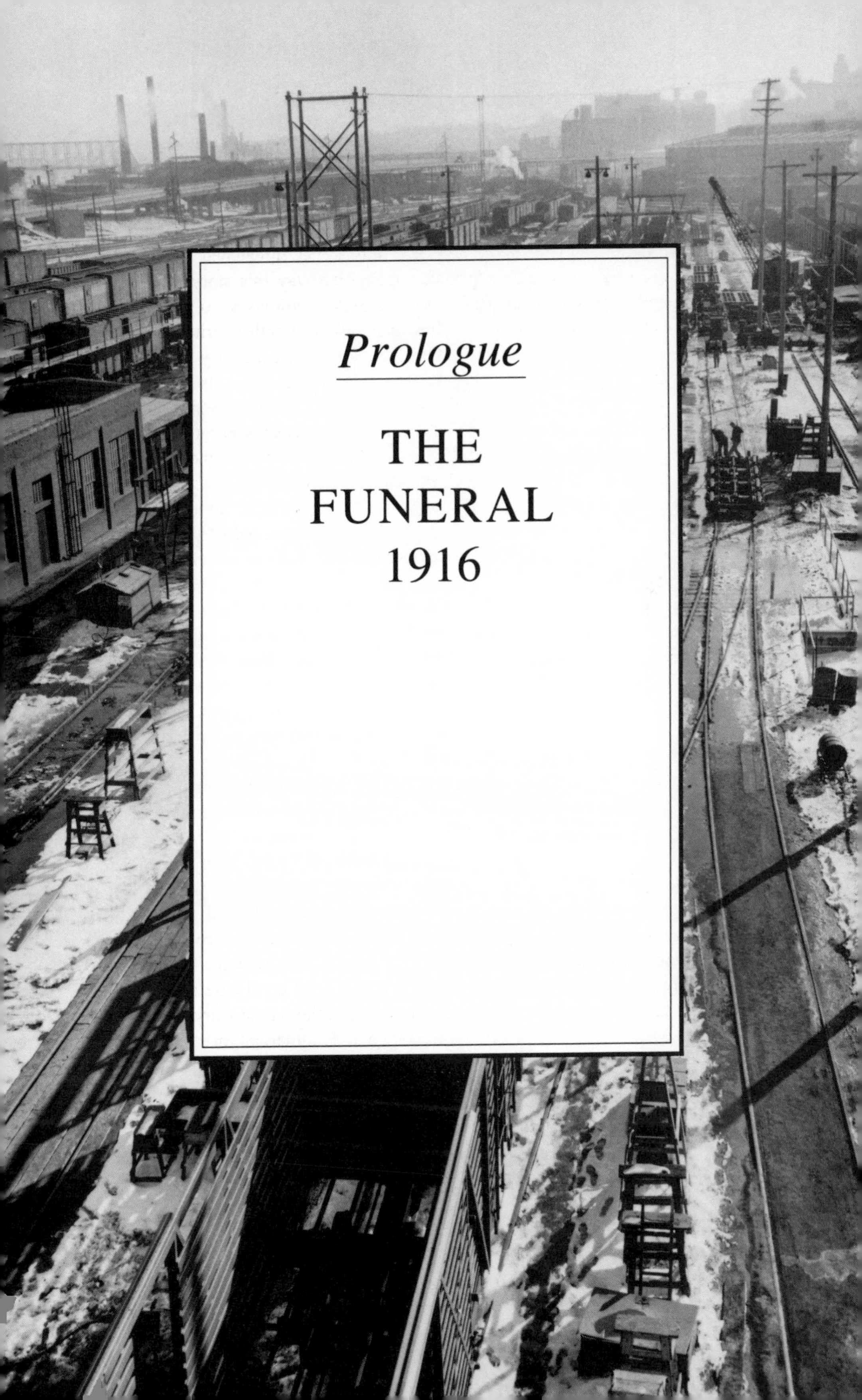

Prologue

THE FUNERAL 1916

On a cold and dreary Thursday afternoon in January of 1916 they gathered by the hundreds to honor the general who, like so many old men, had far outlived his time. Schools and businesses in Council Bluffs and public offices throughout Iowa closed in tribute to his memory. Earlier that day and during the previous afternoon, long lines of citizens had filed solemnly past his body lying in state at the magnificent house on Third Street, from which the view stretched to the river and beyond. Now, as the hour of the funeral neared, they braved a biting wind and single-digit temperatures to pack the streets along which the cortege would move toward Walnut Hill cemetery.[1]

The governor had come over from Des Moines with his entire official staff, and no major business, civic, government, or military organization failed to send a representative to bid the old general farewell. The commander of the local Abe Lincoln post of the Grand Army of the Republic was there along with his chaplain and seventy-three wizened veterans. Only six of their thinning ranks belonged to the Fourth Iowa Infantry or Second Iowa Battery, both of which had been organized by the general. They were joined by twenty-eight officers of the Woman's Relief Corps and Woman's Auxiliary of the Union Veteran League. Nearby stood veterans of the Spanish-American War and eight officers of the Daughters of the American Revolution. The general had been around so long, went the joke, that some youngsters might well believe he had fought in the Revolution instead of the Civil War. A black army veteran named July Miles journeyed over from Glenwood Springs for a last glimpse of the man he had once served as valet. Condolences poured in from all over the country.

Long before his death at the age of eighty-four, Grenville M. Dodge had become Iowa's leading citizen and living legend. His name was indelibly attached to the two most stirring events of his age, the Civil War and the building of the first transcontinental railroad. He had been the last surviving commander of a Union army and the last survivor among the major figures who built the Union Pacific Railroad. Thomas M. Orr, who represented the Union Pacific at the funeral, was an old hand himself but had not joined the company until 1877, a dozen years after Dodge had signed on. Those among the living who actually remembered Dodge from construction days, such as former engineer Fred Hodges, had themselves been youngsters fortunate enough to cut their teeth on the grandest project of their age.[2]

FAREWELL TO AN OLD SOLDIER: The funeral procession for General Grenville M. Dodge forms up outside his home in Council Bluffs, Iowa. (*Historic General Dodge House*)

With the tenacity that characterized his entire career, Dodge had outlived virtually all his friends and foes, had lived long enough to tell his story without fear of contradiction from those who shared it. And tell it he did, again and again. The old general never threw away a scrap of paper or a memory. By the end of his life he had compiled an autobiography that required over a thousand pages to reach 1870 and a documentary memoir that consumed twenty-three large volumes. He had lived long enough not merely to preserve his past but also to arrange it to his satisfaction. Yet, for all his diligence, the story never got told in a way that suited him.

After the services in the parlor of the house concluded, pallbearers from the Iowa National Guard carried the casket outside and settled it gently onto a waiting caisson. As death approached, Dodge had spurned the suggestion that his remains occupy a hero's grave in Arlington cemetery. He wished to be buried at home and asked only that his body be borne to Walnut Hill atop a caisson. It took some scrambling before one was finally located at Fort Leavenworth and hurried to Council Bluffs for the ceremony. Now the caisson with its mournful cargo lumbered slowly toward Willow Avenue followed by a riderless horse heavily draped and caparisoned with an army saddle of the type Dodge used, with the general's boots reversed in the stirrups and his sword strapped in place. Ahead of the caisson marched militia companies with the band and a machine gun unit from the Nebraska National Guard. Behind it a procession of fifty carriages and thirty limousines bearing notables and veterans stretched out nearly a mile along the route. This peculiar mixture of past and present could not have been more appropriate for a man who straddled both ages.[3]

The last years of the old general had not been happy ones. Estranged from his wife and daughters, whom ambition had led him to neglect in his younger days, he dwelled alone among the shadows of the past. His wife, Annie, had continued to live in New York long after the general retired to Council Bluffs. One of his three daughters, Lettie, divorced her husband and returned to keep house for her father; the other two remained more or less loyal to their mother. Over the years the general had survived war wounds, fevers, and a host of illnesses. By any reckoning he had earned the right to die a peaceful death, but even this dignity was denied him. For two years Dodge had been ravaged by cancer which, he complained, was "wearing me out by inches." He had undergone radium treatments and endured an exploratory operation without the use of anesthesia, all to no avail. As he slowly wasted away, a friend observed sorrowfully that "His life should have ended in sleep, or some other quick way. It would have been more in accord with the man."[4]

They buried the general on the highest knoll of Walnut Hill. While the dignitaries and veterans stood shivering in the wind, the Dodge Light Guard fired an honor salute and taps were sounded. The band struck up "The Star Spangled Banner." As the last notes faded against the gloomy sky the mourners lingered, lost in memories and reluctant to leave their posts until the cold drove them at last from the heights.

Behind them lay the man who had seen and made history, had bridged two of its epochs. He had fought rebels in the South and Indians on the plains, declined a chance to fight Spaniards in Cuba and witnessed the outbreak of the Great War in Europe. This last he was quick to deplore, going so far as to praise a Democratic president for keeping the country out of the struggle. Carnage held no appeal for him, being only another form of waste and a grisly one at that. In such matters the world seemed not to have come very far during his long life. Ever the optimist, he found far greater consolation in contemplating that other great episode of his life, the transcontinental railroad.

The Union Pacific had undergone a curious metamorphosis in his lifetime. Leaving the company soon after the road was completed, Dodge had watched it smeared by the scandal of Crédit Mobilier and driven to the brink of bankruptcy in 1873 only to be rescued by Jay Gould. Within a remarkably short time Gould transformed the floundering company into the nucleus of a powerful system, giving it the organization, stability, and sense of direction lacking in previous managements. Under his leadership the road realized the potential envisioned by its founders, but not even Gould's genius and energy could find a way to cut the Gordian knot of the road's relationship with the federal government. Weary of slogging through an endless political quagmire, Gould left the Union Pacific to create a system of his own, the Missouri Pacific. The task of seeking a resolution with the government fell next to the foremost railroad theorist of the age, Charles Francis Adams, Jr., who assumed the presidency in 1884.

Dodge worked long and well with Gould even after the latter left the Union Pacific, and in his inimitable way he worked just as smoothly with Adams, who relied heavily on the general for advice. For all his good intentions, however, Adams failed wretchedly at every aspect of management. He was neither an astute financier nor an efficient manager, and did as poorly at judging men as he did at plotting strategy. By 1890 the Union Pacific was staggering beneath a large floating debt amassed from new construction or acquisitions, and relief from its interminable clash with Washington was still nowhere in sight. Dodge had played some role in Adams's discomfort, not only by supplying advice but by inducing him to buy a road connecting Denver and Fort Worth in which Dodge himself held a large interest as the original builder. The road was merged with some branches and absorbed under a new name, the Union Pacific, Denver & Gulf.

Within months a financial storm swept Adams out of office and brought back Gould, who toiled diligently to revitalize the system he had done so much to create. But Gould was a dying man by then, and his death in December 1892 left the Union Pacific leaderless in the face of an oncoming depression, the worst the country had ever seen. Dodge watched helplessly as earnings plummeted until the company was forced to seek receivership in October 1893. For four dreary years the road's affairs dangled in limbo, its future rendered uncertain by the same political vagaries that had frustrated every management since the line was conceived. As legal actions separated one branch after another from the parent road, including Dodge's pet Union Pacific, Denver & Gulf, analysts predicted that the system would be dismembered beyond repair.

Late in 1897, after many shattered hopes and false starts, the company shook free of its government lien and reorganized. What it needed above all else was a leader capable of breathing new life into it as Gould had done in 1873. To the astonishment of everyone except himself, that leader emerged in the form of E. H. Harriman, a financier of sound if modest reputation. Dodge scarcely knew Harriman and had never worked with him, but he watched with admiration as the little man transformed the Union Pacific from a mediocre carrier with great potential into the most efficient railroad west of the Mississippi River.

Dodge had outlasted them both by a good margin, had seen the best and the worst of what they did. In the end he honored them both for saving and strengthening the railroad he had helped build. Nothing filled him with more satisfaction than his role in realizing the first transcontinental and opening the West to settlement. Soldiering had fulfilled his sense of patriotism, but the railroad was his pride. War was not constructive work even for the noblest of causes, and its results seldom turned out well. In the last pain-wracked months of his life, Dodge again saw the world stumbling down the road to self-immolation. The Union Pacific, however, showed every sign of flourishing despite a rapidly changing environment.

Although Dodge could not know it, his death occurred at the opening of the year that would later be cherished as the zenith of the railroad era. In 1916 the amount of trackage in service exceeded 254,000 miles, the largest figure it would ever reach. New forms of competition, such as the truck, the automobile, and the airplane, had appeared but were not yet ready to challenge the railroad's supremacy. Federal regulation had been around for three decades but was not the strait jacket it would soon become. Labor had long since organized but had not acquired the power it would later possess. Sources of investment capital were drying up but did not yet resemble the Death Valley of later years. New technologies were fast changing the world, but in ways not yet clear even to those who understood their effects. Above everything loomed the war with all its uncertainties and abnormalities.

In a sense, both the general and the railroad he loved were crossing the bar into new and unknown worlds. Like all mere mortals, the old general had seen the best of his times. It remained to be seen in 1916 whether, as many knowing observers predicted, the same held true for railroads—even the mighty Union Pacific system of E. H. Harriman.

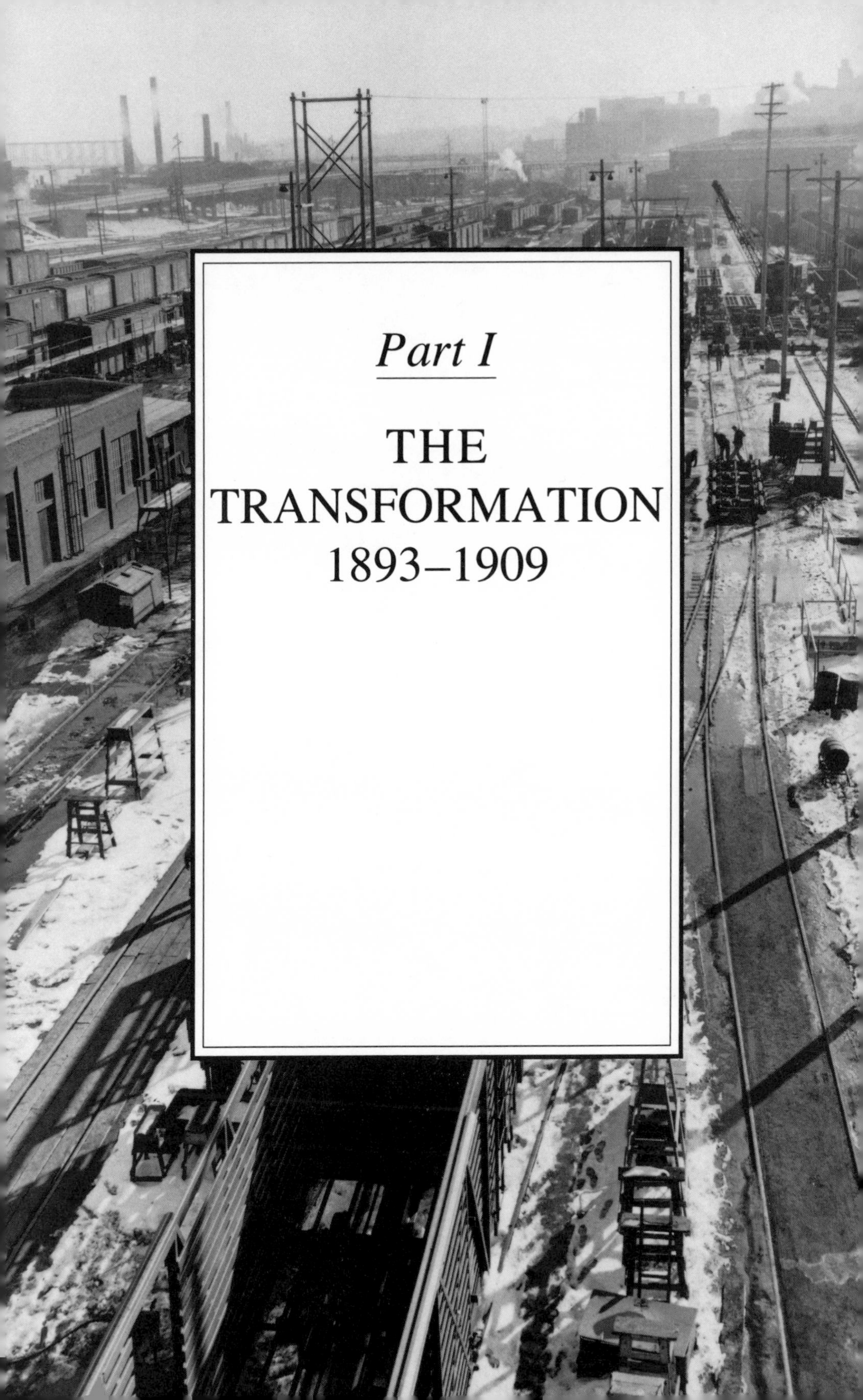

Part I

THE TRANSFORMATION 1893–1909

1

The Receivership

During the summer of 1893 Americans flocked eagerly to Chicago for what many of them would treasure as the excursion of a lifetime: a visit to the Columbian Exposition celebrating the 400th anniversary of the discovery of America. In an age that took immense pride in the magnificence of display, the fabulous White City dwarfed every world's fair that had come before it. "Sell the cookstove if necessary and come," wrote novelist Hamlin Garland; "you *must* see this fair." Most of the twenty-seven million people who toured this "City of Aladdin's Palaces" went home satisfied that it had been worth the expense and trouble.[1]

Outside the Exposition's gates, however, the exhibit was far less comforting. In Chicago, as elsewhere across America, the pall of depression was fast descending. The world's fair kept Chicago prosperous for a time, then left it occupied by an army of unemployed—200,000 of them by the mayor's estimate—their ranks swollen by drifters and vagrants. By the time the fair closed on October 30, the celebration had turned to bitter irony, its gaiety masking the misery of hard times that was fast spreading.[2]

It was the worst depression Americans had yet experienced. The litany of bankruptcies in the newspapers recurred with dreary monotony until by the year's end 583 banks and nearly 16,000 businesses had failed. Textile factories in New England shut down along with steel mills in Pennsylvania and smelters in Colorado, where 30,000 men soon found themselves unemployed. Giant firms, thought to be financially impregnable only months earlier, swayed perilously in the winds of contraction. The huge cordage trust collapsed during the May panic, and both General Electric and Westinghouse were rumored to be in trouble. Nothing shook confidence more than the procession of major railroads tumbling into bankruptcy. The Richmond Terminal, a rickety holding company of southern railroads, had already gone down before the year opened. In May 1893 the Philadelphia & Reading failed and was soon followed by the Erie, the Northern Pacific, the Union Pacific, and the Atchison, Topeka & Santa Fe. Together these five systems controlled more than 21,000 miles of track.

As one failure piled on top of another, jittery foreign investors liquidated their American holdings in record sums. Gold flowed across the Atlantic to Europe in such large quantities as to threaten the legal reserve of $100 million, triggering fears that both the gold standard and currency system were in jeopardy. Hard-pressed banks in the South and West worsened the contraction by drawing heavily on New York banks to meet their own needs. "Everyone is in a blue fit of terror," observed Henry Adams, called home from Switzerland to tend his own precarious finances, "and each individual thinks himself more ruined than his neighbor." On the prairie and plains farmers stared mournfully at bumper crops for which prices had never been lower. In recent years farmers had done well selling food to Europe, which had endured a succession of crop failures, but now their luck too had run out.[3]

For four dreary years the depression dragged on while puzzled Americans exhausted their store of homilies and metaphors searching for clues to its causes. Was it a flood driving everyone to high ground until the waters ebbed, or a storm through which one must hunker down until the skies cleared? Was it the inexorable swing of the pendulum from good times to bad at a speed no one had yet learned to gauge, or the recurring visit of a plague like the locust? Or was it a disease working its insidious way through the body politic, threatening to infect the vital organs unless some remedy was soon found? Socialists and Marxists saw in the depression the first signs of implosion within the capitalist system. In the West a growing number of Populists traced the source to some sort of conspiracy among the crooks and shylocks who inhabited that sink of evil called Wall Street. Public debate on the causes of the depression raged on, convulsing the political system without bringing any noticeable relief from hard times.

Against this backdrop of bitterness and apprehension the fallen Union Pacific was but one more carcass on a littered landscape. Yet it differed from other bankrupt railroads in one crucial respect. Unlike them, the Union Pacific was at the mercy of the politicians in Washington. The same government debt that had been the single most influential factor in bringing the company to ruin now loomed as the greatest roadblock to reorganization. Neither Congress nor President Grover Cleveland showed any sympathy for the company's plight or the slightest sign of comprehending its dilemma. Moreover, both were preoccupied with the monetary issue, which was dividing parties along new and unpredictable lines. When they thought about Union Pacific at all, it was usually in the clichés of Crédit Mobilier.

By the winter of 1893–94 the prospects of all railroads looked bleak, but none faced a darker future than the Union Pacific. A large and complicated system was not only bankrupt but falling apart, and no one seemed to know how to hold it together. The best guess of many analysts was that the system would be dismembered and that its parts would drift into new orbits, triggering a radical restructuring of rail alliances west of the Missouri River. If this realignment occurred, no one cared to predict where it would leave the remnants of the Union Pacific Railroad in the competitive scheme.

Within the councils of Union Pacific management, two problems continued to defy solution. The financial picture showed no signs of improving, and no strong personality emerged to lead the company through its time of trouble.

Earnings for 1893 registered a net loss of $2.6 million, a swing from the previous year of more than $4.6 million. The falloff in gross earnings had been horrendous, plummeting some $7.6 million or nearly 17 percent from 1892. Those hoping for quick relief were devastated by the report for 1894, which showed another 16 percent decline in the gross. For two more years the ledgers hemorrhaged red ink as earnings remained erratic.[4]

Many analysts blamed the Union Pacific's woes on the silver crisis, which had shut down the smelters and reduced the amount of ore being hauled, but the figures didn't bear them out. Although shipments in silver, copper, and iron ores dropped 46 percent between 1892 and 1894, other areas showed equally severe losses. Coal traffic declined 18 percent, coke 45 percent, cement and plaster 31 percent, stone and brick 54 percent, and salt 30 percent. Staple crops were a horror story: wheat plummeted 74 percent, corn 47 percent, oats, barley, and other grains 74 percent. Lumber traffic fell off by 45 percent, hardware products by 54 percent, wagons and carriages by 68 percent, and agricultural implements by 70 percent.[5]

Overall the amount of classified freight hauled declined from 9 billion pounds in 1892 to 5.7 billion pounds in 1895. Despite shifts in individual commodities, the pattern indicated that losses were spread across the board and reflected not merely a collapsed silver industry but generally depressed business conditions. Crops were not moving, construction had slowed, industry (especially smelters) was using less coal and coke, and merchandise orders had dwindled sharply. To alert eyes these figures delivered a disheartening message: the decline was neither localized nor temporary. Traffic would revive only when the economy revived, and no one could predict when that would be.[6]

Until the skies brightened, the Union Pacific management had to find some way of holding the system together. Unfortunately, its leadership corps was as depleted as its income account. The three most dominant figures on the board, Jay Gould, Sidney Dillon, and Frederick L. Ames, had all died within fifteen months of each other during 1892–1893. Dillon had helped build the road and served as its president for a dozen years. The Ames family had been present at the creation and still held a large interest in the road. Fred's father and uncle, Oliver and Oakes Ames, had played major roles in the road's early history. After Oliver Ames's death in 1877, Fred took his seat on the board and became the road's staunchest supporter, sometimes providing funds when it seemed the most dubious of investments. Gould had rescued the company from the brink of insolvency in 1873 and transformed it into a major system. Seventeen years later, despite failing health, he had again stepped forward to bail the road out of a financial crisis and take charge of its management.[7]

Now all three of them were gone, and no one in the Union Pacific management even remotely approached their stature. Silas H. H. Clark, who had replaced Dillon as president, was the first operating man to hold that office; the rest had all been financial men. As Jay Gould's loyal lieutenant, Clark had put in more than twenty years with the Union Pacific and Missouri Pacific. At fifty-seven he was an able operating man but ill-suited by position or temperament to any larger role. Slow, deliberate, cautious to a fault, Clark had always been reluctant to act without the approval of his superiors. For years he had enjoyed poor health and was prone to retire to his couch when the pressures on him mounted. Periodically he threatened to quit and return to the presidency of the Missouri Pacific, only to be coaxed back by anxious directors who had no one else to replace him.[8]

The board possessed able men but no dominant personality. If anything, it resembled an entailed estate in that six of the fifteen members held seats previously occupied by their fathers. The most prominent of them, George J. Gould, had inherited his father's mantle too recently for anyone to know how well or poorly it fit. The other directors were either too inexperienced or absorbed by other interests. Russell Sage was an astute but aged financier who preferred to follow rather than lead. Marvin Hughitt was president of a connecting ally, the Chicago & Northwestern, and Henry B. Hyde the head of Equitable Life. General Dodge was still a director but torn by conflicting loyalties between the Union Pacific and the road he had foisted on it, the Union Pacific, Denver & Gulf. The chairman of the board, banker Alexander E. Orr, displayed his breadth of vision in a squabble over who should pay for his telegrams on company business. "You will please remit me at once forty one (.41¢) the amount which I paid for the dispatch," he growled at company secretary Alexander Millar on one occasion, "and in future if you or any other officials of the Union Pacific expect me to telegraph I shall expect that . . . demand will not be made upon me for their payment."[9]

If Orr was not the stuff of which empire was made, neither were any of his associates. They had been reduced to caretakers of an ungainly property and hoped for little more than to hold it together against the ravages of decay and marauders. In this duty they were driven not by any vision of what the system might become but by the fear of what might be done to it. Their task was complicated by having to work with no less than five receivers. Two of the Union Pacific officers, president Silas Clark and comptroller Oliver W. Mink, represented the company, the other three (E. Ellery Anderson, John W. Doane, and Frederic R. Coudert) the government. The fact that the government saw fit to give its interest a majority of receivers served as warning that a settlement of the debt would not come easily.[10]

Even the role of caretaker was no sinecure, especially when it involved trying to hold the system together against the forces pulling it apart. Every

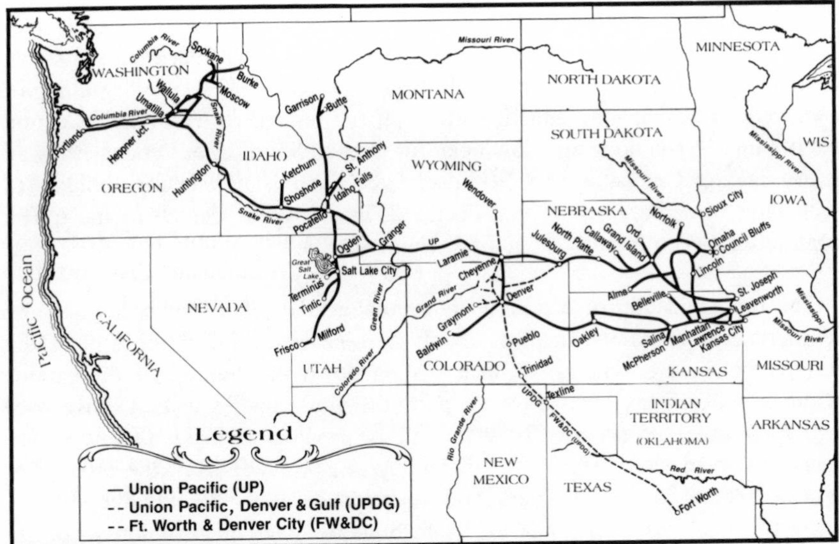

ORIGINAL SYSTEM: The Union Pacific system in 1893, when it went into receivership. Broken lines show the Union Pacific, Denver & Gulf road.

branch road had security holders who, anxious to protect their own interests, might petition the court to separate their property from the Union Pacific and appoint an independent receiver for it. A few lines were such drags on earnings that the Union Pacific would have welcomed the move, but others were vital to the road's future. Once separated from the parent company, they might align themselves with rival lines and become enemies instead of friends. In an age of giant systems the Union Pacific could find itself pared back to the original line from Omaha to Ogden.

The Gulf line, which had always been a creature of maddening complexities, posed the most volatile situation. It was a hybrid created by merging the Denver, Texas & Fort Worth (or Panhandle road, as it was called) with a smattering of Union Pacific branches. But the Panhandle was itself a hybrid bred from two incompatible strains. The Colorado portion of the line had been built by Governor John Evans, the Texas portion by Dodge. For years Evans had regarded the motives of the Union Pacific with dark suspicion, and had reluctantly entered the merger championed so vigorously by Dodge. Events seemed to vindicate Evans's belief that the merger had been a mistake, and the fact that he and Dodge did not get along further dampened efforts to preserve harmony during the hard times of the early 1890s. As early as July 1891 Evans began exploring ways to break up the Union Pacific alliance. In August 1893, two months before the Union Pacific failed, he filed suit seeking a receiver for the Gulf line on the grounds that the Union Pacific had not lived up to the agreement.[11]

The receivership of the parent road gave the Evans suit added impetus. In December 1893 the court granted Evans's request and appointed Frank Trumbull, the young and able manager of a coal company, receiver for the Gulf line. Two months earlier the Texas portion of the line had been placed under its own receiver by a Texas court. Some analysts saw in these moves "the beginning of a movement which may end in cutting all the branch roads from the Union Pacific line." The door was now open for Oregon Short Line, Oregon Railway & Navigation Company, and St. Joseph & Grand Island security holders to seek their own receivers. If that occurred, what would become of the traffic contracts between these lines and the Union Pacific?[12]

The reorganization of a railroad is a complicated affair. In most cases the reordering of corporate finances involves some fierce infighting among the different classes of interests. Since scaling down the company's obligations requires concessions on someone's part, the worst battles usually arise over which group(s) of security holders will be invited to make the necessary sacrifices. And since large sums of money can be made from the process of reorganization, bankers, lawyers, and financiers circle the carcass like vultures eager to snatch off their pound of flesh. Suits by disgruntled minority holders or holdups by predators can delay the work for months or even years. If the company is large and complex, like the Union Pacific system, the process often resembles a maze in which contending groups grope blindly for a way out. The need to resolve disputes with Washington that had raged for a quarter of a century made the maze still more formidable. Even if a plan could be found that satisfied the security holders, who dared hope that it would also be acceptable to Congress and the administration?

For these reasons no one expected a quick solution to the Union Pacific's woes. The press continued to view the road through the unsympathetic eyes of the Crédit Mobilier myth it had done so much to create and perpetuate. "Its history has been a story of nearly continuous swindling," huffed the New York *World*. "The Government practically paid the entire original cost of honestly building the road. If it cost more than the Government gave, it was only because some large fortunes were stolen in the process." A more moderate financial journal looked hopefully to "removing the whole question of the Government's relations with the Pacific roads, which has so long been a source of irritation in the railroad and investment world."[13]

But how to do it? The first of the government bonds would mature in November 1895, the last in January 1899. Although the principal amounted to $33.5 million, back interest swelled the total to about $52 million by the end of 1893. There seemed to be four basic approaches to handling it: (1) the government could cancel the debt; (2) the government could extend the debt and increase payments to the sinking fund under the Thurman Act of 1878; (3) the government could agree to refund the debt at a lower rate of interest: (4) the government could demand payment in cash. No one expected the government to cancel the debt, and it had for years resisted every move to refund at a lower interest rate. Some officials, notably the commissioner of railroads, favored increased sinking fund payments even though the Thurman Act had proved a dismal failure. By far the happiest solution would be to pay the government off and be rid of its influence, but raising $52 million in a depressed market was a formidable task and few bondholders were willing to pay the full amount demanded by the government.[14]

Some security holders thought the government might step in and take charge of the reorganization. This fear at least was groundless. Although the government demanded every last penny of the debt, public opinion was overwhelmingly against its going into the railroad business. A few optimists looked for salvation to banker J. P. Morgan, who was already involved in several other reorganizations, but Morgan took a dark view of the road's prospects and agreed only to chair a subcommittee. Instead the leadership role fell to Senator Calvin S. Brice, chairman of the Committee on Pacific Railroads. The genial Brice, a financier, had some firsthand experience with bankrupt railroads as a major figure in the Richmond Terminal, which had gone to pieces and would ultimately be reassembled by Morgan into the Southern Railway Company. In addition to Morgan, Brice put together a rainbow committee. Dutch banker Adolph Boissevain represented the foreign security holders; Louis Fitzgerald of Mercantile Trust, the Gould interests; Samuel Carr, the estate of Fred Ames; Henry Lee Higginson, the Oregon Navigation Company; and Dodge, the Gulf line.[15]

Through the winter of 1893–94 the Brice committee was content to gather data on the system while gingerly testing the political waters. Collis P. Huntington of the Southern Pacific informed Brice that no bill would pass unless it included a settlement for the Central Pacific's government debt as well. When Brice reported this to the committee, Morgan growled that he could not work with Huntington and wanted nothing to do with him. Brice was of the opinion that the committee could not do without Morgan and so favored going slow until times got better. Others, however, were in no mood to dawdle. In February 1894 Boissevain appeared before the Senate committee to urge a plan calling, among other things, for refunding at a lower interest rate. Shortly afterward three bills were introduced in Congress, two of them punitive, and a fourth appeared in April from Attorney General Richard Olney.[16]

Olney's bill called for refunding the government debt at low interest and a settlement of all disputed claims between the government and the railroad. Although objecting to one proviso, the Brice committee liked Olney's bill well enough to formulate a reorganization plan on the basis of its terms. But the committee dared not make any plan public until it knew exactly what the government would accept. To avoid a blunder that might queer the bill's chance for passage, the committee took the curious step in July of asking stock and bondholders to deposit their securities even though no plan had been announced. Olney's bill went nowhere but that same month the House committee on Pacific railroads reported out a bill by its chairman, James Reilly of Pennsylvania, which incorporated the refunding principle.[17]

No one mustered much enthusiasm for Reilly's bill or imagined it could pass easily. The winter session was short and the obstacles many. A minority member of his own committee demanded that the government foreclose and take over the road. The Populist sentiment for government ownership was rampant in only one part of the country; unfortunately, that part happened to be Union Pacific territory, and the company had made a lot of enemies over the years. An insider complained of "decided opposition to any funding bill, not only among politicians and demagogues, but rival railroad interests [who] will do all in their power to kill it." The government directors of the road muddled matters by offering a plan of their own. By the year's end a frazzled Boissevain despaired of prospects in Washington and turned his energies to holding the system together.[18]

In January 1895 the board roused from its lethargy to offer Congress a plan calling for an assessment on the stock to retire all liens prior to the government bonds if Congress would approve the refunding at a lower rate of interest. The proposal struck some representatives as too little too late and met a cool response. Efforts were made to mount a lobbying campaign in favor of the Reilly bill, but flurries of letters from stockholders could in no way compete with the ghost of Crédit Mobilier. To impartial observers the Reilly bill seemed a clear, straightforward solution to an ancient problem, yet it triggered an acrimonious three-day debate in which the opposition leader set the tone by denouncing the bill as an evil thing. "If we pass it," he warned, "we condone the sins of the men who wrecked this property."[19]

In a time of severe depression, with both political parties falling apart, congressmen much preferred flogging sinners to solving problems. When enough rhetoric had been spilled, the Reilly bill was sent back to committee. A desperate attempt to revive an amended version failed, leaving the Brice committee no basis on which to formulate a reorganization plan. In March the committee disbanded, leaving in the field only the separate committees formed to protect the interests of individual components within the system. One insider, asked his opinion as to what the dissolution of the Brice committee meant, searched for the right word and came up with "Chaos."[20]

It was an accurate choice. Already suit had been filed by the first mortgage bondholders seeking foreclosure and a separate receiver for the main line. Instead the court appointed the existing receivers to serve them as well, but no less than ten foreclosure suits were awaiting action. A discouraged Ellery Anderson voiced his fear that the suits would "result in a general dismemberment of the entire Union Pacific property." The stock sank below 8, the lowest it had touched since the dark days of 1873.[21]

One by one the major branches of the Union Pacific dropped away into the laps of separate receivers. The Gulf system was already gone and the Oregon Railway & Navigation Company followed in June 1894. With a fury born of desperation the company fought to maintain its hold over the Oregon Short Line & Utah Northern, but the battle was in vain. During the summer of 1895 the court appointed a separate receiver for the Short Line, lopping off the last major western branch. The Union Pacific was reduced in essence to a line from Omaha to Ogden, with a Kansas division (the old Kansas Pacific) that reached Denver. Of the 7,691 miles of track that comprised the system in October 1893, only 4,537 miles remained under its control. There was no automatic reason for the defectors to return once the Union Pacific had been reorganized.

They were large enough to form their own system and free enough to make alliances with other roads. Grave doubts existed as to whether Humpty Dumpty could ever be put back together again.[22]

Within the corporate offices a dwindling corps of functionaries plodded through these dreary months of indecision attending to the endless details that accompanied the legal labyrinth in which the Union Pacific found itself. No glimpse of the future could be found among the forms they filled out with dutiful repetition, no reassurance to calm the apprehension that gnawed silently at all of them. Were they presiding over the demise of a once proud system? Was the first national highway across the continent on the verge of being relegated to the dustbin of history? No old-timer with a twinge of loyalty cared to see the Union Pacific dismembered any more than he cared to lose his position in the teeth of a depression. But the prospect of the one, and therefore of the other, had by 1895 become very real.

Along the road this threat was always far more immediate and palpable. Every fall in earnings provoked cries to cut expenses, and every tightening of the belt raised the specter of layoffs or reduced hours. The disaster of 1893 had caused the ax to be wielded with ruthless efficiency; the company payrolls for September showed a decrease of 6,238 employees from the same month in 1892. In some areas the result was overkill. The shops were cut back to thirty-five hours a week until it was discovered that cars and locomotives needing repairs were piling up faster than they could be handled. Reluctantly the hours were restored to forty-eight a week in October 1893.[23]

The rate wars that had plagued western roads for a decade still raged despite feverish attempts to control them. Receivership gave the Union Pacific an edge it did not hesitate to use in the fight for a dwindling traffic. Freed from the necessity of paying interest on its bonds, the company cut rates with a vengeance. An attempt by rival roads to boycott the Union Pacific only intensified the bitterness, especially in the war over passenger rates. "It is believed," reported an analyst when the company ignored a meeting to restore rates, "that the Union Pacific intends to stand out and cause as much trouble as possible." In the spring of 1896 the old Transcontinental Association, which had gone under four years earlier, was revived in an effort to patch up some agreement on rates. Few expected it to bring about the peace that had eluded western roads for so long.[24]

For several months after the Brice committee disbanded in March 1895 the matter of reorganization drifted like flotsam on a tide of discouraging news and developments. Gradually circumstances had forced all interested parties to rethink the whole basis of a reorganization. The failure of the Brice committee left only the committees organized to protect the interests of individual securities, the most prominent of which was Boissevain's group representing the first mortgage bonds. The foreclosure suits already underway, coupled with the intransigence of Congress, dictated that any new plan would have to proceed on the basis of a foreclosure sale. The government was an obstacle in two respects, as sovereign power and as creditor. Nothing could be done to counter its power as sovereign, but its hand as creditor could at least be forced through a sale. Instead of waiting for Congress to act, a new plan could simply reserve some amount of securities to provide for the government debt after foreclosure.[25]

Since the Union Pacific system had already fallen apart, a new plan did not have to worry about holding it together but could instead concentrate on the main line and Kansas division. This offered two important advantages: a new plan did not have to waste time trying to accommodate those with interests in the branch roads, and it did not have to worry about paying off the collateral trust notes of 1891, which constituted a major part of the road's floating debt. The Brice committee had shouldered this obligation because the collateral for these notes consisted largely of securities in the branch lines of the system. Now most of those branches had fallen away from the parent company and were being reorganized on their own; a new plan could allow the notes to default without danger to the Union Pacific.

Circumstances had thus removed several obstacles that had frustrated and ultimately scuttled the Brice plan. Foreclosure would make it far easier to gain approval of a plan and far more difficult to block one, as would the elimination of those seeking to protect their interests in branch lines. Putting off a settlement with the government enabled progress to be made without waiting forever on Congress, and letting the collateral trust notes go removed a host of complications associated with them. The stage was set for another attempt at reorganization on this changed basis, but one vital question lingered: who would undertake the task?

The rumor mill churned furiously. Boissevain seemed a likely choice since Amsterdam owned large quantities of first mortgage bonds and was reportedly buying sizable blocks of stock as well. But Boissevain was in Europe when the first reports of progress on a new plan leaked out. Other fingers pointed to George Gould and Russell Sage, who held large interests, and to the banker who usually represented them, Louis Fitzgerald of Mercantile Trust. Some said Gould had cut a deal with the Vanderbilts whereby he would merge the Kansas Pacific into his Missouri Pacific system while the Vanderbilts added the Union Pacific main line to the Chicago & Northwestern system. The most obvious choice was nowhere to be seen. Morgan had his hands full with the Erie and other reorganizations, and was thought to have written off the Union Pacific as a lost cause. Few other banking houses had the size or prestige to tackle so large a project, and none would touch it unless Morgan clearly signaled his disinterest.[26]

One such house was Kuhn, Loeb, which in its impressive growth of influence had always been careful not to step on Morgan's toes. Its senior partner, Jacob H. Schiff, had done little business with the Union Pacific but a great deal with George Gould's Missouri Pacific. He was also a close friend of Marvin Hughitt, who was anxious to preserve the close ties between the Northwestern and the Union Pacific. Aware that a banker of stature was needed in Morgan's absence, Gould sent his chief counsel Winslow S. Pierce to sound Schiff on tackling the Union Pacific reorganization.

STEPPING OUT OF JUPITER'S SHADOW: The dapper and diplomatic Jacob H. Schiff, the guiding genius of Kuhn, Loeb and Harriman's closest ally. (*B. C. Forbes,* Men Who Are Making America, *Baker Library, Harvard Business School*)

On an autumn day in 1895 Schiff boarded a steamboat of the Sandy Hook line on his way to his country place at Seabright, New Jersey. He was resting in his cabin when Pierce appeared at the door and said he had an important matter to discuss. The surprised Schiff knew Pierce only slightly and asked what it was. Without mincing words Pierce asked him to undertake the Union Pacific reorganization. "That is J. P. Morgan's affair," Schiff demurred at once. "I don't want to interfere with anything that he is trying to do." Not anymore, Pierce assured him. Morgan and Brice had abandoned the task as hopeless; someone new was needed. Schiff agreed to look at some figures on the subject. After examining them, he said only that he would consult his partner Abraham Wolff on the matter.[27]

Before deciding anything, the cautious Schiff visited Morgan to seek his approval. In his forthright way Morgan acknowledged that he was done with Union Pacific and sick to death of all its political intrigues. Schiff was welcome to all of its headaches. Morgan offered what help he could, but was so disgusted with the company's prospects that he declined even to take a share in the underwriting syndicate. These emphatic sentiments must have given Schiff pause; nevertheless, once Morgan signed off, Schiff agreed to involve his firm in the work. He canceled a trip to Mexico early in November, explaining to an associate, "I am forced to direct all the preparations for the proposed Union Pacific reorganization."[28]

At forty-eight Schiff was a decade younger than Morgan but already as well versed in the art of railroad finance. Described by one contemporary as "a patient, skillful man, a suave diplomat with a complex Oriental nature," he had emerged not only as the senior partner of Kuhn, Loeb but also as the dominant figure among what were then known delicately as the "Hebrew bankers." He dwelled in the portly Morgan's shadow literally as well as professionally. Small and lithe, with handsome features set between thinning hair and a neatly trimmed goatee, the dapper Schiff peered at the world through large blue eyes with an expression at once knowing and sardonic. He favored broad linen ties and a fresh flower in his buttonhole. His command of English was excellent but filtered through a heavy German accent and what his daughter called "a certain thickness in his speech."[29]

Although Schiff's tastes were elegant and fastidious, small habits tied him to the ordeal of his forebears. He never wasted notepads but used old scraps of paper for messages. Because he had a Western Union frank, he sent wires instead of telephoning even when time was of the essence. To curtail excessive use of the telephone at home, he kept a book nearby and required everyone to record their calls. In business these idiosyncrasies paled before his intellect, which was as resourceful as his tact. Schiff had learned railroading at the elbow of such masterful practitioners as Marvin Hughitt and James J. Hill, with whom he had become friends during the 1880s. Hill might use Morgan as his banker, Schiff conceded, "but I am his *friend*." While cultivating Hill's friendship, Schiff also made the acquaintance of a newcomer on the Illinois Central board by the name of E. H. Harriman.

Like most financiers, Schiff had a weakness for homilies. To ensure a successful reorganization, he noted, "we would have to paint the whole thing over fresh." In putting together a new committee he included only Louis Fitzgerald from the old one and asked him to recruit Chauncey M. Depew, president of the New York Central. Hughitt of the Northwestern also agreed to serve. His presence and that of Depew spurred rumors that the Vanderbilts would dominate the Union Pacific, an impression Schiff left undisturbed because of its publicity value. Two Bostonians, Oliver Ames II and T. Jefferson Coolidge of Old Colony Trust, were added to represent the large interests still held in that city. Fitzgerald was named chairman and Winslow Pierce counsel, giving the committee a Gould as well as a Vanderbilt flavor.[30]

The changed circumstances noted earlier enabled the committee to produce a refined plan within a remarkably short time. Released in October 1895, it called for a new capital structure consisting of three securities: $100 million in 4 percent bonds, $75 million in 4 percent preferred stock, and $61 million in common stock. First mortgage holders of Union Pacific and Kansas Pacific were to exchange their bonds at par for the new bonds and receive in addition 50 percent of the amount surrendered in new preferred stock. The exchange rate on some junior securities was 80 percent of par but included the 50 percent bonus in preferred. Stockholders were asked to trade their shares for the new issue and pay an assessment of $15 per share, for which they received preferred stock at par. A syndicate headed by Kuhn, Loeb pledged to furnish at least $10 million for purchasing all unpaid coupons and other needs of the reorganization. As compensation, they were to have $6 million of the preferred stock.[31]

Of the new issues, $35.8 million in bonds, $20.8 million in preferred stock, and a small amount of common were set aside for settlement of the government debt and ''extraordinary requirements.'' No details were offered on how this settlement would be arranged, and no provision was made for the collateral trust notes. The committee calculated that average net earnings on the road over the past decade had been $7.6 million, and that it had earned $4.3 million in the worst of those years (1894). Under the new plan interest amounted to $4 million a year and the 4 percent dividend on preferred stock, $3 million. If past earnings were any criteria, the total of $7 million could easily be managed, and the interest alone could be covered by the worst performance of the past decade.

One analyst gave the plan a nod of approval, calling it ''a very clever contrivance . . . containing within it the elements that are likely to ensure its success.'' The ultimate test would be the government's response, which no one dared predict. ''Our legislators,'' added the analyst with vast understatement, ''have been strangely neglectful of the interests of the country in this affair thus far.'' *The Nation* also urged acceptance and asked pointedly, ''What has this generation to do with the sins of the Crédit Mobilier of thirty years ago?'' Others agreed that all the blather about the ghosts of scandals past had no place in the debate. ''The present generation,'' noted the *Railroad Gazette*, ''is called upon simply to solve a business problem.''[32]

By the end of January 1896 enough securities of all classes had been deposited for the committee to declare the plan in operation. Earlier that month Fitzgerald and Pierce informed the congressional committees of the plan's progress and asked for their help in arranging a settlement of the government debt. In March a new refunding bill was introduced. Observers considered the outlook for its passage brighter than it had been in five years. Speculators also sniffed a settlement in the wind and boosted the stock as offering ''greater possibilities on the long side than any stock selling within ten points of its price.'' Although the bill did not pass before the summer recess, the smart money insisted that it would be called up early in the next session.[33]

But 1896 was an election year and featured one of those extraordinary contests that serve as watersheds in American politics. In the swirl of battle between William McKinley and William Jennings Bryan the issue of government ownership of railroads got nowhere near the play of free silver, but it was a hot potato in the plains states where Populism was strong. To advocates of this notion the Union Pacific offered a perfect opportunity for a trial run. Moreover, in an election heated by charges of assorted conspiracies among the moneyed interests of the East, what chance had a major railroad with a tainted past to escape the crossfire of rhetoric among congressmen standing for reelection and eager to do some posturing?

McKinley's victory in the election allowed Republicans to sleep soundly without fear for the Republic, but it also dashed hopes for a spurt in the production of silver. Grover Cleveland gave the Pacific railroad issue a boost in his last annual presidential message, triggering another burst of enthusiasm among analysts and speculators alike. The Fitzgerald committee still hoped to get a funding bill that would save everyone the trouble of a foreclosure, and prospects looked good to many observers. Then mysterious obstacles began to crop up, and slowly but inexorably the momentum behind a settlement slipped. There were problems with some minority holders, with the press, and in Washington—ripples of antagonism that were difficult to isolate but could not be ignored.[34]

The source of this resistance puzzled Schiff and his associates. A friend confided to Schiff that Morgan was jealous of the progress made by the Fitzgerald committee and anxious to take back the reorganization for himself. Schiff did not believe this tale, but it made him uneasy enough to call on Morgan and ask him directly if he had changed his mind about the Union Pacific and now desired a place in the syndicate. Morgan shook his head emphatically; he wanted nothing to do with the Union Pacific. A relieved Schiff told him of the opposition encountered by the committee and asked if Morgan knew whose influence was behind it. Again Morgan shook his head. He did not know, but he promised to look into the matter quietly and see what he could learn.[35]

A few weeks later Morgan summoned Schiff and told him he thought the source of opposition had been located. "It's that little fellow Harriman," he growled, "and you want to watch him carefully."

Harriman. What had he to do with the Union Pacific? Schiff knew him slightly as the financial manager of the Illinois Central, but what interest could the Illinois Central have in the reorganization? Baffled, Schiff went to see Harriman and asked him frankly whether he was behind the resistance to the committee's efforts.

"I am the man," Harriman admitted without hesitation.

"Why are you doing it?" asked Schiff.

"I want to reorganize the Union Pacific myself," Harriman snapped.

A smile flickered across Schiff's polished features. "But how are you going to do it, Mr. Harriman?" he asked. "We have all the bonds in, and what means have you to reorganize this company?"

"The Illinois Central ought to have that property," replied Harriman unsmiling. "In the Illinois Central we have the best credit in the world. I am going to issue $100,000,000 of 3% bonds at close to par and with the proceeds organize the Union Pacific. At the best you cannot get money at less than 4%. I am stronger than you are."

Schiff masked his astonishment at this display of brashness. It was, he later recalled, a "brutal" conversation, and he was not accustomed to such bluntness. "Well, you will have a good time doing it, Mr. Harriman," he said, "but in the meantime, what is your price?"

"There is no price to it. I am interested in the Union Pacific railway and I am determined to take charge of its reorganization."

"Are there no terms upon which we can work together?" Schiff ventured.

"If you will make me chairman of the executive committee of the reorganized road," Harriman answered at once, "I will join forces with you."

"That is out of the question," Schiff countered. "Mr. Pierce shall be chairman. I think he deserves it."

"Very well then, Mr. Schiff, go ahead and see what you can do. Good day."

This was Schiff's version of events, which the known facts neither confirm nor refute. There is, however, a crucial question no one has asked: why would the Illinois Central even be interested in a road with which it had no physical connection? The answer lay in the company's Iowa lines, which reached Sioux City but not Council Bluffs. Stuyvesant Fish of the Illinois Central opposed any settlement of the Union Pacific debt that favored the other Iowa roads and shut his road out of this business. Even more, he wanted to build a direct connector to the Omaha gateway. The Union Pacific had toyed with extending a branch from Norfolk to Sioux City in 1888, and six years later John Doane, who was both an Illinois Central director and a receiver for the Union Pacific, revived the idea. "It seems a little strange to me," Doane told Fish, "that the Illinois Central should run so close to the largest city in this section of the country without getting a slice of the large business that enters here."[36]

Fish agreed and in December 1896 tried to promote a plan whereby the Iowa roads joined to buy the government's lien on the Union Pacific and keep it neutral. During January 1897 Harriman met several times with Schiff on these questions. In these secret sessions Harriman let Schiff know that the Illinois Central wanted "equal facilities with any other line doing business over the Union Pacific in future." Schiff conceded this willingly and even suggested that the Illinois Central put survey parties in the field for its connector. A few days later Fish had men sent out; meanwhile his lobbyists worked against the funding bill then before Congress. The connector to Omaha did get built, but was not completed until December 1899.[37]

By his own admission Schiff walked away from these meetings unsettled by Harriman's overweaning confidence and disturbed by his staccato style. Was he serious? Did he have the ability to back up such bold words? Events did little to reassure Schiff. Things got no better for the Fitzgerald committee. When Cleveland declared that the government would foreclose unless a funding bill passed, Congress responded by rejecting the bill decisively on January 11, 1897. The stock fell sharply on rumors that the defeat meant a larger assessment for the stockholders. The mood within the outgoing administration shifted to the view that better terms could be had through a cash settlement, and a new bill was prepared on that basis. Rumors spread that Fitzgerald's committee was faltering under its financial load and bogged down in internal bickering. An irritated Collis P. Huntington, whose Central Pacific also had to settle with the government, told a reporter the Union Pacific crowd was composed of idiots who did not know what they were about.[38]

Once Schiff realized the government was serious about demanding a cash settlement, he saw no choice but to open negotiations on that basis. Late in January agreement was reached on a foreclosure plan with the committee guaranteeing a bid of nearly $45.8 million for the government's interest. This arrangement would terminate the government's role immediately after foreclosure, but it also obliged Schiff to form a second syndicate for underwriting the funds required for the bid. In return the bankers would receive 100 percent in new first mortgage bonds and 50 percent in new preferred stock. The Fitzgerald committee then modified its plan by reducing the amount of new firsts used in the reorganization from $100 million to $75 million. This was done by asking two classes of bondholders to accept fewer bonds and more preferred stock.[39]

No sooner was this agreement reached than rumors swirled that an unidentified party was prepared to bid $10 million higher for the Union Pacific than the committee. Speculation was rampant on who the challenger might be, but no one mentioned the name that tossed in Schiff's mind. The pattern of resistance to the committee continued, and fresh snags developed with the government. Even worse, Schiff found little enthusiasm for the new syndicate on Wall Street or abroad. A banker observed that Schiff had "a 40 million syndicate for U. P. on hand and its a little slow. he will have to carry a big chunk himself, and use all his friends."[40]

And his foes. Schiff had no way of knowing what role if any Harriman had played in his difficulties, but he was in no mood to take unnecessary chances. Back he went to see Harriman, this time with an explanation of why Pierce should be chairman of the executive committee. It was Pierce, he explained, who had brought the business to Kuhn, Loeb, which put Schiff in his debt. As Gould's counsel, Pierce represented large interests in the Union Pacific, some of whom were cool if not hostile to Harriman. But Schiff had a proposition: Harriman could have a seat on the board and a place on the executive committee. "Then," he added, "if you prove to be the strongest man in that committee, you'll probably get the chairmanship in the end."[41]

"All right," Harriman replied without hesitation, "I'm with you."

As part of the arrangement Harriman joined the syndicate, taking a share of $900,000. It was the only role he would play in the reorganization.

After this bargain was struck, the committee marched steadily toward the foreclosure sale. When the government found fault with a provision for the Omaha Bridge mortgage and threatened an appeal, the committee raised its bid $5 million to avoid the delay. The only formality left was assurance from Attorney General Joseph E. McKenna that he would not appeal the foreclosure sale scheduled for November 1, 1897. No one expected any trouble because, as a committee member observed, "the agreement between the committee and the Attorney General is complete in every detail." McKenna encouraged the notion that more than one bid would be offered but said nothing to suggest that the sale would not be held. However, someone was attacking the committee and

RAILROAD FOR SALE: The Union Pacific is sold out of receivership at the freight depot in Omaha, November 1897.

the Schiff syndicate violently through the press in hopes of delaying the sale. In response the influential *Commercial and Financial Chronicle* declared emphatically that it would be "nothing less than a public calamity to upset the arrangement at this state."[42]

On October 25, a week before the sale, McKenna dropped a bombshell by announcing that he would ask the court to postpone the sale until December 15 so that the new Congress might consider the matter. Speculation was rampant over his motives. Some said the McKinley administration had been swayed by pleas from a rival syndicate allegedly organized by Russell Sage and General Samuel Thomas, an Ohio Republican with political clout. Others saw an attempt by the new administration to protect itself from a deal cut by its Democratic predecessor. There was also the question of some $8 million in disputed claims that had never been resolved."[43]

Whatever McKenna's motives, the last thing anyone wanted was to throw the issue back into the lap of Congress, where it had already died a hundred deaths. An incensed Schiff found himself in a difficult position. The syndicate assumed it had an agreement with the government and had advanced funds, called for assessments, and entered into contracts requiring large outlays such as one with Morgan calling for the purchase of several million dollars worth of securities. All these arrangements would be jeopardized by the delay. Moreover, the deposit of about $7 million in earnest money had to be made within a few days if the sale was to proceed as planned. And he was anxious to get hold of the road, for business was booming. The general manager reported "the most extraordinary revival ever known along the whole line." It was not a time to dawdle or give Congress another oar.[44]

Under the circumstances Schiff saw no choice but to submit to what amounted to a polite form of extortion. Fitzgerald's committee telegraphed McKenna that it would increase the bid another $8 million to include the disputed claims if he would allow the sale to be held as planned. Only the Union Pacific main line would be included; the committee would consent to postponement of the Kansas Pacific sale to whatever date suited the government. In effect the committee raised the white flag of surrender and agreed to pay the entire amount of principle and accrued interest on the bonds. After nearly thirty years of bitter wrangling the government would receive every cent claimed by it. McKenna accepted the offer at once, and the sale was on again.

By eleven o'clock on a gray November morning a crowd of 500 people gathered expectantly outside the Union Pacific freight depot in Omaha, waiting to see if the sale would come off and if more than one bidder would appear. William D. Cornish, the master in chancery, mounted the platform and began reading aloud the description of the property. Forty minutes later, as Cornish neared the end, Louis Fitzgerald stepped onto the platform. Cornish paused, then drew out another document and began reading aloud a protest from Frank Trumbull, the Gulf line receiver, over the sale. That done, Cornish announced his willingness to accept bids. There was a moment's silence before Fitzgerald made his bid. "Are there any more bids?" Cornish asked. Necks craned eagerly in every direction, but no other bids were forthcoming.[45]

The sale was over in minutes, a strange anticlimax to so protracted a fight. The committee paid nearly $58.5 million, less the $18.2 million in the sinking fund, or $40.3 million for the Union Pacific main line. In addition, it had to buy up $27.6 million worth of first mortgage bonds and $13.6 million in other securities for a total of $81.5 million. Some investors, disheartened by the higher price paid the government, sold off their stock during the next few weeks. Wiser heads saw that the stock was among the most undervalued on the market and bought heavily in anticipation of improved earnings. One of them was Harriman, who quietly loaded up on Union Pacific. He joined Winslow Pierce, Marvin Hughitt, banker James Stillman, and Otto H. Kahn of Kuhn, Loeb on an advisory committee named to oversee the Union Pacific until the new company organized.[46]

The sale of the Kansas Pacific was postponed first to December 15, then to February 1898. For weeks the committee and the government haggled over terms before reaching agreement. The sale then went off without a hitch, ensuring that the Kansas division would remain part of the system. The new Union Pacific was chartered in Utah and took formal control from the receivers on January 31, 1898; two months later the receivers handed over the Kansas division. The long night of the receivership was over, yet so complicated had its affairs been and so many details were there to resolve that the court did not finally discharge the last receiver until November 1900.[47]

For months there had been intense curiosity in New York and rampant anxiety in Omaha over what changes would be made in the management after the reorganization. The betting in both places was that Silas Clark would remain as president and preside over much the same staff he had as receiver. But Clark had been ill since summer and so had comptroller Oliver Mink, who was expected to reclaim the vice-presidency. In December, with the sale safely past, Clark announced that he would not become president of the new company because of ill health. Speculation arose at once over his successor. Some thought it would be Horace Burt, an engineer who had risen to third vice-president of the Northwestern and served as Hughitt's assistant. Others boosted Charles S. Mellen, president of the Northern Pacific, whose experience included a controversial stint with the Union Pacific under the regime of Charles Francis Adams, Jr., during the 1880s.[48]

Late in December 1897 the committee named Burt as the new president, declaring that it wanted an experienced railroad man at the helm in Omaha. The Union Pacific would continue to be run as it always had been, with its financial office in the East and its operating head in Omaha. Burt's first executive order confirmed that Edward Dickinson would remain as general manager. John A. Munroe as freight traffic manager, E. L. Lomax as general passenger agent, and John B. Berry as chief engineer. The general solicitor, John M. Thurston, had been elected to the United States Senate in 1895 and surrendered his post to Judge William R. Kelley.[49]

A clear answer to one pressing question still eluded the shrewdest of observers: where did power reside within the eastern management of Union Pacific? Burt's appointment suggested that the Northwestern (and therefore the Vanderbilts) wielded a powerful influence, but the first board was a mosaic of interests. Hughitt was a director and so was Roswell Miller, president of the Chicago, Milwaukee & St. Paul. George Gould took a seat along with Pierce, who served as chief counsel to the company and was also made chairman of both the board and the executive committee. Henry B. Hyde of Equitable Life had long been friendly with the Goulds. Oliver Ames II represented his family's interest. Schiff, Kahn, Fitzgerald, Stillman, and T. Jefferson Coolidge were all bankers associated with the reorganization. George Q. Cannon filled the place reserved for Utah interests, and John Doane of Chicago was a former government director.[50]

That left only Harriman, the mystery man of the board. No one knew why he was there or what role he was expected to play. In fact, no one paid any attention to his presence. He was known only as a broker of moderate means and conservative reputation who had been associated for some years with the Illinois Central Railroad. Not even the shrewdest eyes on Wall Street gave more than a perfunctory glance at the news in May 1898 that the mystery man had been elected chairman of the Union Pacific's executive committee.[51]

2

The Second Coming

To the railroad officers standing alongside the business car on a warm June day in 1898, the New York people were just one more party of official tourists to be waltzed over the road and shown all possible amenities along the way. Veteran superintendents had done the chore a hundred times for eastern officials or government people or visiting dignitaries or friends of the "swells" in Union Pacific's higher management. Like soldiers at parade rest they stood silhouetted against the sun, their leathery faces lined with patience. For them it was a duty that at best got in the way of real work and at worst aroused fears and frustrations none cared to utter aloud.

But this tour was different, clouded by the sense of apprehension that had infused everything since the receivership crashed down on the Union Pacific in 1893. A host of good men who had been with the company for years were already gone, squeezed out by hard times, leaving the survivors to wonder when and where the ax would fall next. The reorganization in 1898 ended the receivership but not the uncertainty over what changes loomed along the line for those who regarded the railroad as their daily bread rather than as part of their portfolio.

This time, however, one of the eastern visitors seemed different—a queer duck who poked into every corner he could find, asking more questions about more things than anybody ever heard asked before, boring in on an officer until he got answers that satisfied him. He was a small, dark man with thick glasses and a walrus mustache. His wiry body seemed always in motion, impatient to get on with the business at hand, radiating energy like a halo about his dumpy appearance. He did not so much talk as fire staccato bursts of words in a brusque tone that startled even tough railroad men. There was in his manner a sense of cold efficiency, a ruthlessness of purpose that kept everyone at arm's length. No one seemed to know much about him, and a few did not even know who he was.

Huddled in front of the depot, waiting with an impassive expression for the next onslaught of questions, one knowing officer nudged J. H. McConnell, the superintendent of machinery, and murmured, ''Joe, did you notice that dark complected man with glasses who seemed to know so much about the price of scrap, and a great deal about things in general? Well, that's the man who is going to have a good deal to say about this railroad.''

''Do you think so?'' McConnell replied dubiously. ''What's his name?''

''That's Ned Harriman. Used to be on the Illinois Central at Chicago. He's a comer.''[1]

In both major periods of the Union Pacific's history there can be found one man whose influence on the company was decisive and whose exploits became the stuff of legend. For the years prior to 1893 that man was Jay Gould; for the era after the receivership it was E. H. Harriman. The case for Gould's pivotal role in the early years has only recently been made, while that of Harriman has been enshrined in myth for eighty years. The fact that Gould was so elusive and controversial a figure has obscured the remarkable parallels between the two men and their careers. In many respects Harriman was the second coming of Jay Gould.[2]

The similarities run at several levels. Harriman was born in 1848, a dozen years later than Gould. Both sprang from humble origins in provincial areas of New York—Gould from upcountry Roxbury and Harriman from Hempstead, Long Island. Little was expected of either man. Undersized, physically frail, the runts of their litters, they each battled every obstacle to achieve great things through indomitable will, fierce ambition, and uncommon genius. Neither man knew how to quit a fight or submit to adversity; setbacks only goaded them into renewing the struggle. In their determination to succeed they never learned how to pace themselves in life. Ill health dogged their footsteps, and overwork put them both in early graves.

Harriman left school at fourteen, Gould at sixteen, to go to work. Both found their way to Wall Street at an early age and cut their business teeth there. Since Gould pursued other ventures first, the two men arrived on the Street at almost the same time, Gould in 1860 and Harriman two years later. However, their paths parted company during these early lessons in finance. Gould mastered the intricacies of Wall Street with breathtaking speed and by the decade's end gained notoriety for his part in the spectacular Erie War and Gold Corner escapades. The younger Harriman followed a slower route as a broker who earned a reputation for being conservative and trustworthy. Where Gould became a national figure in his early thirties, Harriman dwelled in obscurity until he was fifty. In the last dozen years of his life, however, Harriman transformed the American railroad scene in a way rivaled only by Gould before him.

By these different routes Gould and Harriman reached the same destiny as the dominant figure in their industry. At first glance they seemed to defy comparison because their personalities differed so markedly. There was about Gould an intellectuality that Harriman never possessed. Gould was quiet and abstract with a soft voice and insinuating manner, given in his leisure to the perusal of books or paintings and the cultivation of flowers. Harriman preferred the outdoor life and vigorous activity; he was fond of sports and hunting and adventuring in the wilderness.

Like Gould, Harriman was a man of few words carefully chosen, but unlike Gould his words were delivered with an utter lack of tact or charm. He was a bantam rooster, belligerent and combative, bristling with energy, always ready to wager on a good race or election or some other competition. Where Gould was ever courteous and often evasive, Harriman was stiff-necked to a fault and incapable of cajoling or dissembling.

Yet, in a curious way these differences merely underscored the remarkable similarities in their business style. Both were men who cut through the haze of conventional wisdom to see things as they were, not as others thought they were supposed to be. Their minds operated at a speed and on a plane baffling to ordinary men, arriving at conclusions before others had even grasped the question. They possessed a stunning clarity of logic in their thinking, yet were capable of intuitive leaps that no one, least of all themselves, could explain. Associates marveled at their focus, their ability to grasp the essence of a problem without being distracted by extraneous details. Gould and Harriman alike loved nothing better than surmounting obstacles. Otto Kahn thought that Harriman deliberately created obstacles for himself merely for the sport of hurdling them. The greater the challenge, the more eager they were to pit their intelligence against it, pursuing their goals with astonishing perseverance and tenacity.[3]

Not surprisingly, these qualities set Gould and Harriman apart from their fellows. They cared little about appearance or what others thought of them. Both were reticent men who cloaked their acts in mystery and never revealed even to their closest associates the full design of their plans. As shy, unassuming men who disliked ceremony and avoided reporters whenever possible, they became mysterious figures to a public eager to hear about business titans and then targets for newspapers seeking villains to flog for misdeeds real or imagined, Gould was perceived by a hostile press as cold and aloof, Harriman as cold and abrasive. Their careers, sprinkled with controversial episodes, became the stuff of legends that went unchallenged because neither man bothered to explain himself or his actions to the public. As a result, both Gould and Harriman remained misunderstood figures during their lives and long afterward. Indifferent to public opinion, they found solace in their families. Both isolated themselves on vast estates and led exemplary private lives centered around their children.

The nature of their roles in the Union Pacific has long been misunderstood. Legend has it that Gould milked the company for what he could get out of it while Harriman transformed a derelict line into the model of what a modern railroad should be. Actually, Gould's role was no less positive or significant than Harriman's, and without it Harriman would not have had much of a railroad to salvage. Engineer Samuel Felton once said of Harriman that he "built up his fortune, not by speculation but by making more valuable the things he bought." The same holds true of Gould, and the Union Pacific offers a perfect example. Alexander Millar, the company's longtime secretary, was among the few men who recognized Gould's contribution as both constructive and honorable. "Mr. Gould," he insisted, "was (like EHH at a later day) the man who put value in [the] stock."[4]

Both Gould and Harriman bought into Union Pacific at low prices and were accused of doing so for purely speculative purposes. Gould declared repeatedly that the stock was worth par and would get there with hard work; Harriman asserted that Union Pacific was worth as much as Milwaukee stock and would soon surpass it. In each case the prediction was realized, and when both men commenced paying dividends a short time afterward, they were promptly accused of doing so merely to boost stock prices. Both ultimately realized huge profits by breathing life into a moribund property, although they reached that goal by different routes. Gould rescued the road from near bankruptcy and nursed it through the lean depression years of the 1870s; Harriman found it on the threshold of prosperity and brilliantly fulfilled its potential.[5]

So decisive was their impact that it extended far beyond the Union Pacific. Gould and Harriman embodied—indeed defined—two distinct eras in the evolution of American railroads. In most of his work Gould ploughed virgin soil, pushing rails into undeveloped country and following with investments in coal, timber, and other resources. His lightning strokes and relentless energy galvanized competitors into launching their own construction programs. From these clashes emerged the expansion wars of the 1880s, an orgy of track-laying unparalleled in the nation's history. Once-isolated roads evolved into large systems competing savagely for business with other large systems at multiple points.

The wars bred by unbridled expansion lowered rates precipitously, a boon for shippers but disaster for the carriers. The effect on income accounts made it difficult for roads to bear the added costs of expansion, let alone provide adequate funds for maintenance, equipment, and improvements. While their facilities groaned beneath a crush of new business carried at lower rates, dividends were curtailed, the value of rail securities shrank steadily, and new capital grew ever harder to secure. An epidemic of reorganization fights before the collapse after 1893 revealed how deeply troubled the industry was.

Gould and his generation forged the basic rail system that stimulated the development on which Harriman would later capitalize. Two major problems plagued the industry and defied even Gould's genius, although he was hard at work on both at the time of his death in 1892. West of the Missouri River, where so much track had been laid into undeveloped or lightly settled regions, the growth of business had not yet reached a level capable of supporting the roads. The railroad's presence helped ensure future development, but that would take time. Meanwhile, systems fought bitterly for what business there was and aggravated their problems by carrying large volumes of traffic at shrinking rates. The wars spawned by their desperate clashes revealed a need for some mechanism to rationalize and harmonize the rail system.

Although few realized it at the time, the wave of bankruptcies during the depression of the 1890s marked the transition to a new era. Where Gould had pulled for years against hard times and paid the price of all pioneers who open new territory, Harriman caught the rising tide of prosperity that followed the depression. After 1896 the growth of business anticipated by Gould and others burst forth in unprecedented volume. Harriman did nothing to create this flow of traffic, but he anticipated its coming with perfect timing and chose precisely the right course for handling it even though his policy meant spending enormous sums of money just when the Union Pacific had crawled out of bankruptcy.

Gould had built railroads to fit the business requirements of one era; Harriman rebuilt them to conform with the needs of another. Most of the early roads had been constructed quickly and cheaply because little or no business existed to support an expensive road and the object was to get a road in place to develop that business. Later, when the flow of traffic increased, the road and its equipment could be brought up to higher standards. This approach made sense for western railroads and was followed until the expansion wars undermined it. No one could have anticipated the scale and severity of those wars or predicted the extent to which they would devour capital for new mileage that was urgently needed to improve existing track and equipment. As a result, most western railroads failed to modernize their plant at a pace equivalent to the growth of the traffic they carried.

Expansion worsened the problem in two ways: it increased the mileage that had to be maintained or upgraded and triggered rate wars that forced roads to carry a heavier volume of traffic at falling rates. No surer equation for self-immolation could have been devised. While western roads groaned beneath a flood of business that wore out the physical plant at an accelerated pace, lower rates brought less income to repair or upgrade it. The growing clamor for regulation added still more pressure to keep rates down, and attempts by the carriers to maintain rates through pools or other agreements failed miserably.

By 1890 certain harsh truths confronted railroad managers. The industry had just completed its most spectacular decade of growth, yet found itself in the grip of a crisis that threatened its very future. Wiser heads recognized that the age of individual lines had given way to the age of systems, and systems could not afford to fight prolonged wars of attrition or drive rates so low that they could never be brought back. The expansion wars of the 1880s demonstrated the futility of carrying a heavy traffic at low rates over poorly built roads with inadequate equipment. Physical plants had to be made cost efficient, facilities had to be modernized, and some way had to be found of restoring rates and imposing stability. The oldest and most conservative large industry in America had grown tired and was drifting toward disaster. Fresh blood and fresh thinking were needed to revitalize it.

Those who doubted the gravity of the crisis were quick to see the light when the depression swept so many major carriers into bankruptcy. In their usual way railroad managers were as certain of the problems that had brought their industry to its knees as they were helpless to agree on solutions to them. The road to salvation would seem more obvious afterward than it did at the time, when only a select few knew where to look or had the courage to back their convictions. One of those who did was E. H. Harriman.

Surprisingly little is known about the early life and career of E. H. Harriman. As with Jay Gould, the mystery surrounding his early years has created a vacuum that legend rushed to fill with wrong or misleading information. "I have talked to scores of men who knew Harriman before Harriman was rich and powerful," declared one veteran observer of Wall Street, "and not one of them asserts that he detected in those days the signs of greatness."[6]

The Harriman family can be traced back to William Harriman, a London dealer in stationery who came to America in 1795 with enough money to involve himself in the West Indies trade. Of his eight sons only one, Orlando, survived to pass on the family name. Orlando joined his father's business and produced eleven children of his own. His namesake, Orlando Jr., did not follow the others into business but instead attended Columbia University and in 1841 entered the Episcopal ministry. A bright, scholarly man, Orlando possessed a cold, austere manner that kept him at arm's length from his parishioners just as it would distance his famous son from a public intensely curious about him.[7]

Whatever else they achieved in life, most of the Harrimans showed a talent for marrying well, and Orlando was no exception. Shortly after becoming a deacon he married Cornelia Neilson, the daughter of a physician belonging to an old and well-connected New Jersey family. Her cool intelligence and strength of character did much to sustain the family through some lean years and left a lasting imprint on her six children, none more than Edward Henry. A constant struggle to make ends meet drew the family together. For all his erudition, the Reverend Orlando Harriman never mastered the art of earning a living and enjoyed economic security only late in life, when his wife received a small inheritance.[8]

Although Henry was born February 25, 1848, in the Episcopal rectory at Hempstead, he spent most of his childhood in Jersey City. He was a small, kinetic boy with huge dark eyes and a quick mind that bent more toward sports than books. While attending public school in Jersey City he was described by an acquaintance as "the worst little devil in his class, and always at the top of it." When Henry was twelve, his parents scraped together enough money to send him to Trinity School in New York. Every day, in true Horatio Alger style, the boy got up before dawn, trudged two miles to the ferry, crossed the river, and hiked another mile to school. The trip took him through the turf of some street toughs on lower Manhattan who let no newcomer pass without challenge. Necessity taught Henry to be a scrapper early, and he learned the lesson well.[9]

In 1862, at the age of fourteen, Henry made his debut on Wall Street as office boy for DeWitt C. Hays, a broker who held the distinction of being the third member to join the New York Stock Exchange and who later served as its treasurer for thirty years. Soon afterward Henry rose to the position of messenger clerk, or "pad-shover." These were boys who scurried from office to office with current stock prices and buy or sell offers scribbled on pads of paper. A bright, alert boy could learn much from being a pad-shover, and a host of prominent financiers graduated from these ranks. Henry was not only quick but also possessed a remarkable memory; he was perceptive and trustworthy in a place where those qualities counted for everything. By the age of twenty he had mastered the brokerage business well enough to become managing clerk in Hays's firm.[10]

Far from satisfying Henry's ambition, the promotion merely whetted his appetite for striking out on his own. During the Civil War no business arena was more volatile than Wall Street, where fortunes rose and fell on every scrap of news from the front. Young Henry liked to be where the action was, where the challenges were great and victories went to the swiftest of mind. In August 1870, at the age of twenty-two, he took the plunge. Borrowing $3,000 from his Uncle Oliver, a prominent merchant, he bought a seat on the New York Stock Exchange and opened a small office as E. H. Harriman & Company.[11]

Although Henry did well, nothing in these early years offered even a hint of what was to come. A credit reporter described E. H. Harriman & Company as a modest but "good conservative & reliable House" whose proprietor was "not likely to incur obligations he cannot meet." Through the 1880s Henry carefully nurtured his reputation as a sound, trustworthy broker whose fortune grew slowly but surely. He made contacts of the right sort, prominent men like August Belmont, Stuyvesant Fish, W. Bayard Cutting, and James B. Livingston, who provided not only business and access to other opportunities but also social connections. The poor minister's son traveled in the right circles and, true to family tradition, helped himself by marrying well.[12]

Through a close friend, George C. Clark, Henry met Mary W. Averell of Ogdensburg, New York, a small town on the St. Lawrence river. Her father, William J. Averell, was the town's leading banker and also president of a small railroad, the Ogdensburg & Lake Champlain. This chance encounter provided Henry with both a soulmate for life and the doorway to a new career. Mary Averell was, like Henry himself, more intelligent than attractive and possessed of a strong character. Apart from the obvious advantages of a connection to the wealthy Averells, the match was an ideal one for Henry. "His attitude toward her was more than devotion," observed Judge Robert S. Lovett, Harriman's chief counsel and one of his closest business associates. "It was profound admiration, respect and unfailing attention and courtesy."[13]

Their marriage in September 1879 produced six children on whom Henry doted: Mary (1881), Henry (1883), Cornelia (1884), Carol (1889), William Averell (1891), and Edward Roland (1895). His devotion to family was obvious to everyone who knew him at all; it was the center of his universe away from businesss. "No business, however great its magnitude nor how urgent its importance, caused him to neglect his home or his household," insisted Judge Lovett, "or to forget the most unimportant engagement with his wife, or the smallest plans for his children." Harriman's physician declared that he had never seen a more perfect family life.[14]

For their honeymoon William Averell provided the couple with a special train. When they reached the depot at Ogdensburg, a beaming Henry found that the workmen had painted "E. H. Harriman" on the locomotive. Thus his first formal connection with a railroad was purely personal, but not for long. Averell also arranged for his new son-in-law to go on the board of the Ogdensburg road. Although Harriman began involving himself more in railroads, he remained active as a broker. In the years following his marriage he improved his position steadily in both these fields.[15]

But he went slowly. Contrary to most accounts of his life, Harriman did not retire from E. H. Harriman & Company in 1885. For two more years he managed the brokerage house with his younger brother William while also extending his involvement in railraods. Then, in June 1887, he tried a new arrangement. Nicholas Fish was brought in to join William Harriman as general partner, with Henry as special partner. This "limited copartnership" survived only about six months. On February 1, 1888, E. H. Harriman & Company was dissolved and all its contracts transferred to another family firm, Harriman & Company.[16]

On the eve of his fortieth birthday Henry had crossed the Rubicon of his career. He had outgrown his trade and wanted some greater challenge than the buying and selling of securities. He wanted to take hold of properties, build and manage them, watch them grow and prosper through efficient handling. Later some would say he hungered less for wealth than for power, and there was truth in this observation.[17]

For Harriman the change from broker to railroad man came gradually. He tested the waters so gingerly that the transition in his interests went virtually unnoticed even by those few people who bothered to notice what he did. Indeed, he did so little during the 1880s that it never occurred to anyone to regard his presence as the nurturing of genius. Like Gould he kept closed within himself the larger plans and visions that churned inside his head.

The connection with Averell turned Harriman's attention to the northern part of the state, where his eye lit on an obscure, thirty-four-mile road then known as the Ontario Southern. Although situated between the Pennsylvania Railroad on one side and the New York Central on the other, the road did little business and was in shabby condition. It had already gone through receivership once and was about to again. In October 1881 he joined with some other men to buy control of the road and reorganize it as the Sodus Bay & Southern, with himself as vice-president. His partners included Silvanus J. Macy, who assumed the presidency, and one of New York's most proper bluebloods, Stuyvesant Fish.[18]

No association was to have more influence on Harriman's future than that with Fish. They were distantly related, both having Neilsons in their family tree. Their friendship began on Wall Street, where the aristocratic Fish went into banking after graduating from Columbia and serving briefly as a clerk for the Illinois Central Railroad. For five years he toiled in London and New York for the house of Morton, Bliss & Company, leaving in 1877 to take a seat on the board of the Illinois Central and turn his attention to railroads. Three years younger than Harriman, Fish offered a striking contrast to the man who became his close friend. Where Henry was small and dark, Fish was a blond, blue-eyed giant whose handsome features spread easily into a smile. Where Henry was closed and often moody, Fish was open and affable. Together they were the terrier and the golden retriever—the one moody and excitable, bristling with nervous energy and forever alert, the other sleek and graceful, good-natured and open but prone to an indolence born of self-assurance.[19]

The first known venture involving both Harriman and Fish occurred in June 1879 when both were elected directors of the Ogdensburg road. Two years later they left that board and took up the Sodus Bay project, where the object was to sell the little road to one of its giant neighbors at a handsome profit. With the help of Fish and some of his wealthy friends, Harriman improved the road, bought new equipment, and in April 1882 built a grain elevator on Sodus Point to lure Canadian wheat across Lake Ontario. When some stockholders objected to these expenditures, Harriman and friends bought control of the road in October 1883 and Henry assumed the presidency. A few months later he offered it for sale to both the Pennsylvania and the New York Central, using the simple but effective tactic of persuading both sides that neither could afford to let the other gain control of the Sodus Bay because of its strategic position in the growing Canadian trade. Both sides snapped at the bait, and the following June a Pennsylvania subsidiary bought the Sodus Bay. The partners walked away with a nice profit.[20]

In August 1883 Fish brought his friend onto the board of the Illinois Central. It was Harriman's first connection with a major railroad, one he earned by his deft handling of some bond sales for the road thrown his way by Fish. Gradually the directors came to rely on him for advice on financial matters. His presence suited Fish, who as the coming man in Illinois Central wanted a reliable ally like Harriman in a position of influence.[21]

If Harriman was seeking an education in railroads, he had picked a splendid classroom. The Illinois Central was a strong, conservative road—the only major north-south carrier in the country. When completed in 1856 the 705-mile line held the distinction of being the longest railroad in the world. Its Y shape had one arm anchored in Chicago and the other stretching to Dunleith in the northwest corner of Illinois. The arms met just above Centralia with the stem running to Cairo on the Ohio River at the southern tip of the state. Since the Civil War the company had expanded in two key directions. By 1870 it had leased roads in Iowa extending from Dunleith to Sioux City on the Missouri River. More recently it had won a lengthy battle to acquire some roads reaching from the Ohio River to New Orleans, giving the Illinois Central a through line from Chicago to the Gulf. Not until 1882 was this route nailed down through another lease arrangement.[22]

Harriman arrived on the scene at a turning point in the Illinois Central's history; indeed, that was why Fish had summoned him. For years the road had been praised for what one analyst called "the conservative spirit so dominant in the company's affairs." It had honest, capable management, a low debt, an efficient operation, and a tradition of high maintenance standards. Since 1877, a low point in its affairs, the Illinois Central had spent heavily on maintenance and improvements. Newly acquired lines got the same treatment; the New Orleans road was taken over in dilapidated condition and turned into a first-class property laid entirely with steel rails like the parent road. The Illinois Central also adopted a policy of paying for much of the work from income rather than its capital account. This approach was to leave a deep imprint on Harriman.[23]

However, pressures were mounting to redefine this approach. The competitive environment had exploded in an orgy of expansion that forced every major road to reassess its position. On the Illinois Central, as on many other roads, the debate split the board. One group of directors favored a policy of growth; others wanted to go slow. In January 1883 this clash elevated James C. Clarke to the vice-presidency and Fish to the post of second vice-president. That summer Fish got Harriman elected to board, which helped tip the balance toward the expansionists. In August Clarke assumed the presidency with Fish as vice-president, fueling rumors that the new regime might abandon the old conservatism. As the rate wars of the 1880s intensified, Fish and Harriman supported Clarke's policy of building or buying branches as feeders. Analysts questioned the wisdom of this course, noting gravely that the expansion dilemma impaled all major roads and would ultimately drag the most reckless of them into ruin.[24]

But not the Illinois Central. Its new leadership played the expansion game masterfully, adding only about 430 miles of new track in Harriman's first four years on the board and taking care to bring it all up to standard. At the same time it continued the policy of maintaining the entire system in top condition. By 1887 even the journal that had earlier expressed concern had swallowed its doubts. "It cannot be said that the company has abandoned its old-time conservatism," conceded its editor, "but it has developed a somewhat more aggressive disposition."[25]

One vital policy matter either originated with Harriman or captured his attention early. Later it would become the key to his method of financing the huge transactions that characterized his railroad career. For years the Illinois Central had enjoyed excellent credit but had done little with it. Prior to 1880 railroads paid dearly for the capital they needed to lay track. Most roads sold bonds at 7 or 8 percent, and often at prices that cost them 10 percent or more. Everyone saw that interest rates were coming down during the 1880s and many railroad managers were anxious to refund older issues at lower rates, but no one pursued this course with more zeal and imagination than Harriman. In his hands it became not merely sound financial policy but a weapon for expansion as well.[26]

As late as 1886 interest on bonds of the Illinois Central and its subsidiaries ranged from 5 to 8 percent. A plan was devised to refund some 8 percent bonds falling due with 5 percent bonds. Before this was done, however, Harriman saw the company could do even better. Instead of selling the fives, he and Fish used them as collateral for $5 million worth of collateral trust bonds at only 3½ percent interest. These were sold to English investors in August 1886 and the proceeds used to retire $3.2 million of old eights for a savings in interest of 4½ percent. Other bonds were issued at 3½ and 4 percent under an 1874 mortgage and used to help pay for acquisitions. When the company needed $1 million for some grain elevators and double-tracking, it resorted not to bonds but to a new issue of stock that current holders snatched up at a price of 136.[27]

In looking about for other ways to save money, Harriman's eye fell on the Iowa roads. The Illinois Central had leased the Dubuque & Sioux City in 1867 by agreeing to pay its owners 36 percent of gross earnings. These terms worked well until the explosion of railroads in Iowa and the steady decline of rates sent the Dubuque's ledgers into the red. The only way to restore its financial health was to make the road more competitive by extending its two subsidiary lines, but 36 percent of any earnings derived from investment in them would have to be shared with lessors who risked nothing. This arrangement did not appeal to Harriman, who persuaded the board to authorize him to buy control of the road when the lease expired in 1887.[28]

But the stockholders did not care to sell. There followed a bitter fight in which they enlisted the help of J. P. Morgan. Harriman outfoxed Morgan through use of a technicality, and his adversaries grudgingly sold their stock. Once in control of the Dubuque and its subsidiaries, the Illinois Central commenced work at once on 200 miles of extensions. This contest marked Harriman's first brush with Morgan, and it scarred their relationship for years. The banker was furious at being thwarted by what he deemed cheap tricks. Although the Dubuque amounted to small change to him, Morgan came away with his sense of propriety so bruised that he never forgave Fish for it. His anger extended to Harriman, who was in his eyes a nobody. According to his son-in-law, Morgan drew from this episode "a prejudice against Harriman that kept him in later years from cooperating with him when it might have been better had he done so."[29]

The source of his outrage was uncannily perceptive. Harriman had used tactics that would have done Jay Gould proud, and Morgan could not forgive him for stooping to the "Jay Gould method" of taking refuge in "the devices of lawyers and technicalities." But something more was involved, for Morgan actually got along well with Gould and worked closely with him on several enterprises. The difference lay in their personalities. Where Gould's unassuming manner and gift for tact kept him on the right side of Morgan, Harriman's abrasive personality and willingness to challenge the man they would soon call "Jupiter" ensured clashes between them.[30]

Amid the Dubuque fight a momentous change took place within the Illinois Central management. In May 1887 Clarke resigned as president and Fish was elected to the position. Four months later Harriman assumed the office of vice-president. Earlier that year he had closed his brokerage house in what amounted to a decision to devote his full attention to railroad matters. Already he served as president of some Illinois Central subsidiary lines; the vice-presidency gave him a position in which to learn the nuts and bolts of

JUPITER'S WRATH: J. P. Morgan shows his business face. (*Culver Pictures*)

railroading. From this experience he drew lessons that shaped the principles he would apply to all his future rail enterprises.[31]

Fish's election thrust the young Turks of the Illinois Central into a position of dominance. A solid corps of directors supported the new policies even though disagreements sometimes arose over tactics. By 1887 the expansion wars were in full swing, and no company could avoid confronting hard choices. The Illinois Central was building or acquiring nearly a thousand miles of new road, including a line connnecting the Iowa roads with Chicago, nearly 200 miles of branches in Iowa, and a number of southern feeder lines. Rapid growth strained both financial resources and administrative structures. During the spring of 1888 the board engaged in a lively debate over several issues: how best to pay for the new lines, how much to spend on improvements, what reforms were needed to administer the enlarged company efficiently, and how to deal with the worsening rate wars and the changing competitive environment.[32]

As vice-president Harriman played a major role in these debates, and he lost no opportunity to expand that role. In his eagerness to learn, to absorb everything he could about railroads, he stuck his nose into everyone's business. Finance was still his specialty, but now he also dealt with every aspect of management and operations, traffic matters and maintenance, organizational and legal problems, purchasing, and relations with other roads. He swam willingly through a sea of detail work, grasping the essence of each task without drowning in the minutia. If he did not have a photographic memory he did possess something near total recall, and during these years he was cramming his memory with useful data.

Although Fish valued Harriman's advice on finance and other matters, their relationship on the Illinois Central was less one of equals than of leader and protégé. Fish was no slouch when it came to finance, and he had shown genuine ability in rising to the presidency of a major railroad at the tender age of thirty-six. For all his affability, however, he was an imperious taskmaster who could address Harriman as ''My dear Ed'' one moment and scold him for some oversight or fault the next. The tone of their official correspondence left no doubt who was in charge, and Fish never forgot that Harriman owed his position in the company to him. Much of the difficulty between them in later years sprang from Fish's inability to accept how radically their original relationship had changed. During the next two decades Harriman was to grow by leaps and bounds while Fish merely grew older.[33]

In April 1889 the board took a major step toward grappling with the problems of growth and competition. A few months earlier the Illinois Central had declined to join the Interstate Commerce Railway Association, which had been organized to maintain rates. Fish believed the company's charter did not permit it to join such an association, but he vowed to maintain rates anyway. The board supported this position by adding a provision to Bylaw XI that no officer could reduce a rate in Illinois without first obtaining the president's approval. Through a peculiar chain of events this change thrust Harriman into an awkward dilemma.[34]

The new provision outraged general manager Edward T. Jeffery, who protested that he could not conduct traffic matters under such a policy unless the president or vice-president was stationed in Chicago. He offered to resign, which he had done at least twice before for other reasons. Fish planned to summer in Europe, leaving Harriman as acting president, and he wanted no trouble in his absence. For that reason he asked Jeffery to stay on until the end of the year. Later Jeffery claimed that in return Fish promised him a free hand with rates despite the strictures of Bylaw XI.[35]

But two weeks after Fish's departure on July 10, Jeffery announced publicly that he had resigned and would leave the company when Fish returned in October. His motives puzzled everyone. There was no apparent friction between him and Harriman, who spent most of July in Bar Harbor and did not go to Chicago until late August. On the morning of September 2, however, Jeffery stopped by his office to discuss the purchase of some locomotives. Harriman remarked in passing that while he was in Chicago he expected all rate questions to be referred to him in accordance with Bylaw XI.[36]

Jeffery eyed him in silence, then rose suddenly and said, ''If that's your decision, I quit, and will turn the road over to you at twelve o'clock to-day.'' Harriman asked him not to act hastily. ''Well,'' replied Jeffery, ''I quit at five o'clock and turn the road over to you.'' He mentioned the agreement with Fish; Harriman shrugged and said he had no choice but to enforce the bylaw. ''All right, then I quit,'' Jeffery repeated, and left.

This was Harriman's first crisis as a railroad man, and it bothered him greatly. He was a mere caretaker, and an inexperienced one at that, thrust into the position of losing one of the most respected railroad men in the Midwest.

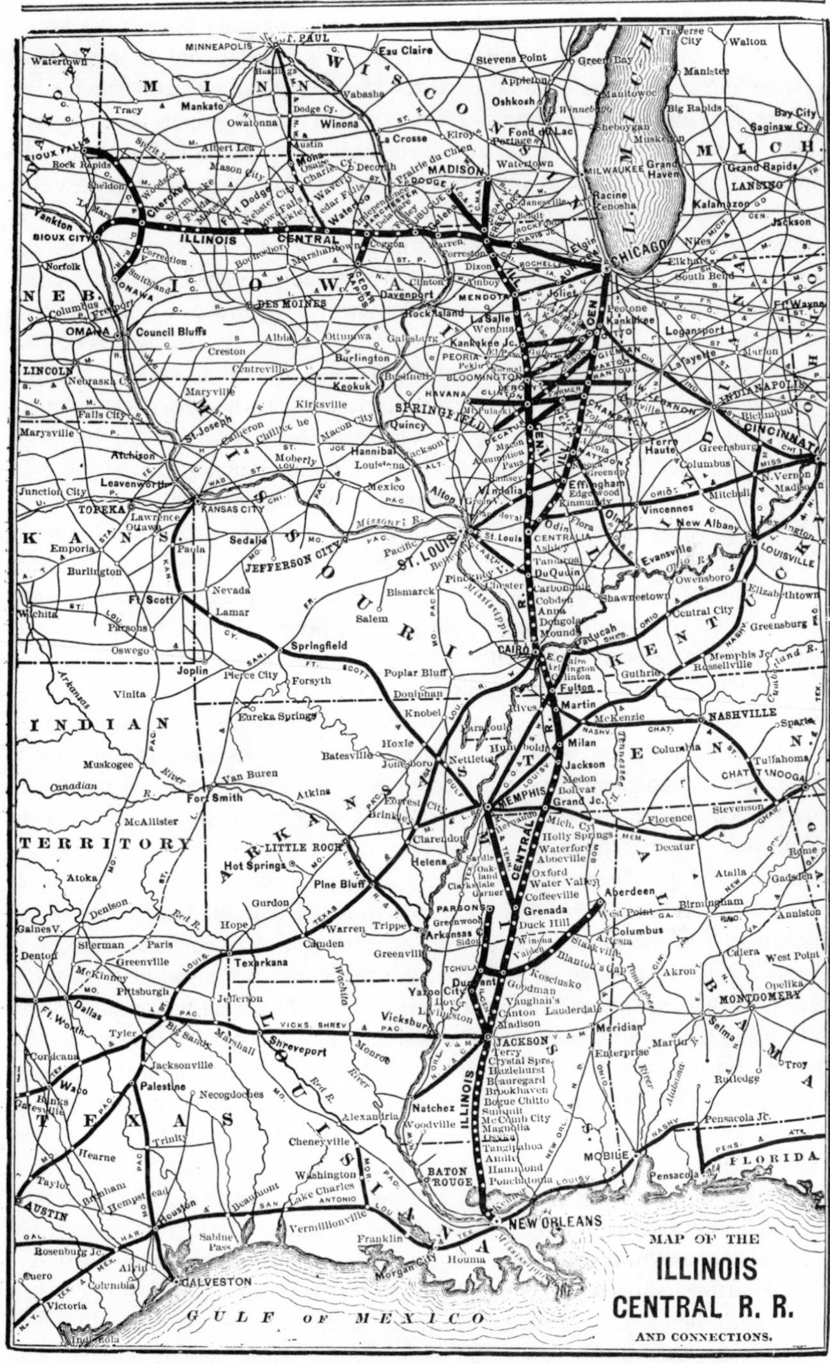

TRAINING GROUND: The Illinois Central Railroad, where Harriman learned the art of railroading. (*Commercial and Financial Chronicle, Investors' Supplement*, 1890)

Jeffery was quick to give the story of his departure to the papers, which showered him with praise and sympathy. Harriman was just as quick to justify his action to the board and to Fish, who wholly supported Harriman's action. He flatly denied any understanding with Jeffery, saying, "I neither agreed to have the By-Law suspended nor in any way authorized its suspension." In fact, he had specifically reminded Jeffery of the bylaw on May 31. The furor soon died down but repercussions lingered, because as usual there was more to the story than came to light in the newspapers or in later accounts.[37]

Jeffery's departure had a liberating effect on Harriman. It was as if he felt free now to move and act without the more experienced Jeffery peering over his shoulder. In the six weeks before Fish's return he worked like a demon on a new organizational plan and several other issues. Gradually it dawned on him that the much admired Illinois Central had long been a stodgy, cautious company standing still while time passed it by. The new board had done much, but much more remained to be done. Harriman was inspired, even obsessive, as he rushed after his vision with an explosive burst of energy.

From his southern superintendent Harriman gleaned the outline for an improved organization. Under Jeffery nothing was done without first getting authority from the general manager or general superintendent, which meant costly delays. "It is absolutely impossible for any General Manager to handle the details of a system like ours," the superintendent told Harriman, "and do justice to the Company and all the departments of its business." The district superintendents needed more autonomy, and Harriman proposed giving it to them. There would be a general manager and general superintendent in Chicago, with district superintendents for the Illinois, Iowa, and southern lines. These proposed changes would move the road toward a division organization.[38]

At the same time Harriman wanted to unify the roads north and south of the Ohio River. The new bridge over the Ohio River at Cairo would help accomplish this, and it was nearly finished. He launched exhaustive investigations of the traffic, operating, and machinery departments, searching for ways to improve their performance. This burst of activity must have puzzled Fish, who was absent for three months during a critical period in the railroad's history. Having lost touch with affairs, Fish found it difficult to catch the pace of events when he returned in October. It did not help that while he struggled to find his footing, Harriman was running full tilt. "The whole machine has now got a fresh start," Harriman exulted, "and we should not allow it to stand still or again to get into such a rut as it has been for some years past." In the next breath he poured out more suggestions for changes.[39]

Fish supported all the proposed reforms, but he sometimes differed with Harriman on details or timing. Although the program of change went forward, clashes between them grew more frequent. Fish and Harriman urged the board to step up expenditures for improvements and were asked to report on how much would be needed during the next three years. In December the board took up the new organizational code and approved it after lengthy discussion. The Jeffery affair made one important point: under the new code the president's office was moved to Chicago. This prospect did not exactly thrill Fish, and it left Harriman to handle affairs in New York by himself. Just as the move was being implemented, however, Harriman fell ill with the grippe and was confined to his house for a month.[40]

During his illness events took an unexpected turn. Months earlier a committee of the board had been asked to study the company's long-term needs and resources. Before submitting recommendations the committee wanted the report requested earlier of Fish and Harriman. With Harriman incapacitated, Fish put together a statement in mid-January strongly urging a policy of increased expenditures for improvements. A few days later the committee cautiously endorsed Fish's argument. Harriman received his copy of the report while lying abed, but he summoned enough strength to fire off a letter strongly opposing the committee's position. "It would be unwise at this time," he declared, "to pass *any* resolution adopting a policy for a large expenditure of money. Our organization is not prepared for it, we haven't sufficient information. It might lead to extravagance. Our whole force should be directed towards *making* and *saving* money."[41]

The five directors who were present at the meeting that received this letter read it and shook their heads in consternation. Why did Harriman suddenly oppose the policy he had always pushed so vigorously? Later he would be credited with remarkable sagacity in anticipating the coming depression, but there is no evidence for this foresight. It did not require genius to see that rates were falling, the competitive wars were worsening, and the bond market was softening. Worried by the financial outlook, Harriman wanted to go slow until it improved. He did not oppose the committee's policy so much as its timing. The new organization was just being implemented and, as he pointed out, was not yet ready to handle so ambitious a program of expenditures.[42]

In February 1890 the board debated the issue at length, then tabled the committee's recommendations until Fish and Harriman submitted a report on improvements. They complied in March with a shopping list totaling nearly $2.5 million for 1890 alone. The board dropped the committee's policy recommendation and, after some wrangling, approved only $612,500 of the items plus an unspecified amount for ballast. It was painfully clear that Fish and Harriman were as split as the directors. This division capped a situation that had arisen since Fish's return from Europe and grown steadily worse. Harriman seemed a different man to Fish, no longer deferential but with his own head of steam, as if he had tasted the power to command and liked it more than he dared say. Their views clashed on one issue after another, and Harriman did not give ground as easily as before.[43]

By March 1890 an open break seemed inevitable. Fish was still groping for some way to seize the reins of leadership that had in subtle ways slipped from his grasp since the trip to Europe. Harriman had plunged back into work after his illness in a way that convinced Fish he was not himself, that perhaps in his excitement he was hurtling toward a breakdown. He broached the matter to Harriman in what must have been a tense and awkward confrontation. Harriman agreed to take an extended leave from his duties for reasons of health and to surrender the vice-presidency when he returned.[44]

All this Fish conveyed privately to banker William Boissevain in Amsterdam. "The affair has been handled very quietly and in a dignified and decorous manner and so to admit of his dropping out with credit," he added, ". . . and I take pleasure in stating the fact that our differences do not relate so much to any personal act or projects as to the general policy and administration of the Company." Only the directors knew of the breach between them, and but a few of them suspected how serious it was.[45]

Fish was right; the affair did not rupture his friendship with Harriman, but it led to radical changes within the company. Harriman resigned as vice-president in June 1890 and thereafter confined himself to being chairman of the finance committee. The auditor was made first vice-president, and a new position of second vice-president was created to oversee the operations and traffic departments. To this post came J. T. Harahan, an officer from one of the subsidiary lines and the man who would later aid Harriman in ousting Fish from the presidency of the Illinois Central.[46]

These changes left the company firmly in Fish's hands while keeping Harriman in the function he performed best. They also refute the myth that Harriman's foresight saved the Illinois Central from possible ruin during the depression. In fact, his warning went unheeded. Although the board junked the committee's policy recommendation, Fish still spent nearly $5 million on improvements. These expenditures continued every year right into the teeth of the depression, even though the dividend had to be cut to 5 percent.[47]

Fish wanted to pay for improvements out of capital rather than earnings, by issuing new stock and asking current holders to subscribe. But an offering in 1890 fell flat. When only $1.5 million of the $5 million was taken, Fish was forced to enlist Harriman & Company to sell large blocks of shares. Two years later the company offered another $5 million in new stock and got subscriptions for a mere 319 shares. Once again the issue had to be sold off slowly. After some rugged going, the Illinois Central sailed through hard times with solid earnings and its 5 percent dividend intact.[48]

What role if any Harriman played in the policy to fund improvements through new stock issues is unclear. Certainly he was instrumental in devising and implementing the policy of funding expansion and refunding old obligations through new issues of low-interest bonds. Bankers appreciated that the Illinois Central's finances were well managed. Much of the credit for this reputation belonged to Harriman, as Fish himself once acknowledged in an expansive mood. "The measure of success which has been achieved by the company in the last twenty years, with regard to finances," he said in 1901, "is due to no man more than to the chairman of our finance committee, Mr. Harriman."[49]

But this praise was rendered after Harriman had burst into the public limelight. Prior to 1898 he dwelled in obscurity, devoting fifteen years to mastering the details of railroading in his own peculiar way that relied less on technical training than on a keen eye, an extraordinary memory, and a brain that worked at lightning speed. In the process he also absorbed a vast knowledge of the details of practical railroading, or more accurately the principles from which those details flowed.[50]

By 1898 Harriman was as well versed in railroading as many men who had spent their entire careers in the field. Many writers have stressed that he came late to this knowledge, but none have pointed out the immense advantage this gave him. Because Harriman entered the business at a time of transition from one era to another, the lessons he absorbed made him unusually well-equipped to deal with the industry at its current state of development. Being new to the game, he had nothing to unlearn before he could begin to learn. His mind was not cluttered with the traditions or shibboleths that shackled so many railroad men. He could look at things as they were rather than as he had once been told they were supposed to be. Those who sneered at him as a newcomer never understood what a great edge this flexibility was in an age of turbulent change.

3

The Reconstruction

The welcome accorded Harriman by the other members of the Union Pacific board during the winter of 1898 was neither cordial nor enthusiastic. Some viewed him as an intruder who was beneath them in terms of wealth, position, and achievement. One doubter was James Stillman, the powerful head of National City Bank, who later became one of Harriman's closest associates. Years earlier a prominent businessman had warned Stillman to "look out for Ed Harriman. He is not so smart as some people think, and he is not a safe man to have business with." The cautious Stillman had heeded this advice. When he encountered Harriman on the Union Pacific board, he remained cool and distant but watchful, willing to revise his prejudice if the evidence warranted.[1]

This reception was hardly surprising for a brash, combative newcomer who had elbowed his way onto the board. If Harriman was bothered by the hostility, however, he gave no sign of it. Instead, he set about earning the other directors' respect with a swiftness that took their breath away. Jacob Schiff had said that if Harriman showed himself the strongest man on the executive committee, he would surely get the chairmanship he coveted. Even that shrewd banker must have been astonished at seeing Harriman installed in the post only five months after the new board took office.

How did Harriman manage this feat? The standard explanation is that during those few months he impressed the other members with his energy and sagacity. No doubt he did this, but there is more to the story. Of the executive committee members appointed in December 1897, Harriman was the least known in business circles. Far from being a handicap, his relative obscurity proved a great advantage. His colleagues were all busy men preoccupied with other affairs. Winslow Pierce was a lawyer whose chief concern was acting as watchdog for the Gould interests; Otto Kahn and James Stillman were bankers who had no time or desire to take charge of a railroad. Marvin Hughitt *was* a railroad man but had his own company to run and could devote only limited attention to the Union Pacific.

Here was a vacuum waiting to be filled, and Harriman alone had the time and willingness to do it. He still played a prominent role in the Illinois Central, but his commitments were nothing compared to those of the other members. Once he impressed them with his knowledge of railroads as well as finance, the job was his by default. It took him only a few months to demonstrate his ability and convince the others he could be trusted. The bylaws provided that Pierce as chairman of the board also served as ex-officio chairman of the executive committee. During the spring of 1898 these were amended to create a separate chairman for the executive committee.[2]

On May 23, 1898, the executive committee elected Harriman its chairman with Pierce retaining his place as chairman of the board. Jubilantly the little man settled into a drab office on the Pine Street corner of the Equitable Building at 120 Broadway. His first act was to summon the Union Pacific's secretary, Alexander Millar, and announce that he had taken charge of the company's affairs.[3]

One of the hoariest myths about the Union Pacific is that Harriman found it in dilapidated shape when he came to the road. In later years everyone from journalists to Averell Harriman spread the image of "two streaks of rust" until it became a staple of the Harriman legend. The fit was too neat. What better way to demonstrate Harriman's masterful influence than to magnify the contrast between the decrepit road he inherited and the splendid property he left behind? Jacob Schiff was not above leaving that impression, and even the meticulous biographer, George Kennan, could not resist observing that "The condition of the property itself was deplorably bad." Averell Harriman put it far more vividly: "Its rusting rails were sinking into mud; its ties were rotted and broken, its rolling stock falling apart."[4]

However, the evidence tells a different tale. Far from being a wreck, the Union Pacific had been reasonably well maintained during the receivership. Silas Clark had no intention of letting it run down, nor did he have to. Since a bankrupt road did not have to pay interest on its bonds, it could apply more of its earnings to maintenance and improvements. Observers agreed the receivers had done just that and would have done more if earnings had not been so wretched. The government directors said as much in their reports, and the *Wall Street Journal* insisted repeatedly that the line was in good condition and ripe for the harvest of better times. "The Union Pacific road," said a typical article in January 1896, "is to-day in better shape than many Western roads which are apparently solvent and paying dividends."[5]

In October 1897, only two months before Harriman became a director, the *Journal* issued its strongest statement yet on the condition of the road:

> Under the receivership the whole property has been put in the most extraordinary fine condition. This was at the expense of the surplus. Just how good a condition the road is in can be accurately known to none but the reorganization committee, but it is no secret that instead of buying a worn-out property, the new company will get a system in as fine condition as anything in the West. New rails, new bridges, new rolling stock, passenger and freight, in fact everything that goes to make up a first-class railroad line.

This account exaggerated the improvements, but its main point was sound. Again and again the *Journal* hammered away at the theme that the reorganized Union Pacific was in good shape and its stock selling at undervalued prices. Harriman took this message seriously, though apparently few other investors did. Nor was the *Journal* alone in its assessment. Knowledgeable men like General Dodge, Alexander Millar, and operating official W. H. Bancroft, who had all been over the road, dismissed the "two streaks of rust" myth and described the line as at least comparable to other western roads. A rail official predicted in May 1898 that "The earnings of the Union Pacific in the next few years are going to be a surprise. . . . The company starts on what may be called the second period of its history with all the advantages it had prior to 1893, but with practically none of the disadvantages."[6]

Discarding this myth does not in the least diminish what Harriman did for the Union Pacific. On the contrary, the myth has long distorted his true accomplishments. Harriman did not find "two streaks of rust" or a broken-down railroad. What he found was a decent nineteenth-century western road that had to be overhauled to meet the demands of the twentieth century. His master stroke was to grasp this necessity before it dawned on other men and to gamble huge sums on his insight without a flicker of hesitation. Events proved him spectacularly right.

A few weeks after becoming chairman Harriman decided to inspect the road and its former branches for himself. He took along the five officers who had the most to tell him: president Horace Burt, chief engineer J. B. Berry, general manager Edward Dickinson, freight traffic manager J. A. Munroe, and passenger agent E. L. Lomax. In typical fashion he made the tour a mixture of business and pleasure by including his daughters Mary and Cornelia as well as a longtime friend, Dr. E. L. Trudeau. Harriman ordered up a special train with the Illinois Central private car *Marion* in front, some Union Pacific private cars and a baggage car in the middle, and the locomotive at the rear. This arrangement provided a cooling breeze to help slake the summer heat. It also allowed him to examine the roadbed, buildings, facilities, and anything else that caught his interest. As the officers soon discovered, nothing escaped his alert eye. For most of the trip the train ran only in daylight.[7]

Leaving Kansas City on the afternoon of June 17, the train ran across the old Kansas Pacific line to Denver and then to Colorado Springs. On the 22nd it returned to Denver and pushed on to Cheyenne, where it picked up the main Union Pacific line. After a short stay for sightseeing at Salt Lake City,

Harriman moved north over the Oregon Short Line, which the Union Pacific was in the process of reacquiring. At Pocatello the train turned north to the mining complexes at Butte and Anaconda. He met the shrewd but genial mining baron, Marcus Daly, and fell to arguing over whose favorite trotting horse was superior. Before parting they settled on a time and place for a race spiced with a wager of $10,000 on the outcome. On the way back the train paused at Boise before heading toward Umatilla and following the Columbia River from there to Portland.[8]

For the next few days the travelers amused themselves by taking in Mount Shasta and other sights along the route from Portland to San Francisco. At Monterey Burt hosted a dinner for everyone at the elegant Hotel Del Monte. After touring San Francisco they went on to Burlingame, where Julius Kruttschnitt, the general manager of the Southern Pacific, welcomed them with a luncheon. Possibly this was Harriman's first meeting with Kruttschnitt, a man who would later become invaluable to him. On July 6 the train left Oakland for the return trip over the Central Pacific and Union Pacific. Three days later it rolled into Omaha, having traveled 6,236 miles in twenty-three days.

On this journey the railroad officers got their first taste of the Harriman style and were dazzled by it. His energy and curiosity were insatiable. His eyes roamed everywhere, catching details others overlooked and forcing even veteran railroad men to ransack their experience on matters that had never occurred to them before. He fired questions nonstop on everything he saw, tough, searching questions delivered in a manner most of the officials thought brusque until they knew him better and realized it was merely economy of motion. Once impaled on his hook of inquiry, no one wriggled free until Harriman got an answer that satisfied him. He could not be fooled or put off because he seemed already to know so much, and smart officials sensed early that he was not a man to trifle with. In reply he said little and offered few opinions, leaving the others to stew in uncertainty.[9]

As the train approached Omaha on the last day of the journey, Harriman announced, "I have today wired New York for 5,000 shares of Union Pacific preferred at 66, and any one of you are welcome to take as few or as many shares as you like plus the interest until paid." This sort of gesture was rare; most financial men shrank from investing their own money in an enterprise until assured of its success. But Harriman was already convinced, and had for months been buying Union Pacific common at prices in the low twenties even though most analysts considered it of little value.[10]

So convinced was Harriman of what must be done that even before his return he telegraphed New York for authority to spend $25 million at once for improvements and new equipment. Everywhere in the West he saw signs of prosperity that promised a huge business if the road was ready to handle it. Labor and materials were still cheap from the depression but would nudge upward once the economy brightened; the time to act was now. In his eagerness to steal a march Harriman let some contracts for improvements and equipment on his own responsibility even though he knew some of the directors would balk at a request of that magnitude.[11]

The board did not merely balk; it bridled in alarm. Staggered by the figure, one director moaned that such extravagance would soon put the Union Pacific back into the hands of receivers. The question was tabled until Harriman arrived to argue his case in person. On July 14 he met with the executive committee for what Kahn called a "long and strenuous argument." After much shaking of heads and wringing of hands the members grudgingly approved Harriman's plan. The cocky little man had put his career and his reputation on the line; if he was wrong, the board would have his head.[12]

This decision marked the turning point in Harriman's career, the moment when the butterfly of genius fluttered from the cocoon of mere competence. It offers a classic illustration of his decision-making style and work methods, both of which have long been misunderstood. There exists a misconception of Harriman as a student of railroads who mastered their intricacies by immersing himself in detail. This image sprang from his uncanny ability to seize on an isolated detail and see flaws or possibilities that escaped other eyes. He once noticed, for example, that engines spent a long time taking on water and asked why the discharge pipes were only four or six inches in diameter. Back came the railroader's stock reply: because they had always been that way, nobody knew why exactly. Harriman ordered the pipes enlarged to twelve inches and crews discovered to their amazement that water stops took a lot less time.[13]

Unlike most men, Harriman's vision never became glazed by experience or convention. He was fond of saying that lack of imagination was a serious defect in any man. Although details gave him insights, they served merely as a point of departure from which he leaped to the larger picture. His genius lay in an ability to master the *principles* of how a railroad should be run and to grasp clearly the priorities for implementing them. There was something frightening, even inhuman, in the way his mind ingested, sorted, and synthesized data with the speed of a computer. That anyone could be so incisive and so quick and still reach sound conclusions awed those who knew him. No one described this ability better than one of his closest friends and associates, Judge Robert S. Lovett:

> His mental processes were unlike any that I have ever known. He never arrived at his conclusions by reason, or argument, or any deliberative process that I could observe. His judgments seemed to be formed intuitively. The proposition was presented to him and he saw it. It was much like turning a flash light on a subject. If interested, he saw it, and did not care and probably did not know how it was revealed. And his vision and measure of it was almost unfailingly clear and correct.[14]

Above all, Harriman possessed vision from which flowed one gigantic plan after another. Those who gasped at what he intended for the Union Pacific were dumbfounded to learn it was but a prelude to projects that would dwarf it. Harriman once remarked to a broker that he laid his railroad plans ten or twelve years in advance, an exaggeration that contained just enough truth to startle people.[15]

Having vision is one thing, implementing it quite another. What separates entrepreneurs from dreamers is their willingness to risk everything on bringing their ideal to reality. Harriman was so utterly fearless in this respect that others thought him reckless. He was not reckless so much as supremely confident of his plans and ability to realize them. Once he saw what must be done, he moved like a juggernaut to accomplish it. No question of cost or magnitude or risk gave him pause if he was sure of his concept, and no obstacle deflected him from his goal.

The money for improvements was not spent all at once but parceled out over time. At the July 14 meeting the only expenditure approved was the purchase of 30,000 tons of steel rail. Nevertheless, a start had been made on a commitment that would reach staggering dimensions. Before Harriman was done he would spend $98 million for improvements and equipment and another $62 million on constructing or acquiring new lines for the Union Pacific.[16]

Harriman's approach to this work utterly refutes the myth of him as a man of detail. The key for him was not how much detail he knew but how well he trusted the officer in charge. He was slow to give men his confidence, but once given he relied heavily on their judgment. "Unless he could trust a man implicitly," observed Julius Kruttschnitt, "he would soon replace him with one he *could* trust." Harriman told his officers what he wanted, asked their advice, looked at their reports, decided what must be done, and left the rest to them. Far from wanting a mountain of data from them, he insisted to their astonishment that reports even on complex matters be boiled down to a page or two at most. Harriman did not like to waste time reading or poring over details. He wanted the essentials of the case, and if the men who provided them did their job well he could make decisions on that basis quickly and effectively.[17]

This was why it was crucial for Harriman to have the right men in key positions. Like Gould, he understood that he could not accomplish large things without reliable subordinates to execute his plans. If the officers did their job well, Harriman left them alone to do it in their own way. "He always said to the railroad people," recalled chief engineer J. B. Berry, "that he looked to them for results and that he did not expect to instruct them in it." Harriman dished out little criticism and even less praise. He never quibbled over costs and never complained when costs overran estimates even by large amounts if he got the results he wanted. Officers felt his lash only when they failed to perform. Harriman made his share of mistakes in appointing men, but they got short shrift when their ineptness surfaced. He expected the officers to pull together and would not tolerate infighting.[18]

According to Samuel M. Felton, who worked ten years in important positions for Harriman, it was never easy working for him. "I say work *for*," Felton emphasized, "because no one worked *with* him. He was always the sole director, and sometimes imperious and arbitrary." He tested a man's mettle thoroughly before giving him free rein, and set an exhausting pace that he expected others to match. In his zeal to save time and energy he used the telephone incessantly, and when it would not serve he used the telegraph like

CLOSE QUARTERS: E. H. Harriman at his crowded and very unpretentious desk, the indispensable telephone at his elbow.

others used the telephone, snapping off inquiries or instructions in his succinct style. In handling correspondence he had his secretary read telegrams to him and usually had the reply framed before the reading finished. He disliked writing letters as much as he did reading them and so kept them to a minimum. One reason he detested letters was the inability of any stenographer to keep up with him.[19]

Felton, who was methodical like most railroad men, could find no system in Harriman's work habits, no manner of proceeding in logical order. He leaped from this project to that one, mixing large matters and small indiscriminately, keeping the whole in harmony by his phenomenal memory. Harriman seldom took notes yet seemed to remember everything in a way that enabled him to recall the smallest detail years later.

What was it in this little dynamo that gripped people and won them to his plans? Stillman thought that of all the prominent men he had known, none excelled Harriman "in his conceptions of vast achievements, and in his skill and energy and daring in bringing his conceptions to fruition." There was genius, a colossal intellect, and something more: a peculiar magnetism that drew even skeptics into his orbit as satellites to his plans. "He would not only convert you but would keep you converted," marveled Felton. "The better you knew him, the more confidence you had in him. He had unbounded confidence in himself, and probably this confidence was so overwhelming that few could resist it."[20]

* * *

Even before Harriman took charge of the executive committee he was busy laying the groundwork for his program. The basic formula for success in the new era was simple but expensive. Payloads could be increased by running longer trains and using larger equipment. This required heavier locomotives, which in turn required straighter track, lower grades, good ballast, and stronger bridges to operate at maximum efficiency. To undertake all these tasks at once meant a huge outlay of funds that few managers were willing or able to make.

During the winter of 1898 Harriman asked chief engineer Berry to gather information on what costs and savings would result from reducing grades, straightening curves, and shortening distance on the line. Few railroads had looked closely at this question, which meant data was meager in general and nonexistent for the Union Pacific. Berry saw he would have to compile it from scratch with surveys, estimates, and careful investigation. As the data came in, he logged it on a one-by-two foot map showing the present and proposed lines with a table itemizing the cost of changes on each section and the savings expected from them. Harriman liked the map and the way it presented everything he needed in concise form. The price tag for the proposed changes was $9 million.[21]

To Berry's surprise, Harriman did not even blink at the cost. He summoned several officers to New York and herded them into a meeting of the executive committee along with the map. After only fifteen minutes of discussion the request for $9 million was referred to the chairman with authority to act. The phrase "referred to the chairman with authority" would soon become a theme song of executive committee meetings, and Harriman wasted no time acting. The officers from Omaha received orders to start the work before they left the room. Berry was astonished at the ease with which so large a sum had been approved. A lesson had been impressed on him: money for improvements would flow if he could demonstrate the savings.

A shorter, straighter, sounder track did more than improve times. It permitted the use of heavier equipment and longer trains, which meant huge savings in costs on much greater quantities of freight. Harriman grasped early the prime imperative of the new era: to make money a road had to haul immense loads at low rates as efficiently as possible. On a western road this could not be done with the older, lightweight engines and small rolling stock. Harriman therefore had to upgrade not only the line but also the equipment as rapidly as possible. He stressed the importance of replacing the old twenty-ton wooden cars with forty- or fifty-ton steel ones. The reasoning was as simple as the conception was bold. A twenty-ton car had a capacity roughly equal to its own weight. An average locomotive, weighing about fifty tons, had less than ten tons of tractive power. Larger cars and more powerful engines, operating on a smooth, straight track, would enable the road to double the capacity of a train with only a minimal increase in operating expenses.[22]

As a first step Harriman ordered many box and stock cars converted into flat cars for construction use by removing their superstructures. He instructed superintendent W. L. Park to spend no more than ten dollars for repairs on any old car. Horace Burt, the Union Pacific's president, was asked to prepare an inventory of existing equipment. His tabulation revealed that 3,597 of the company's freight cars, nearly 20 percent of the total, had been built before 1880. Some 1,180 cars of all types were worn out entirely, as were 43 of the company's 531 locomotives. The Nebraska division still used the old 4-4-0 "American" engine as its standard power. It could haul only twenty or thirty of the lighter cars, making up a train that in Harriman's eyes belonged in a museum. He moved to put it there as speedily as possible.[23]

Even before Harriman returned from his inspection trip the executive committee approved an equipment request for 10 engines, 650 cars, and 2 unusual items: 2 sixty-ton steam shovels and 300 Rodger ballast cars, the latter a design so new the inventor had to come show the men how to unload them. Harriman knew the Rodger cars from his Illinois Central days and wanted them to help rid the Union Pacific of a cruel irony. For decades the road had been poorly ballasted even though it contained a rich supply of excellent ballast—especially the disintegrated granite gravel on Sherman Mountain. The problem had always been lack of heavy equipment to dig the gravel and sufficient equipment to haul it. The new steam shovels could load 200 yards of gravel an hour, and a Rodger car could carry 30 cubic yards of it. Together they soon had entire train loads of gravel for ballast flowing east and west.[24]

Throughout the work of reconstruction Harriman leaned most heavily on Burt and Berry. It helped greatly that the president, a blunt, humorless, rather pompous man, was an engineer who could look at projects with a trained eye even if he and Berry did not always agree on what they saw. Harriman drove them relentlessly, first for advice on what work to undertake and then for results once he decided to go ahead. "He never measured what the capacity of a man might be," Berry moaned, "but just simply piled on work, expecting it to be taken care of."[25]

East of Cheyenne the line needed little straightening except for the infamous "ox-bow" created in 1864–65 by the meddling of Silas Seymour. But it did need ballasting, and before that could be done the skinny shoulders had to be widened. Crews fanned out along the line to strengthen embankments, add new sidings or extend old ones, lay down new ties and heavier steel. Every year the work pressed forward until the entire roadbed from Omaha to Ogden was widened and ballasted with Sherman gravel or slag. Ninety-pound rails took the place of seventy-pound steel that only a few years earlier had been regarded as standard for heavy traffic.[26]

In 1903 Burt and Berry urged Harriman to attack the ox-bow itself. A new double-track line, they argued, would cut twenty-two miles down to twelve, reduce the grade nearly eighteen feet, eliminate 260 degrees of curvature, and do much to relieve the traffic congestion around Omaha. Current business did not fully justify the expenditure, Berry admitted, but an increase of 25 percent would pay for the work. By 1903 Berry had learned how Harriman's thinking always looked beyond present conditions to future growth. The project was approved but progress on the Lane cutoff went forward slowly. Not until May

GOODBYE, OX-BOW: Creating a large fill on the Lane Cutoff, completed in May 1908.

1908 did the new line open on virtually the same route originally surveyed by Peter Dey more than forty years earlier.[27]

The hardest work lay west of Cheyenne in the Black Hills, the Wyoming desert, and the Utah mountains. Berry looked first at the two nearest horror spots, the high bridge at Dale Creek and Sherman summit, the highest point on the line, where a fleet of fifteen helper engines was needed to assist trains up the slopes. Any reconstruction in Wyoming would have to work around the most overtaxed and underpowered operating division on the road, and it would have to battle the climate at altitudes where winter arrived in September and stayed until April or May. Old General Dodge never let anyone forget that he had personally found the original line across the Black Hills. No one had since found a better one, but Berry determined to try. He sent out a force of engineers who poked around for months before reporting that the line he wanted did not exist. Not good enough, replied Berry stonily; go back and try again. The engineers trudged back and searched until they found a line that suited Berry.[28]

The problem for the engineers was less one of location than of vision. They could not at first imagine change on a scale that measured fills in millions rather than thousands of cubic yards or comprehend the immensity of the cuts and tunnels required. Once the vastness of the project penetrated their minds, they had no trouble locating a good line in the most unlikely places. Berry was the first to admit that Dodge and his engineers had done their work brilliantly, but they could never have managed this new route. The original builders had

HIGH LINE: A train snakes through the spectacular Fish Cut near Green River. Original line can be seen just below.

neither the time nor the money to build a better line, nor the amount of traffic to warrant the expense. Even more, they lacked the tools and machinery for so gigantic an undertaking aside from the inconvenience of fending off hostile Indians. The reconstruction was an idea whose time had come, not one that was long overdue.[29]

Berry improved on the Dale Creek bridge and Sherman summit by doing away with them altogether. He crossed the summit at a point 250 feet lower than the original line by relocating thirty miles of track and boring an 1,800-foot tunnel through solid granite. In the spring of 1900 a huge work force landed at Sherman, the vanguard of 131,332 men who would ultimately toil on the cutoff. Eight steam shovels rumbled into place, and behind them fifteen locomotives, each hauling ten to eighteen dump cars. Electric lights were strung up so that the digging could proceed around the clock, and pipes were installed to feed the machine drills run by compressed air. There were pumping stations and blacksmith forges along with all the support facilities needed to sustain so large an army.[30]

The results of all this preparation were spectacular. At Dale Creek a fill 900 feet long and 120 feet high swallowed 475,000 cubic yards of gravel. Lone Tree Creek got the same treatment: a fill 130 feet high and 300 feet long absorbed 350,000 cubic yards of gravel. The changes allowed Berry to impose a new standard grade of 43.3 feet across the Black Hills except for one westbound stretch between Cheyenne and Buford, a far cry from the old grades ranging from 68 to 98 feet per mile. By resorting to one clever device after another, Berry managed to descend gracefully into Laramie with his 43-foot grade only 18 miles long. An immense amount of curvature had been eliminated as well, and all this had been accomplished by adding only a fraction of a mile to the length of the line.

Passengers riding the new route noticed two striking changes besides the smoother, straighter roadbed. The celebrated bridge at Dale Creek was taken down and vanished into history, where it could no longer stop the hearts of travelers, and the great stone monument erected in honor of Oakes and Oliver Ames sat in forlorn isolation at the highest point on the original line, an abandoned relic far from the sight of those who now rode the Union Pacific. Both had become casualties of progress.

Across Wyoming and Utah the engineers brooked no obstacle in their quest to straighten the line. Three cutoffs between Howell and Dana alone consumed 5.4 million cubic yards of fill. The toughest rock work lay three miles west of Green River, where a new line was gouged out of the shale ledges. The longest one drew the name "Fish Cut" after the crews uncovered large deposits of petrified fish in the rocks. So much curvature vanished that in one four-mile stretch the new line crossed the old one seven times. Only in one other place—Weber and Echo canyons—did the terrain defeat Berry's efforts to impose 43-foot grades, and even there he greatly improved the grades and alignment.[31]

A dispute arose over what to do with the old line between Cheyenne and Laramie, which crossed the new line at nearly a right angle. A second track was urgently needed across the summit, but no one wanted to use the old route because it was lefthand westbound and located some miles from the new line. Although Burt conceded that a new second track would be expensive, he objected to having a line "straggling out into the country like a sore thumb." Only Superintendent Park made a case for using the old line as a second track. He was overruled; the matter hung fire for months while crews started work on double-tracking the new line.[32]

In Omaha one day Park learned that word had come to take up the old line. Dejected, he returned to Cheyenne and learned that an important stock train had been delayed two hours at Sherman's hill. Park saw his chance; he wired this news to the general manager and shrewdly sent Harriman a copy. At once an order came from New York to leave the track in place until the executive committee discussed the matter. Later Harriman told Park it took him about one minute to decide that Park's argument was sound. The old route was kept and upgraded to main-line standards.

Everyone from top to bottom felt the pressure to move the work. "Of course, men fell by the wayside," Park admitted. "The pace was terrific; those without brain and brawn got out of the way. The elimination was, however, the survival of the fittest; there was no favoritism; those who made good were remembered, those who did not were forgotten."[33]

This was exactly what Harriman wanted. Performance was all that counted with him. Returning from another inspection trip in July 1899, Harriman declared that the improvements program had not gone far enough, and that much larger expenditures were needed. For the next three years executive committee meetings became an unbroken litany of one large appropriation after another for betterments or equipment. Their approval seemed at times a mere formality. When Harriman received the yearly request for funds from Burt, he told the president to go ahead and arrange the work even though committee approval would not be forthcoming until the next meeting. No obstacle was allowed to slow progress or defeat his plans, no problem was too large or too difficult to be conquered. Not even the Aspen tunnel.[34]

On a particularly troublesome stretch between Leroy and the Bear River, Berry saw a way to eliminate nearly ten miles out of twenty-one, reduce grade from sixty-eight to forty-three feet, and eliminate 1,371 degrees of curvature. To do all this he needed a tunnel 5,900 feet long, which seemed simple enough until the crews attacked the job. The first borings in the spring of 1899 revealed limestone on the east portal and shale on the west. As they pushed inside the headings they found rich seams of coal, oil, and water. They also noticed that openings made one day tended to close up or shift position by the next. Gradually they discovered that carboniferous shale, once exposed to air, swelled with devastating force. The thrust came mostly from below but pushed and squeezed in every direction, its behavior as unpredictable as that of a drunken giant.[35]

The crews braced the opening with twelve-by-ten Oregon pine timbers only to find them snapped like twigs the next day. One engineer swore he saw timbers snapped in different directions within the same four-foot section. Another was standing on a floor of solid planks one day when, to his astonishment, it rose with a fierce cracking noise nearly three feet into the air. Steel I-beams used to reinforce the timbers didn't snap but merely buckled from the upthrust, as if the giant had crumpled them in his fingers. Wall plates fastened in proper alignment twisted overnight into grotesque formations. To hold everything in place the men applied a thick layer of concrete over the beams and timbers.

In August a shaft was sunk three hundred feet, but water and oil flooded in and chased the men out. When they tried again, gas seeped up as well, triggering an explosion that hurled men, mules, and beams out of the heading like a cannon shot. The funerals slowed progress and made some of the men fearful and superstitious enough to leave. Kilpatrick Brothers & Collins, the contractors, braced for a long siege. They had done Union Pacific work for twenty years—Collins was a nephew of former president Sidney Dillon—and they had no intention of losing face to a tunnel. To bolster their depleted work force they sent south for some black men with tunnel experience and summoned Virgil Bogue, former chief engineer for the Union Pacific, as consultant. They procured the best machinery available and ran two level tracks into each heading, one for material cars and the other for a steam shovel mounted on a flat car. No one could remember seeing a steam shovel used inside a tunnel before.[36]

By August 1900 the crews had fought their way 2,260 feet into the headings, leaving another 3,640 feet to go. They were averaging about 13½ feet a day despite water problems that threatened to turn the tunnel into a river, pumping 65,000 to 100,000 gallons daily. Then the west-heading crew struck a flow that overwhelmed their pumps. Despite emptying out 317,000 gallons in twenty-four hours, they watched helplessly as the water rose three feet above the wall plates and forced them to abandon the tunnel. A discouraged Berry feared the work might not get finished until spring; in fact, it took more than another year. The Aspen tunnel, its rails set in a thick bed of concrete, finally opened for business in October 1901, two and a half years after the first borings.[37]

Although most of the reconstruction work was completed by 1902, it never stopped during Harriman's lifetime. By 1909 the Union Pacific had built 253 miles of road on its main line and Kansas division alone. The new line was 54 miles shorter than the old one and had 4,470 feet less grade. Some 9,255 degrees of curvature or nearly twenty-six complete circles had been eliminated and the maximum curvature reduced from 6 to 4 degrees. The roadbed had been widened to a standard of twenty feet and ballasted with gravel or rock. Most of it was laid with eighty- or ninety-pound rail on new ties of uniform size with heavier tie plates. A new, heavier connector, known as the continuous joint, was fast replacing the old chairs and fish plates. During the eight years after 1901 the Union Pacific laid 2,428 miles of new steel, 6,146 miles of ties, and 2,818 miles of tie plates. To veteran railroaders it seemed nothing less than a miracle. An engineer who had worked on the original line traveled over the new one and shook his head in wonder at the difference.[38]

Nor did it stop there. Harriman understood that the transformation he envisioned had a domino effect that did not allow him to launch one project without tackling several others at the same time. If he installed heavier equipment and a wider roadbed, for example, he would also need larger and stronger bridges. Between 1898 and 1909 the Union Pacific replaced 98,603 feet of wooden bridges with embankments or new iron, steel, or concrete spans. Wood was not the only target; older iron bridges deemed too light for modern traffic requirements were also torn down and new ones built.[39]

Double-tracking also posed a problem for bridges, and the rapid growth of business made it an urgent need. "For a long time it has been evident," declared Burt in November 1899, "that the West had outgrown single-track trunk lines and was ready for such roadbeds as are the rule in the East." No other transcontinental road cared to undertake this costly task, yet Harriman plunged into it right in the middle of his reconstruction work. Burt's comments inaugurated a program to double-track the most congested areas of the line and ultimately the entire route from Omaha to Ogden as well as the Kansas division. By the spring of 1910 half the main line had a second track in operation. In addition, longer side tracks were put in, and more of them. Between 1901 and 1909 some 659 miles of new siding was built and 159 miles of old siding taken up.[40]

The old water tanks along the road consisted of huge tubs holding about

25,000 gallons set on frame bents in an inclosed shed with a stove below to keep the water from freezing. The water was driven by windmills or hand pumps, and when the wind failed, section hands or sometimes the train crew itself had to man the pumps. Harriman did more than enlarge the four-inch spouts on these tubs to twelve inches; he replaced them altogether with 60,000-gallon steel vats run by steam or gasoline engines that retired the windmills. In the bad-water districts thirty-six water softeners were erected to keep impurities out of engines, and pipelines were built to carry good water into areas that had none. The larger, thirstier locomotives coming on line got not only more water but better water.[41]

Coal chutes got the same treatment. The older, primitive ones were little more than platforms at intermediate stations where coal was either shoveled onto engines by hand or carried aboard in boxes by the brakemen. During the 1880s a few chutes had been erected at district terminals. Cars were run up an incline by an engine and coal shoveled into pockets from which it was dumped onto the engine. The newer chutes installed by Harriman used a double-track structure that accepted coal from three tracks, two underneath and one at the side. Coal was dumped from cars into a bin and run by conveyor to the top of a chute, where crushers mashed it into proper size for engines. The chutes also had sand bins or pneumatic sanders so that locomotives could take on coal and sand at the same time. Some also had water cranes as well, eliminating another stop.[42]

Block signals became a priority item, as did the elimination of grade crossings. In 1897 the Union Pacific had block signals on less than ten miles of track. Once past the heaviest reconstruction work, Harriman launched an ambitious program in 1904 to install automatic block signals on the entire line. Using a mixture of mechanical and electric signals, the system covered the main line and much of the Kansas Division by 1908, or 1,529 miles in all. A railroad journal noted that Harriman's chief officer had "taken everybody's breath away by his bold expenditures" for signals. Small wonder he was impressed: as late as 1921 only 39,000 miles or about 16 percent of American track had automatic block signals; by 1909 the Harriman system already had more than 5,000 miles. At Council Bluffs the company installed an electric interlocking plant to handle train movements from the east end of the Missouri River bridge to the Omaha transfer station.[43]

Facilities all along the line were upgraded, rebuilt, or enlarged. Omaha welcomed a new union depot in 1899, and the shops there underwent a drastic overhaul that took years to complete. The Omaha shops owned a reputation for innovation before Harriman took charge. In 1890, for example, they began using compressed air for the handling of heavy materials and within six years filled the shops with pneumatic apparatus designed and built right there. But they needed more space and more machinery. New shops were added and old ones enlarged, central heating and electric lighting were installed—all with an eye to making the work cheaper and more efficient. Every addition was planned meticulously with input from those who had to use it. The design of the new blacksmith shop, for example, was not approved until representatives

BRIGHT NEW LOOK: The renovated Omaha machine shop in 1903.

from every department involved had a chance to discuss it and offer suggestions. The *Railroad Gazette* hailed the new car shop as a model of what the "latest practice" should be. Facilities at Cheyenne, Pocatello, Salt Lake City, and elsewhere got similar improvements.[44]

An old idea was revived in 1903 when the company opened two wood treatment plants. The original attempt back in the 1860s to burnettize ties to protect them from decay had flopped, but technology and technique had improved since then. The new plants could burnettize more than two million ties a year and creosote large quantities of other wood fixtures. Still another ancient facility rose from the dead in 1906 when the Union Pacific rebuilt the old Laramie Rolling Mill to handle the huge amounts of iron and scrap accumulated during the reconstruction. The rejuvenated mill produced bar iron, bridge and track material, tie plates, and rail fastenings for current use.[45]

The outpouring of new facilities staggered veteran railroaders long accustomed to penny-pinching policies. In little over a decade the Union Pacific put up 58 new stockyards, a dozen icehouses, 45 section houses, 36 depots, 7 roundhouses, and 274 miscellaneous buildings. The stockyards at major terminals featured two tracks so that one train could be loaded while another was being unloaded, dipping vats, scales, branding chutes, hotels for the buyers and drovers, electric lights for night loading, and trained goats. Why trained goats? Unloading sheep at night proved a problem because the animals were afraid to leave the cars until someone hit on the idea of using trained goats to lead them out of one car into another. On the new railroad even judas goats had to work nights.[46]

Old section houses, most of them weathered shacks made of rough boards, gave way to neat, two-story buildings with stone foundations and plaster walls, built away from the tracks to leave the view unobstructed. Comfortable bunkhouses went up for laborers, maintenance houses for signal maintainers, and trim little cottages with indoor plumbing and other amenities for agents, dispatchers, and other officials. At Green River the sleeping quarters included a recreation building to keep the men from "influences of a different character," as an officer delicately phrased it.[47]

Many old depots were little more than shacks made of boards nailed up right on the framing with the cracks battened. Some still had on their rough, weatherbeaten doors graffiti in the form of horses and wild animals carved by passing Indians. Harriman ordered them torn down and replaced by modern buildings with steam heat and comfortable waiting rooms. He was adamant that they be put in the right place; one depot was moved twice and still did not satisfy disputes over its location. Harriman paused long enough to inspect the scene personally and had it moved to a third spot, where it remained.[48]

Even the telegraph line was spruced up. The original line amounted to two wires strung on small poles of different sizes and powered by gravity batteries placed along with repeating offices (that received messages and repeated them) every 200 miles or so. Under Harriman the line was redone with larger poles and heavier copper wire, 30,000 miles of it, run by dynamos instead of batteries, with circuits every 500 to 1,000 miles. Even a modern telegraph system was not enough to suit Harriman, who was personally addicted to the telephone. At the time of his death the Union Pacific was stringing 2,000 miles of telephone train-dispatching lines along the system.[49]

Harriman wanted not only an efficient line but an attractive one as well. Parks were installed at several terminals and major towns along the line. The barren alkali desert of Wyoming posed a special challenge. During one of his tours Harriman stopped at Rock Springs, one of the top revenue-producing stations on the Union Pacific, and was dismayed by the bleak landscape. "Why don't you put in a little park here?" he asked the superintendent. "The station is of attractive design, and some green grass and a little shrubbery would freshen things up wonderfully."

"Mr. Harriman," interrupted a local resident, "there is not a sprig of grass in Rock Springs; not because we do not want it, but because the percentage of alkali in the soil is an absolute bar to its growth."

"Nothing is impossible," declared Harriman, his eye fixed not on the local but on his superintendent.

The startled officer took his cue. Hundreds of cars filled with the best soil he could find were hauled to Rock Springs and distributed around the depot until there was enough to sow grass and plant shrubs and trees. Nor was Rock Springs the only place to be beautified. Once the officer understood that Harriman was willing to spend money on such amenities, he cultivated parks at Cheyenne, Rawlins, Green River, and other spots. As the plantings spread, section foremen took the hint and began putting in trees and flowers until the line came to resemble an oasis of greenery in the desert. Harriman admired the beauty of the parks and plantings, but he saw in them something more: an example to the employees of neatness, of doing things the proper way and taking pride in the results.[50]

"Going on an inspection trip with him was an ordeal," admitted Samuel M. Felton. "I have been on many of them, and was always glad to get out more or less alive. He noticed everything; he asked you about everything, and he compared what he saw and what he heard with what he had seen and heard on all previous trips over the same line. . . . I have no idea how he did all this; but he apparently did it without effort."[51]

What had Harriman wrought? In little over a decade he spent $160 million, of which $18 million went for line changes, $62 million for the construction and acquisition of new lines, $40 million for rolling stock, $8 million for second track, and $32 million for other betterments, including $2.5 million for new signals alone. For that money he got a modern railroad, perhaps the most efficient of its size in the nation, equipped in every way to handle the flood of traffic that crashed down on it between 1898 and 1910. The line, the roadbed, and the facilities had been transformed to accommodate a new breed of heavier equipment running in longer trains on faster schedules with greater frequency than ever before. The figures below reveal strikingly the gain in performance compared to other roads:[52]

		UNION PACIFIC	MISSOURI PACIFIC	ATCHISON	BURLINGTON	ROCK ISLAND
REVENUE PER MILE	1892	$5621	$5146	$5115	$6043	$5450
"	1902	8167	6680	7528	6634	7309
OPERATING RATIO	1892	66.7	72.6	69.2	68.1	69.9
"	1902	49.9	66.8	57.3	63.2	61.6

Numbers alone barely hint at the Harriman revolution in equipment. During the period 1901–1909 the Union Pacific bought 522 new locomotives, 258 passenger cars, 12,499 freight cars, and 707 work cars. But Harriman did not simply pile up new cars and engines. Between 1899 and 1909 the locomotive fleet on the Union Pacific proper increased only 11 percent from 549 to 660 and cars of all types 20 percent from 16,061 to 17,899. At the same time mileage operated rose 36 percent from 2,422 to 3,306 and tonnage carried more than tripled. How did the company move this crush of traffic with only modest gains in its rolling stock?[53]

The key lay in Harriman's determination not merely to increase equipment but to transform it entirely. A more revealing insight can be found by looking at what Harriman discarded rather than at what he added. In his zeal to rid the company of inefficient lightweight engines and cars with small capacities, he often junked or sold old equipment faster than he acquired replacements. For half the years mentioned above the Union Pacific actually showed a net decrease in equipment. When Harriman got rid of 1,094 cars during his first eighteen months on the job, it proved a harbinger of things to come. Between 1901 and 1909 the Union Pacific system scrapped 343 locomotives and 7,596 cars of all types. In their place came heavier locomotives and larger cars with greater capacities.[54]

The results were impressive. Between 1902 and 1909 the average weight of Union Pacific locomotives (excluding tender) rose from 66.2 to 82.5 tons and the average capacity of freight cars from 27.2 to 37.2 tons. In 1901 the system had 300 eight-wheel locomotives; by 1909 only 104 remained. During those same years the number of 2-8-0 Consolidation engines jumped from 148 to 440. The fleet of Ten Wheelers (4-6-0) used for passenger trains went from 257 to 281, and 44 larger Pacific locomotives (4-6-2) were also added. Nearly all the new cars had steel underframes, and by 1900 Harriman looked to buying all-steel cars of every type from postal and passenger to box and coal cars. Steel cars cost half again as much but were lighter, more durable, lived longer, and cost less to repair. Careful records kept on repair costs showed an average savings on steel cars of about 35 percent.[55]

This upgrading, coupled with an improved line, yielded striking gains. In 1898 an average train hauled 280 tons of freight; eleven years later the figure had nearly doubled, to 552 tons. The rolling stock of 1909 averaged 20.4 tons of freight per car compared to only 11.9 tons in 1898. The number of loaded cars per train increased from an average of 21.5 in 1899 to 27.1 in 1909. Put differently, the number of loaded cars per train rose 26 percent, but the amount of freight hauled soared 97 percent. This combination of new equipment and new roadway drove the operating ratio steadily down from a high of 63.6 percent in 1898 to 47.2 percent in 1909 at a time when costs were rising steadily and rates were being held in check. An earlier generation of railroad men achieved low operating ratios by scrimping everywhere and letting the property go to seed. Harriman did it by investing huge sums in improvements so that trains could run more cheaply. This approach enabled the Union Pacific to carry an enormous volume of traffic at low rates and still reap large profits.

And yet these improvements were barely enough to meet the demand. The traffic pouring onto western lines exceeded the wildest expectations of railroad men. It swamped and outstripped facilities everywhere, even in the East on the mighty Pennsylvania and New York Central systems. Harriman stole a march on most of his rivals by anticipating this deluge. An analyst applauding Harriman's foresight in 1905 noted that "Traffic is so heavy now on all roads that no old car can be spared so long as it hangs together, and the demand for new equipment is so heavy that no road can begin to get what it wants from the equipment companies. The Harriman lines are in better condition in this respect than any others. . . ."[56]

The officers of the Union Pacific got the message early. In 1900 they were instructed to prepare estimates of whatever items their departments would need for the next five years. "We grew so fast," smiled Berry, "that this statement was not worth the paper it was written on at the end of twelve months." They would scramble frantically for a decade trying to keep up with the demand for rail service.[57]

What difference did the reconstruction make in this scramble? In 1897 the company ran fifteen freight and four passenger trains on the main line. By 1909 freight trains had increased 25 percent and passenger trains a startling 70 percent. Serious problems of congestion arose and would have been much worse without the improvements Harriman made. Traffic density (gross ton miles per mile of road) by 1909 had jumped 186 percent since 1896, yet train density (number of trains per mile of road) increased only 82 percent. During that same period the number of meeting points (places where trains meet and one must give way) rose 235 percent. Nothing slowed train schedules or clogged the line more than an excess of meeting points. Despite this rise, the ability to run fewer trains carrying heavier loads instead of more trains with lighter loads greatly reduced the number of meeting points. If the improvements are factored out and the Union Pacific operated in 1909 as it had in 1896, train density would have increased 180 percent and meeting points an astounding 689 percent.[58]

The tide of prosperity on the Union Pacific had been gathering since early 1898. Even before Harriman returned from his inspection trip in July it was a foregone conclusion that a dividend would be paid, and the only question tantalizing speculators was the amount. Trading in Union Pacific stocks grew heavy, some of it on the advice of Harriman and other insiders, who told friends that the company's securities were undervalued.[59]

Harriman's own position on the dividend question is unclear. Berry believed he wished to put all surplus earnings into improvements but was under heavy pressure from the Dutch interests to pay a dividend. Harriman called Berry into his office one day to explain to a Dutch banker why it was essential to plough so much money back into the property. Both the board and the executive committee were divided on the issue. When Harriman proposed a 1½ percent dividend on preferred to the latter, the cautious Stillman threw up his hands in dismay, protesting that it was folly for a company fresh from receivership and with uncertain prospects to even think of paying dividends. But Stillman did not want to divide the committee and so merely abstained on the dividend vote. At the same time Harriman beat back the demand of those who favored a 2 percent declaration.[60]

A few months later the dividend seemed small change as earnings continued to swell. The demand for Union Pacific stocks surged; by the year's end preferred had marched past 74 from a low of 45⅞ in March, and common had jumped from 16⅛ to 44⅝. Those who had bought Union Pacific early reaped their rewards and had yet to see the best of their bargain. As Stillman got to know Harriman better, his suspicion relaxed into trust and then admiration. The entire board was fast coming to appreciate the talents of the man who had been a brash outsider to them only a year earlier.[61]

That appreciation showed itself clearly on December 1, 1898, when the directors abolished the position of chairman of the board. As chairman of the executive committee Harriman now served in that capacity ex officio for the board as well, thereby consolidating his authority. Pierce kept his place on the executive committee and was joined by the man he represented, George J. Gould. The other members—Hughitt, Kahn, and Stillman—stayed on, and no one doubted who was in charge. Schiff had promised Harriman command if he showed himself the best man as an inducement during a tough bit of negotiating, never dreaming for a moment that it might actually happen. But Schiff was not the first man to be surprised by Harriman's phenomenal capacity for growth. For the next decade his colleagues would scramble to keep up with him.[62]

4

The System

Alice Roosevelt, the president's daughter, became good friends with young Mary Harriman but never felt that she knew Mary's father. "He was a small, brown, taciturn man who never seemed to play," she remembered years later. Although Harriman mystified her, Alice glimpsed in him one quality that made his behavior all of a piece to her: "There was little of the pomp and none of the splurge of great wealth about him. What he wanted was power; quietly, deliberately, thoroughly, he worked to get it."[1]

The children knew this influence only too well. No man was a more loving, attentive father than Harriman despite the frantic demands on his time. At home he was more relaxed and playful but no less autocratic. "In everything he did, he took command," recalled his son Averell, "no matter what was going on. Even if we went for a walk, he'd tell us where he wanted to go. He knew what he wanted to do."[2]

Harriman not only craved power, he radiated it. His driving, forceful style allowed no one around him to rest easy or grow complacent. He cared little for money except as an instrument to get things done, and for Harriman there was always something to be done, a challenge to be met or an obstacle to overcome. There was in him a deep sense of purpose, a rage for order that could not tolerate looseness or disarray. Any ship he ran was not only tight but always knew where it was headed and on what course. His vision of an enterprise extended beyond what it could become to what was required to get it there. Harriman made a spectacular success of his rail enterprises because he was the right man in the right place at the right time. He was a man of system

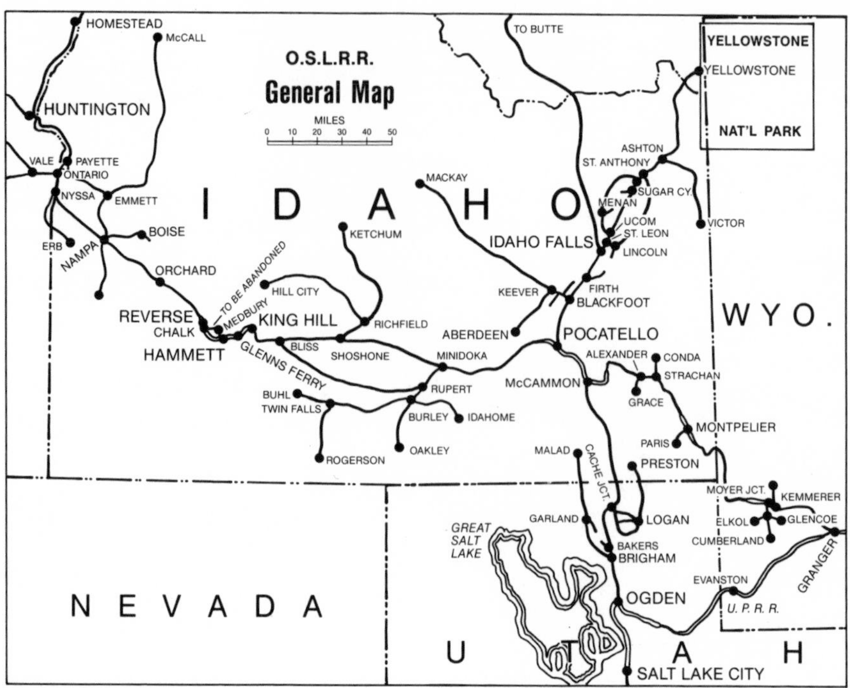

NORTHERN LINK: The Oregon Short Line, which linked the Union Pacific to the Northwest.

come to an industry in transition and desperately in need of someone expert at bringing order out of chaos.

The Union Pacific lacked system in the most literal sense. Bits and pieces torn from the old system during receivership lay scattered about the West like fragments from an explosion. Four years of legal and financial battling had done little to clarify their future, and the Union Pacific could do little until it had put its own house in order. Once in command, Harriman moved swiftly to recapture those properties deemed essential to the system. If nothing else the dismemberment, messy as it had been, allowed him to reassess the value of each component for his own scheme of things.

One road Harriman did not want was the Union Pacific, Denver & Gulf, which still floundered about in a receivership nearly as complex as that undergone by the Union Pacific. An amalgam of twelve roads merged in 1890, the Gulf line had never justified the expectations of its most ardent promoter, General Dodge. The old general clung to the view that its future lay with the Union Pacific even as relations between the two roads deteriorated steadily during the depression. Gradually even supporters of keeping the roads together realized that their destinies lay in separate directions. The Gulf line went its own way, and Harriman did nothing to stop it. In November 1898 it was reorganized as the Colorado & Southern Railway.[3]

But Harriman did want the Julesburg branch, which the Union Pacific had originally built as a direct route to Denver from the main line. After a year of negotiation he pried the 152-mile branch loose from the Gulf's reorganization committee. Early in 1898 the Fitzgerald Committee had purchased enough underlying collateral on outstanding notes to retain 323 miles of small branch lines in the Union Pacific system. That same year Harriman reacquired two other branches he deemed essential: the Omaha & Republican Valley, a 482-mile system in Nebraska, and the 225-mile Union Pacific, Lincoln & Colorado. By the end of 1899 he had bought 1,182 miles of original branch line back into the fold.[4]

In this work Harriman proved a careful shopper, passing over lines that had long been drags on the system. He let the old Central Branch go to the Missouri Pacific, which had leased the road since 1881, and allowed the Denver, Leadville & Gunnison (formerly the Denver & South Park) to remain with the Gulf line. Neither its deficits nor its operating problems in such rugged country would be missed. The Montana Union line, jointly owned with the Northern Pacific, was surrendered to that company, ending years of acrimony over its operation.[5]

For a time Harriman seemed content to let the St. Joseph & Grand Island drift away as well. The Union Pacific's experience in sharing control with the bondholders after its reorganization in 1885 had not been a happy one. In December 1896 the road's reorganization committee bought the road at foreclosure sale and declared their intention of running it as an independent line. By 1900 it had arranged trackage rights into Kansas City and begun to show a modest profit. Satisfied that the branch had potential and bothered by rumors that the Rock Island wanted to buy it, Harriman made his move in 1902. Without warning, his representatives turned up at the St. Joseph stockholders' meeting with enough stock to oust the current directors and install their own men. The new board promptly stopped paying a dividend on preferred stock and embarked on a program of improvements under Berry's watchful eye. Harriman kept personal control of the road until 1906, when he sold his holdings to the Union Pacific.[6]

One important legal change affected nearly all these lines. The Pacific Acts of 1862 and 1864, which served as the Union Pacific's original charter, contained no provision for building branches. Although nothing in their language prohibited branch construction, the company found the political climate so hostile that it never tested the question in court. Instead it resorted to the device of organizing and operating every branch as a separate corporation. The reorganized company operated under a general rather than special charter, however, and nothing in Utah law barred the company from owning or operating feeder lines. This change enabled Harriman to do away with the bother and expense of separate companies. All the branches he reacquired were absorbed directly into the system except for the old Kansas Central, which took the name Leavenworth, Topeka & Western.[7]

And the Oregon lines.

Since the completion of its Oregon Short Line in 1884 the Union Pacific had found itself drawn into growing struggle for supremacy in the Northwest. During the 1880s the fierce railroad wars and byzantine diplomacy that raged throughout the region had utterly demoralized Charles Francis Adams, Jr., who had tried earnestly to stake the Union Pacific's claim to empire. Prior to 1890 his chief rival had been the Northern Pacific and the quixotic Henry Villard, whose visionary belief in the future of the Northwest first opened the region to development. The arrival at Puget Sound of James J. Hill's Great Northern in 1893 opened a new phase of the contest, especially after the depression threw both the Union Pacific and Northern Pacific into bankruptcy. Hard times succeeded only in delaying a fresh round of intrigues and confrontations that would surely come once prosperity beckoned anew.[8]

Before the Union Pacific could even compete in the Northwest, however, it had to regain control of its Oregon lines, which had been cast off during the receivership. Harriman needed little instruction on the value of these lines or the potential of the Northwest. The latter was an open secret, its hold on railroad men's minds so potent that two decades of savage warfare had resolved nothing. Hill had already begun to tap this golden horn, and Harriman was determined that the Union Pacific get its full share as well.

Access to the Pacific Coast depended on two companies, the Short Line and the Oregon Railway & Navigation. The original Short Line left the Union Pacific at Granger, Wyoming, and ran through Pocatello to Huntington, Oregon, where it connected with the Navigation's road into Portland. In 1889 it was merged with the Utah & Northern, a branch running north from Ogden to Butte, Montana. Between these lines lay a potentially rich territory ranging from the mining regions of Montana to Puget Sound.

After building the Short Line the Union Pacific had operated it as a subsidiary through the device of a traffic contract. During the receivership, however, bickering arose over both finances and the division of rates. Although Silas Clark warned that it "would be a great mistake to further dismember the system," he could not prevent the Short Line from being foreclosed and reorganized early in 1897. The Union Pacific's receivers hoped to keep the old traffic arrangements intact but were brushed aside by the new Short Line management, which declared its independence in June by canceling the old contract and proclaiming the Ogden gateway to be open.[9]

The Union Pacific cringed at his threat. Under the old arrangement it had determined all rates and allotments for the Short Line and not permitted it to exchange business with other roads. In theory at least the new policy would open the Northwest trade to the Atchison, Burlington, and Rock Island on terms equal to those given the Union Pacific. These lines could route traffic over the Denver & Rio Grande and the Rio Grande Western to Ogden. However, the Short Line stood to lose something as well. In return for an exclusive contract the Union Pacific had credited the Short Line with 1.75 miles for every actual mile hauled. When the Short Line opted for freedom, the Union Pacific promptly discontinued this allowance, known as "constructive mileage,'' and placed all traffic on a pro rata basis. It also announced that all its Oregon traffic would be routed via Sacramento over the Southern Pacific system.[10]

Since the California route was 491 miles longer than that via the Oregon roads, the boycott antagonized shippers more than it chastened the Short Line. Negotiations for a new traffic contract went nowhere as the Short Line rebuffed every proposal for some modified form of constructive mileage. In October 1897 the Fitzgerald committee bought $8.5 million of the Short Line's $27.5 million outstanding stock, thereby serving notice that the Union Pacific intended to maintain its presence in the Short Line. This purchase gave the languishing contract negotiations the jolt needed to reach agreement. Under its terms the gateway remained open and the Short Line received a less favorable division of rates from the Union Pacific.[11]

''I don't expect the gateway will ever be closed again,'' predicted the Short Line's traffic manager. ''The day is rapidly approaching when all roads will want all of the business they can get from all of their connections.'' The traffic manager also noted that fall business was ''the heaviest that has ever been known,'' a fact that did not go unnoticed by the reorganization committee or by Harriman. Quietly that winter both bought Short Line stock until they acquired a majority. In April 1898 three Union Pacific men replaced Morgan representatives on the Short Line board. By mid-September Harriman could report that ''The Short Line matter has been closed beyond all doubt.'' Off he went with a retinue of officers for a whirlwind inspection of the property.[12]

The Navigation company's situation was more complicated, part of the tangled legacy bequeathed by the erratic Henry Villard. The Short Line owned $16.3 of Navigation's $24 million common stock but did not control the company. There also existed $11 million in preferred stock which, under the terms of reorganization, was held by a voting trust in the joint interest of the Union Pacific, Northern Pacific, and Great Northern. This stock had the power to elect two-thirds of Navigation's board for ten years or until the company paid a 4 percent dividend for five consecutive years. While the voting trust prevailed, Navigation occupied the bizarre position of an independent line under the joint rule of three competing systems.[13]

Jacob Schiff and Charles H. Coster, one of Morgan's partners, perfected this arrangement during the winter of 1897. Their idea was to make Navigation a sort of Switzerland in the turbulent Northwest, independent and impartial, with a management ''pledged to the maintenance of rates, traffic at all times to be directed by the shortest routes.'' The Union Pacific, Short Line, Northern Pacific, and Great Northern would each hold a fourth of the preferred stock. In selecting a president for the reorganized Navigation company James J. Hill vetoed the receiver, Edwin McNeill, because he had ''developed habits of intemperance to such an extent that he should no longer be trusted with the affairs of the Company.'' The post went instead to A. L. Mohler, a tough, stolid railroader who had risen through the ranks.[14]

Hill was sincere in his desire to keep Navigation neutral because it enabled him to reach Portland without having to build there. At the same time, he liked neutrality with an edge in his favor. In this case the edge was Mohler, who had put in fifteen years on Hill's lines before coming to Navigation and was considered Hill's man. Mohler accepted the role willingly and impressed everyone with his efficient, economical handling of Navigation, which rebounded quickly from the depression to do an enormous business. He introduced new methods of promoting traffic and launched a program of improvements that would have pleased Harriman.[15]

As late as April 1898 the prospects for harmony in the Northwest looked bright. Hill knew the Northern Pacific could not legally take control of Navigation because it was a parallel road, and he saw little to fear from the newly reorganized Union Pacific. Even if Union Pacific should gain control of Navigation, he surmised, it would "not see it to their interest to break the present arrangement with the Great Northern Company at least, whatever they might do in regard to the Northern Pacific." All these companies were overcapitalized, Hill reasoned, which meant the Great Northern could build a competing line to Portland at much less cost than the existing roads. This threat was enough to preserve peace.[16]

Hill also wanted Navigation neutral because he hoped to impose harmony by wresting control of the Northern Pacific from Morgan, with whom he shared it in a voting trust. Two men upset his calculations in very different ways. The first was Charles S. Mellen, the Northern Pacific president, whom Hill despised. Indeed, no one seemed to like Mellen except Morgan, who had put him in office. Since the 1880s, when his poisonous influence helped turn the Union Pacific's Omaha office into a cockpit of intrigue and back-biting, Mellen had continued to rise in railway circles through his uncanny ability to fawn on superiors and abuse subordinates. He was, observed another manager astutely, a man who moved up "only by pulling other people down." During 1898 Mellen annoyed Hill constantly by trying to edge his way on one pretext or another into territory belonging to Navigation. Hill finally gave him a stern warning and told Coster bluntly that his firm would be held responsible for any Northern Pacific aggression.[17]

The second man was Harriman, who had just emerged as head of the Union Pacific's executive committee. Hill had not yet taken his measure—hardly anyone had—but was quick to enlist him as an ally against Mellen. Keeping the peace suited Harriman so long as it enabled him to carry out his own agenda, which he had yet to reveal. He recognized that control of the Short Line and Navigation were inextricably linked, and that the first step was to lock up the Short Line. At that road's election in October 1898 the Union Pacific captured the board, and superintendent W. H. Bancroft promptly launched a program of improvements to bring the Short Line up to the parent road's standard. To clinch his hold, Harriman had the Union Pacific exchange nearly $27.5 million in new stock for Short Line stock on the basis of one share Union Pacific for one of Short Line plus three dollars. Since Union Pacific was selling at a higher price and still climbing, most Short Line holders jumped at the chance. By March 1899 more than 85 percent of the stock had come in and the offer was withdrawn. The Short Line had come home to stay.[18]

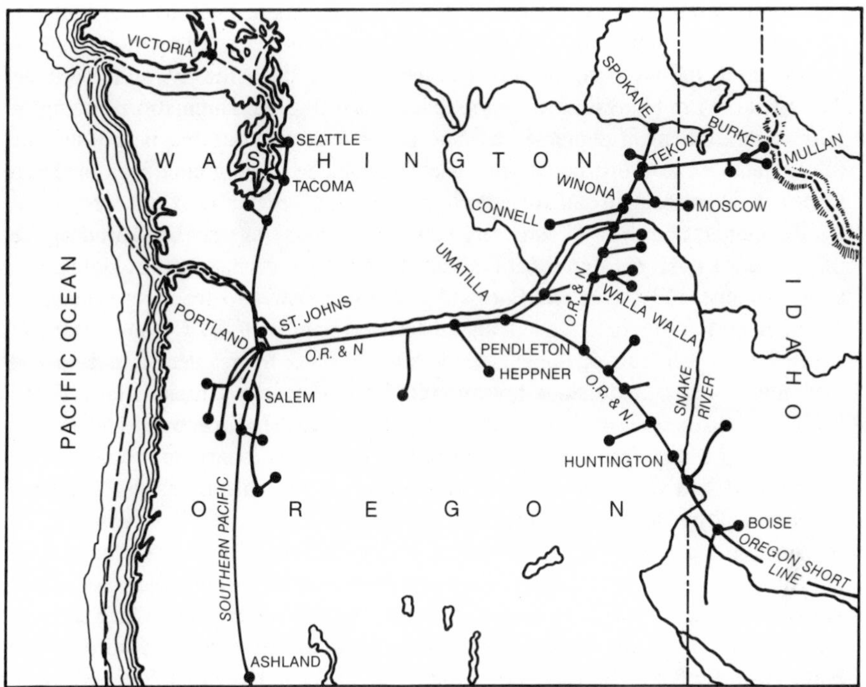

KEY TO THE KINGDOM: The Oregon Railway & Navigation line, which linked three systems to Portland.

"The key to the Pacific Railroad situation is the control of the Oregon Short Line," observed Charles E. Perkins, the venerable chieftain of the Burlington in 1897. He was wrong; the key lay with Navigation. As the rail and steamer system that served as the connecting link for three rival systems, it offered a way to avoid a war of expansion reminiscent of the 1880s in the region where ambitions and dangers ran highest. The prize was the exploding volume of traffic in the triangle formed by Spokane, Seattle, and Portland, as well as in western Idaho. Although both northern roads had penetrated the Cascade Mountains, the best route into Portland remained the low-lying line along the Columbia River occupied by Navigation. At Umatilla on its eastern end the Navigation line forked into a Y. The northern fork ran to a connection with the Northern Pacific, the southern to the Oregon Short Line at Huntington. Between the forks lay a territory hotly contested by Northern Pacific and Navigation for years.[19]

Peace in the Northwest hinged on maintaining a balance of power among the three rival roads, which meant preserving access to Navigation's line on good terms and curbing impulses to expand via branch lines or parallel lines to points served by existing roads. This required cooperation among three ambitious and abrasive men accustomed to getting their own way through very different styles. Two of them, Harriman and Hill, were titans who in 1898 had just begun to circle one another warily. The third was Mellen, an erratic and overweening functionary who smarted at being a mere "hired hand" of the Northern Pacific while the other two controlled their roads."[20]

At bottom the issue boiled down to whether the three roads would fight for the traffic of the Northwest or agree to divide it through some sort of compromise. Any agreement depended on Navigation's staying neutral; if another line to Portland were constructed, the game would be lost. There was also the matter of a connection between Portland and the Puget Sound. The Northern Pacific owned one over a costly and inefficient route. It could be shared by the three companies, or the others could build their own road. A joint line would enable Hill to reach Portland and Harriman to reach Puget Sound. The Union Pacific had signed an agreement with Hill in October 1890 to construct the Portland & Puget Sound, but costs ran higher than expected and the project was abandoned a few months later when the Union Pacific found itself in a financial crisis. It could be resurrected at any time by either or both roads. Meanwhile, the Northern Pacific had its line as a bargaining chip.[21]

The first test came during the summer of 1898. Hill distrusted Mellen's forays into the region north of the Snake River because Northern Pacific presence there would shut out the Great Northern. In July he met with Harriman and Mellen in a futile attempt to mediate the disputes between them. A few days later Harriman wrote Burt that "The most important matter we now have before us is the closing of the purchase of the Oregon Railroad and Navigation Preferred Stock for this company, and obtaining absolute control of that property." Before this could be done, some way had to be found to assure Great Northern and Northern Pacific access to Portland over the Navigation. "My opinion is that any pure and simple trackage arrangement will prove unsatisfactory in the future," he added. Burt was asked to devise some suitable plan with Hill and Mellen.[22]

More meetings followed. At one key session in October, Hill, Harriman, Mellen, banker William Bull, and Schiff gathered with Coster and other Morgan men at the Northern Pacific office on Broad Street with a stenographer present to record what they hoped would be a settlement of the Navigation conundrum. Prominent corporation lawyer Francis Lynde Stetson, who presided, led off by declaring the two issues under discussion to be traffic relations and territorial relations. Coster reminded everyone that the contract of February 1897 defined Navigation as a neutral company "open to all connections and not exclusive to anyone." Problems had arisen to cloud that status, and Coster wanted it clarified anew. For the Northern Pacific, he added, those problems were chiefly territorial in nature.[23]

Hill chimed in with his familiar plea that cooperation was essential because it was folly to build more road or ignore the political hostility in Washington state. The Great Northern wanted only "equal relations and equal terms with the Huntington gateway," but Hill had no specific ideas on how to accomplish these ends. Schiff asked Coster what the Northern Pacific wanted. "Permanent harmony in that territory," Coster replied.

"Now, what do you propose to do to get this harmony?" Schiff pressed.

The solution, Coster insisted at length, must be a division of territory.

Navigation had certain lines north of the Snake River, which the Northern Pacific claimed as its territory; the Northern Pacific had some south of the Snake, where Navigation held sway. Since the river was the natural dividing line, why not agree to keep out of each other's domain? Harriman listened intently, then, after some sparring over terms, said flatly, "I do not want to divide territory. That did not seem to be in contemplation when any of the agreements were made."

A stunned Coster tried vainly to budge Harriman on the point, then confessed to feeling "very apprehensive." When he persisted in arguing for a territorial boundary, Schiff reminded him that "A compromise means a compromise. It does not mean that it would be a compromise for the Northern Pacific to cut across the Oregon Navigation Company's best territory, and cut it out, and get what it has for its own line." Hill repeated his warning that political necessity demanded a viable settlement. "While we are quarreling among ourselves," he added, "there may be somebody come in and establish a line, and give a great deal of trouble."

Harriman conceded that harmony was possible and essential, but thought it "inadvisable for political reasons to agree upon absolute territorial lines."

"The political situation is becoming intolerable in those states," grumbled William Bull.

"There is no question," nodded E. B. Thomas, "but that public knowledge of such an agreement would be a very great mistake."

The talk rambled on without changing anyone's views or producing an agreement. Harriman admitted to having no concrete plan in mind, and he came away no less determined to gain control of Navigation. Another summit conference had flopped, and Mellen resumed his old game of putting survey parties north of the Snake River while dangling overtures of peace to Mohler. Hill saw through this sham and concluded that Mellen's object was "first to get possession and settle conditions afterward." Convinced that the fight hinged on who occupied the disputed ground first, Hill threw his support behind Navigation's effort to beat Mellen at his own game.[24]

With both Harriman's and Hill's blessing, Navigation responded in November 1898 by chartering the Clearwater Valley Railroad to build eight different branches in western Idaho and eastern Washington. A month later the articles were amended to add another ten branches. Heavy work began on some of the lines, leaving no doubt that Navigation was in earnest. Mohler relished taking the offensive. "I am now waiting for Mellen to show his hand elsewhere," he reported to Hill, adding, "I am being well supported by our people in New York." A startled Mellen didn't know what to think. One of his officers blustered that the proposed branches would "take 25 years to do" and posed no threat to Northern Pacific.[25]

In the spring of 1899 Hill renewed his campaign for joint ownership of Navigation on some permanent basis. Once agreed on a general plan "based on conditions that are fair and equitable to all three parties," he told Coster, "the whole question seems to me to be solved." Would Harriman agree to any such terms if they could be defined? While Hill fretted over this question, Harriman was busily laying grand plans of quite another kind. Worn down by the pace of the past year, he had accepted his doctor's orders to take a prolonged vacation. But Harriman's idea of a vacation differed from that of ordinary citizens. Instead of some pleasant, leisurely sojourn, he conceived nothing less than a scientific expedition to Alaska and proceeded to recruit some of the nation's most eminent scientists.[26]

Harriman did not return until August, but his influence was felt even in his absence. In July his representatives managed to dissolve the Navigation voting trust by agreeing to guarantee payment of the required dividend on preferred stock. Control of the company reverted to the common stock, of which the Short Line owned two-thirds. No one doubted that the Union Pacific would take command of Navigation and oust the Northern Pacific directors, but no one yet fathomed what all this meant. Would the long-smoldering Clearwater war break out in the open? Mohler put aside inquiries with the cryptic remark, "I do not like to say anything about our construction operations in this country, because it seems better to follow the scriptural injunction—'by their works ye shall know them.' Our works ought to be showing very plainly by this time, and if not, will speak for themselves in all good time."[27]

The capable Mohler had shifted his allegiance from Hill to Harriman, and Hill was quick to sense the change. His suspicions deepened when Mellen changed front and offered Union Pacific a half interest in the Northern Pacific's Portland-Tacoma line and Tacoma terminals. If a deal was struck, Hill could be shut out on both fronts and forced to build. He complained to Mohler that Navigation was "no longer neutral as between the Short Line and ourselves," but was careful to blame the discrimination on traffic men. Hill demanded equality, nothing more and nothing less. Anything less, he warned, would compel him reluctantly to construct his own lines.[28]

Hill was adept at playing the role of wounded innocent, but his guile proved of little avail here. When Harriman reached Portland, he was met by Burt, Berry, Mohler, and Mellen, who rode across the Navigation line with him. There followed in short order a six-month truce in the Clearwater region and a decision by Northern Pacific to sell its holdings of Navigation preferred to "friends" of Union Pacific. Harriman then moved to increase the Union Pacific's preferred stock by $25 million and its common stock by $7.7 million. These new shares were offered in exchange for some Short Line income bonds as well as outstanding preferred and common shares of Navigation.* Within a few months most of the securities had been exchanged and Navigation joined the Short Line in the Union Pacific stable. At Navigation's annual meeting in September the three Northern Pacific directors gave way to Union Pacific men. Harriman was elected chairman of the board.[29]

The system had been put back together in "the strongest position it has ever held," strong enough to threaten the balance of power in the Northwest. Hill observed gloomily that "the attitude of the Navigation Company towards the

*The Union Pacific exchanged its common stock for Navigation even up and one share of its preferred for one of Navigation plus a dollar.

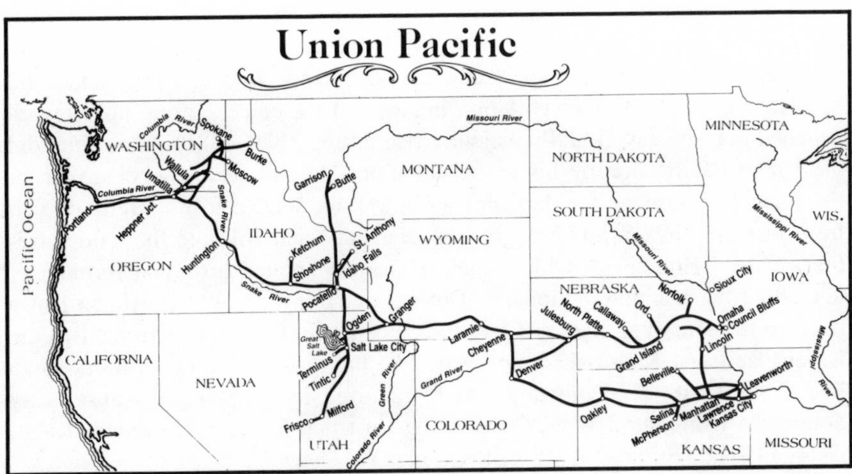

THE SYSTEM RESTORED: The Union Pacific system as put back together by Harriman, 1900.

Great Northern has materially altered in the last three or four months.'' Still, he clung to his belief that some way could be found for the three companies to share Navigation's line to Portland. Doggedly he pressed on Harriman a plan for joint ownership of Navigation on an equal basis. If this were done, the Northern Pacific would surely do likewise with its Portland-Puget Sound road. Harmony could and must be achieved, Hill stressed; if not, he could build a much better road than Navigation's for much less annual interest than he would pay Navigation in rent. The threat was veiled but unmistakable, a red flag that Hill hoped would make Harriman see reason when next they met.[30]

Hill sent his long letter on the subject to Schiff to read before handing it to Harriman. As the friend of both men, Schiff found himself drawn into the role of mediator. It was not a role he relished. Hill was an old and valued friend, but Harriman was fast becoming the mother lode for Kuhn, Loeb's fortunes. Would the day come when he must choose between them? Schiff shuddered at the thought. Dutifully he presented the letter to Harriman and informed Hill of the response. Harriman was impressed by its argument, Schiff noted tactfully, but also irritated by the ''mandatory tone.'' He tried to smooth over the differences and assured Hill there would be no trouble reaching some sort of accommodation, but Hill was not convinced and Harriman himself did not reply. If Harriman could not be brought to terms, Hill concluded, then the Great Northern must draw nearer the Northern Pacific. He wrote Coster that the Great Northern was ready to revive the long dormant Portland & Puget Sound project but that Mellen had offered to share use of his line.[31]

Schiff saw what was happening but was helpless to deflect the course of events. A deep sense of foreboding seized him and would not let go. In the Northwest an irresistible force was hurtling toward an immovable object. If and when they collided, Schiff realized in dismay, the impact would be colossal. And he would be pinned between them.

For most men the reconstruction of the Union Pacific system would have been the capstone of their life's work. For Harriman it served merely as a point of departure for even more spectacular achievements. Between 1899 and 1902 he blazed through the transportation industry like a comet, piling up a record matched only by Jay Gould's meteoric rise during 1879–1881. At no time did the Union Pacific occupy his entire attention. He still served as chairman of the finance committee for the Illinois Central and tended to its affairs on call from Fish. In 1898 Schiff brought both Harriman and Hill into the reorganization of the Baltimore & Ohio, where Harriman applied his usual formula of upgrading the line and equipment. During the spring of 1899 Harriman lent a hand to the bankrupt Kansas City, Pittsburg & Gulf, which connected to the Union Pacific at Kansas City and was, like the Illinois Central, a north-south line to the Gulf. The company was reorganized in 1900 as the Kansas City Southern, with control vested in a voting trust that included Harriman, Kahn, George Gould, Stillman and financier John W. Gates.[32]

During 1899 Harriman also took charge of a road that would plunge him into bitter controversy. The Chicago & Alton was an overgrown local road from Chicago to East St. Louis with a cutoff branch to Kansas City. For two decades it had survived competition with the other Chicago lines by playing the role of maverick: cutting rates, juggling train schedules, shunning most rate associations, and above all refusing to follow its neighbors that were evolving into systems through mergers and construction. Gould had flirted with it for several years, as had the Atchison, but the Alton remained fiercely independent and a constant thorn in the side of larger systems seeking rate stability and harmony.

On the surface the Alton seemed a prosperous, well-managed road. Its dividends averaged 8.3 percent for a quarter century, and in 1898 the stock sold for around 160. The management was praised as conservative; a better term would be reactionary. By standing still through the two most dynamic and tumultuous decades of railroad history, it had allowed time to pass the road by. Gross earnings had dropped nearly 30 percent since 1887, and the dividend was maintained only by letting the property deteriorate physically.[33]

Harriman later claimed that he went into the Alton at the request of John J. Mitchell, an Illinois banker who came to him on behalf of some large stockholders unhappy with the company's management. Once decided, Harriman brought Schiff, Stillman, and George Gould into a syndicate to undertake the purchase. As usual, Kuhn, Loeb handled the financial transactions, and eventually about a hundred individuals and firms joined what became known as the "Alton syndicate." Samuel Felton was installed as president to oversee the usual policy of modernizing the line and equipment.[34]

Why did Harriman undertake the Alton reorganization in the midst of all his other activities? A later investigation condemned the syndicate's financial handling of the Alton, triggering charges that its members had looted the road for their own profit. The fierce controversy that followed has ignored other important elements in the decision. Of course Harriman saw profits in the deal; he was, after all, a businessman, not a professor or a charitable foundation. However, the Alton had become an anachronism in modern railroading. It was a disturber not only of rates but of schedules as well. Nothing was more inefficient than running fast trains on poor track with old equipment. To make speed on high grades the trains had to be short and light, which meant hauling smaller payloads with an excessive number of trains. This practice resulted in greater wear and tear, increased maintenance costs, and soaring expenses.

It also deranged the schedules of roads connecting with the Alton's trains and gave the public false expectations. Shippers and travelers equated speed with efficiency, when in fact the opposite was true for the railroad. On single-track lines a train could make speed only at the expense of other trains, which had to give way for it. Since faster trains carried lighter loads, more of them had to be run. This increased the number of meeting points, which is the dominant factor affecting speed. A meeting point occurs when one train encounters another in the same or opposite direction, and one must lose time yielding to the other. The more trains running, the more meeting points there are, and the figure jumps by the square of the total number of trains involved. That is, one train in each direction produces one meeting point, two trains in each direction four meeting points, ten in each direction a hundred meeting points. A line running many short trains, therefore, lost through excessive meeting points far more time than it could gain in speed. It also wore out its equipment and roadbed at a much faster rate.[35]

For economy and efficiency the best system was to run few trains with heavy payloads at moderate speed. Fewer trains on regular schedules pushed men and equipment less hard, allowed more margin for delays, and reduced accidents. It also meant more reliable connections with other lines, which in turn improved service over long hauls. Passenger service posed a special problem because travelers naturally valued speed above all else, and speed could only be achieved at the expense of siding freight trains, which were the real income producers. This was one reason why the passenger dilemma drove railroad men to despair, and why many of them longed to be rid of it.

The Alton offered Harriman both financial opportunity and a chance to eliminate a competitive dinosaur. It would mark one more step toward rationalizing the industry through the approach that would later be called "community of interest." With that in mind, Harriman suggested putting on the Alton board representatives of the Union Pacific, Illinois Central, Missouri Pacific, Wabash, and Katy roads. "This is all a very big & very important matter," he told Stuyvesant Fish, "& can be turned to good account to bettering the whole situation. Its a great big opportunity for us doing."[36]

The challenge as Harriman viewed it was not only to put the system back in order but also to put order into the system at every level. To the rail industry he was a gust of fresh air blowing through musty closets where the clutter of habit had lain undisturbed for years. His urge everywhere was to rationalize, simplify, and standardize practices. New techniques and technologies were revolutionizing the way things were done, and Harriman insisted that his officers keep abreast of developments lest they miss some advantage that, on the scale of a giant system, could save the company huge sums.

"He was a strong believer in adopting standards and everybody living up to them," observed Berry, "so that the practice would be uniform and that the manufacturer would only have one plan to figure on instead of many." On the Union Pacific Harriman pushed to standardize bridges, buildings, depots, roadway signs, rails, ties, ballast, fencing, engines, rolling stock, air brakes, and a host of other basic items. As the Oregon companies returned to the fold and new lines like the Alton fell under his influence, Harriman brought their officers together with the Union Pacific men to determine standards for everyone. The debates were vigorous and often divisive enough to require set procedures.[37]

The object of this campaign was to unify operations and slash expenses. Unity of command greatly simplified relations between the roads. Every American railroad operated under its own set of rules, which varied markedly from one company to the next. Just as Napoleon codified the laws of France, so did Harriman order his general managers to standardize their rules, thereby putting everyone under the same code. Under Harriman's decree, declared Kruttschnitt, "a uniform policy was followed in all branches of the railroad service on all of the constituent companies. Methods found to be the best on any one of the systems could be applied to all . . . the personnel of the organization was generally improved and unified, duplication of work or of officers being done away with."[38]

Standardization enabled the different lines to exchange equipment easily, and slashed purchasing and maintenance costs. The number of parts stocked was drastically reduced, and heavily used items could be bought in huge quantities for all the roads at once. Few things impressed Harriman more than the advantages to be gained by mass purchases. This policy was applied first to rails and ties. In September 1899 he asked Burt to confer with Mohler and Bancroft on tie purchases. "One party should control the matter for all three companies," Harriman instructed, "and make purchases for benefit of whole system without regard to freight charges by any one of the three as against the other." The same procedure was used for buying rails. Harriman shopped carefully for the best price, using as leverage the size of his order.[39]

This approach was quickly extended to equipment, bridge material, air brakes, and any item that promised savings. It was discovered that the cost of stationery on the different systems ranged from $1.90 to $11.50 a thousand. With the help of a stationer the letterheads were merged into a single form for everyone at a cost of $1.90 per thousand. So too with the lowly telegraph blank, which came in a variety of sizes and headings. Paper is cut in standard sheets known as trade sizes, and considerable waste results unless the telegraph blanks are of a uniform size that uses the entire sheet. A standard size was adopted for all Harriman lines, and headings were simplified to reduce typeset and printing costs. The estimated savings on these blanks alone amounted to more than twenty-five times the cost of installing a central stationer for the system. Moreover, the system could now get better prices by ordering as many as twenty million blanks at once.[40]

The impetus for these reforms came directly from Harriman, who loved to dicker and was fond of driving a bargain. His mind overflowed with fresh ideas, many of them born of his uncanny ability to spot a telling detail or grasp at once the value of someone's suggestion. Much of it amounted to little more than common sense, which may be the most uncommon quality around. Harriman possessed it in abundance and applied it to everything he touched, even the thorny problem of outlaws.

The Wyoming division had long been a haven for bandits preying on the railroad. Some of them, like Butch Cassidy and the Sundance Kid, became folk heroes of sorts, but Harriman was not among their fans. The problem was that a gang could hit a train early in the evening and escape before a posse could be organized by fleeing into the rugged North Park country or Brown's Park or the Hole-in-the-Wall country, where their trail would be hard to pick up so long after the fact. Drawing on his expert knowledge of horses, Harriman devised a clever defense. He suggested giving the special agents horses capable of going a hundred miles in a day, and moving them about the country on trains. This mobile posse could be launched to trail outlaws within hours after a train was hit, and could trail them relentlessly for days if necessary. The cost would be much less than that of organizing a posse belatedly to stalk a cold trail. Not only did the Harriman strike force curtail train robberies on the Union Pacific, but the posse itself became almost as famous as the Hole-in-the-Wall gang. Harriman employed as train guards some of the best known guides and hunters in the West, including Sam Lawson and Joe LeForce, later immortalized as "Whispering Smith."

But there were some bandits even Harriman could not bring to bay. One of them was Harvey Logan, a cold-blooded gang leader who had escaped from prison and was rumored to be holed up in Wyoming. W. L. Park related to Harriman the lurid story of Logan's train robbery, the slaying of a sheriff in charge of the posse, the killing of two bandits and capture of a third, the seizing of Logan near Knoxville, Tennessee, and Logan's bold escape from jail in that town. The word was, added Park, that Logan was planning new robberies or possible vengeance on those who had tracked him so relentlessly.

Harriman listened to this tale intently, then flashed Park a rare smile. "Mr. Park," he said, "there are just two men in these United States upon whom devolves the responsibility for the capture and reincarceration of Harvey Logan."

"Who are these two men?" asked Park.

"The General Superintendent of the Union Pacific Railroad," said Harriman, pointing at Park, "and the President of the Union Pacific Railroad," turning his finger back at himself.

Park knew full well Logan's renowned skill with a revolver and his willingness to use it on human targets. "The General Superintendent of the Union Pacific Railroad [reneges]," he said, shaking his head.

Harriman laughed. "So does the President."[41]

5

The Empire

The rehabilitation of the Union Pacific was a calculated risk at best and a great gamble at worst. The traffic was there and growing if some way could be found to carry it for a profit. Apart from the phenomenal growth of the West, transcontinental business was fed by the dawn of American empire in the Far East. The Spanish-American War had delivered the Philippines into American control, and the Open Door policy was helping American interests improve their foothold in the China market. Japan had emerged as a promising industrial nation and potential trading partner or rival. The flow of goods across the Pacific seemed at last on the verge of fulfilling a century of eagerness to tap the fabled markets of the Far East.

Profits could be made from this traffic by beating the competition or by eliminating it. Harriman pursued both possibilities, the first by upgrading the Union Pacific system and the second by absorbing competitors or cowing them into submission. Sometimes, as in the situation at Ogden, the two overlapped. There the Union Pacific exchanged traffic with the other half of the original transcontinental line, the Central Pacific, a passable road by western standards but in no way comparable to the modernized Union Pacific. The growing disparity between the two lines turned the Central Pacific into a bottleneck and source of frustration for Harriman, who had no other viable route to California. Until he could solve this problem, his realm of reform stopped abruptly at the transfer yard in Ogden.

Harriman had also to worry about the fluid relationships among the rival transcontinental lines. South of Oregon three routes vied for the business: the Union Pacific–Central Pacific line, the Southern Pacific, and the Atchison. The largest and most successful of them was the Southern Pacific, which dominated the flow of traffic on land and sea. It owned the Central Pacific, the Sunset Route to New Orleans, the Morgan line of steamers operating from New Orleans to New York, a road into Mexico, another one north from San Francisco to Portland, and a steamship company working the Pacific trade. This transportation complex gave the Southern Pacific a stranglehold on California business and transcontinental traffic.

Only one other line, the Atchison, entered California over its own track, and it depended on the Southern Pacific for connections to San Francisco and other major points. But the Atchison had its own line to Chicago and could also tap the Colorado market. This once feeble, overbuilt giant had been revived from bankruptcy by a vigorous management eager to flex its muscles in new directions. The Burlington, the Rock Island, and the Missouri Pacific also reached Colorado and could send business over the Rio Grande and the Rio Grande Western to Ogden. For years there had been talk of building a road between Salt Lake City and Los Angeles. Nothing had come of it, yet the rumors would not die and in 1899 took on a new insistence.

During the long night of the depression most of these roads were too weak to do more than fight desultory battles for traffic by cutting rates or exchanging the usual threats. No one had the strength to expand or move aggressively against his neighbors; systems were coming apart, not being put together. As prosperity returned and companies regained their financial footing, the old rivalries reared their heads anew. The transcontinental arena grew increasingly more volatile and alliances more tenuous. Larger roads looked to secure their connections while smaller ones cowered in the shadow of threats to absorb them. Survival depended on an ability to hold a reasonable share of the traffic and carry it efficiently, but any road that succeeded in this opened itself to the threat of invasion or buyout.

It was this cauldron of shifting possibilities that Harriman stirred with such unexpected vigor in 1899. On the map of railroad strategy his revitalized Union Pacific, occupying the center of the continent, was like Germany a power faced with threats on two fronts. To the north lay the Hill roads and the Northern Pacific, both eager to curb Union Pacific penetration of the Northwest. To the south lay a confused and shifting situation in which war might erupt at any time. The Southern Pacific drained the lion's share of transcontinental business to its Sunset Route while its Central Pacific clogged the flow at the Ogden gateway. The Burlington and Rock Island could ignore the Union Pacific by using their connection with the Rio Grande and Rio Grande Western to reach Ogden. Although this route did not yet pose a serious threat, some ambitious figure might try to combine these companies into a more efficient line. And what if someone did build from Salt Lake City to Los Angeles?

Nor were the Iowa roads sitting idle. Their relationships and rivalries were as fluid and shifting as the Missouri River itself. The Burlington thrust a new extension up the North Platte Valley. The Northwestern remained so staunch an ally of the Union Pacific that Marvin Hughitt grew weary of denying rumors that the two roads would merge. As the new Illinois Central connection to

THE MAN IN THE IRON MASK: James A. Stilllman, the quiet, subtle mastermind of National City Bank, who worked closely with Harriman and Schiff. *(B. C. Forbes,* Men Who Are Making America, *Baker Library, Harvard Business School)*

Omaha neared completion in 1900, however, Hughitt could not help wondering how much Union Pacific traffic it would drain. The Rock Island was seeking a connection with the Atchison at Pueblo for California business, and the Milwaukee was looking to expand northward into Minnesota and the Dakotas. South of these roads lay the Gould system, stretching from St. Louis to Pueblo and from New Orleans to El Paso, making it a competitor in one place or another of the Southern Pacific, Atchison, and Rock Island.[1]

That major changes loomed on the horizon was obvious to anyone familiar with railroad affairs. What no one could foresee was the speed with which all these conflicts imploded into a series of clashes during 1900 and 1901 that radically restructured western rail systems into alignments no one had even dreamed of a few months earlier. It was as if a storm gathering momentum for years had suddenly unleashed its fury in one savage outburst that swept away the ruins of the old order and replaced them with the stark, clean lines of a few huge systems bound together by what the press called a ''community of interest.'' The phrase would always be associated with Harriman even though he professed to despise it.[2]

The catalyst for this whirlwind of change was Harriman, whose road stood in the eye of the storm and who alone was willing to tackle this complex tangle of conflicts. Few men possessed a vision of the new order toward which railroads were evolving, and none had the energy or daring to impose it on so grand a scale. Where others shrank from the risks involved, Harriman not only embraced gigantic undertakings but used one deal to vault into another of even greater proportions. It was this activity even more than his transformation of the Union Pacific that burned Harriman's imprint on the public consciousness.

By 1900 Harriman had new allies to help provide the means for his bold visions. The taciturn James Stillman had become transfixed by the sheer dynamism of the little man whose mind knew no rest. He admired Harriman's ability to win others to his views, to make any meeting of directors "synchronized, so that all their pendulums swung together." Harriman's handling of the Union Pacific led Stillman to regard him as a genius in transportation, the likes of which seldom appeared on the scene. Personally Stillman was cold and aloof, yet he developed for Harriman a warm fondness that transcended business and made them lifelong friends.[3]

They made a splendid combination, the truculent, abrasive entrepreneur and the quiet banker whose subtle influence helped tone down Harriman's excesses when feathers got ruffled. Their friendship put behind Harriman the resources of the powerful National City Bank. Stillman also introduced Harriman to a circle of his associates who had immense wealth to tap for any worthwhile project, notably William Rockefeller, H. H. Rogers, and Henry Clay Frick. The presence of Rockefeller and Rogers led reporters to dub this group the "Standard Oil crowd," but that was misleading. The Rockefeller brothers often went their separate ways in investments, and so did their partners. Frequently they disapproved of each other's actions outside Standard Oil, or at least disagreed over their worth. The might of Standard Oil did not stand behind Harriman, but the funds of some of its major figures did, and that was more than enough for his purposes.

No matter how Harriman figured it, the answer always came back to the Southern Pacific. That company was not only a competitor but a bottleneck at Ogden, neutralizing the gains made in efficiency on the Union Pacific. Nothing could be more natural than a merger between the Central Pacific and the Union Pacific; indeed, their separation for so long looked to be the most unnatural of acts. Twenty years earlier Jay Gould and Collis P. Huntington had reached the same conclusion and come within a whisker of pulling off the consolidation only to have Oliver Ames and the other Boston holders of Union Pacific get cold feet at the last minute. Their timidity condemned the two roads to a perpetual life as Siamese twins, joined at Ogden while struggling awkwardly to lurch off in other directions.[4]

Now Huntington was an old man, the last survivor among the Big Four who had built the Central Pacific, sitting alone atop the largest transportation system in the world. His pace had slowed but his grip had not loosened, and he showed little sign of relinquishing authority to younger hands. For years there had been clashes among Huntington, the Crockers, and the estate of Leland

Stanford over the Southern Pacific's affairs. After losing a key battle in 1900, the Crockers sold their stock to banker James Speyer, who allied himself with Huntington.[5]

As the new century dawned, Huntington was busy putting his house in order. He arranged to sell his holdings in Pacific Mail Steamship Company, which he had dominated for nearly a decade, to Southern Pacific, and readied a program of improvements on the rail line. With the Atchison he explored the possibility of a joint line from southern California to Salt Lake. Earlier the two companies had agreed to pool certain kinds of business, and their growing alliance bothered Harriman, who was quick to denounce the proposed line as "unfriendly & antagonistic" to the Union Pacific. Something had to be done about the myriad of threats posed by the Southern Pacific.[6]

In July 1900 Harriman went off to the Adirondacks on a brief camping trip with Huntington and one of his closest associates, Edwin Hawley. Later Otto Kahn would assert that Harriman made repeated attempts to buy the Central Pacific or wring from Huntington some permanent arrangement for their relationship at Ogden. No doubt they discussed these matters at length, but Hawley insisted he had never heard of any offer to buy or other concrete proposals. If Harriman had made any overtures to Huntington, the old man said nothing about them even to his most intimate business associates. The camping trip resolved nothing.[7]

Then suddenly, unexpectedly, Huntington died a month later. No one doubted that his heirs would put the Southern Pacific stock on the market. Fate had decreed some fundamental change in the balance of power among the transcontinental systems, but what was it to be? Harriman grasped at once the danger of allowing the Southern Pacific to fall into the hands of George Gould or the Burlington or another Iowa road, but he also saw how to convert this threat into a golden opportunity. Only one course of action made sense to him: the Union Pacific must buy the Southern Pacific.

In rationalizing this decision years later, Otto Kahn insisted that Harriman acted because he knew George Gould was trying to buy the Southern Pacific. Gould flatly denied this, saying, "I would have considered that disloyal to my associates." If Harriman did not want the stock, Gould added, "I told him if he . . . had no objection, I would take it for our interests." But Harriman did want it. Kahn tried to explain the transaction by saying the object was to secure the Central Pacific and not the Southern Pacific, which no one really wanted because it was not profitable and required heavy expenditures for improvements. His argument convinced no one, then or now. No one who looks at Harriman's activities during these years can doubt that he saw the advantages in possessing the entire Southern Pacific system, or that he relished the challenge of putting it in harness with the Union Pacific system.[8]

The wild card in all these machinations was Gould, whose measure had yet to be taken. At thirty-seven the budding titan still floated on the achievements of his remarkable father, whom he resembled in no way. Where Jay had been silent and secretive, George was open and affable, eager to please and susceptible to flattery. Jay had been a man of bold plans and shrewd, careful judgments based on exhaustive study. George tended to be careless of detail and mercurial in his decisions, as myopic as his father was far-seeing. In his personal life George was extravagant and self-indulgent, fond of sports and parties, in contrast to his father whose tastes were abstemious and always took a back seat to business. Unlike Jay, who was a mystery even to those close to him, George was an open book to the dullest of readers.[9]

To all appearances Gould and Harriman were friends and associates in other enterprises besides Union Pacific. George seemed trusting to the point of naivete; he had offered to pick up the Southern Pacific stock, he said later, because Harriman seemed ''lukewarm'' about buying it. Yet Gould evidently had some plan of his own in mind. During 1900 he had begun buying Rio Grande stock for himself and his Missouri Pacific. Since its bankruptcy in 1886 the Rio Grande had done well under the management of George Coppell, a transplanted Englishman, and Edward T. Jeffery, the man who had quit the Illinois Central during Harriman's brief stint as acting president. The Rio Grande was in turn securing control of the Rio Grande Western. If Gould managed to capture both roads, he would own the only line to Ogden competing with the Union Pacific.[10]

The situation was a ticklish one. If Gould bought the Southern Pacific he would absorb a road that competed directly with his Texas & Pacific between El Paso and New Orleans. He would also be in a position to dictate terms to Harriman at Ogden and to the Atchison in California. If Harriman got the Southern Pacific, he would control every transcontinental line south of Washington except the Atchison. There was also a legal snag in the form of uncertainty over whether Utah law would permit the Union Pacific to own a holding company. Harriman did not hesitate. The combination of danger and opportunity spurred him to move as soon as the stock came up for sale.

In December Harriman opened negotiations with James Speyer and Edwin Hawley, who had been asked by the Huntington heirs to negotiate a sale; late in January an agreement was struck. Although the stock was sold to Kuhn, Loeb, which pocketed a handsome commission for handling the transaction, Harriman did all the bargaining personally. Not until the final meeting at Harriman's house did Schiff even put in an appearance. On February 4, 1901, Kuhn, Loeb formally offered the Union Pacific 677,700 shares of Southern Pacific at a price of $50.61 per share, and agreed to supply another 72,300 shares purchased in the market at the same price. Altogether, this would give the Union Pacific 37½ percent of the Southern Pacific's stock.[11]

To pay for these shares, Harriman devised another brilliant move. At first glance his prospects looked dismal. The Southern Pacific paid no dividends and would likely pay none for years because large expenditures were needed to modernize the road. Somehow Harriman had to raise more than $40 million at a time when he was already spending huge sums on the Union Pacific. The company was only three years out of bankruptcy, and more than one critic predicted it would soon return there.

None of these misgivings bothered Harriman. He had the Union Pacific authorize an issue of $100 million in 4 percent bonds that could be converted into stock any time before May 1906. Convertible bonds were not original with Harriman, but he was to do some very original things with them. Of this amount, $40 million was used to buy the Southern Pacific; the rest was held in reserve for other purposes. Both the acquisition and the bond issue caught Wall Street by surprise, yet subscribers snapped up the new securities within a month.[12]

The burning question was what Harriman would do with the Southern Pacific. The *Railroad Gazette* declared itself "willing to assume for the present that the good will considerably outweigh the harm." The Union Pacific and Northwestern already possessed the shortest line from Chicago to San Francisco; control of the Central Pacific would enable them to tighten their schedules even more. But what effect would it have on the other Iowa roads? Heavy buying in Rio Grande stock that February led some analysts to believe that the Burlington or Rock Island was trying to secure a line to Ogden. They were looking in the wrong direction; the purchases were coming not from the Iowa lines but from George Gould.[13]

While Harriman was arranging the Southern Pacific purchase, Gould was quietly buying Rio Grande stock in the London market so as not to attract attention. He went to Harriman and asked for a half interest in the Southern Pacific on behalf of his roads. Harriman declined the request but did put Gould on the board of the Southern Pacific. By the end of February word leaked out that Gould had gained control of the Rio Grande. In all he acquired 39 percent of its common and 16½ percent of its preferred stock. "You bought that, I suppose, for both interests—Union Pacific and your own," Harriman asked when he heard the news."

"No," Gould replied.

"Well," Harriman persisted, "I would like to have a half interest in it."

That was not possible, Gould said, but he did agree to put Harriman on the Rio Grande board.[14]

To outside eyes this arrangement embodied the community of interest principle. The major players sat on the boards of each other's companies and could keep an eye on what was going on. If nothing else, this provided a forum for discussing conflicts before they erupted into a crisis. The bankers were there, too, to mediate differences and urge harmony on all sides. While some denounced this cosy intertwining as a conspiracy to stifle competition and jack up rates, conservatives applauded it as a reasonable way to avoid the reckless overbuilding and disastrous wars that had plagued the railroad industry a generation earlier.

Those horrors were very much on their minds. In 1907 an Interstate Commerce Commission investigation would seek to prove in ponderous detail what every knowledgeable railroad man already accepted as gospel: that Harriman was bent on eliminating competition among western railroads. Railroad men hungered for a spirit of cooperation with good reason. The bitter wars of the 1880s, followed by the bankruptcies of the 1890s, had frightened them into a determination to prevent such a thing from happening again. Their minds equated competition with low rates, overexpansion, ruinous wars, and perpetual strife, all of which was grotesquely wasteful. The railroad men of Harriman's generation had been to the slaughterhouse in their youth and did not care to go again. It had been their Munich, the pivotal experience that shaped their views of what future policy should be and must never become.

The logical alternative to their nightmare was consolidation on a grand scale along with a strong community of interest among the men who dominated the giant systems that were emerging. Put the rail network in the hands of a select few who would impose order and maintain it with help from the bankers, whose conservative influence would add an element of stability. Harmony among the systems would in turn assure efficient service for shippers and solid returns for investors. However, this approach was vulnerable to attack by the government under the Sherman Antitrust Act, and it required cooperation among strong-willed, ambitious men accustomed to having their own way. How could they get along with each other any better than the previous generation of rail leaders, who had bickered and plotted like petty nobles for every scrap of advantage they could gain?

Harriman offered a perfect example of the difficulties involved. His driving style, indomitable will, and abrasive personality hardly fitted him to play the role of statesman. He wanted to harmonize the roads; others sneered that he wanted to "Harrimanize" them. The older generation didn't trust him and the younger heads feared him, or rather feared his ambition. George Gould once observed that Harriman "aims to dominate, and if he don't like us he'll throw us out." Certainly, in any negotiation Harriman would find it much easier to offer terms *as* the Southern Pacific than *to* the Southern Pacific. Even at this level the major players liked to pose as apostles of peace while watching each other's movements with a wary eye.[15]

"We have bought not only a railroad, but an empire," crowed Harriman after the Southern Pacific purchase. But emperors seemed no better than nobles at reconciling their differences or subordinating their ambitions even though they had the advantage of being fewer in number. Peace was more than a matter of power; it was a matter of attitude.[16]

These were heady times, the first years of the brave new century. "The decade from 1896 to 1906," recalled banker Henry Morgenthau, "was the period of the most gigantic expansion of business in all American history. . . . In that decade the slowly fertilized economic resources of the United States suddenly yielded a bewildering crop of industries. . . . The cry everywhere was for money—more money—and yet more money."[17]

Morgenthau was right. Everything was in motion and moving faster. So much was happening that it was difficult to keep a perspective on events. The spectacular growth of this decade had been nurtured by half a century of wrenching industrial development. Money was needed to spur the trend toward consolidation, the wave of mergers that sought to impose order on growth run amuck, and in some cases (notably the railroads) to upgrade facilities to a level capable of meeting the enormous load thrust upon them. The winter of 1901 was typical. Morgan and his partners were busy perfecting the grand consolidation of the steel industry into what would become the first billion-dollar corporation in America, United States Steel. They also bought the Jersey Central for the Philadelphia & Reading and a coal company for the Erie. Harriman scooped the Southern Pacific and Gould the Rio Grande. The Frisco picked up a major line from Kansas City to the southeast.

The urge toward acquisition and consolidation took a momentum of its own similar to the feeding frenzies that periodically seized Wall Street. In the minds of even the coolest rail managers, fear and reason jockeyed for position in every decision. Whatever sense a merger made on its own terms, there was always the prod that if you didn't do it someone else would. The urge to get ahead or at least keep the pace nagged like a bad headache and was often no more rational. A serious debate arose on how to keep order amid such madness. During that hectic winter of 1901 the masters of merger paused long enough to promote a scheme for imposing stability on the railroad industry.

For fifteen years rail managers had been groping for some way to do this within the strictures of the Interstate Commerce Act. The first efforts in the late 1880s even tried to involve ICC members in the process to ensure their sanction of the final product. In December 1890 the western roads made another attempt by forming an advisory board composed of the president and one director from each road. The idea was to have this board enforce all agreements for maintaining rates, but in 1897 the Supreme Court ruled any such agreement illegal under the Sherman Antitrust Act. For many railroad men this decision killed off any hope of keeping rates stable.[18]

A number of officers, unhappy with the rate situation, persisted in the effort to devise some way of "observing legal and more satisfactory methods in the conduct of traffic." During 1900 a series of meetings resulted in the creation of a new advisory committee composed of Harriman, Schiff, Stillman, Robert Bacon, a Morgan partner, and banker Robert Fleming. In January 1901 these five, along with J. P. Morgan, James J. Hill, Stuyvesant Fish, George Gould, and James Speyer, issued a joint call for a meeting of representatives from all western roads to create a permanent advisory committee. This summons set in motion a wave of concerned scurrying among rail officers. It had come from too formidable a group of heavyweights to be ignored. Those skeptical about the idea had therefore to find some plausible grounds for ducking the call from on high.[19]

General William J. Palmer, builder of the Rio Grande Western, had grave doubts about it. The doughty Palmer, whose long rail career had only another month to run, complained that it was "putting too much influence real or apparent, in one family, over the rate making function. Messrs. Schiff, Stillman and Robt. Fleming are pretty much *Harriman* in this matter." Bacon was a director in Stillman's bank, and two of Stillman's daughters were married to sons of William Rockefeller. Charles Perkins of the Burlington agreed that it "was all done for the aggrandizement of Harriman," and he did not like taking orders from the East any more in 1900 than he had in 1888. "The idea," he huffed, "of the Presidents of all these big western railroads running down to

New York to talk with the bankers whenever the bankers want to talk, seems absurd."[20]

Marvin Hughitt of the Northwestern also had his doubts as did some others, but no one cared to defy the call openly. Perkins suggested to Harriman that "frequent meetings in the west" would get the job done better. When Harriman deflected that argument, Perkins emphasized that the timing was poor because anti-railroad sentiments were stirring in many western legislatures, and a new committee would arouse public wrath. Moreover, Perkins believed the ICC commissioners opposed any such attempt to maintain rates, and were presently seeking indictments of railroad officers who had rate agreements. Why take the risk of forming what might be construed as an unlawful combination?[21]

Like so many attempts at cooperation, the advisory board wasted much time and energy without producing any results. Small wonder that men like Harriman and Hill came increasingly to believe that the only way to attain harmony was to eliminate the small fry through consolidation and reduce the number of players to a handful of giant systems. Perkins and Palmer belonged to that generation of rail managers who gave lip service to the importance of cooperation and were eager to have it so long as they did not have to surrender anything to get it. They were fossils already marked for extinction: by the spring neither would have a railroad to run.

It was only natural for analysts to conclude that the key battlegrounds for rail supremacy lay in the West. They had only to observe the struggles in the Northwest, at the Ogden gateway, and along the southern route. But Harriman was not so careless as to look only in one direction. From the first he recognized the threat posed by the four Iowa roads as their lines leaped across the river at the Omaha gateway. Two of them, the Northwestern and the Milwaukee, occupied the country north of the Union Pacific. The Rock Island had built extensively south of the Union Pacific, and the Burlington straddled the territory on both sides of it. All of them had toyed with the idea of extending their lines westward to the mountains, perhaps even to the coast. Any road doing this would parallel the Union Pacific and have the advantage of owning a line into Chicago as well.

Since the 1880s the Union Pacific had been closely allied with the Northwestern. It posed little danger; the Vanderbilts, who had long controlled the Northwestern, were conservative and unimaginative in their policies. A group of New Englanders still dominated the Burlington, the most efficient and aggressive of the Iowa roads, but its management was old and vulnerable to outsiders. Reckless expansion and undermaintenance had weakened the Rock Island, which was entering a period of transition that made it ripe for takeover. The Milwaukee was the last of the four roads to jump the river and a comer, but its managers too were indecisive. Here was exactly the sort of fluid situation dreaded by seekers of stability. Three of the four Iowa roads had

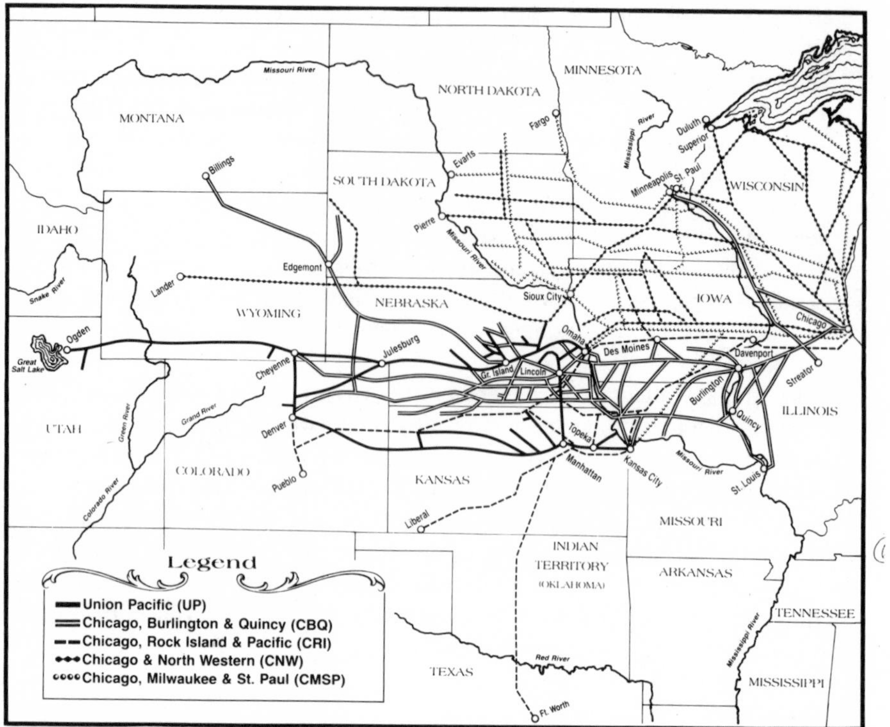

DISPUTED GROUND: The rival lines of the four Iowa roads west of the Missouri River, 1901.

aging managements and were candidates for outside buyers, who might step in and launch aggressive expansion programs.

The unsettled status of these roads injected another note of menace into an already volatile set of relationships. Some progress had been made in resolving the test of wills in the Northwest. Harriman arranged a truce with Charles Mellen of the Northern Pacific over construction in eastern Washington, and directed A. L. Mohler to turn his attention to upgrading the Navigation line between Wallula and Portland. Hill still warbled his tune of peace and harmony based on joint use of existing lines to avoid construction of new ones. Schiff joined willingly in this chorus, but his influence with Hill was fast ebbing away. Mellen still sang mostly sour notes, compounding Hill's frustration.[22]

Hill desperately wanted a settlement of all differences with Harriman in the Northwest. So did Morgan, who was eager to reassure foreign security holders with a broad show of harmony among the western roads. However, in July 1900 Hill learned that Harriman had no interest in reaching an early agreement. "He is very close to Mr. Stillman these days," a friend warned, "and the latter rates him very high as a businessman and a great railroad leader on broad and comprehensive lines—says we have had no such man in the East in a long time; that he is very rich, can command any amount of money, is independent of any man or any banking house and is very ambitious."[23]

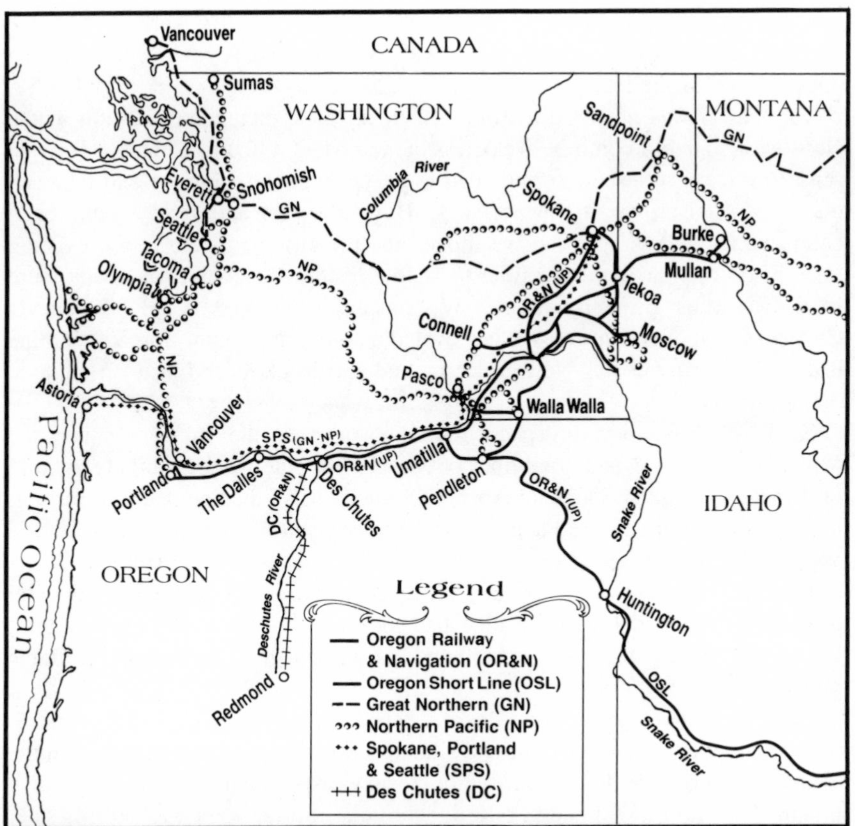

NORTHWEST BATTLEFIELD: The main lines of the three contending roads in the Northwest: the Union Pacific, Northern Pacific, and Great Northern.

These words had an ominous ring to Hill, and events did little to reassure him. A month later Collis Huntington died and the scramble for Southern Pacific began. That same fall Senator William A. Clark announced his plan to build a road from Salt Lake to Los Angeles. George Gould was quietly buying Rio Grande stock abroad. Hill himself mystified Schiff with a cryptic remark that he would soon control the Northern Pacific. In January 1901 Harriman finally offered a proposal to harmonize relations in the Northwest. Instead of a territorial division or even trackage rights, however, he suggested a "close traffic alliance" as the most practical solution.[24]

Hill frowned in dismay. The notion "has a pleasant and assuring sound," he replied wearily, "but how can it be applied? All such divisions or agreements are illegal and cannot be enforced; therefore they are more apt to lead to trouble than to avoid it." The only permanent solution, he insisted, was for each company to control the roads in its own territory. He enclosed yet another plan along those lines with little hope that Harriman would change his views. A new squabble over the line between Portland and the Puget Sound also broke out, leaving Hill sick to death of Mellen's intransigence. By spring everyone expected an explosion in the Northwest; to their surprise, it occurred at the opposite end of the line.[25]

The reason was not hard to find. All three roads dicing for position in the Northwest shared a common weakness: none owned a line to Chicago. It made sense for a true transcontinental road to be anchored in Chicago and to reach the West Coast over its own tracks. Buying a Chicago road would be a defensive as well as an offensive move, and the unsettled state of the existing lines made this an attractive time to shop. Besides the four Iowa roads there were two other possibilities, the Wisconsin Central and A. B. Stickney's Chicago Great Western, but neither owned an attractive route. The Vanderbilts had a firm grip on the Northwestern, and the Rock Island had an inflated opinion of its value.

By far the two best prospects for takeover were the Burlington and the Milwaukee. Both owned good lines out of Chicago and were good bets to build farther west unless checked. In April 1900 rumors flared anew that the Burlington would lay track to the Pacific coast. The company was preparing to invade Wyoming, and its separate depot in Omaha was a stark monument to its "apparent purpose . . . to become an independent factor in trans-continental business." Hill and Harriman alike had long coveted the 8,000-mile system, considered among the best constructed, best managed, and most profitable railroads in the country.[26]

Harriman moved first. His Alaskan expedition in 1899 gave him time to reflect on the entire western railroad situation. That August he had proposed the idea of a merger with the Burlington to a vice-president of that road. Five months later he had sounded Perkins, who told him the road was not for sale. As they parted, Harriman asked Perkins what he thought Burlington stock was worth. At least $200 a share in the long run, answered Perkins. In March 1900 they met again in Chicago, where Harriman offered to pay the $200 per share in Union Pacific 3 percent bonds or $140 per share in cash. Perkins shook his head. Cash only, he declared, and $200 a share. Out of the question, Harriman snapped, but he promised to discuss it with Schiff.[27]

For once the hard-trading Harriman had met his match. The gruff, shrewd Perkins, nearing the end of a distinguished career as president, recognized that the Burlington was not destined to be one of the major systems. Anxious to secure its future, he saw the necessity of tying it to one of the major roads, but which one? The logical choices were the Great Northern and the Union Pacific. Perkins had no doubts about his preference. He had long admired Hill, and the Burlington fit neatly with the Great Northern system. By contrast, the Union Pacific had been his ancient enemy since the late 1870s, when he had been an implacable foe of Jay Gould. The fit with the Union Pacific was not so neat and the emotional fit even worse. Perkins had no love for the company and still less for Harriman, who may have reminded him a little of Gould. But sentiment would not deflect him from wringing the best possible terms from any buyer on behalf of the army of small stockholders he represented. As historian Albro Martin noted, the widows and orphans were in good hands with Perkins.[28]

On April 21 Harriman tried again, this time with Schiff at his elbow to smooth the way. When Perkins again refused to budge, Harriman quietly put together one of his patent "common interest" syndicates of Schiff, Stillman, and George Gould to buy Burlington stock in the market. By July 25 the syndicate had acquired 80,300 shares at an average price of 125⅞. The price kept rising, however, and it soon became evident that control could not be bought in the open market. They had hit what Hill later called a stone wall of small stockholders who would sell only on cue from Perkins. Twice that summer Harriman visited Perkins at his summer place in New Hampshire to ask for a Union Pacific representative of the Burlington board. With control of the stock you get the entire board, came the flinty reply; without it, you get nothing.[29]

All of Harriman's tactics had failed. If he wanted the Burlington, he could get it only by paying $200 per share cash, well above the market price but not excessive for the property and its assets. He was not a man to flinch at the bottom line, yet he did so this time and would long regret it. With only 8 percent of the Burlington's stock and no prospect of getting enough to control the board, the discouraged syndicate began selling off its stock early in November at prices ranging from 130 to 140⅝. When the pool closed up shop on December 21, 60,300 shares had been sold; the remaining 20,000 shares were divided equally among the participants. By then, Harriman was deep into negotiations for the Southern Pacific.[30]

Collis Huntington's death in August 1900 must have distracted Harriman from the Burlington. Ordinary mortals would not even have conceived the idea of buying two huge rail systems at once. The notion raced through Harriman's mind, but the financial requirements were enough to give even him pause. A few weeks later he arranged for the Union Pacific issue of $100 million in convertible bonds, of which only $40 million was needed for the Southern Pacific purchase. The remainder was available for some other giant deal, but Perkins wanted cash, not bonds. Harriman would have to swallow not only a price he thought high but also the additional expense of selling the bonds to raise cash for the transaction—and this at a time when he was trying to close the Southern Pacific transaction.

Harriman's rivals were also busy that autumn. Morgan and Hill had long agreed that both the Great Northern and Northern Pacific needed a terminus at Chicago, but they differed over which road to go after. Morgan favored the Milwaukee because it was cheaper; Hill preferred the Burlington because it let him into territory claimed by the Union Pacific "over better lines and with better terminals than any other road." Especially did he covet a line the Burlington had built northward from Nebraska to a connection with the Northern Pacific at Billings, Montana. When Morgan insisted on the Milwaukee, Hill reluctantly bowed to the great man's wishes and opened negotiations that fall. To his relief William Rockefeller, the dominant holder of the Milwaukee, had no desire to sell. When their discussions fizzled in December, Morgan changed front. "Go ahead," he told Hill, "and see what you can do about the Burlington."[31]

For months the merger mania had been gathering like a vast cloud over the West. Suddenly, violently, it burst in a storm of activity during the winter of 1901. Harriman wrapped up the Southern Pacific, Gould was picking up Rio Grande stock, and Hill took up his pursuit of the Burlington just as Harriman resumed the hunt. At a meeting in Chicago on February 10, Harriman offered to buy half the Burlington's stock. Perkins put him off; his lack of interest may have been influenced by the arrival of a note from Hill asking that they meet the following day. At that session Hill proposed a merger of the Burlington and Great Northern through an exchange of shares. At last Perkins had the suitor he wanted, but he stuck by his terms: $200 a share cash.[32]

Hill demurred but promised another offer. As the price of Burlington climbed in the market, everyone suspected everyone else of buying. Schiff thought it was Hill, who asked Perkins if it was his friends. Perkins put the blame on Kuhn, Loeb, a charge Hill was quick to pass along to Morgan in hopes of goading him into action. Perkins stood firm on his price but left a door open for Hill that he had not for Harriman by suggesting how they might agree on terms. On February 22 Harriman dined with Perkins and two of his directors. Although he noted pointedly that Hill and Morgan were actively buying Burlington, he made no new offer. Instead, he merely asked the board to appoint someone to negotiate with him. Two days later Perkins sat down with two key advisors to weigh the advantages of combining with Hill or with Harriman. "Our unanimous conclusion," he reported the next day, "was that if Hill means also Morgan and the Northern Pacific, as he says it does, that would be the stronger and safer place for us to land."[33]

Meanwhile, Harriman tried to bring indirect pressure on Morgan to arrange a joint purchase of the Burlington by the Union Pacific and the Northern Pacific. To emphasize his point, he demanded new talks on the Puget Sound line controversy, and stalled progress on a settlement in the Northwest. Hill got this news on March 2; that same day he asked Perkins to consider a new plan. Morgan was preparing to embark on his annual pilgrimage to Europe, and Hill wanted an agreement before he sailed. But Perkins rejected the new offer, sending Hill back to confer with Morgan. On March 18 Hill wired Perkins an urgent request to meet in terms so cryptic that Perkins was not sure who had sent the message. Aware that secrecy was crucial, Perkins suggested they meet in Boston at the sedate Victoria Hotel on Dartmouth Street. It was, he noted, "a family hotel, where few people go."[34]

Bitter controversy arose over what happened next. Schiff claimed that late in March he and Harriman grew alarmed over what Schiff called "large and continuous buying, irrespective of price, of Burlington stock, by people known to be close to Mr. Hill." They visited Hill and asked whether he was after the Burlington. Hill denied that he was buying the stock or had any interest in acquiring the road. Schiff took his old friend at his word and felt deeply wounded when events made Hill out to be a liar. In typical fashion the voluble Hill poured out several refutations of this charge and insisted he had told Harriman what he was doing, but his versions of what happened are not

POWERFUL FRIENDS: James J. Hill strolls down the street, arm in arm with two close allies, Morgan partner Charles Steele (*left*) and banker George F. Baker. *(James J. Hill Papers, Hill Reference Library)*

consistent. More likely, he was trying to convince himself that in the heat of battle he had not stooped to deceiving an old friend.[35]

In a series of meetings at the Victoria between March 27 and April 9, Hill thrashed out terms with Perkins. Schiff got wind of the last meeting and sent his son Morti to intercept Hill at the ferry landing in New York. Morti brought Hill to the house of George F. Baker, where Harriman and the elder Schiff were waiting. Why, asked Schiff dolefully, had Hill said he was not buying Burlington and had no interest in the road? Unfortunate, Hill conceded, but necessary at the time. Schiff pleaded with Hill not to close the deal without first coming to some agreement protecting the Union Pacific's interests. Hill refused. The purchase, warned Harriman bluntly, was an invasion of Union Pacific territory that could only be taken as a hostile act. He urged Hill to reconsider. When Hill mumbled some evasive platitudes, Harriman snapped, "Then you will have to take the consequences."[36]

A deep sense of foreboding filled Schiff, who alone understood what awful repercussions would flow from a head-on collision between Harriman and Hill. He hurried to see Morgan but found him on the verge of departing for Europe and unwilling to talk business. Disheartened, he took the matter up with Morgan partner Robert Bacon, who had already told Harriman that nothing could be done until the Union Pacific made some proposal. Schiff warned that the merger "would bring the Northern roads, with their great power, at the throat of all trans-Missouri railroad interests, and would bring about a situation which would particularly be a constant danger to the Union Pacific." To avert this disaster, Schiff offered to take a one-third interest in the Burlington purchase at full price. It was too late, Bacon shrugged; the matter was already closed. In that case, retorted Schiff gloomily, the Union Pacific would have to protect itself. Later Hill claimed publicly that the offer was refused because it was against the law; privately, however, he gave quite different reasons: "the Q directors would not deal with them [Union Pacific] as parties in interest and second, we did not want them."[37]

So much for community of interest.

It is hard to believe that the position of Hill and Morgan did not reflect some degree of payback for the aggravation caused them in the Northwest. Harriman had disrupted the joint ownership of Navigation and seized the road for himself; now he was asking Hill and Morgan to share the Burlington with him. He had resisted all proposals by Hill and Morgan for peace in the Northwest; now he was asking them to swallow his plan for peace on the plains. Only a few years earlier, on hearing the roster of directors for the newly organized Union Pacific, Hill had asked, "Now, who the hell is Harriman?" He had found out the hard way, and it must have given him satisfaction to chasten the pushy upstart with a dose of his own medicine. Morgan had long despised Harriman and, in the words of his son-in-law, resented the request for a third interest as "butting in." He did not want Harriman as a partner, and may well have let prejudice overrule his judgment on good policy.[38]

Schiff made a personal appeal to Hill, but in vain. Perkins, Hill, and Bacon moved briskly to wrap up the details that would divide the Burlington equally between the Great Northern and the Northern Pacific. On April 20 the offer was formally tendered amid rumors that the Union Pacific was chasing the Milwaukee and might unite with it and perhaps the Northwestern as well. Perkins didn't think any such combination could touch the new one, and Hill agreed. "The future," proclaimed Hill, "will justify the value of the trade." To those who thought the price too high, he retorted that in the long run it would seem cheap. But Hill had yet to see the final price tag. Within a week he would discover that the stakes of empire building had shot up higher than anyone dared imagine.[39]

6

The Community of Interest

The basic premise was simplicity itself; it was the scale that boggled men's minds. If they would not sell the colt, Harriman would buy the mare. Denied a share of the Burlington purchase, he would get it by buying one of the buyers. The Great Northern was out of the question, but the Northern Pacific was vulnerable to a lightning attack if one had capital and nerve enough. It had outstanding $80 million in common and $75 million in preferred stock. Of that amount, Hill and Morgan controlled $35 or $40 million, which they assumed was more than enough. Who would be foolish enough to try to buy control of a $155-million property in the market?[1]

On Harriman's order Schiff began picking up Northern Pacific shares early in April 1901, shortly after his frustrating interview with Bacon. The purchases were large but easily masked as the doings of speculators because the market was in turmoil that month. The Burlington takeover was in progress; Gould was gobbling the Wheeling & Lake Erie and the Rio Grande, which was in turn gobbling the Rio Grande Western; and financier John W. Gates was chasing Colorado Fuel & Iron with a zeal that nearly doubled the stock's price. Heavy transactions in the Milwaukee spurred rumors that the Union Pacific would soon own the road, and huge transactions were recorded in Union Pacific itself amid stories that the Northwestern or the Hill-Morgan group were after the company.[2]

All this provided excellent ground cover for Schiff's campaign. By April 15 he had acquired 100,000 shares of Northern Pacific preferred and 150,000 shares of common, which he let the Union Pacific have at 101 and 102½ respectively. Two weeks later he delivered Harriman another 150,000 shares of preferred at 102½ and 120,000 shares of common at 112, giving the Union Pacific in all $25 million of preferred and $27 million of common. Asked to buy another $25 million worth, Schiff came up with 150,000 shares and went shopping for more on a rising market.[3]

At first these heavy transactions aroused no suspicion. Morgan had sailed for Europe on April 4, leaving Bacon and George W. Perkins in charge of his firm's affairs. Hill departed for the Pacific coast on April 15 to show off his Great Northern to an influential English friend. Historian Albro Martin has demolished the myth that Hill, while in Seattle, reacted to sharp movements in Northern Pacific stock by making a mad dash across the continent on a line cleared for him. He did make a record run back to St. Paul just for fun, but then lingered there a week. During that time Northern Pacific attracted little attention until Friday, April 26, when the price jumped three points on large transactions. The next day an analyst linked the buying to Union Pacific, but few took him seriously. Banker Grant B. Schley was negotiating some matter with Harriman and Gould on Hill's behalf. Hill wanted to see Schley in New York that weekend, but Schley left town and Hill did not head eastward until Saturday evening.[4]

Here begins an intriguing mystery. Most accounts have Hill arriving in New York on Friday, May 3, the same date Schiff confirms that he met with Hill. However, Martin has shown that Hill stepped off the train on Monday morning, April 29. During that pivotal week enough happened for Harriman to see his bold scheme come within a whisker of success and to convince Hill that a gigantic conspiracy was in the making. The question is, how early in the week did he arrive at this conclusion, and what did he do about it?

What little is known about Hill's movements after he checked into the Netherlands Hotel on Monday suggests that he had come to New York for other reasons than anxiety over the Northern Pacific. The plan for financing the Burlington purchase had just gone public and had to be promoted. Hill's daughters were going abroad, and he saw them off. Family affairs also occupied Schiff, whose son Morti was married on Tuesday. A reporter spotted the Harrimans and the William Rockefellers among those enjoying the reception at Sherry's, but not Schiff's old friend, James J. Hill. This pleasant interlude was but the eye of a storm that would rock Wall Street for the next two weeks.[5]

The market was going crazy and no one knew why. One sensation followed another as heavy transactions in several stocks jerked prices up and down with a violence not seen in years. On Monday, April 29, Union Pacific shot up eleven points and Northern Pacific ten. "The rise," concluded one baffled analyst, "was a mystery." Charles Perkins, then in Boston, thought he knew. "I see there has been great buying of Northern Pacific, and high prices," he wrote Hill on Tuesday. "Is not that situation the weak link in your chain?" But his letter went to St. Paul instead of New York.[6]

The undisputed leader in the rumor mill was not Northern Pacific but Union Pacific, which on April 24 had set a new record for transactions in one stock as 662,800 of its shares changed hands in a single day. When the price soared from 98½ to 133 in ten days, observers agreed the cause was "buying for control,'' but by whom? On Wednesday, May 1, the New York *Times* stunned Wall Street by proclaiming that a syndicate interested in the Northwestern had snatched the Union Pacific away from Harriman. No one noticed that the syndicate members also had large holdings in Alton and were the same men who had earlier asked Harriman to reorganize that road, or that at least one of them was associated with him in the Illinois Central. Were they buying on his behalf?[7]

Heavy purchases of Milwaukee were also recorded. Was the Union Pacific buying, or was it the same Northwestern syndicate hoping to combine the three roads into one huge counterweight against the Great Northern-Northern Pacific-Burlington system? The mystery deepened when word leaked out that Roswell Miller, the Milwaukee's chairman, had resigned from the Union Pacific board six weeks earlier. To reporters he offered only the bland explanation that he could do the Milwaukee no good in the position. In fact, he was alarmed that the Milwaukee might remain a wallflower as the other systems chose partners in the consolidation quickstep.[8]

Miller's resignation in March had been part protest, part warning. The Union Pacific treated the Milwaukee well on freight traffic but favored the Northwestern on passenger business. If this policy continued, Miller told Harriman, the Milwaukee would be forced to build its own line to the coast. In that case, retorted Harriman, why don't you start tomorrow? On April 9 a distraught Miller, hearing of the Burlington sale, told Schiff that if the deal went through, the Milwaukee would go to the Pacific coast. Schiff was not as cavalier about the threat as Harriman, and both were anxious to prevent the construction of needless lines. This desire reinforced their determination to neutralize the Burlington threat by sharing in the purchase.[9]

After slipping back on Tuesday, Union Pacific jumped thirteen points the next day. Volume on the Exchange hit a record three million shares on Tuesday and flirted with that level all week. As the takeover rumors heated up, Harriman said only that he was not selling Union Pacific and that ''There is no news.'' During Thursday's frantic trading a big run in Atchison stole the headlines, and a sharp break in prices on Friday left the pundits even more bewildered than usual. Pondering these confused ingredients, the *Times* on Sunday, May 5, concocted a wild tale of a gigantic rail combination among the Morgan, Hill, Gould, and Vanderbilt interests.[10]

By the time this fantasy titillated readers, the real story had unfolded with startling swiftness. On Friday morning, May 3, Hill strolled into the building at 27 Pine Street where both Kuhn, Loeb and the Great Northern had offices. Schiff was waiting for him, his face wreathed in a somber expression. He ushered Hill into his private office and confided that Kuhn, Loeb was buying Northern Pacific on behalf of the Union Pacific and had acquired 40 percent of the stock, about $62 million worth. Their object, he added earnestly, was to ''bring about the harmony and community of interest which other means and appeals . . . had failed to produce.''[11]

''But you can't get control,'' Hill exclaimed, thinking of the $35 or $40 million held by the Great Northern and his friends, who would never sell.

Later, to his chagrin, he would learn that some of the stock Schiff bought had in fact come from a Morgan trust fund and from the treasury of the Northern Pacific itself. Both had sold to reap profits, never suspecting that the shares were going to the enemy.[12]

"That may be," Schiff replied, "but we've got a lot of it."

Hill wrote several versions of what happened next. Taken together, they amount to an intriguing conspiracy theory for which there exists no known evidence to confirm or deny. According to Hill, Schiff proposed that the Great Northern, the Northern Pacific, and the Burlington be put together with the Union Pacific and the Southern Pacific under Hill's direction. All Hill had to do was cut his ties with Morgan and join forces with Schiff and Harriman. During this talk Harriman burst into the room several times to say, "You are the boss. We are all working for you. Give me your orders."[13]

Why this offer? "I am sure the main motive," Hill wrote, "was truly expressed by Stillman and others who said they would show the world that Morgan was not the only banker in America, &c, that all other banking houses were nothing more than his clerks, and talked of clipping his wings, &c." To his mind it was not Harriman who pulled the strings but his ally Stillman, and behind Stillman stood William Rockefeller and the huge capital resources of the Standard Oil crowd. Since Rockefeller dominated the Milwaukee, that road could also be brought into the combination. Here was a group formidable enough to challenge even Jupiter.[14]

It is difficult to imagine the cautious Schiff being so indiscreet about Morgan or Harriman's playing the part assigned him by Hill. Harriman was a poor actor and an even poorer puppet. Although Hill did not like Harriman and had yet to take his full measure, he didn't underestimate the threat facing him. The danger to both sides was very real. If the Burlington purchase went unchallenged, the new combination would parallel the Union Pacific on both sides and threaten its local business through branch construction. If the Union Pacific gained control of the Northern Pacific and half of the Burlington, it would pin the Great Northern against the Canadian border and dominate the entire region south of it to the Pacific coast. The stakes were enormous: to the victor went the mushrooming business of the Northwest.

Hill was not tempted by Schiff's offer, but he feigned interest. Hurrying to Morgan's office, he informed Bacon of the threat and puzzled over how to meet it. A check of the stock transfer books gave him the answer: it appeared that Harriman was buying a majority of Northern Pacific common and preferred *combined* rather than of each stock. But there existed a provision that allowed the Northern Pacific's board to retire the preferred stock any time after January 1, 1902. Harriman planned to put in his own men at the annual meeting scheduled for October 1901, but if the present board could delay that meeting until after New Year's Day, it could retire the preferred stock before the Harriman's men climbed aboard. In short, absolute control rested entirely with the common stock, and Harriman had not yet grasped that fact.[15]

But he soon would, Hill was certain of it. The trick was to grab enough common to ensure control before Harriman realized his mistake, say $15 or $20 million worth. Since Bacon could not buy on that scale without Morgan's approval, an urgent cable was dispatched to Aix-les-Bains, where Morgan had gone for his annual visit. That evening Hill went to Schiff's house and lingered past midnight, plying him with assurances that all Schiff had proposed could be accomplished with little difficulty. The most voluble of men, Hill could wear out his welcome even when he was most welcome. More than once he had droned on until Schiff dozed off, ignoring all hints by the butler offering a nightcap or announcing his cab. This night he was buying time by playing possum with his old friend.[16]

On Saturday morning, May 4, Harriman was ill in bed at home, but his mind had not stopped churning. Counsel had assured him that a majority of all Northern Pacific stock was sufficient to control the company, but he knew of the loophole that allowed the preferred to be retired and it bothered him. From his sickbed he telephoned Kuhn, Loeb and told a partner named Heinsheimer to buy 40,000 shares of Northern Pacific common for his personal account. Heinsheimer acknowledged the order, and heavy trading in the stock during the morning convinced Harriman that it had been executed. He settled back on his pillow secure in the belief that Northern Pacific was his.[17]

At the elegant Regina Grand Hotel in Aix-les-Bains, Morgan scowled at the cable handed him but did not hesitate in his reply. Bacon was authorized to buy at any price all the Northern Pacific common needed to assure control. Banker John S. Kennedy, a longtime associate of Hill's, happened to be at Aix-les-Bains then and saw Morgan frequently during the next few days. He was not surprised to see Jupiter's massive brow furrow in agitation over the news reaching him by cable from New York. Hill had notified all his close friends of the battle, and Kennedy was quick to take his place on the ramparts. "*We must stand by [Morgan] to the end,*" he wrote Hill, "*be the outcome what it may.*"[18]

Morgan's cable did not reach Bacon until Saturday afternoon after the market had closed. Nothing could be done until Monday, and no one had any illusions as to what would happen then. Buying on such a scale in an already overheated market amounted to sticking one's hand in a furnace. There was no time for finesse or flanking maneuvers; it had to be a frontal assault, two bulls bashing heads. When the bell rang Monday morning, the Morgan brokers swarmed out with buy orders and the price shot upward. By the day's end it soared 17½ points to 127½ on a volume of 429,900 shares, a spurt that in one analyst's opinion "transcended anything yet seen . . . on this bull market." In a few days it would seem small change.[19]

Harriman noticed the frantic trading and quickly called Kuhn, Loeb to ask Heinsheimer why he had received no confirmation of his Saturday order. The abashed broker replied that before executing the order he had tried to contact Schiff, who was at synagogue. After some difficulty he reached Schiff and was told not to execute the order on his [Schiff's] responsibility. The shares had not been bought, and now the price was marching to the moon. Realizing that little could be done in a market gone mad, Harriman dragged himself downtown to make the best fight he could.[20]

By Tuesday's end the major players had stopped buying. Morgan's men had filled their orders, and Harriman recognized he could do little because the supply of actual Northern Pacific stock had all been corraled. But speculators still tugged desperately at it. Later that day a firm buying heavily for Morgan issued a call for the stock to be delivered, sending short sellers into a panic. While other stocks broke violently, Northern Pacific soared another sixteen points to close at 143½ on a volume of 231,400 shares.[21]

On Wednesday Harriman reported his past purchases to the Union Pacific board and got a rubber stamp to buy or sell as much Northern Pacific as needed. But there was little to do except perhaps sell some shares to the frantic traders who had taken over the market. Turmoil swept the floor of the Exchange as the realization dawned on short sellers that larger forces were at work and no Northern Pacific could be had. The stock had been cornered, but this was unlike past corners on Wall Street. Someone was fighting for control rather than driving the price skyward to sell for profit, which meant they would keep the stock off the market. That day the entire list again fell sharply while Northern Pacific climbed to 160 on sales of only 59,900 shares. Late into the night crowds of brokers and reporters surged anxiously through the halls of the Waldorf Astoria Hotel, talking, craning their necks to overhear conversations, wringing their hands in despair over what the next day might bring.[22]

The market opened ragged Thursday morning as Northern Pacific bobbed up and down between 170 and 210. A strong surge by Union Pacific brought some eager buying. Then suddenly chaos swept the floor as the trapped shorts, unable to beg or borrow Northern Pacific to cover, bid the price up with heart-stopping speed from 320 to 550 and 700 and finally to 1,000 for one 300-share transaction. Meanwhile, other stocks plummeted five to ten points at a time. The army of haggard, ashen-faced brokers milling about the floor gaped in bewilderment, unable to comprehend what was happening around them.[23]

Meanwhile, meetings among Hill, Harriman, and their allies had begun on Wednesday and continued all the next day while panic reigned on the Exchange. Late Thursday afternoon Harriman and Bacon agreed to settle with the shorts at $150 a share and not demand immediate delivery. The traders on the Exchange heaved a sigh of relief, and Northern Pacific closed the day at 325, up 165 for the day. When the story behind the fight leaked out, criticism poured in on Harriman and Hill even though most observers realized they had no role in the panic itself. In his curt way Harriman later referred to the episode as "the supposed contest between Morgan & Co. and ourselves." A weary insider put it more bluntly. "The trouble has grown out of personal feeling between Mr. Harriman and Mr. Morgan," he sighed. "It is an ugly thing all around."[24]

And it was far from over. The panic faded into history, but the battle over Northern Pacific still dangled in limbo. Although Hill and Morgan had secured a majority of common stock, grave doubts remained as to whether the current Northern Pacific board could legally postpone the annual meeting and retire the preferred. Harriman claimed later to have opinions from five eminent lawyers that no such thing could be done. Hill's lawyer assured him that it could be done, but at such high stakes no one cared to test the issue in the courts, where it might remain for months. Nor did they wish to inflame the growing public hostility over what was perceived as a clash between titans indifferent to the fallout on innocent bystanders. The logical alternative was a compromise among men who were accustomed to having their own way and did not even like each other.[25]

Harriman was ready to bargain. He did not want the Northern Pacific or the Burlington so much as a voice in the Burlington's management to protect his system. A compromise might secure this for him and open the door to some larger accommodation that would ensure peace and cooperation among the transcontinental lines. The problem was that Hill did not want to work with Harriman or be associated with him in any way, which made it hard for him to approach the table with an open mind. For the next two weeks he sidestepped Harriman's overtures and tried to pick up any loose shares of Northern Pacific he could find. Harriman too had authority to keep buying, but there was nothing left to buy. Later the two sides would discover that they owned $79 million of the $80 million common stock.[26]

"The Union Pacific ought to combine with the Northwestern and let our combination alone," grumbled Charles Perkins. Here was a typical vision of the future—a few giant systems dominating as separate but equals much as a handful of major roads had done a generation earlier. Hill shared this notion of territorial domination. "It rather looks to me," he told Marvin Hughitt, "as if the future would bring about three groups, a 'Northwest,' 'Middle' and 'Southwest.' " But Harriman's vision transcended the notion of more of the same at a higher level. He wanted not merely consolidation but *integration* on a grand scale. Late in May he informed Bacon that a settlement was possible if he and Hill could agree on "common methods of management and accounting" for all the roads under their control.[27]

Hill viewed this offer more as threat than as opportunity, but he was at least willing to talk. No one could ignore the public rumblings about some huge and sinister monopoly in the making. To lessen the appearance of parallel lines under common ownership, Harriman arranged on May 28 for the Oregon Short Line to buy the Union Pacific's newly acquired shares of Northern Pacific. Three days later Harriman, Hill, Schiff, and Bacon slipped into the exclusive Metropolitan Club in New York to finalize a settlement. The document they produced contained only two major points. The first authorized Morgan to name the new board of the Northern Pacific. In effect, Hill and his friends would control the board while granting the Union Pacific people enough seats to represent their interests.[28]

This deal, made public with assurance that "complete and permanent harmony will result under the plan adopted," was a concession by Harriman to avoid a bitter, protracted fight and obtain the pledge embodied in the second point. Hill agreed to join in devising some plan to establish and maintain uniform methods of management and accounting for the Union Pacific, Southern Pacific, Northern Pacific, Great Northern, and Burlington. A committee of four drawn from these roads (except the Burlington) would formulate the plan, with any point of dispute arbitrated by William K. Vanderbilt or A. J. Cassatt of the Pennsylvania Railroad. The Northwestern, Milwaukee, Atchison, and Missouri Pacific would be invited under this same umbrella, which would also provide for some means of resolving any differences or grievances among the member roads.[29]

In truth, Harriman had little choice but to compromise. He could go only as far as his banking allies Schiff and Stillman would follow, and they were anxious to stop the bloodletting before it drew the public wrath down on all their heads. By contrast, Hill was entirely willing to trade promises of future cooperation to get what he wanted at present, and he had the unwavering support of the most powerful banker in America. Moreover, he was far more sensitive than Harriman to the need of putting a good public face on the deal, and he had long contemplated a plan to secure the properties that comprised his rail empire by locking them up in a holding company. This would ease his current predicament by placing control of all the companies beyond Harriman's reach and reducing him to the role of stockholder.

Hill was careful not to trouble Harriman with this idea during the eventful summer of 1901. Instead he joined in taking the first step toward integration. Traffic policy seemed a logical place to start, if only because rates west of Chicago had again gone to pieces. Early in June Harriman and Hill agreed to try a bold experiment. Each man appointed a traffic officer based in Chicago to represent all his systems, and the two men were told to coordinate all their efforts. Hill named Darius Miller, a genial, moon-faced executive with a rare gift for getting things done without antagonizing people. Harriman chose John C. Stubbs, the gaunt, bespectacled traffic genius of the Southern Pacific. Stubbs had been present since the creation, having come to the Central Pacific in 1870 and handled traffic affairs for Collis Huntington for thirty years. It helped that Miller and Stubbs were old friends who admired and respected each other's work.[30]

On one point Harriman and Hill crossed swords. Oblivious as usual of public opinion, Harriman insisted that the two traffic men be made directors and given the title "Traffic Director." Hill objected that this plan would create the appearance of a commission, which would be illegal, and provoke an inquiry if not an investigation from the ICC. "I fear Harriman loses sight of the danger of arousing unnecessary opposition from the public," Hill confided to Bacon. "I am sure both companies should avoid using the same title." Uncertain as to the best way to handle Miller's appointment, Hill and Bacon let the matter drift for a month after Harriman named Stubbs as his traffic manager.[31]

On July 26 Morgan formally announced his selection of new directors for the Northern Pacific, naming Harriman, Hill, William Rockefeller, banker Harrison M. Twombley (a Vanderbilt man), and Samuel Rea of the Pennsylvania Railroad. "It is remarkable to have a transaction of such importance carried on in the daylight," noted one analyst, "and it is also remarkable as an example of the popular theory of 'community of interest.' " Schiff praised the choices and sailed to Europe for a rest, taking care to warn Harriman before he left to keep an eye on what the new Northern Pacific board did with the preferred stock.[32]

Once Harriman accepted Morgan's choices without a murmur, Hill fretted anxiously over whether he would actually deliver his Northern Pacific proxies for the October election. His unease reeks of irony. Hill worried that his rival might scuttle the whole arrangement with some act of treachery, yet it was he who was scheming mightily behind the scenes to put together a giant new holding company that would reduce Harriman's influence and eliminate "such raids as had been made by the Union Pacific interests." Hill did not even want Harriman in the new company, but Morgan persuaded him that Harriman would be far more dangerous out of the company than in it. In August Morgan met several times with Harriman and Hill, prodding them in his inimitable way to reconcile their differences.[33]

On September 1 Hill visited Harriman at Arden, his estate in the Ramapo Mountains. Their talks convinced Hill that the proxies would be forthcoming, and in fact Morgan received them five days later. Relieved of this anxiety, Hill and his friends hurried their plans for the new holding company. Morgan had suggested that George Gould be invited to join the Northern Pacific board, and Schiff agreed it might "have the tendency of bringing Mo Pac into the grouping." One ominous note marred this swelling chorus of harmony. On the same day that Harriman delivered his proxies, an anarchist shot President William McKinley. Eight days later McKinley died and the presidency passed to the young and unpredictable Theodore Roosevelt.[34]

At the time, however, Roosevelt was the least of Harriman's worries. Hill and Morgan had boxed him into a corner from which he could find no suitable escape. He objected to retiring the Northern Pacific preferred except on his own terms but could not get them accepted short of going to court. He was aware that going into the new holding company would dilute his strength even more, but what was the alternative? The conversion of his Northern Pacific common to holding company shares, he testified later, "was a foregone conclusion unless we were prepared to commence litigation, which would be protracted and which would probably be detrimental to all railroad securities in view of the panic of May 9." Even if he chose to fight, he knew that Schiff had no stomach for it.[35]

Harriman chafed at these harsh realities, but he could not ignore them. Reluctantly he came to terms on a whole range of issues with Hill. He agreed to come into the new holding company, and to accept the sort of territorial agreement in the Northwest he had always opposed. Hill gained trackage rights over the Navigation Company line to Portland and Harriman over the Northern Pacific to the Puget Sound. The old disputes in Idaho and eastern Washington were resolved, with all traffic details left to Stubbs and Miller. No mention of this pact leaked out; the press was absorbed by the far more sensational story of the new holding company. However, the participants considered it vital to ensuring peace in the Northwest. Ever optimistic, Schiff called the arrangement "of the greatest importance and advantage to the Union Pacific."[36]

On November 12 the Northern Securities Company was chartered in New Jersey with an authorized capital of $400 million, making it second in size only to United States Steel. Harriman was allotted three of its fifteen directors; the rest were Hill, Morgan, and Northern Pacific men. Hill was named president, and no Harriman ally was given an office. Harriman exchanged his Northern Pacific holdings for about $82.5 million worth of stock in Northern Securities. To all appearances this represented a smashing victory for Hill. He had not only locked up his properties in the new holding company but also forced on Harriman the territorial agreement he had resisted for so long.[37]

Why then did Harriman acquiesce? Apart from receiving a fifth of the seats on the Northern Securities board, he also gained a concession that has gone unnoticed. The conflict began over the Burlington, and no settlement would endure that did not somehow neutralize the threat it posed to the Union Pacific. To get what he wanted, Hill had to give something. Reluctantly he agreed to create a new company called the Chicago, Burlington & Quincy Railway, which would lease the Burlington system for 999 years. Half the stock of the new company would be owned by the Great Northern, the other half by the Union Pacific. In this way the Union Pacific would be secured from expansion by the Burlington even though it would not manage the road. The last obstacle to harmony would be removed.[38]

Or would it? One shrewd analyst suspected that Hill knew the courts would undo this arrangement because the Union Pacific could not own part of a parallel and competing line. Hill was aware of Harriman's blind spot in this area, and he may well have expected to get back what he appeared to give. But there loomed an even greater question: could Northern Securities itself stand up in court? No one doubted that the test would be made, and it came with surprising speed. Five days after the company was incorporated, Governor Samuel R. Van Sant of Minnesota denounced it as an "open violation of the plain intent and purpose of the law" and promised a suit against it. With the zeal of one looking toward reelection, Van Sant sounded the governors of surrounding states on joining the crusade. Disappointed by the response, he nevertheless had the state file suit against Northern Securities and also vowed to carry the fight to Washington.[39]

There lay the real danger. Hill's lawyers assured him that Northern Securities did not violate antitrust law, but he wanted no chances taken. When Stubbs pressed the need to finalize a traffic agreement for the Northwest, Hill warned Miller to do nothing that would challenge state law or arouse the ICC. He also went about giving speeches defending his actions and promising great benefits to the region from the new order. In one speech he recounted the background to the fight and naturally placed the Union Pacific in the role of villain. His remarks, wrote an associate, put Schiff "very near convulsions," but Harriman shrugged them off as the kind of stump speaking needed to win friends in the Northwest. Hill responded with his own show of faith. When someone enjoined the retirement of the Northern Pacific preferred at the last hour, he assured jittery friends that Harriman was in no way behind the move.[40]

So far the uneasy alliance was holding firm, but the path ahead was strewn with difficulties. The state of Minnesota pressed its suit, and the ICC decided to hold an inquiry on the merger that winter. A Hill associate dismissed the suit as "the most laughable tissue of lies" and predicted a sweeping victory, but the federal government was another matter. Hill warned Harriman that the ICC would miss no opportunity to "go before Congress and increase their [sic] power very materially." And what if the attorney general decided to bring suit under the Sherman Act? No one would have entertained this fear if William McKinley still lived, but he was dead. In his seat sat the dynamic young whirlwind who had never shown himself shy about seizing any center stage at his disposal.[41]

The problem with community of interest was that there were too many interests with too little sense of community among them. To outside eyes, America seemed ruled by tight, conspiratorial cliques that might bicker among themselves but always closed ranks in the face of adversity. In fact, this more perfect unity was less a reality than a holy grail for which the idealists among them searched perpetually but in vain. Some reformers had trouble distinguishing between communities of interest and the old boys' network that had always dominated the business and financial worlds.

The creation of Northern Securities led many observers to conclude that transcontinental railroads had boiled down to three major systems: the Hill lines, the Harriman lines, and the Atchison. The Gould roads remained a wild card with intriguing possibilities, but in 1901 George Gould seemed firmly allied to Harriman and Schiff. On the surface it looked as if all the large roads west of the Mississippi were fast being drawn into the community of interest. Harriman dominated the Illinois Central and the Alton. Of the major Iowa roads the Northwestern and Union Pacific had worked together since the 1880s, and the Burlington was now joined to Hill's roads. The Milwaukee was independent but controlled by William Rockefeller, who was close to Harriman and Schiff, and Kuhn, Loeb had been the Milwaukee's bankers since the 1880s. Only the Rock Island stood outside the fold, just as its tired management had for a decade stood aloof from modernization and allowed the road to deteriorate.[42]

"The community of interest idea does not contemplate or require for its successful working the actual holding of a majority interest," observed one analyst. "It aims merely at sufficient identity of interest to insure harmonious and peaceful arrangements between companies in the same field of operations." By owning a share of each other's roads, rail leaders could put one or more of their own men on the board to keep a watchful eye on what was being done. This early form of on-site inspection was the most common device for keeping faith within the community, and dogged efforts were made to include every major road in the community. During the giddy summer and fall of 1901 everyone seemed to be buying a chunk of everyone else.[43]

Two problems remained unsolved and perhaps unsolvable. There were always ambitious men looking to put together a new system, or marauders assembling the facade of one as bait for a buyout. Both were as abundant as ever in 1901. That summer a quartet of raiders headed by the Moore brothers surprised everyone by gaining control of the Rock Island. The irrepressible

John W. Gates bought some remnants of the old Kansas City, Pittsburg & Gulf road that gave him a triangular line between Quincy, Kansas City, and Omaha. A. B. Stickney was trying to nudge his Great Western into Omaha, while Senator W. A. Clark pushed work on his proposed line between Los Angeles and Salt Lake.[44]

Who was bluffing and who wasn't? Time alone would tell. Meanwhile, the community had to work out the complex relationships among its members. It was one thing to agree that everyone should work in harmony, quite another to devise ways of doing so that satisfied everyone. Harriman and Stubbs were delighted with the traffic plan and eager to get on with it. So was Hill, who had to prod Robert Bacon to approve the sending of Miller to Chicago. "The whole question of relations of the Union Pacific with our three Companies rests upon this action," Hill urged, "and it is necessary that we should lose no time in doing our part. The advantage to all parties is great. . . ." Harriman also showed himself willing to exchange technical and other information.[45]

But there were limits to cooperation. The ancient problem of treating connecting roads equally raged no less inside the community than it had outside it. Stubbs learned that the Burlington had opened a through line to California via Denver with the Atchison, and asked that the latter be dumped in favor of the Southern Pacific. The Burlington still coveted a line deeper into Wyoming to strike coal, especially after its officers heard Stickney was eyeing the same route and perhaps even a connection with Clark at Salt Lake. Harriman found it difficult to serve both the Alton and the Illinois Central. Fish pressed him for closer relations between the Illinois Central and the Union Pacific at Omaha. "Unfortunately," he conceded, "the Northwestern contract stands in the way and I suppose will continue to do so." When Harriman tried to slake the Milwaukee's discontent by granting it improved facilities at Omaha, Fish howled even louder in protest."[46]

"We are finding it difficult to satisfy our connections in the matter of interchange traffic," admitted Stubbs. As always, most connectors were dissatisfied with the share of traffic they received. Disputes arose over the interchange of traffic at Ogden and at Denver. Fish got himself into a row with the Southern Pacific over competing steamer lines and even the interest rate paid on terminal facilities in New Orleans. When a spat in the Columbia River valley arose, Harriman felt obliged to allay Hill's alarm by assuring him that "I have done nothing to antagonize the situation and will not." Concessions made to the Rock Island irritated the Northwestern; for that matter, concessions made in one direction always annoyed someone in another direction.[47]

The community was a house divided and could not be otherwise. The urgent need for harmony did not curb the desire of managers to see their own road prosper at the expense of others. Nor could it eliminate the conflicts that inevitably arose among them. Old dogs did not take readily to new tricks.

Despite all the mergers and frenzied rumors of more consolidation, no one talked in these terms anymore. Only one man seemed to think even remotely on so grand a scale, and he was very adept at learning new tricks. No one yet fathomed the full depth of Harriman's ambitions, but the Metropolitan Club pact offered at least a clue to his thoughts. Was there ticking in the back of his restless brain a concept for some updated version of the One Big Railroad?

The Nevada desert seemed an unlikely battlefield in the clash of empires, but in 1901 long dormant ambitions stirred anew throughout the West. For a quarter century visionaries had dreamed of a direct line from Salt Lake to southern California. The Mormons longed to tap the mineral deposits to the southwest but could not manage it without help. In 1880 the Union Pacific's Utah system had opened as far south as Frisco, 277 miles from Ogden. A clamor to push the branch on to California in 1887 led Bishop John Sharp, who ran the Utah branch lines for the Union Pacific, to urge that the route be staked before the Rio Grande or some other road preempted it. T. J. Potter, then vice-president of the Union Pacific, agreed that the situation was "too attractive to stand unoccupied long" and dispatched two survey parties to find the best line.[48]

As usual, Charles Francis Adams, president of the Union Pacific, felt torn over what course to follow. Several of his officers joined Sharp in urging that the company build 450 miles to a connection with the Atlantic & Pacific road just south of the Nevada border. Adams considered Salt Lake "the place from which all future development is likely to be made," and he was impressed by the route's potential for furnishing coal to the starved markets of southern California and to the Oregon Short Line. "Coal is the bed rock upon which that system has got to be built," he proclaimed, "and until we find just where the bed rock is, and how far it extends, I should not advise doing anything more."[49]

A charter was procured for the Nevada Pacific Railway, and work began on a 145-mile stretch between Milford, Utah, and Pioche, Nevada. But Adams was stretched thin by other projects, and the Union Pacific was heading into deep financial trouble. Nor was he cheered by a report from his chief engineer, who looked over the region and sneered that "There are not enough people on the whole of the proposed line . . . to fill a good sized house." It would earn nothing as a through route, he added, and actually cost the road business by antagonizing the Southern Pacific. As his woes increased, Adams dropped the project in 1890. By that time most of the grading had been completed, some bridges built, and six tunnels driven. Eight miles of track had been laid but were taken up again.[50]

For eight years the route lay neglected like ancient ruins buried in sand by desert winds, oblivious to the violent contraction of depression and its exuberant sequel of prosperity and expansion. In 1898 the Utah & Pacific Railroad Company was chartered to build from Milford to Uvada on the Utah-Nevada border. The Oregon Short Line assigned to this company its rights to the abandoned Milford-Pioche line and agreed to trade some old rails for an option to buy the stock of Utah & Pacific during the next five years. In February 1899 the Short Line created another company, the Utah, Nevada & California, to extend the line from Uvada through Nevada, but no actual work was done. Instead Harriman sent Samuel Felton to report on the value of the Los Angeles Terminal Railway as a terminus for a transcontinental line.[51]

FORMIDABLE FOE: Senator W. A. Clark, who fought Harriman for possession of the Los Angeles-Salt Lake route, then joined forces with him. *(Montana State Historical Society)*

Felton submitted his report late in April, just before W. H. Holabird of Los Angeles sounded Harriman on buying or leasing the line south of Salt Lake as part of a proposed new through road to be built by the Los Angeles Terminal Company. The latter was a collection of interurban lines put together by R. C. Kerens of St. Louis, a Republican national committeeman. For nearly a decade Kerens had been trying to promote the Los Angeles-Salt Lake route, and had tried to interest the Union Pacific in the project. At San Pedro, twenty-two miles south of Los Angeles, lay a good natural harbor that the government had plans to improve. What better port for all the products funnelling down the Union Pacific's Utah system? What better way for the Union Pacific to gain its own outlet to California?[52]

Kerens got nowhere with the Union Pacific, which had little interest and less money in those beleaguered days. Nor could he get past Collis Huntington, who had no intention of loosening his leechlike hold on California's traffic. Huntington was developing his own port at Santa Monica and succeeded in bottling up the bill to improve San Pedro harbor. For years Kerens's vision had languished; now he had a powerful new backer and sent Holabird to see W. H. Bancroft of the Short Line about meeting with Harriman. "I infer from his conversation," Bancroft wired Harriman, "that W. A. Clark of Montana is behind him."[53]

Here was an adversary worthy of Harriman. The grim but dapper Clark had amassed a huge fortune in copper and other minerals before turning to politics and cultural pursuits. Behind his hard, riveting eyes lay a curious mixture of vanity and cold business genius. Small and wiry like Harriman, he possessed the same broad vision and utter fearlessness in marching toward his goals. As Clark grew older, his tastes rarified until he became a hopeless Francophile addicted to social pretensions. He also developed a roving eye for the ladies. In 1900 he was busy erecting a white elephant of a mansion on Fifth Avenue and was embroiled in a scandal charging him with buying his seat in the Senate. Small wonder that Mark Twain wrote of him, "By his example he has so excused and so sweetened corruption that in Montana it no longer has an offensive smell. . . . He is as rotten a human being as can be found anywhere under the flag; he is a shame to the American nation."[54]

Unruffled by his troubles, Clark joined forces with Kerens. His shrewd eye grasped the potential of San Pedro as a harbor and of the Utah desert for mining. The opposition of Huntington made Harriman a natural ally in building the new line, but Huntington's death in August 1900 jumbled everything. The Southern Pacific was in limbo; if Harriman got hold of it, he would have a stranglehold on the shipping arteries through the regions where Clark's mines were located. Scarcely was Huntington cold in his grave when Clark announced that he would build the new road. The following March he chartered the new San Pedro, Los Angeles & Salt Lake Railroad and swept the Los Angeles Terminal lines into the new company.[55]

Clark's announcement caught Harriman at a bad time. He was deep into negotiations for the Southern Pacific and tracking the Burlington as well, to say nothing of his work on the Union Pacific or other roads. Nevertheless, he recognized Clark as a dangerous adversary and moved to counter the threat. John W. Gates suggested that they buy into the Los Angeles road, but Harriman told him bluntly, "I do not care to have even an indirect interest in the affair." At least not right away, not until he knew more. Was Clark acting in concert with some other road? With the Burlington looking west and Gould gobbling up Rio Grande stock, Harriman saw a variety of menaces looming. The old world of transcontinental railroads was dying, the new one struggling to be born. Never was it in more of a state of flux than during that frantic winter of 1900–1901.[56]

As the two men edged toward a confrontation, Clark sprang a surprise. In 1890 the Short Line had graded the forty miles from Uvada, Utah, to Caliente, Nevada, as well as the branch from Caliente to Pioche. It had also surveyed a route through Meadow Valley Wash canyon, on which maps had been filed but no actual work done. The Union Pacific assumed that rights to this route had passed to the Utah & Pacific, but Clark learned that in 1894 the Utah & Pacific had defaulted on taxes and the rights had been sold to Lincoln County, Nevada. He also found that a defunct company called the Utah & California had in 1897 surveyed the same route and asked but not received approval from the Interior Department for the maps. In March 1901 Clark quietly had the Utah & California buy the tax title to the original route and convey it to his new San Pedro line. His engineers also began surveying a route through Meadow Valley Wash canyon, claiming that the old Short Line route had been abandoned. When the federal land office at Carson City ruled in favor of the San Pedro, Clark sent crews onto the old graded route between Uvada and Caliente.[57]

Harriman responded by appealing the land office decision to Washington and having the Short Line exercise its option on the Utah & Pacific stock. Bancroft was summoned hastily to New York and told to build the road to Los Angeles as rapidly as possible. Hurrying back to Salt Lake, he rushed crews and material onto the disputed ground. "We claim the right to the old Union Pacific grade," he told a reporter, "and we . . . will lay track on it as fast as we can, no matter what interests try to interfere with us." Unable to match the forces mustered by Bancroft, the San Pedro crews erected hasty obstacles of barbed wire and filled cuts along the route with rocks and timbers. When the forces confronted each other, the mood was ugly but not reckless; both sides were anxious to avoid violence.[58]

On April 24 the Interior Department reversed the Carson City decision and awarded the old graded route to the Short Line. The fight then shifted to the strategic Meadow Valley Wash canyon, which extended about 110 miles from Caliente to the southwest and was the only feasible short route to Los Angeles. Both sides realized that the outcome turned on possession of this canyon and were determined to seize it. Since no work had been done there, victory would go to the first company that filed its map with the land office. President Horace Burt of the Union Pacific went personally to examine the ground with two of his engineers and a contractor. Bancroft's tracklayers marched relentlessly toward Caliente despite efforts to delay them until the San Pedro's survey parties could run a line through the canyon. The Short Line's engineers arrived belatedly and opened their survey in the narrow canyon.[59]

Here was the sort of spectacle the press loved: two sets of surveyors racing to complete separate lines down a canyon where there was barely room for one decent line. In June a second front opened at Carson City, where the circuit court heard arguments on whether to continue the injunction against the San Pedro's use of the old graded line beyond Uvada. Clark's crews were grading furiously between this line and Caliente, hoping to prevent the Short Line from reaching the canyon. Both sides filled the air with martial rhetoric: the road would be built regardless of any obstacle, legal or otherwise. A showdown loomed, and the threat of violence crackled like thunder over the rival crews sweating in the desert that summer.[60]

Late in July the court sustained the injunction against the San Pedro, but allowed the company to continue working in the canyon. On August 1 Bancroft's first train rolled into Caliente. "This is merely stealing our right of way by brute force," grumbled Clark. Despite their late start, the Short Line engineers rushed through their survey, covering 215 miles in twelve days, and filed their maps first. The San Pedro howled in protest and charged that the maps were simply copies of the 1889 survey. Fresh barricades went up in the canyon to stall the Short Line south of Caliente while the San Pedro crews graded furiously at the other end. Some clashes occurred, but no damage was done. On August 9 the San Pedro triggered a fresh round of litigation by seeking to enjoin the Short Line from any work in the canyon. In effect, this shut down the crews of both sides.[61]

This stalemate left both sides little choice except to negotiate. In September the lawyers drew up a memorandum covering all disputed points and providing for a joint survey of the canyon. Working together, the engineers demonstrated

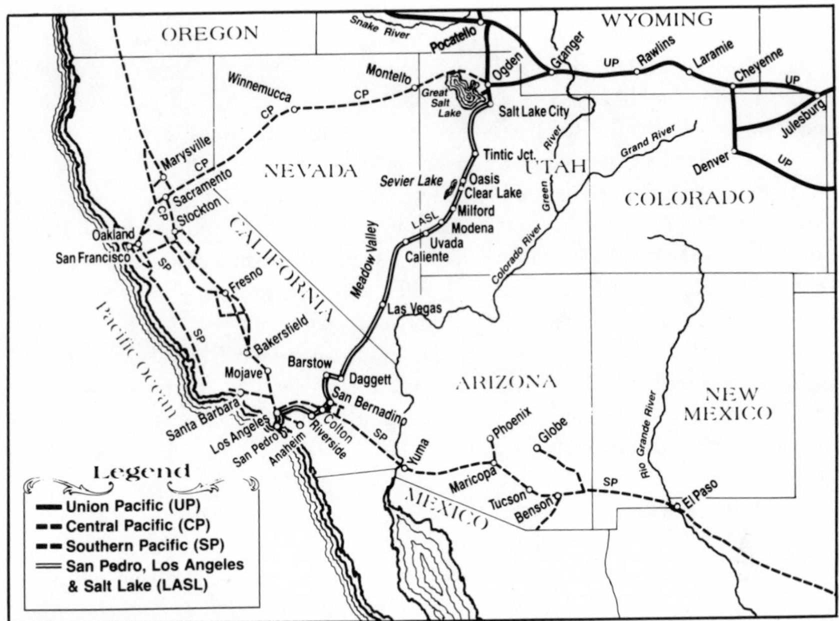

DESERT PRIZE: The Los Angeles & Salt Lake line, which was hotly contested by Harriman and W. A. Clark.

that two separate roads could only get through the canyon by crossing each other more than twenty times. Neither Harriman nor Clark could ignore the obvious fact that the region could not support two competing lines. Harriman owned the Utah end of the line and could use the Southern Pacific to fight Clark in California. Clark had access to Los Angeles and San Pedro harbor but could endure only by building a costly parallel line. He was a fighter but not a fool. The need for compromise was obvious, yet it did not come easily. Through months of hard bargaining, Clark dickered for better terms before signing an agreement in July 1902.[62]

Under its provisions Clark agreed to sell Harriman a half interest in the San Pedro, and to hold the company with him as joint trustees. The Short Line was to sell or lease all its line south of Salt Lake to the San Pedro, which would be pushed to completion. These were the terms that attracted the most public attention, but the agreement contained some other points equally vital to Harriman. The San Pedro agreed not to build any track north of Salt Lake, while the Short Line would not go south of the city. The San Pedro would be operated in tandem with the Union Pacific system and interchange traffic with it "exclusively, in so far as that may lawfully be done." A traffic arrangement would be negotiated with the Southern Pacific so that no road would discriminate against another.[63]

In short, Clark and his San Pedro would join the community of interest. Harriman did not have to own the road to dominate it. The road would be built to his standards and then placed in the care of Bancroft, who found himself managing the Short Line, the San Pedro, the Union Pacific lines west of Green River, and the Southern Pacific lines from Ogden to Sparks, Nevada. Potential conflicts with the Southern Pacific would have to be ironed out, but there would be no race to the sea by rival roads. Construction went forward, and the new road opened for business in the spring of 1905.[64]

The most remarkable feature of the transaction was the secrecy that shrouded it for more than two years. Word leaked out that Harriman and Clark had struck a deal, but on what basis no one knew. "Has Harriman gobbled up Clark?" Charles Perkins asked Hill in January 1903. Not yet, Hill replied. The transfer of the Short Line Utah roads to the San Pedro later that year led observers to believe that Harriman had given up the fight, an image Clark carefully reinforced. The San Pedro, he declared in May 1903, "will be an entirely independent line. I have purchased the entire Oregon Short Line system south of Salt Lake City. It is an absolute purchase, and Mr. Harriman retains absolutely no interest in the property."[65]

This blind concealed the true state of affairs until October 1904, when mention of the San Pedro purchase first appeared in the Union Pacific's annual report. These were troubled years for the Harriman empire, a time when the community suffered serious strains from within and attacks from without. Harriman showed rare restraint in his handling of the San Pedro deal. It never became as conspicuous a target as some other acquisitions, and it proved an invaluable part of the Union Pacific system.[66]

Railroad men liked to describe alliances as one road climbing into bed with another. During the early 1900s the community became a crowded bed in which nearly everyone complained about his place and tugged fiercely at the covers. The independent roads clung to the hope that Clark's line would become their outlet to the sea. But once Clark got in bed with Harriman, the Milwaukee talked again of building to the coast. Harriman soothed its discontent with a new traffic alliance similar to that with the Northwestern, leading Fish to protest anew that the Illinois Central was being treated like an orphan. The Rock Island made a traffic pact with the Southern Pacific while flirting with the Frisco, and Stickney's Chicago Great Western forced its way into Omaha over the Union Pacific bridge.[67]

In Colorado, banker David H. Moffat announced plans to build the long-awaited air line from Denver to Salt Lake by tunneling the Rockies. At Salt Lake Moffat hoped to connect with Clark's road. So did George Gould, whose erratic machinations probably disturbed Harriman most of all. To outward appearances Gould and Harriman were still friends and allies. They sat together on the boards of the Union Pacific, Rio Grande, Alton, and other ventures in true community spirit. But a flurry of rumors in the spring of 1902 hinted that a clash between them loomed. Gould was already deep into a fight with the mighty Pennsylvania Railroad over the system of roads he was patching together east of the Mississippi River. Harriman's scoop of the Southern Pacific had cut Gould off west of Ogden, the terminus of his Rio Grande road. Now

Harriman had snatched away another choice opportunity, the Clark connection.[68]

Although Gould was notorious for rowing to his objects with splashing oars, the full extent of his plans had yet to be disclosed. Some claimed he had an interest in Moffat's road even though it would parallel his Rio Grande. Late in 1902, shortly after the Clark-Harriman deal went public, Gould withdrew from a joint effort with Harriman to capture the Colorado Fuel & Iron Company. In March 1903 a new company called the Western Pacific was organized to build a line from Oakland, California, to Ogden, Utah. Gould flatly denied having any interest in the project, but observers insisted it was to be the final link in his transcontinental scheme. Harriman countered by opening the Denver gateway to the Rock Island, thereby diverting much of that road's freight from the Rio Grande to the Union Pacific.[69]

The Atchison also posed new threats on both flanks of Harriman's system. In 1901 it absorbed a road from Ash Fork, Arizona, to the small town of Phoenix. The local promoter who built this road was eager to extend it southeast to a connection with the Southern Pacific at Benson, Arizona. E. P. Ripley, the Atchison's president, reluctantly agreed to construct a portion of it. A company called the Phoenix & Eastern was formed, and work began early in 1902. Ripley was far more interested in pushing his San Francisco line northwest to the region between the ocean and the Sierra Nevada mountains. Both projects offered potential threats to the Harriman lines. The Arizona road might be extended to the Atchison terminus at Deming, New Mexico, paralleling the Southern Pacific all the way and creating a new through route from Chicago to southern California. If the northwest California line kept going north, it could parallel the Southern Pacific all the way to Portland.[70]

Harriman resented these threats as invasions of Southern Pacific territory. When Ripley opened negotiations for the stock of a small road called the California & Northwestern in the summer of 1902, Harriman grabbed it away from him. That autumn Ripley acquired the tiny Eel River & Eureka to use as a base in northwest California, setting the stage for a construction war unless some agreement could be reached. Harriman told Victor Morawetz, chairman of the Atchison's executive committee, in blunt language that he regarded the Phoenix & Eastern as an invasion. The Atchison, he snapped, should sell him the road and abandon the territory south of Phoenix.[71]

Aware that his company lacked the funds to tackle both or even one of the projects at once, Morawetz tried a game of bluff. The Phoenix & Eastern could be had, he told Harriman, but only as part of a package that included a settlement in northwest California. He suggested splitting the latter properties on a fifty-fifty basis. Harriman rejected this offer, and negotiations dragged on for months. During that time work on the Phoenix & Eastern inched forward while Harriman and Schiff wondered if the time had not come to start buying Atchison stock in earnest.

But how much could they do, and how far could they go? Rumors of new threats sprouted like mushrooms: the Milwaukee would merge with the Katy; the Colorado & Southern was going to Cheyenne; the Burlington was building to Sioux City; the citizens of Enid, Oklahoma, planned a grand line from

Seattle to New Orleans. Some rumors were serious and some silly, but they kept coming in relentless profusion. It was difficult to harmonize this growing welter of interests and still more difficult to ''Harrimanize'' them. The bankers, ever cautious, grasped this fact more clearly than did Harriman himself. There had been a moment in 1901 when Harriman came to Kuhn, Loeb with the news that the Rock Island was being put on the market. It was a good property, he added, and worth the asking price. As Kahn later recounted, he and Schiff dissuaded Harriman with an argument that went straight to the heart of the matter:

> We told him that he was in charge of the Union Pacific and the Southern Pacific, that that was as much as any man could properly attend to, and that even though he was a genius, the burden of administering so enormous a system was, in our opinion, more than enough for any one man to bear; and that even if it were legally permissable to acquire the Chicago, Rock Island & Pacific, we thought there was a limit to the economic advantages of consolidation, of economy of operation, and that limit consisted in the size of the aggregation; that when the aggregation, at the head of which any one man is put, exceeds a certain volume, so as to exceed the human limitations of any one man to give personal and proper attention and direction, that then in our opinion there was no longer any advantage, from the economic point of view, in co-operation, in amalgamation.[72]

It was neither the first nor the last time this issue would arise. The bankers, who most admired Harriman's gifts, had by 1901 begun to grasp the flaws in his genius: his indifference to public opinion, his brusque style that antagonized men whose cooperation was needed, and above all his indomitable drive that led him to take on burdens that would overwhelm three men and still reach out eagerly for more. He was an engine that knew only one speed and would run until its last drop of fuel was drained. Hill listened to the engine's incessant roar and drew his own conclusion. ''Mr. Harriman's own people,'' he noted with satisfaction, ''are beginning to grow tired of him.''[73]

This was wishful thinking on Hill's part, but Harriman's friends were growing concerned about him. How long could his fragile health stand the pace he set? How long could he (and they) hold together a community of interest riddled with inner strains and weakened by increasing attack from without? If its members would not be harmonized or Harrimanized, how long could they survive these attacks? From every angle Harriman held the key to whatever answers emerged. His genius made him the right man to lead the rail industry into a new era, but his abrasive personality ensured that too few of his peers would follow. He was the wave of the future lapping against a society that had not yet assimilated the past and was unprepared for the daring vision he offered. Like all prophets, he would pay dearly for the seeds he managed to sow.

7

The New Order

Charles Perkins had no doubts as to who was the prophet of the new era. "The truth is," he once observed, "Mr. Hill has seen more clearly than any of us that the fittest to survive would be the railroad which could work at the lowest rate per ton mile. That has been his central idea." This tribute to Hill was deserved, but Perkins, like most men with strong convictions, had his share of blind spots. Just as earlier he had failed to see the positive side of Jay Gould, so in his twilight years did he miss the immense contribution made by Harriman. No man did more than Harriman to usher the rail industry into the twentieth century, and no one implemented the principle cited by Perkins faster or more fully on whole systems.[1]

Harriman's vision began with upgrading a system and running it in a systematic way. Then he took the process one step farther by integrating the systems under his control as thoroughly as possible—not only their operations but their accounts, purchasing, traffic solicitation, and other elements as well. The drive everywhere was to obtain economies of scale through standardization. Julius Kruttschnitt, the vice-president and general manager of the Southern Pacific who would later be called the "von Moltke of transportation," had this principle impressed on him in a typical way. He was walking the road one way with Harriman when the latter noticed a track bolt and asked why so much of the bolt protruded beyond the nut.

"It is the size which is generally used," Kruttschnitt replied.

"Why should we use a bolt of such a length that a part of it is useless?" Harriman persisted.

"Well," shrugged Kruttschnitt, "when you come right down to it, there is no reason."

They walked a little farther, and Harriman asked how many track bolts were in a mile of track. When Kruttschnitt gave him a figure, Harriman's dark eyes gleamed in calculation. "Well," he said, "in the Union Pacific and Southern Pacific we have about eighteen thousand miles of track and there must be some fifty million track bolts in our system. If you can cut an ounce off from every bolt, you will save fifty million ounces of iron, and that is something worth while. Change your bolt standard."[2]

The Southern Pacific was a holding company into which Collis Huntington had swept the largest collection of transportation properties in the world. It owned 9,441 miles of railroad extending from New Orleans to Portland and 16,186 miles of water lines plying routes from New York to New Orleans and from San Francisco to China. The rail lines outearned all rival roads and also cost more to operate, as the figures below indicate:

COMPARATIVE DATA
ON TRANSCONTINENTAL ROADS,
1898–1901
(All figures averages)

CATEGORY	UNION PACIFIC	SOUTHERN PACIFIC	ATCHISON	NORTHERN PACIFIC	GREAT NORTHERN
MILES OPERATED	5,427	7,676	7,322	4,686	4,789
GROSS EARNINGS PER MILE	$7,162	$7,889	$6,172	$5,967	$5,357
COSTS PER MILE	$3,706	$4,900	$3,925	$2,905	$2,690

One major source of expense was the high cost of fuel in a region lacking its own supplies of coal. To remedy this problem the Southern Pacific experimented early with locomotives that burned oil, of which the Southwest possessed huge amounts. One analyst predicted that the change in fuels alone could save the company as much as $4 million annually.[3]

The traffic of the Southern Pacific was richly diversified: lumber, grain, fruit and vegetables, cotton, and manufactured articles. No western road had a better mix or was in better shape to make money from its local business. But it also had a funded debt of $350 million and had never paid a dividend, which made it suspect to investors. Once Harriman gained control, analysts agreed that dividends would be even longer in coming because the surplus would be spent on improvements. From a financial point of view the purchase looked dubious: a heavy outlay for a sprawling system that required large expenditures for upgrading.[4]

In 1901 the Southern Pacific was a good nineteenth-century road in "suitable condition for its traffic," as chief engineer William Hood noted. Plans for

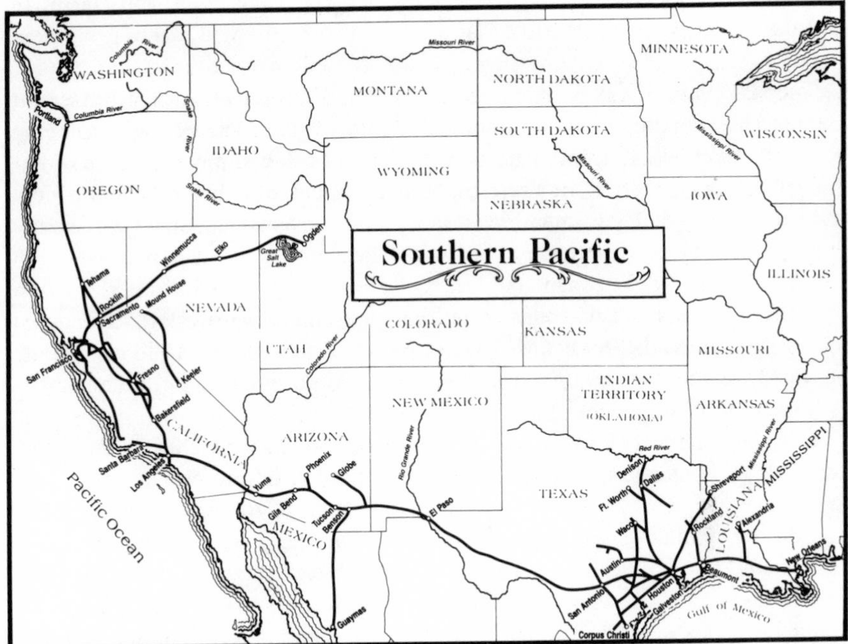

THE OTHER HALF: The Southern Pacific system, which Harriman acquired in 1901.

modernizing the line were on the drawing board but had yet to be implemented because of the expense involved. Few of the road's officers had reoriented their thinking to changing conditions. One incident illustrated the contrast with the Union Pacific. In modernizing its equipment the Union Pacific steadily increased its fleet of cars larger than forty tons only to have the Southern Pacific announce in February 1899 that it would accept no cars for California business larger than forty tons. "The rapidly increasing size of cars," explained traffic chief John Stubbs, "is a growing evil because it increases costs and risk without increasing revenue." Fifty-foot cars were in his opinion "unnecessary and unprofitable."[5]

Stubbs's reasoning fit the Southern Pacific, which was not in condition to handle larger rolling stock efficiently, but not the Union Pacific. Harriman acquired the Southern Pacific not only to eliminate friction with it and assure himself of its business but also to integrate the two systems at the same level of performance. His first task, therefore was, to bring the road up to the standards of the new Union Pacific. Kruttschnitt assumed the role played by J. B. Berry in reconstructing the Union Pacific and got the same eye-popping introduction to the Harriman style. One evening Harriman took Kruttschnitt to his house for dinner. Afterward he hauled out the maps, blueprints, and sheets of statistics on reconstruction in Utah and Nevada, firing questions nonstop at Kruttschnitt, often before the reply to the last one was finished, and always getting at the crucial points. "The swiftness with which he covered the ground," marveled

Kruttschnitt, "was astonishing." In two hours they were done, and Harriman told the dazed railroad man to be at an executive committee meeting the next morning.

Since the plans involved spending $18 million for improvements, Kruttschnitt assumed the meeting would be long and argumentative, with perhaps grudging approval given some small part of the plans. To his surprise Harriman explained in concise terms the projects, their cost, and what benefits would flow from the work, and got unanimous approval for everything. This was something very new to Kruttschnitt, as it had been to Berry. He left the room wondering what kind of man could in such short time digest $18 million worth of work along a thousand miles of railroad and outline it so clearly as to gain immediate approval from his associates. As Kruttschnitt prepared to head west, he asked Harriman cautiously how fast he should go in spending the money.

"Spend it all in a week if you can," came the reply.[6]

Thus began the reconstruction of the Southern Pacific. During the years 1893–1900, Huntington had put about $12.4 million into improvements. Over the next eight years Harriman expended $30 million for line changes, $115 million for purchase and construction of new lines, $46 million for new equipment, $14 million for terminal and other real estate, $2.7 million for second tracking, and $39 million for other betterments, including $3 million for automatic block signals. The outlay totaled a staggering $247 million to make the Southern Pacific a matched pair with its parent road.[7]

Everywhere the work echoed that done on the Union Pacific. On the Central Pacific 373 miles of line were replaced by 322 miles of new track, shortening the route by 51 miles. Maximum grades ranging from 53 to 90 feet were reduced to 21.1 feet, and 16,625 degrees of curvature shrank to 3,889 degrees on the new line, a savings of more than 35 complete circles. The reduction in grade rise, heading east or west, amounted to about 3,000 vertical feet or the equivalent of over 60 miles of continuous 50-foot grade. No curve on the new track exceeded 4 degrees, compared to the 8- and 10-degree curves on the old line.

The engineering challenges were formidable. In 1901 the Southern Pacific still entered San Francisco via its original route—a steep, winding single track on the slope of the San Bruno Mountains. The city had grown too much for anything to be done with the line, and Harriman didn't like it anyway. Instead he built a new one along the water's edge. The Bay Shore cutoff cost $9.3 million and required five tunnels, but it knocked 2.65 miles off the original 11-mile line and ran double track at water level straight into improved terminal facilities. A bridge was erected at Dumbarton Point to allow trains from the east to cross San Francisco Bay by rail instead of transferring to ferries. The crooked line with choppy grades between Montalvo and Burbank gave way to one with low grades and little curvature.[8]

Impressive as these changes were, they paled before Harriman's two most ambitious projects. The first sought boldly to eliminate nearly all the snow sheds in the Sierras by blasting a tunnel through the mountains. It would have to be a giant among tunnels, at least five and possibly seven miles long. After two years of surveys and studies, Harriman reluctantly abandoned the idea and instead built a new line over the Sierra Nevadas from Rockland to Colfax with good alignment and a 1½ percent grade. This became the uphill track; the original line served downhill traffic, giving the company a double track over the mountains.[9]

The scale of the second project probably helped dissuade Harriman from tackling the tunnel. For years Huntington had toyed with the idea of avoiding the heavy grades and extra miles of the original route around the north end of Salt Lake by running a new line either around the south end or directly across the water. Both ideas had been present at the creation. The southern route had been rejected for several reasons, and the lake was too foreboding an obstacle for the technology of 1870. Soundings had been taken since the 1860s, but disputes still raged over what they meant. Where was the bottom and what was it? How could a bridge withstand the heavy waves whipped up by storms? What if the water rose? What would the salt do to building materials?

In recent years the lake had receded several feet. Huntington believed this trend would continue because more irrigation projects were tapping its feeders. After rejecting a southern route, he ordered William Hood to survey the cutoff in November 1899. The following June a company was organized to build the line; two months later Huntington was dead. The project dangled in limbo until Harriman came aboard. He was anxious to get rid of the Promontory bottleneck but uncertain of the best way to do it. Hood argued for the cutoff; Berry filed a report opposing it. Salt Lake City interests, who had been striving to get their city on the main line since the days of Brigham Young, revived their arguments in favor of the southern route. Fresh surveys of that route were ordered, and plans were announced to make Salt Lake City the new terminus.[10]

Still Harriman hesitated. Hood's thorough report impressed him, and Stubbs pointed out that the southern route would add sixty-seven more miles to the road than the cutoff, giving the rival Atchison an advantage in the fight for transcontinental traffic. No doubt the challenge of so immense a project also roused Harriman to battle. Brushing aside protests from Salt Lake City, he gave approval in January 1902 for what became known as the Lucin cutoff. Both companies would be involved in the work. In his usual way Harriman delegated responsibility to Burt and Kruttschnitt, with Hood and Berry as their lieutenants, and told them to work together. When Burt sent suggestions to Harriman, he was ordered to take them up with Kruttschnitt.[11]

The project was, observed a knowledgeable writer, "perhaps the most noteworthy engineering achievement ever attempted in bridge-and-fill work." Apart from being 44 miles shorter, the new 103-mile line would save 3,919 degrees of curvature and 1,515 feet of grade, enabling passenger trains to run faster and freight trains to haul much heavier loads. It ran west from Ogden across Bear River Bay to the tip of Promontory Point and over the large western arm of the lake to a point called Lakeside. From there 58 miles of track connected it to the main line just beyond Lucin. In all, the cutoff required 78

miles of regular track, 11 miles of permanent trestle, and 16 miles of temporary trestle to be filled.[12]

Hood laid his plans carefully, but he could not have gone far without the resources of the Harriman system behind him. The need for lumber alone was staggering: a forest of piles, 25,000 bents, stringers, caps, and timber for stations, boarding houses, sidings, and the steamboat under construction. These needs would have overwhelmed the Sierra supplies, but large amounts came down from the forests along the Short Line and Navigation roads. In San Francisco twenty-five giant pile drivers were constructed. To haul the mountain of fill, the company built four hundred special steel dump cars with capacities of 110,000 pounds and pressed into service every spare dump car and flat car it could muster. Eight giant steam shovels scooped out the loads of rock and gravel from nearby quarries, and eighty locomotives hauled the endless rows of cars to the lake.[13]

To do the work the company recruited an army three thousand strong of laborers, carpenters, mechanics, bridgemen, and engineers who worked ten-hour shifts around the clock seven days a week. At each station a boarding-house was built on piles high above the storm waves; the company provided cooks and charged four dollars a week for meals. A camp of outfit boxcars was set up on sidings at Lakeside and elsewhere to house men with families. Fresh water, half a million gallons daily, had to be hauled in by train for the men and equipment. Coordinating the logistics of so gigantic an undertaking kept every-one scurrying frantically, yet they managed to work together smoothly and safely. Only one serious accident occurred beyond the usual rash of smashed hands or broken limbs.[14]

The engineers discovered early that regular fill simply floated away in the heavy salt water, forcing them to dump thousands of tons of rock into what seemed an insatiable maw before dirt and gravel could be used. Day after day, as the trestle extended farther into the lake, the line of dump cars followed it like an endless caravan. Occasionally a storm smashed one of the log booms, sending timber cruising about the lake in all directions, but the heavy salt waves caused far less damage than had been feared. In March 1903 the temporary track was completed across the entire length, and the first engine chugged forward from Ogden. Two places had proved especially difficult to fill: one in Bear River Bay and the other at a spot on the west arm of the lake called Rambo. As the locomotive reached the first of these sites, the embank-ment suddenly dropped out of sight, leaving the engine in two feet of water. She was hauled back with a cable.[15]

Wearily, the engineers realized that the lake's mysterious crust had simply cracked under the weight of the fill and sunk; no one could predict where,

SHORTEST DISTANCE BETWEEN TWO POINTS: View of the Lucin Cutoff from Lakeside, Utah.

A JOB WELL DONE: Dignitaries and workers pose at the opening celebration of the Lucin Cutoff. Harriman stands inconspicuously at the far right with Horace Burt to his right. The burly Julius Kruttschnitt, with white handkerchief in his breast pocket, stands in the middle of the track. William Hood, the engineer who oversaw the project, is just behind Kruttschnitt's left shoulder. John C. Stubbs, holding his coat and hat, has his right foot on the rail.

when, or how much. A week after the track was raised and refilled it sank again beneath a work train, giving the crew a good fright, and it kept settling—always to a point just above the fill. Thus began a fight that would last twenty-one months, always with the same dreary pattern: the line would sink and have to be filled, again and again. Around the clock twenty-five hundred men dumped rock and gravel into a seemingly bottomless pit while the engineers shrugged helplessly. "We know what it ought to do," grumbled one of them, "but what we don't know is why it doesn't do it."

Gradually the sinking slowed, then stopped everywhere except at the two trouble spots. The permanent trestle was completed and the roadbed laid on three inches of asphalt roofing over heavy planking ballasted with fourteen inches of gravel. On Thanksgiving Day 1903 Harriman led a party of friends and railroad men to celebrate the formal opening of the cutoff, but not until March 1904 did trains begin running over it. Even then passenger trains continued to use the old line. Bear River Bay finally stabilized after one last drop of eight feet, but Rambo gave the engineers fits. In 287 days, starting in April 1904, careful records showed 482 incidents of settling and only 19 days when nothing occurred. During August there were 84 incidents, 7 of them in one day, all in different places, averaging 2 to 4 feet.[16]

Wild rumors flew about the country of locomotives swallowed up by the lake's bottomless pits. If it had gone on much longer, Utah might have had its own lake monster, Briny Nessie or Sesquatch with fins. But the fill kept coming, 70,000 carloads of it at Rambo alone, until small islands of congealed debris began to form near the trestle. Through it all, freight trains rolled over the cutoff, and in September 1904 the first passenger train breezed across the water. After a final drop in December, the fill held firm; Rambo had been tamed. A woman making the trip with one of the engineers saw the offshore debris and exclaimed, "How fortunate it was that you found those little islands!"

"Found them!" cried the engineer. "It took us two years to make them!"[17]

Four years later the *Railroad Gazette* congratulated the cutoff for standing up so well "that to-day unless the traveler looks out of the window he would not know from the motion of the train that he was on a bridge." Every day five passenger and seven freight trains in both directions used the cutoff, and one official estimated in 1917 that it had saved 172 million car-miles by then. Small wonder that it was praised not only as a great feat of engineering but also as "one of the most profitable investments ever made by a railroad."[18]

Elsewhere, the pattern of improvements followed the Union Pacific model. Kruttschnitt noted that the first question Harriman asked of any proposed work was "whether the device or plan recommended was absolutely the best that could be gotten. That seemed to be the criterion." Shoulders were widened, heavier rail laid down, and more miles ballasted. More siding was added, and busy stretches of the line were double-tracked. Heavy iron bridges replaced lighter wood or iron spans. New buildings went up and existing structures were spruced up. In six years 1,213 miles of automatic block signals were installed. An obsolete fleet of equipment was retired in favor of newer, heavier models. Between 1901 and 1909 the number of locomotives jumped 41 percent and their relative hauling power 45 percent. Freight cars increased by 25 percent while their average capacity went up 40 percent. As a result the average tons of freight per train soared 51 percent, fulfilling Harriman's demand for fewer trains with bigger payloads.[19]

These expenditures turned a good railroad into an efficient money-making machine. Although earnings were phenomenal, Harriman plowed them back into the property and paid no dividends on common stock until 1906. Within a year the rate jumped from 2½ percent to 6 percent, where it remained. No amount of criticism deflected Harriman from his dividend policy. In 1902 one of Wall Street's best known speculators, James R. Keene, devised a plan to buy large amounts of Southern Pacific common and force Harriman to declare a dividend. Keene tried first to lure Harriman into the scam as a partner and then to intimidate him with litigation. Neither tactic worked, and Keene ultimately beat a retreat with heavy losses.[20]

The improvements paid another kind of dividend in the form of safer operations. Accidents and safety are not popular topics with either railroads or their historians, who seldom even mention them. But they were live issues early in the century, when the number of accidents and casualties took an explosive upturn. During the decade 1897–1907, some 97,373 people were reported killed and 745,992 injured on American railroads; the actual figures were doubtless higher. The trend marched steadily upward: total deaths increased 58 percent and total injuries 202 percent from 1897 to 1907. Passenger deaths and injuries shot up 175 percent and 367 percent, those for employees 168 percent and 217 percent respectively. Put another way, death claimed one out of every 395 and injuries one of every 22 employees during the decade.[21]

These grisly figures peaked in 1907, a year when everything went wrong for the railroads. They were handling record volumes of traffic on lines where operating routines were disrupted constantly by improvement work. It was like trying to rebuild a busy expressway at rush hour or, as Howard Elliott of the Northern Pacific quipped, "attempting to force a three-inch stream through a one-inch nozzle." Every man and piece of equipment was pressed into service, often without regard for how fit they might be or how poor their past performance had been. A record 610 passengers and 4,534 employees (or one out of every 369) died in accidents, and one out of every 19 employees suffered an injury. Newspapers splashed lurid accounts of accidents across the front pages even as their editorials complained of delays caused by the congestion of traffic.[22]

Safety has always been a public relations problem for railroads, but it assumed a new dimension in the age of regulation. Congress had already intervened in 1893 with the Safety Appliance Act eliminating hand brakes and couplers, and a new ICC investigation loomed in 1907. However, the growing mania for safety was no sudden response to a situation that had been neglected for years. It was rather an old problem blown into crisis proportions by the swelling density of traffic that swamped even those roads spending millions on improvements. Not every road invested heavily in safety, but even those that did found it impossible to keep pace with the demands placed on their lines.

Harriman was unique among rail leaders in his relentless pursuit of safety. Where others demanded it and spent some money on it, he invested millions and hounded his operations people with the zeal of a vigilante. Kruttschnitt estimated that during 1898–1907 the Harriman lines spent $12 million on block signals, double-tracking, steel cars, and other improvements for safer operations. No system in the country installed more automatic signals, which were expensive to install and maintain, and no western system spent more per train-mile on routine maintenance than the Harriman roads.[23]

Physical improvements made roads safer but could not rid the company of accidents caused by human error or carelessness. Harriman could not tolerate negligence and badgered his officers to instill safety awareness in the men. On this subject he was a perfect ogre, demanding immediate details of all accidents and explanations on the causes as well as a monthly summary. After one collision caused by the failure of a flagman to protect a stalled train during a blizzard, Harriman fired off a telegram telling Burt that "Something must be done to enforce the Company's regulations [and] someone who has force of character should be put on this particular matter, and see that the rules are carried out.''[24]

The hapless Burt felt Harriman's lash after every misfortune. ''Would like you to administer severe penalty on all those responsible,'' growled Harriman after an ice train switched onto the main line without orders and collided with a passenger train, ''and would also like special report from you.'' Averell Harriman recalled an inspection trip with his father on which the train hit some rough track and nearly derailed because a work crew failed to post a flagman. A furious Harriman ordered Burt to discharge the entire crew. ''That's rather cruel,'' protested Burt. Perhaps, retorted Harriman, ''but it will probably save a lot of lives. I want every man connected with the operation to feel a sense of responsibility. Now, everybody knew that the man hadn't gone back with the flag. They could see it. And if he's responsible, that sort of thing won't happen again.''[25]

On another inspection trip Harriman summoned the superintendent to his car late one evening, sat him down, and said, ''About four or five miles east of Green River, I noticed a block signal not burning. Now, I want you to tell me what the trouble is; and, before you answer, I want to say to you that I am willing to expend millions in improvements . . . if—now mark you—if we get the benefit of them; but I am unwilling to expend one dollar for any purpose whatever if the result we are trying to accomplish is not brought about. Now, sir, what is the trouble with that signal?''

It might be any number of things, replied the superintendent; he promised to investigate and find out. Then he added rashly, ''Mr. Harriman, as you know, this is a single track railroad, and there are two sets of signals, one each for east and west bound trains; is it not just possible that you noticed the back of the east bound signal instead of the face of the west bound?''

Harriman fixed him with a steely expression. ''I said the signal was not burning,'' he said coldly; ''that is all, except that I want to know the cause.''

Next day the superintendent found that the signal was indeed not burning because the lamp tender had neglected it.[26]

Inquiries into accidents had long been a scandal among railroads. ''Not a few railway accidents are whitewashed in the investigation to the extent that the officials deceive themselves,'' conceded superintendent W. L. Park. The ''science'' of railroading, he added, ''is the art of shifting responsibility.''[27]

The troubles of 1907 induced Harriman to attempt one of his boldest experiments. Four years earlier he had set up boards of inquiry to look into all accidents; now he announced that in future ''outsiders of local reputation and standing'' would be invited to sit on these boards and participate fully in their investigations. Harriman hoped that going public would give findings more credibility than could be obtained from a board of insiders. As the first railroad to adopt this policy, the Union Pacific ''approached it with no little timidity,'' Park admitted later. ''Our legal department said it would . . . throw open to legal 'shysters' information upon which claims would be made.'' Kruttschnitt understood that doctors could say little of value on the composition of boiler steel or merchants on train dispatching but added, ''whatever we do get in these reports, we will get no whitewashing. We will get the responsibility put squarely where it belongs. This is what I want.''[28]

Experience did much to convert the lawyers and other skeptics. Under Kruttschnitt's ironclad rule that the cause of every accident must be ferreted out, employee discipline and operating efficiency improved and newspaper misrepresentation of accidents decreased. The new policy had superb public relations effects, and it produced results. In one case a board with two bankers as the outsiders found a conductor and a brakeman negligent in an accident that killed ten employees. When the findings were protested, the company convened a second board with two brigadier generals and a retired Northwestern superintendent as the outsiders. This group probed deeper and found an engineer's ''improper manipulation of air'' to be the cause.[29]

The combination of physical improvements and unremitting vigilance made Union Pacific the industry leader in safety. At a time when national accident figures were climbing, the rate on Harriman lines declined sharply. Between 1904 and 1909 the average number of train accidents per million locomotive-miles dropped from 20.0 to 9.2 on the Union Pacific, from 20.1 to 14.3 on the Short Line, from 29.4 to 24.1 on the Southern Pacific, and from 22.7 to 15.3 on the latter's Sunset and Overland routes alone. It was altogether fitting that, after Harriman's death, his widow endowed the Harriman Medal to be awarded by the American Museum of Safety. No rail leader did more to leave his mark on this least popular area of the industry.[30]

The challenge of transforming one railroad into a model of efficiency paled before that of welding several giant lines together into a smoothly functioning system. To a surprising degree, genius consists of an ability to see the obvious with fresh eyes. Harriman showed this gift in the ease with which he moved from overhauling the Union Pacific to integrating the Union Pacific, Southern Pacific, Short Line, and Navigation roads. Here truly was the new order in transportation. To old railroad men seated comfortably in tradition, Harriman's principles seemed breathtaking in their scope and boldness; in fact, most of them were ideas that had been kicking around for a long time. What Harriman did was convert theory into practice with characteristic force and vigor. In the process he revealed to the railroad industry what its future should and would be.

The first step toward this new order came in the settlement of the Northern Pacific fight, when Harriman and Hill agreed to delegate all traffic matters for the roads under their control to one representative of each system. In addition, both sides agreed in the Metropolitan Club memorandum of 1901 to devise some plan ''for the establishment and maintenance of uniform methods of management and accounting'' for their systems and, hopefully, the other transcontinental lines as well. This concept proved too radical for Bacon, Hill, and those suspicious of Harriman's intentions, but Hill at least had the foresight to grasp the advantages that would flow from the traffic pact.[31]

The appointment of Stubbs by Harriman and Darius Miller by Hill created traffic czars who bypassed the presidents of each line and reported directly to

THE GREAT TECHNICIAN: The redoubtable Julius Kruttschnitt, who took charge of operations on the Harriman lines and later headed the Southern Pacific.

Harriman or Hill. Both men took offices in Chicago even though all the lines Stubbs served were west of the Mississippi River. This arrangement shocked many railroad men. One western president sneered that no road could be run by two heads and argued that big railway systems "ought to be operated by men on the ground and not by financial people a thousand, or perhaps three thousand, miles from the seat of war."[32]

The creation of a traffic manager for the combined Harriman systems was no isolated event. Everywhere Harriman moved to reorganize and consolidate his organization. The authority of Erastus Young, the crusty general auditor, was extended over all the lines. William V. S. Thorne, the assistant secretary in New York, was named director of purchases, and William Mahl of the Southern Pacific became comptroller for the Harriman roads. Robert S. Lovett, who had long served the Southern Pacific, reluctantly moved to New York to take charge of the legal department. In 1904 Harriman made his most daring move by appointing Kruttschnitt director of maintenance and operations for the entire system, with offices in Chicago. Railroad veterans blanched at the idea of consolidating authority for these crucial functions on so many miles of road in one official stationed off-line.[33]

In effect the two most important aspects of railroading, operations and traffic, had been centralized in the hands of two officials above the presidents of individual needs. They made an odd couple, the gaunt Stubbs whose spectacles and severe expression gave him a scholarly cast, and the burly, ham-handed Kruttschnitt, who resembled a prosperous brewmaster. A native of Ohio, Stubbs had apprenticed on an eastern road before coming to the Central Pacific shortly after it opened. He rose to the position of third vice-president in charge of traffic with the Southern Pacific. For nearly a quarter century he had handled transcontinental traffic, and no one knew its intricacies better.[34]

Kruttschnitt hailed from New Orleans, where his merchant father lost everything in the Civil War. By dint of hard labor he earned a degree in civil engineering from Washington & Lee in 1873, but the onset of depression forced him to teach school for five years. His first railroad job came in 1878 with Morgan's Louisiana & Texas road and tested his mettle early. Placed in charge of a survey party working its way through some swampy wilds, he had a chainman collapse with yellow fever. The rest of his men fled in terror but Kruttschnitt stayed on, tending the sick man for weeks with supplies obtained by posting his list of needs on a board planted some distance away. Finally the man died. Kruttschnitt dug a grave, read the service, filled the grave, and only then went home to recover from his own case of the fever.[35]

When Collis Huntington leased the Morgan roads in 1885, he got Kruttschnitt as well. At the time of Huntington's death Kruttschnitt was serving as vice-president and general manager of all Southern Pacific lines. Like Stubbs, he was known for his intelligence, fierce loyalty, and utter dedication to duty. He became a pioneer in the generation and proper use of statistics on railroads; one observer credited him with doing "as much as any other railway executive to make railroading into a science." Kruttschnitt had only contempt for men who wished to start at the top and coast through their careers. "The only way I know in which anyone can have an easy life," he once said, "is to *earn* it by the hardest possible kind of work during the formative years."[36]

Harriman gave him all the work he wanted. The new order taxed officers on every system in two ways: it demanded hard work and strict accountability, and it forced radical adjustments in their thinking. Railroad men were used to hard work but not to new ways of doing things in what was the most hidebound industry in the nation. Those who could not adapt fell by the wayside, and the casualties started coming early. One of the first was Charles M. Hays, the president of the Southern Pacific, who resented the erosion of his power by Stubbs's new position and Erastus Young's authority over Southern Pacific accounts. In July 1901 Hays resigned impetuously, then tried to reclaim his position. "He evidently feels terribly mortified," Schiff reported, "& is prepared, I feel, to do almost anything if he is spared the consequences that he has brought upon himself."[37]

But Harriman did not want Hays. The only issue was who would replace him. Most of the rumors centered on Burt or Felton, but Harriman and Schiff agreed that Burt was not suited to run both companies and Felton was still needed at the Alton. Schiff went off to Germany still fretting over the dilemma. In his absence Harriman imposed his own solution: he took the job himself, with Kruttschnitt as vice-president and assistant to the president in charge of actual operations. Schiff was so appalled when the news reached him that even his legendary tact melted from his response:

> The present state of affairs is unjust both to you and the Company. I know of no other Company which so greatly needs a strong local management than the Southern Pacific. In California it is anything but popular, & as Mr Rea tells me he was informed that some of the Company's employees simply use their positions to further their own political ends & that of their friends. In Texas & California the Company's territory is constantly menaced by its rivals, & from one end to the other of the system a watchful eye is needed *urgently* & *constantly*. . . . I cannot but say that the existing situation fills me with anxiety and misgivings & I would not be loyal to you if I did not express this to you in entire frankness.[38]

Even those close to Harriman regarded the move as another example of his tendency to take on too many tasks at once regardless of the burden imposed on his stamina. However, even Schiff came to see the method in his madness. Harriman recognized that no traditional rail president could abide the curtailment of authority required by the centralized system he was putting together. Unless he could find the right man, it made more sense to take the post himself and leave operation of the road in the hands of a vice-president. The trend toward separating financial and operating control of roads had long been underway—indeed, it had always existed on the Union Pacific. Harriman was now leaping ahead another step by creating a new intersystem organizational structure above the individual roads.

Horace Burt lasted only a little longer under the new regimen. He had always been a good soldier if not an imaginative one, and the strain eventually wore him down. When he quit in January 1904, stories circulated that Harriman had forced him out through a series of humiliations, the most savage of which was summoning him to New York and letting him cool his heels for days outside Harriman's office while the latter occupied himself with other matters. Critics hammered at the parallel to Hays's departure and wondered just what kind of man could work for so overbearing a master. There was enough truth in this charge to make it plausible. Harriman banged away at subordinates with supreme indifference to their feelings or stamina, and he sometimes shot from the hip.[39]

General superintendent W. L. Park learned firsthand how these episodes wore Burt down. On an inspection trip in the fall of 1903 he and Harriman met Burt in Cheyenne, and Park saw at once that relations were strained. Harriman wanted to visit the shops because he had heard that his orders on abolishing piecework were not being carried out. After he went off with the master mechanic, Burt grabbed Park's arm and walked him up and down the platform. "When Mr. Harriman comes back to his car I am going to tender him my resignation," he muttered softly. "I want you to know it now, so that later it cannot be said that I was dismissed."[40]

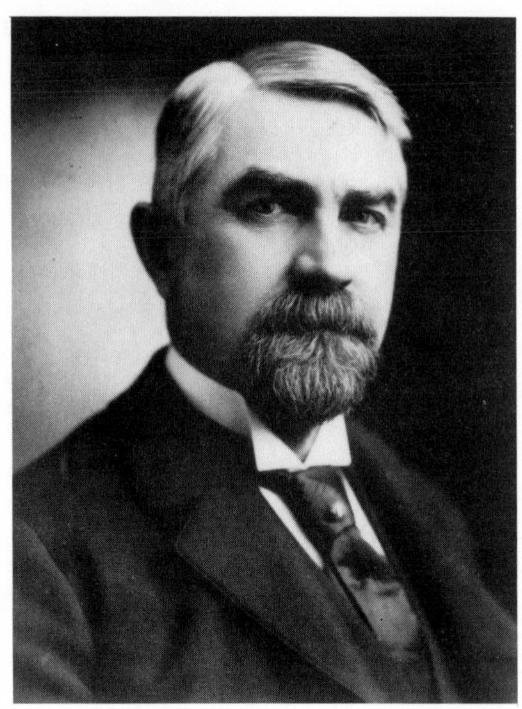

THE GOOD SOLDIER: Horace G. Burt, first president of the newly reorganized Union Pacific, who quit the office after being worn down by Harriman's demands.

Park tried to talk him out of it, but Burt would not relent. "I cannot be humiliated in this way," he said bitterly. "These men around us know what is going on." Harriman soon returned from the shops and started up again on Burt. That evening Burt handed in his resignation, to take effect in January.

A few years later, on Harriman's last trip over the road, Park heard the other side. In a lengthy conversation Harriman said he had not fired Burt and praised him for his reconstruction work. But he had constantly to urge bolder plans on Burt and others, who never seemed to grasp broader visions. He had practically forced new equipment on Burt, and even then the road was swamped by the great increase in business. Harriman grew as tired of pushing as Burt did of being shoved. Even so, their parting was amicable despite the rumors. "The press dispatches, saying that there was friction between us," Burt wired Harriman, "were entirely gratuitous, and of course entirely wrong." He accepted an invitation to visit Harriman in New York, but noted plaintively to William Mahl that "it is a source of very sincere regret that I am compelled at this time, to retire from [Union Pacific]."[41]

Burt's departure opened the door to a series of changes. Two months later, in March 1904, Kruttschnitt assumed his new post in Chicago. Harriman added the presidency of the Union Pacific to his collection of titles and brought A. L. Mohler from Navigation to become general manager (and soon vice-president) in Omaha. A longtime Union Pacific man, E. E. Calvin, who had been assistant general manager of the Short Line, went to Portland in Mohler's place. C. H. Markham, vice-president of the Houston & Texas Central, succeeded Kruttschnitt as operating head of the Southern Pacific. Bancroft remained in charge of the Short Line but had his jurisdiction extended to all lines west of Green River, while Mohler commanded those east of the river.[42]

With Kruttschnitt and Stubbs in Chicago, Harriman could perfect his scheme to place all systems under unified and standardized control. Both Gould and Huntington had envisioned such an arrangement in the late 1880s but were never in a position to make it happen. Harriman marched toward this goal from the very start in matters large and small. In December 1898 the general manager launched monthly meetings with all the superintendents "to secure greater uniformity and harmony as well as the adoption of the latest and best known methods for handling the business of the Operating Department." Harriman had Burt install new systems for use of motive power and distribution of cars, and ordered a comparative study of coal use. The accounting system was revised, and the duties of all officers were shuffled into more efficient arrangements.[43]

Everywhere Harriman demanded efficiency even if it meant doing things in unorthodox ways. By 1902 he was ready to extend this vision upward from the Union Pacific to all the roads under his control. Operating rules were standardized for the Union Pacific, Short Line, Navigation, and Southern Pacific. The superintendents of motive power met to establish uniform standards for car and engine construction. Other equipment and structures were also standardized; in one case, fifty patterns of switch frogs were reduced to four. A plan was devised to purchase supplies jointly for the four companies. By lumping orders for such things as coal and rails, Harriman could shop carefully for the best price. He introduced a new authority for expenditure (AFE) procedure embracing the Alton and Kansas City Southern as well as his other companies.[44]

The idea for common purchasing, noted Union Pacific secretary Alex Millar, "came to Mr. Harriman's attention incidentally through a recommendation for an increase of salary at Salt Lake City." That was exactly how his mind worked. There was no master plan for efficiency but rather a laser beam of intelligence that fastened on a detail and drained from it larger insights for making things work smoothly. Centralized purchasing and common standards lowered unit costs or most items, reduced inventories, and lowered downtime on equipment by making interchangeable parts more readily available. Apart from his own ideas, Harriman impressed on everyone in the organization the need to "devise ways and means for handling the largest possible business at the least possible cost."[45]

Kruttschnitt's promotion inaugurated the final phase of that development. Shortly after arriving in Chicago he organized a clearing house to pool all cars on the Harriman roads, as if the systems owned all their equipment in common. Officers were held strictly accountable for utilizing them to full capacity, and special tracers followed their movements. To wring full value from locomotives, trains were loaded on the basis of a formula that included tonnage rating, tractive power, and speed requirements. Heavier cars were kept on long-haul runs to maximize their capacity, and shipments were combined to save equipment. Elaborate statistics on these matters poured into Kruttschnitt's office and were studied closely to monitor the level of efficiency. Kruttschnitt calculated that in the first two years alone the new system saved more than fifty-three million miles in empty cars hauls.[46]

The chief engineers and superintendents of motive power reported directly to Kruttschnitt. The former took charge of all construction, maintenance, and certain facilities; the latter handled the shops and all matters relating to equipment, tools, and power plants. All requests by general managers and superintendents for improvements or expenditures had to be approved by Kruttschnitt, which sometimes slowed progress but gave him an overview of work on all the systems. On traffic movement he consulted with Stubbs to find the most efficient routings. In general, traffic moving south of a line through Buffalo, Pittsburgh, Cincinnati, and Cairo was shipped via the Sunset Route while everything north of that line went through the Ogden gateway.[47]

Harriman's new order shattered tradition in the way it tackled the old conundrum of organization. "There are essentially two different methods practiced by large railroad systems," observed Charles Perkins. "One method is to spread the working organization . . . over the entire system; the other makes a number of different working organizations, or units of management, each complete in itself." This was the old "department vs. division" dilemma over which thoughtful railroad men had argued since small roads became large ones. The department method organized the road by function and gave each department authority over the entire system. This highly centralized structure had two major flaws: it grew unwieldy as the system expanded, and it hampered the development of junior officers, who tended to become dependent not on their own initiative but on their superiors.[48]

The division method carved enlarged systems into separate spheres and put them in charge of a general manager or superintendent, who ruled his domain and was responsible for its performance. J. Edgar Thomson of the Pennsylvania had pioneered this method in the early 1870s, and his road had utilized it with brilliant success. Curiously, few companies copied this model, preferring instead to spread the centralized department method over their expanding systems. Perkins adopted it for the Burlington, and Charles Francis Adams had tried it on the Union Pacific in the 1880s. The division method solved the flaws of the department approach but posed some new ones, most notably a tendency for fierce rivalries to develop among the division heads, who often concentrated on a good showing for their realm regardless of what happened to the overall system. It required not only able general managers but skilled diplomacy to make the division method work.

Harriman's new order sought to retain the best features of the division method while eliminating its drawbacks. Above all, it provided a level of management charged with monitoring, coordinating, and integrating the combined systems for maximum efficiency. Six general managers presided over what amounted to self-contained systems. Beneath them, twenty-six superintendents each had charge of a "miniature but complete railway." Kruttschnitt clothed them with "the same authority as is exercised by the Vice President and General Manager over the entire property. . . . The control over all matters under their jurisdiction shall be complete.'' Harriman believed fervently in delegating authority and demanding results. He did not want Kruttschnitt interfering in the autonomy of these divisions, but he did expect the director to be out on the road checking the results of their efforts. He warned Kruttschnitt not to let his office become a ''correspondence bureau'' and urged him to go ''out over the various lines and keep things smooth.''[49]

In the last year of Harriman's life Kruttschnitt tried an experiment on the Nebraska division by abolishing all duty titles (master mechanic, division engineer, trainmaster, etc.) and designating officers as either superintendent or assistant superintendent. Although everyone retained their former duties, they occupied a common office and covered it on a rotating basis. All correspondence (except personal) to the division was addressed to the title, not the individual, and was handled by the man on duty at the time. The object of the unit system, as it was called, was to reduce ''government by chief clerks'' and avoid the tendency of men kept behind a desk to develop ''academic tendencies.'' It aimed to cut internal correspondence in half, thereby freeing officers to spend more time in the field.[50]

Obviously this system required able managers, who were always in short supply in the rail industry. Harriman was quick to tap every system for its best talent, and it happened that the other systems had more talent than the Union Pacific. Four of his top officers (Kruttschnitt, Stubbs, Lovett, and Mahl) came from the Southern Pacific, Bancroft from the Short Line, Mohler from Navigation. At every level, those who could not attune their thinking to new ways soon left for other jobs. J. H. McConnell, the superintendent of motive power who had been with the Union Pacific for thirty-three years, quit in 1901. His successor, brought in from the Lehigh Valley, lasted little over a year before being replaced by the capable W. R. McKeen, Jr. Late in 1902 Edward Dickinson, the veteran general manager, fled to a position with a smaller road.[51]

Those who worked for Harriman conceded that he was demanding but fair. In taking over a new road he never replaced officers with his own pets but gave the old hands a chance to show their stuff. Throughout the ranks he was more admired than loved. ''They don't dislike Harriman like the Great Northern men dislike Hill,'' observed Edwin Lefevre. ''The trouble seems to be that everybody is afraid of Harriman. . . . They do not exactly cringe nor kowtow before him. They act rather as though they recognized the existence of a vast gulf between his brain and theirs.''[52]

Which, of course, there was.

Harriman treated his men well and gave them every opportunity to advance. The visionary labor schemes of Charles Francis Adams, Jr., had died aborning, casualties of his own failure as a manager and of the depression. Harriman rooted his innovations in more practical soil. In 1909 the Union Pacific created its own Bureau of Information and Education to train employees in all aspects of railroading. Employees could enroll for training in any area they chose and take courses at the company's expense. The applicant was asked to list any previous education and state "what he desires the bureau to do for him; the information he wants; what line of work he wants to advance in, and what (in reason) he is ambitious to become."[53]

Workers could also submit to the bureau any question they had on matters related to their jobs, and an advisory board would answer them on an anonymous basis. The object of these programs was to improve the men's efficiency, keep them abreast of changing methods and technologies, and target likely candidates for promotion. At bottom it was a bold attempt to cut through the hoary railroad tradition of old hands teaching young hands to do things the way they had been taught to do them. It also offered the lowliest worker a ladder for self-advancement. Nothing better exemplified Harriman's determination to wrench the rail industry into the new century. Within three weeks after the program began, it had 157 applicants.

Earlier Harriman had extended a helping hand to older workers. During the fall of 1902 he approved a pension plan modeled on those used by the Illinois Central, Pennsylvania, and Northwestern roads. Under its provisions an employee had to retire at seventy but could leave earlier if incapacitated. If he had put in at least twenty years with the company, he would receive an amount per month equal to 1 percent of his average monthly pay for his last ten years of service multiplied by his number of years of service. Thus, a man with thirty years service who had averaged $75 a month during his last ten years would receive a pension of $22.50 a month. Those denied by the pension board could appeal to the board of directors, which granted occasional exceptions to men who had served the company well but did not meet the other criteria. The system went into operation in January 1903 and by 1910 had 188 retirees on the rolls at a total cost of $51,798. "It is a noble thing for the Company to do," wrote one old hand after receiving his first check.[54]

The company had every reason to encourage the men to improve their skills. The great explosion of business taxed the labor force no less than the equipment. Veterans had to work longer and harder than ever, and more greenhorns than usual filled the ranks to handle the traffic that swamped the road. The volatile mix of raw and seasoned workers meant more accidents and lay behind the drive for increased safety. Everywhere the demand was for greater efficiency, more productivity, smoother coordination, with results that sometimes backfired. The worst labor strife of Harriman's career erupted in reaction to one such campaign.

In June 1901 the company decided to install the piecework system in its shops. The machinists, boilermakers, and blacksmiths refused to accept the change and went out on strike. At first the unions confined the walkout to the Union Pacific, where Burt managed to keep the shops running on the piecework plan despite the strike. That winter a truce was patched up and the men returned to work, but in June 1902 negotiations broke down when the boilermakers demanded more money as well as rule changes. Burt stood firm, and the shopmen walked again. Once the strike began, Burt moved to install the piecework system among the boilermakers and blacksmiths who remained.

"If there were no strike, it would require from two to three years, under pressure, to fully introduce piece-work," he observed, "but of course with the opposition of a strike it is more difficult; but there is no doubt about it being accomplished."[55]

The strikers failed to get the carmen, who comprised about half the shop force, or any other unions to join them, yet they held out month after month. "The Union Pacific has a hard fight on its hands," warned a general manager, "one that means a great deal of money, to all of the Harriman lines; if we lose it, we practically lose control of the shops." Burt agreed. Having staked his reputation on the outcome, he declared that "With such efficient and loyal service on the part of officers and employes [sic], there is no such word as fail." Neither the duration of the strike nor scattered outbreaks of violence shook his confidence. By January 1903 negotiations had resolved all differences except that of piecework. Burt insisted that most of the strikers actually favored piecework, a view the union leaders laughed away.[56]

The worst situation was at the Cheyenne shop, where a work force augmented by 227 strikebreakers was doing poorly under the piecework plan. The master mechanic tried to improve things by recruiting apprentices from the vicinity but had little luck. Meanwhile, scab workers were attacked at Cheyenne, and the unions threatened to extend the strike to the Southern Pacific. Until then Harriman had left the handling of the strike to Burt, but he dared not let the strike spread just as the time when James R. Keene was about to launch his attack on Southern Pacific stock. It galled Harriman to back down on vital issues, and he never swallowed defeat easily. Nevertheless, he agreed in June 1903 to withdraw the piecework system gradually from the shops and grant the shopmen a 7 percent pay increase.[57]

Under the settlement union men returned to the old system while the nonunion men continued piecework until October, when the issue would be discussed. Burt noted in September that nonunion men comprised 73 percent of the total shop force compared to only 25 percent before the strike, and insisted that they preferred the piecework system. But during Harriman's visit in October 1903 the shopmen complained that the system was not being removed as promised, and Harriman gave orders to abolish it. This was the final blow to Burt, who had felt betrayed and humiliated by the settlement; that very night he handed Harriman his resignation. His departure, coupled with the abolition of piecework, left the nonunion men uneasy, and gradually they began to leave or shift over to the union.[58]

In handling its labor force the Union Pacific for most of the Harriman era belonged to a small group of roads that used "Brown's discipline system." Railroads had three levels of punishment for rule violations: reprimand, suspension, and dismissal. Most companies suspended a man without pay for infractions and posted his name for others to see. The Brown method suspended men only on the books and in private. A record of demerits was kept for each man (one demerit equal to a day's suspension). The accumulation of a certain number of demerits meant dismissal, but a clean record for several months or a year removed demerits accumulated earlier. Monthly lists of offenses for which demerits had been given were still posted at division headquarters, but without any names.[59]

Some figures for the six months ending June 30, 1902, suggest how the system worked. On the Union Pacific proper 4,624 employees were subject to discipline by record. Of this number 3,846 (83 percent) maintained perfect records and 5 were commended. Another 43 were reprimanded, 748 were suspended on the books for five to sixty days, and 235 were discharged. Of the latter 56 were dismissed for intemperance, 34 for unsatisfactory service, 33 for negligence causing damage, 23 for hazard of accident, 22 for other forms of negligence, 21 for insubordination, and 15 for failing to report for duty. Other men were reprimanded or suspended for all of these offenses except intemperance, for which discharge was automatic.[60]

Labor too had entered a new era, and no one yet knew what to make of it. A leading journal chided that the Harriman lines, in using Brown's discipline, "tolerate the characteristic weakness of the system—the practice of continuing leniency too far." But it also emphasized that "good discipline cannot be had merely by the operation of a machine; some strong man must put his personality into it; and he must do a lot of hard work." In the new order that strong man was more than ever some line officer, who needed solid training and close watching himself. "We cannot restore the conditions of 30 years ago," noted the editor wistfully, "when so many managers were personally acquainted with their employees, therefore the only alternative is to increase the efficiency of the deputy managers."[61]

This was true in the larger sense as well. The railroad industry could not restore the order of thirty or even ten years earlier, and it was heading into another era of rapid change. To Harriman went much of the credit for pointing the way to a future based on something more than the past.

8

The Storms

To the officers who served him he was known simply as "The Chairman," and The Chairman presided over so many systems and companies that those around him struggled to keep straight which chairman they were addressing at any given time. He sat astride the largest and most complex transportation system in the world, one in which the individual systems were larger than most other railroads. His influence kept spreading, first into other roads and then into other industries. To outsiders he was a marvel of brilliance and efficiency, and a ruthless engine of raw power as well. His indifference to public opinion and his cold, aloof business style earned him more than his share of enemies. The very size of his empire, the sheer scale of his success, made Harriman a choice target in an age growing increasingly disturbed by the influence of large enterprises on society.

A prudent man could see that storms of great intensity were brewing and recognize the need for diplomacy and tact. But this had always been Harriman's blind spot. In time he would do much to mend it, but not before one fierce storm after another raged over him and his empire. Like all conquerors who rise so swiftly to power, Harriman found himself thrown on the defensive by the enemies he had accumulated and the fears he had aroused. And like Gould before him, he endured these storms with remarkable stoicism, content to ride out their violence in the hope that calmer days would vindicate his course. Gould emerged with his empire more intact than his reputation, while for Harriman the reverse proved true. Both men paid dearly in the coin of broken health for their determination.

* * *

Months of negotiation with the Atchison failed to break the impasse in Arizona and California. Harriman insisted that the Atchison sell him the Phoenix & Eastern and abandon its invasion of Southern Pacific territory. Atchison chairman Victor Morawetz doggedly refused to deal in Arizona without a settlement in northwest California as well. Personally Morawetz thought the branch of little worth for the Atchison, but he saw its value as a bargaining chip and played it to the hilt. In December 1903 the struggle took an ominous turn. Until then the Eastern was viewed only as a cutoff line giving the Atchison connections into El Paso. Suddenly, however, its crews crossed the Gila River and headed toward the strategic Gila Canyon, the only suitable route for a low-grade line between Phoenix and El Paso. The Southern Pacific had long coveted this route and intended to build on it as soon as funds permitted. Now a dangerous rival threatened to snatch it from them.[1]

News of this change was hurried to Harriman, who responded by sending engineer Epes Randolph to form a new company, the Arizona Eastern, and commence surveys for a route through the canyon. There followed an instant replay of the struggle for Meadow Valley Wash in Nevada. Survey crews from both sides rushed into opposite ends of the canyon with indecent haste. By March 1904 the engineers had given way to grading parties who cheerfully blasted rock onto the line claimed by the other. Before any serious violence could erupt, the fight was transferred to the courts.[2]

While the lawyers haggled, Harriman tried another tack. That summer he and his associates bought 300,000 shares of Atchison and asked Morawetz for representation on the company's board. Morawetz refused, saying he did not believe directors of one road should sit on the board of another. After some sparring he agreed to give Harriman two seats only if the new directors were not officials of the Union Pacific and all outstanding differences between the Atchison and the Harriman roads were resolved first. This brought Harriman back to the bargaining table, and within a few weeks an agreement was thrashed out. The competing northern California lines were put into a new company jointly owned by the Atchison and Southern Pacific. In return the Atchison sold the Eastern to the Southern Pacific and agreed to share a proposed through line from Mojave, California, to Deming, New Mexico. The Gila Canyon suits were dropped, and in February 1905 two "friends" of Union Pacific were elected to the Atchison board.[3]

Both sides could parade the outcome as a victory. Morawetz had kept Harriman off the board and secured the Atchison's place in northern California. Harriman had neutralized the Atchison in a way that enabled the two roads to remain friendly if not cozy for some years despite occasional spats. Observers not privy to the agreement hailed the new California company as another Harriman coup, but it was rather a triumph for the community of interest principle. Unfortunately, its gains were more than offset by losses on other fronts.[4]

For two years the fate of Northern Securities hung like a Damoclean sword above the Harriman and Hill camps. The Minnesota suit against the holding

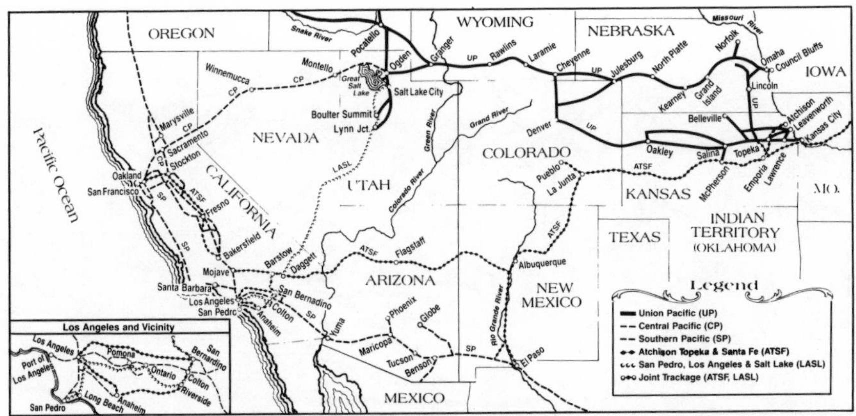

SOUTHWEST BATTLEGROUND: The region contested by the Union Pacific-Southern Pacific and the Atchison, Topeka & Santa Fe systems.

company had been removed to a federal court where neither Harriman nor Hill lost much sleep over it. However, in January 1902 the ICC held an inquiry on the community of interest question. Two months later Theodore Roosevelt stunned everyone by having his attorney general file suit against Northern Securities for violating the Sherman Antitrust Act. While his motives for this action have been widely debated, historian Albro Martin makes a plausible case for political expediency as the driving force. To writer Hamlin Garland, Roosevelt boasted of having "taken down the fences of a very great and very arrogant corporation." From this one action he would gain an inflated reputation as "trustbuster." Like any good politician he recognized that timing and gesture counted far more than deeds.[5]

The federal suit posed a much greater danger. Only two cases had yet applied the Sherman Act to railroads: in both decisions the Supreme Court struck down agreements to maintain rates. This suit was the first challenge against one of the companies created by the recent merger frenzy. For that reason it commanded widespread attention as a precedent for the court's attitude toward not only railroads but other giant amalgamations such as United States Steel. In April 1903 a special panel of four circuit judges ruled unanimously that Northern Securities had the power to restrain trade and was therefore unlawful whether or not it actually used that power. In September, however, the judge hearing Minnesota's suit decided that the company had broken no state laws. Both decisions were appealed to the Supreme Court.[6]

While the legal fight dragged on, less publicized clashes kept Hill and Harriman embroiled inside the company, where both were still maneuvering for advantage while steadfastly denying they were doing so. The uncertain future of Northern Securities only intensified their efforts to protect their interests whatever the outcome. In November 1901 all parties had met again at the Metropolitan Club and produced a new memorandum to cover the traffic and territorial matters mentioned in the May agreement. But final approval of this

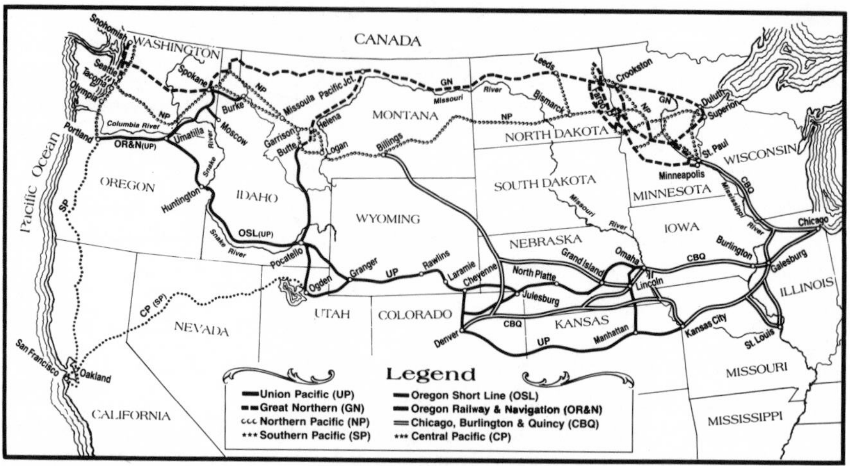

CLOSE ENCOUNTER: The disputed ground of the Northwest, where Hill and Harriman clashed.

draft encountered one delay after another. It did not help that Harriman and Hill had styles that could not have been more opposite. The younger man was all speed and motion, the older one a monument to deliberation. The impatient Harriman wanted all issues wrapped up and all proposed projects launched; Hill preferred moving with caution, especially with the legal waters so murky. This clash of styles did much to heighten their mutual distrust.[7]

The most sensitive flash point remained the southeast corner of Washington, where both sides had agreed tentatively to joint construction of several lines radiating from the Snake River. Harriman wanted one key branch built at once and bristled with impatience over Charles Mellen's delays. There was also trouble around Portland, where Hill suspected Navigation of being behind some lines heading toward the Nehalem Valley and north of the Columbia River. Hill complained to Harriman and Schiff, who both assured him that the charges were groundless, but Hill would not relent. "I cannot disregard evidence which is so direct and strong that your people are practically behind the North Shore enterprise," he snapped at Harriman. "The work should be stopped at once as only safe plan."[8]

The memorandum of November 1901 was supposed to resolve all these traffic and territorial matters, but new disputes arose before approval was even in sight. Harriman questioned some surveys made by Mellen on the north bank of the Columbia, and pressed a claim for $50,000 against the Burlington. He grew positively livid when Mellen tried to buy a small Cascades road without first informing him. Clearly he was strung out from overwork, and the more tired he was, the more suspicious he grew. "He continues his outbursts about breaches of faith of which he imagines himself about to become the victim," reported W. P. Clough, one of Hill's closest associates. "He should go off and rest a month."[9]

Negotiations over the November 1901 memorandum entered their second year with no agreement in sight. Hill, in his usual style, kept insisting that he was honoring the Metropolitan Club pact while Harriman was trying to gain more than the agreement gave him. When Stubbs and Miller could not agree on a division of rates in the Northwest, Hill told his man to "give them ultimatum and be done with it." Like most railroad men, Hill presumed himself to have a monopoly of virtue if not of traffic. He was tired of the Harriman style of negotiation in which "Mr. H. has pronounced himself satisfied, and agreed, only to have his representatives appear the next morning, and demand things that could not be conceded."[10]

The harder Harriman pushed, the more Hill growled that if differences "cannot be settled on a fair basis, the whole thing can go by the board." Both sides knew the letter of the memorandum, but they took different views of its spirit. Miller seemed more intent than Hill on nursing the negotiations along, but little progress was made. By the winter of 1903 peace reigned in the Northwest through what amounted to an informal truce, but its future looked bleak unless some agreement could be reached on the Metropolitan Club memorandum.[11]

Unfortunately, Harriman endured a series of personal misfortunes that distracted him from business. His younger brother William, who was very close to him, had long suffered from Bright's disease. When his condition worsened in the fall of 1902, Harriman sent him to Florida in the care of a doctor and a nurse. Through long stretches of the winter Harriman journeyed south to be with his brother. In the spring William was brought back to New York, where he died on April 4. A few days after the funeral, laid up with another of his innumerable colds, Harriman felt obliged to pen an apology to Hill that "family matters" had prevented him from looking closely into the Snake River dispute.[12]

Once out of bed, annoyed that he was behind in everything, Harriman rushed west to tackle a variety of problems. On the way back he agreed to meet a delegation of shopmen in Omaha about the settlement of their strike. However, in Utah he fell ill with what was finally diagnosed as appendicitis. Samuel Felton, who met Harriman in Cheyenne, found him lying in bed, his face drawn and wracked with pain. But Harriman refused to go on to Chicago until he had met the shopmen as promised. Knowing from experience that Harriman would not budge, Felton quietly ordered the trainmaster to send the train on to Chicago without attaching a car for the committee.

Still, Harriman insisted on seeing the shopmen in Chicago before receiving treatment or returning east. Only the doctor's firm stand persuaded him to leave at once for New York. On May 20, four days after reaching New York, he submitted to an operation. That same day, once revived from the ether, he wired Hill that the doctor "took out the useless thing this morning. I am in fine shape." By early June he was well enough to take his family abroad for an extended vacation.[13]

Hill was solicitous of his rival's health, but not to the point of conceding anything on their differences. In England Harriman took care to visit and woo two of Hill's associates, banker Gaspard Farrer and Lord Mount Stephen. Both came away deeply impressed. "He *appeared* to me to be an exceptionally able & clearheaded man and a man to be trusted," reported Mount Stephen. Their enthusiasm did not sit well with Hill. "Privately speaking," he was quick to inform Mount Stephen, "he has a reputation of being able to turn a very sharp corner where he thinks it to his interest to do so." After Harriman's return in September, negotiations resumed on all the old issues. The outlook brightened in one respect that fall when Mellen left the presidency of the Northern Pacific and was replaced by the able Howard Elliott.[14]

In January 1904 Harriman offered some new concessions, but neither side seemed able to break the stalemate. On March 14 the whole matter went into eclipse when the Supreme Court upheld the government's position by a five to four vote and ordered Northern Securities dissolved. Justice John M. Harlan's majority opinion argued that *any* combination with the power to restrain trade was illegal even though it had not actually used that power. No case better illustrated the confused attitudes of Americans toward the new corporate giants that had become so significant a part of their economic life. Northern Securities had not yet done anything, but it might, and what might it do? It would promote "monopoly" by restraining "competition." The fact that this might be the most desirable state of the rail industry never entered their thinking. Competition was good, monopoly evil, and concentrations of power a menace regardless of their purpose. Or so most Americans believed.

"Great cases like hard cases make bad law," wrote Oliver Wendell Holmes in his dissent. He was only half correct. Certainly the decision was bad law in that it pointed Americans in the opposite direction from where their economic life was tending. But Northern Securities proved not so much a great case as a loud one. "The nearer one gets to the core of the matter," sneered one analyst, "the more narrow and inconsequential is the item of fact and law that is found to be settled." Not one major element of the decision endured except as a bad example. The railroads torn asunder in 1904 finally got back together in 1970 as the Burlington Northern. The "rule of reason" urged in vain by Justice David J. Brewer was embraced by the Court in 1911. Through a series of acts Congress soon replaced competition among roads with a straitjacket of regulation, including the power to set rates.[15]

However, all this lay in the future. The immediate effect was to deal a death blow to the fragile alliance between Harriman and Hill. The failure to ratify the Metropolitan Club memorandum already had both sides edging toward open conflict in the Northwest. Now a fight loomed over how to dismember Northern Securities, which could be done in one of two ways. The first was simply to return to each Northern Securities holder the stocks in subsidiary lines he had held in the first place. The second was to distribute pro rata the holding company's assets without regard for what each stockholder had turned in originally. Harriman preferred the first plan because he would walk away with a majority of Northern Pacific stock; Hill favored the second because it would leave his rival with armloads of stock in the underlying companies but control over none of them.[16]

Since Hill and his friends dominated the board of Northern Securities, there was little doubt about which plan would be used. On March 22 the Northern Securities board unanimously approved the pro rata plan with Harriman abstaining. A circular went out to stockholders offering them $39.27 in Northern Pacific stock and $30.17 in Great Northern stock for every share of Northern Securities surrendered. Ten days later Harriman filed suit to intervene. When the court denied his request, he asked for an injunction to halt the pro rata distribution. Hill was infuriated by the suit and insisted that Harriman had agreed to the plan, then gone back on his word. Aware that Harriman and Stillman were going to London that summer, Hill churned out some angry warnings to his English friends. "For myself," he raged, "I would not, under any circumstances, be associated with them in any business. All they want to make them crooked is an opportunity to cheat some one."[17]

Hill was right to worry, for once again his friends in England were impressed with Harriman's ability and his refusal to deal in personalities. "The head and font of his complaint is the menace to Union Pacific interests of the Burlington in your undivided control," Gaspard Farrer reported; ". . . it is not the present but the future that Harriman fears; it is not Gould or the Moores but *you*." Mount Stephen echoed Farrer in arguing for a peaceful solution and added that Harriman seemed unwell, "having a tired worn look for so young a man." Their plea for harmony drove Hill to more diatribes against Harriman, each one nastier and more personal than the last. There would be no community of interest in the Northwest.[18]

In August 1904 Hill appealed Harriman's case to the circuit court of appeals, which dissolved the injunction the following January. Harriman then appealed to the Supreme Court and lost again. Even this complete victory could not ease Hill's bitterness. When Schiff ventured to congratulate him, Hill snarled, "I do not agree with you that the fight was a fair one. I think it was the foulest and most unnecessary fight that I have ever known.[19]

Aware that a dangerous vacuum now filled the Northwest, Farrer and other Hill associates pleaded for peace and compromise. But neither seemed likely in 1905. Harriman surveyed the ruins and told reporters sagely, "We are going to run into an era of competitive railroad building just as we have passed through an era of competitive buying." This widely-quoted remark impressed analysts deeply as events unfolded. Hill scoffed at the idea even as he prepared to launch an ambitious plan to construct his own line along the north bank of the Columbia from Spokane to Portland and on to Astoria at the river's mouth. This would forever free the Great Northern and Northern Pacific from dependence on Navigation.[20]

"Concealment is no longer possible," noted a Portland paper gleefully, "of the intentions of the Hill and Harriman interests to wage the bitterest warfare of recent years." Nor was the fight limited to one front. On the heels of Harriman's prediction came word that the Milwaukee, after much waffling, would build to the Pacific coast, thereby taking the first fateful step toward the most spectacular railroad bankruptcy of the next generation. In Colorado David Moffat vigorously pushed his plan to tunnel the Rockies, and the long smolder-

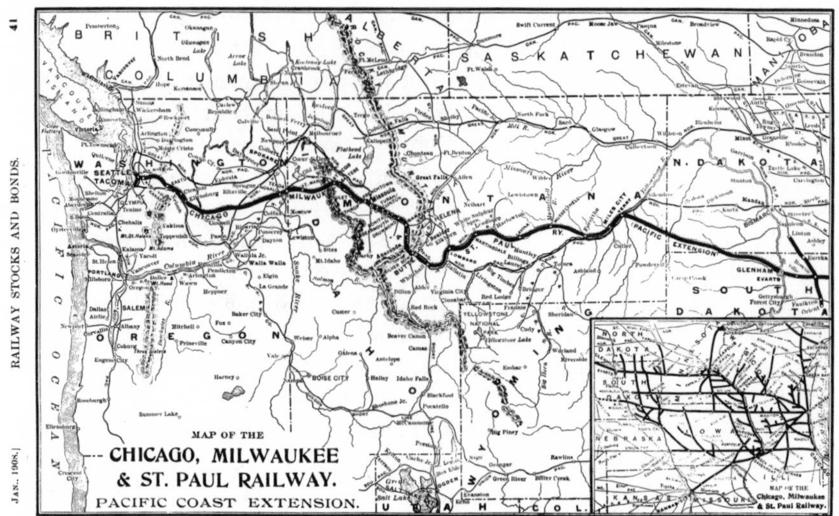

LATECOMER: The Milwaukee's extension to the West Coast, with the parent system in the inset. (*Commercial and Financial Chronicle, Investors' Supplement,* 1908)

ing tension between Harriman and George Gould flared into the open when Gould finally admitted that he was behind the Western Pacific, a new line projected from Oakland to Salt Lake City.[21]

Gould's activities had undergone some strange convolutions in recent years. On the surface he and Harriman embodied the community of interest principle, sitting on each other's boards and joining in syndicates on various enterprises. Yet beneath this amiable gloss they tugged strenuously in opposite directions. Gould had watched Harriman snatch the Southern Pacific and San Pedro lines from him, while he in turn had grabbed the Rio Grande and Rio Grande Western, giving him a line from St. Louis to Ogden. By 1903 Gould had acquired a patchwork quilt of roads (the Wabash, Wheeling & Lake Erie, and Western Maryland) with the potential of forming a through route from St. Louis to the Atlantic seaboard. All he needed to complete a true transcontinental system was a road from Ogden to California. Such a line had been his father's dream, and some said the son sought to realize it.

The idea of a railroad through Feather River Canyon had been kicking around since the 1860s, but not until the new century did it get beyond the talking stage. In 1900 a California lawyer named W. J. Barnett decided to extend his investment in a local road to one reaching eastward from Oakland. By 1903 Barnett had organized three new companies and picked up valuable properties for the project. He disclosed his plans to Gould, who was already scouting possible routes for a road to the Bay area. In February 1903 they joined forces, and the Western Pacific was incorporated a month later. Although Barnett and his friends dominated the new company, several papers from the first pointed to Gould as the power behind the throne.[22]

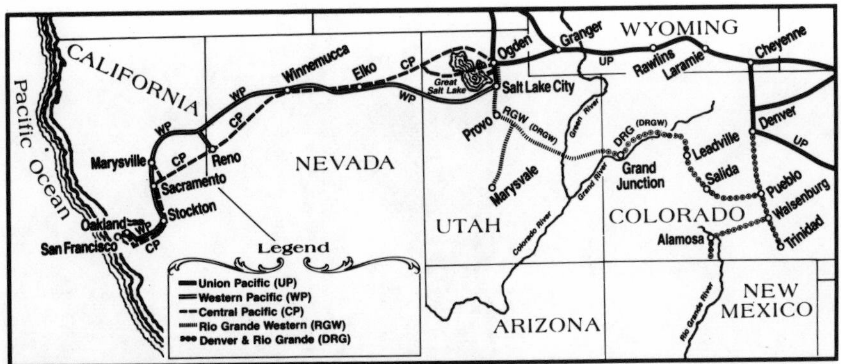

FEEBLE THREAT: The Western Pacific, Denver & Rio Grande, and Rio Grande Western systems, which George Gould hoped to make into a rival line between San Francisco and Ogden.

Gould steadfastly denied any involvement, as did E. T. Jeffery, the Rio Grande's president and Gould's closest advisor. For a year Gould's role remained a favorite guessing game of the press. In March 1904, after the Western Pacific filed a mortgage with a trust company headed by his brother Edwin, George declared solemnly, "I have not put a dollar into the undertaking, nor have I any intention to do so. I am not interested in the Western Pacific directly or indirectly, nor are any of the officials of the several roads with which I am connected." Six months later Jeffery became a director of the road because, he explained, "of the traffic relationship that will naturally exist between the Denver & Rio Grande System and the Western Pacific when completed." He was joined by Edwin Hawley, a larger holder in the Colorado & Southern, who had just fought a bitter battle with Harriman for control of the Alton.[23]

Meanwhile, surveys went forward under the charge of Virgil Bogue, former chief engineer of the Union Pacific, and preparations were made to start construction work. In December 1904 Jeffery was made vice-president of the Western Pacific, and no one doubted Gould was behind the road. Harriman watched this gathering of enemies with a wary eye, amazed that Gould persisted in denying his involvement. As late as March 1905, after a meeting of the Western Union board, he told Harriman and Schiff that he had no interest in the project. On April 25 he finally admitted his role and resigned from the boards of Harriman's roads. Harriman in turn left the Rio Grande and Rio Grande Western boards. The die was cast, and Wall Street braced expectantly for a clash of titans.[24]

Gould placed Jeffery in charge of the project and, through a series of elaborate contracts, dumped the burden of financing the Western Pacific onto the Rio Grande. Once construction got underway, Harriman did everything he could to delay progress. Legend has it that the Southern Pacific charged exorbitant rates for Western Pacific construction materials and promised labor-

A FISH OUT OF WATER: Stuyvesant Fish walks the streets around the time of his falling out with Harriman. (*Culver Pictures*)

ers high wages to lure them away from the construction area and then set them adrift, but none of these tales are documented. A fierce clash over terminal space in Oakland did erupt and was finally settled by an agreement signed in April 1907. In fact, Gould had all the problems he needed without help from Harriman; the Western Pacific proved a monstrously difficult and costly road to build.[25]

By 1906, then, Harriman found himself engulfed in storms everywhere. He was at war with Hill in the Northwest and Gould in the West. Fresh threats arose from the Milwaukee in the Northwest, the Rock Island in the Southwest, and Moffat's road in Colorado. Minority holders in Wells, Fargo challenged Harriman's domination of that company. Hawley made a determined bid to wrest the Alton from him, and troubles in the Illinois Central management led to a bitter clash with his old friend and mentor, Stuyvesant Fish, who was ousted from the presidency in a blaze of publicity. An ugly fight within the Equitable Life Assurance Society board, of which Harriman was a member, plunged him into the center of a major controversy. The ensuing investigation dragged his name through yet more muck.

Amid these difficulties Harriman brought yet another storm of public indignation down on his head with his handling of the Union Pacific dividend. By 1906 the combination of improved efficiency, shrewd financing, and a rush of business had boosted Union Pacific to new heights of prosperity. Gross earnings soared from $39.1 million in 1900 to $67.3 million in 1906, a gain of 72 percent, while net earnings jumped 69 percent from $19 million to $32 million. "It has become common," gushed one analyst, "to see the gross and net earnings of the Harriman lines increase month by month at a phenomenal rate." In addition, income from other investments went from $2.7 million to $10.3 million, giving the company a net income in 1906 of $31.8 million compared to $12.6 million in 1900.[26]

The returns from Harriman's transformation of the company surpassed the wildest fantasies of investors, who watched its stock vault from a low of 16⅛ in 1898 to a high of 195⅜ during 1906. For years he had resisted their clamor for more dividends while he overhauled the Union Pacific and Southern Pacific, keeping the rate at 4 percent despite the growth in earnings. So adamant was he on this policy that one critic labeled it "conservatism run mad." As earnings continued to swell, Harriman upped the rate to 5 percent in July 1905 and then to 6 percent early in 1906. These jumps only whetted appetites for more. When Gaspard Farrer urged Harriman in March 1906 to put the rate still higher, Harriman replied that "The property will have to husband its resources for protection against & aggression of its neighbors both north & south as well as in the middle."[27]

Those resources were growing in some interesting new ways. The dissolution of Northern Securities left the Union Pacific with piles of valuable securities that produced a large income, and the time was near for the rejuvenated Southern Pacific to commence dividends. A large portion of these payments would go to the parent Union Pacific, which owned $90 million worth of Southern Pacific common. Together these sources accounted for most of the "investment income" that supplemented the earnings from operations, and speculation was intense over what would be done with the huge surplus arising from these forthcoming bonanzas.

Later in the year Harriman would astound the financial world with his use of the surplus. As a first step he decided to increase the Union Pacific dividend again and to pay a first dividend on Southern Pacific common. In July Harriman told the board that earnings had surpassed all expectations and asked them to mull over the idea of a dividend increase. At the August meeting the directors were handed figures showing a surplus of $25.2 million after paying all charges and a 4 percent dividend on the preferred stock. Moreover, the Southern Pacific board, which had just concluded its meeting, had declared a 5 percent dividend, giving the Union Pacific another $4.5 million. On this basis the directors voted to hike the dividend to 10 percent.[28]

Although this level was unprecedented for the company, the figures warranted it. But several directors were absent from the meeting, and Harriman wished to notify them before announcing the news. The board then authorized the executive committee to determine the timing of the notice. Normally that body met the next morning, but Harriman had to attend the funeral of an old friend and the meeting was delayed until three in the afternoon. By then Harriman had passed the word along to the absentees, but the New York Stock

Exchange was closed before he, Stillman, and Lovett (the only members present) finished the meeting. If the news was released at once, the London market would get it before New York. "We decided," Harriman later testified, "that it was best to have the announcement . . . made in New York before it was in London; that is, while the New York markets were open."[29]

For these reasons the news of crucial decisions made on the afternoon of August 15 was not released until the morning of August 17. But traders had been boiling with anticipation over rumors of another dividend hike since early August. Two dozen reporters milled about the company's office waiting vainly for the news on the 16th; that day, 40 percent of the activity on a busy market was in the shares of Harriman roads. Nearly 300,000 shares of Union Pacific changed hands as the stock reached a new high, and 190,000 shares of Southern Pacific were traded. The delay in announcing the dividend not only infuriated speculators but also unleashed a stream of gossip over the motives. When at last the word came next morning, an angry chorus of accusations filled Wall Street. Sentiment was strong "in almost every banking or brokerage house," noted the *Wall Street Journal*, that the directors had delayed the announcement to profit from "tremendous stock market operations by individuals and by a pool."[30]

"THE INSIDERS MADE MILLIONS," blared the New York *Times* along with a guesstimate that Harriman had personally cleared $10 million. The *Times* clinched its charges with a form of circular logic that would later be perfected by government spokesmen:

> That the opportunities that were presented by reason of the delayed announcement were profited by on a scale perhaps never before attempted in Wall Street was accepted as a fact with a unanimity that was hard to explain on any other ground than that the supposition was based on fact.

Although Harriman had some defenders, criticism poured in from all sides. The *Railroad Gazette* labeled it "a wrongful use of corporate power," while *Forum* found it surprising that "a management which for years had been notably conservative not only in its action on the rate of dividends, but in its statements as to future policy, had suddenly changed front and indulged in what to the eye of Wall Street and the investing community amounted to reckless promising." More than one observer labeled the episode a throwback to the days of Gould, Fisk, and Drew.[31]

No one doubted the dividends had been earned. The storm of criticism centered around two points: the delay in announcing the dividends and the sharp reversal from past policy. Together they created what more cautious heads like Schiff and Kahn considered an untenable situation, one in which Harriman's past conservatism came back to haunt him with savage irony. Suddenly Harriman's name, unknown to the public only a few years earlier, splashed across the headlines with a notoriety reminiscent of Gould a generation earlier. Like Gould, he was portrayed as greedy and grasping, hungry for power and ruthless in his use of it. Unlike Gould, he made some effort to defend himself, but his version of events seldom got the play given the other side. For a brief time in mid-decade he assumed Gould's old role as chief target for the storm of public wrath crashing down on giant corporations and businessman who were changing the structure of economic life in ways unfathomable to most Americans.

These attacks threatened not only Harriman but also the companies under his command. Surviving them required all the strength he could muster. Unfortunately, they commenced just at the time when his always fragile health had begun to fail, and their toll hastened its decline. If in these bleak months Harriman thought the world had turned against him, he had good reason to think so, for nature as well as man joined in the assault.

At 5:13 A.M. on the morning of April 18, 1906, a series of violent tremors shook the Pacific coast from Oregon to Mexico, inflicting their worst shocks on the San Francisco Bay area. The earthquake itself did not destroy the city, but it triggered a wave of fires that spread relentlessly until they combined in one raging conflagration. The chief of the fire department lay dead in his bed, a victim of falling bricks, and most of the city's water pipes had been ruptured, stripping the firefighters of both their leader and the means to combat the flames. Desperate attempts to halt their advance by setting back fires and dynamiting buildings in its path failed. Finally, a jerry-rigged string of fire engines with hoses drawing water from the bay stopped the fire at Broadway, Franklin, and Gough streets. Miraculously the waterfront and docks escaped damage, giving the city an outlet for rescue and supplies. However, more than five square miles of the business and residential area lay heaped with rubble and smoking ruins, the skyline broken only by the skeletons of structures that survived the shock.[32]

Despite the chaos in the streets, E. E. Calvin, then general manager of the Southern Pacific, managed to reach the company's offices in the Merchants Exchange Building at nine that morning. Other officers had already arrived and, finding the structure little damaged and apparently safe from the fires, hurried home to take care of their families. Calvin dispatched a messenger to Oakland, the nearest open telegraph station, to apprise Harriman and the Chicago office of the disaster. Orders were given to move all equipment out of reach of the spreading fire. Calvin visited the office that afternoon and found it still secure; he returned again at five and was sent away by soldiers because the fire was marching toward the area. There were no men or teams to retrieve anything from the building anyway. At eleven that night it succumbed to the flames.[33]

Harriman got the news at home that same morning and rushed to the office, where he gave orders to spare no expense in hooking up communications with San Francisco. Working through a telegraph line to Oakland Pier, he received full reports from his officers and ordered them to do everything possible to relieve the crisis. Supplies were to be hauled in and people evacuated at no charge; all company facilities were to be made available to local authorities. When Harriman finished, he jumped up and told his secretary to be ready to leave for the coast at daybreak.[34]

The special train sped across the continent in three days, arriving in Oakland on Sunday morning, April 22. Along the way Harriman kept in constant touch by telegraph, prodding officials that were already doing yeoman duty in handling the crisis. The city had 225,000 homeless people who had to be evacuated or supplied with shelter, food, water, clothing, and medicines. Money was being raised all over the nation, but Calvin could not wait. He ordered officials at major points along the line to buy carloads of provisions with company funds and rush them to the city, where troops helped distribute them to the needy. So rushed was the procurement that Calvin could not keep account of it, but he estimated that $18,000 was spent on food the first day alone.[35]

One way to relieve the pressure was to evacuate people to nearby cities or farther east. The Southern Pacific ferries to Oakland were still running; in fact, the company had set up headquarters at the Ferry Building on the docks. Every available ferry and steamer was recruited to carry people to Oakland Pier at no charge and with a free meal to boot. Trains running south also hauled refugees out of the city. Using automobiles and horses, the company opened information centers at nine points throughout the ruined city and posted schedules elsewhere. These centers, which operated for three weeks, furnished information on missing persons, relief supplies, and other necessities as well as transportation. As the crush of humanity flowed out of the city, connecting lines agreed to ticket passengers to distant locations at no charge. On the 19th alone 1,073 cars of refugees moved out to supplement the thousands leaving by ship.[36]

When gasoline for automobiles ran short, the company supply at Union Ferry Building was offered to civil authorities without charge. Explosives were donated to the fire department to fight the raging flames, and all facilities were opened to the homeless. The company hospital on Mission Street, which survived the quake with no injury to any of its 150 patients, was pressed into service to aid the casualties. The chief surgeon and most of the staff reached the hospital within an hour after the tremors and worked without relief for six days. More than 250 victims were brought there the first day, of whom 13 died. When the fire approached the hospital that evening, everyone was hurriedly moved fifteen blocks to the car barns of the local trolley company, where the patients were put in the cars or on platforms between the pits.[37]

In this makeshift setting the doctors and nurses toiled furiously until the next afternoon, when they learned that the fire would reach them before dawn. No part of the city burned more fiercely than the Mission Street district, where people fleeing the fire jammed the streets with vehicles piled high with whatever goods they could salvage. Amid the confusion, officials threw together a patchwork train from cars that had been hauled nearby to get them away from the fire. An engine was procured, and the police somehow found enough wagons to get the patients to the train, which took them to San Mateo. Later they were transferred to the company hospital at Sacramento. Calvin had nothing but praise for the dedication of the doctors and nurses, "who could not be driven to rest but worked unceasingly—some of them until, fainting, [they] fell into the pits at the car barns."[38]

All this happened before Harriman's arrival on the morning of April 22. Parking his private car alongside Calvin's at Oakland Pier, he went at once to meet with a committee of prominent local citizens and in his usual way offered a number of suggestions that were accepted. He stayed on until May 5 to direct the company's efforts, living out of his car, handling the barrage of telegrams that swamped his secretary, and issuing relentlessly upbeat statements of the progress being made to local and distant papers alike. It was as if he determined to let his own supreme confidence inspire everyone else to their best efforts. His dispatches were widely quoted in the papers; he managed to upstage the media and become a major spokesman for the disaster.[39]

Here was Harriman at his best: the man of action at the scene, conquering all adversity by sheer force of will. No other major figure rushed there so quickly or stayed so long; he had center stage all to himself. A few critics questioned his motives, but even skeptics conceded that "The almost lavish generosity of the Harriman system assumes a new economic importance. . . . The Harriman monopoly, if it be so called, has proven itself in the hour of need the strongest and most faithful friend that the city of San Francisco could have had." The notorious "Octopus" appeared in a new guise as public servant, prompting a company officer to chirp that "Mr Harrimans coming here was exactly the right act at the opportune moment, and it has won him the golden opinions of all—even our old livelong enemies."[40]

On the return trip Harriman celebrated with a record run, crossing the continent in just under three days. The reason, he told his secretary, was to be home in time for Mrs. Harriman's anniversary, but that was not true; their anniversary was in September and her birthday in July. To the gaggle of waiting reporters he explained that he had important engagements in New York, then launched into another tribute to the spirit of San Francisco. These were anything but easy times for Harriman. Apart from the fights in which he was embroiled and the attacks by what Kahn called the "Harriman Extermination League," he suffered incessantly from one illness after another. Later he told Kahn that not a single day of 1906 passed without his being tormented by pain.[41]

Even as Harriman grappled with the San Francisco disaster, nature was preparing another nasty surprise for him. The southeastern corner of California had undergone a stunning transformation in recent years. For centuries it had been an arid desert scarred by the capricious Colorado River, which formed the border between California and Arizona. In ancient times the river flowed into a Gulf of California that extended a hundred miles farther north than it does now. Gradually, however, the huge deposits of silt carried by the fast-moving river built up a dam that cut the Gulf in half, creating an inland salt lake as large as the Great Salt Lake in Utah. Over the years this sea evaporated into a depression later known as the Salton Sink, a hundred miles long, thirty-five miles wide, and a thousand feet deep at its lowest point.[42]

Over the centuries the Colorado emptied into the lower Gulf until its rushing waters deposited enough sediment to create a delta that diverted it back into the sink. As this process continued, it reversed itself and again flowed into the

Gulf, leaving behind a huge alluvial plain ranging from 80 feet above to 280 feet below sea level, in a desert region where scarcely any rain fell and temperatures climbed as high as 120 degrees. This combination of soil and heat offered an ideal hothouse environment for farming if some way could be found to irrigate the region. The Salton Sink had been dry for ages, and its bed was being mined for salt. The Colorado was a promising source but a dangerous river to tamper with because of its swift current and unpredictability during the flooding season. A visionary attempt to finance such a project during the 1890s was quashed by the depression.

As late as 1900 not a soul inhabited this ancient sea basin. That year, however, the California Development Company, a New Jersey corporation chartered in 1896, secured enough money to begin digging an irrigation channel. The company also controlled a Mexican subsidiary, enabling it to extend the work below the border. Since a series of sand hills stood between the river and the valley, the first heading was cut opposite Yuma and a canal dug in Mexico parallel to the border until it reached the dried bed of the Alamo River, which carried the water northward into the valley. The first water rushed through the head gate in May 1901, and the Development Company was in business. Although it sold only water rights, the promoters quickly formed a land company to attract settlers and gave the region the beguiling name of Imperial Valley.

Their efforts proved spectacularly successful. Settlers flocked in from all parts of the country, and a network of irrigation ditches spread across the basin. About 120,000 acres were cultivated, with another 200,000 acres covered by water stock. Towns sprang up as what once resembled Death Valley turned magically into a Garden of Eden boasting a population of ten thousand by 1905. The Southern Pacific main line happened to cross the eastern rim of the Salton Sink on its way to Yuma, which made it easy to throw a branch into the burgeoning valley. Prosperity shone like the blazing summer sun on this newest garden spot of America.

Only one cloud darkened this serene sky. The demand for water grew steadily, but the capacity of the canal and ditches declined as sediment from the rapid waters began to clog them. A professor estimated in 1900 that the turbulent river carried 60 million tons of matter past Yuma every year, and the company had spent nothing to dredge, sluice, or provide settling basins for the canal. Instead it decided rashly in 1904 to increase the flow by tapping the river with two new cuts in Mexico. The first, made just below the border, was small and silted up quickly like the original head north of it. The second was made about four miles south at a point where the river divided around an island. Here the water flowed across the quarter-mile heading with enough velocity to scour the canal effectively.

No head gates were installed on these cuts. The engineers counted on the pattern of recent years in which winter floods were rare. Nor did they want to close the cuts until the summer flood season in order to gain maximum benefit from the scouring action. But their luck ran out that dismal winter, for the volatile Colorado battered them with two floods in February 1905. Hurriedly

RUNAWAY RIVER: The Colorado River opens a huge new channel as its falls cut rapidly upstream. (*Smithsonian Report, 1907*)

they threw a dam of brush and sandbags across the lower cut only to have another flood sweep it away in March. A second dam suffered the same fate as the surging waters enlarged the channel, overflowed its banks, and spread rapidly toward the Salton Sink. Along the way it carved new beds in the soft, powdery soil, creating falls that grew steadily larger and threw torrents of water into the Sink.

By the spring a crisis loomed even though few realized it. Early in 1905 the financially strapped Development Company sounded Kruttschnitt on a loan from the railroad and were rebuffed. The promoters then went to Harriman, who had no investment in or connection with the project. Grasping at once the potential of Imperial Valley for generating business, Harriman ordered an investigation made and, against Kruttschnitt's advice, loaned the Development Company $200,000 on condition that the Southern Pacific hold 51 percent of its stock as collateral and also take charge of its management. Through this convoluted and often misunderstood arrangement, Harriman injected himself into the Imperial Valley muddle just as disaster struck.

The winter floods foretold the coming of an unusual season for the river. Normally its rise began in the spring, peaked in July, and subsided some time in August. However, in 1905 the floods came early and kept rising until by June water was lapping at the railroad embankment skirting Salton. Before granting the loan, Harriman had been assured by the Development Company engineers that the cut could be closed for about $20,000; the rest of the money was to be used for improving the canal and ditch system. He put Epes

Randolph, an engineer then overseeing Southern Pacific lines in Arizona and Mexico, in charge of the Development Company.

Randolph looked the situation over and saw at once that it was far more serious than anyone admitted. The original cut, forty feet wide and eight feet deep, had already expanded to a hundred feet wide and twenty feet deep, and the fast-flowing water was still scouring furiously. If the cut was not closed, the entire river would soon pour through the gap and spread across the valley to the Sink. He informed Harriman that it would be hard work to save the valley, and that far more than $200,000 would be required.

''Are you certain you can put the river back into the old channel?'' Harriman asked him.

''It can be done,'' Randolph replied.

''Then go ahead and do it.''[43]

So far the overflow had found its way to the bottom of Salton Sink, where it flooded out the salt works but did no other damage. In July an attempt to divert the river around the opposite or eastern side of the island failed to deflect the current. The cut grew steadily wider, forcing Randolph to try another tack. In October a 600-foot barrier dam was erected at a cost of more than $50,000 across the west fork of the river from the heading to the island. Although the river was much higher than usual, the dam made good progress. Once in place, it would lessen the flow enough for the cut to be closed.

Unfortunately, this plan did not reckon with the Gila River, which drained into the Colorado at Yuma and was notorious for violent floods that, in the words of one engineer, were ''far more to be feared and reckoned with . . . than anything coming down the Colorado River proper'' because they were so unexpected. Late in November the Gila unleashed a furious flood bearing huge masses of driftwood. Without warning the Colorado's discharge soared from 12,000 to 115,000 cubic feet per second. The raging waters ripped through the dam, swept away large chunks of the island, widened the cut to six hundred feet, and surged into the Imperial Canal on its way to the Sink, where the earlier overflow had already created a large lake.

In effect the mighty Colorado had changed course and was seeking out its ancient basin. The Salton Sink had once more become the Salton Sea. If the heading could not be closed before the next flood season, the river would menace the entire Imperial Valley and its irrigation system, fields, towns, and rail facilities. The irrigation system was a lifeline not only for the crops but also for the residents, who had no other source of fresh water. Some way had to be found to control the river without shutting it out altogether.

A plan was devised to erect a steel and concrete head gate at the original heading north of the border and to construct a special dredge for cleaning the silt out of the old section of canal abandoned when the lower cut was made. Once completed, this gate could divert enough water to supply the valley and enable the lower heading to be closed. A second head gate, made of wood, would be installed at the lower cut to shunt water away while a permanent dam was erected. All work was rushed to get it done before the spring floods, but nothing went well. The concrete head gate was not installed until late June.

Even though crews toiled day and night on the wooden head gate, it was not ready until April 18. That same day the earthquake struck San Francisco, where the special dredge was being built.

Meanwhile, the river remained at near record levels throughout 1906, a year when its total discharge was twice the normal amount. While Harriman was in San Francisco grappling with the catastrophe that threatened the major terminus of his entire system, he authorized Randolph to spend another $250,000 in restraining the Colorado. Randolph went back to fight what by then had become a runaway river. As flood season peaked late in June, the cut had grown to half a mile in width, through which the entire river poured before spreading over an area nearly ten miles wide and then splitting into onrushing streams toward the Salton Sea. At its height the flood sent 75,000 cubic feet of water through the gap every second or 6 billion cubic feet per day. The Salton Sea rose at the astonishing rate of 7 inches a day over an area of 400 square miles.

By this time the hapless salt works lay beneath sixty feet of water. Two towns were badly damaged and thousands of acres of crops inundated, with thousands more so badly eroded that they could not be cultivated. Five times that dreary summer the Southern Pacific had to move its tracks to higher ground. The flood swept away irrigation flumes, leaving some 30,000 acres in the western part of the valley without water and therefore uninhabitable. More danger loomed from the cutbacks carved by the torrents rushing across the delta soil, which was soft and fine like powdered sugar. As this soil washed out, the flow became a rapids, then a cascade, and then a cataract if not a waterfall. Some of the gorges made by this action stood eighty feet deep and a thousand feet across. An engineer calculated that the amount of soil swept into the Salton Sea was four times that excavated in the digging of the Panama Canal.

If one of these cutbacks pierced the irrigation system itself, it could divert the water into a deep gorge and leave the entire valley dry. There was cruel irony in the two threats facing the Imperial Valley: it might be buried under water or it might lose all its water and die of thirst. No precedent existed for reversing the course of a major river under such conditions. When the engineers could not agree on the best plan of attack, Randolph decided to follow his own plan of a rock dam even though the others heaped objections on the idea. But Randolph cared little for their criticisms as long as he had Harriman's support.

This time the preparations were massive. In August a spur line was run down to the lower heading and two trestles thrown across the river. The Development Company provided three steamers and some barges for the river work, and the Southern Pacific sent ten work trains along with three hundred of the oversized side-dump cars that had been used to fill the Lucin cutoff. Every quarry within a radius of four hundred miles was tapped for rock, and a new quarry was opened near the concrete head gate north of the border. Trestles and timber poured in from Los Angeles, supplies came from the railroad, and laborers were rounded up wherever they could be found—including large numbers of Indians, Mexicans, and drifters looking for a few dollars.

Randolph hoped to dam the channel enough to shunt most of the water to the bypass where the wooden head gate had been installed, and then close the breach permanently. Two shifts of men working around the clock toiled twenty days to construct a brush mattress as a base for the dam. Once this was installed in September, the caravan of dump cars, or "battleships" as the men called them, rolled across the trestle heaving their loads of rock onto the bed much as they had done at Lucin. As the dam rose, more water shifted to the bypass, where the wooden head gate had been enlarged to handle the flow. But on October 11, just when success seemed certain, the combined pressure of the water and accumulating driftwood snapped the head gate and sent two-thirds of it floating downstream. The river then rushed through the bypass, leaving the new dam high and dry.

The only good news was that Randolph's controversial rock dam had held up well. Undaunted, he decided to erect another one at the bypass and connect the two dams with a levee, creating a barrier half a mile long. For three more weeks the "battleships" rumbled over the trestles with their loads, three thousand carloads in all, while gravel and clay was plastered into the rocks to stop leaks. The levee was extended in both directions from the dams, using works built earlier by the Development Company. The cost was as massive as the project. "In sixty days," declared one of the engineers, "a million dollars was put into that hole and into the levees." On November 4 the crews cheered as the river veered back into its original bed.

Their jubilation was short-lived. Early in December, heavy rains sent another flood roaring down the Gila into the Colorado. The dams held firm, but on December 7 the water undermined the levee at a point half a mile south of the dam and carved a passage that widened until the whole river was again pouring down the slope of the basin toward the Salton Sea. A bitterly disappointed Randolph talked it over with the engineers and agreed that closing the gap was the smallest part of what needed to be done. Safety required an immense levee fifteen or twenty miles long and very deep, "the most expensive levees per mile that had ever been built for anything like that distance." Gloomily Randolph advised Harriman to give up the effort and seek aid from the government.[44]

Harriman had already poured $1.5 million into the fight, and Randolph figured it would take at least that much more. This was far more than the total traffic garnered from the valley. The tracks of the Southern Pacific could be moved to safe ground for about $60,000. However, apart from the ledger sheet there remained a sticky moral and legal issue. The Development Company had caused the fatal break before the Southern Pacific took charge of its management, but that detail could easily get overlooked when blame for the catastrophe was handed out. The Southern Pacific was stuck with at least the appearance of being responsible for the Development Company's blunder. Harriman was rarely sensitive to matters in this vein, but he always responded to a challenge and was not likely to back down.

On December 13 Harriman informed President Roosevelt of the situation in a lengthy telegram. "In view of the above," he concluded, "it does not seem fair that we should be called to do more than join in to help the settlers." An exchange followed in which Roosevelt held Harriman and the Southern Pacific responsible for closing the break and exhorted them to do the work because the government could not act until it received authority from Congress and official permission from Mexico. Let the Development Company do its duty, Roosevelt added, and then the government would take up its claim for restitution.[45]

The timing of this exchange could not have been worse. A political controversy had ruptured the longtime friendship of the two men; only a few weeks earlier Roosevelt had referred to Harriman as an "undesirable citizen." The President was known to be behind the ICC investigation of Harriman roads that began in 1907. Moreover, Harriman was again ill and on December 31 underwent minor surgery that would keep him confined for a month. But his mind was alert and as fiery as ever. On December 20, the same day he received Roosevelt's telegram, he shot back a reply denying that the Development Company was a subsidiary of Southern Pacific but agreeing to proceed with the work, "trusting that the Government . . . will assist us with the burden." Epes Randolph always believed that Harriman would have done the work "even had Roosevelt pointedly denied any aid."[46]

By then the gap in the levee was eleven hundred feet wide and forty feet deep at some points. Two trestles were erected over the breach even though the torrents ripped out the ninety-foot piles three times in a month. The first one was ready on January 27, 1907, and the parade of "battleships" rolled across the break, dumping its load of rock. For three weeks two divisions of the Southern Pacific were virtually shut down to feed equipment and supplies to the crews in Mexico; San Pedro found itself without any flatcars for two weeks. On February 10 the river was finally pushed back into its bed and work began on a double row of dikes behind the dam. Altogether the dam and levees required 10,960 carloads of rock and gravel, 1,200 ninety-foot piles, and 16,000 feet (more than three miles) of pine stringers. Nearly 900,000 cubic feet of earth was moved, and the cost reached $1.6 million, making the total outlay for the fight $3.1 million.

This time the works held firm, and Imperial Valley was spared any further threat of extinction. Confident that the river would stay home, more settlers poured into the region, swelling its population to 40,000 by 1917. The valley became a garden spot of the West and, as a bonus, the newly filled Salton Sea did not evaporate as many experts predicted. For this herculean achievement Harriman deserves great credit, but few outside the valley or his own companies honored him. Although Roosevelt (and later his successor, William Howard Taft) urged speedy handling of the Southern Pacific's claim for reimbursement, Congress dawdled and finally refused to pay anything on the grounds that the work had been for the benefit of the railroad.* Nor did it even bother to pass a resolution thanking Harriman or his men for their heroic efforts.

Those who lived in the valley were more generous. There, Randolph noted with satisfaction, "I never visit . . . the Imperial Valley that I do not hear Mr.

* The Southern Pacific asked the government only for the $1.6 million spent on the final dam and levees.

Harriman's name mentioned with little short of reverence.'' In 1916 they gave the Southern Pacific land and irrigation bonds to cover part of the cost incurred. Harriman himself took immense pride in having halted the runaway river. ''I used every ounce of driving power I possessed to hustle the job as I have never hustled any job before,'' he told Otto Kahn. ''. . . That was the best single bit of work done on my authority and responsibility.''[47]

9

The Reckoning

While the brilliance of Harriman's strategy in modernizing the Union Pacific was obvious to anyone with a cursory grasp of railroad affairs, fewer people understood the extent to which the company also owed its prosperity to his masterful handling of its finances. The Harriman system raked in profits because it was well managed in every respect. Some attributed its success to Harriman's remarkable foresight and wondered what elixir enabled him to peer into the future. Only a few understood that Harriman's vaunted foresight was at bottom merely an unbounded confidence in his ability to make things turn out the way he envisioned them.

The $100 million of convertible bonds issued in 1901 offers a classic example. Harriman used the proceeds to buy Southern Pacific and Northern Pacific stock. Although the bonds could be exchanged for common stock at par anytime before May 1906, no one expected a stampede toward conversion. They paid 4 percent interest; at the time the dividend on common was also 4 percent with no sign of an increase even on the distant horizon. Apart from being a cheap security to fund major acquisitions, the issue had two other benefits. Conversion on a large scale could produce a dramatic reduction in fixed charges within a few years. Meanwhile, the Kuhn, Loeb syndicate could use them as a check against anyone looking to snatch control of the company away from Harriman and his allies.*[1]

This last objective was very important in 1901 amid the fight with Hill and the steady stream of takeover rumors. A pool composed of Harriman, Schiff, Stillman, and friends held a call on the syndicate bonds for two years, and Schiff did not want to let them go "until we are absolutely certain that our rear is safe & that no attempts are likely to be made by others to get control of U. P." Liquidation must therefore be "necessarily slow, assuring us for a long time the control of a considerable amount of the bonds *in case of need.*" In the

*The cost of the two purchases exceeded the bond proceeds by $27 million. This was carried as floating debt until July 1902, when the Short Line covered it with a new bond issue. After May 1906 the convertibles could be redeemed at a price of 102½.

madcap Erie War of 1867–68, Drew, Fisk, and Gould had used convertible bonds to keep Commodore Vanderbilt from gaining control of that road. The approach of Harriman and his friends may have been more sophisticated, but the idea was the same: keep a reserve of stock on call to repel any unexpected raid on the open market.[2]

During the fall of 1902 Harriman and Schiff switched tactics by letting the convertible pool go and forming a new pool to control $50 million or half the outstanding preferred stock for the purpose, in Schiff's delicate phrase, "of having in friendly hands concentrated holdings of Union Pacific stock."* This eliminated any threat of a hostile takeover. Meanwhile, the steady climb in earnings sent the common stock upward and spurred new rumors of a dividend increase. Any such hike would make the cost of conversion more expensive to holders and thereby push the exchange process, but Harriman was in no hurry. By July 1904 only about $12.7 million worth of bonds had been converted as Harriman held the line on dividends.[3]

However, the phenomenal prosperity of the company during the next two years boosted earnings to levels that made an increase in the dividend impossible to resist. A reverse effect took place as holders rushed to convert their bonds before the dividend went up; by March 1905 the amount exchanged had risen to $48.1 million, $21 million of it within the past six weeks. Harriman then announced that the Union Pacific would issue another $100 million in new preferred stock to be used for purchasing stock in "other companies." A guessing game arose at once over what other companies he had in mind, with the New York Central being one favorite candidate. In the same breath Harriman all but promised an increase in the dividend.[4]

While analysts rushed to praise Harriman's management, few grasped how radically he was transforming the asset base of the Union Pacific. So rapidly did bonds pour in during 1905 that full conversion became a foregone conclusion, which meant that $100 million in interest-bearing obligations would soon be reduced to equity at a saving of $4 million in fixed charges annually. The new preferred provided an equity basis for future capital needs without resorting to bonds; it also expanded the stock to a point where outside buyers could not gain control of the company. This fear faded to the point where Stillman could advise Harriman in April 1906 that he thought it "wholly unnecessary for protection" to hold so much Union Pacific common.[5]

By July 1906 all but $550,000 of the bonds had been exchanged. When the 10 percent dividend was announced a month later, the ensuing uproar distracted attention from Harriman's real achievement of creating a new and stronger asset base for his system. Conversion also released those securities used as collateral for the bonds, giving the company treasury free assets on about 858 miles of road. By 1907 the Union Pacific system held unpledged $83.4 million worth of its own bonds and owned free of all debt 1,650 miles of auxiliary lines. Nor was this all. In 1905 the Short Line had issued $100 million in new 4

*Members of the new pool were Harriman, Schiff (for Kuhn, Loeb), Stillman, William Rockefeller, H. H. Rogers, W. K. Vanderbilt, James Hazen Hyde, Henry Clay Frick, and P. A. Valentine. Schiff, Harriman, and Stillman were to manage the pool, which was to last for five years.

percent bonds. Part of this issue went to retire some earlier bonds, and part was used to subscribe to $18 million worth of new Southern Pacific preferred. The latter company in turn used the proceeds from this stock to repay Union Pacific for the sums advanced to reconstruct its line.[6]

Another major benefit flowed from this new Short Line issue. It released as collateral all the Great Northern and Northern Pacific shares received in the breakup of Northern Securities. Altogether the Short Line held 216,521 shares of Great Northern, 281,829 shares of Northern Pacific, 7,249 Northern Securities stubs, and 90,364 Great Northern ore certificates. During 1905 and early 1906 the price of these stocks rose steadily until the dividends paid on them averaged only about 2.8 percent. Since the Short Line did not own enough of either stock to gain control, Harriman decided to sell off most of these holdings. During the last half of 1906 Kuhn, Loeb disposed of 163,601 shares of Great Northern at an average price of $304.41 and 281,829 shares of Northern Pacific at $208.76. Gradual selling continued until June 1910, when all the securities except the stubs had been sold.[7]

The outcome of these sales cast a radically different light on Harriman's losing fight with Hill. Altogether Union Pacific had invested $89.4 million in Northern Securities and received back $144.4 million for a whopping profit of $55 million or 62 percent. Those who stress the price of victory might look closely at Harriman's gift for making defeat pay so handsomely. In 1907 a noted rail expert, asked to name Harriman's most noteworthy achievement, replied, "I think it was this, to get licked in a fight and pull out of it with a colossal fortune as the result."[8]

Remarkable as this coup was, Harriman eclipsed it with his handling of the proceeds from these transactions. The sales in 1906 alone fetched the company nearly $100 million, which he decided to invest in the stocks of other railroads paying higher dividends than those he had sold.* By January 1907 he had acquired an impressive list of holdings:

RAILROAD	SHARES PURCHASED	COST (MILLIONS)	PERCENT of ISSUE
Atchison preferred	100,000	$10.4	7.61
Baltimore & Ohio pref.	72,064	6.7	21.23
B & O common	323,342	38.8	12.01
Illinois Central	186,231	32.6	29.59
Milwaukee common	36,900	6.0	6.34
New York Central	142,857	19.6	7.97
Northwestern common	32,150	5.9	3.32
Railroad Securities Co.			
preferred	18,984	1.9	na
common	34,154	6.9	na

*The total of these acquisitions exceeds the $100 million received from stock sales in 1906. The Union Pacific issued short-term notes to make up the difference.

The Railroad Securities Company was a corporation controlled by Harriman that held stock in the Illinois Central. By selling his interest in the company to Union Pacific, he gave the latter road altogether a 30 percent interest in the Illinois Central. Harriman also bought nearly 40 percent of the securities of the St. Joseph & Grand Island, returning control of that former subsidiary to the Union Pacific. Earlier the Union Pacific had also purchased 103,431 shares of Alton preferred.[9]

Harriman insisted that he acquired these stocks to earn the Union Pacific a higher investment income than it received from the shares sold. On that basis his judgment once again proved astute; the company's income from such investments soared from $7.5 million in 1906 to $15.8 million in 1909. But what was good business proved to be bad politics. The new holdings had a valuable fringe benefit in providing Harriman with a potent community of interest in all the roads. Unfortunately, he made these purchases just as the ICC was girding up to investigate his activities, which amounted to throwing down a gauntlet to an administration already hostile to him.[10]

From a political point of view, the stock purchases looked less like investment strategy than a bald attempt to forge a gigantic rail monopoly. For that reason Kahn called them "the one serious mistake of his management of Union Pacific affairs." Harriman admitted the timing was poor but insisted the action was correct and proper for the company. He was dealing with a problem of great delicacy, one unknown to most businessmen or politicians: how to handle a cash fund of $100 million to the best advantage of the company. The purchases were neither secret nor illegal; they were merely suspicious to eyes inflamed by generic fears of monopoly.[11]

Whatever critics thought, investors smiled on Harriman's financial policy. Anyone holding Union Pacific stock since 1900 would have reaped 60 percent in dividends by 1909 and seen the price of common jump from 44⅜ to 219. They would also own one of the most modern, well-equipped railroads in the country. Financially it was rock solid, with all of its bonds funded at 4 percent. Although $220 million worth of bonds had been sold between 1900 and 1908, fixed charges increased only about $3 million while net income jumped 125 percent and the surplus 188 percent. During 1908 Harriman launched a new issue of convertibles intended to shrink obligations ever further while providing for future capital needs.[12]

"I wish I had known this a month ago," smiled a Union Pacific director after the dividend increase in 1906.

"No reason why you should not have known it," retorted Harriman in his inimitable way. "I knew it years ago."[13]

Analysts poring over their maps confirmed Harriman's prediction that a new era of competitive railway building had commenced. Four new lines eyed the Pacific coast: the Milwaukee, the Western Pacific, the Grand Trunk, and the Canadian Northern. If all were completed, they would bring to eleven the number of lines reaching the West Coast. Since the first two posed direct threats to the Union Pacific, Harriman took steps to disarm them in advance. He bought a large block of Milwaukee stock and had little trouble persuading his friend William Rockefeller that the two companies should thrash out an agreement well in advance of construction.[14]

On the Western Pacific George Gould was building a road that would have done Harriman proud. He had enough sense to realize that the day of putting down flimsy lines had passed; only a first-class road could vie with the established, modernized lines surrounding it. The Western Pacific boasted heavy steel rail, steel and cement bridges, and a maximum grade of 1 percent compared to 2.25 percent on the other transcontinental lines. It had minimum curvature and ran through the mountains rather than over them, at an elevation with a summit two thousand feet lower than that of the Central Pacific. The road featured spectacular views of Feather River Canyon and reached Salt Lake City by skirting the southern end of the lake.[15]

But a first-class road cost money, in this case far more money than even the Cassandras forecast, and Gould was struggling to piece together his system east of the Mississippi River at the same time. He hoped to complete the Western Pacific by September 1908 for an estimated $39 million, but by January 1908 the road was barely 75 percent finished and costs had soared to nearly $80 million. Apart from the usual logistical nightmares, fires, floods, and the San Francisco earthquake slowed progress. There were forty-one bridges and forty-four tunnels to build, some of them long and expensive, which helped delay the last spike until November 1909. Even then the road was far from finished and did not open fully until the following August.[16]

So monumental a project needed a driver like Harriman or Jay Gould. Instead it had son George, whose attention span was much shorter. He refused to allow decisions to be made without him, yet thought nothing of leaving his key officers in the lurch to dash off somewhere. E. T. Jeffery filled the vacuum created by George's indecision and inattentiveness until he became a sort of *éminence grise* for the Gould empire. But he lacked authority to do all that was needed.

It was painfully obvious that Gould's reach exceeded his grasp, and that his grasp was slipping. "The last four or five years of George J. Gould's career in railroad finance," noted a New York *Times* reporter in October 1905, "have been so crowded with contradictions, and the 'Gould policy' has become so inscrutable to Wall Street, that members of the financial community refer nowadays to the Gould situation only in terms of bewilderment." The financial panic of 1907 dealt Gould's empire a blow from which it never recovered. One by one his eastern properties tumbled into receivership. Eventually so did the Rio Grande, which staggered under the huge financial load of the Western Pacific, and the once proud Missouri Pacific. Ironically, it was Kuhn, Loeb that helped reorganize the road.[17]

Harriman's dilemma over the Western Pacific was quite different from that portrayed in myth. He feared Gould less than he feared what stronger hands might do if they got the road. Gould's wobbly position created an instability dangerous to all transcontinental roads. They might all wish his empire to remain weak, but none wanted it to collapse. By 1908 good feelings between the two men resumed as Harriman and Schiff stood ready to lend financial support if the Gould empire neared disaster. For his part Gould welcomed their help, at least on the surface.[18]

The Western Pacific never posed a serious threat to Harriman. Apart from its crushing financial load and long-delayed completion, the road had no branch system to feed it and was therefore dependent on highly competitive through business. Moreover, its efficiency hit a bottleneck at Salt Lake City, where it exchanged business with the Rio Grande, a line that had not yet been transformed into a first-class road. In that sense the Western Pacific resembled the Union Pacific in 1900, when service on its improved line ended abruptly at the interchange with the Central Pacific. However, a superior line always posed the threat of falling into the wrong hands, which prompted Harriman to keep it in weak and/or friendly hands as long as possible.

Farther north the threat was more dangerous. The prize there was lumber, huge amounts of it, 365 *trillion* board feet by one estimate, at a time when the supplies in eastern forests were dwindling. For a quarter century the Northwest had been a cockpit of struggle among the roads seeking dominance of its lucrative traffic. Over the years rail diplomacy grew more tortuous and clashes fiercer until the region gradually replaced the Omaha gateway as the primary battlefield among western lines. The creation of Northern Securities in 1901 had provided at least the illusion of stability, but the Supreme Court had swept that away in 1904 with a finality that promised renewed warfare. At the time Hill had brushed aside Harriman's prediction of competitive building with a remark that "There is no struggle. Nothing of that kind." This was pure smokescreen. Aware that the weak link of his thriving system lay at the western end, Hill had already resolved to build the line to Portland along the north bank of the Columbia River that he had threatened to construct for years.[19]

The Spokane, Portland & Seattle would be built jointly by the Great Northern and Northern Pacific. Hill tried to get the jump in secret, but the veil parted in September 1905 and Harriman's men did what they could to delay the project. Before Hill was done, he completed 550 miles of road and another 229 miles of subsidiaries. It cost him a lot of money—$10 million more than his original estimate of $45 million for the line, a price that appalled even his staunchest banking friends. A branch extended the road to Astoria, where it connected with a line of coastal steamers that Hill hoped would cut into Union Pacific traffic. When this splendid, low-grade road opened in 1907, it found business hard to come by for several years.[20]

While Hill pushed this project along, Harriman did not sit idle. Apart from strewing obstacles in Hill's path, Navigation was busy laying rail on several branches. The long-delayed joint line up the Snake River from Lewiston, Idaho, to Riparia, Washington, finally went forward in 1905, and several feeders were constructed in northeast Oregon. Improvements were stepped up to make the line more competitive with Hill's. The Short Line started work on a branch to Yellowstone Park, thereby staking its claim to the tourist traffic dominated by the Northern Pacific. The major piece of unfinished business was access to Seattle and Tacoma without relying on the Northern Pacific. In 1906 Harriman organized a new company, the Oregon & Washington, to reach the Puget Sound. "Seattle has a future that can scarcely be realized at this time," he told its citizens, "and the extension of the Union Pacific . . . will assist in its upbuilding."[21]

For twenty years rail diplomats had scrambled to avoid duplicate lines in the Northwest through treaties. Hill's north bank line and Harriman's Puget Sound road sounded the death knell to those long and futile efforts. Although analysts predicted the region would shake with the wrath of titans, the fight that followed was surprisingly tame. Some writers have tried to pump more blood and guts into this last gasp of the rail wars than was actually spilled. Hill and Harriman were tough, hard-nosed dealers, but neither shot from the hip. For them war was always an extension of diplomacy.

Their struggle proved a fitting coda to the Northwest clash. Harriman laid down a covering fire of lawsuits to get himself into Seattle and keep Hill out of Portland. At the same time he made a great show of marching to Seattle, ordering surveys, planning grand tunnels, spending large sums for terminal sites and right-of-way. It was in military terms a feint, a grand demonstration designed to avoid committing the assault troops until absolutely necessary. Hill met every thrust in kind, taking his casualties in cost overruns while pushing the north bank line forward. The new road opened in 1908 but did not get into Portland's Union Station until 1920. The fight for Seattle raged until May 1909, when Hill agreed to let the Union Pacific share the Northern Pacific line from Portland to Tacoma, thereby coming full circle to the agreement first sought by Charles Francis Adams two decades earlier. There would be no second road to Puget Sound.[22]

One other battlefield occupied their attention. Central Oregon had yet to be tapped by rail, partly because it was not easily reached except through the narrow, twisting confines of Deschutes Canyon. On a vacation trip to Oregon in 1908 Harriman, smarting from criticism that he had not "opened up" central Oregon, promised that a road would be built from Navigation's line at The Dalles 130 miles down the Deschutes River to Madras. Hill decided the following year to grab the canyon route for himself and perhaps even turn it into an inland line to San Francisco. Seizing the charter of a moribund project called the Oregon Trunk Line, he sent his best engineer to buy right of way and run a line through the canyon ahead of the Harriman forces.[23]

The result was one more spirited contest for an obscure but strategic bit of real estate that writers of the purple prose were quick to call "The Deschutes Canyon War," the last in a series of canyon wars that spilled far more ink than blood. This one occurred in the last summer of Harriman's life and was settled after his death in the usual way of joint occupation. The compromise was but one episode in the process of adjustment by which the major systems in the Northwest accepted the obvious truth that no one of them would own the region. With the Milwaukee about to join them and the old generation of forceful, dominant entrepreneurs giving way to a new breed of managers and caretakers, the time had come to practice coexistence if not brotherly love.[24]

Through these turbulent years Harriman and his railroads withstood the fiercest blows of man and nature. However, in 1907 they had to reckon with quite another formidable storm, the wrath of Theodore Roosevelt. The dynamic young President was a man incapable of sharing center stage; it was once said of him that he had to be the bride at every wedding and the corpse at every funeral. No public figure matched his energy and ambition or his gift for self-serving and dissembling.

Although Harriman and Roosevelt had been friends for many years, their relationship endured only as long as they moved in separate spheres. An ardent Republican, Harriman had furnished Roosevelt and the party in New York with money and advice whenever asked to do so. In recent years, their relationship had endured some rugged strains, notably the Northern Securities fight, the sensational publicity surrounding the investigation of Equitable Life, a clash over the ICC's role in regulating rates, and the Colorado River dispute. However, the incident that finally drove them apart concerned a fund of $250,000 raised by Harriman for the campaign of 1904. When a controversy arose over the fund, Harriman felt that Roosevelt put him in a bad light to make himself look better. This resort to righteousness, a common tactic of Roosevelt's, stung Harriman deeply. In December 1905 he poured out his views in a letter to longtime friend Sidney Webster. When James S. Sherman of the Republican Committee asked Harriman for a contribution in October 1906, Harriman whipped out a copy of the Webster letter and read it aloud to explain his refusal.[25]

A few days later Sherman reported this incident to Roosevelt. That very day the President sat down and wrote a position paper disguised as a letter to Sherman, recording their interview and stating Roosevelt's views on the disputed points. Among other things Sherman claimed that Harriman had said he did not care if the Democrats won the election because "those people were crooks and he could buy them; that whenever he wanted legislation from a State legislature he could buy it; that he 'could buy Congress,' and that, if necessary, 'he could buy the judiciary.' " Roosevelt professed to be horrified at such cynicism and labeled Harriman a "wealthy corruptionist" who was "as undesirable a citizen as Debs, or Moyer, or Haywood [all radical labor leaders]."[26]

This controversy, which had not yet gone public, might have remained one more tempest in the political teapot except that five weeks later the ICC launched an investigation into "Consolidations and combinations of carriers, relations between such carriers, and community of interests therein, their rates, facilities, and practices." By some curious coincidence the only roads investigated were those controlled by Harriman; no attempt was made to present it as anything else. By an even stranger coincidence the commission focused most sharply not on existing conditions but on the controversial reorganization of the Alton seven years earlier. Indeed, its final report devoted eight of twenty-four pages to discussion of that one incident. The Alton played no role worthy of notice in the existing relations among carriers and was a minor line in the modern rail network. However, its reorganization was by far the most questionable episode in Harriman's career, the Achilles heel of his reputation as a financier.[27]

The question naturally arises as to whether Roosevelt in some way prompted the ICC to undertake just this investigation at just this time. He denied the charge with his usual indignation, and no known evidence exists to confirm or deny. If he did not make his influence felt, directly or indirectly, the timing made for an extraordinary coincidence. Whatever the source, the chain of events that flowed from this decision was to leave a deep and fateful imprint on the Union Pacific. Ultimately it resulted in a government suit to dissolve the merger with the Southern Pacific.

The ICC hearings opened in December 1906 and droned on through the winter, drawing steady headlines despite having to compete with the sensational murder trial of Harry K. Thaw, the slayer of Stanford White. The excitement created by Harriman's appearance as a witness on February 25 inevitably reminded observers of Jay Gould's performance before the Pacific Railway Commission twenty years earlier. Where Gould had been "meek, low voiced and suave," Harriman gave the impression of "frankness coupled with stubbornness." Where Gould had spun artful webs of repartee, Harriman fought his inquisitors "both offensively and defensively, nothing being too small to call for a contest, and it was apparent that he looked upon the entire investigation as only one more engagement in what has been a ten-year battle for his way."[28]

For three months the newspapers crowded their columns with revelations gleaned from the testimony, much of it distorted to the point of fantasy. Roosevelt evidently took an interest in what Harriman had to say; a copy of extracts from his testimony can be found in the President's papers. While the hearings proceeded, several people made vigorous efforts to heal the breach between Roosevelt and Harriman. Schiff tried in his tactful way to persuade the President that he was moving too fast on railroad matters, and Harriman himself went back to Washington in March 1907 to meet with the ICC. While there he asked lawyer Maxwell Evarts, one of the few who knew the inside story of the Webster letter and Sherman interview, to arrange an interview with Roosevelt. The President threw up his hands in response and cried "How can I do it? What will the newspapers say?"[29]

Finally, Roosevelt agreed to meet with Harriman on the condition that a stenographer was present. Unfortunately, he told a newsman that Harriman wanted to see him, and the story promptly got into the papers. Morgan, who was about to leave for Europe, saw the report and hurried to Washington to confer with the President. At his urging, Roosevelt decided to meet with four other leading rail presidents as well. "We will wait until after these other fellows get through," Harriman told Evarts, "and then, when the matter quiets down, we will go down on our trip."[30]

But the quiet never came. The day after Morgan's hasty visit, the governor of Illinois arrived to discuss with Roosevelt the possible indictment of Harriman on the Alton transaction. A parade of rail presidents tried to impress Roosevelt that his attack on railroads was ruining their credit at home and abroad. Harriman himself startled observers in March by ending his policy of silence and talking to reporters. "It has never been my idea to concern myself much about the relations of the public to the railroads," he admitted, "but I propose hereafter to give the public information, to take it into my confidence as to matters it is entitled to know about." He followed this declaration with one of the longest and fullest interviews he had ever given.[31]

Roosevelt was assured that no case could be made against Harriman on the Alton transaction. Nevertheless, one editor predicted that Harriman would "become to the United States as black a figure as was Jay Gould in a former era." Senator Shelby M. Cullom of Illinois visited the President and told reporters afterward he thought Harriman should be put in jail for his part in the deal. Shown the text of Cullom's remarks and asked to comment, Harriman made good on his new policy of openness. "If Senator Cullom said that," he snapped, "he could not have been sober."[32]

Before the proposed meeting with Roosevelt took place, something wholly unexpected happened to dash all hopes of a reconciliation. A stenographer discharged by Harriman a year earlier sold his notes of the Webster letter to Hearst's New York *American*. When the latter did not print the letter at once, the stenographer sold it again to the *World*, which splashed it across the issue of April 2, 1907. Harriman tried to minimize the damage by asking the other papers to print a notice that the document was stolen and garbled and not published by his authority, but it was to no avail. Roosevelt reacted in his usual wrathful way by giving to the press in rebuttal the letter he had so carefully composed after his interview with Sherman, which denounced Harriman in vigorous language and contained charges that Evarts had earlier shown him to be patently untrue.[33]

The uproar that followed did Roosevelt little credit as his denials grew louder and more harsh. Harriman responded with a statement written for him by Melville Stone that repeated the facts and affirmed everything he had said in the Webster letter. The remarks attributed to him by Sherman were false, and Roosevelt had been told this "by a mutual friend [Evarts] who was present at the interview." More than that Harriman refused to say, except to insist that time would vindicate him. No meeting between the two men took place.[34]

Virtually all of Harriman's friends agreed that Roosevelt had behaved badly if not dishonestly, and some doubted he ever intended to meet with Harriman. Diplomat Willard Straight, then stationed in Havana, heard in mid-March that Roosevelt was "especially down on him and is thought to intend to 'break' him." Evarts noted that Morgan's conference with the President was "simply a specimen of the way that Morgan tried to block Harriman whenever an opportunity offered." Otto Kahn went even farther. "The Harriman Extermination League," he later wrote, ". . . played its trump-card by poisoning President Roosevelt's mind against Mr. Harriman."[35]

Other men, especially one as ill as Harriman, might have heeded advice to duck the storm and flee to Europe for his health until the skies cleared. But

Harriman would not budge. He uttered no complaints or pleas for sympathy despite his failing health and the strain imposed on it. Ignoring the pleas of friends to ease up, he stubbornly went on about his business. A brief but sharp panic that fall left the business climate and financial markets unsettled, giving Harriman another worry in an already tough year.

The appearance of the ICC's final report on July 13 sparked a new round of condemnation of Harriman over the Alton reorganization, which occupied a third of the document. Even before the report was issued, Roosevelt and his cabinet wrestled with the question of bringing suit against Harriman. Their mood was heady, inspired by the recent action of a federal court that had hit Standard Oil of Indiana with an unprecedented $20 million fine. Attorney General Charles J. Bonaparte declared haughtily that "a better moral effect would be produced by sending a few prominent men to jail than by a great deal of litigation . . . against the corporations they controlled." Unmoved, Harriman denounced the report as "a political document and part of a personal pursuit of me."[36]

During the ICC hearings Harriman and Kahn had refused to answer any questions about their private transactions in Alton securities. In August 1907 Bonaparte filed suit asking that they be compelled to respond, but the Supreme Court upheld Harriman's position. Regarding this as a mere skirmish, Bonaparte asked the court in January 1908 to dissolve the Union Pacific merger with the Southern Pacific. "In logic and as a measure of public policy," grumbled the New York *Times*, "the suit is senseless and without warrant," the child of an "outworn and misdirected statute." But it would go forward, and with it a new round of hearings.[37]

The government suit exposed anew a glaring contradiction in public policy on rail transportation. Even critics of Harriman agreed the Sherman Antitrust Act was obsolete and ought to be replaced, but Congress in its dawdling way had not done so. As a result, the government now found itself trying to dissolve the most logical of mergers for reasons that made no sense to anyone. The idea that the Union Pacific and Southern Pacific formed a monopoly was, declared the *Chronicle*, "absurd on its face":

> These acquired properties cannot be said to serve the same territory. The most that can be affirmed is that they lie in the same geographical division. They do not traverse the same or even contiguous territory, and the area between them is of enormous extent. Moreover, these lines, instead of being parallel lines . . . are lines necessary to round out and complete the Union Pacific system. Both the Northern Pacific and the Great Northern are complete systems in themselves. On the other hand, neither the Union Pacific nor the Southern Pacific is complete in itself.[38]

The *Railroad Gazette*, always a perceptive journal, put its finger on the essence of the contradiction. "Our national law has definitely taken two positions which are absolutely irreconcilable with each other," it noted. "Through the Sherman law it has required competition; through the rate law of 1906 it has made it impossible." The problem lay in the government's determination to enforce competition even though a mountain of evidence demonstrated that attempts to legislate competition had failed miserably. If the Union Pacific-Southern Pacific union was illegal, asked the *Saturday Evening Post*, what about the New York Central's control of its Lake Shore system and the roads parallel to it, the Nickel Plate and West Shore? Such examples could be multiplied almost at will. Any attempt to apply the Sherman Act vigorously would "throw into confusion a considerable part of the transportation system of the country."[39]

Like the Northern Securities decision, the "unmerger" suit marked a giant step backward in the process of rationalizing the rail industry, one that would leave deep and permanent scars. Harriman did not live to witness the outcome of the suit; it remained for his successors to cope with this latest example of public policy as the triumph of faith over experience. Time has confirmed an obvious truth of 1907: Harriman knew more about railroads but Roosevelt knew more about politics. Although historians have done much to revise the hoary legend of Teddy the Trustbuster, too few have followed the lead of Albro Martin in showing the incalculable damage done by his erratic policies to the nation's railroads just at a time when they had entered an era of crisis. No system was to suffer more from Roosevelt's misguided influence than the Union Pacific.

Everyone, it seems, knew that Harriman could not go on forever except Harriman himself. The little man piled up projects even faster than dollars, and his ambition seemed to grow in inverse proportion to the decline of his health. The old indomitable spirit still flourished: the harder the road and tougher the obstacles, the more eager Harriman was to run it. By 1908 his friends Schiff and Stillman were edging toward retirement even though both were in far better health than Harriman, and they urged him to join them or at least cut back on his commitments. As early as 1904 or 1905 Stillman told Harriman that he intended to retire soon from active business and that Harriman should do the same so as to have more time to enjoy himself and his family. Unfortunately, this well-meaning advice only made Harriman suspicious and caused him to grip the reins tighter.[40]

Harriman could not quit because he could not imagine life without challenge, and retirement offered no challenge that appealed to him. There was also the delicate problem of succession. Where Schiff and Stillman had groomed able men to follow them, Harriman had not. In May 1905 it was rumored that Harriman would retire from the presidencies of his roads and manage them as chairman of their boards, but nothing came of it. Kuhn, Loeb and National City Bank had become greater than the men who dominated them. As Stillman put it, the bank "was one of the great organisations in the world, where every man had obliterated self, and made themselves part of one great machine." But the Harriman roads were still Harriman above all else. As Felton had said, you worked for Harriman, not with him.[41]

The troubles of 1906–1907 riveted Harriman even more into his place while draining him of the strength to carry his enormous burden. Once he began buying stocks in other roads, talk arose of converting the Union Pacific into a holding company to separate its investments from its transportation assets. Such a company, analysts agreed, would be a "mighty power in [the] financial world." If nothing else, the move would enable the road to show that its high dividends came from profitable investments, not exorbitant rates. The ICC investigation slowed progress toward creation of the new company until the fall of 1907, when a committee was formed to arrange a plan. Although the rumor mill churned on the subject for another two years, the idea was one whose time would not come for another six decades.[42]

During the spring of 1907, amid the uproar over the ICC hearings, an attempt was made to reduce Harriman's load by strengthening the executive committee and its responsibilities. "The system," noted one observer, "is now so vast and ramified, and so prominently fixed in the public eye, that it is desirable . . . that the responsibility . . . be divided among as many strong men as possible." Harriman did not oppose the idea but made it clear that any impetus for change would come from him, and he was in no hurry. The men most likely to share power with him didn't want the job. In January 1908 Stillman surrendered his seats on the Harriman boards to Frank Vanderlip, who would soon succeed him as president of National City Bank, and took to spending most of his time in Europe. Schiff and Kahn had gone off the Union Pacific board in 1906.[43]

Schiff added his voice to those imploring Harriman to cut back on his commitments. While testifying before the ICC in February 1907, Harriman had celebrated his fifty-ninth birthday and remarked that he would retire at sixty. Later that year, before departing on an extended vacation abroad, Schiff pressed Harriman anew to give up the presidencies and content himself with "the chairmanship of the boards & executive committees, placing moreover men of experience on the boards & executive committees to share responsibilities with you."[44]

But Harriman could not let go. He could not retire with the unmerger suit still pending and so much yet to do elsewhere. A trip to Japan in 1905 had filled him with a vision for building railroads in China and Manchuria as part of a vast system of rails and steamers circling the globe. After many setbacks the project had sprung to life again, and others demanded his attention. Reminded of his vow when he turned sixty in February 1908, Harriman replied, "Well, it isn't a case of changing my mind, but of not having had time to think about retirement . . . there are too many moves yet to be made."[45]

His friends understood this logic all too well. They smiled ruefully at reports that Harriman was about to form a consulting board to help relieve his workload. The problem with this idea, quipped one of them, was that "it would be unconstitutional for him to do it, his constitution being so constructed that he consults nobody except himself."[46]

Unfortunately, the sieges of illness that had always plagued Harriman grew steadily worse. On the last day of 1906 he underwent a minor operation that kept him abed for more than a month. The malady was never disclosed but may have been hemorrhoids, from which he suffered constantly. In September 1907

TIRED BUT GAME: A worn and aged Harriman meets the business leaders of Omaha in this extract from a 1908 picture. Roland (*left*) and Averell sit at their father's feet. The man to Harriman's left is Euclid Martin, president of the Omaha Chamber of Commerce.

he had surgery again for the same ailment. His absences from the office became more prolonged, the vacation trips more frequent, leaving in their wake intense speculation about his health. Back trouble added to his agony, yet he would not relent. During the spring of 1908, while confined with a painful back ailment, he saved the Erie Railroad from default by agreeing to personally take up $5.5 million of the road's notes falling due.[47]

There was rich irony in this generous action by Harriman. He had saved from default the railroad so long associated with the most notorious phase of Jay Gould's career, and he had done it when Morgan and the other Erie directors adamantly refused to lend the road another penny even though the Erie was widely regarded as a Morgan road. Nor would they consent to lend Harriman any of the funds needed to save the Erie. Only George F. Baker, who was not involved in these negotiations, showed a willingness to let Harriman have as much as $3 million. Harriman's prompt response to the crisis earned him widespread praise on Wall Street and helped swing public opinion back toward him after the Roosevelt debacle.

By 1908 the Harriman Extermination League had collapsed. "The more generous of its members frankly acknowledged his great qualities, admitted he had been wronged, and became whole-hearted adherents," Kahn observed;

"others, from self-interest, made haste to climb on his bandwagon; only a few irreconcilables continued to sulk and frown, but no longer dared attack him." Shortly after the Erie crisis, in a letter to Schiff, Harriman permitted himself a rare moment of introspection:

> To me it is the greatest satisfaction that we "still stand together" & are looking forward as well as back. Of course it has been nerve wearing, & taken some of our vitality, & sometimes I have questioned whether it has been worth while. Maybe it would not have been had only the UP & ourselves been the gainer. Where would have been those whom it serves had we not straightened, improved, & improved again, enlarged, made better, & so increased its capacity that it permitted the enlargement of every enterprise, & establishment of new ones in all the territory adjacent to it & the systems under its influence. Besides its method introduced like methods by other important systems. Where would we all now be without them? It has all made for advancement in civilization & will someday be understood. . . .

It would be hard to find a more fitting epitaph to Harriman's career, yet he was looking forward as well as backward. "There is much in the future to be worked for improvement," he wrote Schiff in the next breath, "& I hope we will still be found standing together when the opportunities & responsibilities present themselves."[48]

To outward eyes Harriman did not resemble a man ill or contemplating retirement. He pushed vigorously the building of Southern Pacific track in Mexico, followed developments in his Far Eastern scheme, took a seat on the board of the New York Central, and talked of expanding the Central of Georgia system. Especially did he talk; the once reticent bantam rooster waded into his new policy of openness with gusto, giving talks and interviews as freely as a politician. Everywhere he went the reporters were waiting, and seldom did he fail them. "The greatest violator of the Sherman Act," he snapped to one reporter, "has been the Government itself."[49]

In December 1908 Harriman fell ill with what was labeled ptomaine poisoning. Through the dark bottom of winter he kept at home while insisting that he would be downtown any day. By early February he was confined to bed, wracked with pain yet transacting a steady stream of business over the ever-present telephone. Vanderlip, who visited him several times, found the sight of him "little short of tragic . . . the telephone in his hand, his brain as active as Napoleon's at its best."[50]

Marvin Hughitt took a less charitable view. On a bleak February day he and Vanderlip found themselves the only members present for an executive committee meeting. Harriman had promised to be there but called at the last moment to say that it had taken the combined efforts of three doctors and his wife to keep him from leaving home. In his usual way he boasted of the fight required to hold him at bay. Hughitt snorted that he needed no new evidence of

Harriman's obstinance, and with that he launched into a tirade against the little man that astonished Vanderlip.

The whole Harriman system was drifting badly, Hughitt raged, and he was worried because of the Northwestern's dependence on the Union Pacific. Important questions were piling up that needed more attention than a sick man could give them, but there was no vitality in the New York office, no one with any force except Judge Lovett. It had been a fatal error to vest so much responsibility with Kruttschnitt and Stubbs in Chicago, so far removed from the scene of action, and leave no one else with authority to act decisively. Vanderlip dutifully reported this outburst to Stillman, who merely said that matters were "not really as bad as he thinks." There would be a reorganization of executive staffs once the unmerger suit was decided, he was certain of it.[51]

In February Harriman finally left on a prolonged trip to the South and West in hopes of regaining his strength. For a time he installed himself in a tent outside San Antonio with a large entourage and a private telegraph line. In New York special meetings of the Union Pacific and Southern Pacific executive committees were called. Rumor had it that a large issue of Southern Pacific bonds would be approved. "In that respect the Street has the advantage of the Executive Committee," noted Vanderlip dryly. He and Hughitt knew nothing about the proposed issue, but he did know Harriman's style and was therefore not surprised when the rumors proved true. At the same meeting, Lovett was elected vice-president and director of both roads.[52]

Early in April, Harriman returned to New York, but something was clearly wrong. His stomach grew worse, and the frail little man could muster no appetite. He decided to go abroad for rest and medical help, telling Vanderlip that he felt fine but Mrs. Harriman suffered from nervous prostration. While she got attention, he added, he might as well see what he could do for himself as well. What he needed was a change of habits—simple meals, proper hours, a routine he could bring back to America with him.[53]

On May 28 Harriman held a special meeting of the Southern Pacific executive committee at his house, during which several large expenditures were approved. Three days later he sailed for Europe. Once on the continent he paused a few days in Paris to visit Stillman, who found him looking much better than he had expected. Harriman begged him to stay on in Europe awhile, but Stillman was itching to leave and had only delayed his departure for their meeting. Disappointed, Harriman took a train to Vienna, where he placed himself in the care of Dr. Adolph Struempell.[54]

The weather was cold and rainy, the news no better. Struempell told him what would not become public until September and would always be denied publicly by the family: Harriman had cancer too advanced for an operation to remove. He went on to the resort town of Bad Gastein, taking the baths and hating every moment of it. During his visit with Stillman he had recalled the banker's earlier advice to retire and said with a rueful shake of his head, "You were right Stillman all the time. I ought to have quit and laid back. But it is too late now. I am in deeper than ever, and must go on, on, on."[55]

By August he had lost ten pounds from his already gaunt frame and determined to come home, telling his friends that the ''German hotels and food are not the kind on which I would thrive,'' and that ''the good food and air of America'' would restore his strength. Harriman paused again in Paris for a couple of days. While his daughters shopped, he endured a sitting for Rodin, who was obliged to finish his work from memory. There were also business meetings, necessarily short, devoted mostly to his Far Eastern project.[56]

The family sailed from Cherbourg on August 18 and reached New York a week later. Aware that the reporters were waiting for him, he insisted on walking down the gangplank without assistance, and submitted to an interview in his private rail car while lying on a sofa. Despite his friendly tone and willingness to give them time, the reporters were shocked at his haggard, wizened appearance, his ''parchment-like skin, yellow and hanging; his weak and faltering step, and his lustreless eye.'' Mary Harriman and Judge Lovett tried to cut the session short, but Harriman insisted on answering all questions before the train pulled away.[57]

Home he went to Arden and the still unfinished house atop a hill, where he rested, watched the workmen, and conducted what business he could by telephone and letter. To friends and the public alike he tried to leave the impression that he was on the mend and would soon be back in harness. Schiff and Stillman came to visit and found Harriman full of talk about tomorrow and the projects it would bring. Only six days before the end, Schiff talked to Harriman on the phone and was astonished at how well he sounded and how full of curiosity he was about business conditions. ''I myself almost believed he would recover,'' he noted afterward, and Stillman had the same impression. But on Sunday, September 5, 1909, Harriman collapsed, and four days later he died quietly in his bed.[58]

At the family plot in a far corner of the churchyard at Arden parish, the ceremony on a quiet Sunday afternoon was simple and private, attended only by the family and old friends with six men from the estate as pallbearers. For one minute during the funeral, trains on all the Harriman lines across the West paused in silence wherever they stood. ''When we laid the little man into the grave near the quiet village church,'' wrote a sorrowful Schiff afterward, ''a power was buried which it will hardly possible to replace.''[59]

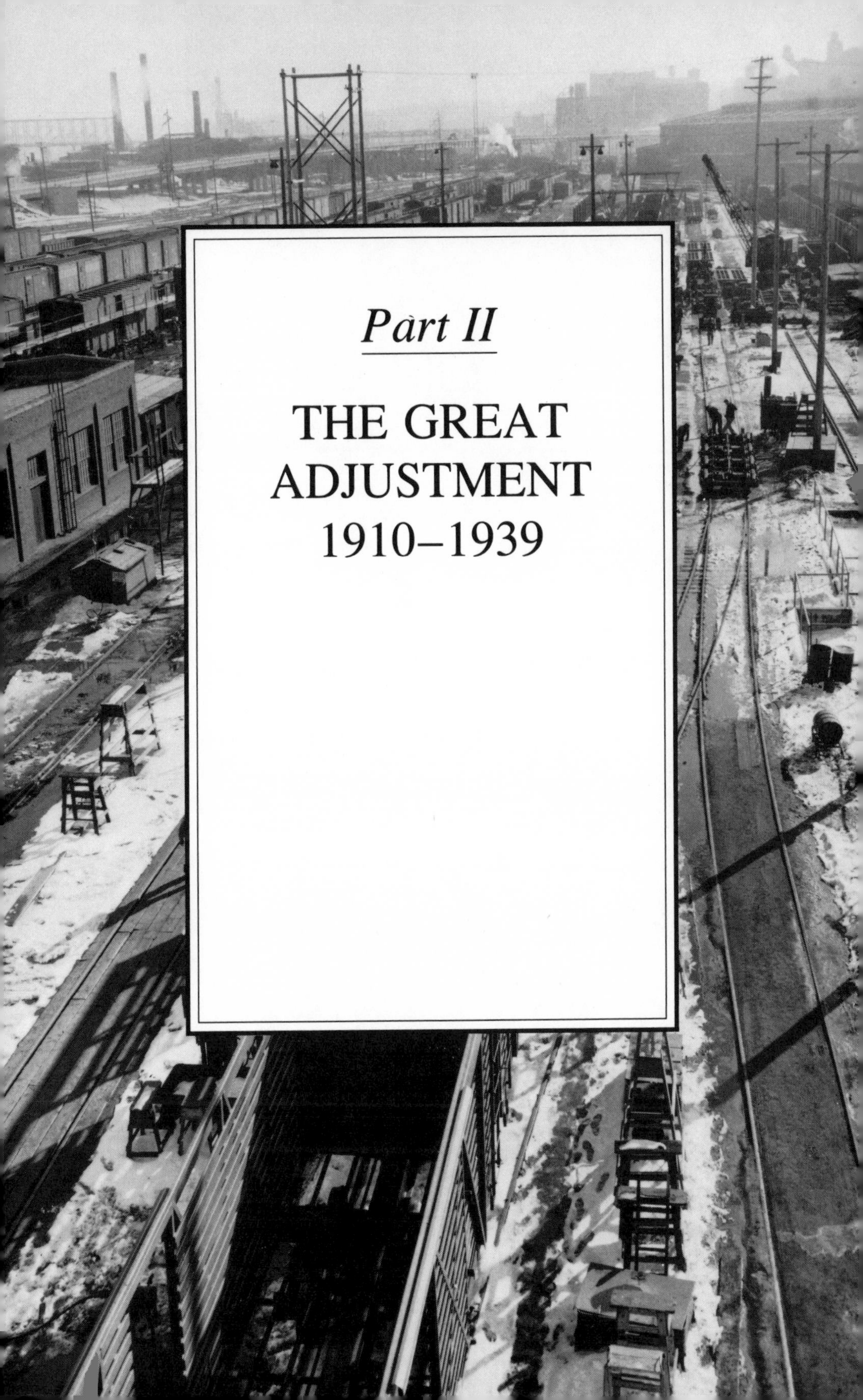

Part II

THE GREAT ADJUSTMENT 1910–1939

10

The Stewardship

"Who is to be Mr. Harriman's successor?" a reporter asked Alex Millar, the venerable secretary who had served both Gould and Harriman.

Millar chewed thoughtfully on a pencil, his brows furrowed above piercing gray eyes. "There will be none," he said finally. "His work will be divided. There is no man in the country who can fill the shoes of that little giant. And, besides, his intentions have been so thoroughly mapped out that there really is no necessity for one at present."[1]

Millar was right. The Chairman was gone, and there would never be another like him. He had left behind a magnificent and prosperous system along with a blueprint for its continued development. What the property required now was stewards capable of realizing the destiny conceived for it by Harriman. Those who complained that he had groomed no successor were right; what they failed to notice was that he had left behind one of the smoothest and most effective management teams to be found in any company. He had built as solidly within as he had without. No one man could equal the Chairman's gift for managing everything from finance to operations, but the men capable of handling these fields together were already in place.

Speculation on the line of succession was intense, especially in Wall Street. Rumors circulated that J. P. Morgan would step in to manage the empire financially, but no such thing occurred. Kuhn, Loeb remained the banking partner of the Union Pacific, a point emphasized by Jacob Schiff's return to the board a few days after Harriman's death. The move was clearly symbolic; Schiff lingered only until January, then surrendered his seat to Otto Kahn. William Rockefeller also joined the board, and Frank A. Vanderlip, who had succeeded James Stillman at the head of National City Bank, was already there. Three key positions remained unfilled: chairman of the executive committee and presidents of the Union Pacific and Southern Pacific railroads. The names bandied about most frequently were two men considered Harriman protégés: L. F. Loree of the Delaware & Hudson and Frederick D. Underwood of the Erie. To the surprise of many analysts, neither one was tapped.[2]

The company had no need to go outside its own ranks. Thanks to Harriman's novel organization, the system still ran with clockwork efficiency under the watchful eyes of Julius Kruttschnitt and John Stubbs. Despite rumors to the contrary, neither man was a likely candidate for promotion. Stubbs was nearing retirement, and Kruttschnitt had attained the level for which his talents were best suited. Where Harriman had been a great virtuoso, Kruttschnitt was the technician who kept the instrument in perfect tune. He had "absolutely no imagination," Vanderlip said of him. "His implements were facts; he was a living index of all railroad facts." Both men were also splendid team players untainted by blind ambition or prickly egos. "They worked like a baseball team in pennant stride," wrote one admiring reporter of the men who presided over Harriman's empire.[3]

But who should manage this team? The logical candidate was the man who in recent years had grown close to Harriman as both friend and trusted adviser, one who had been reluctant even to live in New York, let alone sit astride the mightiest rail empire in the world.

They called him the judge even though he had never been one except for a brief stint as a substitute. It was one of the few conceits indulged in by Robert Scott Lovett, whose life was in every respect a reflection of his upbringing. He was born in June 1860 in San Jacinto, Texas, north of Houston, to strict Scotch-Irish parents whose dour, stern manner left a deep imprint on him. In later years the judge would be hailed as the model Horatio Alger hero, but his parents were not dirt poor as was often proclaimed. They did reasonably well at farming and did not hesitate to give the boy large doses of responsibility; once at an early age he was sent to fetch quinine on a journey that took seven days.[4]

Lovett learned early to work for everything he wanted. Between chores he attended Billy Wood's School at Big Creek but quit school at seventeen against his father's wishes and ran away from home. He found work grubbing stumps for the Houston, East & West Texas Railway, a road some called "Hell Either Way You Take It," then clerked at a commissary. His sister married an East & West agent, who got Lovett a job at Normanville, where the depot was an old box car. He followed his brother-in-law to the Houston depot where, in his spare time, he studied law on his own and later in the office of a local attorney. At twenty-three he passed the bar and was hired by the East & West, which in 1885 sent him to look after its interests in the small town of Nacogdoches. He excelled as a "cow coroner," handling suits over slain livestock and other damage claims. The railroad noticed how well he did with local juries and in 1886 brought him back to Houston.[5]

NO ROOM FOR FRIVOLITY: The stern visage of Judge Robert S. Lovett.

In 1889 he moved to Dallas as assistant general attorney for Jay Gould's Texas & Pacific, but returned to Houston three years later to join the law firm that became Baker, Botts, Baker & Lovett, which handled the business of the Southern Pacific's Texas lines. Lovett grew expert at dealing with the state's notorious railroad commission, the most hostile and oppressive in the nation. At this early stage in his career he mastered the intricacies of regulatory statutes and policy before many lawyers even understood their general thrust. His appetite for hard work and thorough grasp of detail made him invaluable to the Southern Pacific and later to Harriman when he acquired that system. "They are perceiving [a word dear to Lovett's vocabulary]," he once remarked of the authority given him in a case, "that the handling of such matters as this had best be done by the men on the ground rather than by the men in New York."[6]

Lovett was content to remain on the ground. In October 1890 he had married Lavinia Abercrombie, who bore him a son five years later. They lived in a fine old Victorian house with a wrap-around porch in Houston that the boy remembered fondly all his life. As an old man himself, Robert Abercrombie Lovett still recalled his father as "the finest man I ever knew." He was the quintessential east Texan: tall, lean, reserved, austere, hard working, and a stickler for good behavior. The judge did not hesitate to spank young Robert soundly for any breach of manners, but a dry, quiet sense of humor leavened his stern sense of rectitude. He was the soul of honor and integrity, a man devoted to principle and seriousness of purpose without being somber or overbearing in his righteousness.[7]

Legend has it that Harriman summoned Lovett to New York, but in fact he went originally to help with a Southern Pacific stock suit and stayed on reluctantly because Harriman and Winslow Pierce decided he might be needed if new proceedings arose. The more Lovett did, the better Harriman liked his soft-spoken intelligence, cool judgment, and methodical ways. Like Harriman, he had the facts at his disposal and knew how to put them together. He was made counsel for the Union Pacific and then, after the death of W. D. Cornish, vice-president. But he did not want to leave Texas. In New York he put up at the Hotel Majestic overlooking Central Park, saying he liked to be "close to nature," or what passed for nature in the big city.[8]

There would be no return to Texas because Harriman drew Lovett ever closer to him as both adviser and friend, especially during the troubled years after 1906. His calm, deferential manner was the perfect complement to Harriman's excitable style. The Chairman was notorious for summoning men peremptorily to his office on the fourth floor of the Equitable Building, but when he wanted Lovett he often hiked up to the judge's office on the fifth floor. Finally, Lovett conceded his destiny and brought his family north, but not to the city. Instead, he found a place at Locust Valley, Long Island, which offered some larger semblance of nature than Central Park. The two families grew close, especially the boys. Young Robert came to regard Roland Harriman as the closest thing to a brother he ever had.[9]

Lovett was the ideal steward and the logical choice to oversee the empire when Harriman died. He would never fall into the trap of trying to be Harriman or anyone else but himself, and his uncommon gift for common sense made him a steady navigator in rough seas. Even Wall Street trusted Lovett, who had earned a reputation for being the only man who had not lied about the state of Harriman's health. Never a man to sacrifice principle for expediency, he had shown his mettle in 1908 when several members of the Texas legislature asked him as president of the Houston & Texas Central to stop employing blacks as switchmen and brakemen and give the jobs to white men. Such a move, it was suggested, would help create a "better feeling between the people of this state and the railroads."[10]

The judge badly needed this better feeling in Texas, but not at the price offered. He rejected the demand in a temperate but firm letter that echoed Abraham Lincoln. "Being a southerner," he added, ". . . no one is more opposed than I am to the Negro in politics, and to all his aspirations to 'social equality.' . . . But, if, with his political rights, we take away his right to do any work he is fitted to do; if we deny his equal right to earn by any honest labor the necessaries and comforts of life for himself and family—the day the North realizes that this is the attitude of the intelligent white people of the South will be an evil day for the South."

For the judge, legality and integrity were cut from the same cloth. On one occasion he praised the Omaha office for its part in defeating a taxation amendment to the Nebraska constitution. "This seems a wise business move," he added, "provided nothing illegal was done. . . . We cannot be too careful, however, to avoid doing what is illegal in such matters." Not to worry, responded the chief officer in Omaha, A. L. Mohler. Nothing was done without consulting the law department, and the lawyers could not be more cautious. "This Legal feature has been so repeatedly drilled into them," Mohler emphasized, "that it takes precedence over the 'Lord's Prayer.' "[11]

On the day after Harriman's funeral in September 1909, Lovett was elected chairman of the executive committee. Later he was also made president of the Union Pacific and Southern Pacific. The executive committee was expanded from five to six members and included Jacob Schiff (later Otto Kahn), William Rockefeller, Frank Vanderlip, Marvin Hughitt of the Northwestern, and Henry Clay Frick. One of them confided to a reporter that policy for the next few years would be "one of extreme conservatism, even to the extent of laying the management open to the charge of 'old fogyism.' " This had not been possible while Harriman was alive and forever bristling with fresh plans that gave him a reputation as a speculator and disturber of stability. The image was dead wrong, but it existed and had to be counteracted. "Henceforth," predicted an analyst, "the crest on the door at 120 Broadway will be 'Reliability.' "[12]

Schiff put the matter more delicately. "Although the companies are apparently organized in excellent fashion," he told a close friend, "the keen eye and almost reckless energy of a Harriman cannot be replaced at once. For this reason alone, and probably also for other weighty reasons, more quiet methods will necessarily have to be pursued, and they must be chosen very carefully." No one was better suited to finding quiet methods than Lovett. He had inherited one of the strongest, most prosperous companies in the nation, which in a sense made his task even more difficult. If he did well, little would change; if not, he had nowhere to go but down. "In all the history of American railroads," marveled one analyst, "no man before has been called upon to fill a position of such vast responsibilities as the present executive of the Union Pacific."[13]

Some thought it too big. The more Vanderlip saw of Lovett, the more he liked him, yet he could not escape the "absolute conviction" that the judge did not measure up to the position. "Indeed," he conceded, "I doubt if any human being is big enough for the job. Evidence comes up with great frequency that, in his later days, Mr. Harriman certainly was not equal to the job. The job really is not a one-man affair." Lovett was in his view a fine man, more judicial than acute. The problem, thought Vanderlip, was that he had some subordinates "who should be supervised by acuteness."[14]

Whatever apprehension investors felt over the change in management faded quickly. During Lovett's first year in office gross earnings hit a record high of $88.5 million. Although earnings rode a roller coaster for several years, the dividend rate remained at 10 percent until July 1914, when it returned to 8 percent. In December 1916 the 10 percent rate was restored with the increase labeled an extra dividend each quarter because of the abnormal conditions wrought by World War I. Investment income stayed high even in years when railroads did poorly. In December 1911 analysts noted that the Union Pacific had $75 million in ready money after meeting all obligations. Kahn obtained figures showing that the company had spent nearly $94 million on improvements for which no capital had been created and possessed more than $209 million in free assets.[15]

Financial success did not mean smug or fossilized management. Lovett was the most attentive of stewards, poring over figures, analyzing prospects, and examining the organizational structure to see where improvements could be made. The first change came at once and pleased directors like Vanderlip, who hated Harriman's style of holding private executive committee meetings over which he cracked the whip. Under Lovett they became full meetings with "real discussion of many important matters." The judge understood that the system devised by Harriman had worked best with Harriman at the top, and that major changes were needed to make it work without Harriman. For nearly two years he did little more than study the problem; then, in April 1911, he moved to implement his reforms.[16]

The key to his plan lay in the belief that western officers needed more autonomy in responding to their prospects and problems. The trick was to find an organization that centralized functions affecting the entire system while "localizing the management with respect to local matters." Lovett's solution was to effect a cleaner separation between New York and Omaha. It had always been true that Omaha proposed and New York disposed, but Harriman had blurred the distinction by serving as both chairman and president of the major roads, and by centralizing operations and traffic functions under chiefs located in Chicago. His chain of command ran from the chief operating and traffic officers of each road to Kruttschnitt and Stubbs and then to himself, making some decisions cumbersome and time-consuming.[17]

As a first step, Lovett surrendered the presidencies and confined himself to the chairmanship of the executive committee. A. L. Mohler was named president of the Union Pacific, William Sproule of the Southern Pacific, and J. D. Farrell of Navigation. Under the new system the presidents regained control over their operating and traffic organizations, which formerly reported to Chicago. Kruttschnitt and Stubbs moved their offices to New York, where they acted more as advisers than administrators. To emphasize the change, Lovett also announced plans to move the Union Pacific's offices from the Equitable Building to a larger structure at 165 Broadway. Unfortunately, the change did not take place quickly enough. On January 9, 1912, shortly after the move commenced, a fire gutted the Equitable Building and destroyed many valuable company records.[18]

Lovett did more than devise a structure to separate the functions of New York and Omaha; he prodded the new presidents to use their new autonomy. When Mohler continued to deluge him with piles of information, Lovett sent him a gentle but clear reprimand:

> I cannot undertake to deal with the details of freight train schedules of your own or of connecting lines. Detailed reports to me of negotiations or discussions respecting such matters between connecting lines will only consume my time and may mislead you by assumption that I am giving the same attention, which I cannot do. I can only reiterate the general instruc-

> tions, heretofore given from time to time, to meet competition. The details you will have to work out yourself and every purpose will be served without passing them on to me.

When Mohler failed to get the message, Lovett told him bluntly, "You are getting more and more into the habit of enclosing, in your letters to me, copies of voluminous correspondence, and many long statements. . . . I wish you would first digest all the matter yourself, and then write me your final decision, or specific recommendation, stating your reasons in a short, but clear manner."[19]

Always a good organization man, Lovett knew how to delegate authority. In his own role as chairman he was as careful and exacting as he was in the practice of law. When earnings slumped, he demanded corresponding reductions in expenses or precise explanations of why this was not possible. Having learned from Harriman's experience, the judge took care to give the public full information about the company's activities. He expected the financial press to be as meticulous as himself and was quick to protest when a publication mangled his statement.[20]

In another respect Lovett showed himself the perfect steward for Harriman's vision. During 1911 he announced a program of improvements costing $98 million that included double-tracking the entire main line, installing more block signals, reconstructing the Omaha bridge, and building several extensions. Lovett estimated the second track alone would cost about $75 million, and the other work also required large expenditures. Wall Street and Main Street alike gasped at the news. From distant Paris Stillman labeled it "almost folly." The remarkable feature of the decision was not merely its price tag but also its timing. A major rail system had decided to invest huge sums in the future even though the government was investigating it, Congress had recently passed adverse legislation in the form of the Mann-Elkins Act, the ICC had just denied carriers a rate increase after long and bitter hearings, and a major strike threat loomed on the horizon.[21]

"True, the outlook in many respects is unsatisfactory," the judge conceded. But this was, he hoped, a temporary condition, and meanwhile the West continued to grow. "If we wait until all difficulties are out of the way," he added, "we shall probably find our lines falling behind instead of doing their share in the development of the growing country." To the disheartened rail industry and financial observers, Lovett's bold move was, in the *Chronicle's* words, "an inspiring exhibition of courage in the face of many Governmental obstructions."[22]

Explaining his priorities to an inquirer, Lovett declared that "Our first object is to improve our track and keep it, not only safe, but make it comfortable. Then we want to update engines and cars, and plenty of them, automatic signals and other improvements that make for safety and reliability and comfort. . . . Stations are designed only for getting on and off trains. Hence they are not more than secondary in importance to track, equipment, etc." He assured Mohler that no appropriation "which you believe proper consideration for safety requires" would be denied.[23]

But no authorization for an expenditure, however small, went unnoticed by the judge. He jumped on Mohler for excessive cost overruns and items that seemed unwarranted, such as a new depot for Burley, Idaho. It cost only $1,850 but had not appeared in Mohler's original budget and so was sent packing. Scanning Mohler's budget for 1916, Lovett noted that it seemed to be "made up with the idea that it would be cut quite liberally, which is not the way that it should be prepared; and which is anything but helpful to me." Unwittingly the judge had glimpsed the future of the budget process and wanted no part of it. His old-fashioned hackles were easily raised by sloppy procedures and careless work. "Our people must realize," he decreed, "that money can be obtained only for necessaries."[24]

Although the extensions garnered less publicity than the improvements, they were no less important. The years prior to World War I were the sunset of railroad expansion in the United States, and sunset lingered longer over the Union Pacific than over most lines. Only two weeks after Harriman's death Kruttschnitt had announced a massive program calling for 2,000 miles of extensions evenly divided between the Union Pacific and Southern Pacific systems. Between 1910 and 1916 Lovett put even this ambitious goal to shame, constructing 1,849 miles of new track for the Union Pacific alone or three times the 600 miles of second track laid during those same years.[25]

For both programs the pace of progress was uneven: 75 percent of the extension mileage and 86 percent of the second track went down between 1910 and 1913. The European war created uncertain conditions and abnormal prices that made Lovett reluctant to spend money on betterments, and long before the war broke out, the Union Pacific found itself once again in battle with its ancient nemesis, the federal government.

By 1910 the government's suit had assumed a life of its own. The ICC investigation that had spawned it had been forgotten, Harriman was dead, and Roosevelt had reluctantly yielded the presidency to William Howard Taft, but the suit droned on under a new attorney general, George W. Wickersham, whom Vanderlip suspected of having developed political ambitions that were coloring his view of issues. Lovett and his lawyers appealed to Taft to drop the case, arguing that the evidence collected during the past year had proven nothing, but Taft ordered it to proceed. The president, snapped Lovett, was "trembling between two fears—the fear of the return of Roosevelt and the fear of a panic." In February 1910 the taking of testimony resumed and dragged on through the spring; after a summer recess final arguments were presented in October.[26]

In essence, the case amounted to the next chapter of the fight begun in the Northern Securities clash. The government argued that the Union Pacific and its managers had acquired the Southern Pacific to monopolize trade and suppress competition, and that it had bought the Los Angeles & Salt Lake and shares in the Northern Pacific and Atchison for the same purpose. It asked that the Union Pacific be forced to divest itself of all holdings in these roads. The issue once again was competition as defined under the Sherman Act, the ambiguities of which continued to confuse businessmen and enrich lawyers.

Much depended on how competition was defined. The government argued that "active competition" had existed at Ogden and other points before the Union Pacific bought the Southern Pacific. The two roads were "naturally competing lines, and but for the control the former exerts over the latter would be competitive now." From this logic emerged a classic legal syllogism of the Progressive era: competition between the two roads existed; after one road acquired the other, competition ceased; therefore, one road acquired the other to eliminate competition. No other motives were taken into consideration and no other avenues explored, such as the possibility that competition had little to do with matter or what was actually meant by competition.[27]

As had happened so often in previous investigations, the government chose to ignore the historical context. Harriman had other reasons for grabbing the Southern Pacific after Collis Huntington's death. He was anxious to secure his entrance into San Francisco, which meant buying the Central Pacific before George Gould or someone hostile to the Union Pacific beat him to it and shut him out of California. To get the Central Pacific he had to buy the Southern Pacific, which Otto Kahn claimed he did not even want at first. There was another compelling reason to acquire the Central Pacific: it was a bottleneck at Ogden, wholly unable to handle efficiently the flow of traffic pouring across the modernized Union Pacific. Harriman could eliminate the problem by improving it as he had the Union Pacific. The little man also happened to believe he could do things with railroads no one else could.[28]

There was both history and logic behind the notion of combining the two roads. The original Acts of 1862 and 1864 had decreed that they should be operated as "one continuous line," and Gould and Huntington had tried several times to merge them. As the defense emphasized, the Union Pacific and Central Pacific could hardly compete with each other because they were *connecting* lines. The government argued lamely that the Union Pacific had its own line into San Francisco via Portland and therefore did not need the Central Pacific, but traffic men knew that convoluted route had never been a serious competitor. To what extent, then, did the Union Pacific and Southern Pacific actually compete for transcontinental traffic, which was the only business at stake in the case?[29]

Prior to 1900 there were five basic routes between California and the Atlantic seaboard: (1) the American-Hawaiian steamer line via the Straits of Magellan; (2) Pacific Mail steamers via the Panama isthmus; (3) the Southern Pacific's Sunset route; (4) the Atchison rail route; and (5) the overland rail route via Ogden. The merger gave Union Pacific control over three of these routes, and Harriman's later purchase of Atchison stock gave him some influence over a fourth route. Traffic from the Mississippi Valley could reach California via the Ogden gateway, the Southern Pacific's El Paso gateway, or the Atchison route. After the merger the Atchison remained independent, and competition from the Gould roads still existed at both Ogden and El Paso.

The defense contended that the Union Pacific and Southern Pacific competed for a tiny amount of traffic—less than 1 percent of the Southern Pacific's total tonnage for 1901, and 3.1 percent of the Union Pacific's tonnage—and that the merger itself had little effect because the Southern Pacific virtually monopolized California traffic before the merger. The Union Pacific's role in the competitive struggle started and stopped at the Ogden gateway, where it connected with the Southern Pacific. After the merger the two roads consolidated their agencies, which meant they no longer vied for traffic from certain areas, notably the Midwest and Northwest. However, the chief effect was to rationalize the flow of business in a way that maximized returns to the overall system. The elimination of competing agencies allowed traffic to move along the lines of least resistance to one or the other of the lines, which had the effect of increasing the freight routed via the Omaha gateway.[30]

In June 1911 the circuit court accepted most of these arguments and ruled in favor of the Union Pacific. Violation of the Sherman Act, noted the judges, required "a contract, combination, or conspiracy in restraint of interstate or international commerce. This restraint must be substantial in character and the direct and immediate effect of the transaction complained of." Three of the four judges agreed that none of these criteria had been met. In their opinion the Union Pacific was not "a substantial competitor for transcontinental business with the Southern Pacific in or prior to the year 1901." Moreover, the small amount of competitive traffic involved was a "controlling and decisive consideration." The charges involving other roads were also dismissed.[31]

Another factor influenced the judges. Two recent Supreme Court cases involving Standard Oil and American Tobacco Company had produced formal recognition of what was called the "rule of reason." By this doctrine a combination in restraint of trade was declared illegal only if it was unreasonable or against the public interest. After repeated rebuffs the reason rule seemed finally to have been accepted by the court. Although the judges in the Union Pacific case did not formally invoke it, observers viewed the decision as an example of its influence. If so, it was a crucial precedent, for the earlier decisions concerned industrial combinations; this was the first case involving railroads. "The decision," noted one analyst, "declared legal what may be called the life and soul of modern railroad development." Another doubted that any court could have found this particular merger an "unreasonable" restraint of trade because it was "perhaps more conclusively defensible than almost any other merger of roads."[32]

There was consensus too that the decision vindicated Harriman and his policies. "The suit upon which it once was fondly hoped to send Mr. HARRIMAN to jail has failed," observed the New York *Times*. Hopes that the issue had at last been laid to rest remained strong even after the government filed an appeal. The hearings before the Supreme Court took place in March and April 1912. When they had finished, the justices did not rush to judgment; the decision was not rendered until December, conveniently after the election. Maxwell Evarts, who had handled the case, assured Lovett that he could rest easy about the decision. "My judgment," predicted the confident Evarts, "is that the case will be decided unanimously in our favor."[33]

Evarts was half right and dead wrong: the decision was unanimous but against the Union Pacific. The justices looked at exactly the same set of facts as their brethren of the circuit court and reached entirely opposite conclusions. The decision was astonishing enough; that eight justices joined in it was enough to send chills shuddering down the spine of every rail executive in the nation.[34]

The court, while giving a nod to the rule of reason, took a position that consciously roused the ghosts of decisions past. It reaffirmed that the Sherman Act prohibited any combination placing railroads in a position "whereby natural and existing competition in interstate commerce is unduly restricted or suppressed." The circuit court had accepted the argument that the Union Pacific and Southern Pacific were more partners than competitors prior to 1901; the Supreme Court, impressed by the testimony of shippers, found them to be "in competition, sharp, well-defined and vigorous." Where the lower court had considered the amount of premerger competition to be negligible, the Supreme Court declared it to be "large in volume, amounting to many millions of dollars."[35]

On the key issue of competition the court retreated to the protective armor of the Northern Securities case by reaffirming that it was not the actual deeds of defendants but "their power to suppress or stifle competition or create monopoly which determines the applicability of the act." The court acknowledged that railroads competed in two broad arenas: rates and service. An earlier decision had declared the consolidation of competing systems in violation of the Sherman Act because it resulted in higher rates and less satisfactory service. Yet the fact that in this case rates had not advanced and huge sums had been spent to improve service did not sway the court. What the merged systems had actually done during the past decade mattered less to the justices than their possession of the potential power to do something else.[36]

The beauty of law, at least to lawyers and judges, is that it can be dealt with in terms of the private world of its own inner logic regardless of its fit with social realities or its repercussions on society. In this decision, however, even the logic was forced if not spurious. It denied that Harriman's motive for the merger was to avoid being shut out of San Francisco partly on the grounds that the Union Pacific already owned such a route via Portland and the sea. Where the lower court recognized that this line could in no practical way compete for California business, the Supreme Court decision declared it "a factor in rate making to the coast" despite repeated testimony that it had never been used since opening in 1884.[37]

Nor did the court's logic ever strike at the heart of what really constituted competition in transcontinental business. On eastbound traffic the two roads could not compete because all California business originated on the Southern Pacific, which could use its own Sunset route exclusively or divide the rate with the Union Pacific and one of the Chicago roads. Westbound traffic could be solicited by both roads, but the Southern Pacific would get part of the rate on whatever the Union Pacific carried. In effect, the Union Pacific competed to get part of a transcontinental rate that might otherwise go entirely to the

Southern Pacific. As a combined system this competition would cease, but few if any shippers would suffer. The real competition was with the Atchison and the Gould roads, and that was not affected by the merger. Indeed, the merger spurred the construction of a new competitive line to California, the Western Pacific.

Finally, what would the unmerger accomplish? Of course, the court had only to interpret the law, not worry about the consequences that would ensue. As the *Railway Age Gazette* observed in a perceptive critique of the decision, "A perfectly valid law in the constitutional sense may be a very bad law in an economic sense. The consequence of its economic defeats will be to do harm. And this is what will be the result in this instance." If the object was to restore active competition between the two roads, the chances ranged from slim to none. Aside from the fact that little competition existed between them, much had happened since the Sherman Act's passage in 1890.[38]

Rate competition had been legislated out of existence through the Hepburn Act of 1906 and Mann-Elkins Act of 1910. Since no rate competition currently existed between the transcontinental lines, the unmerger would have no effect on the situation. This left only service, an area in which the two roads could indeed compete. "There probably is keener competition in service between the transcontinental lines today than there ever was before," the *Gazette* noted. It was, however, difficult to see how the unmerger could improve the situation. Virtually no one complained about the service offered on the combined system; indeed, the fact of their being run as one road had wrought dramatic improvements in service. What would happen if they tried to outdo each other? "The more competition in service there is," reasoned the *Gazette*, "the more it costs to render the service; and the more it costs the railway to render the service, the more in the long run the shipper and traveler are going to have to pay for it."[39]

None of these considerations moved the court, which enjoined the Union Pacific from using or voting its Southern Pacific stock until a plan for its disposal was prepared and approved. The other charges were dismissed, leaving possession of the Los Angeles & Salt Lake undisturbed, and the court took pains to impose no obstacle in the way of the Union Pacific acquiring the Central Pacific after the unmerger. Attorney General Wickersham favored this arrangement as the fairest solution, but it added one more obstacle to devising an equitable plan. No one expected the unmerger to be thrashed out quickly.[40]

While Wall Street reeled in shock at the outcome, Lovett and his colleagues tried to mask their disappointment with only partial success. "This is poor reward for all the beneficial and constructive work done by you and your predecessor," cabled Kahn from London. The judge himself, normally the most imperturbable of men, could not resist a jab at the inequity of it all. In a telegram congratulating one of the government's attorneys he added sardonically, "It was genius rather than justice."[41]

The court gave the Union Pacific three months to devise an acceptable plan or it would intervene to dispose of the stock through receivership sale. In fact, the question had been pondered since September 1910, when Lovett, Schiff,

William Rockefeller, Vanderlip, Morti Schiff, and the three lawyers defending the company held a meeting to discuss what should be done if it were lost. The elder Schiff had a definite plan in mind: he wished to revive the holding company scheme of a year earlier and dump all the Union Pacific's investment holdings, including Southern Pacific, into it. The holding company would exchange its stock for the investment securities and have a board of people friendly to the Union Pacific but not directors of it.[42]

The major consideration, countered Lovett, was what effect such an action would have on the suit. All three lawyers agreed it would have an adverse effect and might lead to charges of subterfuge. If the lawyers insisted, Schiff sighed, then the plan must be dropped. "It may be good law," he muttered in protest, "but it is bad business." Some plan had to be adopted in advance, he emphasized, to separate clearly in the public's mind earnings from operations and earnings from investments. But nothing was done, and the suit was lost in a most unexpected way.[43]

For the Union Pacific the problem went beyond devising a plan to dispose of the stock. It also had to separate the management of the two systems and decide what officers were going with which road. Many of the Union Pacific's top executives, including Lovett himself, had come from the Southern Pacific. Who would return and who would stay? As a financier quipped, "How can you unscramble an egg?"[44]

The unscrambling moved smoothly if sometimes painfully. Lovett chose to remain with the Union Pacific, while the redoubtable Kruttschnitt returned to the Southern Pacific as chairman of the executive committee. Separate boards were created for each company, and a massive sifting of files got underway to determine who should receive what records. In this task, at least, the Equitable fire proved a godsend to overworked clerks. Joint traffic agencies were dissolved and separate ones opened in February 1913, and the joint equipment pool that had served the system so well was laid to rest in April.[45]

Where these efforts proceeded briskly, the stock plan bogged down in controversy. Lovett wanted to distribute the stock exclusively to the stockholders of the Union Pacific on the grounds that they had a vested right to it. Not so, countered Wickersham: "They have a vested right in the *proceeds* of that stock when disposed of in a manner best calculated to terminate the illegal combination." The attorney general rejected the plan, and the court sustained him. He also took a strong stand on the Central Pacific, declaring that no dissolution plan would be approved unless it transferred that road to the Union Pacific. By adding this provision, Wickersham forced the company to devise two plans: one for disposing of Southern Pacific stock, and one for the Central Pacific transaction.[46]

Through the dark, dreary weeks of winter the bargaining proceeded in what amounted to a race against the calendar. On March 4 a new Democratic administration would take office, and no one cared to leave the unmerger to the whims of a new cabinet. Tough, dogged negotiating produced a workable plan by early February. The Southern Pacific stock would be offered to stockholders of the two companies. The Southern Pacific would transfer to the Union Pacific all stock in the Central Pacific and its lease of the Central Pacific's lines in return for proceeds of the stock sale, estimated at $83.5 million, plus $14 million cash and $5.4 million in Southern Pacific obligations owed the Union Pacific. Part of the Central Pacific's line would be sold or leased back to the Southern Pacific to maintain its unbroken line from Portland to the Gulf, and terminals owned by either company were to be used jointly.[47]

Wickersham endorsed the plan, but obstacles arose on every front. French bankers, who had loaned the Central Pacific money, worried over their collateral and insisted the lease be maintained. Some European holders of Southern Pacific wanted better terms. The Western Pacific demanded important concessions if the Union Pacific acquired the Central Pacific, and the San Francisco *Chronicle* launched an editorial tirade on the theme of home rule versus New York domination. Even these objections paled before one procedural fact: several of the plan's provisions had to be approved by the California railroad commission.[48]

Fearing that the state under the proposal would, "instead of securing two strong competing lines, secure one dominant line and one much impaired line," the California commission withheld its approval unless certain conditions were met. If the Union Pacific got traffic rights over the Benicia cutoff, which saved the Central Pacific eighty miles between Sacramento and Oakland compared to its own line, the Western Pacific and any other road must receive them as well. Any terminals used jointly by the Southern Pacific and Central Pacific must also be opened to the Western Pacific. If the parties could not agree to terms for these rights, the commission would fix them.[49]

The commission imposed these conditions not only to protect the Western Pacific but out of concern that the Southern Pacific might be too weakened to compete with the Union Pacific. It also deplored the disruption of "a well-built system of local lines . . . into two disassociated sets of branches." Here was irony of vast proportions, a monument to the schizophrenic attitude that characterized public policy toward railroads. For years Californians had blasted the Southern Pacific as "something unholy . . . organized and operated for the sole purpose of extorting huge revenues from the California public." Since the appearance of Frank Norris's scathing novel in 1901, it had been the "Octopus" whose greedy, grasping tentacles spread corruption into every corner of public life. The commissioners themselves had been appointed by Hiram Johnson, the progressive governor sworn to keeping the Octopus at bay.[50]

Instead, the commission found itself defending the Octopus against the intrusion of a competitor. Even more, it feared that hacking off some of the Octopus's tentacles into competing lines would disturb their efficiency and convenience. This was in microcosm a classic example of the public dilemma over rail policy: it wanted the convenience and service of monopoly and what it presumed to be the lower rates of competition even though the latter no longer existed. It assumed that restored competition might somehow improve service without changing the existing structure of things where the existing structure was found to be suitable.

Although the commission insisted otherwise, its objections had the effect of scuttling the plan. As Kruttschnitt emphasized, the conditions imposed had been deemed unacceptable all along by both the Union Pacific and the Southern Pacific. Lovett, who had already fought the battle over the Benicia cutoff and other branches with Wickersham, found himself impaled on a nasty dilemma over the purchase. The French bankers continued to demand that the Union Pacific lease the Central Pacific even though any such lease required approval by the California commission, whose terms were already anathema to the Union Pacific. Nor was that all. An international syndicate formed to underwrite the $126-million transaction expired on March 15. If the plan was not operative by that date, the Union Pacific stood to lose $1.3 million in guarantees given the syndicate.[51]

A frantic effort was made to modify the plan. Lovett thought the new provisions satisfied the commission's objections, but after his arrival at St. Louis on March 15 for the court hearing, he received word that the commission had rejected the modifications without giving its reasons. There was no choice but to abandon the plan and pay the underwriting guarantee. The unmerger found itself back at square one except for one notable change: Woodrow Wilson's administration had taken office with a new attorney general, James C. McReynolds, who had to approve any new version. Wearily, Lovett undertook yet another pilgrimage to Washington to sound the newest player's views on the subject and impress on him the importance of leaving the Central Pacific with the Union Pacific.[52]

The situation was growing critical for the Union Pacific, which had $126 million worth of assets tied up in such a way that it could neither vote nor collect dividends on them. McReynolds rejected a revised plan to dispose of the stock but agreed that sale of the Central Pacific to the Union Pacific must be a part of the final arrangement. Lovett gained from the court an extension of the unmerger deadline to July 1 and made further concessions to expedite the transaction. But the California commission remained obdurate, the French bankers still balked, and the Southern Pacific showed a growing reluctance to part with the Central Pacific. As the difficulties mounted, Lovett decided to concentrate on the stock disposal and leave the Central Pacific issue for later negotiation.[53]

As the search began yet again for a suitable plan, Lovett masked his frustration with characteristic restraint. "If all the interviews Judge R. S. Lovett ever gave out were combined into one," grumbled one reporter, "the writer would still be short of matter to fill out a column." Filling columns did not interest the judge; filling the vacuum created by the government did. Late in May he offered the court two different plans for disposing of the Southern Pacific stock. McReynolds looked them over and again shook his head. His objections, which one critic called "fanciful in the extreme," led observers to wonder if any way could be found out of the impasse.[54]

Fortunately, one possibility had emerged in April. Morti Schiff and Paul Warburg learned that the Pennsylvania Railroad wished to sell its holdings in the Baltimore & Ohio lest it be attacked for owning stock in a competing line. They suggested to Lovett exchanging the Pennsylvania's B & O shares for part of the Southern Pacific stock, which would reduce the amount to be disposed of and perhaps make one of the latest plans more palatable to the court and McReynolds. All sides found this solution acceptable, and in June the details were thrashed out. The court gave formal approval on June 30, just under the deadline it had imposed for disposal of the stock.[55]

Under the agreement the Union Pacific swapped 382,924 shares of Southern Pacific stock for 212,736 shares each of preferred and common in the B & O. This gave the Union Pacific nearly 39 percent of the B & O's stock while the Pennsylvania acquired about 14 percent of the Southern Pacific. The remaining 883,576 shares of Southern Pacific were put in trust until certificates of interest representing them could be offered to all stockholders of the Union Pacific and Oregon Short Line. Although this was a modified version of one of the plans McReynolds had rejected, he agreed to it this time because the swap reduced the amount of stock to be dispersed by nearly one-third. The decree expressly forbade the Union Pacific or its subsidiaries from buying back any of the stock.[56]

The long fight was over. An exhausted Lovett heaved a sigh of relief and sailed for Europe on July 1, leaving behind intense speculation on what the future held for the unmerged roads. Some analysts saw in the stock swap the seedbed of two coast-to-coast systems. One editor noted shrewdly that the trade had been made possible by a radical change in conditions. "The law is now doing for the railways what they assumed to do for themselves," he declared. "The stocks were acquired to establish that community of interests which was to prevent rate wars. Now rate wars are impossible, since all rates are regulated by law."[57]

If the law had stopped there, the railroads might have been grateful. The unmerger suit offered a striking illustration of the growing intrusion of government into railroad affairs. Rail executives worried over how far this intrusion would extend, and to what degree it would take control of corporate affairs from their hands. The unmerger experience offered them little comfort, and it was not yet finished. Nothing had been done about the Central Pacific, over which a fresh fight was brewing. Time had stiffened the position of Sproule, who served notice that the Southern Pacific would "resist any attempt of the Union Pacific to gain possession . . . even to the extent of going to court." The government called his hand by filing suit in February 1914 to compel divestment of the road. Both sides might have hesitated had they known that nine more years of struggle lay ahead.[58]

A more pressing concern to interested parties in the fall of 1913 was what the Union Pacific would do with the proceeds of the stock sale. Talk of an extra dividend "melon" fueled speculation in the stock. The sale itself was a smashing success, with subscriptions totaling $220 million for the $88 million worth of stock. Profit to the Union Pacific on the combined sale and exchange of Southern Pacific shares came to about $20 million, which would amount to a dividend of more than 9 percent if it were distributed. Lovett delayed action on the matter until he was sure of his ground and had a plan that was "legally bomb-proof." It was not, he remarked dryly, the first time the company had had a large sum of money to dispose of.[59]

Lovett was concerned about not only a dispersal but also the regular 10 percent dividend, which he regarded as financially sound but politically vulnerable. The board deferred action at the October meeting, and Lovett took pains to assure reporters that no increase in the present rate was being contemplated. In January 1914 the board finally released a plan giving stockholders $12 in B & O common, $22.50 in B & O preferred, and $3 cash for each share of Union Pacific owned. The package was thus worth $37.50 per share, but at the same time the regular dividend was reduced to 8 percent, lowering the net value of the distribution to $32 at current market prices.[60]

If Lovett thought this plan would deflect criticism, he was quickly undeceived. Several senators denounced the extra dividend as stock watering and demanded that the $100 million in convertible bonds originally issued to buy the Southern Pacific be retired because they represented no actual property. A precise, careful man like Lovett could not help but be appalled at such sloppy thinking and reckless charges, but he also knew the political game well enough to grasp the motives behind the rhetoric. Dutifully he and the company lawyers explained to the senators that the extra dividend was derived entirely from *nontransportation* income and had no effect whatever on rail earnings or rates.[61]

Still the uproar continued. To Lovett it must have seemed as if trying to do things the proper way brought more trouble down on one's head than doing them improperly. "There are so many wild statements made in the papers," sighed a discouraged Alex Millar, "that it seems almost hopeless to correct them." The controversy died down only to flare up again in February 1916, when another senator took up the cry. By that time, Lovett understood more clearly what was not yet apparent in 1914: the furor over the unmerger and the extra dividend were not isolated occurrences but symptoms of a much larger problem. The relationship between the railroads and the government, in a state of flux for a decade, was on the verge of dramatic and far-reaching changes.[62]

11

The Turning Point

During its early history, nothing had plagued the Union Pacific more than its tempestuous relationship with the government. The receivership of 1893 had come in large part because of failure to reach a settlement in the thirty-year war over the government loan or to find solutions for a host of other conflicts. No railroad endured more public investigations and political censures. The tarnished reputation born of the Crédit Mobilier scandal was reinforced by the Pacific Railway Commission and prolonged by the constant howl of critics, demagogues, and sharks looking to snatch prey from the wounded company. During the reorganization the government had extracted a final pound of flesh for giving its consent.

In taking charge of the Union Pacific as a Utah corporation, Harriman might well have thought he was rid of the federal government, but it was not to be. His transformation of the road coincided with what has long been known as the Progressive Era, a confusing period about which historians have written much but still understand little. One of its most striking characteristics was a growing resentment against the dominant role of big business in American life. As instruments of change in the transition from an agrarian to an industrial society, large corporations were easy to blame for its painful dislocations and upheavals. Movements arose to curb their power lest they destroy smaller producers, if not a way of life that Americans had cherished for more than a century.

The railroads were a natural target for these movements. They were the first large corporations and by far the most visible of the giant enterprises dotting the American horizon. They furnished services that directly affected every citizen who traveled or bought goods. No industry had a higher or more vulnerable profile. To the public the railroad was a middleman, selling transportation to shippers who could blame the high price of their wares on the freight rates they had to pay. Since rail rates were as arcane a subject as theoretical physics to most people, they were easily exploited by politicians offering simple answers to complicated questions. As shippers grew larger and more powerful, they mastered the art of posing as victims and helped foster the image of the rail problem as a clash between greedy carriers and a helpless, exploited public.

The railroads could not duck these attacks because the apparatus for public control was already in place. As the only industry yet regulated by the federal government, they were at the mercy of any increase in power Congress handed the ICC, any restrictive legislation it passed or judicial interpretation of antitrust law. At the state level railroads faced an even more ominous situation. Prior to 1900 fourteen states had commissions with authority to prescribe rates; by the time of Harriman's death in 1909, the number had risen to thirty-three, and by 1915 all but Delaware and Utah had joined the list. For a system like the Union Pacific this meant dealing not only with the ICC but also with thirteen state commissions, to say nothing of state legislatures seeking to impose higher taxes and other measures.[1]

As the movement limiting the ability of railroads to manage their own affairs gained ground, those who possessed a sense of history could only shake their heads at the bitter irony of this trend for the Union Pacific. The company had failed once because it could not shake free of the federal government. Harriman's genius had transformed it into a powerful and flourishing system only to find its destiny once more being taken over by Washington. This time, however, federal interference was not unique to the Union Pacific; it was generic to the rail industry.

Federalism had been creeping into railroad affairs at a quickening pace since the turn of the century. Three landmark pieces of legislation—the Elkins Act (1903), Hepburn Act (1906), and Mann-Elkins Act (1910)—had transferred the power of making rates from the carriers to the government. Railroad men had mixed feelings about this change. On one hand, it rid them at last of the fierce rate wars and rebate controversies they had for forty years tried vainly to eliminate among themselves. On the other hand, it delivered their chief source of revenue into the buzzsaw of politics. The new process for obtaining rate hikes was long, cumbersome, and blatantly political, with the burden of proof for any raise resting entirely on the roads. Carriers got their first taste of its perils in 1910, when the ICC flatly rejected a request for an increase.[2]

Railroads also felt the scourge of the Progressive notion that big is bad. Two major efforts had been mounted to wield the Sherman Antitrust Act against rail combinations. Both the Northern Securities and Southern Pacific unmerger cases set precedents that frightened rail managers, and both had profoundly altered the destiny of the Union Pacific. Judge Lovett might well have felt that Washington had singled out his company as a scapegoat, but that was not his way. On these broader questions the judge was not only a meticulous legalist but a deep thinker on policy as well. His early career representing railroads in Texas had given him considerable experience with a regulatory commission that was implacably hostile to carriers. During his years with the Union Pacific he had seen the tide of resentment against railroads rising at both the state and national levels.

Like most rail executives, Lovett had no desire to return to the rate wars and cutthroat competition that had bled many roads into bankruptcy. But he saw clearly that no one yet understood the changed role of railroads in the new age then dawning. Vast confusion reigned over what competition was to be and how it would take place. As the rate hearings in 1910 revealed with painful clarity, few people grasped how difficult it would be for railroads to raise capital without some control over their rate structures.

How far would federalism creep into railroad affairs? Even conservatives like Lovett conceded that regulation had a proper role. Many rail managers had their own wish list of legislation, topped by a national incorporation act to free them from the costly struggle with so many state regulatory bodies. For decades the railroads had fought less to obtain favorable legislation than to kill hostile bills. During the Progressive era the fight grew steadily more intense over a widening range of issues. The worst clashes took place over taxation and valuation, but dozens of other bills hit the railroads directly or indirectly: the creation of commissions, employers' liability, labor rights, arbitration of strikes, full crew requirements, train size restrictions, to name but a few. One Kansas bill made it illegal for railroads to repair equipment without first erecting sheds to protect workers from inclement weather.[3]

To fight what it deemed obnoxious bills, the Union Pacific monitored elections closely to see which way the legislative winds were blowing, sent lawyers to work the legislature, handed out passes liberally until the Elkins Act cramped its style, and joined forces with other roads to oppose threatening bills. Company attorneys with a taste for politics thrived on this work, but even they grew weary of the grind. "I am sincerely glad that the whole thing is over and that I can get back to ordinary business again," sighed Nelson Loomis, the general solicitor in Omaha, after one tough session of the Kansas legislature where he had beaten back some thirty or forty bills. For nearly a month he had stood vigil at the state house from dawn until late into the night. Some of the bills had to be killed three or four times. Loomis distributed passes freely to get the work done, but offered little else besides a few meals to choice legislators; his lobbying expenses did not total seventy-five dollars.[4]

During that same winter of 1903 the company beat back sixty bills in Nebraska, where the Real Estate Board led a campaign for higher valuations on railroad property, and a large number in Utah and Wyoming. A decade later the situation had worsened. Buoyed by Progressive enthusiasm, a tidal wave of bills dealing with rates, full crews, workmen's compensation, crossings, passes, fifty-car train limit, maximum work hours, and other issues rolled into state houses throughout Union Pacific territory. The box score submitted to Omaha of wins and losses in each legislature seemed to be tipping away from the company's favor.[5]

As these fights multiplied along with the number of state commissions, the carriers found themselves looking desperately to Washington for relief. One analyst, who had adamantly opposed giving the ICC power to make rates, reversed his position when he discovered that the Hepburn Act, far from settling the issue, only spurred state commissions to more vigorous reductions in defiance of federal authority. A national incorporation act would help reduce federal-state conflicts, and there were other areas in which federal regulation might prove useful.[6]

But there was grave danger as well. Lovett and his peers knew full well that federalism might creep into areas where it was not wanted. Already Congress showed signs of taking a hand in the sensitive realm of labor relations. Most railroad men agreed that nothing would prove more disastrous than thrusting labor negotiations into the political arena. The tiger uncaged could not be counted on to eat only one's enemies.

The political scene was unusually volatile in 1912. Progressivism was approaching high tide as Woodrow Wilson swept into the White House over a divided Republican Party, and the Democrats captured both houses of Congress. A lifelong Democrat like Lovett should have relished this victory, but he was troubled by what the reform mood boded for the rail industry. No one, it seemed, was satisfied with the existing state of federal regulation. Changes were clearly in the air, but what direction would they take and how far would they go?

Informed public opinion seemed finally to grasp some of the railroad's real problems. The Hadley Commission, appointed in 1910, stressed in its final report that "The building of additional mileage will be far less rapid . . . but the capital needed for the development and the improvement of the mileage already existing is enormous." Where was it to come from? The current rate of return on rail securities, added the commission, would make it difficult to raise large sums. A New York editor blasted the ICC for possessing "a maximum of power, but a minimum of responsibility." A Baltimore editor agreed that the time had come "for a stop to be put upon punitive legislation" such as full crew laws requiring extra brakemen on trains already equipped with automatic air brakes.[7]

Attitudes within the industry were also shifting. Lovett joined the procession of rail leaders who spent larger amounts of their time writing for and talking to public bodies on railroad issues. The judge was no spellbinder, but his thoughtful, fair-minded approach on policy matters impressed even critics. In 1912 he returned home to appear before the Texas Welfare Commission as one of several witnesses seeking to ease that state's hostility toward railroads. Such invitations came more frequently, and Lovett felt obliged to accept them, even seek them out.[8]

Rail managers realized at last that the time had come to stop squabbling among themselves and join forces to defend their interests. After some clumsy early attempts at self-promotion, a few executives had organized to provide more sophisticated public relations for the industry. In 1910 they founded the Bureau of Railway Economics, which soon attracted support from most large roads. The Bureau assembled a staff of economists and a library of materials on railroad matters.[9]

The next logical step was to create a body to represent the industry on policy matters. Railroad men were forever organizing into committees but seldom effectively; in the past it had been more a substitute for action than a prelude to it. In 1910 they also formed what Frank A. Vanderlip called "an extensive and compact organization," the Railway Executives' Advisory Committee on Federal Relations, which represented about 60 percent of the roads. Lovett was among the nine top executives named to the committee, and Frank Trumbull of the Chesapeake & Ohio was made chairman. For the next several years the Advisory Committee lobbied Congress and the White House in a dignified but strenuous manner. In February 1914, for example, it presented Woodrow Wilson with a position paper on the antitrust bill pending in Congress.[10]

Despite an improved public opinion and earnest efforts to mobilize the industry, the outlook remained bleak for the carriers. The departing Congress in 1912 left behind two presents in the form of the Panama Canal Act, which barred railroads from holding interests in any competing water carrier that operated through the canal, and the Norris Act limiting the width of right-of-way to two hundred feet, or half of what the Union Pacific had been granted in Norris's home state of Nebraska. The company challenged the law in court, but George W. Norris had in 1913 been elevated to the Senate and did not look to be any friend of the railroads there.[11]

Neither did that group of diehards characterized by Albro Martin as "archaic Progressives" because they had never ceased flogging the railroads for sins committed a generation earlier. Never mind that the world had changed and the railroads with it; these men clung doggedly to old shibboleths for which they demanded legislation: the railroads were vastly overcapitalized, and no rate increase could be valid until the "real" value of their property was determined; the roads cheated on their rate schedules by shifting items from lower to higher classifications; and a small, powerful group of men controlled the roads through interlocking directorates.[12]

In March 1913 the departing Congress and President honored one of these complaints by passing the Railroad Valuation Act, empowering the ICC to fix the physical value of railroad property as a basis for determining rates and reasonable profits. This amounted to undertaking a census of the chicken population to figure out how much to charge for a dozen eggs. Conducting this census required a new bureau with a staff and budget that soon dwarfed the rest of the ICC. Even critics of the railroads pounced on the act as an exercise in futility. "While the results will be interesting," scoffed one editor, "they will be of no value whatever for any useful purpose."[13]

Those promoting the valuation bill reckoned that it would cost $3 or $4 million and take several years to carry out. After passage one observer hiked the price tag to $15 million, which turned out to be not even a down payment. Ultimately the project consumed twenty years and several hundred million dollars to determine that the railroads were neither grossly overcapitalized nor making lavish returns on their investment. Even by American standards this seemed a steep price to pay for puncturing myths. Moreover, nothing in the final report overrode what railway experts like Henry Fink had tried to tell Congress all along: that the true value of any railroad was its earning capacity.[14]

While a generation of lawyers, accountants, and clerks toiled at the valuation mountain, some congressmen sought a more immediate solution. William C. Adamson of Georgia, chairman of the House committee on interstate commerce, thought overcapitalization could be curbed by authorizing the ICC to regulate the issue of securities by carriers. Frank Trumbull called on Adamson in February 1914 to discuss the matter. To his surprise the congressman abruptly stopped and dictated to his secretary a statement dealing with a grievance over railroad rates and policy in his home district. He handed the statement to Trumbull and asked that it be fixed up, adding that it was "pretty hard for him to help the railroads when he has been stabbed in the back in his home town."[15]

The securities regulation bill got through the House only to die an unmourned death in the Senate. A more serious threat loomed in one of the major pieces of legislation before Congress, the new antitrust bill that would become the Clayton Act. One section of the bill banned interlocking directorates among corporations. If applied to railroads, where directors routinely sat on the boards of many subsidiary lines, the result would be, in Lovett's words, "the greatest shock to railroad securities that has been felt in years." Systems would be torn apart, undoing several decades of rational organization. In explaining what harm would be done, Lovett hammered at a point that seemed constantly to escape lawmakers. "Railroads and industrial corporations," he emphasized, "are fundamentally different."[16]

The obvious solution was to exempt railroads from the proviso, but railroads were not in good grace that season thanks largely to the headlines generated by the New York, New Haven & Hartford Railroad bankruptcy. This debacle had prompted Adamson to bring his securities bill, and influenced the views of those who supported the antitrust bill as well. The ICC report, released in 1914, condemned Morgan's management of the New Haven as "loose, extravagant and improvident." Railroad men regarded the New Haven as an exception; reformers saw it as the rule, a flagrant example of how the carriers behaved. The Clayton Act passed Congress intact but was not scheduled to take effect until October 1916. During the interval Lovett urged the Advisory Committee to get it modified. The bankers would have to leave all boards, Lovett conceded,* but he didn't believe Congress meant to dismantle whole railway systems.[17]

In the delicate area of labor relations the carriers took a more positive role. In 1898 Congress had passed the Erdman Act authorizing the chairman of the ICC to mediate labor disputes if one of the parties so requested, and allowing him to invoke arbitration if mediation failed. The law remained dormant until 1906, when it sprang to life in a flurry of cases, sixty-one in all by 1913. The

*The act barred bankers who handled issues of securities for a road from sitting on its board.

unions had done well under it; in 1907, for example, western conductors and trainmen won a 10 percent wage hike and reduction of hours from twelve to ten per day—in effect, another pay raise. In 1912, however, a major strike by engineers in eastern territory exposed the act's defects. Neither side was willing to place the outcome of a strike involving more than fifty carriers and thirty thousand men in the hands of a temporary board with a single neutral arbitrator.[18]

All sides agreed that the Erdman Act was flawed. A new bill was drafted under the auspices of the National Civic Federation, the executive committee of which was a blue-ribbon panel drawn from business, labor, and the public. The process was an impressive display of democracy in action, an orderly harmonizing of interests enacted into law as the Newlands Act in July 1913. Although the final version differed from the Civic Federation's draft, it gained support from both labor and the carriers. A permanent mediation board with four members was created, and provision was made for a board of either three or six arbitrators if mediation failed.[19]

W. C. Brown of the powerful New York Central wanted (and got) the new act in place before his system entered negotiations with the conductors and trainmen. So did President Wilson, who was anxious to avoid a strike. His obvious concern reinforced two lessons the unions were fast learning: there was strength in joint action against the carriers, and union influence could be wielded effectively in the political arena. Lovett and his peers had their own causes for disquiet. Labor negotiations were becoming more rational, but they were also slipping away from the railroads. Already they had lost control over their chief source of income; now they were losing control of their major cost factor as well. If that should happen, the roads would find themselves entirely at the mercy of the political process.

The result would be to detach costs from income by allowing adjustments in one without any concern for the other. The left hand would grant pay hikes while the right hand virtuously kept rates down. One commissioner had already said testily that the ICC "could certainly not permit the charging of rates for the purpose of enabling railroads to pay their laborers extravagant compensation." This was no abstract concern for the Union Pacific, which was a logical target for any strike. "It is an open secret," noted an analyst in 1911, "that the Federation of Labor has picked out the Union Pacific as the road with which to begin its fight for higher wages precisely because that road reports larger earnings on its common stock."[20]

Much more was at stake in this threat than higher wages. The 1911 conflict ushered in a new era in labor relations for the Union Pacific and the industry as a whole. The shopmen issued a long list of demands for wages, hours, abolition of piece work, restrictions on number of apprentices, and changes in work rules. These were unacceptable to the Union Pacific in themselves, but the men added a new wrinkle: they wanted a closed shop. The five trade unions representing the shopmen—machinists, blacksmiths, boilermakers, car repairers, and sheet metal workers—had banded together under the auspices of the American Federation of Labor. All future negotiations, they insisted, must be with the federation rather than individual unions. In addition, all present or future shop employees who were not members must join the appropriate union within thirty days.[21]

The federated unions went after the Union Pacific and the Illinois Central, which was still deemed a Harriman road. Through the dog days of August and September the two sides sparred, with the strike threat hanging in the air like a thunderstorm on the edge of a heat wave. Neither Kruttschnitt nor C. H. Markham of the Illinois Central had any intention of recognizing the federation or conceding wage and hour demands totaling 36 percent. Since both sides were anxious to avoid a strike, they nursed the negotiations along even though the Union Pacific laid off two thousand men because of a decline in business. But no one could find a face-saving compromise. The sticking point was not unionism but federation. Although the carriers did not formally recognize the unions, they had dealt with them for years. The idea of negotiating with them in concert, however, was anathema to rail leaders.[22]

By October the railroads had not budged and the unions saw no choice but to call the general strike they had hoped to avoid. In all, 3,042 men on the Union Pacific and 5,189 men on the Southern Pacific walked out. The roads filled their places with unskilled recruits, which meant months of patient waiting for them to learn their jobs and heavy outlays for guards to protect men and facilities from violence. Although some of the union men returned to their jobs, the strike dragged on in desultory fashion through the long months of the unmerger and changing political climate. Lovett was adamant that nothing be done to "modify to the least extent whatever the position and policy taken at the outset of the strike." When Markham showed signs in April 1913 of making some minor concessions, Lovett warned him sharply that "it would be a mistake, amounting almost to a calamity, for any of the lines affected by the strike to recede in the least degree. . . . Any sort of concession would be taken as a surrender by the company."[23]

Some labor leaders recognized the bind in which the carriers found themselves. In August 1911 an A.F. of L. official was quoted as saying, "It is patent to every well-posted railroad man that either rates must go up or wages must come down. So-called scientific management and efficiency cannot overcome the steadily decreasing margin of profit that the roads are able to make under present conditions." But the public did not want either the inconvenience of a strike or the price of a rate increase. "We seem to have settled upon three propositions as passed beyond discussion," sighed the *Chronicle;* "that a glass of beer and a trolley fare shall remain five cents and that fares and freights on railroads are not to be raised."[24]

Despite the failure of the 1911 strike, the unions grew so confident of winning disputes through joint action that even the four operating brotherhoods, long the elite among rail unions, came around to this tactic.* In 1912 the engineers, going it alone, were disappointed by the arbitrator's award. A year later, heartened by the gains trainmen had made against the western roads under the Newlands Act, the engineers and firemen joined forces to press for

*The four brotherhoods were the enginemen, firemen, trainmen, and conductors.

higher wages. A. L. Mohler growled that it was "unreasonable and unfair for these men to make such demands at this time, but we have been more or less helpless with Public opinion, Courts, and everything else, to resist these things successfully without a Strike."[25]

The dispute still hung fire in the summer of 1914, when a cataclysm in Europe launched the war that was to be the requiem for nineteenth century civilization. Although the United States was officially neutral, the repercussions hit here with violent force. Capital markets and foreign trade were paralyzed to an unprecedented degree. On July 31 a financial hurricane ripped across the floors of European bourses, shutting them down with stunning swiftness. This abrupt closing of overseas markets sent waves of panic through the New York Stock Exchange, forcing it to suspend to avoid a ruinous collapse. It did not fully reopen until December 15.[26]

During the fall of 1913 the economy had begun slipping into a recession. The dislocations wrought by the outbreak of war turned this decline into a headlong fall. The loss of European markets, on which Americans depended heavily, sent shivers down the spines of businessmen and politicians alike. As export volume dropped, so did rail traffic. Woodrow Wilson found himself peering uneasily over his shoulder at the ghost of the last Democratic president, Grover Cleveland, who had taken office in 1893 to preside over the worst depression in American history. Wilson himself was at low ebb that fateful summer, distracted by a long, wrenching vigil at the bedside of his dying wife, who finally succumbed early in August.

But the rush of events allowed no one peace. Railroad strife hounded Wilson incessantly. Despite declining traffic and rising costs, the ICC granted only a token rate increase to one territory. The engineers and firemen happily accepted the recommendation of a mediator that only their wage demands (and none of the carriers' grievances) go to arbitration. At the same time, the Advisory Committee launched another effort to cut through the jungle of state regulation by getting a federal incorporation act. Thoughtful observers saw a major transportation crisis looming if solutions could not be found to the conflicts hurtling toward one another on a collision course. Even some shippers were beginning to see the light. J. Ogden Armour, the meat magnate, told a reporter bluntly, "All railroad rates should be increased, and at once."[27]

On the labor front most of the western roads stood firm, saying they would endure a strike rather than arbitrate only issues the engineers wanted. Lovett disagreed. He favored backing down on the arbitration issue if a strike could not be avoided, believing strongly that all the engineers would walk out, "and that consequently we simply could not operate the railroads because we could not get the skilled enginemen necessary for the purpose." Lovett was merely being practical, but another conviction lay behind his position. "The railroads . . . are practically helpless against the demands of employes [sic] as now organized," he stressed, "and . . . sooner or later this situation will have to be recognized by the public and the government; and that, while exercising the power of fixing rates, the government will have to assume responsibility for the regulation of the demands of labor."[28]

Events would soon make Lovett swallow those words. The distraught Wilson, aware that a strike was the last thing a depressed economy needed, summoned the railroad men and pleaded with them to accept arbitration on the mediator's terms as a concession to the abnormalities wrought by the war. When the managers agreed, the relieved President praised their patriotism and public spirit. Privately, he left them with the impression that the award of the arbitrator would be modest, which proved to be the case. Once again intervention had produced the worst of both worlds. The railroad men, who had opposed one-sided arbitration, were not hurt by the award but did not get their case heard. The unions, which had wanted arbitration, came away disappointed and vowed never to be lured into that trap again.[29]

In September a committee of railroad presidents asked Wilson's help in convincing the country that the carriers needed improved credit and additional income to meet wartime conditions. Wilson was amenable, calling their plea "a lucid statement of plain truth" and their need "very real." The ICC extended its recent rate increase to a second territory, and some prominent senators agreed the roads needed help. Encouraged by these developments, Lovett drafted a national incorporation bill and sent copies to Kahn, Trumbull, and two rail counsels for criticism.[30]

The judge had arrived at a clear sense in his own mind of what the future held. "Complete and exclusive Federal control," he concluded, "is the only solution to the railroad problem." It could come in one of two forms: federal ownership or regulation through comprehensive legislation. Since Lovett vastly preferred the latter, he thought "railroad men ought to get their views upon the subject settled; and then . . . endeavor to educate the public." More than a national incorporation act was needed. The ICC was overwhelmed by the growing burden of responsibilities thrust upon it, and urgently needed enlarging or reorganization. None of this could be done unless the carriers were freed from the shackles of state control. "The present conflicting control and regulation, through the various States," declared Lovett, "is intolerable and worse than stagnation."[31]

That a conservative state-rights Democrat like Lovett could arrive at these remarkable conclusions only demonstrates how profoundly American life had changed since the 1890s. The federal government had become a dominant force in society as it had never been before except during the Civil War. The Congress that adjourned in March 1915 had stayed in session an unprecedented 654 days in two years and appropriated a record $1.1 billion while incurring a $103 million deficit during the past fiscal year alone. It had created the federal reserve system, the federal trade commission, an income tax, a new antitrust act, and a lower tariff. Creeping federalism was fast becoming galloping federalism.[32]

Railroads too had changed. As they evolved into giant systems and therefore creatures of interstate commerce, the tortuous maze of state regulation grew ever more intolerable. The steady intrusion of Washington into their affairs had compounded this problem, forcing thoughtful men like Lovett to the belief that only Washington could remedy the conflict. During 1915 the railroads pursued their agenda of reform. Wilson was still sympathetic to their plight, but the recession and mounting criticism of the "radical" legislation pouring out of Congress made him more cautious. Nor did he appreciate the grumbling of railroad men over recent rate decisions. The railroads, he suggested coldly at one point, should "get together to help out prosperity rather than to be grouchy."[33]

Unimpressed, the western roads filed claim in the winter of 1915 for a rate increase amounting to a mere 2 percent of gross revenues. Clearly this was a token request; what the carriers really wanted was a signal from the ICC that reasonable requests would be treated reasonably. After four months of hearings and six weeks of deliberation the ICC readily conceded the financial plight of western roads, then granted a meager increase of about .3 percent. Wilson was shocked at the decision, and even Congress was roused to action. Senator Francis Newlands reiterated his belief that a national incorporation act would solve many of the problems, and promised a thorough investigation of rail regulation. A year passed before the inquiry got underway; as events revealed, the congressmen could not have picked a worse year to waste.[34]

"The trouble is not with regulation in itself," observed one thoughtful critic, ". . . the trouble is with the particular policy of regulation that has been followed." The need to rationalize national transportation policy was painfully obvious. There was widespread agreement that the ICC was the proper body to undertake that mission, yet so far the commission had ignored the problem despite the pleas of railroad men and one or two of its own members. One crucial question had yet to be answered decisively, although railroad men were not encouraged by the evidence they had seen so far: could federal regulation proceed without being warped by the tug and haul of politics? During 1916 rail executives got an answer that chilled them to the bones.[35]

During the winter of 1915–16 the four brotherhood leaders thrashed out their own agenda for the coming year. After vigorous debate they agreed to unite behind efforts to win an eight-hour work day. Convinced that the strike threat was their most potent weapon and mindful of past disappointments, the unions declared early that they would reject arbitration on the question. The carriers also presented a united front by creating a new organization called the General Conference of Railway Managers headed by Elisha Lee of the Pennsylvania. The lines were drawn for what loomed as the first real attempt at collective bargaining across the entire industry.[36]

The eight-hour issue was more complicated than most people realized, especially for railroads. No restriction on the length of workdays existed until March 1907, when Congress imposed a limit of sixteen hours in any twenty-four-hour period. Most railroad men worked a ten-hour day, with terms for overtime varying widely from road to road. For roadmen, however, the issue took on another dimension. Their work could not be measured conveniently in hours because a run had to be completed. Those assigned to prime runs such as deluxe passenger trains often finished a run in less than eight hours; others seldom made their trip inside ten hours because of the time lost waiting on sidetracks for priority traffic to pass. An eight-hour law would therefore not likely shorten their workday but, coupled with time and a half pay for overtime work, it *would* give them a generous raise in pay.

Railroad managers were convinced the issue was merely a ploy for higher wages, especially after the unions demanded the same pay for the shorter workday. On the Union Pacific the brotherhoods divided sharply. The engineers voted against joining the movement and promptly found themselves embroiled in a nasty dispute with the national leadership; the firemen and trainmen voted in favor of support, but 60 percent of the conductors were opposed. Mohler was confident that in a pinch two of the unions would reject a strike call. He had also to contend with the telegraphers, who had been in negotiations with the company for a year and a half over a number of issues including work hours. If that were not enough, all thirteen janitors in the Omaha headquarters struck for higher wages.[37]

"The whole country in the west seems to have the strike fever," groaned Mohler. The building trades were out in Omaha, the miners in Montana, and the longshoremen in the Northwest. Conservative editors howled in protest against the prospect of a major rail strike or the huge price tag that would accompany the eight-hour day. Teddy Roosevelt, languishing in political eclipse, spoke out strongly for curbing state authority with national regulation as a measure of national defense. Before anything could be done, however, the confrontation that everyone hoped to avoid took place. In June the brotherhoods and rail spokesmen came to an impasse over the eight-hour day and time-and-a-half issues. The rail managers appealed for federal arbitration; the unions spurned it. "This is indeed the most ominous cloud on the horizon," noted Woodrow Wilson.[38]

Wilson would have dearly loved to duck this fight. He was worried that summer for good reason. The European war was inching steadily closer to the United States, thanks in large measure to his own policies. Moreover, this most idealistic of presidents was deeply committed that season to the ideal of being reelected in the fall. The two gravest perils to that hope were the war and a downturn in the economy, which could well happen if a major rail strike tied it into knots. But intervening in the dispute could be just as disastrous as ignoring it. "The poker is hot at both ends," warned Josephus Daniels, one of the President's most trusted advisers, who suggested letting the two sides fight it out themselves.[39]

In August the combatants assembled in New York to act out the ritual of mediation, which reached its predictable failure on the 12th. The carriers again asked for arbitration; the brotherhoods rejected the call, announced that they would walk out on September 4, and waited to see what Wilson would do. Reluctantly the President sent his private secretary to summon both sides to Washington, telling them that a strike at this time would be disastrous. The two leaderships hurried to catch trains while making a show of standing firm. "This fight is to industry in America," intoned a rail spokesman, "what the war is to Europe."[40]

The rail leaders had tried to anticipate this meeting. One of them reminded Lovett that history must not repeat itself:

> Two years ago, when considering the demands of the engineers and firemen of the Western lines, we came hastily and abruptly to the same point as we are now approaching in this controversy, and because of the same fear on the part of the President and the public, the President hastily interested himself and took immediate steps toward the adjustment of the case. This is what I feared would be the result in the present negotiations . . . we were wholly unprepared to meet such an issue, as the railroads have never properly . . . stated their position to the Administration or the public. . . .

The Union Pacific had already hired an advertising man from Chicago to promote opposition to the eight-hour day in towns along the company's routes. Ballard Dunn, a former lawyer and editor, had in Mohler's opinion done so well at this work in Nebraska that he was kept on to tour thirty towns in Kansas "where public education friendly to transportation interests, is badly needed."[41]

Unfortunately, the President was something of a missionary in his own right and not readily susceptible to the blandishments of others. On August 14, two separate tribes of officials, sweating heavily in the summer heat, arrived in Washington to plead their cases with Wilson. That morning the brotherhoods told him solemnly that their members had been thirty years preparing for this final battle. In the afternoon Elisha Lee and seventeen rail presidents informed Wilson that the eight-hour day would cost them $100 million annually and, with time and a half, would simply bankrupt them. The President urged both groups to keep the national welfare paramount, and offered a proposal to the executives: accept the eight-hour day in principle, leaving overtime and other issues to arbitration.[42]

Next day, both groups saw Wilson again and refused to budge from their positions. The frustrated President then hinted to reporters that he would draw up his own compromise and ask Congress to approve it. On August 16 he typed up and dispatched to Lee a memorandum that included concession of the eight-hour day, postponement of the overtime issue and all demands of the carriers until experience showed the actual effects of the eight-hour day, and the creation of a commission to study and report those effects without recommendation. A dejected Lee polled the presidents three times on the proposal; it met with a crushing defeat every time. Despite Wilson's appeal for silence, some of the executives vented their bitterness to reporters. The President was playing politics, they charged, spending their principles to serve his own interest. "It will be a hot day," growled one sweltering executive, "when we ask Washington to help us out again."[43]

Once again relations between government and the railroads wore the thick glaze of irony that had become their natural patina in recent years. Enlightened observers had long hailed arbitration as the rational solution to such disputes. But arbitration, like the old railway pools, was a game that worked only if everyone agreed to play by the rules, which they seldom did. In this case, one side insisted on arbitration while the other absolutely refused it. Who then arbitrated disagreements over arbitration? Wilson took that burden on himself, largely because he saw no other choice. The heat was on in every sense of the word.

On August 17 Wilson sent telegrams asking the presidents of every large railroad to come to Washington. That same day he welcomed on the White House lawn some six hundred division leaders of the brotherhoods, whom he had also summoned to Washington. He urged them to accept his compromise, extolled his belief in the rightness of the eight-hour day, and spoke passionately of the public suffering that would accompany a strike. The union men retired to the Bijou Theater where, after fierce debate that afternoon and again the next morning, they agreed to support the compromise. On the morning of the 18th they marched back up Pennsylvania Avenue to the White House. Beneath a merciless sun the President again greeted them on the lawn, thanked them profusely for their support, endured their cheering and whooping, and hurried back inside to await the rail executives.[44]

They began arriving by car a short time later and were ushered into the Green Room, where the blinds had been drawn tight against the torrid sun. Standing in the darkened room, fanning themselves profusely, the executives were startled when a portière at one end of the room was drawn back. There in the doorway stood the President, framed in bright sunlight, immaculately clad in a white duck suit, lacking only a golden halo to resemble an inspiration of Fra Angelico. He thanked them for braving the summer heat to answer his call so promptly. Hale Holden of the Burlington stepped forth from the murmuring flock and said in a hushed voice that the railroads were fighting for the principle of arbitration and could not accept a proposal that undermined it. How could any future issue be negotiated if the unions were granted so large a concession as the eight-hour day without debate?[45]

Wilson replied coldly that he had to deal with a condition, not a principle. A national crisis loomed and must be averted. If the presidents would cooperate, he would do everything possible to relieve any financial burden from the eight-hour day with a rate increase from the ICC. He then told them a story of his teaching days at Princeton, when a student who had failed his course pleaded that his mother was in precarious health and might collapse at the news of her son's failure. If she died, the student added, Wilson would be responsible. Nonsense, snapped Wilson; her death rested squarely with the boy's failure to master the course, not with its teacher. Pointing a stern finger at the executives, Wilson spelled out the moral for them: "If a strike comes, the public will know where the responsibility rests. It will not be upon me."

The portière was drawn shut as abruptly as it had opened, leaving the dazed executives to realize that their audience had ended barely twenty minutes after it had begun. As they filed out onto the lawn the tone of their conversation was something less than reverential. "What in hell did the President mean?" muttered one supplicant. "I suppose," shrugged another, "he means it is up to us to settle the strike."[46]

But they could not settle it. Wilson fired off telegrams urging those rail presidents not already in Washington to come at once, then issued an appeal to the country saying, "I have recommended the concession of the eight-hour day . . . because I believe the concession right." The change should be adopted "even where the actual work to be done cannot be completed within eight hours" because society now sanctioned the idea. On August 21, a steamy day when the temperature climbed past a hundred degrees, Wilson met again with the rail presidents, now swollen to fifty in number thanks to his call. For an hour he lectured them earnestly on the need to avert a crisis, stressing national defense and "the extraordinary situation that will immediately emerge out of the European war."[47]

The presidents listened intently, then returned to the Willard Hotel where they released a statement denouncing the eight-hour day as a cynical grab for a wage hike and Wilson's demand to settle without arbitration as "inconceivable in a democracy like ours." Their position had hardened, but they could find no suitable course of action. The next day, August 22, a delegation of rail leaders visited Wilson and offered a deal: they would surrender the eight-hour day in return for arbitration of the overtime issue and the President's guarantee of a rate increase, however he managed it. Wilson spent the rest of the day closeted with Francis Newlands and W. C. Adamson, the two interstate commerce committee chieftains of Congress. But Congress could make no such promise; all the chairmen could deliver was a vow to consider reorganizing the ICC by adding two members, and that would take time. The deal fell apart before it had even come together.[48]

"Matters rapidly approaching crisis here," Lovett reported early on the morning of August 26, "and break is liable to occur at any time." Two days later the executives delivered their formal reply to Wilson, making some concessions but standing firm in their demand for arbitration. The four brotherhoods, proclaiming that they had $15 million in their war chest, issued a strike order for September 4. An incredulous Wilson begged them to recall it and was told that was not possible. The president now saw no choice but to go before Congress and request legislation. A joint session assembled hastily on the afternoon of August 29. Dressed nattily in a blue blazer, white flannel trousers, and white shoes, the first president ever to appear before Congress in informal garb according to one observer, Wilson looked curiously at odds with the grim purpose of his mission.[49]

After summarizing the crisis and declaring a strike out of the question, Wilson itemized the legislation he wanted: the eight-hour day for railroad employees; a commission to study the effects of the eight-hour day; immediate enlargement of the ICC; approval for the ICC to consider rate increases if operating costs increased; amendment of the law to require arbitration; power for the President to take control of the railroads and draft its workers if conditions warranted. The applause was thunderous, the response predictable. Congressmen let Wilson know his package was too large to pass by September 4; at best he could get the eight-hour day and the commission, with the rest postponed until the next session. The President hesitated briefly, then agreed to this strategy.[50]

The railroad presidents were furious but helpless to deflect events. E. P. Ripley of the Atchison growled that Wilson's appeal for the eight-hour day proved how ignorant the President was about the subject. Unmoved by angry rhetoric, Adamson drafted a brief bill that went before Newlands's Senate committee on the morning of August 31. Lovett was among those who testified during that frantic session, and his remarks unfolded a grim vision of an emerging future that no railroad man cared to glimpse whole.[51]

In his professorial way Lovett reminded the senators that railroads had entered a new age where they were "essentially public institutions" no longer owned by individuals but by diversified stockholders. Their funds for development came not from bankers but from investors who bought securities from bankers. To punish them for past sins, therefore, was only to harm the public, who would have to bear the cost of any increase in wages. The railroads must either raise rates or cut back expenses in the form of reduced maintenance. Since the roads differed widely from each other, the effect could be disastrous for poorer lines with weak credit. The cost of Adamson's bill would be $60 million, which would go to the men who were already the best paid railroad workers in the nation.

"What they really want is an increase in pay," the judge insisted. "That is the real issue." If the brotherhoods could gain $60 million under duress, "why, that will be an attractive method for dealing with the question of time and a half overtime." Was it to be, Lovett asked, "that one hundred millions of people are going to be absolutely tied, hand and foot, and put at the feet of 350,000 skilled, highly paid, and highly organized workmen?" He could not believe the people would allow four men, from Wall Street or anywhere else, "to keep within their hands power to paralyze the national life." And what was the great rush? Why must the bill be passed before such large and grave questions could be investigated by a commission or some competent body?

Senator Newlands asked the same question of the spokesman for the four brotherhoods. Why the need for such haste? Could not the strike be delayed to avoid working under such pressure? A tearful A. B. Garretson, spokesman of the combined unions, replied that he would be denounced as a traitor by his men if he did so. He recalled his days as a railroad man in Mexico, when vultures followed the train in hopes that it might hit a cow. "Now the public is the carcass," he added mournfully. "And we are all, perhaps, the vultures. . . . The country will pay."[52]

He was right. The hearings amounted to little more than a formality. That afternoon the House committee received the bill and reported it favorably the next morning. On the afternoon of September 1 the House voted approval; the Senate followed suit the next day, enabling the bill to reach the White House at 7:10 p.m. The brotherhood leaders sent out messages at 8:35 p.m. rescinding the strike vote, and Wilson signed the bill next morning aboard his private rail car. A passing yard engine greeted him with several long whistle blasts. The eight-hour bill was law; the other issues would have to await the next session of Congress. "It is," declared the President, "the climax of a very happy day."[53]

Not everyone shared this feeling. Ripley served notice that the Atchison would not comply until "ordered to do so by the court of last resort." A disgusted Lovett left Washington just after the hearings, convinced that Congress would enact the bill "to please the Unions and avert a strike." The burden for the railroads would be heavy: a twenty percent wage hike at once, and the certainty that the eight-hour day would spread to other classes of workers. "I never before felt as much ashamed for the Government of the United States," the judge raged privately. "If Congress had had any backbone, it would have immediately passed a law prohibiting a strike until the controversy could be investigated . . . instead of being driven . . . under whip and spur by these leaders."[54]

A historic turning point had been reached in both government-business relations and labor negotiations, and its influence would reach deep into the twentieth century. Wilson saw the Adamson Act as imperfect but necessary to avert a strike that would have amounted to a national calamity. "All here recognized that the strike would be the greatest catastrophe that ever befell our country," wrote a southern congressman. "Another thing," he added, "if the strike had not been averted, the present Administration would have been destroyed."[55]

But the price had been high. What some people saw as a protective umbrella of government influence struck others a spreading web. To avoid the strike Congress had snatched from the railroads control over the wages paid their workers, which was by far the largest single factor in the cost of operations. By 1916, then, the government had taken over both sides of the ledger, income and expenses, and the mechanisms for regulating one were in no way coordinated with those for adjusting the other. Ahead lay even more drastic controls, but they served merely to confirm what had already taken place by 1916: the railroads could still manage their affairs, but they could no longer manage their destinies.

12

The Takeover

On a fine January afternoon in 1916 the portly A. L. Mohler, seeking relief from the cares piling up in his office, motored to a park in Omaha with his wife and mother-in-law to do a little skating. He wobbled onto the ice and tried a few strokes. Suddenly he lost his balance and flopped backward, striking his head hard. Too heavy for his wife and chauffeur to lift, he lay on the ice ten minutes before help arrived and got him to a hospital, where he did not regain consciousness for several hours. Three weeks later he returned to work and scorned all suggestions that he stay away longer, feeling more embarrassed than injured. "There is no fool like an old fool," he told a well-wisher mournfully, "and I have been a good example."[1]

But he was in worse shape than he knew. At sixty-six the burden of responsibility had worn Mohler down, and the pace was quickening just as he was slowing. Still weak from his accident and dead tired, he came to terms with Lovett over his pension and retired from office. Lovett was sincere in regretting his loss and anxious to make his remaining years comfortable. To his place Lovett named the loyal and hard-working E. E. Calvin, a lean, taciturn Indianian who at fifty-eight had already put in thirty-four years with the Union Pacific and Missouri Pacific. Like most rail officers of his generation, Calvin had learned the railroad from the bottom up. He had returned to the company after a ten-year absence in 1914 to replace the retiring Bancroft as vice-president and general manager of the Short Line.[2]

Mohler's departure ushered in an age of transition for the Union Pacific, one accelerated by the rapid changes that swept through the rail industry as a whole. Those eager for portents might have taken a closer look at Mohler's

SOLID AND RELIABLE: A. L. Mohler, the tough, hard-working president who served both Harriman and Judge Lovett well until a skating accident undid him.

accident. Like that unfortunate officer, the railroads were skating into trouble and would suffer a fall from which they would never recover their former place.

Man and nature alike conspired to make the winter of 1916–17 one of the most miserable on record. Low temperatures and massive snowfalls gripped the nation, and no section suffered more than the West, where storm after storm raged across the mountains. As always, the flash point for the Union Pacific was the fifth district between Cheyenne and Laramie, which boasted some of the roughest weather on the continent. The first blizzard struck in mid-November, pushed by howling winds that buried cuts in snow and sent thermometers plunging to thirty degrees below zero at Sherman. So vicious was the wind that switches and flagmen protecting trains could not be seen, forcing crews to block trains a station apart. Unfortunately, this caused many engines to freeze up, blockading traffic between Hermosa and Buford, one of the last remaining single-track stretches on the line.[3]

There had been trouble on the Union Pacific even before the storms hit. In 1916 the war overwhelmed railroads with business as orders poured in for food and other goods. The Panama Canal closed, thrusting on western roads a huge volume of eastbound business that formerly moved by water. Atlantic ports also felt the pinch as some ships shifted to more profitable routes. On the Union Pacific revenue freight tonnage soared 25 percent, ton-miles carried 44 percent, and average distance per ton hauled 15 percent. Freight revenues jumped 33 percent, but money alone was helpless to move the flood of traffic skewered so heavily in one direction.[4]

By April the glut of grain at Chicago was so great that the Union Pacific lent other lines fifty cars it could not spare. In July the Southern Pacific put a freight embargo on its Sunset Route to reduce congestion at Galveston. A month later the Union Pacific was forced to the same extreme despite J. D. Farrell's fears that the embargo would be "seized upon as an excuse by the President and Congress to enact drastic legislation." Gradually this crisis eased, but on November 1 a severe shortage of boxcars tied up the Short Line. The heat for this snarl fell on a tough, burly Irishman who had just become general manager in June, William M. Jeffers. Never one to dodge a bullet, Jeffers called the situation "indefensible" and blamed it on the failure of pumping and coaling stations "due largely to lack of maintenance and failure to provide proper supplies to keep pumping stations in service."[5]

Jeffers managed to untangle the bottleneck only to have the blizzard paralyze the line days later. Once the line began to clear, some two thousand cars a day moved through Laramie, far more than that terminal could handle. Jeffers had to hold back trains to get the cars through the yard. He desperately needed good weather to clean up the backlog, but in December another killer storm blockaded the line completely for the first time in twenty years. Reluctantly Lovett approved an embargo on competitive freight while crews struggled to open the road. Oregon apple growers fired off angry protests, as did other shippers. Lovett did what he could to appease them, but relief was nowhere in sight.[6]

All winter long the howlers kept coming, pushed by winds that smashed all previous records. In Wyoming the wind *averaged* over forty miles an hour for most of January and reached as high as eighty-one miles an hour on one day. Calvin called the conditions at Rock River the worst he had seen in forty years' experience there. "The storms at times came up so suddenly that trains were caught between stations, and were so terrific that men simply could not live in them. The snow and dirt drifted into the cuts faster than it could be thrown out." Twenty dead engines sat at Rock River, where the temperature rose above freezing for only three days between November and April. The same pattern continued in February as the men dug out of one blockade only to be hit by another blizzard. During one crisis near Hanna, Wyoming, Jeffers and a livestock agent toiled for two days alongside the crews, digging furiously with little to eat and no change of clothes.[7]

The storms raged on into spring, climaxing with a sleet barrage late in April that knocked out 1,500 telegraph poles. For Calvin the battle with nature compounded the growing crisis over cars. A distraught Farrell reported the Huntington yard, the meeting point between the Union Pacific and the Short Line, to be completely blocked in mid-January. "We estimate 15,000 cars or

60% of grain is still on hand at stations on our line awaiting movement,'' he added, ''10,000 cars of which [is] destined east of Huntington.'' Calvin reckoned that the Union Pacific had only 12,520 of the 22,274 boxcars it owned, and was losing them to other lines at the rate of 85 a day. ''The situation is serious on all three lines of the System,'' he concluded grimly, ''and it will probably be necessary to adopt unusual measures to protect ourselves.''[8]

But what measures? Lovett, his presidents, and B. J. Winchell, the director of traffic, wracked their brains for a way out of their dilemma. Winchell suggested telling shippers frankly that they should use other lines until the Union Pacific got free of the storms and car shortages because their complaints had grown so bitter. Calvin admitted in March that he could not restore normal service for at least a month even if good weather returned, which it did not. All their remarks rubbed Lovett the wrong way. The December embargo still rankled, a grave mistake in his mind, and he wanted no more of it. The company, he snapped, would not be disgraced by another one unless forced into it by abnormally bad weather. Other roads were having similar problems; why should the Union Pacific advertise its difficulties? Farrell too came down hard against an embargo even though his shippers were screaming and he had no cars to move local business.[9]

Despite these handicaps, the road acquitted itself well that dismal winter. Once escaped from the clutches of the storms, engines on all main lines made round trips every twenty-four hours. The power was holding up but, as Calvin admitted, ''Our men are generally pretty well worn out.'' In a detailed and incisive analysis of the train service, Jeffers did not hesitate to single out the weak points while lavishing praise on the men. ''When it is taken into account that the past five months has been one continuous storm in Wyoming,'' he concluded, ''with the track singled and current of traffic reversed almost daily at one point or another, due to either one or the other of the main lines being blocked, it is a remarkable performance.''[10]

Nor was the Union Pacific alone in its misery. Business continued to pour forth in unprecedented volume, much of it war orders bound for eastern ports. The return of Germany to unrestricted submarine warfare in February 1917, however, shut down Atlantic shipping lanes. Rail cars piled up in eastern yards and turned into temporary warehouses, clogging every available track in long strings until the eerie silence of gridlock fell across usually bustling terminals. It was as if the continent had tilted and all the nation's rail cars rolled eastward. Here was the chief source of the car crisis apart from the weather. ''Cars, cars everywhere, and not a ship to load,'' mused one spectator.[11]

Then, in April, the United States entered the war and the tempo of industrial output quickened without any regard for how goods were to be moved or how the gridlock in eastern ports would be unraveled. The carriers agreed on some rules for handling the reconsignment and diversion of freight only to have the ICC suspend them because shippers protested so vehemently. On April 11 the carriers, with ICC blessing, formed a special committee known as the Railroads' War Board to coordinate their efforts. They would need all the help they could give each other, for ahead lay the gravest transportation crisis in the nation's history.[12]

The railroads had no intention of obeying the Adamson Act without a court test, and the unions vowed to walk out if the act did not go into effect as scheduled on January 1, 1917. Some hectic dealing produced an agreement to wait for the Supreme Court to rule, which it did in March. By a narrow five to four margin the court upheld the act, and the two sides negotiated a way to implement it, thereby averting a strike at a time when the rail system was all but paralyzed anyway. Earnest calls for efficient transportation as a patriotic duty rang through the halls of Congress and the agencies. The problem was that no one had yet figured out how to translate the rhetoric of good intention into the reality of policy.[13]

Many rail executives saw the Newlands Committee hearings as their last best hope, but it proved too little, too late. Although Wilson had called for an investigation in December 1915, the hearings did not get underway until November 1916. After two weeks they were suspended and did not resume until March 19, 1917. By that time the rail gridlock was producing severe shortages of food and coal in the East and Midwest, and the public mood was turning ugly. By one estimate, some 50,000 empties sat amid the loaded cars trapped in eastern terminals while the West pleaded for 60,000 cars to move freight. Attempts to relieve the congestion bogged down in futile efforts to skirt the laws against pooling and demands by state commissions that roads keep their cars at home.[14]

When the hearings resumed in March 1917, the first witness called was Lovett, whose views interested the committee enough to keep him before it for a week. The judge repeated some familiar themes, and warned that "if the present system or lack of system of regulation is continued there will be stagnation in railroad development." Asked if he favored pooling, the judge said no. "I believe in competition in railroad service," he added, "but not competition in rates. That is impossible without discrimination and rebates." Throughout the long ordeal he fended off questions from hostile congressmen with extraordinary patience. An admiring friend likened him to "a great St. Bernard dog, set upon by a crowd of very small mongrels, who considers it beneath his dignity to take a bite at any of them, in spite of all the yelping and snapping going on."[15]

By 1917 an ominous situation had emerged. Railroad management had become more a prisoner of politics than it had ever been. The politics of rail operations had become a three-cornered hat dance among managers, shippers, and labor in which the shippers had captured the ICC and labor had gained the backing, however unwilling, of the administration. The carriers, with no one in their corner, had lost control over both rates and wages at a time when war orders sent prices rocketing upward and the crush of traffic wore down their physical plant at an alarming rate. Money for maintenance and improvements was urgently needed, but where was it to come from? The capital market was gorged with government issues, and rail securities held little appeal for investors as long as the ICC held their revenues in check and prices continued their upward spiral.

Even prosperous roads like the Union Pacific faced a nasty dilemma. When the war erupted in 1914, Lovett ordered all capital expenditures suspended at once except where safety or necessity demanded. The war was such an extraordinary event, he explained, that "any forecast of the future is unreliable except that opinion here is unanimous that for several years demand for money abroad will be so great and interest rates will be so high that money will not be available for industrial development, and large improvements works." Frank A. Vanderlip, president of National City Bank, urged the company to keep its funds liquid. Soaring costs only confirmed Lovett's reluctance to spend money on improvements at prices he deemed excessive and unreasonable.[16]

Weak roads had no money for betterments or way to get it; stronger roads hesitated to spend their funds when costs were high and income low. The fact-minded Kruttschnitt marched a parade of pregnant statistics past the Newlands Committee to demonstrate that *real* freight rates, still a novel concept in 1917, had dropped steadily since 1899, and that railroads had absorbed about $8 billion in real rates during that time thanks to increased efficiency. His message was plain: shippers and labor had reaped the benefits of efficiency, not the carriers. On the subject of labor Kruttschnitt was equally blunt. "Labor no longer looks to the carrier, to its employer, as being in charge of its wages and destiny," he declared, ". . . it looks to the state legislatures and to Washington."[17]

Whatever help Washington rendered others, it left the railroads out in the cold. The Newlands Committee hearings drifted on into December 1917, then adjourned subject to a chairman's call that never came. The war simply passed the committee by, and its chairman as well. Hard at work in his office on the afternoon of Christmas Eve, the senator collapsed and died later that night. "He was not showy," mourned the *Times*, "he was useful."[18]

To relieve the financial crunch the railroads decided to try yet again for a rate increase, asking in March 1917 for 15 percent across the board. Lovett was reluctant to join in the request until an urgent appeal from his traffic director changed his mind. His instincts proved sound, for the hearings amounted to little more than a rehash of earlier ones, and in July the ICC denied the request except for coal, coke, and iron. The naive belief that increased war business would provide railroads the cash they needed was quickly shattered as prices kept rising, profits shrank, and several roads hemorrhaged red ink as winter approached with its threat of another gridlock.[19]

The carriers applied for a rehearing, but events outflanked them. Late in July Lovett was appointed to the government's newly created War Industries Board; the following month he was put on an important purchasing committee and also given charge of the priorities system created to expedite war traffic. A tag system had been devised for government agencies to mark priority shipments, but it broke down at once as officials applied the tags indiscriminately until more cars bore them than not. Lovett did little to untangle the snarl. He shared

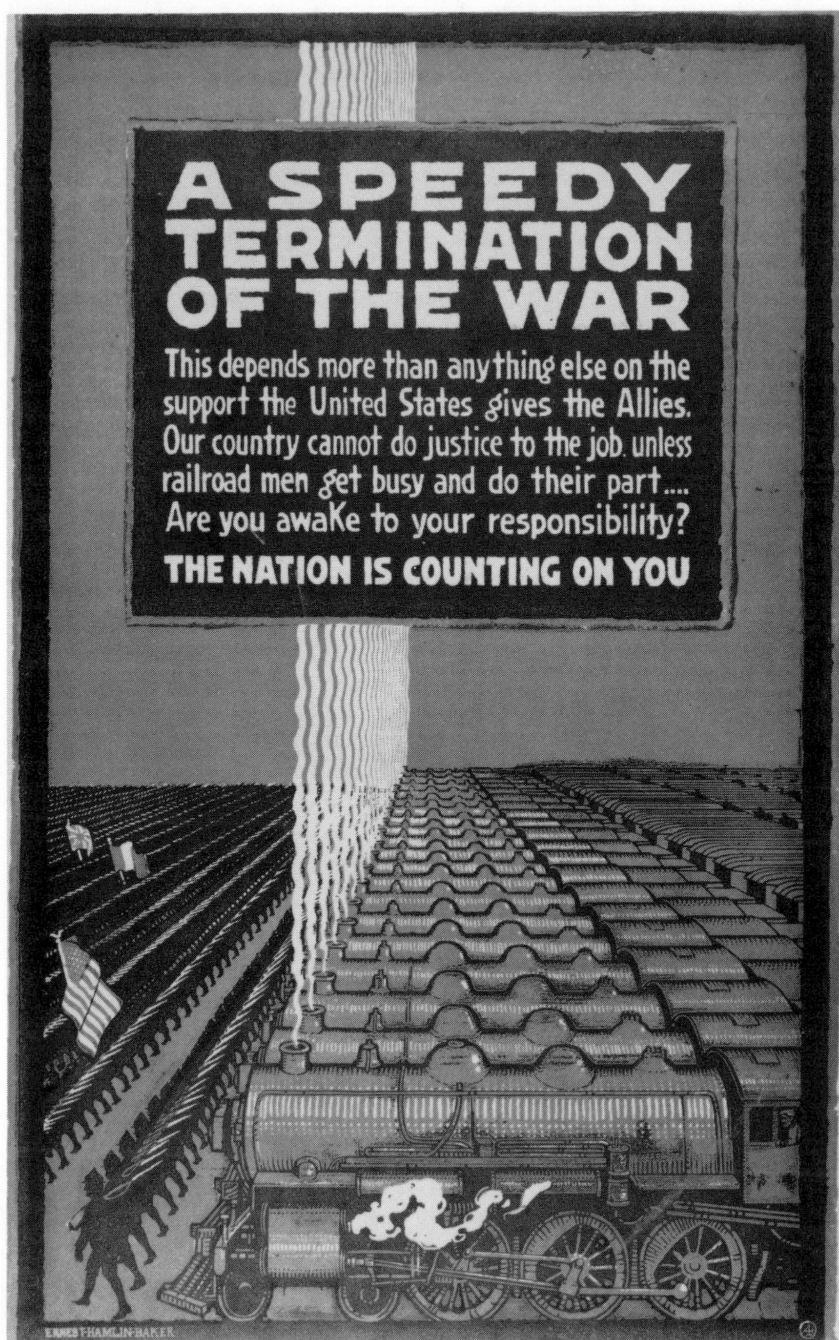

WINNING THE WAR: A World War I poster exhorts railroaders to do their duty.

the view that he lacked the authority to cancel priority orders, and he was reluctant to issue new ones except in dire emergencies. As a result, the lack of coordination in transportation worsened steadily.[20]

Shortages of equipment and labor along with bungled allocations of coal aggravated the traffic snarl. The carriers found themselves losing unskilled workers to war industries that paid higher wages. "Situation regarding labor is becoming acute all over the West," E. E. Calvin had warned in April 1917. The B & O was already hiring large numbers of women to fill vacancies, and the Union Pacific followed suit. By September more than three hundred women were working in the Omaha offices, which caused some scrambling to create such amenities as rest rooms and lunch rooms for them. The mandatory retirement age for mechanics and other skilled employees was postponed for the duration.[21]

Despite vigorous efforts, the railroads were utterly swamped by the rush of war orders and continued pileup of goods in eastern ports along with the normally heavy flow of autumn business. A growing cry to unify the rail system must have made managers weep with frustration, especially since some of the loudest howlers were those who had done so much to bar the carriers from operating in a unified way. The War Board simply lacked the authority to impose such a system, and it was undermined by petty bickering among some of the roads. On December 5 the ICC issued a report to Congress calling for unified operations during the war period. This could be done in two ways: by suspending the antitrust laws and antipooling clause in the Interstate Commerce Act or by nationalizing the railroads.[22]

On December 26 Wilson released a proclamation placing all rail and water systems under federal control. Under the circumstances he made the correct if not the only choice. The President's message showed that he had learned much about the railroad problem since taking office. He acknowledged that the War Board and its member roads had tried diligently but lacked the power to accomplish what was needed. "In mere fairness to them the full authority of the Government must be substituted," he added, if only because the measures needed to create that authority were even more difficult to forge than the complexities of federal operation.[23]

"The strong arm of government authority," declared one approving ICC commissioner, "is essential if the transportation situation is to be radically improved." No doubt the irony of this statement eluded him entirely. What federal control did above all else was free the railroads from both the coils of state regulation and what Albro Martin has aptly called "the palsied hand of the ICC." Once the government took charge, no more was heard of clashes over rate regulation or other disputes that had hamstrung the carriers.[24]

One of Jay Gould's favorite market tactics when someone attacked one of his companies had been to sell enough of its stock to the enemy that they dared not let the price fall too far. In effect the railroads had accomplished the same thing without any effort on their part. Now that the government was responsible for their performance, it could not help but view their problems in a more sympathetic light. Another analogy impressed itself on one observer, who noted that the government was seeking the very objective of unified, efficient transportation Harriman had endeavored to create until he ran against "the impossible snag of public opinion."[25]

What no one yet realized was the extent to which Wilson's decree marked the passing of the era dominated by the railroad. Contrary to the belief of many people, the takeover was not an aberration of wartime conditions but one more episode in the radical transformation of the place occupied by the railroads in American life.

Even before Wilson's proclamation the war had come home to the Union Pacific in several ways. A threat to blow up the Omaha bridge in August 1915 prompted Mohler to find out quietly "exactly how many Germans and Austrians we have in the service." The following June, when Wilson called up National Guard units, the executive committee gave any employees engaged in military service an indefinite leave at full pay for married men and half pay for single men. Once the United States entered the war, the sleepy post at Fort Riley, Kansas, mushroomed into a major training installation, Camp Funston. To service its needs, the Union Pacific built twenty miles of second track from Manhattan and thirteen miles of new running and side track. The company also promoted Liberty Bonds to its employees and took $5 million worth itself in the first drive.[26]

None of these activities prepared the Union Pacific or any other road for the changes that followed Wilson's proclamation. A new federal agency, the United States Railroad Administration (USRA), was created with William G. McAdoo as its director general. Since McAdoo was also secretary of the treasury and preoccupied with the bond drives, much of his work fell to his assistant, Walker D. Hines of the Atchison. The new organization included divisions for law, finance and purchasing, operation, traffic, labor, public service and accounting, capital expenditures, and inland waterways. At first the roads were divided into three regions: eastern, western, and southern, but in June 1918 the eastern was split into two and the western into three regional groups. Under this arrangement the Union Pacific found itself in the central western group except for its lines north of Huntington, Oregon, which were placed in the northwestern group.[27]

In March 1918 Congress passed the Federal Control Act authorizing the President to make agreements guaranteeing each railroad compensation based on its average net operating income for the three years ending June 30, 1917. The act contained provisions for maintenance, special circumstances, and claims disputes; it also authorized the President to fix rates and require additions or betterments on any line where needed. Wilson delegated these powers to the director general of the Railroad Administration, which was to (and did) function as a nonpolitical agency. However, it was staffed chiefly by executives from the railroads, laying the agency open to charges that it was little more than the rail industry lobby come to power for self-serving purposes.[28]

Oblivious to these rumblings, McAdoo in March 1918 simply made the president of every road its chief executive for federal control, thereby bypassing board chairmen and committees. When controversy continued to rage over the rail executives promoting their self-interest, McAdoo responded with an order in May requiring each road to appoint a federal manager who must sever all official connections with the railroad company. While this ended the furor over conflict of interest, it forced managers on every road to choose between service to company or government. The result was a frantic shuffle of personnel that would have some interesting repercussions in the postwar period.[29]

Lovett was the first to leave the Union Pacific on what everyone hoped would be a temporary absence. He resigned from both the road and the War Industries Board to join USRA as head of the capital expenditures division. His post as chairman went to C. B. Seger, the vice-president and comptroller, who had begun his career on the Southern Pacific in his native Louisiana and gone with the Union Pacific after the unmerger. In July Seger also assumed the presidency as Calvin left the company to serve as federal manager of the Union Pacific. J. D. Farrell, however, decided to remain as president of the Navigation lines rather than enter government service.[30]

Every corporate officer agonized over which way to go. In that sense the war experience helped reshape the Union Pacific's management, but the company's officers left their own mark as well. One of them beamed at a rumor that the Railroad Administration was "Unionpacificizing" the nation's railroads. As an accountant he swelled with pride when told that the company's accounting organization was "far ahead of any other railroad in the United States." Whatever the Union Pacific's influence, USRA created what one ICC commissioner called a "mild revolution in transportation," one that reversed trends of the past two decades.[31]

For most of the century shippers had dominated transportation policy through their influence with the ICC and Congress. During this brief interlude their dominance waned as USRA took command of both operating and regulatory functions. It transformed the railroads into an efficient system by doing what individual carriers could never do: bypass the ICC, ignore the antitrust and antipooling statutes, and brush aside the interference of state commissions. The ICC had for two decades specialized in negative policy, but negativism could not make the railroads run as a unified system or respond effectively to an emergency.[32]

Under the Railroad Administration the roads could do things never before possible. They could pool equipment, share terminals, yards, depots, and other facilities, repair cars and engines in the nearest shop, create joint agencies, consolidate shipments, standardize designs, curtail marginal service, and eliminate such abuses as cross-hauling. And they could raise rates. In May 1918 McAdoo issued an order hiking freight rates about 28 percent and passenger fares about 18 percent. Ironically, the freight increase came to just about what the railroads had sought in their last three supplications to the ICC. With the commission dropped into limbo by the takeover, shippers lost their usual forum for complaint. "There was not even any formal consultation with the Interstate Commerce Commission," said Hines with a smile. "There was no consultation with the State commissions."[33]

WAR VETERAN: A spruced-up 4–6–2 Pacific locomotive makes its pitch for the Liberty Loan Drive, 1918.

The increases were unprecedented and wholly unappreciated by shippers and travelers, who also resented every change in operations that made service more efficient at their expense. USRA unraveled the priorities tangle by creating a permit system that controlled traffic at its source. Cars could not be loaded until assurance came that they could be promptly unloaded at their destination. To lessen the shortage of cars, shippers were prodded to load cars more fully, resulting in an increased average load per car of 2.2 tons or 8 percent during the first ten months of 1918. Engines, also in short supply, were allocated to wherever need was greatest, and the shopmen agreed to increase their hours so that more repair work could be done on the overtaxed power supply. Some shops moved to work weeks of sixty or seventy hours.[34]

The transcontinental roads had been wrangling for months over where and how to reduce passenger service in order to facilitate freight movement. Passionate objections were raised over everything from schedules to the consolidation of trains. The Milwaukee on its own initiative discontinued a Chicago-Denver sleeper run jointly with the Union Pacific, then admitted it had acted rashly. Even the high-minded Lovett found himself drawn into the fray. As the Atchison, Western Pacific, Southern Pacific, and Rio Grande pulled off trains, pressure mounted for the Union Pacific to eliminate its premium fare Overland Limited or consolidate it with the Los Angeles Limited. "Each of these two trains is a high class, widely advertised, transcontinental train," protested the judge, "and after all these years ought to possess a very valuable 'good will.' Why should this be destroyed . . . ? If there is some great public necessity for it, I have not heard of it."[35]

On any such issue, railroad managers had to walk a delicate line between patriotic duty and loyalty to company. In June 1918 Seger instructed one of his accountants to handle matters "FIRST as the corporation may be interested; and SECOND as the Federal Managers may desire your assistance." Lovett could not refrain from giving Seger occasional advice on policy matters, and Federal Manager Calvin found himself in the strangest position of all. While still managing the road he had been associated with for decades, he was expected to act temporarily as if his loyalty belonged elsewhere. It was a tough balancing act for all of them, yet this format worked surprisingly well during 1918, when everyone's attention was focused on the war effort and differences were submerged beneath that goal.[36]

The results were impressive. Carl R. Gray, who headed the division of operations for the Railroad Administration and later became president of the Union Pacific, recalled with pride moving nearly 6.5 million troops in eleven months, most of them eastward into the region already congested with traffic. In July alone the roads carried 1.1 million men an average of 748 miles each, a remarkable feat considering that one division of troops required 59 trains for the men and 59 more trains for their equipment. The car shortage, which had reached 150,000 in November 1917, dropped to 15,000 a year later as the accumulation of cars, which totaled 200,000 in February 1918, was cut to 40,000 by November. Afterward McAdoo told Gray that he had never seen a group of men "who so measured up to what the emergency required as the railroad officers."[37]

The armistice ending the war in November 1918 changed things entirely. At once the energy and dedication that had gone into the war effort turned toward a long agenda of unfinished business. How long would federal control last? What would be done with the railroads? What policies would be formulated to deal with the host of prewar issues interrupted by the takeover? Railroad managers shuddered at the thought of returning to the horrors of prewar conditions, shippers bitterly resented how the USRA had ignored their interests, and labor pressed its demands anew. Wartime inflation had hurt all three groups deeply, though in different ways, and all looked to the government to remedy their ills. But each group wanted something very different from Washington.

For two decades the "railroad problem" had inched its way toward the center stage of public policy. The problem, of course, was not so much the railroads as the public attitude toward them and how that attitude was to be expressed through the instrument of regulation. Few issues were more vital to the national welfare than resolving the transportation question in some rational way, and the stakes went even higher. Here as in so many areas the railroads broke new ground for Americans; this first experience with federal regulation and control would certainly provide a model for later attempts in other fields. Unhappily, it was to be a badly flawed one.

Small wonder, then, that interest in the railroad problem was intense and widespread during the turbulent period after the armistice. The need to do something about the specific issue of federal control set the stage for addressing the whole range of problems that had boiled up during the past decade. The result was an unprecedented outpouring of books, articles, and speeches on the subject, and a public debate that was to define the future of railroads in

American society at the very time when they were beginning to lose their place as the dominant mode of transportation in the nation.

The armistice forced every railroad man who had gone to work for the Railroad Administration to reassess his position in light of the uncertainties hanging over that agency's future. Events pushed Lovett into a quicker decision than most of his colleagues. McAdoo resigned his offices and left public life in January 1919. Lovett was high on the list of possible replacements, but he too quit and declared his intention of returning to the Union Pacific after a two-month rest. Apart from being worn out, the judge had a leadership vacuum to fill. Seger had been made president of United States Rubber Company and was preparing to leave the railroads he had served for thirty-six years.[38]

The most obvious question was how long federal control would last now that the war was over. Both McAdoo and his successor, Walker Hines, asked that the government either give USRA three to five years to carry out a rational, orderly transition or return the railroads at once to private hands to relieve the paralyzing uncertainty of their status. Congress rejected both options, insisting that federal control continue until legislation could be framed to provide for the transition. Wilson, preoccupied with the epochal peace negotiations at Versailles, summoned an extra session of Congress in May 1919 to deal with the railroad issue and told the members he would return the roads to private control at the year's end.[39]

McAdoo and Hines hoped to take the railroad question out of politics for a time, but that was wishful thinking. The Senate interstate commerce committee opened hearings on the tenure of federal control early in January and, with some interruptions, kept at it until October. The House committee joined the fun in July as the twin hearings broadened into consideration of several proposals for legislation. Virtually everyone except the shippers agreed that any return to the prewar situation was unthinkable. But what should take its place? McAdoo had a plan, as did Hines, the ICC, several ICC commissioners, the Association of Railway Executives (ARE), two organizations of railway investors, the National Transportation Conference (called by the National Chamber of Commerce), and the brotherhoods.[40]

So did Judge Lovett, who started with the premise that no thoughtful person cared to return to the overburdened prewar ICC with its negative approach to policy. He rejected permanent government ownership because it would eliminate competition, create a gigantic pork barrel, saddle the government with an enormous debt, turn labor into a dominant political force, and drive out skilled managers. What Lovett wanted had changed little since the prewar years. "I believe profoundly in the competitive principle," he wrote McAdoo. "In railroads it can and should extend only to competition in *service* and *facilities*, since competition in *rates* inevitably leads to rebates and discrimination, which are atrocious." If there must be regulation, and Lovett believed there must, then the best solution was "*exclusive federal control* and regulation of *private* ownership."[41]

In taking his views public the judge was by no means alone in the field; several other rail executives produced their own statements on what should be done. If nothing else, the industry's leading lights had learned in recent years the necessity of working together even if they did not always agree on what should be done. During the long and intense struggle to define the postwar status of the railroads, the ARE emerged as the chief vehicle for unified action by the carriers.

Late in 1918 ARE appointed a committee of twenty-five to consider a platform the carriers could support. A subcommittee of five headed by Julius Kruttschnitt met in Philadelphia to draft a set of principles the ARE hoped to get enacted into legislation. Borrowing heavily from Lovett's ideas, the Philadelphia plan included among its proposals a return to private ownership; regulation exclusively by the federal government; creation of a Department of Transportation to relieve the ICC of most administrative and executive functions; strengthening the ICC as a quasijudicial body; giving the ICC power to prescribe minimum as well as maximum rates; amending the antitrust law to permit pooling of equipment, facilities, and services; federal incorporation; and federal supervision of rail securities.[42]

A discouraged Frank Trumbull looked over the plan and could not muster any enthusiasm for it. In particular he was bothered by what he saw as a requiem for private enterprise and initiative in the rail industry. "I am not in favor of Government Ownership," he told Lovett. "I believe, however, that the Philadelphia Plan, so-called, will lead us directly into it within a few years unless it is supplemented by more definite and specific assurances to investors."[43]

What could the railroads do? They needed capital urgently, and needed to raise it through issues of stock rather than bonds. As a prominent banker put it, "The railroads need fewer creditors and more partners." But uncertainty did not attract partners, and neither did the shackles imposed by rate legislation. Trumbull raged at the Mann-Elkins Act of 1910 for requiring the carriers to "*publicly* show the necessity for higher rates which is equivalent to showing that they are 'needy.' In other words, they must put up a hard-luck story in Washington (and be criticized by the Commission for doing it) and do the best they can in the matter of telling good-luck stories to bankers and investors." The future looked bleak to him from any angle:

> Under the regulatory system, or lack of system, developed in this country—so-called private initiative is like a race horse tied to a post and the Philadelphia Plan proposes to shorten the rope without getting anything in return. No one is attempting to repeat the private initiative of a Huntington or a General Dodge or a Harriman—for regulation, so-called, has blighted all that. We are—particularly under the Philadelphia Plan—no longer to be navigators but simply pilots or trustees and if whatever private initiative is left cannot be preserved under some profit-sharing arrangement, it seems to me there is nothing left of it worth talking about.

Trumbull was not alone in his pessimism within or without the rail industry. Gloom was abroad in the land during that turbulent year of 1919. The inflation-ravaged economy was already feeling the dislocations of the war's end. A record number of strikes plagued the country as restive workers, who had lived with low wages during the war effort, tried to gain ground on the relentless climb in prices. The peace negotiations at Versailles turned sour and erupted into an ugly political controversy that upstaged the railroad problem. The public mood was tense and volatile, teetering on an edge of hysteria that exploded into the Red Scare. And if that were not enough, the global flu epidemic that claimed ten million lives had just begun to loosen its deadly grip.

These were hard times to preach the gospel of sweet reason on the most controversial domestic issue before the public. Or to keep it free from politics. The Republicans had captured both houses of Congress in the fall elections and were already eyeing 1920. Late in February William McAdoo abandoned all hope for getting federal control extended and urged Wilson to return the railroads to private hands as soon as possible. ''This Congress,'' he told Wilson in disgust, ''is going to do nothing about railroads.'' On that point he was wrong. By spring a host of plans had entered a crowded field vying for the attention of the Senate committee.[44]

Like the ARE plan, most of these proposals centered around the goal of making the railroads more efficient and better managed. They also differed sharply on how to achieve these goals. Senator Albert B. Cummins, chairman of the Senate committee, believed the key lay in merging ''weak roads with strong ones, to the end that the resulting systems, and they will be comparatively few in number, may do business upon substantially even terms.'' Cummins added that his plan would also require some government guarantee of return on capital. The consolidation scheme won support from Walker Hines, among others, and a group called the Association of Railway Security Owners was already pushing the guaranteed return idea vigorously.[45]

Most shippers lined up behind those members of the ICC who argued that the problem could be solved merely by enlarging and strengthening the agency. This was a conservative if not reactionary position in that it sought to roll back the changes wrought by the wartime emergency. It was also a defensive posture because shipper organizations never devised a coherent plan to advance. Not so the brotherhoods, who put forth the most radical proposal. Known as the Plumb plan after their general counsel, Glenn Plumb, it advocated government ownership and operation by a private corporation, the stock of which would be held in trust for the exclusive benefit of railway employees. Plumb grounded his plan in the conviction that railroads were a public utility cursed by a ''low degree of managerial skill'' because they had always been exploited by Wall Street financiers.[46]

Lovett shrank in horror from the worst features of these proposals. The Plumb plan he denounced as an attempt to ''Russianize the American railroad industry,'' and he had equally harsh things to say about a scheme advanced by S. Davies Warfield on behalf of the National Association of Owners of Railroad Securities. Warfield, a Baltimore banker, advocated a guaranteed return to the railroads of 6 percent, with all net earnings above that amount distributed among the government, employees, and shippers. Lovett also objected to Senator Cummins's consolidation plan and to certain details of the proposals advanced by his banker friends.[47]

The Plumb plan bogged down early as the trainmen withdrew their support and the conservative American Federation of Labor joined the railroads in attacking it. At a time when the Red Scare was fomenting public hysteria, opponents jumped gleefully at the chance to smear the plan with radical tar. A more formidable threat lay in the growing support for some combination of federal guarantee and cap on profits. In Lovett's view such a policy would prove a disaster for the railroads, especially if wedded to the kind of consolidation scheme pushed by Cummins.[48]

Wearily, Lovett undertook his own campaign to sway public opinion on these issues. The time had come, he told ARE general counsel Alfred P. Thom, for rail executives "to stand firmly until the end for a system of regulation that will be effective and to leave with the Congress the responsibility of enacting any plan that is foredoomed to failure." During the summer the judge produced an expanded version of his earlier pamphlet on the railroad problem. To give his views wide currency, the executive committee of the Union Pacific allocated $25,000 to distribute 200,000 copies. Ivy Lee, a giant in the emerging field of public relations, outlined a publicity campaign that made the reticent Lovett blush. Still, he agreed to it, aware that the industry's future was at stake. As the pamphlet drew praise from all sides, Lovett amplified his points in appearances before the committees of both houses and in interviews given to reporters.[49]

In all this work the judge hammered away at familiar themes, many of which had been incorporated into ARE's plan. For him, the restoration of credit *was* the railroad problem and the crux of the controversy. All the proposals Lovett disliked had the effect of weakening rather than strengthening credit. The consolidation scheme offered the worst of both worlds by punishing strong lines for their efficiency and rewarding weak lines for their incompetence. In the process it ruined the credit of strong roads by saddling them with the financial burden of roads that could not survive on their own. The guaranteed return and limit on net earnings would also destroy railroad credit, especially if the earnings of strong roads were used to shore up weak ones. "A man would be a fool," concluded the judge, "to put his money into railroads under such a system."[50]

These views drew Lovett into a testy dispute with the nervous, intense Warfield, who took them personally. But Lovett would not be deterred. He told the House committee bluntly that it was "no time for the popular Washington sport of 'passing the buck.' " The ICC in his view had been conceived in hostility to the rail industry and had always acted to repress and punish it. The spirit of its rules and the statutes on railroads was "unrelieved by a single helpful constructive encouraging provision which I can now recall."[51]

The best remedy for this negativism, Lovett believed, was the creation of a department of transportation headed by a secretary with cabinet rank who could bring problems directly to the president. Both the ICC and the war experience had shown that executive and administrative functions could "not be efficiently exercised by boards, commissions or committees.'' The ICC had reorganized in 1917, and its rapid growth was a harbinger of Big Government to come. Even so, it was still too swamped with duties to move promptly or efficiently. Stripping the agency of its administrative duties, which required fast response, would in Lovett's opinion enable it to perform its judicial functions more effectively.[52]

''I am glad to see that you 'uncorked yourself' before the House Committee,'' wrote an appreciative Frank Trumbull, who was in England trying to repair his broken health. But his pessimism ran deeper than ever. ''I think the procession has gone by private ownership under strict regulation, with no assurance in return,'' he added gloomily. ''I am glad to think that my railway career is about over, instead of just beginning.''[53]

Had the procession gone by? Lovett wasn't sure, but he had to keep chasing it. When the hearings closed in October, sharply contrasting bills were reported out of the two congressional committees. The House's Esch measure, written largely by an ICC commissioner, amounted to a classic exercise in time-warp politics. It sought to restore the *status quo ante bellum*, with the roads run privately under strict ICC regulation. This approach added little and solved nothing except to please shippers hoping to roll back the influence of the wartime experience. ''We did not incorporate in the bill new and strange features and untried plans,'' explained John J. Esch. ''. . . We did not think that this was a good time for experimentation.''[54]

The Senate's Cummins bill was far more positive and innovative. It allowed for minimum as well as maximum rates, changed the rate-making procedure to guarantee a return on investment, placed regulation of securities under federal control, and contained a flat prohibition of strikes. Alfred Thom of the ARE hailed it as the first real effort ''to abandon the theory that regulation should be repressive only.'' But it also harbored some objectionable features, notably a reasonable return limit that confiscated all net earnings above 6 percent of the ICC's valuation of the property. Still, Thom found much to encourage him, especially the attitude of Congress. Both committees, he reported happily, ''want to do what is best for the country, and neither is actuated by hostility to the railroads.''[55]

All sides recognized that something had to be done fast; the deadline for return of the roads to private control was fast approaching. On December 23, 1919, Wilson signed an order delaying the return until March 1, 1920, but the President had ceased to be a factor in the issue. Caught up in his struggle to win support for the Versailles Treaty, he had suffered a stroke on October 2 and lay virtually helpless while the debate raged in Congress. The economy too was paralyzed by the abrupt shift from war to peace. In February 1919 the Railroad Administration had found itself burdened with the greatest surplus of cars in its history and groped frantically for places to store them. Yet by fall record crops, a surge in lumber use, and stockpiling of coal in anticipation of a strike led to a huge outpouring of traffic for which the roads scrambled desperately to find enough cars.[56]

The coming of peace stripped USRA of its ability to handle these dislocations effectively. Without the wartime emergency it could no longer ignore shipper routing designations or compel pooling or impose heavy demurrage charges. Discontinued passenger trains were restored and cross-hauling of coal resumed. The result was a decline in efficiency and a mounting deficit aggravated by the relentless climb in prices. Aware that return to private control lay ahead, Hines resisted most wage and all rate demands despite the inflationary spiral, leading disgruntled shopmen to stage an unauthorized strike in August 1919. In effect the Railroad Administration found itself in limbo, unable to formulate cohesive policy and unwilling to take chances because of the uncertainty surrounding its future.[57]

As the Esch and Cummins bills stumbled through Congress, Lovett had no doubts about which he preferred. Although he did not think the ARE plan was ideal, he supported it as the most practical one available. "Unless a substantial part of the plan of the Railway Executives is adopted," he told Trumbull frankly, "I see no solution of the problem except Government Ownership." The Cummins bill embodied portions of the plan, while Esch's measure went in quite another direction. Accordingly, the judge sent a statement to every member of Congress praising Cummins's bill for having "the merit at least of recognizing the facts of the railroad situation and the courage of grappling with them."[58]

The Esch bill passed the House on November 17, 1919, but Cummins's measure ran into trouble. When it reached the floor in December, Senator Robert LaFollette of Wisconsin left no Progressive cliché unused in denouncing it as the "worst drawn in history." Charging that "the whole system was honeycombed with inside graft" when the government took over the roads, he demanded extension of federal control for two more years. His three-day harangue drew only eleven votes for the amendment he sought.[59]

While LaFollette raged, Lovett and the ARE steamed for quite another reason. Despite vigorous efforts, Cummins came out of committee with only half a loaf: the bill lost its provision giving roads a guaranteed return but kept the confiscation of earnings above 6 percent. It passed the Senate on December 20 and headed into joint conference, where a tough fight was expected. The Union Pacific set aside another $11,000 to give Lovett's newest pamphlet wide publicity, but pessimism ran deep among those hopeful of a fresh approach to railroad policy. A gloomy McAdoo told Lovett, "Personally, I do not see anything in the Esch bill, or the Cummins bill, or the Plumb plan, that is a solution of the railroad problem."[60]

The two bills had some key provisions in common. They returned the roads to private hands, kept existing rate schedules, and allowed roads to receive the guaranteed standard return from the government for as long as six months. Both bills authorized the ICC to make minimum as well as maximum rates, and explicitly recognized the supremacy of federal over state authority in rate disputes. The government was vested with power to order acquisition of equipment and facilities, and could regulate car service. But the bills differed radically in four major areas, and therein lay the fight many observers predicted would determine the future of railroads.[61]

The first concerned administrative machinery. Instead of a new cabinet post, Cummins offered a transportation board of five members to be appointed by the President and vested with extensive power over such crucial matters as the proposed consolidations, railroad securities and credit, administering of safety legislation, acting as final appeals board in labor disputes, and conduct of all inquiries into transportation needs and facilities. The Esch bill merely piled more duties onto the ICC. The proposed consolidations were voluntary under the Esch bill, mandatory under Cummins's in line with a plan to be devised by the transportation board.[62]

The Esch bill created no new principles or machinery for rate-making but simply restored the ICC's traditional methods. The Cummins bill ordered the ICC to divide the country into rate districts and the carriers into rate groups. The roads in each group could earn an aggregate net operating income of 5½ percent on the total value of their transportation property, and could also retain another half percent to invest in nonproductive improvements that could not be capitalized. In addition, each road could accumulate a reserve fund from excess earnings to support its credit. Any excess earnings above these requirements would go into a general reserve fund to be used by the transportation board for the "furtherance of the public interest" in the industry.

Finally, the measures diverged sharply on the labor issue. The Esch bill created three boards of adjustment to hear disputes, and three commissions on labor disputes to make final decisions on all matters referred to them by the adjustment boards. Railway management and labor were to have equal places on all boards, but the process remained at bottom a voluntary one. Not so with the Cummins bill, which created a committee on wages and working conditions along with three regional boards of adjustment, all staffed equally by management and labor. Most important, strikes and lockouts were flatly declared illegal.

The conferees had the thankless task of harmonizing these incompatible features within the two months remaining before federal control expired. All sides resorted to a lobbying blitz, with the shippers lined up behind Esch and the ARE behind Cummins. A month of stormy meetings produced nothing as both committees dug in their heels. Despite heroic efforts, Cummins had to abandon mandatory consolidation and the transportation board to save his financial program. Nor could he budge the House on his tough antistrike provision. Calling his foes "weak-kneed upon the subject," he watched helplessly as it was stricken out of the bill.[63]

A compromise measure emerged on February 18, sailed through Congress in five days, and was signed by Wilson on February 28, the last day before the end of federal control. Like all compromises, the Transportation Act of 1920 tried to please everyone and satisfied no one. By any standard, however, the final product was more Esch than Cummins. It terminated federal control on March 1, 1920, and guaranteed railroad earnings for six months thereafter. Rates then in effect could not be changed during that period without ICC approval. A host of other provisions addressed the knotty problems of disintangling the roads from the government.[64]

On the broader issues the act dumped the transportation board idea in favor of an ICC enlarged from nine to eleven members and clothed with new powers. In the area of rates and finance, which Thom called "the most important subject in this legislation," the carriers got something of what they wanted. The ICC could make minimum or even exact rates to ensure adequate earnings, and it was instructed to favor weak lines in joint rates. But the act also included the one innovation by Cummins that the railroads disliked most. It prescribed a "fair return" of 5½ to 6 percent on the physical value of the property. Half of all net earnings above that amount would go into a reserve fund to be used only for paying interest, dividends, or rentals; the other half would be recaptured by the government and placed in a special fund for loans to other railroads.[65]

The railroads also got half a loaf in their efforts to curb the state commissions. Federal incorporation was dropped from the act, but the ICC was given power to regulate the issue of securities, thereby removing the states from this sensitive area. The commission could also regulate intrastate rates that discriminated against interstate rates. The consolidation proviso remained but was made voluntary; the act required the ICC to prepare a plan for unifying roads into a limited number of systems in such a way as to preserve competition. On the sensitive labor question, the act created the Railroad Labor Board and the boards of adjustment, but it did not prohibit strikes and rested its hopes for compliance on the force of public opinion.

In the area of service the ICC gained considerable new muscle. It was given a mandate to require adequate transportation service even to the extent of ordering lines extended. It could unify the roads in emergencies, and was given supervision over car distribution, joint terminal use, safety appliances, and other aspects of operations. No carrier could extend or abandon lines or combine with another road without ICC approval. But roads were allowed to pool or combine if their action improved service and did not restrain competition.

A chorus of indiscriminate voices sang hosannas to a bold new departure in transportation policy. Even Thom, who knew better, called the act "an achievement in constructive statesmanship almost without parallel in our legislative history." More careful observers like I. L. Sharfman, who saw it as "eclectic in spirit," were closer to the mark. In essence the act restored the old Progressive system of regulation with all power vested in the ICC. At the same time it attempted to convert the ICC's traditionally negative mission into a more positive one. Whether the commissioners would accept this change in venue remained to be seen.[66]

Predictably, Lovett took a dim view of the outcome. The two chief defects, he noted, were sins of omissions. The act left the power of state commissions over rates "practically unimpaired," which meant rate reductions would soon follow, and it failed to create a transportation board. Some such agency, Lovett insisted, was "absolutely necessary to relieve the Interstate Commerce Commission of the vast executive and administrative duties devolving upon it under the old law and continued and enlarged by the new law.'' The proper business of the commission, he added, was determining rates, and it should not be burdened with other responsibilities.[67]

In one stroke the Transportation Act of 1920 closed one era in railroad history and opened another, the character of which no one could yet foresee. The takeover had ended, yet in a sense the takeover was now complete. Outright federal control had been relinquished, but the carriers found themselves more in the control of Washington than ever before. Not for another half century would they regain from the government some hold over their destinies. The enlarged role of government in their affairs troubled most rail executives. More than any other railroad in America the Union Pacific knew from bitter experience the perils and pitfalls of that relationship.

13

The Fresh Start

The Transportation Act of 1920 was supposed to give the railroads a fresh start in the postwar era, but the past lingered on in the form of disputes over the terms of settlement ending federal control. When the director general of USRA expressed a desire to wind up the affairs of his agency quickly if the railroads would cooperate, Judge Lovett smirked knowingly. The carriers were willing, he said, but the transactions involved were so large it would take months to settle them. He was right. Like most roads, the Union Pacific spent nearly two years haggling with the government.[1]

Since the spring of 1919 the Union Pacific had been embroiled in a fight with the Railroad Administration over maintenance policy and claims. The federal contract required the government to return the roads in "as good repair and in substantially as complete equipment" as it received them. But labor and materials had been in short supply during 1918, which prevented even basic work from being done on some lines. When the government agreed to provide funds for any maintenance not performed for roads with valid claims, every carrier scrambled furiously to prepare and negotiate claims.[2]

The Union Pacific joined the line, but Lovett made it clear that he wanted a straight, unbloated claim. He threw out one version because he considered the theory on which it was based untenable if not unsound. When a revised claim reached him, he rejected half of it as well. A final version was not completed until the winter of 1920–21, by which time a familiar complication had arisen. Warren G. Harding had won the 1920 presidential election in a landslide vote and decided to take the settlement issue under his erratic wing. The new

President, reported some bankers who had dined with him, "showed a good deal of feeling, if not pique, because the Railroad Presidents had not called on him. Indicating that he alone was authorized to settle claims, he reiterated several times that he would be glad to sit across the table with the Railroad Presidents and come to an immediate settlement of their claims." A surprised Lovett, like most railroad men, had assumed that USRA's director general was in charge of settlements. Dutifully he joined other members of the ARE steering committee in meeting with the President, who promptly warned them that most of the claims were excessive and unreasonable.[3]

While the political bickering dragged on, the Union Pacific came to terms with the Railroad Administration by accepting $8 million for its $13 million claim. In all, the carriers submitted claims totaling $678 million for alleged undermaintenance during federal control and ultimately settled for $203 million. By that measure the Union Pacific did very well, but no one came away happy either with their settlement or with the new mood in Washington, which promised a long row over the Transportation Act.[4]

An embittered Julius Kruttschnitt hauled out his beloved statistical cannons and fired a parting salvo at federal control. The root of the problem in his view was forcing the carriers "to spend more in increased wages than they were able to earn from increased rates." Using adjusted prices, still a novelty to many people in his day, Kruttschnitt came up with some revealing figures. Between 1900 and 1917 wholesale prices rose 120 percent while freight rates *declined* 1 percent. By July 1920 both wholesale prices and railroad wages were 240 percent higher than in 1900; freight rates had risen only 30 percent. An increase granted in September 1920 pushed rates up to 74 percent, and prices had fallen to 180 percent higher than 1900, but the gap was still huge.[5]

Nothing rankled Kruttschnitt more than the charge that the business depression of 1921 was caused by high rail rates and inefficient railroad management. He blasted those businessmen who failed to see the burden thrust on the carriers by the legacy of federal control. "Never before in the history of railroads has the pressure for advanced methods been so great as now," he insisted, "and never before have managers, imbued with the sentiments of the late Mr. Harriman,—'Never dissatisfied, always unsatisfied,'—responded more heartily." Most railroad managers shared these views to some extent, and most felt as much on the defensive in 1920 as they had during the Progressive era. Amid the confusion and cross-currents swirling through Washington, the fresh start looked anything but fresh.[6]

Even before the war Lovett was dissatisfied with the Union Pacific's organization, which seemed to him expensive and unwieldy. Despite his earlier efforts, it still concentrated in New York too much activity that in his opinion did not belong there. Harriman had created this system to serve his unique style of management, but he was dead and the company needed an organization that did not require a genius at its top. More authority had to be delegated to Omaha, a policy that Lovett had followed consistently since coming to office, but this required a strong leader in the West capable of administering the various roads as a unified system.

The unmerger gave Lovett a golden opportunity to revamp the New York forces. In 1913 he had asked all officers to submit their ideas on the "most efficient and economical manner" of reorganizing the administration once the separation had occurred. Director of purchases W. V. S. Thorne responded with an elaborate scheme that Lovett brushed aside with the rebuke, "I have been rather disappointed that your plans do not seem to involve a substantial reduction of your office force." Apart from the expense involved, the plan went in the wrong direction. "I am anxious," Lovett emphasized, "to avoid an organization that will be inclined to take out of the hands of men on the lines the work that can better be done there than in New York; and the larger and more expensive the New York organization, the more it will be inclined to do this."[7]

The same message went to western officers. In April 1914 Lovett asked presidents A. L. Mohler and J. D. Farrell to undertake a "critical examination of the different departments to determine whether we have drifted into expensive habits that can be rectified." To expedite the process he sent west two young men from his office, both of them sons of men prominent in the Union Pacific: Chauncey Stillman and W. Averell Harriman. In New York Lovett kept the pressure on Thorne. The judge had never been entirely comfortable with the centralized purchasing system devised by Harriman, and he was annoyed at Thorne's failure to reduce the expenses of his operation despite a mandate to do so. A year after the unmerger the purchasing office still cost the Union Pacific as much or more as it had when handling the Southern Pacific as well.[8]

His patience worn thin, Lovett ordered Thorne in May to cut his expenses in half. Thorne responded by submitting his resignation. The vice-presidency of purchasing he coveted went instead to Averell Harriman, but in revised form. Lovett used the change to shift all preparation of drawings, specifications, and other materials for bids to the West instead of centralizing it in New York, as Thorne had wanted. Averell Harriman, asked by Lovett to make a careful study of the operation, demonstrated that centralized purchasing for all the lines did make sense for many standard items, and the judge continued to hammer away at this theme of economy through unification within the system. "I want the dining car service handled," he said in one squabble, "precisely as if a single company were operating the three lines."[9]

The disruption of federal control gave Lovett a golden opportunity to revamp his organization for the postwar era. The changes wrought by the war and by the Transportation Act required a new approach as well as a new breed of manager. A president still had to know how to run a railroad, but he also had to be more of a political animal. The old days of rail presidents dealing with one another like rival monarchs were gone forever. They might still be despots, benevolent or otherwise, within the company, but their external negotiations were less with each other than with unions, agencies, political bodies, and other organizations. Problems were increasingly handled on a generic basis. More than ever before, the rail president was a spokesman for his company, and often for his industry as well.

Federal control had scrambled both the organization and its personnel by forcing officers to choose between working for the government or their company. Lovett grasped at once the leeway this gave him in putting Humpty Dumpty back together after the war. It happened that the Union Pacific was already passing through a transition from one generation of officials to another. W. H. Bancroft, long ailing, had retired from the Short Line in 1914 and died a year later. Alex Millar, who traced his service as secretary back to the Gould era, left in July 1917 because of ill health and lived less than a year thereafter. J. A. Munroe, who had been in the traffic department since the 1880s, retired in 1919, giving Lovett a chance to revise that operation. Treasurer F. V. S. Crosby died in 1920, completing the turnover in the New York office.[10]

The board had also undergone major changes even though seats tended to stay in the family much as they had in the 1890s. Among Harriman's closest allies, James Stillman went to his grave in 1918, Jacob Schiff in 1920, and William Rockefeller in 1922. The venerable Marvin Hughitt of the Northwestern surrendered the seat he had held since 1890 to his son Marvin Jr. in 1918. By 1920 the sons of directors occupied six of the fifteen seats: Averell and Roland Harriman, William G. Rockefeller, Oliver Ames, Mortimer Schiff, and young Hughitt. Stillman's place was taken not by his son but by his protégé, Frank Vanderlip. Kahn still served but gave his seat the next year to fellow banker Paul Warburg. Most of the newcomers deferred to Lovett's experience in such matters as reorganization.

The judge was clear in his own mind about what he wanted. Earlier there had been two presidents, one of Union Pacific and the Short Line, the other of Navigation, each with his own staff, as well as officers who served all three companies. To unify the Union Pacific System, Lovett wanted a single president presiding over all the roads. The traffic, accounting, and other officers, who had reported to New York in Harriman's day, would instead report to the president in Omaha. "New York would be limited to financial matters and very large matters of policy," he explained to an officer. "I was and am still convinced that we handled too much detail in New York, though this was unavoidable under the organization previously existing."[11]

Obviously the key to this scheme was finding the right man for the presidency. Although Lovett held the office nominally, he had no intention of keeping it. Indeed, given his increasingly fragile health, he regarded the lessening of his duties as a major bonus of the plan. The government takeover in 1917 had freed his hands in this area. Of his two presidents, Calvin had become federal manager of the Union Pacific and Farrell had been reassigned as vice-president of all three system companies. Both wished to remain with the Union Pacific but could be placed elsewhere in a new organization. The judge regarded Calvin as a fine operating man but not one suited to the other duties required of a president in the postwar era. He tended to shy away from public

WILLING TO WORK: E. E. Calvin, who moved from president to vice-president, stares pensively from behind his desk near the end of his long career.

appearances, partly because he had a slight speech defect. And he was old, not so much in years—he had turned sixty just before the armistice—as in attitude. Calvin was an old-fashioned railroader and so was Farrell.[12]

Happily, Lovett's tenure in Washington had brought him into contact with just the man he wanted for the presidency. Carl R. Gray had served as director of operation and maintenance for USRA, a difficult post in which he had done a superb job. "I do not think any of us did anything which measured up to what he accomplished," marveled B. F. Bush of the Missouri Pacific. "I cannot now recall one single decision he made which, in the light of later events, did not seem to be justified." What impressed Bush about Gray was not only his ability but also his grace under pressure, and his patience. Walker Hines praised Gray as "one of the ablest railroad operating officials in the country."[13]

Gray was a southern puritan whose parents migrated from Maine to Arkansas, where he was born in 1867. His father taught mathematics at the state university in Fayetteville and lived in a house near the tracks of the St. Louis & San Francisco. The boy developed a fascination for railroads and hung around the depot until he was put to work doing odd jobs. "I cleaned stoves and spittoons, rustled baggage and between times learned telegraphy," he recalled. "My wages were nothing a month, and I paid the telegraph operator to teach me what he knew." In 1883 he landed a job as an operator and worked his way

IT MIGHT HAVE BEEN: Carl Gray *(right)* confers with James J. Hill, who tapped Gray to be president of the Great Northern Railroad. (*James J. Hill Papers, Hill Reference Library*)

up the ladder until he became senior vice-president of the Frisco in 1909. Three years later James J. Hill thought well enough of Gray to make him president of the Great Northern.[14]

At forty-five Gray seemed to have reached the pinnacle of his career, yet for some unknown reason Louis Hill, who had been made chairman by his father, decided he could not work with Gray. In 1914 Gray left the Great Northern and became president of the Western Maryland, which had been reorganized after its debacle as part of George Gould's ill-fated scheme for a transcontinental line. The war plucked Gray from this position and into a new destiny. Once named president of the Union Pacific, a post he assumed in January 1920, he remained with the company for the rest of his life.

The youthful Gray had once been described as "six feet tall and thin as two clapboards nailed together." By middle age the clapboards were spread to generous proportions over a large frame topped by a kind, fatherly face and a mane of prematurely white hair. An affable man utterly lacking in pretense or arrogance, Gray won friends easily with his open, sincere manner and consideration of others. A writer described him as "one of the most lovable men in the business." He was a devout Baptist and somewhat prudish, but not in a righteous or overbearing way. Friends and foes alike found him impossible to dislike or distrust, and Gray was clever enough to use his charm to advantage. Behind his genial nature lay a shrewd mind and an ability to get things done with a minimum of fuss. The term most often applied to him, and it fit well, was "fine Christian gentleman."

Government officials and other railroad men admired Gray for his integrity no less than his ability. To the employees he looked and acted the part of the sincere, benevolent leader who worked with his people and was accessible to them—a valuable quality in a changing era of labor relations. During the war he had served on a board created to oversee wages and working conditions. This experience only strengthened Gray's belief that employees would respond to an attitude of fairness and genuine concern. One incident typified his way with the men. Eugene McAuliffe of the Union Pacific Coal Company was riding in Gray's business car when the engineer hit the brakes hard at slow speed, pitching his distinguished cargo forward. The conductor rushed back at once, burbling apologies for the engineer, who was too embarrassed to do it himself. After a painful moment of silence Gray flashed his beatific smile and told the conductor to go back and tell the engineer the story of a young private who, hurrying across the parade ground at dusk, overtook a man in uniform and greeted him with a sharp whack between the shoulder blades. To his horror the face that greeted him belonged to the colonel of the regiment. The ashen-faced soldier tried to blurt out an apology, certain that the guardhouse awaited.

"That's all right, my boy," said the colonel. "I don't mind the mistake in the least, but be sure you don't try slapping a second lieutenant."[15]

But Gray could also be tough. In 1933 a woman complained that she had been unjustly dismissed by the assistant treasurer in Los Angeles. Gray sent the general auditor to examine the case and received convincing evidence supporting the complaint. He promptly ordered the woman reinstated. The official did so in a rude, intimidating way that prompted the woman to take another job. Gray got wind of this and wrote the man a blistering rebuke. "Your handling of this case from first to last has been quite a shock to me," he concluded, "and has had the effect of shaking the confidence which I ought to have in an officer . . . it will be necessary for you by your future handling of your work, your employes, and your public contacts, to overcome this impression."[16]

With Gray aboard, the rest of the organization fell quickly into place. Calvin returned as vice-president of operations for the system, while Farrell became a vice-president of the Navigation Company. During the war C. B. Seger had brought to New York a talented accountant named F. W. Charske, who now assumed the position of comptroller for the entire system. Henry W. Clark served as general counsel, H. M. Adams as vice-president of traffic, and E. E. Adams as consulting engineer for the system. G. E. Bissonnet became general auditor in Omaha, and each company had its own auditor as well.[17]

Under the new arrangement the New York office held only Lovett, Clark, Charske, E. E. Adams, Thomas Price, who replaced Millar as secretary, and the treasurer E. G. Smith. The judge succeeded at paring it down to the basic functions of policy and finance. The reorganization was a fitting capstone to his stewardship. He had taken a company made in Harriman's own image and restructured it to function smoothly without Harriman. And he was not yet done with his tinkering.

After 1920 the Union Pacific System, as it had been called since before the war, began to emerge as a reality. In October 1910 the Short Line had absorbed seven subsidiary lines. Two months later another thirteen lines were merged with the Navigation Company into the new Oregon-Washington Navigation & Railway Company. In 1921 Lovett tightened the organizational structure another notch by purchasing the half interest in the Los Angeles & Salt Lake road still held by W. A. Clark. The Union Pacific paid Clark $20 per share for his $12.5 million in stock and traded him a mix of Southern Pacific and Navigation bonds for his $29.5 million in bonds. Once in complete possession of the Los Angeles line, Lovett installed Gray as president but left it as a subsidiary company.[18]

One loose end remained in the form of the Central Pacific, which had dangled in legal limbo since 1917. After protracted delays the Supreme Court in May 1922 reversed the lower court by ordering the Southern Pacific to sever its control of the Central Pacific through stock ownership or lease. Staggered by this decision, Southern Pacific officials launched a publicity campaign designed, in the words of one directive, to "Raise as much 'cain' as possible in California." In their desperation the road's managers hit upon a bold and ingenious tactic: they attempted to bypass the court's decision by asking the ICC to legalize their hold on the Central Pacific.[19]

The Supreme Court had declared ownership of the Central Pacific by the Southern Pacific to violate the Sherman Antitrust Act in review of a suit brought by the government in February 1914 and concluded before passage of the Transportation Act of 1920. Section 407 of the latter law, however, authorized the ICC to permit consolidations in the public interest and to render them immune from the Sherman Act. If the Southern Pacific could persuade the ICC to approve some form of merger with the Central Pacific, it would confer legality on what the court had ruled to be unlawful. Since the newer legislation had not been mentioned in the court decision, ICC approval might be construed as both fulfilling and superceding the court's wishes rather than defying them.[20]

The Union Pacific got wind of this scheme in June 1922, when a company lawyer in Los Angeles warned Gray that the Southern Pacific was "actively engaged in spreading propaganda to create a sentiment in favor of their retaining control of the Central Pacific by authority of the Interstate Commerce Commission." Caught by surprise, the Union Pacific allowed itself to be pulled into a war of words that did neither side credit. Before the air cleared, even such level-headed men as Gray and Kruttschnitt said things they were later to regret. "The fight got started," Lovett recalled, "and many agencies were employed . . . some of them strangers to us. [I realized] mistakes might be made and some things were done which we wouldn't do. I also saw things on the other side that I thought the Southern Pacific officers would not have approved. But it was a good deal like a war or a political campaign."[21]

The object was to win support among shippers, businessmen, commercial organizations, bankers, and others who might testify before an ICC hearing or bring pressure on their congressmen. Despite its resources, the odds were stacked against the Union Pacific. There was always discontent for an enemy to play upon, especially among shippers eager to secure lower rates or new lines. The Traffic Bureau of Salt Lake City had been hostile to the road for years, and the Commercial Club still harbored resentments over an attempt by the Short Line to control it a decade earlier. Both were willing converts to the Southern Pacific's lavish promises of expenditures for extensions and improvements. Supporters of the company in Utah demanded an open gateway at Ogden as the price for their loyalty.[22]

A parley among Union Pacific officials in September revealed that most of Nevada and much of Utah had lined up behind the Southern Pacific. Strong support could be found elsewhere. From the first, Lovett made it clear that he was unwilling to sacrifice any "permanent interest for any local public sentiment" in the fight. The goal, he wrote privately on June 9, was "the absolute independence of the Central Pacific; unless sold to Union Pacific, with suitable feeders and terminals." Gray stated this position publicly the next day. Some observers dismissed the call for independence as a smokescreen for seeking outright ownership, but the judge was sincere. Events over the next several months reinforced his conviction that some other suitable arrangement was preferable to ownership by the Union Pacific.[23]

The sparring before the ICC opened in November and continued until December 13. A wrathful Kruttschnitt, having all but broken with his former colleagues, defended the Southern Pacific's position with righteous vigor. Attempts to cross-examine him got nowhere, Gray reported glumly, because "he insisted upon reading a stump speech in reply to every question, most of which was far afield, and a large part of it vituperative and bitter." But Gray conceded that the Southern Pacific had "made the very best of their case, and have really made a fine presentation."[24]

In his testimony Lovett emphasized the shift of business to the Sunset Route along with the original intent of the Pacific Railway Acts that the roads be operated as one continuous line. At every turn he was firm in his views but never critical of his rivals, saying, "I would do the same in their place." The ferocity of rhetoric had diminished for good reason. A few days after the hearings closed, top officials from both roads met and thrashed out an agreement leaving the Central Pacific with the Southern Pacific under terms that preserved Union Pacific use of it as one continuous line.[25]

After the "peace conference," as Lovett termed it, the ailing judge headed west for a lengthy rest in Santa Barbara. On the train he jotted down detailed suggestions for Gray. Once an agreement was made, the key lay in getting the ICC and the court to accept it. In these negotiations, he stressed, "we must not under any conditions or at any cost get in any questionable or equivocal or *unethical* position with the Commission." If the ICC rejected the deal, Gray should oppose any plan that made the Central Pacific "free under conditions which would make it another Western Pacific."[26]

There remained the problem of how to approach the ICC, which had scheduled final hearing on briefs and arguments for January 19, 1923. After some delicate maneuvering, two commissioners were apprised of the deal and proved receptive to it. Early in January the bargaining took on fresh urgency for Gray. Poring over the four thousand pages of testimony and more than a hundred exhibits disclosed to him that fully half the business interchanged at Ogden originated on the Central Pacific itself, and that the latter's major north-south traffic moved from Ashland to Fresno and Goshen. All this business would be diverted if the Union Pacific got the Central Pacific, leaving only what Gray called "a fearfully over-capitalized railroad." It would be invited to pay an inflated price for a devalued line.[27]

Gray was chagrined not to have grasped this truth earlier. "The only excuse I can offer is to plead unfamiliarity," he told Lovett, "which does not satisfy me." He now recognized the importance of not being saddled with the Central Pacific stripped of its north-south feeders on terms that left the Southern Pacific and most California shippers hostile. Lovett brushed this contrition aside and prodded his lawyers to counter objections from other roads to a contract giving the Union Pacific preferred connections at Ogden by "eternally hammering on the Pacific Railroad Acts, pushing them to the front and emphasizing . . . our peculiar and vested rights under them."[28]

The California sunshine had reinvigorated the judge, rid him of the severe headaches that plagued him. "As the Coue-ites say," he smiled, " 'Day by day, and in every way, I am getting better and better.' " His renewed zest showed itself in the detailed suggestions he forwarded to the lawyers in Washington, where negotiations were fast moving to a climax. Gray and the attorneys discussed his suggestions at length but did not feel bound by them when the bargaining grew complicated. A long session with the Southern Pacific produced some changes that general counsel Henry Clark assured Lovett would give the company "not only everything to which we are entitled but also everything we need."[29]

The ICC accepted the modified agreement and secured approval from nearly all those who had intervened in the case. Under these terms the Southern Pacific retained the Central Pacific while agreeing to solicit business actively for the route and to equalize rates at the Ogden, El Paso, and Portland gateways so that no one route would have an advantage. The Southern Pacific then struck a deal with the Western Pacific, removing its objections, and the court approved the package, thereby closing a dispute that had raged for more than a decade. Gray conceded to Lovett that the final product, "which I believe represents the maximum of our abilities to secure, is not entirely satisfactory to you." He was right. The fresh start for the one continuous line turned out to be the same old symbiotic connection.[30]

The ICC took the Transportation Act as a mandate for a fresh start by again reorganizing itself. To handle its mushrooming workload, an act in October 1917 had increased the number of commissioners to nine and created three rotating divisions (valuation, rates and long/short haul cases, and formal cases not argued orally), and changed its old offices or divisions into bureaus. Under the new act the eleven commissioners added two divisions for financial supervision and service. The bureaus too were overhauled. Two new ones were created for administration and finance; the eleven existing bureaus, some with changed names, dealt with accounts, formal claims, informal cases, inquiry, law, locomotive inspection, safety, service, statistics, traffic, and valuation.[31]

A sprawling bureaucracy had sprung up in remarkably short time. The ICC started life in 1887 with eleven employees and expenditures of $113,000; as late as 1904 it had 150 employees and spent only $325,000. By 1919 it boasted 2,206 employees and an outlay of $5.8 million, with more to come because of the Transportation Act. Yet the ICC still could not cope with the duties thrust on it. Increasingly the commissioners had to rely on their staffs to originate and prepare casework along with recommended decisions. In 1928, for example, Division 4, which handled finance and also helped out with rate cases, decided a total of 1,017 cases or about four each working day. This kind of workload did not encourage an already fragmented commission to ponder broad policy.[32]

Despite all its new responsibilities, rates remained the commission's staple fare. Under the new law the ICC prescribed minimum as well as maximum rates, and had to provide an adequate return to the carriers. The old Progressive negativism that had so blatantly favored shippers gave way to a more balanced and positive policy. Unfortunately, this meant seeking a course that pleased all sides and tried to define new principles at a time when the commission was scrambling frantically just to keep up with its routine work. Amid the thousands of rate cases handled by the ICC during the 1920s, only three dealt with the level of rates for all roads.[33]

The first chance to apply the new rules came in the summer of 1920, when the need for a rate hike was glaring. To determine what level of rates would provide a 6 percent return, however, the ICC needed some estimate of the worth of the railroads, and the valuation project still plodded onward. Rejecting the carrier's plea that book value be used, the ICC chose almost capriciously a different set of figures: $8.8 billion for eastern roads, $2 billion for southern roads, and $8.1 billion for western lines. On this basis the commission granted a 40 percent increase to eastern, 25 percent to southern, 35 percent to western, 25 percent to Mountain-Pacific roads, and 33⅓ percent on interterritorial freight.[34]

Just three years earlier the ICC had denied a request for an increase of 15 percent. Why the change of heart? One reason was obvious: nine days before the rate hike was authorized, the Railroad Labor Board had approved wage increases totaling $618 million, which the carriers could not meet without more money. In 1921, however, a sharp recession sent revenues tumbling and caused the commission to rethink its action. A widespread clamor for reducing rates helped convince the ICC that lower tariffs might actually improve railroad income by stimulating business. The carriers disagreed vehemently; above all, they insisted that no cuts should be made unless wages, which comprised 60 percent of rail expenses, were slashed as well.[35]

Brushing these protests aside, the ICC cut the advances of 1920 by 14 percent for eastern roads, 12½ percent for southern and Mountain-Pacific lines, 13½ percent for western roads, and 13⅓ percent on interterritorial freight. The Union Pacific imposed some cuts on its own, and increased traffic resulted in only a 2.1 percent decline in freight revenues. But an old dilemma loomed anew: carrying more traffic at lower rates caused operating expenses to soar and wore out the physical plant faster. And when the Labor Board ordered a 10 percent cut in wages, the unions responded with a strike in which 91 percent of Union Pacific's mechanical department workers walked out.[36]

Whatever the outcome, the ICC had at last assumed a bold, positive role. It had initiated an inquiry to meet a problem, taken forceful action, and sought to harmonize the conflicting interests of shippers and carriers. The agency's most sympathetic historian called it the "high-water mark of the Commission's performance in the regulation of railroad rate levels." Unfortunately, the water receded at a rapid pace. For the rest of the decade the ICC kept general rates at about the same levels. A petition by western roads for higher rates in 1925 ran into a stone wall of repeated demands for reductions. Earlier that year, Congress had passed a resolution asking the ICC for lower rates to aid depressed industries, particularly agriculture. The commission resisted pressure from both sides, recognizing glumly that shippers could not afford higher rates nor railroads lower ones.[37]

The rate puzzle had always been a delicate balancing act among discriminations so intertwined that the ICC hesitated to disturb them. Unable to resolve its contradictions, the commission failed to lift rates to a level that provided railroads the income guaranteed them by the Transportation Act. Despite this shortcoming, both Lovett and Gray defended the ICC from critics who sought to reform it. "The present system, unsatisfactory as it is," declared the judge, "is infinitely better for the railroads themselves than the former system of arbitrary and irresponsible rate making by individual lines and officers who were subject to irresistible pressure by shippers even if they did not have other motives."[38]

Gray agreed. "The need of the hour is not legislation but surcease therefrom," he told a congressman eager to revamp the ICC in 1926. "The situation is very much better than it was at the time of the passage of the Transportation Act in 1920." He pointed to a procedure adopted three years earlier that allowed large numbers of cases to be disposed of without formal hearing and therefore at greatly reduced cost. But the recapture of excess earnings provision, in which Senator Cummins had placed such great hope, never got off the ground. Although the Supreme Court upheld it, the fierce controversy over valuation and ploys by the carriers to bury excess earnings in other categories kept the fund low. Between 1920 and 1931 the railroads reported excess earnings of $23.5 million; the ICC estimated the real figure to exceed $300 million. Litigation tied up much of the money that did reach the fund, and the provision was finally scrapped in 1933.[39]

The consolidation plans fared no better. A stunning reversal in policy, they were as loosely applied as competition had been earlier. The ICC had two distinct charges: to approve all mergers, and to prepare a plan for consolidating the nation's roads into a limited number of systems. No merger could be approved unless it fit the commission's grand consolidation scheme. This seemed reasonable in theory, but in practice it left all merger proposals at the mercy of consolidation plans that were voluntary and controversial if not bitterly opposed by the railroads. The result was more confusion of policy that entangled the Central Pacific settlement and nearly scuttled it.[40]

The preliminary plan released in August 1921 called for nineteen systems including one combining the Union Pacific and Northwestern. Lovett bared its flaws at once. Congress had imposed an impossible task in proposing to aid weak roads by combining them with strong ones. Even if this were done, he predicted, "it will be but a few years thereafter until we have 'strong' systems and 'weak' systems again, just as now, differing perhaps in the size of the systems, which in case of failure will only add to the magnitude of the disaster." Strong and weak lines were an inevitable result of private ownership, he concluded, "and we may as well choose first as last between private ownership with strong and weak lines and other incidents of competition, or government ownership with all that attends it."[41]

What nettled Lovett (and other rail leaders) most was the notion of saddling strong, well-managed roads with weak, poorly managed ones. This had the effect of penalizing the strong lines for good management. The act also stipulated that the systems have their service, rates, and rate of return equalized as much as possible. How could a well-built and well-maintained line like the Union Pacific be equalized with an undermaintained road with a circuitous route, steep grades, and a single track? Inevitably the result would be to weaken the strong roads while improving weak roads only marginally. And since the consolidations were voluntary, what strong road would willingly adopt stray dogs? How could security holders ever agree on the relative value of their holdings? "It is evident," the judge emphasized, "that here is occasion for almost endless negotiation."

When hearings opened on the consolidation plans for western roads in January 1923, the Central Pacific controversy and rate clashes were still in the headlines. "It would look to me," declared Morti Schiff, "as if there should be four great western systems based on the Union Pacific-Southern Pacific, on the Hill roads, on the Atchison and on what was formerly the Gould roads." The northern lines had already approached the ICC in November 1922 with a plan to reunite the three roads torn asunder by the Northern Securities decision. Led by Hale Holden of the Burlington, a skilled, persuasive advocate, the Hill roads faced two major obstacles: their proposed combination had earlier been dissolved by the Supreme Court, and their plan differed from that of the ICC, which wanted to put the Great Northern with the Milwaukee.[42]

Between April 1922 and December 1923 the consolidation hearings piled up 12,000 pages of testimony, much of it conflicting, and 700 exhibits. The commission emerged more puzzled than ever. Staggered by the complexities of the question and the fierce objections raised, it did not produce a final consolidation plan until December 1929. Meanwhile, it reverted to old habits by considering merger requests on a piecemeal basis without regard to their place in the grand scheme of consolidation. Through a variety of devices the ICC consented to 298 combinations involving 51,000 miles of track. Holden and Ralph Budd of the Burlington pushed the merger of the Hill roads until even Gray confessed to being fed up with their being "so obsessed with the subject that they seemingly could not think or talk of anything else."[43]

Their efforts moved the ICC to grant permission in 1930 for the Great Northern and Northern Pacific to merge only on condition that the Burlington not be included. Preferring to retain their half interests in the Burlington, the two roads withdrew their application to await a better day. It would finally arrive forty years later, amid an explosion of merger mania that took the American railroad system back in the direction it had been tending at the turn of the century. Fresh starts came in many forms, few if any of which were really new. In this case it merely took the country fifty years to catch up with the thinking of E. H. Harriman.[44]

During these years another ghost of legislation past, the valuation project, plodded onward, a legal and accounting equivalent to the Great Wall of China, extended each year by faithful legions of accountants and clerks toiling away at arcane matters whose origins seemed lost in the mists of history and whose conclusion lay too distant to be glimpsed. Even the project's most ardent supporters lost their way in the maze of technical hairsplitting that resembled the finer points of medieval theology more than anything else. The doughty Charles A. Prouty, who as a commissioner had pushed hard for the Valuation Act and then resigned to become head of the project, possessed a fine grasp of accounting, but the act was too much for him. "I would rather undertake to recite the Chinese alphabet backward than read the thing anyway," he grumbled four years after taking up his new post, "because it does not mean anything after you have read it."[45]

Railroad executives agreed, but they could not ignore a project that hung like a Damoclean sword over the heads. Once final valuation figures emerged, they would serve as the basis for both rates and the return on capital promised each road by the Transportation Act. In that sense the valuation numbers held the key to every road's financial destiny regardless of the extent to which they did or did not reflect any palpable reality. The real snag remained a sharp disagreement over what basis should be used to appraise a carrier's property. Railroad managers, lawyers, and accountants had been grappling with the problem since a landmark court decision, *Smyth v. Ames* (1898), raised it in language that confused more than it clarified.[46]

The law asked the ICC to generate three sets of figures for each road: its original cost, the cost of reproduction, and the reproduction cost minus depreciation on existing structures. Apart from the difficulties of getting and computing these data, there arose savage debates over their actual worth as well as their definition. The dispute over what depreciation should be, for example, dragged on for years. To complicate matters, the valuation work was pegged to prices for the period prior to 1914 and ignored the effects of wartime inflation. Every road had to create a valuation department at considerable expense to handle this work and oversee what the government did with it. On the Union Pacific H. A. Scandrett, an able lawyer, became the valuation counsel, devoting most of his time to that task alone.[47]

The carriers had trouble presenting a united front on the issue because the same approach to valuation did not benefit roads in different regions. Two solid days of wrangling in March 1920 produced a uniform recommendation to the ICC, but the agreement hung by threads. "The southwestern group advocates are well organized and determined," reported a weary Henry Clark, "and there are threats of further splitting up if they persist." The Union Pacific found itself on the front line of the fight by mere chance. In 1923, ten years after the project began, the ICC issued its first full single-sum report, which happened to be on the Los Angeles & Salt Lake. At once, all sides viewed the contest over this report as a vital precedent for future battles.[48]

In his testimony Lovett had placed the road's worth at $73.5 million. After pondering the data and rejecting again the road's own claims, the ICC fixed a value of $45 million on the Los Angeles road. A friendly commissioner suggested applying for a rehearing, but Scandrett demurred because of "the almost total lack of consideration that the majority of the Commission pays to evidence offered in support of a protest." The commissioners split as widely on the decision as the analysts who scrutinized their report. "This great problem of valuation," groaned *Railway Age*, "is very far from solution."[49]

Lovett saw no choice but to file suit to annul the ruling on grounds that the method of valuation had been improper. The railroad won in the lower court, but a test case meant little until the Supreme Court passed on it. To wage that battle the Union Pacific engaged Charles Evans Hughes, a once and future justice of the Supreme Court as well as former secretary of state. His prestige and erudition proved inadequate if not irrelevant, for the decision announced in February 1927 disappointed everyone. It upheld the ICC's order on the narrowest of technicalities and did not touch the substance of the case. "To use familiar slang, the court did not 'Leave us a leg to stand on,' " Lovett sighed to Gray. "True, the numerous errors committed by the Commission which impressed you so much upon reading our brief, are not excused or justified. The court simply refused to consider them upon the ground that it had no jurisdiction to do so."[50]

By then the valuation project was fourteen years old, and the end was nowhere in sight. It had yet to make a final valuation of any major road, and the validity of its approach remained an unsolved bone of controversy. In debating the original bill, Senator LaFollette among others had predicted the work would cost only a few million dollars. By 1927 it had already drained the government of $30 million and the railroads of $90 million. When the final story of valuation was written, noted one close observer, it would make "one of the most interesting, important and paradoxical chapters in the history of property."[51]

Property was very much on the players' minds during these turbulent years. "We hear, everywhere, the statement that private ownership and operation of the railroads is now being subjected to its final test,'' said C. H. Markham of the Illinois Central in an address to the Transportation Club of Louisville. If this were true, he added, then ''it is equally the fact that American institutions . . . are also on trial.'' The people must realize they have common cause with the carriers because ''if the railroads fail, other lines of industry must go down.'' The president of California Barrel Company agreed. ''It is the people of America who are under trial,'' he told the Railway Business Association.''It is we who represent the practical leadership of America who are under trial.''[52]

Amid the squabbles over policy, the legal probing of the new act, and the jockeying for position under the new rules, the specter of government versus private ownership still loomed ominously against the backdrop of the Russian revolution that had so unsettled Americans. Markham was right; the Act of 1920 was widely viewed as the last stand of American railroads to remain in private hands. Even so staunch a defender of private property as Herbert Hoover, the proud author of *American Individualism* (1922), was disturbed enough by 1923 to warn rail executives that ''unless the railroads could get together upon a definite program of co-operation . . . Government Ownership was the only alternative.''[53]

Lovett wrinkled his nose at Hoover's complaints. ''His lack of experience with railroad operations,'' sniffed the judge, ''has made his meddling with the railroad problem anything but helpful.'' But the fear of another takeover lingered like an unwelcome guest. A friend of Lovett's defended it as ''the only thing that is politically practicable.'' Rumors swirled that McAdoo was seeking to get the Democrats to adopt it for the 1924 campaign. ''I hope he will not do it,'' Lovett said wearily. ''It would be even a greater mistake than free silver, and not half as popular.''[54]

The need was urgent for a constructive dialogue on the problem, but antagonisms corroded every effort. Union leaders, fighting to keep wage gains, accused the railroads of inefficient management and banker domination. Their attacks drew sharp rebuttals from Lovett and Kruttschnitt among others. The powerful eastern roads grew shrill in demanding the right to handle labor negotiations without government interference. Their cry struck Lovett as futile, ill-timed, and wholly unrealistic. ''Without national authority to keep them going,'' he snorted, ''their railroads can be tied up tighter than a knot any time the brotherhood leaders want to tie them up.''[55]

During these critical years railroad managers had trouble keeping their own ranks closed against common adversaries. Some, like Kruttschnitt, were content to vent their spleens at the ill treatment afforded the carriers while brushing aside legitimate complaints about the industry. More thoughtful men, like Lovett and C. H. Markham, conceded that the roads had failed to address their shortcomings until forced to do so by public pressure. ''Why was Railroad Management so long in attaining the extraordinary degree of efficiency which has characterized their operations since Federal control?'' Lovett asked. ''Why was it not attained before Federal control? Does not the present Management prove that the past Management of American railroads was inefficient?''[56]

Take the newfound economy of increasing engine runs on some lines from two to five hundred miles. The Union Pacific had started this practice in the early 1920s. "Why was it not initiated generations ago if it accomplishes what is claimed?" demanded Lovett. Two years earlier Markham had argued along similar lines. "There is no denying the charge," he said bluntly, "that the railroads have been derelict in providing the shop facilities necessary to take care of their equipment." As a whole, he added, "there is less efficiency in operation of the railroads than in any other large industry. I don't think it is wide of the mark to say that the average railroad shop is using antiquated tools and machinery to an extent unheard of in industrial plants."[57]

The divisions among rail executives spilled over into the ARE, which by 1922 was on the verge of breaking up. A. H. Smith of the New York Central had long complained of the association's expense. Other presidents joined the chorus and suggested merging the ARE into the American Railway Association (ARA). Lovett vigorously opposed this idea and reminded Smith that ARE's expenses had grown largely because it had "become the clearing house for many organizations that we have long supported." If nothing else the debate revealed the extent to which the rail industry had in fact become a society of organizations. In 1920 the Union Pacific System paid out nearly $390,000 in dues to various associations, an increase of 82 percent over 1916. While a small part of this went to civic organizations like chambers of commerce, most of it was devoted to transportation groups, sixty-six of them in all.[58]

For many years the ARE and the ARA had served separate functions, with the former handling policy issues and the latter more practical questions such as car service and per diem rules. Put another way, the chief executives of railroads staffed the ARE, while vice-presidents and general managers belonged to the ARA. At the end of federal control, however, the ARA was reorganized with a board composed of presidents, including many who sat on the ARE executive committee. It was, therefore, possible to transfer the policy functions of the ARE to the ARA.

Some executives also frowned on the work of T. DeWitt Cuyler, the chairman of the ARE, and Alfred P. Thom, the general counsel who had charge of the crucial Washington office. Lovett, Markham, and others defended them and the organization, but a showdown loomed in the fall of 1922 when several major western lines threatened to withdraw from the ARE. They were willing to support the Washington office under Thom but wanted Cuyler's New York office abolished and its functions transferred to the ARA. To Lovett fell the thankless task of informing Cuyler of this mounting discontent.[59]

A twist of fate made the judge feel even worse. On November 12, only twelve days after Lovett had broached the issue, Cuyler died suddenly on his way back from giving a speech in Rochester. His unexpected death eased the task of those seeking to overhaul the ARE. Cuyler's position and the New York office were abolished, and many of the ARE's functions were transferred to the ARA. The Washington office remained intact under Thom, but the ARE itself was reduced to a "voluntary association . . . without any power or authority . . . to bind any member-road with respect to any matter whatever."[60]

Although the ARE limped along for another decade as a useful clearinghouse for policy, it never again provided a forum for unified action. The railroads still cooperated on a wide range of problems, but regional differences, personality clashes, and underlying suspicions kept them from acting together in many crucial areas. Too few executives appreciated that the carriers could no longer afford the luxury of rugged individualism. Those who had grown up in an age when the railroad dominated the transportation arena fell easily into the belief that it would always be so, but progress played a cruel trick on them. Just as competition from within had finally been tamed, new forms of transportation emerged to challenge the carriers from without. In less than a generation the golden age gave way to a struggle for survival.

14

The New Competition

During the summer of 1919, while debate over the railroad problem raged, a veteran import-export man paused from his own labors to ask Judge Lovett a question. No one seemed to him to be discussing "the inroads which the constantly increasing number of automobiles have made in cutting down both passenger and freight business for the Railroads. Have you any idea of the tonnage that is carried by automobile trucks within a hundred miles from New York, or any other large distributing point in the United States? Or of the millions of people who have automobiles and hardly ever use a train now, except for very long distances?"[1]

Yes, replied the judge, the impact of automobiles had been a grave concern for several years, but not one much talked about. The automobiles had taken some traffic from the railroads, but they had "compensated to some extent by wider development and settlement of the country as well as through the creation of a freight traffic of their own."[2]

A dozen years later, while the depression-wracked carriers pondered whether to seek a rate hike, Carl Gray took the measure of his own competitive situation in tones that had grown considerably less detached. The Union Pacific could not get more for fruit and vegetables because "on the present rate basis we are losing more and more fruit to the steamships." A hike in lumber rates would send more of it to the boats as well. Coal rates could not go up because of an invasion of pipelines throughout the territory, and an increase in merchandise rates would "further stimulate inroads from trucks," as would any move on livestock tariffs.[3]

On every side Gray found himself hedged in by forms of competition that had scarcely existed before the war. The inroads on passenger business were even greater than that on freight, thanks to the machine that was transforming American life in this century on the same grand scale as the railroad had done in the last. "Today, the automobile is the most popular form of transportation," crowed a General Motors executive in 1932. "It has taken its place beside the railroad, and as far as passenger transportation is concerned, has in many cases supplanted it. . . . The automobile is today the most popular vehicle for carrying passengers the world has ever known. The motor truck in its field becomes daily more efficient and adaptable. The freight train suffers from inflexibility and must be assisted by the truck."[4]

Nor was the motor vehicle the only threat. As Gray noted, two old adversaries, pipelines and shipping, had become greater menaces, the latter due in large part to the Panama Canal. Commercial aviation was still in its infancy but developing fast and already nibbling at one of the railroad's most lucrative prizes, the mail service. A new age of intermodal competition had dawned in which the railroads found whole domains of their business carved away within a remarkably short time. To survive this challenge, the railroads had to redefine their place in an expanded transportation industry.

One of the most striking characteristics of industrialization is the way technology has telescoped the process of change. Where the railroad took half a century to revolutionize transportation in the United States, the newer forms worked their magic in only a decade or two. The evolution from the early steam locomotive to the diesel engine consumed more than a century; the airplane leaped from the primitive glider at Kitty Hawk to jet propulsion in half that time. Small wonder, then, that the railroads were caught off guard by the sudden, even explosive rise of these challenges to their supremacy. With the hubris of all who hold the center stage of history, they thought their time would never end, and certainly not so abruptly.

In most cases this foreshortening of the time needed for the next advance worked against the older technology. The automobile, for example, was a new development seeking its place in the transportation industry. The railroad had already defined its role, which had to be adjusted in the face of changed conditions. Put another way, the older technology had to unlearn or escape the burden of its past. In the nineteenth century railroads had been catalysts for change in the American economy. By the twentieth century they had become the most traditional of industries and found themselves struggling to respond to constant change.

Prior to the war, the Union Pacific System regarded the new Panama Canal as its major competitive threat, but not a serious one. When the canal opened in August 1912, Julius Kruttschnitt predicted that the transcontinental business lost to it would be offset by greater local development. "If the Panama canal means anything it is the building up of the West," he asserted confidently. "The building up of the West is Southern Pacific's gold mine." But the gold mine didn't quite pan out that way. The canal sent rates tumbling and deranged traffic patterns. Marvin Hughitt cited one instance of furniture being shipped from Rockford, Illinois, east to New York and then to San Pedro via the canal.[5]

The canal forced transcontinental roads to depend more on short-haul traffic just when new forms of competition for that business were emerging. Moreover, the Panama Canal Act of 1912 forbade any road from operating a water line that used the canal. This took the Pacific Mail Steamship Company, a Southern Pacific subsidiary, out of the lucrative coastal trade. The Union Pacific managed to keep its water routes in the Northwest, but the inability of the railroads to use the canal greatly increased the damage done by it. By 1921 Kruttschnitt had changed his tune and was complaining loudly about competition from the canal.[6]

He had good reason to sound an alarm. After the war's end the growth in transcoastal shipping was spectacular if little noticed by the public, being obscured by the more dramatic rise of the automobile. A report made in September 1921 confirmed that all-rail lines could hope to get "only that meager portion" of transcontinental business "which through its perishable character or some other urgent needs requires a quicker and superior service." Already boats were snatching traffic from points 500 to 700 miles inland on both coasts. Shipments from such industrial centers as Pittsburgh that once went by rail to the West Coast were now going by rail to the Atlantic seaboard and by boat to the West. Flour milled in the Northwest was moving by sea to Gulf and South Atlantic ports, from which it reached interior points formerly supplied by Minnesota.[7]

And the ships were multiplying. The 1921 report listed ten companies with sixty vessels running between San Francisco and Atlantic ports; eight companies with fifty ships reaching European ports from San Francisco; six more lines connecting San Francisco with Cuba and South America; and fourteen with steamers running to Atlantic, Gulf, Hawaiian, and Far Eastern ports with cargoes that were "formerly handled at San Francisco and transported by rail lines across the continent." Los Angeles boasted eight companies with fifty-eight ships operating to Atlantic and Gulf ports, eight companies with thirty-one steamers sailing directly to Great Britain and the continent, seven companies with fifty-one vessels linking the Puget Sound to Gulf and Atlantic ports, and five ships serving Cuba and South America.[8]

These ships were already carrying an estimated 80 percent of the tonnage from San Francisco and 85 percent of the goods bound for Europe. Of the all-rail traffic for the year ending June 30, 1921, 78 percent was fruit, vegetables, canned goods, and sugar. This dismal situation only grew worse. Between 1921 and 1929 the transcontinental tonnage passing through the canal soared from 1.4 million to 10.1 million tons, a gain of 637 percent. By contrast, overall shipments via the canal grew 164 percent from 11.6 million tons in 1921 to 30.6 million tons in 1929. During that same period traffic moving over inland waterways (excluding the Great Lakes) nearly doubled, going from 83 to 161 million tons.[9]

Between 1921 and 1930 oil-carrying pipelines increased their mileage 61 percent to 88,728. Two aspects of this growth greatly disturbed the Union Pacific management. Where earlier pipeline mileage serviced the eastern oil fields, most of the new lines were being constructed west of the Mississippi in territory served by the Union Pacific. By 1930 California, Oklahoma, and Texas were producing 85 percent of the nation's oil. Since the same companies that produced the oil also owned or controlled much of the pipeline, this traffic was lost to the railroads.[10]

Pipeline expansion was merely part of an even more ominous trend. As an analyst noted, "Both fuel oil and natural gas have been supplanting coal for fuel purposes progressively during recent years." He estimated that natural gas was displacing coal at the rate of 28 million tons a year. The refineries themselves sent a clear signal: their use of coal dropped from 6.15 million tons in 1925 to 1.95 million tons in 1930. Coal was a staple of Union Pacific traffic, and earnings would suffer if less of it was being hauled shorter distances. Natural gas traveled exclusively by pipeline, and more oil moved that way every year. An expanding network of electric transmission lines also hurt coal shipments.[11]

Clearly an energy revolution was underway, and its most obvious effects seemed to be working against the railroads. The same could be said of the transportation revolution wrought by the internal combustion engine. As early as April 1921 President Warren G. Harding declared that "the motorcar has become an indispensable instrument of our political, social, and industrial life." Indeed, the very swiftness with which the automobile swept to center stage blinded many Americans to what was happening. Between 1920 and 1930 the number of automobiles registered leaped 183 percent from 8.13 million to 23 million. In 1920 there was one car for every thirteen Americans; in 1930, one for every five. Robert and Helen Lynd, in their classic study *Middletown* (Muncie, Indiana), found in 1923 that the town had 6,221 cars or about two for every three families, and the number was growing rapidly.[12]

Whole industries shifted their output or emerged from nowhere to serve the automobile. During the 1920s motor vehicle manufacturing consumed 20 percent of national steel production, 80 percent of rubber, and 75 percent of plate glass. Gasoline replaced illuminants and lubricants as the primary product of the petroleum industry, and highways became the most gigantic construction project in history. Car dealers, garages, filling stations, motels, restaurants, and a host of other ancillary businesses sprang up. While these phenomena were nationwide, the hotbed of automobile development lay west of the Mississippi River and was led by California—a fact that did not bode well for western railroads.[13]

The new wonder permeated American culture no less deeply than it did the economy. "As, at the turn of the century, business class people began to feel apologetic if they did not have a telephone," wrote the Lynds, "so ownership of an automobile has now reached a point of being an accepted essential of normal living." A working-class mother of nine put the matter more graphically when she cried, "We'd rather do without clothes than give up the car." The summer vacation emerged as a national institution, giving workers a set period to roam about the country seeing the sights. The Sunday drive quickly became a favorite recreation. The Lynds noticed that the automobile "appears to be an important agency in bringing husbands and wives together in their leisure." Car salesmen played unabashedly on this theme. "Holding the family together," proclaimed *Automobile*, ". . . is an argument that has sold thousands of cars."[14]

The effects of this revolution hit the railroads at once. In 1920 rail passenger travel reached a peak of 1.27 million passengers and 47.4 billion passenger-miles. Over the next decade the numbers slid steadily downward to 707,987 passengers and 26.9 billion passenger-miles in 1930. No one doubted that the automobile was fast stripping the railroads of their short-haul passenger business, and it was only a matter of time before the long-haul business suffered large losses as well. Automobile travel proved to be remarkably self-generated, piling up billions of passenger-miles that would not have happened if the traveler had to rely on commercial transportation.[15]

An offshoot of the private car, the motor bus, also made its appearance in small but growing fleets. It did not take long for bright young people to find profitable opportunities in the flexibility offered by the motor car. In 1912 a mine worker named C. S. Wickman of Hibbing, Minnesota, noticed a lack of transportation between there and South Hibbing. Rigging a crude passenger body on a truck chassis, he began hauling passengers on what may have been the first intercity bus. Form this experiment grew the Greyhound Corporation with Wickman as president. Between 1926 and 1941 intercity bus travel increased 212 percent, and average runs grew steadily longer.[16]

Another child of the internal combustion engine took aim at the heart of rail income, freight traffic. The motor truck revealed yet again the American genius for improvisation. In 1914 Henry C. Kelting stripped the rear seat from his Ford roadster and converted it into a van for hauling light freight between the docks and shops in Louisville, Kentucky. From this small acorn grew Union Transportation Company, which went broke, and then Central Truck Depot, which demonstrated the flexibility of trucks by cutting three days off a four-day rail delivery schedule and offering responsive, personalized service no railroad could match. In a fast-changing society, this proved to be a decisive advantage.[17]

Stories similar to Kelting's were repeated in many places because trucking, like the automobile and unlike the railroad, was very much an individual enterprise. Trucks were versatile and ubiquitous in what they could carry. They could haul cargoes of varying sizes from door to door without the large terminal costs that saddled short-haul rail delivery. Like the automobile, they could go to places that had no rail service. "The flexibility of the vehicle enables the motor carrier to adapt its service closely to the needs of its patrons," conceded a study sponsored by the railroads. "Private and contract carriers can accommodate their movements to any hours desired by the shipper. . . . The possibility of routing a shipment by motor vehicle to its destination without delays in transit expedites delivery."[18]

By 1930 at least sixty-two industries, ranging from the Post Office to general contractors to bakeries, relied heavily on trucks, most of which were still lightweight models. The number of trucks jumped from just over one million in 1920 to 3.4 million in 1929. Newer models grew steadily larger and heavier. Although the amount of freight they hauled was still fairly small, the trucks hurt the railroads by carrying premium goods that fetched high rates rather than bulk cargoes that brought lower rates. The railroads found themselves caught in a squeeze play, with trucks muscling in on high-value traffic and water carriers taking away transcontinental bulk business.[19]

The automobile revolution required the development of a national road system, which proceeded at a staggering pace during the 1920s. Total mileage of roads and streets increased about 100,000 miles, or 3 percent, but the amount of surfaced highway doubled during the decade and would do so again in the 1930s. By 1930 the country had nearly 3.26 million miles of road, of which 694,000 was surfaced. Only about 329,000 miles of this total could be called intercity road, 73.8 percent of it surfaced.[20]

The new roads took a bite out of the railroads in a literal sense. Many of them were built on land leased from railroad right-of-way. In Nebraska the Union Pacific rented the outer 66 feet of its 400-foot right-of-way for the Lincoln Highway. The lease was approved in May 1919; eight years later the county asked for another 34 feet to handle the ever increasing flow of traffic. "What on earth can they do with 100 ft. highway right of way?" asked an incredulous Henry Clark. "Allowing ten feet on each side for drainage, the remaining 80 feet would provide for 8 streams of traffic. Of course they could never afford to build and maintain this width." Nevertheless, the extra land was given, and similar arrangements were made throughout Union Pacific territory—for instance, the Golden Belt Highway in Kansas. In this way a major portion of the highway system came to be located alongside the railroads.[21]

To pay for this mushrooming system, the federal and state governments poured $1.8 billion into highway construction between 1922 and 1930. As the cost mounted, state and local officials looked for new sources of income. They found the ideal solution in a tax on gasoline, which by 1929 had been imposed in every state; that year it raised a total of $431 million at rates of three or four cents a gallon. "Never before in the history of taxation," noted a modern authority, "has a major tax been so generally accepted in so short a period." It spread the cost fairly among those who actually used the roads, and soon became neatly hidden in the cost of gasoline at the pump. Here was graphic evidence of the public's willingness "to pay for the almost infinite expansion of their automobility."[22]

Two aspects of the new competition especially infuriated the railroads. All these modes were subsidized in some way by the government, and none were subject to regulation. Shipping benefited from the canal (to say nothing of the rivers and harbors pork barrel), motor vehicles from roads. Railroads had to run the competitive race in a straitjacket of regulation while the other contestants ran freely. Without the flexibility to adapt to rapidly changing conditions, the railroads could not compete effectively with any of their new challengers. From these complaints arose a set of demands that would become the clarion call of the railroads for two decades.[23]

The railroads demanded an end to all government subsidies to competing forms of transportation. They also wanted trucks, buses, water carriers, and pipelines made subject to regulation comparable to that on rail lines. At the same time they wanted the freedom to operate truck, bus, and water lines of their own. This would enable them to extend their own service by competing directly with rival modes. The end result, argued the carriers, would be an improved national transportation system. Finally, they wanted relief from the tendency of both federal and state regulators to impose conditions that cut rates and increased expenses. Without some flexibility in these areas it was difficult for the railroads to compete with other modes.

Every item on this wish list faced a political gauntlet that would make passage bloody if not fatal. The odds against success on any of the demands were formidable, yet the railroads had no choice but to try. As an industry they had already begun to bleed badly during what was supposed to be an era of prosperity. Between 1921 and 1929 the rate of return of class I railroads averaged only 4.28 percent, well below the amount called for by the Transportation Act. The reasons were not hard to find. During the 1920s freight receipts per ton-mile declined 15.6 percent despite an impressive 22.7 percent reduction in expenses and an outlay of $6.86 billion for improvements. Passenger revenues fell from $1.17 billion in 1921 to $731 million in 1930, a drop of 37 percent, with no end in sight.[24]

From any angle prospects looked gloomy for the industry. The carriers were being squeezed long before anyone even dreamed that the worst depression in American history lurked just around the corner. Weak roads seemed a poor bet to survive, and strong roads would endure only if they adjusted to rapidly changing conditions. The time had come for this most traditional of industries to redefine what it did and how it did it.

What business was the Union Pacific in? By the 1920s this was no longer a silly question. The Union Pacific had been a diversified company from the beginning with its subsidiary land, coal, water, rolling mill, and resort interests. More recently, E. H. Harriman's mass purchases of securities in other railroads had given the company a diverse portfolio from which it drew a sizable income that ensured a surplus for dividends even when railroad earnings drooped. This strategy came close to being formalized in 1908 when the bankers nearly persuaded Harriman to create a holding company that would separate the investment assets from the railroad.

This history suggested a logical answer to the question, and the new competition helped ram it home. The Union Pacific had to think of itself not merely as a railroad but as a transportation company selling a service that could take many forms. Obviously the railroad was the heart of that service, but other modes could be used to extend or in some cases substitute for it. The new competition could neither be ignored nor driven away, but it could be challenged on its own turf. Motor vehicles had used their advantage of flexibility to exploit the weaknesses of a fixed-track carrier. Railroads could not change the basic limitations built into them, but they could graft the advantages of motor vehicles onto their own service.

The logic of it was compelling; the question was whether the government would allow such an arrangement. The need for a new approach was urgent. Between 1917 an 1925 passenger revenues on the Union Pacific fell 27 percent, passengers carried dropped 61 percent, and the average distance traveled per passenger fell 42 percent. On one route, Omaha to Fremont, ticket sales were down a staggering 85 percent. In August 1925 Gray took the first step by replacing an Oregon passenger local with bus service. The results were gratifying. During the last quarter of 1924 the train had lost $3,708; for the same period in 1925 the bus cleared a profit of $4,174.[25]

The Union Pacific was no pioneer in this tactic. So much interest had been aroused that in February 1926 *Railway Age* launched a new section called the "Motor Transport Section: Coordination of Railway and Highway Service." That March seven roads joined the Union Pacific in asking the ICC for the right to issue joint through fares for travel by a mixture of train and bus. At October hearings by the ICC on the possible regulation of motor vehicles, vice-president of traffic H. M. Adams stated his belief that the railroads would jump into bus and truck service in a big way if regulatory laws were put into effect. But the ICC was slow to recognize the impact of the new competition, and federal regulation was not forthcoming until 1935.[26]

Undaunted, the Union Pacific expanded its bus lines. In 1927 it added service from Portland to Pendleton, Oregon, and to Walla Walla and Yakima in Washington. A subsidiary named Union Pacific Stages was created for the bus operations. Here was a classic example of the American tendency to make new technology more familiar by giving it an old and comfortable name. Headquartered in Pendleton with its own superintendent, Union Pacific Stages became the hub for a growing network of routes that by 1929 extended into Idaho as well. For some years the Union Pacific had run buses to its Utah Parks resorts; that summer it also picked up Beehive Stages, which operated out of Salt Lake City. Although local passenger train service was reduced, the buses did not so much replace trains as supplement them. Customers had a choice of using their ticket to ride either way, a real bonus in scenic country. In May 1929 the company opened a combination rail and bus depot in East Los Angeles to facilitate transfer from one mode to the other.[27]

By 1929 the new operation looked good enough to require a major decision. One officer, J. L. Haugh, was deeply impressed by the potential of bus service. An engineer by trade, Haugh had worked for the Northwestern before going to Washington during the federal control. There he met Gray and followed him to Omaha as vice-president and assistant to the president. At first Haugh worked on the unfinished business of federal control. When that was wrapped up, Gray put him into industrial development and never regretted it. Haugh showed a knack bordering on genius for finding land and buying it cheaply for later development. He persuaded the company to buy several hundred acres of cornfield across the river from Kansas City that became the lucrative Fairfax

IDEA MAN: J. L. Haugh, who convinced management to go into buses and industrial development.

Industrial District, and did nearly as well with property in Omaha, Salt Lake City, Denver, and especially Los Angeles. A colleague called Haugh "the most resourceful man I ever knew."[28]

The same kind of instinct that steered Haugh to good land brought him to the bus business. Haugh liked the future it promised if, like the land, it was developed vigorously. He was not just thinking defensively; the buses would eliminate some costly passenger trains and, Haugh believed, would be profitable once past the stage of early development. In February 1929 he persuaded the cautious but open-minded Gray to jump into the business, and New York went along. The Burlington had already staked its claim with a bus line from Omaha to Lincoln. The Union Pacific could form its own line to run along its tracks, but Haugh had more ambitious plans in mind.[29]

Haugh's eye lit on a bus company called Interstate Transit Lines, which had recently brought up two smaller lines and now operated eighty buses across Nebraska and connecting points in neighboring states. The company had been created by an ambitious young man named Russell J. Walsh, who had earlier built a successful trucking firm before turning his attention to buses. Haugh persuaded Walsh to sell out to the Union Pacific and stay on as manager of an expanded operation. In July 1929 the Northwestern agreed to share in the purchase and become a partner in Haugh's scheme.[30]

Using Interstate Transit as the hub, the Union Pacific launched a series of interstate bus routes from North Platte to Denver, Salt Lake City to the Northwest, St. Louis and Kansas City to Denver, and (with the Northwestern)

Chicago to Denver. Late in 1929 it inaugurated the nation's first transcontinental route from Chicago to Los Angeles and Portland along with a line from St. Louis and Kansas City to Denver. In effect the company paralleled all its major rail routes with bus service. By then the Union Pacific had poured $3 million into its bus subsidiaries and was running three million miles a year over seven thousand miles of road.[31]

The Union Pacific, proclaimed the *Deseret News*, was entering "on a new phase of its history as one of the country's great transportation agencies by paralleling its railroad lines with bus service." By 1931 the company had taken off passenger trains totaling nearly 2.3 million miles a year. It was running 10,216 miles of bus line and had created a new subsidiary, Union Pacific Stages of California, to handle the lines radiating from the new depot at East Los Angeles. In addition, the Utah Parks Company operated sixty-five buses linking the railhead at Cedar City, Utah, to several nearby national parks.[32]

Rival bus companies, alarmed by this aggressive expansion, tried to halt it with legal blockades. Early in 1930 the Pickwick-Greyhound Lines complained to the ICC that Union Pacific control of Interstate Transit violated both the Interstate Commerce and Transportation acts. As the first test of railroad-owned bus operations, the case was followed anxiously by the carriers and bus firms alike. In February 1932 the ICC dismissed the complaint, leaving the railroads squarely planted in the bus business.[33]

Truck service posed a different set of problems. By 1931 the Union Pacific had explored the possibilities but done nothing because, as Haugh admitted, the situation was changing so rapidly that a coherent policy was hard to formulate. Union Pacific Stages had ventured into the express business in a small way, carrying automotive parts, laundry, and ice cream between towns. Haugh realized the company could not afford to hang back much longer. The highway system was expanding and improving, allowing trucks to grab larger slices of business, especially less-than-carload (lcl) freight, which they could handle far better than the railroads. In 1929 trucks also moved 30 percent of the livestock reaching the Omaha market.[34]

The Southern Pacific, Texas & Pacific, and Cotton Belt were already using trucks to supplement their delivery service. In April 1931 Union Pacific Stages followed suit by launching a pickup and delivery service from depot to store on certain Northwest lines. A month later the operation made its debut in Nebraska for lcl shipments. An employees' organization called the Booster League eagerly began soliciting traffic, and local draymen who had been put out of business by the trucks found new work making deliveries for the Union Pacific. Still the road faced an uphill fight. Trucks hauling livestock to Chicago and Omaha quoted absurdly low rates on cargoes to avoid returning empty. The Union Pacific had to deal with a mix of through and local rates once shippers put pressure on the road to extend the service to interstate hauls. In September 1933 the ICC dealt the company a blow by prohibiting a rail trucking subsidiary from quoting rates below the published schedule to meet cuts by truckers.[35]

On a broader scale Railway Express Agency (REA), the company created by all the railroads to handle their express business, faced an even graver crisis

WAVE OF THE FUTURE: An early Union Pacific truck gears up for duty.

than the roads that owned it. By 1929 an internal survey showed that there did "not now exist a distinctive field within which the express company has a monopoly," and that it was no longer even competitive in fields it had once dominated. The advent of parcel post service in 1913 with its much lower rates had swept away the small package market, and trucks had cut heavily into short-haul traffic since 1917. In recent years REA had begun to lose long-haul business to the lower rates offered by trucks.[36]

In response, REA acquired what was by 1930 the largest private fleet of trucks in the nation, yet it still struggled to meet the challenge. Many railroads hesitated even at that late date to venture into buses or trucks. As one of those that had seen the light, the Union Pacific could by the early 1930s legitimately be called a transportation company. Nevertheless, at bottom the railroad could not escape certain inherent limitations: its huge capital investment in fixed routes, excessive regulation that made quick or creative response to rapid changes in the environment virtually impossible, and the weight of a long tradition that prevented most railroad men from seeing the world with fresh eyes.[37]

The Union Pacific did not overlook an old tactic for dealing with competition. Unlike many roads, it continued building new mileage right through the 1920s. Kruttschnitt asserted this policy less than two weeks after Harriman's death, when he stunned the industry by announcing that the Union Pacific-Southern Pacific would spend $100 million to construct 2,000 miles of extensions. Although much of this work was in Mexico, 600 miles of it was in Union Pacific territory and another 390 miles in the Northwest. This program marched steadily forward prior to the war, then went into hibernation until the roads were returned to private ownership. By then the position of railroads had changed radically.[38]

The new conditions slowed but did not stop extension work on the Union Pacific. A project begun before the war of building up the North Platte Valley into Wyoming was pushed to completion because irrigation had opened up large areas there for cultivation. In 1923 Gray had his eye on a region north of Fort Collins, Colorado, where irrigation permitted the growing of sugar beets. Then Union Oil blew in a mammoth gas well on land leased from the Union Pacific, and oil men flocked to the area. Gray got the jump on the Colorado & Southern by laying a branch eighteen miles north of Fort Collins. Two more miles were added in 1925 to serve a new cement mill. Three years later, the company decided to build a north-south cut-off from its North Platte branch to the main line near Burns, Wyoming, thereby giving Denver direct access to the North Platte region.[39]

In the Northwest the Short Line concentrated on developing branches in southern and western Idaho. The largest project, a ninety-four-mile extension from Rogerson, Idaho, to the Southern Pacific at Wells, Nevada, gave Idaho more direct access to San Francisco and tapped some new copper mines. The Navigation Company did little more than construct a thirty-mile branch to Burns, Oregon, to reach some timberland.[40]

The biggest furor arose over a road Navigation didn't want to build, and illustrated again the great advantage enjoyed by the new forms of competition that were not regulated. For decades the citizens of central Oregon had agitated for an east-west line across the state. Harriman had flirted with the idea but concluded there was not enough business to justify the cost. Two decades later Gray agreed despite strong pressure from local interests. In 1929 the Oregon Public Service Commission forced the issue by asking the ICC to require a carrier to build the line. The commission endorsed the idea and singled out Navigation as the lucky company to undertake the 185-mile project at an estimated cost of between $9 million and $11 million.[41]

The issue at stake was a critical one. "If the commission can make its order effective," warned *Railway Age,* "there is practically no limit to the extent to which it can control the policy of the railways in developing their properties. . . . Has the government the power to make the owners of the Union Pacific subsidize people in Oregon by incurring losses on a line which they do not want to build?" A recent Supreme Court decision had held that the ICC could not compel the railroads to construct a joint union depot in Los Angeles. Would the court extend this logic to new mileage? The case was closely watched as a precedent.[42]

Unfortunately, the legal struggle got upstaged by a macabre sideshow. Three federal judges heard arguments late in September 1930. On October 2 one of them died in an automobile accident, forcing a second hearing in December. Early in January 1931 another of the judges dropped dead of a heart attack. A second replacement was brought in, and the court managed to enjoin the ICC order late in January. Judge Frank Rudkin, who wrote the order, had replaced the accident victim; four months later he was dead of heart disease. One observer spoke ominously of a "Man-Killing Injunction." The ICC promptly appealed to the Supreme Court, which in January 1933 ruled that the commission lacked authority to compel construction. All the justices survived the decision, and the railroads breathed a loud sigh of relief. By 1933 they had quite another set of problems on their hands.[43]

The Los Angeles & Salt Lake posed a different difficulty. Just before becoming its president in July 1921, Gray went over the line and the region it served. The condition of its branches left on his mind a very sorry impression; they had to be improved and new ones built. After driving around Orange County one day and the San Fernando Valley the next, Gray concluded that "The former has promise . . . but the latter is our opportunity." Future business, he was convinced, would come to and from San Bernardino and points west. That autumn two new branches totaling thirty-six miles were commenced southwest of San Bernardino.[44]

In Los Angeles itself the company invested $1.75 million in a new shop and terminal complex. The new facilities bordered a parcel of 750 acres intended for industrial development, making it one of the largest such projects then available. It also received one of the first giant sewer lines installed by the city. One innovation in the new terminal branded it indelibly as southern California: part of the delivery system for supplies included a counterman who flashed up and down the long aisles on roller skates.[45]

The biggest project revolved around an old controversy, the development of Long Beach as a major port for Los Angeles. For years local interests had sought some plan for routing the Union Pacific and the Atchison into the harbor over one line. In 1924 the city council approved a plan estimated to cost $3 million, but the Southern Pacific fought a long and successful battle to block the Atchison's access to the proposed line. Finally, in 1932 the Union Pacific constructed a $2 million cutoff on its own, one of a precious few such projects in the depths of the depression.[46]

In Utah two more branches were added to tap very different markets. A thirty-one-mile extension from Fillmore to Delta opened up 100,000 acres of irrigated land for cultivation, while a thirty-two-mile branch from Cedar City to Lund created a new railhead for tourists visiting the Grand Canyon and other national parks in the region. Although tourism was a growth industry in the 1920s, it was old hat for the Los Angeles & Salt Lake. One of the road's original components, the Los Angeles Terminal, had handled tourist traffic to Terminal Island, Verdugo Park, and Long Beach since the 1890s. In those days the Glendale train formed the habit of stalling briefly in the middle of a vineyard so the passengers could scramble out and pick grapes.[47]

Even Nevada got some new track of a very specialized kind. The decision to build Hoover Dam on the Colorado River created a huge demand for supplies. In 1931 the Union Pacific completed a 30-mile spur to the site under an unusual arrangement. The company kept 22.4 miles of line, the government purchased the 7.3 miles nearest the dam, and a third of a mile for switching was shared. This little branch and the Long Beach cutoff were virtually the last gasp of expansion for the Union Pacific except for industrial spurs. The great tide of

DEPRESSION TEMPLE: The new Omaha Union Station, which opened in January 1931 just in time to catch the bottom of the Great Depression.

new construction that had surged forward since the dawn of the industry crashed on the beach of depression and rolled back out to sea. In the reports of every company the section once devoted to new mileage began instead to list abandonments.[48]

During these transition years nothing posed a thornier problem than passenger depots. Their story reflected the history of the roads that had built them. In the golden age of railways, passenger stations served as imposing gateways to every major city, welcoming travelers with a display of magnificence that advertised the dominance of the owning lines. By 1930, with passenger traffic dwindling and costs rising, they were fast becoming white elephants, monuments of grandeur whose impressive facades masked an empire in decline. But they could not be let go, especially in the big cities. The railroads still owned most of interstate travel, and their tactic for keeping that business increasingly stressed comfort and elegance. It would not do for rail managers to show the public a shabby face or themselves a mirror in which to view the decline of their industry.

Not only did stations have to be kept up, some new ones had to be built. Topeka got a new depot in 1927, and two years later the Union Pacific invested $3.4 million in an impressive new complex at Omaha. The new depot opened in January 1931, with double the car capacity, a much larger waiting room, vastly improved facilities, all the modern conveniences, and a striking design across its Tenth Street entrance. Six other major roads also used the station, which handled eighty-two trains every day. Only one other project rivaled the Omaha depot, and it was one the Union Pacific did not want to build.[49]

Since 1911 the city of Los Angeles had been trying to force the Union Pacific, Southern Pacific, and Atchison to build a union station in a designated downtown site that would eliminate grade crossings, collect many scattered facilities, and help showcase an ambitious civic center plan. The three roads disagreed with each other, the ICC, and the city on what to do, and none were eager to spend money on a major depot. For years the battle raged, going several times before the state commission and courts, five times before the ICC, and twice to the Supreme Court. In May 1931, however, the case got a third crack at the Supreme Court, which upheld a state supreme court decision affirming a 1927 order by the California State Commission. When the smoke of legalisms cleared, the railroads found themselves compelled to erect a new union terminal estimated to cost $10 million.[50]

Having lost at last a battle they had won so many times before, the three roads began work in 1933. The city of Los Angeles chipped in $1 million, which about covered the cost overrun. For its effort the city got a beautiful and spacious facility in striking Mediterranean design highlighted by a 125-foot clock tower. The decor and detail produced an impressive mix of beauty and efficiency. One feature unique in passenger station construction, the South Patio, was an open area paved in five shades of brick and landscaped with olive, pepper, and palm trees. Dining space on the North Patio featured a garden delight of orange, jacarandas, eucalypti, fig, avocado, and oak trees.[51]

The new union station opened in May 1939, one of the last passenger depots to be erected in a major city. As the product of a shotgun wedding among the participating roads, it was not the most apt of symbols for the railroads' struggle to keep their dwindling passenger business. As a thing of beauty it might well have served as a model for depots of the future—if passenger depots had a future.

While battling the challenge of new modes of transportation, the railroads had also to contend with each other. The old days of bitter, protracted wars waged by slashing rates and invading each other's territory had passed to the extent that even the hint of a showdown invoked banner headlines trying to rekindle the old excitement. Railroad wars had been relegated to the dustbin of nostalgia, but rivalries still existed and disputes still flared that required careful diplomacy to settle. It helped that the carriers had drawn closer together in recent years, and recognized that division among themselves only played into the hands of their common enemies.

Major shifts had taken place since Harriman's day in both the relative strength of western roads and the alliances among them. The Hill roads remained powerful along with the Burlington, which had long since established itself as the strongest of the Iowa roads. The Northwestern had lost some of its bloom, and the Rock Island, newly emerged from receivership, maintained its proud tradition of short-sighted management. The Milwaukee, as the newest and weakest transcontinental line, needed all the friends it could get and drew nearer the Union Pacific. Farther west the once debt-riddled Atchison had emerged as a powerful rival to the Union Pacific and Southern Pacific, while the bankrupt Missouri Pacific still struggled to recover from the legacy of George Gould.

COMMAND PERFORMANCE: The front of the beautiful Los Angeles Union Passenger Terminal, built in 1939 after a lengthy court battle compelled its construction.

Once competition among the roads was reduced to service, schedules and interchanges loomed more important than ever. Even before the war these questions were straining traditional alliances. When the Northwestern, long the Union Pacific's closest connection east of the Missouri River, joined with the Northern Pacific in a new passenger service to the West Coast in 1912, the Union Pacific countered at once by putting on new trains with the Milwaukee. A year later the Atchison demanded certain concessions as its price for joining a general agreement on freight schedules. Denouncing their position as "absolutely unreasonable," A. L. Mohler switched tactics by installing new schedules to teach the Atchison an object lesson.[52]

The contrast in styles between Mohler and Gray reflected clearly how times had changed. Where Mohler was brusque and imperious in his dealings with rival lines, Gray was deft and smooth, a genial diplomat who understood well the appeal of honey to flies. Railroad officials were a proud, prickly lot, quick to take offense and to personalize issues. Misunderstandings were much easier to remove when the presidents of the roads involved were good friends. In 1921, for example, James E. Gorman of the Rock Island appealed directly to Gray to help curb growing distrust among their lieutenants over relations between the roads. Gray did so at once.[53]

Two years later L. J. Spence of the Southern Pacific went directly to Lovett with a list of grievances against vice-president H. M. Adams. Lovett passed the complaint along to Gray, who talked to Spence and found him convinced that Adams had deliberately snubbed him by handling with other officers matters that should have gone to Spence. In laying the affair before Adams, Gray emphasized that it had "affected Mr. Spence's pride." The thing to do, he suggested, was "convince Mr. Spence of your attitude toward him personally." Gray arranged a meeting at which the two men openly thrashed out their differences with himself as mediator.[54]

Diplomacy also assumed a grander scale during these twilight years of rail supremacy as the last gasp of expansion played itself out. After the Milwaukee had installed itself in the Northwest, rumors persisted that the Northwestern would build to the coast because of its disagreements with the Union Pacific over traffic issues. Stories popped up regularly about some new project, but railroad men took few of them seriously. Attention shifted instead to the realignments posed by the ICC consolidation scheme, which hung like a specter over all the carriers. Throughout the 1920s major systems maneuvered cautiously in search of possible acquisitions that would both strengthen them and win approval from the ICC.[55]

Another factor heightened interest in new connections. The brothers Van Sweringen, two Cleveland real estate operators turned railroad promoters, were busily erecting a Tinkertoy empire of rail systems held together through a maze of holding companies in the style so fashionable during the 1920s. Ultimately they swept together the Chesapeake & Ohio, Nickel Plate, Erie, Wheeling & Lake Erie, Pere Marquette, Kansas City Southern, and Missouri Pacific. In the summer of 1929 they were buying the Missouri Pacific and rumored to be after the Katy, but had not yet acquired the Kansas City Southern.[56]

Gray was concerned because he had long believed the Union Pacific's strength in the Southwest lay in the independent lines—the Frisco, Katy, and Kansas City Southern—that competed with the Rock Island, Southern Pacific, and Atchison. But the Van Sweringens might tie one of them to the Missouri Pacific, and the Frisco had bought heavily into the Rock Island, which had acquired a chunk of the Cotton Belt. The mighty Pennsylvania had gained control of the Wabash, giving it lines west of the Mississippi for the first time. The Atchison was expanding aggressively, throwing out extensions and picking up smaller lines, including the 735-mile Kansas City, Mexico & Orient in 1928.[57]

The major systems were uneasy because so many smaller lines were lying around loose, as had been the case half a century earlier. But times had changed in a big way. Railroads were no longer a growth industry, and most of them didn't have the money to go shopping. Moreover, they couldn't do anything without government approval, and the consolidation scheme hung over every ICC deliberation. The Southern Pacific discovered this when it tried to acquire the Cotton Belt in 1930 only to be denied by the commission on grounds that astonished even Union Pacific officials. They had agreed with the Southern Pacific to sanction the merger provided the Cotton Belt was made subject to the same traffic agreement governing the Central Pacific. Those terms still held in 1932, when the ICC reversed itself and approved the takeover.[58]

The depression cut the heart out of the most ardent expansionist. Even before hard times hit, however, the Union Pacific pursued a cautious course, resisting attempts to foist the bankrupt Alton and the moribund Chicago Great Western on it. In 1931 the Pennsylvania had second thoughts about the Wabash and abruptly sounded Gray on whether the Union Pacific wanted the lines west of the Mississippi. After consulting with Lovett, Gray urged the Pennsylvania to keep the lines and stay in Kansas City, where it acted as a stabilizing force. The Union Pacific did not need to buy Wabash track; it had long been a preferred connection of both the Wabash and Missouri Pacific. Nor was it seriously tempted by the Kansas City Southern, a stronger and more desirable road. On all these questions Gray was content to play a waiting game.[59]

One project continued to haunt Gray as it had western roads for three decades. Denver interests had never forgiven the Union Pacific for running its main line through Wyoming and relegating their city to a branch. Many roads ran to Denver but none included it as part of their main line. During the 1880s David H. Moffat, who had made a fortune in mining and banking, resurrected the idea of a direct line from Denver to Salt Lake. As president of the Rio Grande he tried vainly to get that company to build such a road. After resigning the office in 1891, he pursued the idea until it became an obsession with him. Moffat let the depression run its course, and by 1902 had secured enough money to commence his Denver, Northwestern & Pacific, which would always be known as the Moffat Road.[60]

Moffat's line snaked to the northwest toward Steamboat Springs over forbidding terrain through Rollins Pass, 12,000 feet high and blanketed with blizzards, toward a region with fewer inhabitants than a good-sized town. His dream was to run a straight line toward Salt Lake City by tunneling through James Peak, shortening the distance between the two cities from 735 to 525 miles. Plans were made to connect with Clark's San Pedro road at Salt Lake City. If Moffat succeeded, he would shatter the existing structure of transcontinental relations. For that reason alone, all the major players watched him closely. George Gould, then in the midst of piecing together his own line to the coast, actually underwrote some of Moffat's bonds but opposed the project vigorously. For years rumor also accused Harriman of trying to block it, a charge Judge Lovett later denied in vigorous language.[61]

As news of the Western Pacific trickled out, Moffat found himself caught amid the battle of the titans. ''By God,'' he roared defiantly, ''the road will be built, if I have to go out and drive spikes myself.'' He tried desperately to get backing from the Burlington, which stood to gain most from completion of the line. Hill was interested, but ultimately he and Burlington president George Harris thought it a poor investment and told Moffat in 1904 there was ''no prospect of our Company taking an interest with him at present.''[62]

Discouraged, Moffat later went to Harriman and importuned him to take an option on the project. The challenge of tunneling the Rockies could not help but rouse Harriman's fighting blood. He sent William Ashton, the Short Line's chief engineer, to make an inspection. Ashton did a thorough job and prepared a report advising against involvement. When Kruttschnitt and Stubbs also entered strong objections, Harriman reluctantly let the option go. Moffat never did find financial backing. He poured his own fortune into the road, which straggled into Steamboat Springs at an appalling cost of $75,000 a mile. Worn out and financially ruined, Moffat died in March 1911.[63]

But the idea lived on. William G. Evans, son of former governor and railroad pioneer John Evans, had long been associated with Moffat in the project. Shrewd, energetic, determined, Evans commanded wide influence in Colorado's financial and political circles. In 1911 he pressed Mohler for support and won him to the cause. Mohler had long believed someone would eventually build the road and tunnel. ''As an ally or a direct ownership,'' he told Kruttschnitt, ''it is more valuable to the Union Pacific Railroad than to any of the other Lines operating through the City of Denver.'' A company attorney there added that it would erase decades of antagonism toward the Union Pacific in Denver and produce a close alliance ''with the most powerful influences in this community.''[64]

Lovett, who had personally drawn up the papers for Harriman's option, studied the proposition carefully. He read Ashton's report and got hold of another one by J. B. Berry, former chief engineer of the Union Pacific, who was then with the Rock Island and had looked at the project for the owners of that line. Berry's conclusions were even more unfavorable than Ashton's, and Lovett could not get past one crucial factor. ''When Mr. Harriman refused to buy a railroad,'' he told Otto Kahn after ticking off all his other reasons for rejecting the project, ''. . . the presumption is pretty strong that the line is an undesirable acquisition.''[65]

The road terminated at Craig, Colorado, where prospects for extension were nil without a tunnel. Undaunted, Evans turned to the public coffers. A bill to construct the tunnel with state funds was voted down in 1911, then gained approval in 1913 only to be challenged in court. While the fight dragged on, the Moffat road twice sank into receivership and was saved only by the federal takeover. A new scheme to get federal money was trotted out in 1918. When that failed, Evans and his friends again went after the state of Colorado, enduring setback after setback until they got a tunnel act in 1921. After surviving a legal challenge, the project that wouldn't die finally became a reality in 1927 as the longest tunnel (six miles) in the country.[66]

During the fight to revive the project, the old rumors that the Union Pacific was blocking the effort surfaced anew. An annoyed Lovett assured Evans that he was "very tired" of these tales, which were "absolutely false." Nor did the Union Pacific want the Moffat road other than as a connector. But the judge followed events closely. He still thought the line was a white elephant even if the tunnel was built, and told Gray emphatically, "The time is past when railroad companies can buy a property for its 'nuisance value.' " The tunnel legislation, however, meant that the Union Pacific as taxpayer would again be asked to subsidize a competitor. Then, in 1924, the idea of building to Salt Lake City was challenged by a plan to construct a cutoff to the Rio Grande's station at Dotsero, Colorado.[67]

Suddenly the long-neglected Moffat road found itself at the center of a strategic maze. Once reorganized and with the tunnel completed, it would force a realignment of transcontinental business. The Rio Grande line across the mountains, which was high, circuitous, and 130 miles longer than the Union Pacific, would be devastated by a through line from Denver to Salt Lake. If the Dotsero cutoff were built, however, the Rio Grande could obtain a superior line into Denver. But the Rio Grande was controlled jointly by the Missouri Pacific and Western Pacific, which together utilized the Pueblo gateway and could only lose business to a route favoring Denver. Nor was this all. Railroad investor Arthur Curtiss James, who held large interests in the Burlington and Western Pacific, cast his eye on the Moffat road as the final link of a new through line from Chicago via the Denver gateway.[68]

A delicate situation had arisen. Without the cutoff the Rio Grande would bleed to death. If it were built, the Missouri Pacific would be hurt badly. Either way the Union Pacific would lose the Moffat road as a connector and have to compete with its shorter route.

"There are potentialities about this line which we cannot afford to ignore," concluded Gray in 1927. From his Western Maryland experience he knew the Moffat road could haul coal at a profit with the tunnel open. He also knew the road ran through some of the finest coal in the country. A fight loomed in which the Union Pacific could be little more than spectator. Having passed so many chances to acquire the road, any attempt to do so now would enrage the company's friends in Denver.[69]

Gray was anxious to keep the road as an independent connector, but he knew the Rio Grande would be in deep trouble without the cutoff. Moreover, the goal of the Moffat road had always been to connect Denver with the western part of the state, which the cutoff did better than any alternative. Fortunately, Hale Holden of the Burlington antagonized the interests behind the Moffat road and cost his company any chance of acquiring the road. Gray did what he could to keep the road out of the hands of the Rio Grande. He wanted the business that its local stations brought into Denver, and he feared any construction into Salt Lake Valley, which he thought would soon be attractive territory.[70]

In August 1928 Averell Harriman learned that the Rio Grande was about to build the cutoff in return for a joint rental agreement on the Moffat line. He rejected an overture to take the stock at a price he deemed absurd but passed the news along to the New York office. General counsel Henry Clark doubted the company could legally own the stock, but Gray determined to look into it anyway. His efforts proved too little too late. By early 1930 James had pressured the Missouri Pacific into going along with Rio Grande acquisition of the Moffat road. The Rio Grande purchased more than half the road's stock only to be stalled by legal wrangling from building the cutoff. Not until September 1931 were the obstacles removed, and by then a new one loomed in the form of the depression.[71]

Wallowing in debt, the Rio Grande could find no way to build the cutoff until the summer of 1932, when a long and acrimonious struggle culminated in a loan from the Reconstruction Finance Corporation. Although bickering dogged every step of the way, the Dotsero cutoff opened in June 1934. By that time the long night of depression had settled on the land, and in 1935 the Rio Grande sank yet again into bankruptcy. It would be years before rival roads felt the real influence of the new route.[72]

15

The Counterattack

The board room of the Union Pacific floated in the clouds on the thirty-second floor of the Equitable Building, its windows overlooking downtown Manhattan and the bay beyond. Like most board rooms it wore an air of muted opulence, a plush aerie high above the clamor of the streets. At the same time it possessed one feature not found in other board rooms. All the chairs lined one side of the table, facing a wall on which hung a map ten feet high and thirty feet long showing every mile of the Union Pacific System along with its stations, shops, grades, and projected construction. An electric switch controlled the movement of the giant map, rolling it from the plains to the high country to the Northwest while the directors followed the course of developments.[1]

The map was a tool, a chessboard on which the players plotted strategy. Half a century earlier the map had changed faster than the players, sometimes so fast that they despaired of keeping up with it. By the 1930s the reverse was true: the map remained stagnant while the players came and went with increasing rapidity. Between the wars the Union Pacific underwent yet another transition of leadership at every level of management. Part of the change was simple attrition; another part reflected Judge Lovett's continuing efforts to improve the organizational structure and diminish his own role. The judge, whose health had long been frail, was wearing down.

In 1924 Lovett completed his restructuring work by reviving the position of chairman of the board, which had been abolished on Harriman's rise to power in 1899, and moving into it. A finance committee was created in place of the executive committee and given charge of all financial matters. To emphasize the point, the controller was elevated to a vice-presidency and put in charge of

MAN OF FIGURES: C. B. Seger, the first accountant to rise to a top position in the Union Pacific management.

the New York office. The president in Omaha was cloaked with new duties, giving him command over all properties in the West. Under this arrangement the board handled policy and the finance committee money matters, with the controller serving as liaison between the president and the committee. As board chairman Lovett planned to devote his time to two key issues: valuation and mergers. He told the press he was quitting his executive duties on the advice of his doctor.

"Is your health really poor?" asked a reporter.

"My physicians have told me," replied the judge in his dry manner, "that if I cut down the amount of onerous work with which I have been saddled for years I may die of old age. That is my plan. To die of old age. Think it is a good plan?"[2]

But Lovett had an unspoken agenda as well: completing the transition to the post-Harriman era. The industry had entered its mature phase in which lawyers and accountants replaced the entrepreneurs who had built it. A clear division of power had been drawn between the president, who was czar of all operations, and New York, which still clutched the purse strings firmly. The structure was in place, the system functioning well; all it needed was good men in the key posts. Carl Gray certainly fit that bill, and so did F. W. Charske, the controller, who gained important new duties.[3]

Longtime director Charles Peabody, president of Mutual Life and chairman of the Illinois Central executive committee, became chairman of the finance committee but found the burden too great at the age of seventy-five. In August 1924, only eight months after taking the post, he relinquished it to C. B. Seger, who had remained on the executive committee after becoming president of U. S. Rubber. The fifty-seven-year-old New Orleans native had always been a railroad man. He began as an office boy on the Louisiana & Texas in 1883, then worked as an auditor on Southern Pacific roads until moving up to the parent system in 1910. After the unmerger, Seger stayed with the Union Pacific and was soon made comptroller and vice-president. His presence as finance chairman, along with that of Charske, whom Seger had brought to New York, put the eastern office in the hands of two former auditors who worked well together.[4]

The board also underwent some major changes. In 1921 a long-deferred provision of the Clayton Act, designed to prevent interlocking directorates, had forced Kahn and Morti Schiff off the Union Pacific board. They were replaced by Newcomb Carlton of Western Union and Paul Warburg of Kuhn, Loeb. Both joined the new finance committee along with Seger, Peabody, Averell Harriman, and Lovett. Warburg's presence kept the Kuhn, Loeb connection alive but in attenuated form; when Seger replaced Peabody, Otto Kahn found it "disturbing to reflect that we did not know a thing about the whole episode until after it had been consummated, when Seger came in to tell us." William Rockefeller's namesake son died in 1923, only a year after his father, and Frank Vanderlip left the board the following year.[5]

The election in 1923 of Heber Grant, president of the Mormon Church, restored the old tradition of a Mormon director begun with Bishop John Sharp shortly after the road was built. But finding the right men to serve as directors had become a difficult task. When Marvin Hughitt, Jr., left the board in 1926, Seger was stumped on a replacement and had to push Henry Clark onto the board temporarily. Part of the problem involved filling seats for so many subsidiary companies within the system. This was but one of several difficulties in the existing organization that Lovett proposed to rectify in his new post. The time had come, he believed, to make the Union Pacific System a true system by merging its separate lines into one company.[6]

The best way to accomplish this, Lovett believed, was through a series of long-term leases prior to the merging of each subsidiary with the parent company. In April 1924, while relaxing in his favorite vacation spot, southern California, the judge drew up a detailed plan using the Southern Pacific as his model for the leases. He hoped large savings would result from centralizing such activities as accounting, auditing, freight offices, and other corporate functions. He realized loud protests would come from Salt Lake City, Portland, and Los Angeles, which would be affected most by the cutbacks, but shrugged that "the controversies that will grow out of the merging of our own lines must be faced sooner or later."[7]

Gray agreed there would be an outcry in all three cities, but he was willing to endure it for the savings, estimated conservatively at $412,508, to be made by closing and consolidating offices. The closer he looked at the Southern Pacific plan, however, the less convinced he was that this would occur. "They encounter just as much clerical work in this respect as we do," he told Lovett, the major difference being that "they concentrate this detailed clerical work in the main office while we have it segregated between four offices." If the savings were substantially less than projected, Gray concluded, he preferred leaving things as they were.[8]

Nothing could be done quickly because the proposed leases and mergers had to be approved by the ICC, and nothing could be done on the mergers until the commission issued its final consolidation plan. Lovett thought this would be forthcoming by the winter of 1924–25 and was anxious to have the leases in place before then. He needn't have hurried. The ICC did not release its plan until December 1929, and the Union Pacific did not submit its merger request until May 1932. By that time a great deal had changed in the industry and in the world.[9]

Working up his contribution to the annual report proved a much harder task than usual for Gray in December 1929. "Have never known a time," he apologized to Seger, "when it was so hard to visualize future prospects."[10]

Like everyone else, Gray had been shaken by the collapse of the stock market that autumn, and he had no idea what it portended for the future. His cautious, moderate soul had not yielded to the giddy euphoria that swept so many others along on the back of the big bull market. What goes up comes down, and the higher the flight, the greater the fall. All this Gray understood well, yet he could not imagine how devastating the impact would be on the larger world of business. Hardly anyone guessed that the economy would sink to the bottom like a broken ship and lie there for more than a decade despite repeated attempts to salvage it.

The shock hit with stunning swiftness because the 1920s had been prosperous for the Union Pacific as they had for many roads. The company had come into the decade with the distinction of having earned more for the government during its period of control than any other road. It was in better physical and financial condition than most roads. Analysts soon pounced on its stock as undervalued. One noted in August 1920, when the common was selling at 115, that its asset value was $171.[11]

Since Harriman's death the stock had remained the bluest of blue chips, paying a consistent 10 percent dividend except for the period from 1914 to 1916, when the rate was cut to 8 percent because of the extra dividend in B & O stock. Through the turbulent teen decade the annual swing between the stock's high and low exceeded 28 only twice, in 1914 and 1917. Despite the company's consistent performance, the generic woes of the industry helped drive the price downward from a high of 204¾ in 1910 to a low of 110 in 1920. But earnings stayed strong during the 1920s, reaching record heights in 1928 and again in 1929. Prosperity sent the stock steadily upward again from a high of 129½ in 1920 to 297⅝ in 1929, a gain of 130 percent. This was an impressive climb but small change compared to more glamorous stocks that soared three or four times this amount during the bull market.[12]

The big difference was that Union Pacific had long since ceased to be a speculative stock and become a favorite of investors. Few other stocks paid a 10 percent dividend every year. The bonds too were highly regarded; one analyst called them "the premier investment in the railroad class." Throughout the decade the company was able to sell new issues at premium prices. In 1923 it peddled $20 million in 5 percent bonds at the lowest cost any railroad had managed since before the war. Much of the credit for this belonged to Charske, who continued the Harriman tradition of buying money at the cheapest rates. Partly for this reason the Union Pacific enjoyed a striking advantage over most roads. During the 1920s only 44 percent of its net operating income went to paying interest compared to an average of 68 percent for all railroads.[13]

There was no secret to the company's success. Management still followed the Harriman formula of a well-built, well-maintained road keeping its plant and equipment ahead of the demand for business. This formula enabled it to cut expenses in lean years without impairing the physical condition of the system, as was the case with poorer roads. The zeal for upkeep and a steady flow of long-haul business allowed the company during the 1920s to maintain an average operating ratio of 70.9 percent, significantly lower than the industry average of 77.8 percent. High earnings and efficiency of operation also permitted the Union Pacific to spend more on new plant and equipment than other roads. By 1927 the company ranked as one of five rail systems among the ten American corporations with assets of more than a billion dollars.[14]

One other factor accounts for the Union Pacific's continuing role as a giant in a declining industry. It too was a Harriman legacy, and long a controversial one. Since the breakup of Northern Securities the Union Pacific had put the proceeds of that transaction (and later the Southern Pacific unmerger as well) into outside investments, mostly the securities of other roads. Harriman's successors continued the policy despite severe criticism. The old charge that the Union Pacific was seeking to dominate connecting lines still echoed, but a new and more powerful fear emerged. "The Union Pacific," predicted one analyst, "will never be sure of an unprejudiced hearing of its cause in either labor or rate controversies as long as the stream of its investment income is allowed to mingle with the stream of its transportation earnings in such a fashion that only a few bespectacled academicians are able to remember the difference."[15]

Although the outside investments produced $139 million in income between 1909 and 1919, they looked to have all the makings of a white elephant by 1921. Harriman had bought railroad stocks at peak prices, but the industry's woes since then had badly eroded values. Illinois Central had slipped from 163 to 91½, New York Central from 136 to 70, Northwestern from 168 to 65, B & O from 120 to 39, and Alton preferred from 161 to 8. Bonds and notes had also depreciated a staggering $115 million in face value thanks to a depressed market. The future of railroads remained uncertain under the Transportation Act, especially with new forms of intermodal competition emerging. Events seemed to confirm Otto Kahn's belief that the investments were "the one serious mistake" of Harriman's management.[16]

He could not have been more wrong. The political damage caused by the policy may have justified Kahn's views, but not the financial performance. A better assessment came from one analyst who called the investments "one of the brilliant spots in the history of American finance." During the flush times of the 1920s the portfolio reaped an income of $169 million, an amount only $6 million less than all interest charges for the decade. Put another way, this income reduced from 44 to 31 percent the proportion of its combined earnings the Union Pacific had to pay for interest, leaving ample funds for dividends and improvements. Moreover, the bull market boosted the value of stocks in its portfolio. By the summer of 1929 B & O had rebounded to 145, Northwestern to 108, Illinois Central to 153½, and New York Central to 236.[17]

In 1922 the ill-starred Alton went into receivership, and the Union Pacific wrote off much of its investment in the road. Such losses posed no danger because the company had long ago established a reserve fund of $50 million for depreciation of securities. The outside investments gave the Union Pacific an earnings edge no other road could match. Between 1920 and 1929 combined operating and investment income *averaged* $15.74 per share of common, and reached a peak of $20.36 a share in 1929. Outside investments provided 49 percent of total net earnings for the decade, which is to say they doubled the company's income.[18]

Impressive as this performance was, it looked even better during the depression as railroad earnings fell to pieces. Forty years earlier a similar economic blow had knocked the Union Pacific into receivership along with many other roads. This collapse was far more severe than that of the 1890s, and once again a procession of railroads fell by the wayside. In 1894 a record 40,819 miles of road had gone bankrupt; during the 1930s the amount of mileage in receivership *averaged* 49,176 and peaked at 77,013 in 1939. None of it included the Union Pacific, which showed a strength in hard times comparable to that of good times. Instead of the disaster that ruined so many other roads, the depression ultimately proved to be one more stunning monument to the Harriman legacy.[19]

It helped to have the railroad with the longest average haul and densest traffic in the West. Gross earnings on the Union Pacific for the 1930s dropped 27 percent from the 1920s compared to 37 percent for all railroads. Net earnings reversed this difference, falling 44 percent on the Union Pacific and only 34 percent on all roads—showing among other things that the company did more business and spent more on upkeep than other lines. It could afford this policy because investment income declined only 9 percent despite the loss of virtually all dividends on railroad securities in the portfolio. Income from bonds, government securities, and equipment notes still flowed in; as a result, combined net income fell only 33 percent compared to the 44 percent drop in transportation net earnings alone.[20]

Nor was this all. Shrewd financial handling enabled the company to cut its interest payments by 12 percent. During the 1930s the Union Pacific paid 69 percent of net transportation earnings (41 percent of combined net earnings) for interest compared to 103 percent for all roads. The investment income alone covered all interest charges for the depression decade. While other roads canceled dividends and struggled frantically to meet fixed charges, the Union Pacific merely reduced its payment from 10 to 6 percent in 1932. Never did it miss a dividend even in the worst of times. By 1934 only four other railroads in the country could boast of having earned a surplus above their dividend.*[21]

Nothing vindicated the Harriman legacy more strikingly than the performance of the Union Pacific during the long night of the depression. It had the reserve strength to endure a lengthy siege of financial illness that consumed more sickly roads. The past policy of high maintenance standards enabled it to cut expenditures on improvements by 54 percent from the previous decade and still keep the road in good shape. Unlike weaker roads, it had no catching up to do. A property that had never been allowed to run down was far easier to maintain in lean times, and times were much less lean for the Union Pacific than for the vast majority of railroads. A tradition of high standards could not be continued without money, but the money was always there when it was needed.[22]

For thirty years the Union Pacific had held its place among the leaders of the industry. During the 1930s, while other roads faltered and fell—some never to regain their place—the company emerged as one of the giants of the industry. Where the devastating blows of the depression forced most other roads onto the defensive, the Union Pacific had the resources to mount a counterattack. Instead of hunkering down and waiting for the storm to pass, the company took the offensive, searching for new opportunities amid the debris of hard times with a more potent arsenal of weapons than most other lines could muster.

"I have great hopes for the railroad business," Carl Gray said in 1937. "I have been in it more than half a century and in all that time Old Nick has been just around the corner. Several times we have seen a piece of his tail, and sometimes a hoof but he has never got around the corner yet. I don't believe he is any nearer around it now than at any time in that period."[23]

Harriman would have loved it. He relished a good fight and hated being back on his heels. Seizing the offensive suited his temperament perfectly. In a way he was still there to wage the battle, not only through his legacy but also through his sons, who were increasing their role in Union Pacific affairs. So was the namesake son of Judge Lovett taking on added responsibilities. A new generation of leaders was emerging in the ordeal of the depression.

The changing of the guard in management accelerated as retirement and death emptied the ranks with brutal swiftness. A long link with the past was severed in 1929 when Oliver Ames died; he was the last member of the family who had helped build the road to serve as a director. Two years later the venerable Charles Peabody, Morti Schiff, and Paul Warburg all died, and Otto Kahn followed in 1934, the last survivor of the Kuhn, Loeb group that had

*The Norfolk & Western, Pennsylvania, Chesapeake & Ohio, and Bangor & Aroostook.

SOMETHING OLD, SOMETHING NEW: The four indispensable members of Union Pacific management during the 1930s pose in front of a system map. (*From left*) Carl Gray, Averell Harriman, Woody Charske, William M. Jeffers.

worked so closely with Harriman. Seger turned sixty-five in 1932 and retired; secretary Thomas Price, who had been ill, left in 1933. In Omaha E. E. Calvin reached the mandatory retirement age of seventy in 1928, and general solicitor Nelson Loomis retired three years later.[24]

When Judge Lovett turned seventy in 1930, the board voted to waive the mandatory retirement rule and asked him to stay on as a chairman. The old gentleman was grateful but very tired. Apart from poor health, the spark had gone out of him after the death of his wife in 1928. His only son was put on the executive committee of the Union Pacific in 1930. The judge could rest content. He had been a most successful steward and a sound pilot as well, steering the Union Pacific through two turbulent decades, using the Harriman legacy as his beacon but not following it blindly. Through his efforts the Union Pacific emerged stronger than it had ever been, a powerful giant in a faltering industry. Worn down by his labors, the judge died in June 1932, shortly after entering the hospital for an operation.[25]

Where many companies would have been decimated by the loss of so many key figures in so short a time, the Union Pacific was fortunate to have an impressive array of talent waiting in the wings. In Omaha Gray remained a tower of strength in the twilight of his career, and Calvin's place was taken by the burly Irishman who amazed everyone with his vigor and toughness, William M. Jeffers. In New York Woody Charske quietly emerged as the man who held the operation together. He had replaced Peabody on the executive committee and become its chairman after Seger's retirement. On the board the chairmanship passed to Averell Harriman; his brother Roland and young Robert A. Lovett also served as directors.[26]

The second generation of these two close families had already united in business outside the Union Pacific. During the 1920s the Harrimans formed two banking firms, W. A. Harriman & Co. and Harriman Brothers & Co., while Robert Lovett became a partner in Brown Brothers, a venerable house that traced its origins back to 1818. With several of the Brown partners nearing retirement, some of the younger men, including Lovett, were amenable to a merger with the Harrimans. They were all friends, most of them classmates at Groton and Yale. As Roland Harriman later said, it was "a joining of forces by people who thought alike and liked each other." The new firm of Brown Brothers Harriman was created in 1931 and remains the only large commercial bank in the nation that is still a partnership instead of a corporation. Although the Harrimans provided most of the original capital, the new firm made no distinction between junior and senior partners.[27]

The entry of the Harrimans into banking could not help but affect Kuhn, Loeb's position with the Union Pacific. In 1927 the brothers asked for and got half of the railroad's time and call loan business formerly handled exclusively by Kuhn, Loeb. Five years later the Union Pacific decided to sell part of its holdings in New York Central and invest the proceeds in Pennsylvania Railroad stock. The executive committee heard that Kuhn, Loeb was buying New York Central stock for another party, which meant it could not sell for the Union Pacific. Instead the business went to Brown Brothers Harriman just after Averell had become chairman of the board.[28]

The timing proved unfortunate. Kuhn, Loeb was not buying the stock, and its partners became upset after learning the transactions had gone to Harriman's firm. "I thought we were the Union Pacific bankers," said one of them pointedly." Charske assured him that they were and turned the rest of the transactions over to Kuhn, Loeb. Averell helped soothe their feelings, and Kuhn, Loeb continued to handle the larger Union Pacific issues.[29]

Nevertheless, the message impressed early on Kuhn, Loeb soon became clear to everyone else. Paradoxically, change within the Union Pacific management produced a continuity unique in major public corporations. Since 1898 Harriman and Lovett had dominated the Union Pacific. The election of Averell Harriman to succeed Judge Lovett perpetuated that tradition. Indeed, the younger generation of the two families would rule the company for another thirty-seven years.

The counterattack on the depression began internally and affected every level of the corporate structure. The Union Pacific did not achieve its impressive financial record during the 1930s without taking heavy casualties. As earnings dropped, cutbacks were made with ruthless efficiency. An energetic young officer named E. J. Connors, who had come to the Union Pacific in 1923 after service with the Railroad Labor Board, had the unhappy task of compiling the boxscores of attrition. In November 1928 the Union Pacific System had 54,297 employees on its payroll. Three years later the number had dwindled to 29,254, the lowest number in service since 1905. The layoffs continued until the force bottomed at 23,781 in March 1933, a drop of 56 percent since

November 1928. Across the industry as a whole, employment fell 41 percent between 1928 and 1933.[30]

Maintenance of way, which had the most transient labor force, suffered the severest loss in personnel, 65 percent between March 1929 and March 1933, but every area felt the ax. Staff officials, clerical forces, and shopmen were all slashed 49 percent, the transportation department 42 percent. Some of the layoffs proved temporary; employment crawled back to 28,741 by March 1935 and 32,135 by the following March, a figure still 33 percent below that for March 1929. Those who kept their jobs had to take wage cuts, leaving no doubt that hard times hurt the strong roads as well as the weak. Four major western roads* exceeded the Union Pacific's total payroll reduction, but none matched its cuts of staff, office, and clerical forces. By 1933 the company's front office was leaner if not meaner than that of its competitors.[31]

One reason for the scale of attrition was simply that prosperous roads like the Union Pacific had more employees to cut than poorer lines. In part, however, the cutback was achieved by pushing through Judge Lovett's plan for unifying the system into one company. The petition, submitted shortly before the judge's death, met what had become for the company a typical reception in the ICC. The commission approved the merger provided the Union Pacific agreed to buy two small lines it didn't want and couldn't use. The company refused this proviso and appealed for a rehearing. A former commissioner wrote in disgust, "Either the Commission *has* authority from Congress to compel one railroad system to purchase another—or it has not." If so, he added, it need not attach the order to another, wholly unrelated request; if not, it had even less reason for doing so.[32]

The ICC denied the appeal, ignoring the argument that buying two useless lines would negate the economies projected in unifying the system. Caught between its boiling resentment at the order and the urgent desire to carry off the merger, the executive committee spent twenty months dickering over terms with the owners of the two roads. In December 1934 agreement was reached, and the commission approved the merger leases the following July. On January 1, 1936, the separate corporate identities of the Short Line, the Navigation Company, the Los Angeles & Salt Lake, and the St. Joseph & Grand Island passed out of existence. The Union Pacific System had become the Union Pacific Railroad.[33]

In that moment five boards and five sets of books became one, with savings estimated at $472,000 a year. Of the 400 clerks staffing offices in four cities, 137 lost their jobs and received a year's "dismissal pay." The rest were moved to Omaha, with the company paying their expenses and reimbursing them for any loss suffered in the sale of their homes. This enlightened policy was so well received that it became the model for a general agreement between the unions and the Association of American Railroads for handling any consolidation among carriers. Averell Harriman was delighted at the praise heaped on the company by the press.[34]

*The Burlington, Illinois Central, Milwaukee, and Northwestern roads.

The top level of management underwent some trimming as well. After Charske replaced Seger, his former position as vice-chairman of the executive committee was abolished. In Omaha the vice-president of operations was changed to an executive vice-president with Jeffers moving from the one post to the other. He also picked up two assistants, the labor expert E. J. Connors and a bright if somewhat quixotic accountant named George F. Ashby. The change nudged Jeffers up the organizational chart past Gray's own two assistants, fueling reports that he was the heir apparent—a rumor Averell Harriman had to deny as early as 1933.[35]

In the realm of finance Charske pursued with quiet efficiency the policy of cutting costs wherever possible. Interest payments struck him as a logical target. With corporate bonds selling at near record lows, Charske thought it possible for a strong company like the Union Pacific to refund issues at reduced rates. He waited until April 1936 to refund $26.8 million of older 4½ percent bonds with a new 3½ percent sinking fund debenture. The offering startled Wall Street. No railroad had sold an unsecured bond at that low a rate since the turn of the century; indeed, only one secured issue had gone at 3½ percent, and it had been guaranteed by both the Pennsylvania and New York Central railroads. If successful, the issue would save Union Pacific an estimated $5 million.[36]

Kuhn, Loeb took the bonds at 97 and, to the surprise of many pundits, had no trouble selling them at 99. Encouraged by the results, Charske tested the waters again in September with another $20 million in 3½ percent debentures to refund an outstanding issue of fours. The new bonds, sold to Kuhn, Loeb at 97½, were also snapped up by investors, and the company saved another $2.52 million in interest charges. The Union Pacific also saved money by reducing the amount of its long-term debt from a high of $415.7 million in 1923 to a low of $343.7 million in 1935. These tactics enabled the company to slash interest payments by 12 percent during the 1930s compared with the previous decade, while weaker roads bled themselves into bankruptcy trying to meet their obligations.[37]

On the road itself the new economy meant lower expenditures for improvements and equipment. For a few years the drop was severe. For the period from 1926 to 1930 the company spent an average of $8.8 million annually on improvements and $6.3 million for equipment. During 1931 to 1934 the figures dwindled to $2.8 million and $803,000 respectively. At the trough of the depression in 1933 the expenditures were cut to an astonishing $785,000 for improvements and $100,000 for equipment.[38]

Lovett had been a most dutiful steward in preserving the Harriman tradition of aggressive maintenance and improvements. By 1920 the company had replaced the main spans of the Missouri River bridge, extended its block signal system, enlarged yards, put in some experimental concrete snow sheds, and commenced double-tracking the rugged terrain between Wasatch and Emory in Utah—part of the original line laid so well by Samuel Reed in 1864. Some ninety-six miles of single track remained on the main line, all of it in difficult mountain country. The heavy wartime traffic spurred the company to eliminate the last bottlenecks. It took until 1926 to complete the double track from Omaha to Ogden, whereupon the company turned its attention to other lines in the system. Gray also believed firmly in this policy, and the prosperity of the 1920s let him practice it with record outlays until hard times slowed him down.[39]

The road got leaner in another sense as the historic trend of railway expansion was reversed. By the 1920s railroads cost too much to build and no longer paid a good enough return to warrant the investment, especially in competition with other modes of transportation. Construction of new mileage nationally fell off to 5,637 miles during the 1920s and a paltry 1,808 miles the following decade, most of it prior to 1934. Between 1934 and 1936 a total of 99 miles was built; in 1939 exactly one mile of new track was laid. Offsetting this collapse was a counter trend toward abandonment. The 6,973 miles of main track retired during the 1920s paled before the 15,414 miles dumped during the depression decade. These figures produced a net loss of 14,942 miles for the period between the wars. It was as if a major system and its subsidiary had been wiped off the map.[40]

Of course, the missing track was scattered across the map rather than concentrated in one region. Much of it had originally been built to serve mines or other resources that had been exhausted. The Union Pacific did not hesitate to follow this policy, although it preferred to use the euphemism of "retiring fixed property" without replacing it. Altogether the company owned 137 branches totaling 5,142 miles, of which it had abandoned only 14 miles prior to 1930. The sagging economy caused it to study the entire branch system closely to see what lines might be let go. In each case Gray paid no attention to number of cars, tonnage, or length of haul; rather he looked at the gross revenues contributed by the branch measured against its own expenses plus the cost of the system line haul.[41]

By this yardstick Gray retired 62 miles of branch line as of November 1931 and marked another 57 miles for abandonment. Although the ICC denied some applications, the company managed to lop off 432 miles of track during the 1930s, most of it small industrial spurs except for a 143-mile branch in Kansas and a 71-mile line in Oregon. Service was also cut on many branches, reflecting the decline in business and growing inability to compete with highway vehicles for short-haul traffic. By 1929, even before the depression hit, daily regular freight service had vanished from 65 branches totaling 1,051 miles, some of which were later abandoned. These trends did more than reveal the impact of a major depression; they also pointed to an industry in the throes of a profound transformation. The future belonged to the systems with a long haul.[42]

There was much of the father in the son, though not in his looks. Averell Harriman was tall and handsome, with dark hair and a lean, athletic build. Where E. H. had been educated in the rough and tumble of Wall Street, the son went to Groton and Yale. Although his manner was far more polished than his father's, there was a slow, almost plodding quality about it. But the same intensity was there along with the explosive energy and insatiable ambition. Decades later an admiring aide would say of Averell, "he's the only *ambitious* seventy-seven-year old I've ever met." But the ambition was not blind; it was rather a voracious drive to achieve, to succeed at whatever he took up, whether it be polo (at which he was good enough to earn an eight-goal rating) or business or diplomacy. He was no less competitive than his father; he simply handled it with far more grace and tact.[43]

Averell was at once a man of his social class and beyond it. He had come of age at a time when society was being nudged out of the headlines by a new breed called the celebrity, a synthetic creature of the entertainment field that was fast taking its place among the nation's giant industries. To the surprise of many, Averell moved as easily among this new breed as among those of his own class. So strong was his sense of self that no amount of rubbing against the wrong elbows could erase it. Nor was he averse to the limelight. "I was brought up with the instinct to avoid publicity," he once told Arthur Brisbane, but he learned early to curb the instinct that had brought so much grief to his father. In this area he possessed gifts and strengths that E. H. Harriman never had.[44]

Nevertheless, the father's imprint was strong and indelible. As a boy at Groton, Averell struggled to overcome a problem with stammering. Told by his father that it would be a good thing to overcome some difficulty each year, he worked on his spelling as well as his stammering with some success. Although very close to his father, he did not get to enjoy his company for very long. E. H.'s death in September 1909 occurred just as Averell was preparing to enter Yale. That same summer, while his father was seeking relief in European spas, Averell did his first stint on the railroad with a survey gang between Ashton and Victor, Idaho, at the base of the Tetons.[45]

After his father's death Averell drew closer to Judge Lovett. He was an earnest, rather awkward youth who felt comfortable around the judge despite their difference in age, and looked forward to visiting him during the latter's vacations in southern California. Lovett saw to it that Averell did a cram course in railroad work during his college summers. He toured the system on a track motor car with a rail inspector, sat at the elbow of the master mechanic in the Omaha shops, followed auditor G. E. Bissonnet over the system to see how he analyzed the accounts of each department. In 1913, the year of his graduation from Yale, he went on the Union Pacific board along with Frank Trumbull as part of the reshuffle following the unmerger. A year later he was made vice-president in charge of purchases, becoming at twenty-two a prodigy among rail officers.[46]

Although he started at the top, the job was no sinecure. On one level he mastered the finer points of how many calendars and towels to order for the system each year; on another he got involved at Lovett's request in a close study of the entire central purchasing operation. From the first Averell showed himself to be bright, quick, and incisive in the mold of his father, whose shadow might have crushed a less talented son. In 1918 he moved up to the executive committee, destined in his own mind and in the eyes of others to make his career in railroading. But appearances were deceiving. At twenty-six he had already begun branching out in other directions, notably banking and shipping. He remained a vice-president of Union Pacific but in July 1918 requested that his salary be dropped because virtually all his time was being devoted to other interests.[47]

Shipping offered extraordinary opportunities during the war. Averell gained control over a number of shipyards, built vessels for the government, and emerged from the war as the dominant figure in the industry. In 1920 he stunned observers by opening a shipping link to Hamburg, the first such arrangement with a German line at a time when war feelings against that country still ran high. Brushing these sentiments aside, Harriman contended it was crucial that Americans control enough of their own commerce to remain independent of foreign shipping. He had gone into the industry because he considered it "the most important matter connected with the growth and well-being of the United States." One impressed analyst described him as occupying at thirty a position in shipping similar to that held by his father in railroading fifteen years earlier.[48]

But shipping was merely a point of departure. Within a year Harriman formed his banking firm, and soon entered mining, aviation, and other fields. In 1924 he headed an investment group that obtained a concession from the Russian government to mine manganese in western Georgia. Four years later the new Harriman Building opened at 39 Broadway with the banking house occupying five of its thirty-six floors. He had become an international figure; his banking and other interests sprawled across the globe, yet still he searched for new challenges. The impact of the depression, coupled with an appeal from the failing Judge Lovett, lured him back to railroads.[49]

In a sense he had never really left them. Harriman had kept his place on the Union Pacific executive committee, but it had not been central to his concerns. Since 1913 he had also been a director of the Illinois Central, in which the Union Pacific still held a large interest. The depression nearly sank the Illinois Central. At Lovett's request, Harriman became chairman of its executive committee in 1930 and the following spring gave the judge a report on the property and its officers. Although the road had to scrap its dividend, which did not resume until 1950, it managed to stay afloat through the decade. Harriman's influence with the bankers did much to ease the financial pressure. While undertaking this work, he suspected that Lovett was grooming him as his successor on the Union Pacific.[50]

A year later the judge was dead and Harriman took his seat as head of the board. His appointment was no surprise; the Harriman family still held the largest interest in the company. He was forty-one years old, a decade younger than his father had been when the destiny of the Union Pacific fell under his control. Like his father, Averell would never be content to confine himself to one field. He was still an international banker with far-flung investments of his own, and soon the New Deal administration would lure him to Washington for what proved to be a career in politics that superceded all his other activities.[51]

* * *

Where E. H. had caught the road on the rebound from a depression, Averell found it in one not yet touched bottom. The Union Pacific had the longest average freight haul of any road in the nation and the highest traffic density of any western road. The traffic was diversified but more dependent on agriculture than most of its rivals, which made it vulnerable to shifts in crop output. In most years between a fourth and a third of its business came from the farm, with manufactures and miscellaneous products comprising another fourth. Behind these two categories came coal, oil, other minerals, lumber, livestock, and lcl (less-than-carload) shipments.[52]

For decades the company had run special trains composed entirely of high-value import products such as silk and tea. In recent years this had extended to vegetable oils, copra, and even local commodities like canned salmon, canned goods, and forest products. The signs of changing times could be read in the waybills: in 1922 the Union Pacific carried a full train of washing machines consigned to A. A. "Washer" Wilson in Los Angeles. Six years later, amid a chorus of wisecracks from the agents and hands, it hauled an entire carload of silk hosiery and lingerie to Salt Lake City, of all places. Averell was anxious to increase traffic from the Orient and Australia as well as from conventional sources.[53]

He was also eager to develop new ways to exploit existing business. When Clarence Birdseye was developing his newfangled notion of frozen foods, he made contracts for vegetables and then sent in his freezing machines to move from field to field. Harriman suggested having the railroad promote the development of vegetable growing along its line to regularize the supply. If the industry grew, it would create a more orderly marketing process for fruits and vegetables that normally had to be sold quickly or else canned or dehydrated. In other areas the bankers were not shy about lending a hand; James P. Warburg tried to hustle business from Lockheed, and Knight Woolley of Brown Brothers Harriman wooed some shippers of large pipe.[54]

But Averell was not content merely to renew the company's strength. In a move that would have made his father proud, he decided to counterattack the forces of depression at the road's weakest point: its passenger traffic. The business had slipped to 60 percent of 1920 levels by 1929, and to an alarming 23.6 percent by 1932. Prior to 1930 attempts to reduce passenger service had been thwarted by the ICC and state regulatory agencies. Their reluctance eased when the depression hit, but even then cuts in service did not match the loss of revenue.[55]

The point was rammed home to Averell on a trip west during the bleak winter of 1932–33. His private car was hitched aboard the *Los Angeles Limited*, or what was left of it after business dwindled. Gray was with him, and so were Jeffers, traffic vice-president Frank Robinson, and some other officials. At one point Harriman left his car and walked through the train. It was a ghost town, so empty "you could shoot a cannonball through the train and not hit anybody," as one of those present described it. After returning to his car Harriman asked Gray if there was any reason they couldn't just get out of the passenger business. Gray shook his head. Apart from the regulatory straitjacket, he explained in his patient way, the people along the route had no other way to get their supplies or mail. There were no roads yet, no other access to the outside world. In that case, said Averell, we had better do something to get people back on these trains.[56]

The "something" was already underway: an intensive study to develop a new type of passenger train. It was one of two dramatic projects Harriman would promote in his inimitable style to turn the disaster of passenger business around.

16

The Projects

The decision came partly by chance, as many decisions do. Averell was still learning, still seeking the right path to strike. Unlike the blunt, abrasive manner of his father, he had a smoother style of doing things that made them seem simpler than they were. "I really had a great deal to do with saving the Illinois Central from bankruptcy," he explained years later. He had imposed ruthless economies on everything from maintenance to the payroll. "It was pretty hard to lay people off, but you had to do it. I think that was one reason why, when I assumed chairmanship of the Union Pacific the next year, I wanted to do something creative."[1]

Nothing offered more room for creativity than passenger travel, which had been stagnant for years. As an old man, Harriman still wrinkled his nose in distaste at the recollection of the drafty, noisy old coaches with green plush seats used by most roads. "They made life about as uncomfortable as it could be, and the Pullman car had not been changed." One incident revealed to him the difference between the stodgy rail industry and the fledgling airlines. "In those days Pullman had blankets that were almost pieces of board—they were the color of a piece of board—brown and hard blankets." Harriman pointed out to the Pullman salesman that the airlines used attractive, light-colored blankets and asked if Pullman avoided them because they got dirty too fast.

"Oh, no," replied the salesman, "we don't mind washing them. We wash these blankets every six months, whether they need it or not."

New technology was required along with new thinking. To revolutionize travel, a train had to be much faster and therefore lighter. It required a design to cut wind resistance and a self-contained engine that would eliminate stops

WE DID IT TOGETHER: William R. McKeen, Jr. (*center with beard*) poses with some of the men who helped him build the fabled McKeen car. The man on McKeen's right is Arthur H. Fetters, who was instrumental both in designing new power and guiding the Union Pacific through its early diesel and streamliner work.

for fuel and water, produce more power within a smaller space, weigh much less, and run cheaply. In other words, the train of the future.

Advances in two areas made this kind of thinking even possible: improvements in internal combustion engines, and research in aerodynamics and lightweight metal alloys spurred by the rise of aviation. The Union Pacific had been active in both areas for years. Indeed, E. H. Harriman had been a pioneer promoter of new engines for railroad use. As early as 1905 the company shops had built a gasoline-powered car designed by W. R. McKeen, Jr., the superintendent of motive power and machinery. So impressive were the results that the Union Pacific formed the McKeen Motor Car Company to produce more of them.[2]

What Harriman had wanted was a self-propelled vehicle capable of replacing more costly and cumbersome steam power on branch and interurban routes. The enterprising McKeen came up with a prototype that was cheaper than electric vehicles, more flexible than steam, and could do forty to sixty miles an hour on sustained runs. The first car, produced in March 1905, was thirty-one feet long and mounted on a single four-wheel truck. After testing out well on

PIONEER: An engineer poses proudly in the window of McKeen Motor Car no. 4 with trailer no. 1, December 1905.

runs between Omaha and Valley, Nebraska, it was replaced by a fifty-five-foot car made entirely of steel and seating fifty-seven. This became the prototype for several more cars, all of which performed well in Nebraska. One traveled under its own power to Houston and was put into service on the Southern Pacific; another went to Los Angeles and saw duty there.[3]

By April 1906 a revised prototype emerged as car no. 7, also fifty-five feet long but seating seventy-five and equipped with sealed porthole windows that kept out the elements and permitted stronger body construction. A bemused reporter said it looked like a submarine on wheels but was really an automobile on rails. When the gleaming red car headed east for a test run over the Erie, an exuberant Harriman climbed aboard at Arden to join a covey of Erie and Union Pacific officials for the trip.[4]

Before the new competition had even emerged, Harriman had seized on a way to meet it. Encouraged by the test results, the company put the McKeen cars on regular routes throughout the system and ordered more built by the new company. Gasoline motor cars were also used as section cars, but these were bought from outside suppliers. By 1915 the McKeen engines had been hiked from 100 horsepower to 200 and 300 horsepower, and seating capacity to seventy-eight. The war interrupted progress and helped kill the McKeen Motor

Company, which did little work other than repairs and was dissolved in 1920, with the Union Pacific absorbing its assets. But the company continued to buy motor cars with power plants furnished by the Electro-Motive Company.[5]

Despite its short life, the McKeen car left behind an imposing legacy. It ushered in a new era of rail technology; some of the 150 cars built were still operating in the 1930s. It also influenced two people who would play key roles in developing the streamliner. Edward G. Budd, one of the foremost passenger car builders of the era, cut his teeth working on the McKeens. Budd freely conceded in 1934 that E. H. Harriman and McKeen "foresaw the engineering principles which have recently been embodied in the Zephyr type of railway train." The sleek contours with porthole windows, the gasoline engine mounted in front, and other features anticipated the streamline concept.[6]

A veteran mechanical engineer for the Union Pacific named A. H. Fetters, who helped design the first McKeen car, grew particularly interested in the fuel problem. To reduce both costs and the fire hazard, Fetters began in 1914 to develop carburetors for the larger McKeens that could use low grade fuel. Two years later he and a local manufacturer produced a car running on kerosene, which became the standard fuel until distillate was substituted in 1922 because of its cheaper price. Fetters's work on fuels was to have considerable influence on the company's prototype streamliner.[7]

In this field as in so many others, E. H. Harriman showed himself a man ahead of his time. So was McKeen. "We know that the development of the internal explosion engine is in its infancy," he wrote in 1906, "that our experience with these engines is more or less limited, as compared with other means of developing power, and that the future use of these engines will be enormous as compared with the present day."[8]

By the 1930s, however, much had changed. The internal combustion engine had leaped forward along several lines of development, the most promising of which was an engine patented in 1892 by Rudolf Diesel in Germany. If certain problems could be solved, the diesel engine offered railroads an ideal blend of power, compactness, endurance, and economy. For years the Union Pacific had monitored progress on the diesel. In 1926 Gray sent Fetters, who had designed all the company's locomotives in recent years, to Europe, where Averell Harriman arranged to get him into all the major companies doing research on diesels. Fetters's report gave management its first full account of the state of the art.[9]

The key to successful adaptation, Fetters realized, lay in finding some way to transmit the power of the engine with its nearly constant speed to the varying speed torque requirements of a locomotive. And the weight of the engine would have to be reduced without sacrificing power or reliability. None of the plants he visited had yet solved these problems. Engineers were tackling the variable speed obstacle along six lines: electric, hydraulic, geared, compressed air, compressed steam, and compressed exhaust gas. Of these Fetter considered electric transmission the only one suitable for the high-horsepower needs of railroad use. It was reliable, flexible, had high starting torque, and offered good average efficiency for all speeds and loads. Moreover, the technology of electric transmission was well known by 1926.[10]

Fetters saw that the Europeans were far ahead of the Americans in this research. Only American Locomotive Company and two associates, General Electric and Ingersoll-Rand, were even building diesel locomotives, although several others were licensees of European firms. The reason was obvious: European trains ran lighter loads and needed less power. No existing diesel engine was compact enough even to fit the clearance requirements on American tracks, let alone haul heavy-tonnage trains. Nor was multiple unit use deemed practical. The construction cost of diesels per horsepower was nearly double that of steam locomotives, but the return was impressive. Nothing could match its high available heat efficiency. Recent technical advances had increased the thermal efficiency of steam locomotives to 10 percent, nearly double what it had been only a few years earlier but paltry compared to the 33 percent level of the diesel.[11]

"So many minds are working on the problem of perfecting the Diesel locomotive," concluded Fetters, that it would be unwise to generalize on its potential. He was exactly right. Progress on the diesel moved rapidly, but it had not come far enough by 1933 to convince the Union Pacific that it was suitable for an experimental train. Instead, Fetters commissioned from Winton (a subsidiary of General Motors) a 600-horsepower electric engine that ran on distillate, using the carburetors he had developed earlier. "After 15 years of experience in operating rail motor cars with low grade fuel," he had said in 1929, "we have faith in the future of the distillate engine."[12]

Technology had leaped forward in other areas as well. Rapid growth in both the automobile and aviation industries spurred development of aluminum and steel alloys that could be used to radically lighten passenger cars without reducing their strength. Aircraft builders had turned aerodynamics into a science and developed new techniques for welding lightweight metals to endure great stress. Borrowing heavily from the technical advances of these rival modes, the Union Pacific in 1932 launched an intensive effort to develop an experimental "super train" to recapture lost passenger traffic. Extensive tests were conducted with models in the wind tunnel at the University of Michigan to find the ideal design for reducing wind resistance by streamlining exterior surfaces. The idea, explained a publicist, was to "open a clean hole through the air and let it close in again with the least possible fuss or turmoil."[13]

The goal was to create a train that could knock a whole day off the schedule between Chicago and the Pacific Coast. A preliminary report showed this could be done at less than half the cost per mile of existing trains if the power problem could be solved. Weight projections ran a third lighter than a German train already in use, the *Flying Hamburger*, and had the engineers shaking their heads in disbelief. By May 1933 research had gone far enough that Harriman could let contracts and announce the project publicly. The basic design was in place, lacking only final decision on some details pending further tests. Pullman would build the three-car train, called M-10000, with Winton providing the engine. It was expected to be ready in six months at a cost of $200,000, a modest price tag for the train of the future.[14]

After some trial runs between Chicago and Niles, the M-10000 rolled out of Pullman's yards in February 1934 and was engulfed in an avalanche of public enthusiasm that not even its most ardent promoters had anticipated. It was more than a new train, a bold display of modernism; it was an *event*—something wholly unfamiliar and bewildering to traditional railroaders who had not yet grasped the curious ways in which the world was changing.

Nothing like it had been seen before. The three cars, made entirely of aluminum alloy, weighed a total of 85 tons, the equivalent of a single Pullman sleeper; by comparison a ten-car conventional steam train weighed 1,000 tons. Where the latter required 4,500 horsepower to reach 90 miles an hour, the M-10000 could achieve that speed fully loaded with 116 passengers, crew, and 25,000 pounds of mail and baggage, using only 500 horsepower. In place of the usual steel underframe the new train was tubular in shape and formed a stiff beam, giving it maximum strength from a minimum of material. Between an inner and outer sheathing of aluminum alloy plates could be found two inches of a new insulating material called "Rokflos," which was fireproof and sound-deadening as well as very light.[15]

The train hugged the rails like an automobile hugged the road, a mere 9½ inches above them and 11 feet high or 2 feet less than conventional cars. The cars were articulated or hinged together with one truck between each two cars instead of a pair for every car. Eliminating trucks reduced costs, track resistance, and weight. The twelve-cylinder Winton engine was made of wrought steel with a crank shaft of chrome molybdenum steel; no cast iron was used except on the cylinder sleeves. The engine connected to a 425-watt Westinghouse generator that ran two General Electric 300-horsepower traction motors mounted on each axle of the front truck. There was also a 25-kilowatt auxiliary engine for other uses and a backup 8-kilowatt unit in the baggage compartment for use when the main power plant was shut down.

The entire power plant with all auxiliaries weighed only 20 tons, a stark contrast to the 316-ton steam locomotives used in passenger service. The distillate fuel, stored in tanks built into the floor, could take the train 1,200 miles or *twelve* times the distance a conventional passenger train could run on a load of coal. No stops were needed for water or refueling. New types of rubber were used for cushioning on the trucks and antifriction bearings for the journals, generators, and ventilation system. To stop this high-speed train safely and comfortably required a whole new braking design. A dual system with an electric circuit parallel to the pneumatic circuit was devised, which synchronized and accelerated all braking.

Close attention was given the interior decor as well. The sealed windows needed for streamlining were made possible by a ventilating system that heated or cooled through thermostats and kept air moving enough to permit smoking anywhere in the car. All lighting was indirect and had three levels of brightness. The colors ran through a variety of metallic blues to a white ceiling, and the floors used cork tile to deaden sound. A new type of adjustable seat with footrest and attachable tray was installed, and the overhead baggage rack was eliminated in favor of space beneath the seat. In place of a diner there was a buffet built into the last car from which waiters served passengers on what they called a "kiddie car," a sort of glorified tea wagon with steamtable on top and shelves below. Even the crockery was custom-made from a new lightweight material that reduced the 530 pounds of standard china service down to a mere 189 pounds.

The windows were also specially made of shatter-proof glass and coated with a formula that removed glare. As a final touch the train was painted a high-gloss brown on top and bottom and canary yellow on the sides. The yellow was chosen after tests showed it to be the most visible color from a distance. Even before M-10000 made her debut, the shopmen had their own nickname for her: "Little Zip."

All the brass were on hand in Chicago when the train was formally delivered on February 12, 1934. Joining them were officers from Pullman, Winton, General Motors, Electro-Motive, and Aluminum Company of America. A souvenir coin made of the same aluminum used on the train was distributed. NBC announcer Ben Lyon passed through the train describing it in hushed tones for his radio audience. In accepting the train, Harriman also announced a new order for one six-car and two nine-car streamliners with sleepers for Pacific coast service. This was made possible, he added, by General Motors's recent development of a new two-cycle diesel engine with new alloys light enough to install in a train. Having at last found the right combination of power and weight, General Motors could provide a 900-horsepower engine for the six-car train and 1,200-horsepower engines for the nine-car trains.[16]

This new engine had already been adopted by the Burlington for the streamliner it was rushing to completion. For years confusion and disputes have raged over which of the two companies developed the first streamliner. The answer is in fact simple and indisputable. The Union Pacific's train went public in February, the Burlington's in April, giving the former clear title on that basis. However, the Burlington's *Zephyr* included the newly perfected diesel engine from the start; the Union Pacific originally used the Winton before switching to the diesel, enabling the Burlington to claim rightly that it developed the first diesel-powered streamliner. The two trains had one other major difference: Pullman built the Union Pacific cars of aluminum; the Burlington had E. G. Budd make their cars of stainless steel.[17]

The controversy is both silly and unnecessary to anyone not a diehard partisan of the roads. Both roads deserve credit for being pioneers in the development of "tomorrow's train," and there was glory enough to share. After its unveiling, Little Zip was sent east for a series of display stops beginning in Washington. Huge crowds flocked to see it in every city, including President Franklin D. Roosevelt and many of his official family. On the run from Baltimore to Pittsburgh, Gray marveled at the crowds packed along the line in Harrisburg, Johnstown, Altoona, and other cities, all waiting for a glimpse of the super train. "From Johnstown to Pittsburgh it was a solid mass of people," he reported, "and . . . although we ran very slowly past them my

CROWD PLEASER: Eager throngs wait in line for a close look at the M-10000 streamliner on her maiden tour.

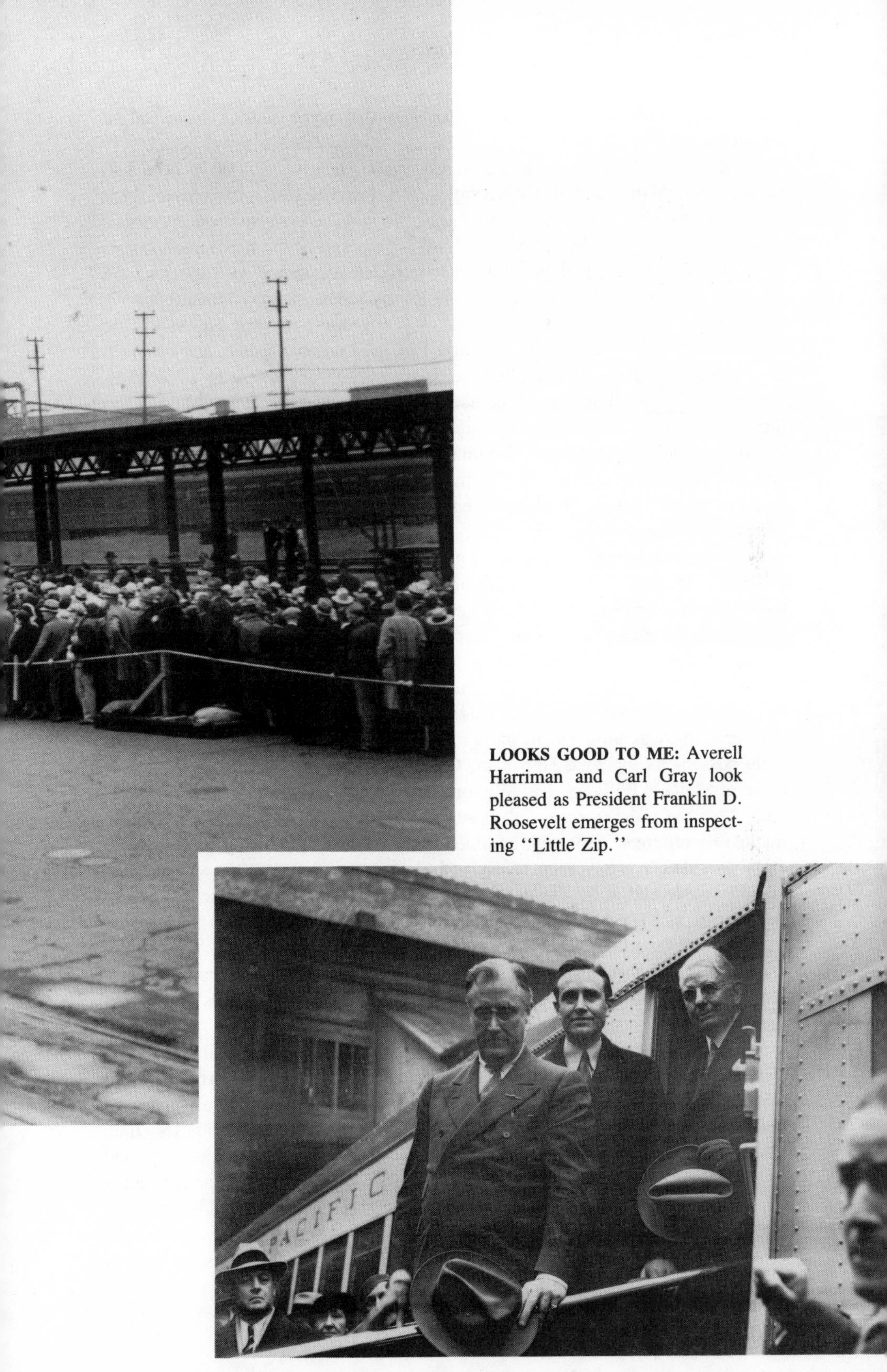

LOOKS GOOD TO ME: Averell Harriman and Carl Gray look pleased as President Franklin D. Roosevelt emerges from inspecting "Little Zip."

heart was continually in my mouth for fear that some sudden surge might produce a calamity.''[18]

By the time Gray disembarked in Cheyenne, nearly 300,000 people had passed through the train in fifteen cities. West of Cheyenne the crowds kept coming all the way to Los Angeles. The Burlington *Zephyr* also drew enormous crowds, showing that the public could not get enough of the new streamliners. When the *Zephyr* reached Washington, Harriman was quick to inspect it. An Illinois Central official who rode the train briefly sent back a favorable report.[19]

The jokes poured forth at once. ''They really don't run this Union Pacific train,'' went one, ''They just aim and fire it.'' When a passenger orders a three-minute egg, ran another, he gets it six miles from where he ordered it. ''At present no sleeping car is included,'' brayed another. ''The public is too jittery just now to sleep on a projectile.''[20]

All this attention delighted Harriman, who understood better than most the value of promotion and publicity in the new era. No opportunity to cultivate it was overlooked; Little Zip visited the Chicago World's Fair and Boulder Dam. When the second streamliner arrived in October 1934, it was sent to Los Angeles for display and to prepare for yet another coup: a transcontinental run to shatter the speed mark of seventy-one hours and twenty-seven minutes set by E. H. Harriman in May 1906. The six-car M-10001 boasted a new 900-horsepower Winton diesel and three sleeping cars. At the suggestion of director James H. Perkins, each one had two sections with extra-long berths for tall people like Harriman and himself. Charske loved the idea. It was quite a stunt, he chirped, ''to have 'Four long beds for long men'!''[21]

Everything was arranged to garner maximum publicity. The roster of fifty-eight passengers included Harriman, Charske, Gray, Jeffers, the presidents of General Motors, Pullman, and Winton, and a select gaggle of reporters. After some tests the train commenced its run at ten p.m. on October 22. The media tracked its progress across the continent with breathless intensity; radio broadcasts provided live coverage at every fuel stop. On the plains a wild broom-tailed horse reared at the strange sight and galloped away. ''If it scares one of those critters,'' laughed Harriman, watching the pony flee, ''this is indeed a new era in railroading.'' The train reached Chicago in under thirty-nine hours, clipping six hours off the fastest previous run from Los Angeles and a whopping nineteen hours off the fastest current schedule. Huge crowds watched it hurtle through every city.[22]

At ten o'clock on the morning of October 25 the M-10001 rolled into Grand Central Station, greeted by a band of redcaps playing ''California, Here I Come.'' It had demolished the old record by making the run in just under 57 hours, 14½ hours less than E. H. Harriman's 1906 run and 23 hours less than regular transcontinental schedules. Equally impressive, the entire trip had consumed only $80 worth of fuel compared to $280 for a similar run using coal. On the stretch between Cheyenne and Omaha it had averaged 84 miles an hour, the fastest time ever recorded for a run exceeding 500 miles. Amid the crowd of dignitaries, the popping flashbulbs and blinding klieg lights, the battery

ON ITS WAY: The M-10001 *City of Portland*, looking like an angry caterpillar, rounds a curve.

of microphones, the engineer fainted from the excitement while an unflappable Harriman made a short speech.[23]

Afterward the M-10001 remained on display in New York, then visited cities that had not seen its predecessor. Some changes were made in details of the design, larger streamliners were ordered, and the two prototypes were put to work. M-10000 was always intended as an experimental train—a "laboratory on wheels"—of a size too small for anything more than commuting runs. After spending the fall on display at the World's Fair, Little Zip underwent more tests during the winter. It crossed mountains and deserts on fourteen different lines, endured temperatures ranging from ten below to a hundred above, survived snow and dust storms on every type of grade and curve. At the end of January 1935 the M-10001 was renamed the *City of Salina* and put into service between Kansas City and Salina, Kansas.[24]

After its record-shattering trip the M-10001 underwent more tests before becoming the *City of Portland*, which was the first diesel streamliner with sleepers. Equipped with a new 1,200-horsepower diesel engine and a dining car-lounge, it commenced a forty-hour schedule between Chicago and Portland in June 1935. The two new trains on order were also given more power, double units totaling 2,100 and 2,400 horsepower, and two more cars. Except for some axle trouble that Jeffers pinned down to faulty design work by Pullman, the new trains ran smoothly. As passengers flocked to them in record numbers, other lines ordered streamliners until by 1936 the addition of new trains and the making of record runs had become almost commonplace.[25]

A funny thing had happened on the way to the future: the iron horse was no longer iron or a horse. The hot breath of steam and the galloping surge of power that had always been a part of the romance of railroading had been set on the road toward extinction. The puffing, panting growl of the steam locomotive, with its insatiable appetite for coal and water, could not long endure a race against the quiet, tireless whir of the electric diesel. Efficiency had marked romance as an endangered species.

The future had arrived, and Harriman knew it. He was seeking the modern traveler, who had to be wrenched forcibly from his or her familiar images of train travel. A preliminary report on the streamliners had looked carefully at the market problem, trying to determine who would and would not ride the new train. For business people, it concluded, speed mattered more than cost. "The precise reason why Americans are always in a hurry is a problem for the future," it noted astutely, "but the fact remains that they are—or they think they are." On that basis airplanes alone could beat the proposed new trains, but they were neither as safe nor as comfortable. The railroad offered more convenient terminals and far nicer amenities.[26]

Vacation travelers fell into two broad groups: those who went to one place to stay, and those who stopped at several places along the way. The automobile had created the latter type, had in fact created the modern breed of vacationer called the tourist. "The railway may offer attractive rates to carry him to the chosen destination," observed the report, "but it deprives him of the use of his car and so robs him of his independence in visiting the points which interest

Now-2 Streamliners
CITY OF SAN FRANCISCO
A SAILING EVERY THIRD DAY
SF-4
WITH another 17-car Streamliner placed in service between Chicago and San Francisco, supplementing the present 17-car "City of San Francisco," there will be fast 39¾-hour service *every third day* from each terminal. This additional Streamliner replaces the "Forty Niner". • These ultra-modern Diesel-powered trains represent the last word in rail transportation for Coach and Pullman passengers. • On the inside pages are diagrams of cars comprising the Streamliners "City of San Francisco." • The Streamliners are not only thoughtfully designed for passengers' comfort and convenience, but also are outstanding examples of interior decoration. Harmonizing and individual color treatments have been carried out in each car.
EFFECTIVE JULY 26, 1941
CHICAGO and NORTH WESTERN · UNION PACIFIC
SOUTHERN PACIFIC

COME RIDE WITH US: The cover of a pamphlet advertising the newest addition to the streamliner fleet.

him and in distributing his time advantageously." Although the automobile had snatched huge numbers of passengers from trains, the report found a surprising ray of hope. Figures from Yellowstone National Park revealed that rail travel there had remained constant; the automobile had not taken business away but merely brought more people who would otherwise not have come at all. For certain types of pleasure travelers, the new train would prove a real attraction.[27]

For all its remarkable insights, the report overlooked a subtle but no less compelling factor that had emerged in the 1920s. The streamliner aroused such wild enthusiasm because it was a dazzling blend of old and familiar associations with futuristic technology. Where the airplane was something new out of the blue, the streamliner was something stunningly new in a familiar setting where the leap of progress from its predecessors could easily be measured by one's own experience. The streamliner was not merely fast, though speed was one of its prime appeals. In this first age of chic it was sleek, glamorous, and thoroughly modern, offering amenities once reserved only for the rich.

The modern transcontinental traveler was well-to-do if not rich, and liked nothing better than to be fussed over, to be made somebody for however brief a time. The elite had always valued their prerogatives and still did, but the membership roster had in recent years grown confused. Great changes were taking place in American life, one effect of which was a blurring of class ranks. In any such time of transition, there is a tendency for people to define who they are by what they have and what they do. Money talks in a louder voice than usual and plays a larger role in defining status. Even during the depression, more people in corporate America could afford to travel in both speed and style, which was precisely what the streamliner provided. It was one more thing to set people apart from the crowd at a time when the crowd was increasingly submerging traditional distinctions.

In some intuitive way Harriman seems to have understood these forces at work. This product of aristocratic upbringing always displayed a gift for being of his class and yet unbound by his class. He grasped who the clientele would be for the new trains, what their tastes and desires were, and how to gratify them. He had enabled them to get places in a faster, more luxurious way than ever before. The next logical step was to provide them with somewhere new and exciting to go.

This time the idea came from calling on his fellow bankers in Europe and often finding them away at some ski lodge in the Alps. Harriman did not then ski, but he noticed the smart set had been abandoning the Riviera in favor of St. Moritz, Davos, Kitzbuhl, and other fashionable mountain resorts, where new hotels were going up to handle the rush of visitors. In the United States, however, resort hotels were places people went in the summer. The Union Pacific had developed an impressive summer tourist business at Yellowstone and the Utah Parks, but it had never found a way to utilize what had always been its natural liabilities: the mountains, the snow, and the cold. Ski resorts offered a way to transform them into assets. The sport was far more popular in Europe than at home, but the winter Olympics of 1932 at Lake Placid, New York, had triggered a modest boom that Harriman believed would grow rapidly if the right facilities could be provided.[28]

And what better place for those facilities than on the line of the Union Pacific? Ski trains already ran out of several cities for local enthusiasts, but no mountain resort existed where people might spend a week or two skiing. In September 1935 he broached the idea to Gray. "Some day," Harriman predicted, "there will be established a ski center in the mountains here of the same character as in the Swiss and Austrian Alps." While it might be years away, the time to start looking was now. Gray had some officers look into it and reported that the only site with a reliable supply of snow was Yellowstone Park, which was inaccessible most of the winter. Harriman brushed the objection aside. He knew a young Austrian ski expert who was willing to go over the territory in search of the right place for nothing more than his expenses. Let him see what he could find.[29]

Count Felix Schaffgotsch, a thin, handsome skiing enthusiast who had once clerked at Brown Brothers Harriman, arrived in December and set out on his search for the St. Moritz of America. His quest took him to places that would later become centers of winter sports but which to his discerning eye had flaws that ruled them out for the present. Lake Tahoe had blizzards that would keep skiers indoors; Aspen had too many trees and was not on the Union Pacific line; Jackson Hole was too remote and windy; Alta was too near Salt Lake City, which would make it a haven for weekend skiers rather than a detached resort living in its own world. Working his way east from California, the count was fast running out of possibilities as he headed toward Idaho in January 1936.[30]

At every stop Schaffgotsch had the assistance of local Union Pacific agents. In Boise his man was William J. Hynes, a former state legislator who knew the area but not the assignment. "I didn't know a damn thing about what the hell a ski resort was," he recalled. "I kind of thought it was a waste of time and money." But he dutifully took the count around the area, going first to Jackson Hole. It was magnificent country, the count agreed, but to get there required leaving the railroad and plodding 185 miles through the numbing Wyoming winter. Next he tried Spencer, Idaho, a small town on the Montana border, but it was not right either. He thanked Hynes and said he wanted a second look at one site in Colorado before giving up the search. "If you find anything," he added, "let me know. Wire me at the Brown Palace in Denver."[31]

After the count left, Hynes retreated to the Locker Club in Boise for a drink with his friend Joe Simmer, director of highways. He told Simmer of his adventure, dragging a load of ski gear around the country in search of the perfect location.

"Did you look in the Hailey and Ketchum area?" Simmer asked quietly.

Hynes set his drink down hard. "By God no, I forgot."

Off went a telegram to Schaffgotsch, who met Hynes at Shoshone, forty-five miles from Ketchum. The road to Hailey was closed, but Simmer sent along an engineer and a snowplow to get them through to Hailey, eleven miles from Ketchum. Once a prosperous copper mining district, Hailey had fallen on hard times. Only half of Ketchum's 270 inhabitants stayed around during the winter; the local grocery was open only two hours a day. Schaffgotsch went there after slogging into Ketchum and asked for a young man who could ski and was willing to show him the area. A boy arrived with skis that were nothing but two slabs of wood with canvas footholds. The count choked back a smile and offered him a pair of his own skis. Hynes watched them head for the distant hills and settled in comfortably by the stove.[32]

For three or four days they explored the area. Everything looked right to Schaffgotsch, especially a small valley surrounded by untimbered slopes. The place stood at the edge of a desert and at the foot of the craggy Sawtooth Range, which shielded it from harsh northern winds and storms. The sun shone brilliantly, making it uncommonly warm regardless of the temperature. The hills to the left were much lower than those on the right and bare of snow, while the opposite side was full of snow. Best of all, the snow was plentiful and perfect for skiing: dry, light, powdery, with no surface crust.

"It's the ski heaven," Schaffgotsch telegraphed Harriman from Ketchum. "When are you coming out?"[33]

Idaho was familiar ground to Harriman. His father had bought a 14,000-acre ranch there (later called the "Railroad Ranch") which the boys still owned. In February Harriman and his wife went to Ketchum with some close friends, William S. Paley of CBS and his wife. Hynes scrounged up an old covered wagon and rigged it with a portable stove for the trip into Ketchum. The Paleys found it an amusing vacation. Harriman was entranced; later he called it "the most beautiful site I've ever seen." He opened negotiations at once to buy 3,500 acres of grazing land from a local rancher, who in the tough times of the depression was glad to sell out while holding on to the grazing rights for awhile. By working fast, Harriman could have the new resort open in time for the next winter season.[34]

Harriman had in mind erecting a small lodge as a test, and he realized that anything put up in the wilds of Idaho would go unnoticed unless it was well promoted. He took the idea to Steve Hannagan, a public relations man who had boosted the virtues of Miami Beach and Florida sunshine with enormous success. If you build a lodge, Hannagan told him, no one will pay any attention because everyone builds lodges. But if you build a luxury resort in the wilderness, that will be news. Harriman grasped the point at once and shifted his thinking to a grander scale. He engaged a Los Angeles architect named Gilbert S. Underwood to design the hotel, and had preliminary plans in April. That same month the portly, stoop-shouldered Hannagan, who looked as if he got most of his exercise at the dinner table, went out to inspect Ketchum.[35]

Wearing a light tweed suit, a warm-weather creature when he ventured out of doors at all, Hannagan endured the car and sled ride to Ketchum with misgivings. "We got there and looked around," he recalled, "and all I could see was just a goddam field of snow. I thought they must be crazy. 'This is strictly ridiculous,' I said, but we walked around some more, with my shoes full of snow, and then the sun came out. It began to feel pretty good, so I opened my coat. Then I took it off." By the time Hannagan finished his stroll, he had the germ of an idea for a promotion campaign. The first poster would feature a handsome young man on skis in the snow, stripped to the waist and wiping the sweat from his tanned forehead, his huge smile conveying the theme: enjoy winter sports and stay warm while you do it.[36]

"When you think of winter sports, you usually think of cold, don't you?" smiled Hannagan. "Well, I always believed in a good name." In a very short time the new resort had one: Sun Valley.[37]

Moving quickly, Harriman got the executive committee to approve an expenditure of $685,000 for the project with the understanding that costs would ultimately reach $1 million. To provide estimates, he brought in fellow banker John E. P. Morgan, a ski enthusiast who saw great promise in the project. The moribund Idaho economy sprang abruptly to life as workers flocked to Ketchum in hopes of getting jobs. Ground was broken in June and construction proceeded rapidly, but one thorny problem remained: how to get skiers up the nearby mountains for their runs. At Hannagan's suggestion Harriman asked the company engineers to find a solution. "Our approach," he told chief engineer H. C. Mann, "should be to develop as inexpensive a method as possible with a capacity of say one hundred people an hour."[38]

Harriman pointed them toward the devices used elsewhere, but none of these fit the new resort's needs. The older hands in the department were stumped, but a young engineer named Jim Curran had earlier worked for an iron company in Omaha that had made davit-and-hook devices for a fruit company to load bananas onto ships in South America. He adapted this lift to a cable system rigged with chairs to carry skiers up the mountain in a continuous flow. His superiors dismissed the sketches as too dangerous, but Curran got them into the hands of Charles Proctor, a former ski star at Dartmouth who had been hired to lay out the runs. Proctor liked the idea; so did John Morgan and Harriman, who ordered it pushed to final development. Thus was the modern ski lift born.[39]

Morgan went personally to Omaha to test the prototype, an old pickup truck with a chair hanging from its side. The first chair moved four feet a minute; in short order the speed was advanced to 450 feet a minute. Two low hills within walking distance of the lodge were chosen for the first lifts. The formidable Bald Mountain was left alone. Schaffgotsch knew it offered a rich variety of runs, but few skiers would be skilled enough to use them at first. When the lifts were delivered in August, crews led by bridge engineer William Castagnetto toiled for nearly three months snaking them into place. Apart from solving a difficult problem, they had great publicity value.[40]

Luck favored the project in one important way. The harsh weather and lack of firefighting units forced the builders to cast the hotel in cement. Once the cement hardened and expanded against the pine forms, however, it emerged with a color and texture that looked like wood. The hotel housed 250 guests and included such amenities as a game room with everything from slot machines to billiard tables, an elegant dining room, a dance floor, a beauty parlor, a barber shop, and a branch of Saks Fifth Avenue. Outside the hotel could be found a swimming pool with heated water—another promotion for a winter playground without shivers—a skating rink, stables, and sledding runs. Harriman understood that people settling in for a week or two of vacation had to be entertained with more than skiing.[41]

Busy as he was elsewhere, Averell let no detail escape his alert eye. He hired Marjorie Oelrichs Duchin, a Newport socialite who had been an interior decorator before marrying bandleader Eddie Duchin, to handle the decor. But Harriman personally approved everything from the plaster finish of the game room to the furniture design to which parts of every door should be painted what color. Ski expert Hans Hauser and five other Austrians were hired as instructors and a Canadian as skating master. A band was engaged along with cooks, waiters, valets, and a staff that eventually totaled four hundred.[42]

Despite the short time available to cope with so many problems in so remote a place, Harriman decided to target December 21 as the opening date. The already hectic pace grew frantic in the rush to meet this deadline. To make the resort accessible, sleepers left Chicago and Los Angeles on Friday nights for direct connection to Ketchum, where buses met the guests. Harriman also jumped on an offer by Harold Crary of United Airlines to boost Sun Valley in drumming up business for his company. ''More people will come to Sun Valley by rail if they feel sure of being able to return home rapidly in case of emergency,'' Harriman explained to Gray. ''Some will come to the hotel by air where they would not come by rail.''[43]

The key was not merely to get people there but to get the *right* people there for the opening. ''Society is like a band of sheep,'' wrote gossip columnist Nancy Randolph, who was in real life Boise native Inez Callaway Robb. ''Get a few bellwethers . . . headed in the right direction and the rest will surely clamber after.'' Harriman needed bellwethers from two directions to put Sun Valley on the map: socialites from the East and celebrities from Hollywood. Both were circles in which he moved easily and had many friends, all of whom he hustled with indefatigable good nature. One of them, producer David O. Selznick, offered to recruit a carload of stars if Schaffgotsch would help him. ''Could it be arranged to have a through car direct to Sun Valley,'' he wired Harriman. ''If so believe I could turn my publicity department loose and really get some free space for Sun Valley. Don't know how far you want me to go on this but . . . I can't think of any better opportunity to get the place quickly established with Hollywood people.''[44]

Harriman prompted a befuddled Gray to give Selznick what he wanted, explaining that the publicity would be crucial because ''we will have few nationally known names from East until after New Years.'' This line of work was new to Gray's long railroad experience, but he adjusted to it as best he could. Harriman furnished the names of prominent people who had already made reservations to another syndicated columnist and turned Hannagan loose on a promotional blitz. One of his efforts drew a cry of protest from Selznick, who asked that nothing go out without his seeing it first because ''if wrong things get out I will have to leave town.'' An indirect approach would work best, he assured Hannagan, adding that he was ''counting on your good taste to see to it that this isn't handled like a Billy Rose special to the Dallas Exposition but rather as casual photographs of stars en route and at American St. Moritz, etc.''[45]

The chastened Hannagan backed off, but only slightly. Within days he came up with another coup. Paramount director Wesley Ruggles was making a film called *I Met Him in Paris* that included some winter Alpine sequences. The alert Hannagan lured Ruggles up to Ketchum to inspect the place as a possible location. When Ruggles decided to shoot the scenes at Sun Valley, a delighted Harriman ordered him given every cooperation. This coup brought in Claudette

Colbert, Robert Young, and Melvyn Douglas to join the stars who arrived with Selznick. The sixty-foot circular swimming pool inspired Hannagan to come up with a new breed, the winter bathing beauty, and to coin a new term, "snow tan." From day one a relentless stream of publicity poured forth from Sun Valley. It was, admitted Harriman much later, "an extraordinary job of promotion."[46]

As opening day neared, workmen scrambled frantically to get the last details in place. Harriman, held prisoner in New York by his daughter's debut, choreographed events by telegraph. As the guests poured in, one problem arose that was beyond Harriman's power to control: there was not enough snow for skiing. St. Moritz without snow. Here was an image that smacked of disaster, and it drove hardened railroad veterans to an act utterly alien to their nature. All their working days they had fought snow, cursed snow, hated snow; now they prayed fervently for snow.[47]

Opening night, an elegant dinner followed by dancing and a live radio broadcast, went smoothly with William Jeffers presiding, but Christmas came and went beneath clear skies. The real crush of celebrities was due to arrive that week for the gala New Year's Eve celebration, but there was a limit to how far a ski resort could go without snow. An unruffled Harriman promptly informed the guests already there to stay on at no charge and told expected arrivals, "No snow here. If you are a good gambler come on out and be our guest till it arrives." In this clever, gracious way he turned a liability into an asset that reaped more publicity than normal snow conditions would have. On Sunday, December 27, Hannagan went to midnight mass and prayed for snow. When flakes began to fall, he stationed himself at his window with a bucket of champagne to await the dawn.[48]

Or so he later claimed. With Hannagan the line between fact and promotion was always fuzzy, but this was an occupational hazard. "Delighted to hear the sun is shining in more ways than one and that one worry is behind us," wired Harriman two days later. The stars flocked in for New Year's Eve—Selznick, Errol Flynn, Joan Bennett, Claudette Colbert, and Madeleine Carroll among others—and they kept coming. Ruggles came and shot his alpine sequences, transforming the Ketchum depot into a Swiss one with a few props. Behind the stars came the socialites, or "bluebloods" as a columnist called them. Sun Valley had its bellwethers, and the sheep flocked eagerly after them. During its first year the resort drew 3,900 guests.[49]

An audacious gamble had worked, and in the bargain created what might prove a useful model for the industry. "The railroads as a whole," noted an approving *Railway Age*, "as the Union Pacific has done individually through its winter sports development, can create new demands for rail transportation by stimulating interest in those pursuits which require travel."[50]

And Harriman was by no means finished. In the spring of 1937 he reevaluated the project with an eye to making it a year-round resort. Sun Valley closed April 1 only to reopen July 1 because the demand was there for fishing, swimming, horseback riding, hiking, and other summer fun. In the rapid-fire way of his father Harriman swept through Sun Valley, leaving in his wake

SUN VALLEY SERENADE: Lunch on the front porch of the Challenger Inn, complete with a musical trio, under the baleful eye of "Bingo," the resident St. Bernard.

dozens of ideas in remarkable detail for improvements. He wanted the Proctor lift moved to a location that offered more challenging runs, picked a site for damming Trail Creek to create a lake, added a ski jump, arranged an area for visitors who came by car to watch winter sport exhibitions, laid out a scheme for landscaping to give the place "a Western atmosphere, with as little sophistication and formality as possible."[51]

The major addition was a second hotel with more moderate prices and services. Harriman saw that Sun Valley, once established, did not have to remain a playground only for the rich and famous. It would also attract middle-class vacationers who relished not only its pleasures but its glamorous clientele. Recently, in another bold innovation, the Union Pacific had put on a new low-price passenger train called the *Challenger*. Its success helped inspire Harriman to erect at Sun Valley the Challenger Inn aimed at a similar clientele. The Union Pacific appropriated another $1 million for the lodge along with $65,000 for a rodeo arena. Despite this latter facility, the western motif soon gave way to a more European atmosphere.[52]

The new inn became an imitation Swiss alpine village with a lodge capable of handling four hundred people, a guest cottage that could accommodate twenty, a dining room, a "weinstube" called The Ram, a large general store, several small shops, a drug store, a movie theater with five hundred seats, another outdoor swimming pool, and tennis courts that could be flooded in winter for skating. When it opened on December 21, 1937—exactly a year after the first hotel made its debut—Harriman arranged another big splash. Combining his two pet projects, he had one of the company's brand-new streamliners, the *City of Los Angeles*, make its maiden run from New York to Sun Valley with a cargo of vacationers including himself. The seventeen-car train dashed across the continent in time to make the opening ceremonies and become the first streamliner to visit Idaho. Harriman loved the publicity it garnered, but after a stay in Sun Valley he flew home on United Airlines.[53]

During 1938 the number of guests increased to 4,120 and more amenities were added, including a nine-hole golf course, a third ski lift, skeet shooting, and a steady parade of special events. Celebrities like Gary Cooper and Ernest Hemingway made Sun Valley a regular stop, and more film makers brought their crews to shoot winter scenes. More important, behind the celebrities and socialites came flocks of ordinary vacationers. "The average new arrival," observed one reporter, "is not *soigné* at all." A New York couple, he figured, could enjoy two weeks at the resort for about $500 including train fare. The Union Pacific also ran special excursions for its employees, giving them 20 percent discounts.[54]

As the popularity of Sun Valley soared, Harriman continued to immerse himself in the details of its operation. Although deep into political work in Washington as well as his business activities, he insisted on involving himself in every aspect of the resort's management. No one could doubt that it was his pet project, perhaps his pet pleasure as well. He monitored every detail of the Challenger Inn; after the opening, he handed the man in charge of construction a list of a dozen items to be changed, some of them on his own private chateau. He devoted a four-page letter to the proper handling of tow-line buses, offered a scenario for a film he commissioned on the resort's ski school, demanded that the school itself be improved by bringing in top skiers, and arranged the schedule for a three-day visit to Sun Valley by the Business Advisory Council, of which he was chairman.[55]

Clearly Sun Valley had become something to Harriman that transcended the bottom line of company profits or even his own triumph in making it work. It was his mark on the railroad, like the streamliners, and his own playground as well. The resort was a place he sent his friends as well as himself to have a good time, and he insisted that it be all he had promised regardless of cost. Some of the improvements or details made no sense from an economic standpoint, but Averell wanted everything just right because any shortcomings would reflect on him. What could be more perfect: a resort that made money and at the same time satisfied his craving for a vacation paradise for himself and his crowd?

Nothing proved more revealing in this respect than the appointment in 1938 of W. P. "Pat" Rogers as manager of Sun Valley. Rogers was exactly the kind of man Harriman wanted at Sun Valley. Genial, big-hearted, less a manager than a host, Rogers was an oldtime hotelman who stopped at nothing to ensure his guests a good time. He burrowed into details and let nothing slip when it came to maintaining standards. "He didn't care much about profit-and-loss statements or money," recalled an employee. "He would just give away the whole place, and of course he was loved by everyone, guests and employees."[56]

As long as Harriman held sway over Sun Valley, Rogers was the perfect manager. His value as host overruled his managerial shortcomings. Under his rule Sun Valley enjoyed its golden years as a resort between 1938 and 1941, and Harriman's involvement remained as deep as ever. In June 1939, only two months before the Nazis invaded Poland, Averell was concerning himself with the details of the dresses to be worn by waitresses in the lodge. The coming of war shifted his focus abruptly and brought an end to the first era of winter paradise. For Felix Schaffgotsch the change brought tragedy. Caught at home, he found himself fighting willingly or otherwise for the Third Reich. In the snowy hell of the Russian front, a long way from Idaho, the count died in combat against the country where his old friend Harriman was then serving as ambassador.[57]

17

The Trimmings

The Union Pacific had always been more than a railroad. From the first, it had engaged in land operations and coal mining, both of which were vital to development along its line. It was involved in the express business, dabbled in the mining of other minerals, owned a rolling mill for a time, and had even gone modestly into the resort and tourist field. E. H. Harriman added still another dimension by giving it investment holdings that provided a major source of income. The company had always been a diversified enterprise, but it had never found a satisfactory way to integrate its several activities or clarify the relationships among them. To old-time rail men the Union Pacific was a railroad, and all the rest of it was trimmings. To more thoughtful officials the "trimmings" were precisely what made the railroad a success, and they wondered why more could not be done with them.[1]

Attempts had been made to spin off nonrail assets into a holding company, but these involved only the investment securities rather than the whole range of enterprises beyond the railroad. The status of the land, coal, oil, water, and other resource operations remained as nebulous as ever. Pushed by the new competition, the Union Pacific moved steadily toward redefining itself as a transportation company. Most of the trimmings, however, were ancillary or sequential investments that fed the railroad in one way or another. What place should they occupy structurally in the company? How would they be treated by officers who were railroaders first and last? Most took it for granted that the trimmings were the tail and the railroad the dog, but arguments flared over how important the tail actually was.

IF YOU CAN'T BEAT THEM . . . Union Pacific Stages shows off one of its new streamlined transcontinental buses, October 1937.

And, as always, there lingered the larger question of what the government would and would not let the Union Pacific do with its nonrail assets. Two kinds of restrictions limited what could be done: those imposed on excursions into other forms of transportation and those on holdings outside the field altogether.

For a select few officers like vice president J. L. Haugh, the vision of Union Pacific as a transportation company had already become a driving force. The bus lines were doing well and expanding rapidly despite occasional clashes with state or federal regulatory bodies. The company owned all the stock of Union Pacific Stages, which operated between Salt Lake City and Portland, and 71 percent of Interstate Transit Lines, which ran between Chicago and Los Angeles. During the period from 1936 to 1940, it modernized the fleet by buying 155 new streamlined coaches and air-conditioning 140 older models. More commuter service went into the fast-growing hub at Los Angeles, and new equipment was added to the mountain tourist routes.[2]

An echo of past fights reverberated in 1940 when the ICC allowed a bus subsidiary of the Atchison to operate between Denver and Los Angeles on the grounds that a 1932 agreement between Union Pacific, Southern Pacific, and Pacific Greyhound amounted to a monopoly on the territory. Haugh saw at once that the ICC was "establishing the precedent that it will not grant exclusive franchises over long routes." He fretted only a little over the decision, believing that the Union Pacific had built up a strong, alert operation against which the Atchison and Burlington could not compete. But it would be a struggle much like the not-so-good old days. "The competition under which our bus lines have been built and developed," he observed, "has been as keen as any that we will ever encounter."[3]

The trucking industry took an ominous turn during the mid-1930s. For a decade or so it had supplemented the rail system with short hauls. As trucks grew bigger and faster, and as more people jumped into the business, they began competing for long-haul traffic. Some consolidation was taking place, but the vast majority of trucks were owner-operated or "gypsy" vehicles. Three types of trucking emerged by 1932. Common carriers, who served the general public, comprised only 5.5 percent of all trucking firms, with contract carriers, who served specialized customers, accounting for another 8.7 percent. The remaining 85 percent were private carriers, of which 65 percent were estimated to be solo gypsies.[4]

Since entry into the business was cheap, trucking was a growth industry during the depression years, when other forms of transport were struggling to stay alive. Regulation scarcely fazed truckers. The Motor Carrier Act of 1935 brought common and contract carriers under federal scrutiny, but nothing touched the gypsies, who roamed at will, defying state regulations in their efforts to scratch out a living. The gypsy syndrome was something new to the transportation game. Railroads, with their need for large capital investment, had maverick lines but not lone operators. Traces of it could be found in the bus and air travel sectors, but growth and capital needs for updated equipment were fast squeezing out the little players. The trucks remained a moving target, a swarm of locusts, each one harmless in itself but capable in toto of taking large and painful bites out of the traffic.[5]

The railroads learned early that the only way to beat the trucks was to join them. Three approaches were tried. By 1940 virtually every major system had its own fleet of trucks for pickup and delivery service as well as some short-haul work. The Union Pacific started this operation in Oregon as an experiment in April 1931 and quickly extended it elsewhere. At first Union Pacific Stages handled the operation in Kansas and Nebraska, but protests by shippers forced the railroad to take it over in 1933. In addition, seventy major railroads jointly owned the Railway Express Agency (REA), which by 1940 owned 14,000 trucks, the largest private fleet in the nation. This kept in the family some revenues that would otherwise have gone to trucks, but on a shared basis.[6]

The third avenue was to enter the trucking business directly, just as the company had done with buses. Late in 1935 the Union Pacific undertook a bold venture in tandem with the Burlington and the Northwestern. To dominate the Omaha trade market, the three roads agreed to buy jointly three existing truck lines and merge them into a single concern to be run independently of the railroads. Other roads in the territory served by the new company would be offered a share of the ownership as well. The object was to develop a "complete and comprehensive trucking system" to coordinate rail and motor operations in the territory. Haugh admitted the company would look to acquire other truck lines as well.[7]

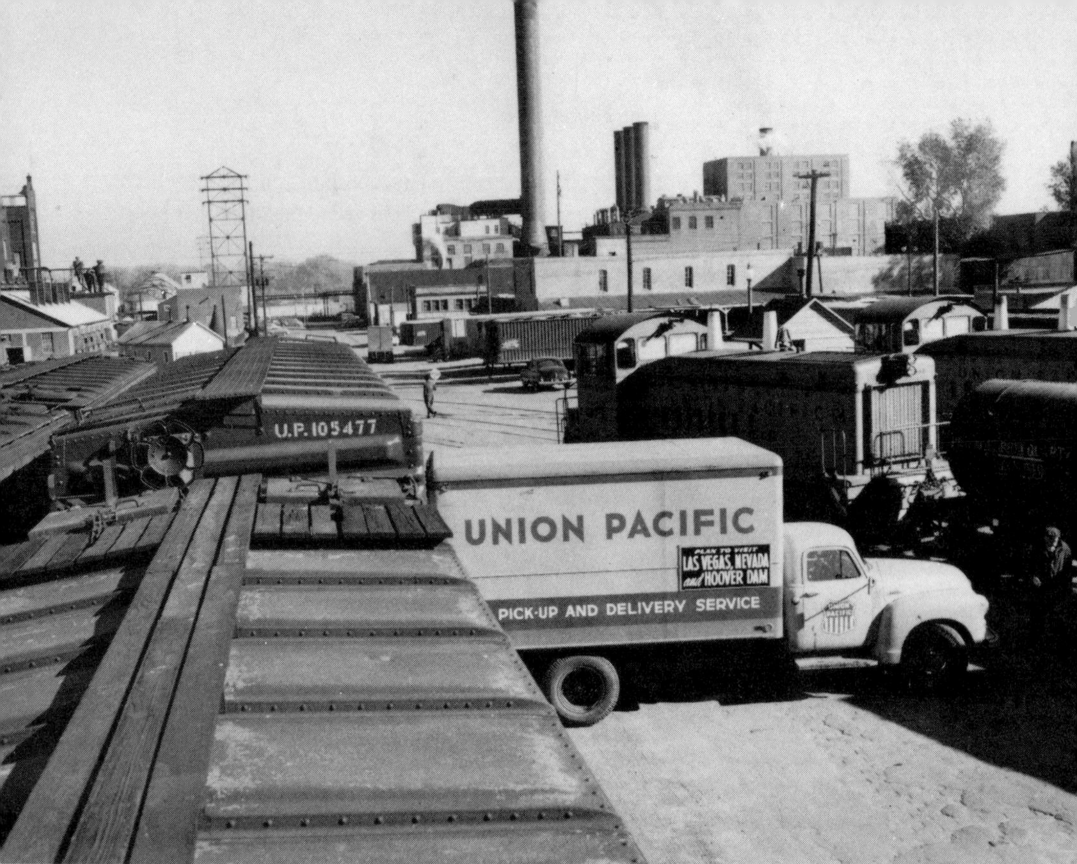

IT PAYS TO ADVERTISE: A Union Pacific truck carries not only goods but a message for tourists.

Predictably, trucking firms rushed to oppose the application before the ICC, and they were joined by the trustees of the bankrupt Milwaukee as well. In their complaint, the trustees declared that the offer to share in the plan amounted to little more than subsidizing a competitor, which made no sense to them. The examiner who took testimony in the hearing recommended approval only to be reversed two years later by Division 5 of the ICC. "The time may ultimately come for a considerable degree of union between these rival branches of the transportation industry," concluded Joseph B. Eastman, one of the commissioners voting against the application, "but I am not persuaded that it has yet come." The reason he offered was an old and familiar one: the union presented "possibilities of unfair competition which it would be difficult to guard against."[8]

Thwarted in yet another lengthy bout with the government, the company looked to find a more perfect union in a much more improbable place; the aviation industry. No one expected the oldest transcontinental road to develop an interest in the newest form of transportation, but the Union Pacific had two managers with close ties to flight. One was Averell Harriman himself, who in 1929 had helped organize the Aviation Corporation, or AVCO as it became known. This move gave Harriman a straddle in three major transportation arenas: railroads, shipping, and aviation.[9]

THE TORCH PASSED: Robert A. Lovett and Averell Harriman, the second generation of Union Pacific leadership, chat with two unidentified young men.

The other figure was Robert A. Lovett, who had developed a passion for flying at an early age. Growing up on Long Island, where two of the early aviation plants were located, Lovett watched the planes come and go in fascination. He left Yale during his sophomore year in 1916 to help organize an Eli squadron for the war threatening with Mexico. The following year he joined the Naval Air Service and received pilot's license number sixty-seven. When the United States entered the war, Lovett was sent to France to patrol the coast. Later he flew dangerous night bombing missions against German submarine bases, for which he earned the Navy Cross in 1919. His parents bore the ordeal of exposing their only son to such high risks with an air of stoic patriotism. The judge's only interest in airplanes, Lovett later quipped, was "that I shouldn't kill myself in one."[10]

Bob Lovett came home from the war a devout believer in the possibilities of aviation, an attitude that would later benefit both the Union Pacific and the nation. Somehow he still managed to graduate with his Yale class of 1918 and entered Harvard Law School. He expected to follow his father in the law but discovered that it didn't suit him and switched briefly to the Harvard Business School before going to work as a clerk for the National Bank of Commerce. In April 1919 he had married a neighbor, Adele Quartley Brown, whose father was senior partner of Brown Brothers. James Brown brought his new son-in-law into the firm while sending his own son to apprentice at Harriman & Company. When the firms merged in 1931, Lovett found himself once again partners with the Harriman boys who had been his close friends since childhood.[11]

The presence of Averell Harriman and Robert Lovett in the Union Pacific management ensured an open mind toward aviation. In June 1929, shortly after AVCO was formed, Harriman prodded Gray to discuss the possibility of joint transcontinental schedules with another Yale product, William Boeing, who had started his own aircraft company and recently subsumed it into a large holding combine called United Aircraft. The transportation component of United Aircraft was United Airlines, which was staking claim to the same transcontinental route used by the Union Pacific. Boeing was interested but unwilling to consider such a move until he had a reliable plane to fly; at the time he was experimenting with a twelve seater.[12]

In September 1932 banker Frederick M. Warburg suggested to Woody Charske that the Union Pacific buy United Airlines if the parent company would sell. Passenger travel was growing; United's business had jumped 106 percent for eight months of 1932 compared to the previous year. Ironically, United Aircraft had the backing of National City Bank, which had earlier been E. H. Harriman's close ally. "This is just one of my pleasant day dreams," Warburg added, "and if it sounds like bunk to you, you can throw the whole thing in the scrap basket." A few months later, Charske was invited by an officer of Lockheed Aircraft to buy some of their planes. He urged Charske to forget the air mail subsidy that had sustained the industry so far. "We can prove that our planes can be installed and operated on your railroad at a profit, with or without a subsidy."[13]

Nothing came of these offers, but in 1934 the situation changed radically with passage of the Air Mail Act. Among other things, the new law forced aircraft companies to separate manufacturing from transport. As a result, American Airlines spun off from AVCO, United Airlines from United Aircraft, and Transcontinental & Western (TWA) and Eastern Airlines from North American Aviation. Averell Harriman let the dust settle, then asked Haugh in June 1935 to make a study of the current state of air transportation. The indefatigable Haugh visited three major manufacturing plants on the West Coast and talked with officers of three airline companies along with several other people knowledgeable about the industry.[14]

Haugh found the business in the throes of a severe transition. The controversy over air mail that had spawned the 1934 act obscured a far more important change looming on the horizon: the switch from small- to large-capacity aircraft. In 1935 the largest plane flying the transcontinental route carried only fourteen passengers, but both Boeing and Douglas had plans for new planes capable of carrying thirty-two passengers and sleeping sixteen that could be operated at about the same cost as the smaller current models. Projected cost per plane was $95,000 compared to $65,000 for existing planes. Haugh calculated that the new versions could break even with a 30 percent load at current fares against the 70 percent load of smaller planes. And the airlines were constantly driving down their costs.[15]

The new planes would carry more people in better comfort at higher speeds, which did not bode well for the railroads. Three routes between New York and Los Angeles were already in operation. American flew the southern arc via Washington and Dallas, TWA occupied the middle route through Pittsburgh, St. Louis, and Albuquerque, and United held the northern lane via Chicago, Omaha, and Salt Lake City. Competition was fierce and would get worse as more people screwed up their courage to fly. Some interlocking already existed; Haugh noted that General Motors held the controlling interest in TWA, while the Pennsylvania Railroad owned a minority interest large enough to gain representation on the board.

"The Union Pacific is a major transportation company," Haugh asserted, "and should, in so far as it can, control the transportation field in its territory. . . . If the Union Pacific can control air transportation in its own territory it will to a large extent be able to influence the passenger rate structure." In this one revealing statement Haugh defined how the world had changed, and with it the industry, in sixty years. Earlier the Union Pacific had been a railroad defending its territory against other railroads; now it was a transportation company defending its turf against all comers on land and sea and in the air.

Control could be managed in two ways: start a new company or buy an existing one. Since the railroad knew nothing of the aviation business, the first option would cost too much and take too long; it made more sense to buy into a major airline while it could be done cheaply. Despite Harriman's ties with AVCO, the logical choice was United, which flew routes parallel to those of the Union Pacific from Omaha to Seattle, and of the Central Pacific from Salt Lake City to San Francisco. Another line, Western Air Express, operated between Salt Lake City and Los Angeles and was bound to United by a traffic contract. Encouraged by United's earnings outlook, Haugh recommended that the Union Pacific buy 40 or 50 percent of its stock.[16]

The stock was then selling at about $7.50 a share. In November the executive committee authorized the purchase of 20,000 shares at no more than $11 per share. After buying 2,000 shares, however, the price rose past 12 and the company sold its shares for a profit. By February 1936 United was selling at $16 a share. At $7.50 the cost of half United's stock would have been just over $3.9 million; at $16 the cost soared to $8.4 million. Haugh estimated the stock's asset value at $7.47, making it a poor buy at the higher price. Turning his attention back to the first option of starting a new company, he worked up figures on the costs and submitted them without recommendation. The management continued to watch and wait.[17]

A pattern was unfolding in aviation that would soon become numbingly familiar to businessmen in many fields: advances in technology changed the basic ground rules faster than outsiders (and sometimes insiders too) could absorb their implications. Clearly the airplane was going to revolutionize transportation, but in what ways? How should rival forms like the railroads respond? The questions kept coming, kept knocking insistently at their doors. In June 1938 Douglas Aircraft approached Averell Harriman with an offer to sell the Union Pacific some of its new DSC cargo planes, which it predicted would open a new era of air freight. William M. Jeffers, who by then had succeeded Gray as president, took a dim view of the idea. "To secure freight for one railroad," he argued, "planes would have to invade the territories of other transportation systems, and this would lead to such other railroads providing competitive service." If anyone offered the service, Jeffers thought, it should be Railway Express.[18]

That same year Congress passed the Civil Aeronautics Act, which gave the industry a sharp boost as well as creating a regulatory agency for it. In the troubled world of the late 1930s, it was fast becoming apparent that aviation possessed an enormous advantage over competing forms of transport, especially the railroad. The government was eager to see it advance, not merely to improve mail service but because modern air technology was deemed vital to national defense. For that reason the government remained the largest customer of the aircraft companies, subsidizing their research and development in areas that had commercial application as well. The railroads were also crucial to national defense, but wars were not fought between competing locomotives. They were not a form of military hardware caught in a spiral of technical escalation to stay ahead of the other side.

One form of government subsidy especially rankled railways. At the very time the ICC compelled the Union Pacific and Southern Pacific to build a new depot in Los Angeles, other agencies were spending millions in public funds on airports all over the nation. There seemed no way to resist this favoritism while the threat of war loomed. As railroad men watched the relentless progress of aviation technology, it was hard for them to know whether they were practical souls laughing off the fantasies of dreamers or dinosaurs witnessing the approach of their own extinction.

One thing was certain: as planes grew larger and faster, air freight service was a revolution waiting to happen. By 1940 it was a very small nose nuzzling under a very large tent. Most eyes were on passenger traffic, which had soared 46 percent in 1939 from the previous year, but the Union Pacific's management was no less concerned about freight. The first air cargo line had commenced operations in May 1940 out of Dallas; the following month two railroads applied for authorization to operate an air transport service. With the Nazi blitzkrieg storming through Europe, American defense spending rose sharply, which meant more orders for airplanes. From then on, the cloud of war hovered over everything that was done.[19]

Prodded by Robert Lovett and James P. Warburg, the executive committee resumed discussions that summer over the feasibility of buying into United Airlines. The lawyers thought the company might acquire airline stock as an investment so long as they did not exercise any control through it. Debate arose over the extent to which the Civil Aeronautics Act forbade ownership or merger. For that matter, disagreement raged over whether to do anything at all. The debate heated up in July 1940, when a report on the subject commissioned by Harriman Ripley & Co. triggered a sharp division among the management.[20]

From Omaha, Jeffers opposed any "joint fares or close working relations" with United. Warburg disagreed. The report confirmed his belief that the airlines "will sooner or later take away from the railroads all but a small part of their so-called first class long haul passenger traffic, and that residue . . . will become increasingly expensive." What was true today of passenger service, he added, would soon be true of express and then of freight. Warburg thought a merger would benefit everyone, and that the Civil Aeronautics Board (CAB) could be persuaded that it was in the public interest. Costs could be driven even lower if United could use Union Pacific ticket offices, buses, and other facilities. The railroad had a large investment in passenger service to protect, Warburg insisted: "The UP has spent more money *only* on streamlined trains than the UAL has spent in toto on its equipment which operates over the UP territory."[21]

The rebuttal to Warburg's argument came from Harriman, then in Washington on government service. "I cannot see," he countered, "how ownership would assist the Union Pacific in reducing unprofitable rail passenger expenditures." Nor did he think United would make much money under such an arrangement. The company's experience with buses, he noted, showed that it was impractical for different modes of transport to share the same ticket offices. Most important, Harriman believed "the odds are 100 to 1 that no approval could be obtained from the present board [CAB]." Harriman dispatched a copy of his letter to Robert Lovett, who mulled it over and produced in August a searching memorandum of his own.[22]

During that hot, ominous summer of 1940 Lovett peered coolly into the future with the surgical precision that became his trademark. For years he had perceived the Union Pacific as a transportation company that already utilized two modes of travel, rail and bus, and should take to the air as well. Air travel had grown enormously—70 percent in the first three months of 1940 alone—and the new technology of airplanes made it clear that express and freight service was "merely a matter of time and proper organization."[23]

Lovett believed the time had come when it was politically feasible and economically desirable to attempt a "test operation" in the field of joint air freight. A model for this service developed on a national scale could be sold to the government as being in the public interest and useful as part of any national defense program. "The Union Pacific has pioneered in the development of many aspects of transportation," he stressed, "and the present time may be a most appropriate one for it to blaze the trail again."

The railroads derived about 80 percent of their revenue from freight. Some of this, notably bulk shipments, was safe from air competition, but high-tariff goods were vulnerable. Once air freight began to grow, two factors would pose critical dangers to the railroads. The first was the "vital necessity for a ground-collection and ground-distribution system." Air freight required ground support, which trucks could perform easily and well. The railroads, warned Lovett, would look very foolish if air freight developed out of collaboration between the airline and trucking firms. A second question, which had been entirely neglected, concerned the origination of traffic. Most existing air express and freight was concentrated in a very few major cities, leaving many freight centers virtually untouched by air traffic solicitation. This condition would not last long once the industry began to grow rapidly.

To Lovett's mind, these two areas offered precisely the arena for joint effort between the railroads and airlines. Together they would provide a public service by eliminating wasteful competition and duplication. The railroads already knew how to solicit business and had a system of ground distribution in place. Union Pacific and United could plan the venture as a model for a national system in which all railroads and airlines shared. The experimental "National Air Freight Co." might function along the lines of Railway Express, with Union Pacific traffic men taking care to keep the air solicitors from invading the territory of competing railroads.

Why should the Union Pacific do this? Air freight was surely coming to its territory; the railroad had the choice of sharing in it or losing it. Getting involved early would avoid the embarrassment of having some other railroad snatch the territory away. Moreover, a coordinated air-rail-ground system offered another great advantage. "The establishment of proper master tariff schedules is of cardinal importance," Lovett noted, "as these rates may very well affect the entire rate structure of all transportation companies." Even if the venture lost money, he concluded, it would be well spent for the peace of mind resulting from proof that air freight wasn't profitable.

Lovett's incisive memorandum defined the issue with stunning clarity and foresight, but his vision remained unfulfilled. Apart from skeptics within the company, there would be opposition from Railway Express, which had dabbled in air service as early as 1910 and currently operated air express at 216 airports across the country. That same summer its officers had bristled at another plan suggested by General American Transportation Company that REA turn its air service over to an independent organization. Lovett thought this problem could be handled, but there was another grave difficulty beyond anyone's power to control: the growing world crisis.[24]

No progress was made before world events swept the issue into the limbo created by the abnormalities of wartime. In December 1940 Lovett was tapped for duty in Washington, where he played a pivotal role in strengthening American air power. There was a touch of irony in the brilliance of his performance for the war department. Having failed to create the Union Pacific Air Force, Lovett did much better at bringing into existence the United States Air Force as a separate service.[25]

The Union Pacific had been in the resort business long before Sun Valley. It had begun in a modest way at one of the most popular attractions on the road, the Great Salt Lake, by putting up a few bathhouses and a pavilion in the 1880s at a place called Garfield Beach. At the same time it looked for ways to reach another scenic wonder, Yellowstone Park. The Northern Pacific carried most of the tourist traffic from its line above the north entrance to the park; few visitors entered from the south or west, which required a stage ride of a hundred miles from the nearest railway. A branch from the Utah Northern could open this gateway into the park to a large tourist trade. But attempts to get a bill through Congress bogged down, more urgent projects took priority, and the onset of depression kept the idea in limbo until E. H. Harriman took charge of the road.[26]

Harriman had his hands full with more important work, but by 1905 he was ready to undertake the Yellowstone branch. Construction went slowly over rugged terrain, snaking through Warm River Canyon and Rea's Pass at an elevation of 7,000 feet en route to a terminus at the Madison River. Not until July 1908 did the St. Anthony branch, as it was called, begin carrying tourists into the southwestern corner of the park. The line stopped nineteen miles from the Fountain Hotel in the Lower Geyser Basin. At first the Union Pacific was content to provide only transportation to Yellowstone, but it soon found that its business was at the mercy of those who hauled travelers by stage to the hotels and operated the hotels.[27]

Both were doing a poor job and had a history that complicated the present situation. Originally the Northern Pacific had owned the hotels, and had tried to get the Union Pacific to share the investment. When this failed, the road later sold out to a private operator, who also controlled the stage line into the park from both entrances. Both roads agreed the hotels were mismanaged but still could not agree on what to do about it. One option was to take the hotels back and operate them jointly, but the two roads could not agree on terms. The Union Pacific then considered building its own hotel only to have the Short Line's officers split over whether the place should be leased to a private operator or run by the railroad. Although Judge Lovett thought the hotel should be built, he would not impose a decision on officers who would have to be responsible for the project.[28]

Not until 1916 did president E. E. Calvin and traffic director B. J. Winchell join in supporting the hotel idea. Plans were drawn only to be scotched when the country entered the war the following spring. In June 1917 the Burlington joined the other two roads in lending the operator of the transportation company enough money to motorize his service. The hotel idea surfaced again in 1919 when Congress finally authorized land for the project. Lovett delayed action until the end of federal control, by which time conditions had changed in another way. More and more tourists were flocking to Yellowstone, but an increasing number of them were coming by car. During the summer of 1920 nearly two-thirds of the 77,871 visitors drove to the park.[29]

Of those who came by rail, the Union Pacific carried more than half, but it was clear the company could not hold the business without offering more than a ride to the park. As early as 1903 the road had created a department of tours for bringing people to the scenic spots on an all-expense basis. Joining with the Northwestern, it created the "Bureau of Service National Parks and Resorts" for organizing and conducting escorted tours through Yellowstone and Rocky Mountain National Parks. So successful were the first offerings that the company added winter tours to California. Gray recognized that vacations were a growth industry, and that for most motorists, "the automobile trip itself is the principal inducement, the visit to the park being secondary to that."[30]

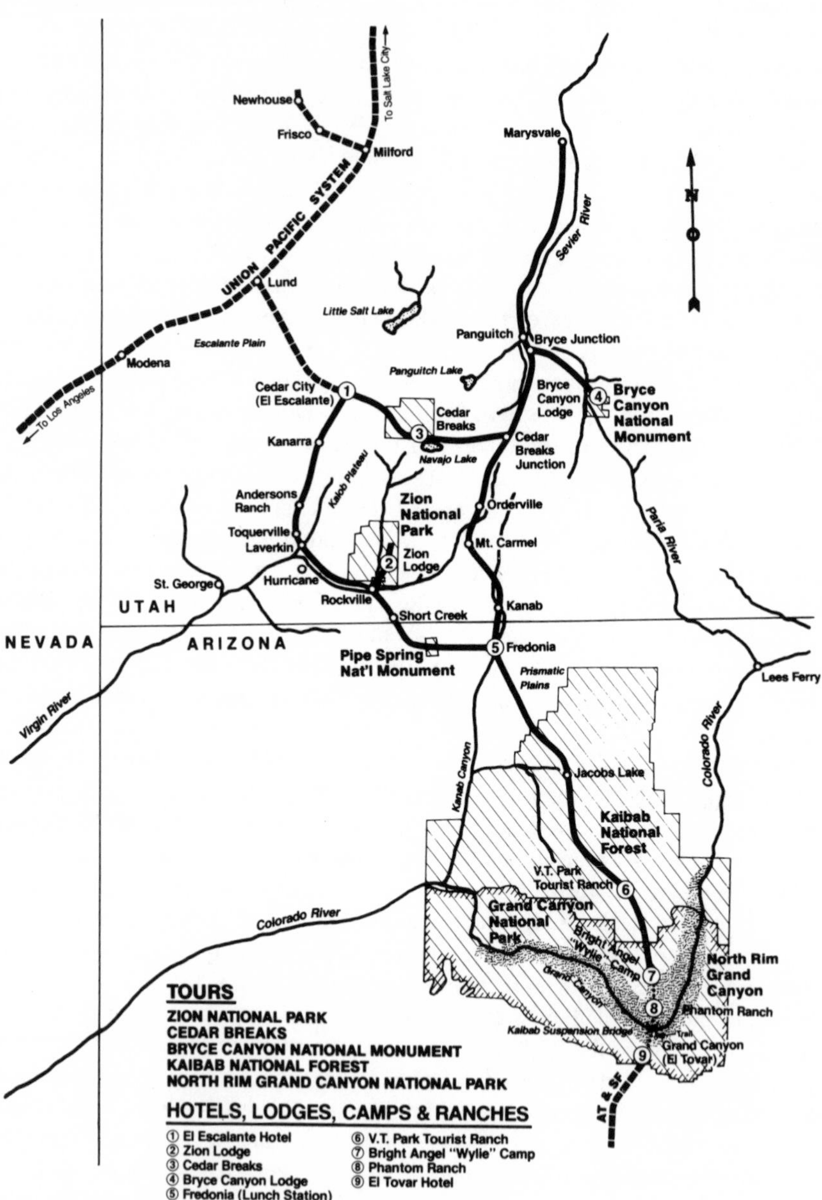

VACATIONLAND: The Utah Parks complex, first developed in the 1920s.

For those who came by train, the answer was to offer package tours relieving travelers of all responsibility for details that got in the way of their sightseeing. Gradually the Union Pacific moved from merely carrying vacationers into the larger business of arranging their trips and operating the resorts they visited. The extent of the company's involvement varied from using private contractors at Yellowstone to a mixed operation in the Utah Parks to complete ownership at Sun Valley. In each case the object was to make the tourist a captive audience of the railroad and its facilities in a pleasant, entertaining way. By providing services itself, the Union Pacific could avoid putting its reputation at the mercy of private contractors.

The Utah Parks operation evolved along these lines. Southern Utah and northern Arizona held a treasure trove of scenic wonders: Zion Canyon, Bryce Canyon, Cedar Breaks, Kaibab forest, and the north rim of the Grand Canyon. By 1920 Grand Canyon and Zion had become national parks and the National Park Service had been established. Gray visited the region in July 1922 and saw at once the possibilities for a tourist operation. If the right facilities were provided, all these wonders of nature could be combined in a single package. Some locals had already set up crude camps at Zion, Bryce, and the north rim; they could be worked with, but much more was needed. By autumn the company had decided on a major development program.[31]

As a first step, Gray had a thirty-three mile branch built on the Los Angeles & Salt Lake from Lund to Cedar City. Completed in June 1923, the line opened new territory for agriculture and iron mining as well as bringing travelers to the doorstep of scenic wonders. Gray persuaded local interests in Cedar City to join in erecting a new hotel for the tourist trade. New roads between the attractions were needed along with lodges at the sites and car or bus service. In March 1923 the company formed a new subsidiary, Utah Parks, to handle the operation. Three months later Utah Parks signed a contract with the Interior Department for installing facilities at Zion. Plans were made to build hotels at Zion, Bryce, and the north rim, camps at other sites, lunch counters, and concession stands.[32]

None of these improvements came easy in the wilderness. Bryce needed a pipeline for water before anything could be done. No maintained roads existed between Cedar City and Bryce, and only a rough road reached Zion or Cedar Breaks. The first lodge and cabin facilities went up at Bryce and Zion in 1924 and were added to in succeeding years as business increased. During the winter of 1927 Utah Parks won the concession for the north rim from the government and by June 1928 had erected a central lodge, seventy cabins, power and pumping plants, a garage, and other facilities at Bright Angel Point.[33]

To get the facilities ready, construction went right through the winter as convoys of four-cylinder trucks with high wheels, called ''iron horses'' by their drivers, bumped over frozen semi-roads behind a rotary plow following a trail of boards nailed to trees to show where the road was. To get heavy machinery over the vertical cliffs of Bright Angel Canyon, a cable tram line was transported from an abandoned mine and rigged by men with steel nerves along fifteen wooden towers built down the steep cliffs. When finished the cable was

ROUGHING IT: An early view of Zion Lodge.

three miles long. All the machinery for the pump and power station were lowered into the canyon this way. The power lines were strung by two linemen sent in from California. Both arrived by mule, one tied to the animal because he was dead drunk.[34]

About 125 men toiled through the harsh winter and muddy spring to get the north rim ready for tourists. Some brought their families with them. A school was run in a lumber building heated by a wood stove, with classes taught by the wife of a stonemason who was later denied a salary by the state of Arizona because she was not certified. Most lived in tents with wood floors and ate in a large mess tent much as the original construction crews on the railroad had done. At north rim the past sprung to life with a vividness the workers would long remember. For their remarkable feat the masons and carpenters got eighty-five cents an hour, the truck drivers seventy-five cents, and the laborers fifty cents, with nothing extra for overtime.[35]

For three more summers work continued on new buildings. In September 1932 a fire destroyed the main lodge and two cabins. The lodge was not rebuilt until 1936, but the tourist trade continued during its absence. Utah Parks offered a variety of packages topped by a six-day 489-mile motor bus tour of all the sights. There were also side trips for those with the stamina and the wallet to include them. The hardy could even buy a ticket for viewing Grand Canyon by plane, a service begun by other parties in 1929. As a scenic wonder, the Utah Parks itinerary offered a spectacle matched by few places on the continent. Like Yellowstone and Sun Valley, it did a thriving business until the war came along. Nevertheless, the Union Pacific gained no profit from its tourist business beyond a vast amount of favorable promotion and publicity.[36]

Some of the trimmings had been present at the creation, especially land and coal. In 1900 a surprisingly large chunk of the original land grant remained to be sold. After the reorganization in 1897 the old land department was dissolved and a new subsidiary, the Union Pacific Land Company took charge of the six million acres still belonging to the main line alone. Since most of the land was arid and suitable only for grazing, E. H. Harriman adopted the policy of selling it in large tracts to ranchers or irrigation projects that promised to make it productive for farming. The object was, as it had been since Jay Gould first emphasized the policy in the 1870s, to fill up empty country and provide more long-haul business on a permanent basis.[37]

But the old policy also took on some new wrinkles. While the company still did everything possible to encourage the growth of agriculture, it was also promoting other types of land usage. Since 1886 the company had reserved the mineral rights on all the land it sold. In 1912 it ordered all lands sold with this reservation examined to determine which parcels should be explored for their "prospective oil, coal and other minerals." The object was to weed out land that had no mineral value so that all rights on it could be waived. This idea gained fresh urgency when Wyoming began taxing the company for mineral reservations held on land sold to other parties.[38]

Gradually there evolved a policy of leasing mineral rights to outside parties for development. If coal or oil or other minerals were found, they would provide traffic for the railroad. Since mineral traffic had always been important to the road, this was less a new approach than a shift in emphasis. The most novel change in land policy came in the area of industrial development. Here the company reversed its role entirely; instead of selling land, it began buying large parcels for the creation of industrial parks along the line. The indefatigable J. L. Haugh pioneered in this work, beginning in 1923 with the 919-acre Fairfax district in Kansas City and following with a large development in Los Angeles.[39]

Although it was not yet apparent in the 1920s, the company had reached a turning point in its approach to mineral and industrial development. In the past it had been content to play a passive role, making its land available to those who wished to use it. Only in agriculture had it pursued settlers aggressively. By the 1920s, however, virtually all the arable land was occupied, and agricul-

FEEDING THE IRON HORSE: The No. 1 coal mining town at Hanna, Wyoming.

ture was anything but a growth industry. Driven by the need to find new sources of development, and by the new competitive pressures, the Union Pacific switched to a more active role in luring new business to its lines. In time these first tentative steps would become separate enterprises on a scale that would dwarf earlier efforts.

The one exception was coal, which the company had operated directly since Gould seized the mines from an outside contractor in 1874. Coal was in a special category because the railroad had to assure itself of a reliable fuel supply. For years the company struggled to realize Gould's vision of mining coal at a price cheap enough to supply the road its fuel and service a growing commercial market as well. If done efficiently, the profits from commercial sales would in effect pay for the fuel. But coal mining was a world unto itself, and problems plagued the Union Pacific mines from the start. In 1890 the company had organized a subsidiary, Union Pacific Coal Company, to oversee the Wyoming mines. It also owned mines in Colorado, which were swept into another subsidiary, Union Coal Company.[40]

After the 1897 reorganization Union Pacific Coal again took charge of the operation. The long depression and troubles encountered prior to it left the mines wholly unprepared to cope with the flood of traffic that soon came pouring over the Union Pacific lines. Of the thirteen fields opened in Wyoming, Utah, and Colorado before 1891, only five were still producing coal, and three of these were nearly played out. Most of the coal came from one of the oldest fields, Rock Springs, and the newest, Hanna. By the end of 1896 the work force had dwindled to 1,969 men of more than twenty nationalities. About 26 percent were Finns, nearly 22 percent came from the British Isles, and only 10 percent were Chinese. More miners were desperately needed; as an assistant superintendent reported in December 1898, the men were working twelve-hour days and could not endure the pace much longer.[41]

Labor posed a special problem in the closed, specialized, still primitive world of mining. Intent on avoiding unionism at all costs, the company had deliberately imported different ethnic groups in hopes they would segregate themselves from each other and thereby resist organization. This policy had succeeded in keeping the unions out; it had also led directly to the infamous Rock Springs massacre of 1885. Since then racial and ethnic friction had toned down, but the company still looked to "average up nationalities" in recruiting new men. Superintendent D. O. Clark wanted 400 more miners, at least 80 of them married, to provide stability. As an experiment he brought in about 125 black men to Hanna, where he also imported 60 whites from Texas and Missouri.[42]

Within a few months many of the black miners left. Only about a third of the blacks brought into Rock Springs stayed on. Some could not endure the harsh climate; others were good miners, Clark reported, "but we cannot get them to work as many hours per day nor as many days per week." By 1899 the demand for black workers was so great that Clark could not induce many to come so far west. He denied a newspaper story that he was also looking for more Chinese. Thanks to the Exclusion Act he couldn't get them anyway, so he did the next best thing: he brought in Japanese, who were smuggled across the border at Vancouver. Their diligence pleased Clark immensely.[43]

To get more coal, the company had to acquire or open new mines. This meant it also had to recruit more miners, which in turn meant building decent housing, a store, and other amenities. Union Pacific paid more attention to these details and treated the men better than most because it was difficult to attract workers to the wilds of Wyoming. Clark looked personally into one grievance about a weighman and found that, "while his weights were all right, he was surley [sic] and ugly with the men." Clark promptly replaced him and allowed the men to have one of their own check the weights. "These men are not at all bad men," he sighed, "they are more like a lot of children and very sensative [sic]."[44]

Sometimes the miners themselves helped recruit newcomers. One brought eighty Germans from Pennsylvania to Hanna and Rock Springs. Clark had the new men sign a pledge not to join a union. "While this may not be any good legally," he admitted, "it has a moral effect." He still took care to balance ethnic groups "and not allow any nationality to predominate, and no member of a labor organization is knowingly employed." Unfortunately, half the Germans skipped out after the company had paid their fare to Wyoming. "Men get here in debt from 50 to 80 dollars," complained Clark, "and knowing they can get work anywhere they leave and we have no recourse, even when they go to work for the railroad company."[45]

By 1902 the Union Pacific was heading into serious trouble over coal. The growth of the West increased the demand for commercial coal, and the over-taxed railroad system consumed more fuel than ever. An anthracite strike in the fall shut off eastern supplies from western markets. Commercial orders jumped sharply, forcing the Union Pacific to run its mines at full capacity. Two new mines had been opened in Wyoming but production costs were rising at the older mines as the men burrowed deeper for coal. Horace Burt urged Harriman to buy a large tract of coal land in Iowa, Missouri, or Kansas to protect the company's supply. Rock Springs and Hanna coal were lignite, which deteriorated when stored; it was therefore better suited for the commercial market. New mines farther east could be used for locomotive fuel and would need a shorter haul.[46]

For some reason Harriman rejected this suggestion. At the same time he asked sharply why the company discouraged other coal companies from opening on the Union Pacific line. "It does not seem to me," he growled, "that we should allow our interests as a transportation company to be interfered with by our interest in our coal properties, or that we should not do what we can to develop proper industries along our line." Thrown on the defensive, Burt could not budge Harriman. The company sold coal lands in Colorado that were too remote to be utilized effectively. During the winter of 1902–1903 the shortage grew worse. In June 1903 a disaster at Hanna's number-one mine killed 169 men and forced sealing of the mine until early the next year.[47]

By October 1903 a crisis loomed. The miners were stretched to their limit of endurance and still the company could not produce enough coal to meet its needs or the commercial market. "The difficulty is," reported Burt glumly, "that we have neither mines nor miners enough to anywhere near take care of the business which properly belongs to this Company." As shortages arose, Burt contracted to buy coal for fuel from mines in Colorado and Kansas. "This Company should open more mines in Wyoming," he told Harriman, "and should, as I have before suggested, have mines of its own or that it can control in Missouri River country." A strike in Colorado during November underscored Burt's message even though it did not affect the Wyoming mines.[48]

Still Harriman moved slowly. A new company, Superior Coal, was formed in 1906 to tap some seams northeast of Rock Springs. Its output soon rivaled those venerable mines. That same year Union Pacific bought some coal lands in Colorado, but by 1907 the shortage grew so acute that the company bought coal from Australia as well as Illinois, and resorted to paying freight on coal cars to get them back from the East. Labor too was scarce, and wages shot up. In March 1908 another calamity at Hanna's number-one mine claimed fifty-nine lives, forty-one of them rescuers trying to reach the men originally trapped. That same year the government charged the Union Pacific with using coal from lands not belonging to it. The company chose to settle by ceding 4,500 acres of Wyoming coal land back to the government.[49]

In 1911 the company opened more new mines north of Rock Springs and created the town of Reliance. The labor situation, intensified by a series of bitter and bloody strikes in Colorado, grew worse. World War I put added pressure on the coal company, forcing it to stop the sale of commercial coal at Rock Springs because of the rising demand for locomotive fuel. Early in 1917 E. E. Calvin had to advise the Navigation Company to buy its fuel from other companies because Union Pacific Coal could not fill its needs. After the war

MINERS' MAN: Eugene C. McAuliffe, who gave the Union Pacific Coal Company fresh, imaginative leadership.

western miners got caught up in the tensions and turmoil that brought on a number of national strikes and unleashed the notorious Red Scare.[50]

When the coal miners issued a strike call for November 1, 1919, Judge Lovett went west to examine the situation for himself. He found that miners on the Union Pacific lines had no grievances and wanted no conferences, but planned to honor the strike. "Wages, living and working conditions of Union Pacific System miners are good," he reported, ". . . and miners are generally satisfied." But those eager to work feared violence if they did, and would not return unless guaranteed protection. This was done, and three weeks into the strike Union Pacific mines were working at 80 percent capacity. The split left little room for compromise; on December 2 Rock Springs and Superior worked normal shifts while Hanna, Reliance, and Cumberland stood idle.[51]

The recurring cycle of labor disputes left all the mines unsettled and the company as dissatisfied as its workers. Gray took a hard look at the coal conundrum after coming to the Union Pacific. In the past the president of the railroad had also served as head of the coal company. Gray held the job less than two months before turning it over to Calvin, then made the break complete in January 1921 by giving the post to E. S. Brooks, who had spent most of his long career with Union Pacific Coal. Two years later Gray took the final step of bringing in an outside president, Eugene McAuliffe, relegating Brooks to the vice-presidency. For the first time the coal operation became a separate organization under its own president.[52]

McAuliffe proved an inspired choice. The son of a British engineer who had survived the Sepoy Mutiny and migrated to America, he went early into railroading with the Northern Pacific before taking a new job as fuel agent. For some years he worked at developing mines in the Midwest for a utilities company. He was employed on special assignment with the utilities firm when Gray tapped him. During the war McAuliffe had served as director of the fuel conservation section for USRA. Most likely, Gray first met him in government work because one of McAuliffe's strengths coincided with Gray's: labor relations. The need for a fresh approach in this area may well have been what led Gray to seek McAuliffe out.[53]

When McAuliffe took office in March 1923, the company was producing 16,500 tons daily from seventeen mines. All were small, slope-driven mines with wooden tipples, narrow-gauge cars, and small pit cars. The miners, spread across forty-nine nationalities, were entirely unionized but transient, with a turnover of nearly 125 percent annually due to the policy of stockpiling men to get out a heavy tonnage in anticipation of strikes. Absenteeism was high and morale as low as earnings. McAuliffe recognized that miners had always been fiercely independent, and that they resented paternalism of any kind. The trick was finding a way to stabilize their position without impinging on what he called "the last stronghold of labor individualism." He also had the urgent task of increasing output and efficiency.[54]

The course McAuliffe chose seemed at first glance to be one that guaranteed labor strife rather than harmony. He persuaded the company to undertake an extensive program of mechanization, beginning with loaders. The object, of course, was to replace men with machines, but not directly. No man would be let go to make way for a mechanical loader; the machines would be introduced gradually as natural attrition of the work force permitted. McAuliffe took care to introduce the new technology as helpmate rather than threat to the men, a way to increase productivity and therefore earnings. As a sign of his good faith, McAuliffe in 1929 appointed former United Mine Worker president John P. White as umpire for any differences between the men and the company. This shrewd move helped draw the union into a relationship based on mediation instead of antagonism.

"Whatever the crimes committed in the past by the Unions," he declared in print, "such have in our opinion been fully paralleled by many abuses put upon mine labor by many employers. The Union Pacific Coal Company decided to give the Union the widest possible chance to establish itself upon the property, on a business-like basis, asking only that the extreme element . . . be shaken out, all theories of 'wobbly' propensities to be eliminated."[55]

Prior to McAuliffe the company had made some efforts to mechanize and improve safety. Cutting and drilling machines run by compressed air had been introduced at Rock Springs as early as 1882. Punchers arrived during the 1890s, and a decade later electricity replaced compressed air, enabling the company to put in more undercutting machines. The newer Superior and Reliance mines got electric undercutters from the start, while Hanna did not get its first one until 1913. As early as 1901 the company experimented with safety explosives, but it took several years to perfect permissible powder.* The first electric mining locomotive made its appearance in 1892 but the breed was never effective until loading machines and larger cars arrived.[56]

Under McAuliffe the last black blasting powders, which some miners preferred, gave way to permissibles and the old carbide lamps to Edison electric cap lamps. Loading machines and shaking conveyors were installed as fast as attrition allowed, and locomotives with capacities reaching fifteen tons replaced the venerable mules that had long served the mines. The company also launched a program of building more modern housing, bath houses, schools, and other facilities. McAuliffe also organized the Old Timers' Association and spurred publication of an employees' magazine to help strengthen the sense of community among the miners. No less than the mechanical loading program it was, he admitted freely, "an attempt at human engineering." Sometimes the engineering took novel twists, such as a $1,000 contribution to an Eastern Christian Orthodox Church for Greek and Slav miners run by a minister who was, in Gray's words, "of the very greatest value to us in the handling of labor matters among this very difficult class of people."[57]

The results confirmed McAuliffe's fondest hopes. When he arrived in 1923, only about 3 percent of the coal was loaded mechanically; five years later the figure exceeded 51 percent, and by 1935 it reached 99.8 percent. The miners worked shorter days but more days every year, earned less per hour but more money per year. Extraction per acre rose from 40 percent in 1900 to 80 percent by 1940. Costs declined along with wages, and production stayed level despite the gradual reduction in work force. Safety improved steadily, thanks in part to the required use of hard hats and goggles. Mine fatalities dropped from 68 during 1923–1929 to 39 during the 1930s, while man-hours per accident soared from 15,101 to 62,274.[58]

Like the railroad, however, the coal company solved many of its internal problems only to find that it could not escape the growing tug of external pressures. During the 1930s the cockpit of mining labor strife lay in the Appalachian fields, but the strike calls affected western mines as well. So did the settlements, although some of the terms scarcely affected Union Pacific Coal. When another strike loomed in April 1939, John L. Lewis of the United Mine Workers promised the western operators that they would not be shut down while he negotiated for the Appalachian mines. But Lewis was engaged in a power struggle with a rival union, and in May the western miners walked out in support of the strike call.[59]

Another external factor was to have a more enormous impact on the coal industry than the government and unions combined. The Union Pacific mine at Spring Valley, Utah, felt its effects in a literal sense. Opened in 1900, the mine ran into trouble from oil seepage. At first the oil was used to lubricate the

*Permissible powders are consistent with samples tested for safety by the U. S. Bureau of Mines and approved for use in gaseous or dusty mines.

hoisting engine; then pools began to accumulate in the low places. Behind it came explosive gas in such quantities that the company ordered the mine sealed in 1905. Oil and gas had closed it down.[60]

It would have taken extraordinary vision to read Spring Valley's fate as more an omen than a fluke. By 1905 oil had long been a giant industry, but its true potential had yet to reveal itself. The automobile was in its infancy, the diesel locomotive and airplane not yet born. Not until the internal combustion engine was perfected did the petroleum industry commence its monumental shift in primary use from illuminants to fuel. The Atchison and Southern Pacific already used oil-burning locomotives because coal was so scarce in the Southwest. Tests on these roads in 1901 showed 170 gallons of fuel oil equal to a ton of bituminous coal, which meant cheaper costs, cleaner fuel, and longer runs. The only drawback was the horrendous noise made by the forced draft of the burners.[61]

These tests interested the Union Pacific, which knew it had large oil deposits in Utah and Wyoming. The company was anxious to stimulate mineral development as a means of increasing business. In 1899 it offered free transportation to any scientist wishing to explore for minerals in Wyoming. Prior to World War I the Union Pacific leased exploration rights to oil companies seeking new sources. No thought was given to going directly into the business because the presence of oil in large quantities was not yet proven.[62]

As the market for petroleum expanded with the rocketing use of cars and trucks, the Union Pacific continued its policy of encouraging other companies to explore and share any finds on a royalty basis. Good finds were made in Colorado and Kansas, but no major finds occurred until 1936, when a sudden turn of events set in motion a dramatic shift in policy and direction for the company. That year three promising wells were brought in near Medicine Bow, Wyoming. More important, a private driller struck oil in vast quantities at Long Beach (California) harbor on land owned by the Los Angeles & Salt Lake. Thus began the fabulous Wilmington oil field.[63]

Other producers with rights on adjacent lands in Long Beach rushed in to drill their own wells. By April 1937 they had sunk eighty-one wells, of which twenty-nine were already producing oil. Averell Harriman realized that quick action was needed to protect the company's fields from drainage. Since certain obstacles made the usual lease and royalty arrangement with other parties untenable, Harriman decided to put the Union Pacific directly into the oil business by drilling wells on its own. By the year's end the company had sunk seventy-two wells, all of them producing, and had eighteen more underway. That first year the wells fetched a net income of $429,000.[64]

Suddenly the company found itself in the oil business, and confusion reigned supreme. The state of California promptly filed suit to recover the fields by virtue of its sovereignty over tidelands, and some taxpayers in Long Beach challenged the railroad's title to the lands. These suits put the company in limbo. If it continued to produce and lost the suits, it would be liable for any oil already produced; if it closed down the wells, other producers would drain much of the field. Convinced that the litigation would be protracted and that the company would win, Harriman decided to risk keeping production going. In March 1937 he brought in an outside man, William Reinhardt, as vice-president in charge of oil development.[65]

Meanwhile, the lawyers scrambled about frantically trying to revise the form of their leases for mineral exploration. "In view of the fact that new mineral values, previously unheard of, are continually springing up," stressed one officer, "and that the rapid development of mining and manufacturing methods is resulting in the extended use of newly discovered minerals, no one at this time can even guess what the future may develop in the way of mineral values or where such minerals may be discovered."[66]

He was exactly right. The venture into oil may have been precipitate, but it was also the wave of the future. Minerals would play a vital role in the company's future, none more so than oil, and would be instrumental in determining what direction its affairs would take. The trimmings were slowly but inexorably turning into essentials.

18

The Family

The course of labor relations, like that of true love, never did run smooth for railroads. During the nineteenth century disputes remained a family affair to be settled between the company and its employees. Gradually the unions elbowed their way into the process until their role grew strong enough to draw in the federal government as well. By 1920 a new set of relationships had emerged in which the ground rules had yet to be fully clarified.

The basic parameters had been set. Negotiations had become generic, taking place between spokesmen for the industry and the unions rather than between representatives of a specific road and its men. As a result, they had also become heavily politicized because collective voices talked much louder and could not be ignored by elected officials. In this way the revolution that was fast transforming American life into a society of organizations swept through the industry that, as creator of the first large private corporations, had done so much to bring it into existence.

Within these bounds, however, the players were still groping for a workable set of rules. The old problem of how to instill loyalty to the company in workers took on fresh urgency in this framework. It was difficult enough to impose policy on a giant organization; how could spirit be diffused as well? The Union Pacific came up with the same answer as many other railroads: it tried to promote the image of the company's officers and employees as one big family working and playing together for the common cause.

Since the dawn of industrialism society had been bedeviled by the question of what obligations attached to the wage relationship. In its earliest phase none was involved; the employer was beholden to a worker for nothing except his or her pay. Yet a certain loyalty to the firm was expected, which required some kind of bond between organization and employees. One major influence of the Civil War on railroad men revealed itself in the way they described themselves as being "in the service" and obliged to perform their duty. This sense was reinforced by the fact that railway organizations were structured on the military model with its hierarchy of ranks in which every man knew his place.

As this model grew larger and more sophisticated, the old indifference gave way to a sort of benevolent despotism. The company might reward loyal and dutiful workers for their service in ways above and beyond their pay if it pleased, but this largess was strictly voluntary. In this casual way such benefits as pensions, sick leave, death and injury compensation, and hospital funds first crept into existence. The company handled these matters strictly on a case-by-case basis, insisting always that it was not obliged to do any of it.

The Union Pacific became interested in employee welfare sooner than most because of its need to attract a stable work force to remote, harsh places. During the 1880s Charles Francis Adams, Jr., had installed libraries and other facilities on the rugged Wyoming and Idaho divisions to give the men an alternative to saloons. In 1886 he went even further by devising a visionary plan for a full-blown welfare system for Union Pacific workers. His ideas struck officers in this most conservative of industries as dangerously radical and were quickly dropped.[1]

By 1920 striking changes in this one-way relationship had taken place. As unions gained more power on their own and in collaboration with the government, the bargaining process grew more formal. Workers no longer negotiated on their own but rather through organizations; benefits once bestowed or not at the company's pleasure also became formalized and eventually got thrown on the bargaining table along with wages and working conditions. In this new age neither fear nor paternalism could bind workers to the company. Something more was needed, especially as the organization grew larger and more specialized, and its work force more diverse. During the 1920s, that something was the extended concept of the organization as family.

The visionary welfare scheme of Charles Francis Adams died aborning, a casualty of his own failure as president and of the depression of the 1890s that weeded out the ranks like a scythe. Harriman did little to improve matters; labor relations were hardly his strong suit. Although he tried to be fair, he was hard on everybody and was more feared than loved.

Harriman's drive for efficiency ground men down in ways that were not always obvious. During the first winter after reorganization the work force was slashed 10 percent beginning with the shops. This did not endear the new management to the men, and neither did a seemingly more humane policy of limiting shop work to forty hours a week. The superintendent soon discovered that men were leaving because they could earn more money on roads that ran their shops forty-eight or sixty hours a week. Reluctantly the old hours were restored.[2]

The shops remained the flashpoint for clashes between the old ways and the new, as the bitter strike of 1902–1903 demonstrated. Ironically, it was Horace Burt who stood firm on the issue of piecework and Harriman who ultimately backed down. Unwilling to buy piecework at any price, he agreed to abolish the system so despised by the old workers. The fight over piecework struggled for another decade, and the shop unions remained at the forefront of labor discontent. In 1911 they struck again, this time demanding not only higher wages but the right for all five shop unions to bargain jointly. A prolonged fight failed to gain this concession, but the issue had come to stay.[3]

There followed the long and dreary chain of events that culminated in the Adamson Act, which marked a new departure in labor relations for the railroads. Negotiations were taken out of the railroads' hands and thrown into the political arena. The federal takeover accelerated this process by forging a direct link between labor and government in its new role as manager. Wartime conditions produced a host of striking changes for labor no less than the carriers.

On every front the government sought to standardize and unify policy. Since the easiest way to deal with labor was through the unions, the Railroad Administration encouraged their growth. By the end of 1918 unions represented nearly every class of rail worker on the vast majority of roads. Rules governing everything from grievances to promotion were devised for most classes of workers. Boards of adjustment were created to handle disputes and discipline cases. The eight-hour day was extended to virtually all classes of workers, and time-and-a-half pay for overtime was granted shopmen and some others.[4]

Wages were standardized on a national basis for everyone except engineers and trainmen. Women received the same pay as men for the same class of work, and black firemen, trainmen, and switchmen gained equal pay with whites in the same jobs. Piecework was eliminated from shops, closing at last that long battle. The government also granted wage increases totaling $784 million in 1918 and another $181 million in 1919. As director of USRA's labor division, Carl Gray had taken part in some—but not all—of these fundamental changes.[5]

Much of the program that had worked well while the war still raged came unraveled after the armistice in 1919, when no one knew how or when government control would end. The decision was made to eliminate all overtime work, a severe blow to workers' income already ravaged by wartime inflation. A wave of strikes swept the railroads as well as the rest of the nation as bitter disputes over wages erupted. USRA, unable to get Congress or the President to act, entered into what became known as national agreements for the duration of federal control. These involved concessions for working conditions in lieu of wage hikes.[6]

Thus did all sides enter the new era under the Transportation Act of 1920 in a suspicious, combative mood. Managers believed the men had gained huge wage increases and liberalized working conditions that would remain a burden for years. The new Railroad Labor Board added fuel to this sentiment by granting wage adjustments totaling $618 million in July 1920. Despite these gains, the unions still felt cheated because inflation outstripped pay raises in many cases, especially without the overtime pay on which many people had come to depend. Some classes of workers like switchmen actually lost ground in the government's effort to impose uniformity on wages, and many received less pay than workers in other fields.[7]

Judge Lovett shared this grim view. In November 1919 he had asked Jeffers to summarize what he called "unjust and obnoxious results of all wage rules and regulations issued during Federal control." Several wildcat strikes on the road that winter did nothing to temper his outlook. The newly arrived Carl Gray took a more moderate view. Having been deeply involved in the process, he understood the labor problem more thoroughly than most railroad men. In April 1920 he took part in an Association of Railway Executives meeting to define a position on the labor boards of adjustment mentioned in the new Transportation Act. The sessions revealed how divided among themselves the railroad presidents were on the labor issue.[8]

The act did not require the boards but said they could be established if the carriers and unions agreed on them. Gray's wartime experience with the boards had been so positive that he favored them unequivocably, as did several of the more liberal presidents. A strong faction led by W. W. Atterbury of the Pennsylvania adamantly opposed the boards, insisting that all labor disputes be left to the individual roads. The New York Central favored some kind of regional boards but in the end went along with Atterbury. This was not the old split between the eastern and western roads; something more was involved.

Gray saw at once that the opposition lured to it everyone who disliked USRA by casting the debate as "a Railroad Administration crowd Vs. the Corporation Interests" fight. To his surprise, several key western presidents such as Howard Elliott and Hale Holden wavered, then helped vote down the report to take part in creating the boards. "To my mind," sighed Gray, "it smacks of opera-bouffe."[9]

Five months later the presidents met again to consider the issue. During the long and heated debate the choleric Atterbury wound up his passionate statement by asserting that "Our duty is clear. Make no contract with Labor Unions." Another president chimed in with the ringing declaration that "we must handle our own men, on our own railroad in our own way." Gray shook his head in disgust. These men, he snorted, "have the most charming disregard of actualities and are seemingly not able to comprehend that the Transportation Act has ruthlessly provided against any management handling their own men in their own way."[10]

Unable to agree, the presidents passed a limp resolution authorizing their labor committee to negotiate the matter with the Railroad Labor Board. On his own road Gray deplored the methods of the striking switchman but insisted to Judge Lovett that the men had legitimate grievances. The policy of uniformity had worked against them; their pay no longer exceeded that for less skilled and hazardous work, and compared poorly with wages outside the industry. "The great difficulty," he explained, "is that the mass of American people are convinced that the Railroad Administration allowed profligate increases in wages.'' Except for a few freak cases, Gray emphasized, rail workers merely got the same increases given other industries.[11]

Lovett accepted Gray's explanation, but the dispute lingered on. Jeffers handled matters in his own inimitable style: when some trainmen at Cheyenne followed the switchmen out, he rushed to the scene and informed them he had come to break the strike, not settle it. His tough stand won immediate support from the regular union men who had opposed the wildcat strike, and even the strikers respected Jeffers enough to listen to him. The episode demonstrated to Gray that the Union Pacific had ''a very strong sub-strata of pure loyalty among its employees.''[12]

But tapping it was difficult because Gray himself was torn on several key issues. In his view the basic problem over wages traced back to the Lane Commission report of April 1918, on which USRA wage orders had been based. The Lane Commission devised a sliding scale to equalize wages, giving the lowest paid workers the highest increase and vice versa. This approach had two glaring flaws: it blurred existing distinctions between different types of work (i. e., switchmen vs. clerks), and it ignored entirely the market demand for labor in competing industries. As a result, shopmen, who were well off thanks to prewar raises and could find work in other industries that paid better than railroads, got short shrift under the Lane formula.[13]

Gray had vehemently opposed the Lane approach, but no one in USRA ever got to discuss the matter. Somehow a New York paper got hold of the report and published it before director general William McAdoo and his people had even seen it. With the report made public, McAdoo thought it impolitic to disappoint the workers given the larger increases, and the recommendations were put into effect. The result, as Gray had feared, was wholesale discontent among several classes of workers. McAdoo also put into effect orders recognizing the eight-hour day for all workers and giving equal pay to women and blacks despite objections by Gray.[14]

To make matters worse, McAdoo issued his order abolishing piecework while Gray was in Florida and unable to join in the discussion. When he took McAdoo's place, Walker Hines compounded the difficulties by entering into the so-called ''national agreements'' that became the flashpoint for criticism of USRA policy. Gray had hoped to avoid introducing any new work conditions and deal only with wages, but Hines scuttled that approach. A short time later the railroads returned to private ownership, leaving managers to cope with unions anxious to preserve and extend wartime gains in a radically changed postwar atmosphere.[15]

The worst damage occurred in the shops, where the abolition of piecework rates led to a startling drop in efficiency. By 1921 man-hours in the boiler shop at Omaha had increased 31 percent while output dropped 24 percent; in the blacksmith shop hours were up 36 percent and output down 26 percent; in the wheel shop hours rose 32 percent and output declined 24 percent; in the paint shop hours were up 42 percent and output down 30 percent. Similar figures were reported from other shops on the Union Pacific and on other systems across the country.[16]

As the postwar economy staggered through a brief but severe recession, the shops once again emerged as the battlefield for labor strife. During the winter of 1920–21 the Union Pacific joined other western roads in laying off large numbers of men and seeking wage cuts. In May 1921 the Labor Board approved a general reduction that totaled about 10.6 percent for the Union Pacific. The brotherhoods responded with a strike threat, which Gray thought privately was a bluff. To his surprise, a majority of Union Pacific men voted to support the proposed strike.[17]

Lovett was shocked by what he considered a lack of loyalty. It was evident, he snapped, "that the insurance plan and the other things we have done, including clubhouses, etc., have failed to make our men any more appreciative of their positions with the Company than are employes [sic] of other companies which have done nothing comparable for their men." Gray shared his disappointment. "If this strike occurs," he said mournfully, ". . . it will explode every theory I have ever made with respect to the response of employes to considerate and liberal treatment."[18]

The hearings before the Labor Board narrowed the clash to the wage reduction order. To Gray's surprise, the board stood firm behind its decision and warned that any strike against one of its orders would cost the unions all benefits from existing contracts and previous orders. Gray had urged this stand but did not expect it to be adopted. On the Union Pacific Jeffers once again did yeoman service, holding meetings at every division point and, as Gray put it, talking to the men "without gloves."[19]

The unions backed down and the strike threat passed, but everyone knew the respite would be brief. Early in 1922 Lovett stressed that the public demand for lower rates ruled out higher wages. Secretary of Commerce Herbert Hoover injected himself into the picture by exploring with the presidents some way to separate the four brotherhoods from the other unions and deal with them outside the Labor Board. At the board's hearings in March 1922 a row erupted during what was supposed to be a routine presentation of data. The explosion was not long in coming.[20]

In June the Labor Board reduced the pay of clerks, signalmen, and stationary firemen by a total of $27 million. Cuts were also imposed on the shopmen, who promptly walked out and demanded wage increases. In less than a month Gray had enough returned strikers and new men to cover 43 percent of the work force. As this figure climbed past 60 percent early in August, the strike looked lost and the men ready to return to work. But they could not, for a new issue had arisen in a way that illustrated dramatically the changed nature of labor relations.[21]

Both the Labor Board and the railroads warned the shop unions that any men going out on strike would lose all rights and privileges, including seniority. Gray promised loyal workers and new employees alike that their rights would be protected in any settlement. In essence this meant they had seniority and were now the bargaining members of the recognized shop unions. The strikers wanted their seniority restored if they returned; this was the one thing Gray could not and would not give them.[22]

Gray and Lovett alike were adamant on this issue. It was for Gray a question of honor: "Our guarantees to these men were that we would not agree to any settlement which would jeopardize their positions and the rights which they had secured." Lovett felt the same way. "The sole inquiry with me," he said, "is whether we are keeping faith with the men now in service." But how could they keep faith when the decision was not entirely in their hands? If the Labor Board ruled that the strikers were entitled to their seniority back, the Union Pacific must obey or violate the law. To complicate matters, President Harding had proposed a vague plan to settle the dispute with little thought to its wider ramifications on such matters as seniority.[23]

Abruptly the strike shifted from one over wages to one over seniority rights and the rights of strikers in general. If the men returned to work and petitioned the Labor Board to restore their seniority, the Union Pacific was legally obliged to respect the decision. Lovett saw the danger at once. "It will set a precedent for all time," he observed, "that men on strike are not out of the service."[24]

To Lovett's chagrin, a majority of the presidents favored Harding's plan, which took the expedient view that seniority would not be a problem because there would be ample work for all. Most of them were concerned about the seniority question but willing to let the Labor Board decide it. Lovett and Gray were not, and the men they were protecting organized an association to fight restoration of seniority to the strikers. In settling with the different unions, Gray offered wages slightly above what the Labor Board sanctioned. Once the shopmen's cause looked hopeless, he offered to restore all pension rights but would not relent on the seniority issue.[25]

By late September the Union Pacific shops had returned to 98 percent of normal employment, and Gray negotiated an agreement containing some novel features with the new association. The strikers held out doggedly, growing ever more desperate, appealing finally to Mary Harriman for help in ending the dispute. Meanwhile the new association basked in higher wages than the Labor Board had set and their new seniority rights protected as promised. Not until October 1923 did the old shop unions formally terminate the strike that had long since been lost.[26]

The unions were quick to view the Labor Board as a friend of the carriers, and attempts were made in 1924 to push through legislation abolishing it in favor of the old mediation-arbitration system that had proved such a disaster in the Adamson bill fight of 1916. The railroads opposed the bill despite some internal clashing, and managed to defeat it. Two years later Gray created an adjustment board for the Union Pacific System, thereby reinforcing a trend for carriers to take back the handling of labor problems as much as possible. But they could only go so far, and sometimes progress marched backward when the rules imposed by the Labor Board proved less liberal than the company rules they replaced.[27]

For the rest of the decade labor relations remained smoother than usual but not dormant. Most of the unions gained modest wage advances, some of them granted by the Union Pacific on its own. A dispute with the firemen in 1927 raised a strike threat, but the four brotherhoods were too divided among themselves to worry Gray deeply. Once a sense of stability returned to the work force, he was far more concerned about restoring a sense of loyalty and team spirit to the ranks as a way of healing old wounds and preventing new ones.[28]

As the first giant, far-flung business enterprises, railroads learned early that the task of winning employee loyalty was not easy. There were in reality two work forces, the permanent and the transient, the latter a product of shifts in seasonal employment and business swings. Adams saw that each required a different approach, and hoped the one could serve as an apprenticeship to the other. Nothing came of his plan, and in the end Adams had to compete with the unions for his men's loyalty like other presidents.

How to bind employees to the company? After the Civil War the railroads emphasized every man's sense of duty—a strong appeal to ex-soldiers who had been taught to obey orders and perform whatever tasks were assigned them. As the work force grew larger and more diverse and the power of unions increased, railroad managers had to offer the men something more than wages to gain their loyalty. From this need arose a second approach: the concept of the corporation as family.

At bottom this was an updated form of paternalism. The basic premise was simple. A large organization was impersonal by nature, but its members could create a web of relationships, formal and informal, to give it meaning and even a semblance of warmth. The notion of the corporation as family was obvious and irresistible. A family looked after the welfare of its members, did things together, shared ties of experience and loyalty. It created a sense of identity and mutual purpose that might otherwise not exist.

This approach took root slowly and in piecemeal fashion, nudged along by the growing threat of union influence. The most immediate need of men in so dangerous a business was medical attention. The Union Pacific had instituted its hospital fund in 1882, and supported the deficit it often ran. By the 1910s, however, the fund on the Navigation lines had accumulated a large surplus, prompting the unions to demand control of the fund or at least a voice in its management. Caught by surprise, the company agreed readily to publish annual financial reports and to add employees to the committee.[29]

The complaints dried up as services were improved. At Gray's request the company quietly donated $10,000 toward a new hospital in Cheyenne and installed a dispensary in the shops at Salt Lake City. Coverage was extended to new types of maladies ranging from basketball injuries to automobile accidents, and to conditions originally excluded, such as the recurrence of long dormant venereal disease. Judge Lovett took a conservative approach to the fund, refusing to invest its proceeds in securities and allowing it interest on money deposited with the company.[30]

By 1927 the surplus had turned into a deficit that mounted steadily during the depression as staff attrition whittled away the base of contributors. Although the company continued to expand coverage under the fund through the 1930s, all sides realized that a major reorganization could not be avoided.[31]

No benefit mattered more to workers than the pension plan. Management had long regarded it as crucial to developing loyalty to the company, but changing conditions dealt this role a fatal blow. The plan had grown steadily since its creation by E. H. Harriman in 1903, forcing several amendments to the rules as complications arose and the number of requests for exceptions increased. By 1916 there were 456 pensioners on the Union Pacific System, about 1.15 percent of the average number of employees, collecting an average of $30.31 per month at a total cost to the company of $171,106 for the year. Two-thirds of them had retired before the age of seventy, and half that number before the age of sixty-five because of physical or other incapacity.[32]

The company had started the pension fund with an appropriation of $100,000, and added $50,000 a year. By 1916, however, the cost had outstripped this amount and required larger contributions. Wartime inflation also hurt the pensioners, especially those at the bottom of the scale. Unlike the Atchison, the Union Pacific had no minimum or maximum amount of monthly payment. To create a minimum of $30 per month and apply it to current as well as future pensions, Gray told Lovett, "would be a very graceful thing." At the time 57 percent of the pensioners received less than that sum. The judge agreed to $25, which helped about 40 percent of those on the lowest rung of payments.[33]

Lovett shared Calvin's view that "one of the strongest ties on the men in many cases was their pension rights." At the same time he began wondering where it would end. He believed in giving liberal treatment to special cases, but the large wartime increases in wages had also caused pension costs to soar. The trend was ominous: more people were retiring at higher pensions every year.[34]

To Lovett's dismay, the trends continued. By 1931 the company had 1,370 pensioners collecting an average of $58.16 per month at an annual cost to the Union Pacific of $963,569. The average pension figure was misleading, for 52 percent of the retirees got less than $50 a month while officers got much higher sums. Since 1903 the company had paid out nearly $8.2 million to 2,566 pensioners. Despite the upward march of these outlays, the Union Pacific did not follow the lead of the Pennsylvania and other roads by cutting pensions as well as wages in 1932. Gray pleaded with executive committee chairman C. B. Seger to leave the pensions alone, arguing that the effect on morale was worth far more than the reduction in costs. His plea fell on sympathetic ears; Seger himself retired that year with an annual pension of $25,000.[35]

The pension problem took a new turn in 1934 when the New Deal Congress passed the Railroad Retirement Act. The act was struck down by the Supreme Court a year later, but a revised version passed in August 1935. It took until February 1937 for the railroads and the unions to agree on a way to fold existing pension plans into the government plan. Another federal retirement act in 1937 implemented this agreement, and the Union Pacific formally abolished its pension plan in May 1937.[36]

Although workers gained the advantage of having their pensions regularized within a federal plan, they also had to pay into it along with the railroads. The company suffered a less obvious loss in having one more direct tie between it and its employees severed, and one more function taken over by the impersonal agency of government. If Lovett and Gray were right in their belief that the pension and other benefits bound workers to the company, what would replace them in creating a sense of identity and loyalty among the employees?

Sometimes the company itself faltered in keeping up the ties it created through benefits. Insurance offered one such example. Since the reorganization the Union Pacific had made accident insurance available to its employees. The worsening inflation and labor upheavals of 1916 moved the company to more liberal action. In December it gave all workers earning $1,800 a year or less an extra month's pay as a bonus; at the same time it introduced a new life, sickness, and accident insurance plan for all employees earning $4,000 or less at no cost to them.[37]

The policy written by Equitable, which had done its first group offering only four years earlier, was billed as the largest ever made. It covered about 35,000 employees for $30 million worth of life insurance alone; another company handled the accident and sickness policy. The Atchison had adopted a similar plan in July 1916 intended, as its president told Lovett, "to place a premium on long and continued service" by providing for the families of those who had toiled many years at low wages for the company. The Union Pacific policy covered all employees with at least one year's service for an amount equal to a year's wages, and continued after retirement. Calvin thought the older men valued it even more than they did their pensions.[38]

The new plan drew wide praise and a stream of inquiries from other roads interested in how it worked. Cardinal Gibbons hailed it as "the practical putting into effect of the principles of Christian charity." Like rail managers, the cardinal viewed the pension and insurance plans as devices to strengthen the loyalty and sense of mutual interest in employees toward the company. And it did not come cheap. In March 1920, for example, claims under the group plan totaled nearly $72,000.[39]

Although some complaints arose about the plan's operation, Gray called it a "handsome and thoughtful gratuity" that had done much to keep morale high on the Union Pacific System. He wanted it extended to employees above the $4,000 level, and suggested that the company take it over from the insurance companies. Lovett preferred leaving it in the hands of independent outside firms, but in October 1921 this debate got upstaged by the labor unrest culminating in a vote by Union Pacific workers to join a strike if called.[40]

This strike vote shocked Lovett into rethinking his whole position on benefits. The cost of the insurance plan, like that of the pensions, had been swollen by wartime inflation. By 1921 it cost the company around $1 million, and he wondered whether it was worth the price anymore. Gray canvassed his officers about the value of the program to the men in their departments, and the response helped him persuade the judge to continue the plan. But the costs kept mounting to the point where, as Gray explained, "we simply had to take in sail." In January 1923 the company dropped the accident and sickness policy while continuing the life and permanent disability insurance plan.[41]

The depression pushed the company into retreating even farther. In July 1932 the free life insurance was dropped in favor of a revised plan allowing employees to buy coverage at sixty cents a month per thousand dollars. The contributory rate was still a bargain but no longer a gift. Another benefit was also winnowed out by hard times. In 1916 Lovett had also explored profit-sharing plans as a way of "establishing closer relations between the Company and its employes." Four years later he approved instead a plan allowing employees to buy stock in the company on an installment basis. Like the stock market itself, the plan proved popular during the 1920s only to collapse after the crash in 1929. The company suspended it for lack of interest in 1932.[42]

The Union Pacific also ventured into education. It had been a priority since the Harriman era, partly because it benefited the company as much as the employees. The UP's Bureau of Information and Education, created in 1909, grew impressively before World War I, thanks largely to the leadership given first by W. L. Park, the superintendent highly regarded by Harriman, and then by D. C. Buell, a mechanical engineer who was doing fuel work until tapped to become head of the bureau. During its first two years the bureau handled nearly 3,000 students, about 80 percent of whom remained in good standing by keeping up with their lessons.[43]

No benefit offered the ambitious worker more potential than the bureau. The object was not merely to make the men more knowledgeable but also to identify candidates for promotion and advancement. Other roads had created special programs for training men, but the Union Pacific was apparently the first to establish a bureau directly under its major officers to give all employees instruction in whatever field or branch of service was required. All courses were done by correspondence, enabling the men to work their normal jobs. The cost to the company was surprisingly low, an estimated ten dollars per student.

Predictably the largest proportion of applicants came from the offices rather than the field. A survey of the first 1,800 students showed that about 27 percent of the general clerks enrolled, and 20.5 percent of the accounting department. Only 6.5 percent of the engineers, firemen, and trainmen signed up, but 16 percent of the track department took courses—a gratifying number at a time when railroads were wringing their hands over the general deterioration in track work.

One reason for this decline was the transitory nature of the labor force, and the fact that most of the workers were immigrants who spoke no English. The bureau tried to attack this problem directly. A special branch dealt solely with Japanese trackmen, 27 percent of whom enrolled for studies that were provided in both Japanese and English to help them learn the latter as well. They were deemed among the best students in the program. The bureau also prepared an edition of the Book of Rules in Greek. Section foremen also signed up in impressive numbers, many of them seeking to climb a rung or two on the occupational ladder. Buell entered into a plan for University of Cincinnati engineering students to spend summers as laborers on track gangs.[44]

By 1913 the program had grown enough to require reorganization. The educational bureau served not only the Union Pacific but the Illinois Central and Central of Georgia as well. It also handled the apprentice schools for all three roads and, under the new arrangement, concentrated on these programs. A separate organization was created to handle the correspondence courses, and a charge of one dollar a month imposed on those who enrolled. To that extent, the company took a step backward in the benefits it provided.[45]

Gradually the correspondence programs fell more into the shadow of the apprentice schools, which were the bread and butter of training for the road. By 1913 the schools were experimenting with motion pictures as a teaching tool. One film on locomotive firing was installed in a display car for showing all along the line. Another covered proper and improper ways of handling baggage and of getting on and off trains—complete with thrilling scenes of dummies being crushed beneath the wheels. The dining car and hotel department subjected every dining car crew to a complete course of instruction and called them back periodically for review. Vocational education programs were also run jointly with the states of Nebraska, Kansas, and Colorado for improving the skills of engineers and firemen on the road.[46]

It was no accident that these benefits sprang into existence at a time when good labor was scarce and becoming more expensive, and when the hold of the unions over the men was growing stronger. Like most forms of corporate paternalism, the programs were a blend of goodwill and self-interest. That they served the Union Pacific made them no less valuable to the employees, but as a mortar for binding the workers to the company they achieved only partial success. The survey done on the first 1,800 men to enroll in the correspondence courses, for example, turned up one intriguing statistic: only 23 percent of those who signed up belonged to the unions.[47]

By 1928 most public attention went to the apprentice schools, which took boys of seventeen or more with at least an eighth-grade education and turned them into railroad men that it was hoped would serve the company well for years to come. In words that might have come from Charles Francis Adams, Jr., the company emphasized that it was "good business to develop high-class men."[48]

Francis Lynde saw it coming even before the turn of the century. He had put in thirteen years in the Union Pacific shops before going on to a career as writer and publicist. "Throughout that period I saw with increasing regret," he told Judge Lovett in 1919, "the gradual extinguishment of the most valuable asset that any industrial combination can possess; namely, the esprit du corps of the working force." What had caused it? Lynde believed it was "the growth of the great corporations, the necessary result being a more complete isolation of the managing officials and the consequent impossibility of anything like the personal touch between them and the rank and file."[49]

It was to recapture something of this spirit in the uncertain world after 1920 that the corporate family movement arose on the Union Pacific. The employees felt this need no less urgently than the company. Change was sweeping through every corner of American life, unsettling old ways, threatening traditional roles and identities. In response to these forces, Americans became even more a

THE FAMILY ALL TOGETHER: The Old Timers at Columbus, Nebraska, whoop it up at a party.

nation of joiners during the 1920s as the organizational revolution surged past our economic and political institutions into the fabric of everyday life.

Here was yet another reason why Carl Gray proved the right man in the right place at the right time for the Union Pacific. Who was better suited to preside over the quest for family than a benevolent father figure, stern but just, the soul of honor, a giant teddy bear of a man with a ready smile and ''just plain folks'' manner? Gray embodied the very personal touch that was fast disappearing from American business organizations. His presence did much to defuse the impersonality that had become a way of life in corporations.

Gray himself did not take the lead in cultivating the family spirit, but he sanctioned and encouraged its growth. There already existed a system-wide Family League that held dances, picnics, and other social events as well as doing relief work for members. In February 1922, for example, the league's general committee handled 201 relief requests. Since 1913 there had also been a Retired Employees Association that held social outings and gathered every year in Omaha for a reunion.[50]

Another organization emerged almost spontaneously in May 1924 to become the center of the family movement. Some two hundred men who had served twenty years or more in the Union Pacific System gathered in Cheyenne to honor a pair of retirees with a banquet. At the ceremony engineer J. C. Williams proposed forming an organization for employees with twenty years or more experience in the company. From that simple gesture was born the Old Timers Association. William Jeffers was present and said at once that management would welcome such a group. Wisely he urged that no company official be allowed to hold office in the association. Gray later seconded these views; any officer attending an Old Timers meeting, he quipped, should check his brass collar at the door.[51]

The idea struck a responsive chord throughout the system. By November eight chapters had been organized and a central committee formed. The one at Marysville, Kansas, boasted 158 members still in active service who had put in a total of 4,649 years with the company. By any measure these were the bedrock of the Union Pacific, the employees who had served longest and identified closest with the company. The prospect of an organization arising spontaneously among its most loyal workers delighted management just as it dismayed the unions, who for years condemned Old Timers' activities as a medium for discrimination in favor of some employees. But the unions could do nothing; officers of the road got into the Old Timers only if they had served enough years to qualify.[52]

By 1929 chapters had been organized on the entire system, and a monster celebration took place in June at Salt Lake. The Old Timers proved invaluable in providing a sense of continuity amid turbulent change, stability in an age of flux. The very requirement of its membership gave the association an attachment to the company that management could never have provided on its own. An assistant yardmaster in Armstrong, Kansas, offered up a poem called ''Old Timer'' with this closing verse:

Through twenty years of friendship and
association
We've turned the wheels of U. P. trans-
portation.
Twenty years of life; loss balanced with
the gain;
Twenty years, Old Timer, shake! Let's
go again![53]

Even before the Old Timers organized, Gray had moved to encourage the growth of family spirit. In January 1922 he provided a useful tool in the form of a company magazine that went to every employee. The *Union Pacific Magazine* was part social calendar, part spiritual uplift, part sermon, and part information on who did what throughout the system. The tone was relentlessly upbeat; every social function was well attended, and no one ever had a bad time. There were reports of doings on every division, profiles with a Horatio Alger slant, articles on safety, social gossip, and series like the one in which different workers such as yardmen, dispatchers, and porters explained their jobs to the readers.[54]

One type of activity appeared early and often in the magazine: athletics. By the 1920s the longtime zeal among the employees for baseball had exploded into a wide program of sports. Baseball still held top place among and within the system terminals as the men found any excuse to stage a game. The freight office in Kansas City got its team ready for the coming season by pitting a nine

THE FAMILY STEPS OUT: The Union Pacific employees' band and majorettes show their style.

of single men against one of married men. Teams played each other within divisions with the winners taking on the top teams from other divisions in a playoff series.[55]

Other sports got their due as well during the sports-crazed decade of the 1920s. Workers in Las Vegas organized an "Athletic and Welfare" club to "bring employes and their families into a closer social relationship." The club featured tennis, basketball, handball, and other sports along with baseball. In November 1925 the Union Pacific System Athletic League was formed to run sports programs within the four units of the system: the main line, Short Line, Navigation, and Los Angeles & Salt Lake. Each unit staged its own leagues and meets, with the winners meeting in a system-wide meet that climaxed the season.[56]

All this was done by the employees themselves. With company approval they organized the local clubs and raised money for equipment and facilities by paying dues, holding dances, and staging entertainments. From an original 12 clubs and 1,500 members the league grew by 1930 to 52 clubs and 18,000 members. Some of them owned gymnasiums, golf courses, swimming pools; nearly all had athletic fields embracing five to thirteen acres at major division points. Junior and senior competition was held in baseball, track, tennis, golf, shooting, horseshoes, bowling, basketball, billiards, soccer, handball, swimming, and even battles of the bands. The all-system meets in August 1930 drew

600 athletes and 4,000 other employees and their families to Ogden to watch the contests in several sports.[57]

A few clubs published their own papers. The Council Bluffs club issued one called *The Diamond* with the subhead "Clean, Sparkling Sport of the Council Bluffs Athletic Club, U.P.R.R." The paper extended well beyond sports, and so did the activities of all employee organizations. There was a Union Pacific band, a quartet, a men's chorus, a women's chorus, and even a drum and bugle corps composed of employees' children. When the depression hit, the rank and file formed a booster organization to solicit traffic for the line, while the Family League asked members to contribute one percent of a month's salary for five months toward a fund for unemployed members. In less than eight months the league collected $150,737 and helped 3,892 families and individuals.[58]

A family took care of its own. The Family League tried to do just that, especially during the depression, and so did management. Apart from policy, there were many small acts of kindness that involved officers in everything from domestic quarrels to widows left poor to men down on their luck or stricken ill or ravaged by drink or insanity.

The imaginative Eugene McAuliffe of the coal company went one step farther with an act of kindness that helped to heal old wounds. By 1925, forty years after the Rock Springs Massacre, few Chinese remained in the mines, and most were at or near retirement. When several expressed the wish to spend their last years in their native land, McAuliffe arranged for them to do so.[59]

In November 1925 the UMW locals in Rock Springs gave nine retired Chinese a farewell banquet. The mayor was there along with coal company vice-president George B. Pryde to exchange tributes and toasts that seemed finally to banish a half century of racial animosity. White miners who had themselves grown old in the ranks traded anecdotes with the men whom time had transformed from foes to friends. The Chinese responded in kind and presented written notes of thanks to the unions and the company. Afterward they boarded a train for San Francisco in the company of two officials, and were put aboard a ship to China after a day of sightseeing. Four more Chinese returned home in 1927.

The Chinese were given enough money to live comfortably at home, but by 1929 war and inflation had left most of them destitute. They appealed to Pryde for help, and were each granted pensions of $10 a month. This small sum enabled them to live their remaining time in dignity, although one complained that he preferred America to China because his village was "very hot and too much trouble [sic] by the thieves." McAuliffe and Pryde maintained an interest in the old pensioners, happy in their own minds at least to have laid the ghosts of Rock Springs to rest.[60]

Throughout the Union Pacific system the family spirit endured, but it never fully captured the hearts of the rank and file as management hoped. Like all attempts at family unity it had to compete with harsh realities imposed by the outside world, and these realities have seldom been harsher than they were after 1930. They included depression, unemployment, changing technology, a demoralized world economy, and ultimately world war. The impact of these forces drove unions to resort ever more to adversarial rather than cooperative tactics to gain their ends.

Nor did the Union Pacific itself stand still during these years. By an unhappy coincidence changes within the company, coupled with pressures from without, ushered in a period of transition that squeezed the notion of family from both sides. Nothing characterized the changed mood more than the fate of *Union Pacific Magazine,* which died in the 1930s, a victim of the depression era's ruthlessly cost-effective budgets.

19

The Operation

With the war over and return from federal control imminent, Union Pacific management was anxious to know how well the road had survived the ordeal. During 1919 Judge Lovett, engineer E. E. Adams, and a consultant all toured the line, followed by the newly-arrived Carl Gray in 1920. To their relief the road had held up even though the government had not maintained it to company standards. The rail renewal program begun before the war had been let go, as had the ballasting and the general appearance. The main line had been ravaged by heavy rains, and the track west of Pocatello was in the worst shape of all. Nevertheless, Gray was generally pleased except for the Los Angeles & Salt Lake. Once the Union Pacific got full control of that line, he spent five years bringing it up to company standards.[1]

The Harriman legacy of high maintenance standards became even more crucial as new competitors emerged. The tradition would have been useless without money to carry it out, but management understood that to save money they had to spend it. Efficient operations and effective cost control both depended on having a modern physical plant. What Gray proposed Lovett usually disposed, but not blindly. Railroad men, he told Gray, were too ''inclined to jump to conclusions and adopt rules as to the life of a tie or a rail or a bridge'' when they should instead ''feel its pulse and take its temperature, as it were, before it is thrown out as worthless.''[2]

Gray's officers did not go quite that far, but they did some impressive work in maintenance and operations. An engineman named W. L. Richards won a national competition for the best paper on fuel economy. O. S. Jackson, the superintendent of motive power and machinery, gained national attention by

HITTING THE ROAD: A track crew rides to work on a flat car equipped with a ballast spreader underneath.

revamping the handling of locomotives at terminals. Jackson created specialized gangs to do maintenance work on each class of engine at regular monthly intervals, thereby catching minor defects and sharply reducing power failures. The results showed in better keeping of schedules; between December 1925 and July 1928, for example, the main line handled 8,000 fruit trains without a single one arriving behind schedule.[3]

The rhythm of maintenance revolved around the seasons: a frantic scramble to get the road and equipment ready for the fall crop movements, followed by a frenzy of work to put everything in shape for surviving the winter. Like all roads with heavy agricultural traffic, the Union Pacific had wild swings in the demand for cars, depending on how well the crops turned out. In 1906 Harriman had done much to rationalize the handling of the vital Northwest fruit crops by creating a subsidiary called Pacific Fruit Express. Jointly owned by Union Pacific and Southern Pacific, Pacific Fruit answered the need for a system to get perishable fruits quickly to market.[4]

To start the new company, Harriman ordered a fleet of six thousand new refrigerator cars. These forty-foot cars each had a capacity of 30,000 pounds and were cooled by 11,500 pounds of ice stored in bunkers at both ends. All surfaces were insulated with panels of degummed flax, then the best material available (by 1926 the same size reefer held 70,000 pounds of perishables and was insulated with hair felt). The purchase was another of Harriman's bold gambles. Observers wondered what he would do with a fleet of reefers needed only two seasons of the year.[5]

They found out soon enough. The demand for fresh fruit and vegetables proved so voracious that western growers found ways to produce crops all year round. Pacific Fruit survived the unmerger to become a reliable cash cow for its owners. "In the summertime," boasted an officer, ". . . we'd have one fruit train after another coming to us from the SP at Ogden."[6]

In 1907 Pacific Fruit had 6,600 cars that hauled 48,900 carloads of perishables; by 1921 it owned a fleet of 19,200 cars that carried 170,000 loads. So rapidly did business expand that by 1922 a dozen artificial ice plants had been added to the company's five natural ice facilities. As the fruit trains grew longer and more frequent, ways were found to pack the bunkers with incredible speed. The North Platte station iced an average of a thousand cars every day during one period in the fall of 1927. One train got seventy-three of its eight-seven cars iced in only half an hour; another iced eighty in only thirty-five minutes.[7]

Through the lean depression years Pacific Fruit continued to pay handsome dividends to its owner roads and to expand its fleet. Some new cars ordered in 1936 were still forty-footers but were the first to have steel sheathing and use kapok and fiber glass for insulation. Their capacity had jumped to 80,000 pounds, but they still used ice bunkers despite the lower temperatures required by a new source of business: frozen foods. The number of ice plants increased, but new technology was slow to infiltrate Pacific Fruit until the 1950s.[8]

Change came faster to the parent road, where railroaders found themselves pushed to find new ways of doing old things. More than technology threatened the habits of a lifetime; the pressure was mounting to improve performance at every level by taking no function for granted. The fuel economy drive launched in 1921 reduced transportation costs; longer engine runs improved schedules while cutting terminal costs; extensive programs for rail welding and tie and timber treatment lengthened their lifespan; the introduction of labor-saving devices like an automatic wheel counter on the Missouri River bridge cut expenses while releasing men for other work. Chemists found ways to improve the treatment of boiler water. This was no small item; tests showed that a mere sixteenth of an inch of scale on a firebox or boiler tube increased fuel consumption 15 percent.[9]

The system for servicing locomotives introduced in 1923 worked so well that four years later it was augmented by one concentrating on intensive repair of a relatively few units. As a result, shop time on heavy power was trimmed by more than half for most repairs. Labor-saving devices and techniques that proved their worth in one shop were installed elsewhere on the line. Reducing shop time enabled the company to carry larger volumes of traffic with fewer locomotives at lower cost.[10]

All this was done before anyone knew a depression lay over the horizon. Efforts to centralize operations had been underway for years. The water treatment service, which had been scattered across the system, was reorganized around a central staff in 1916. Forced by expanding business to enlarge its terminals after 1917, the company concentrated much of the growth in two major shops, Omaha and Cheyenne. Where the Omaha shop had been overhauled in 1910, Cheyenne got an entirely new layout with the most modern design and equipment. Efforts had been made to centralize the stores operation

HEADQUARTERS: The Union Pacific office building in Omaha, taken in 1940. Note the ticket office at the corner and *Challenger* sign on the roof, billed as the largest electric sign west of Chicago.

since 1922 by installing such innovations as uniform stockkeeping and unit piling.[11]

A major drive to reorganize the transportation department in the name of efficiency and economy was also well along before the depression spurred it to greater heights. The goal was to control operating costs through more centralized supervision. Although the four components of the Union Pacific System were not formally consolidated until 1936, the process of merging their separate organizations began in November 1928. The twelve-story main office building in Omaha, which had opened in 1912, was enlarged 25 percent in 1928–29 to house the growing work force in Omaha. Within three years the entire operating structure was overhauled with results that impressed New York if not the employees who lost their jobs or were transferred into Omaha.[12]

Under the new structure four of the fourteen divisions were eliminated along with 143 officials and 3,000 clerks. The mechanical, stores, engineering, maintenance of way, telegraph, and freight claim departments were all consolidated into central organizations that handled the work previously done by four separate offices. One chief mechanical officer replaced four, as did one storekeeper, with staffs slashed along similar lines. Instead of four unit chief engineers, there was one. Accounting, timekeeping, and payroll operations once performed by division and local officers were folded into central bureaus for the entire system. Extending the districts of dispatchers cut dispatching costs 35 percent. A form survey committee abolished nearly 1,500 reports deemed no longer necessary at a huge saving in time, printing, and paper.[13]

''There is no question as to the permanency of these consolidations,'' wrote labor expert E. J. Connors, who cranked out detailed reports on the progress of the campaign, ''nor the permanency of results of centralized supervision and detailed control of expenses that has resulted.'' An officer who had started his career as an apprentice in the Pocatello shops took a less charitable view of the changes. ''Things were pretty rough at the Pocatello shops,'' he recalled. ''. . . They kept on cutting and cutting . . . there was a lot of dissatisfaction about it because after all, they broke up an awful lot of people. . . . Say you was living at Pocatello, you had to go to Omaha. People out at Pocatello didn't have a damn bit of use for Omaha.''[14]

Like it or not, they went to Omaha because jobs were hard to come by in the 1930s. To their dismay the cuts kept coming. Jeffers reported in 1933 that one hundred stations had been closed since January 1929 and forty-seven diners withdrawn from service. The shop force was laid off for short periods, then given floating schedules to spread the work. Railroaders found their ranks shriveling and barren like the topsoil in the Dust Bowl, part of which lay along the Kansas Division. The survivors were expected to do more work, and no one felt secure in his place or knew how much work there would be. As one veteran put it years later, ''it was on and off for some of those old heads for a long time.''[15]

But the cuts did not mean stagnation. The company's budget for 1931 included $70 million for maintenance, improvements, and capital outlays. That same year it chose to upgrade its rail weight standards from 110 to 131 pounds on the main line and 90 to 112 pounds on certain branches. New projects included a freight cutoff line between Topeka, Kansas, and Gibbon, Nebraska, and some lesser improvements. In 1935 the company launched a major rail-relaying program that continued for several years. Even during the depression large sums were expended for equipment.[16]

Especially passenger service. Like other major roads, the Union Pacific made a determined bid to recapture the passenger business lost during the 1930s. The streamliners were merely the flagships of a larger campaign. The passenger business had always been a tug-of-war between quality service and cost control. Although passenger service produced only a small portion of the overall revenue for transcontinental roads, it aroused the fiercest competition in everything from schedules to service to rates to amenities. The reason was not hard to find. Passenger service touched the public directly, and was therefore the basis for judging the railroad. Shippers might measure a road on how reliable it kept to freight schedules, but for the traveling public a railroad was its passenger trains.

The schizophrenic battle between service and cost control had raged long before the new competition emerged. Judge Lovett kept a sharp eye on both. He had no choice; complaints often came directly to him. One tempest over whether a bottle of Poland water had been refilled before it was served took over a month to resolve. Another arose over the fact that the Union Pacific charged an extra dime for bread and butter while other roads did not. In 1915 the weary judge found himself going over a list of requested additions to dining car equipment that included ice tea spoons, stem goblets, crumb trays, and enlarged celery troughs. The attention demanded by such minutia drove Lovett to push for standardization of furnishings, which did not exist as late as 1915.[17]

Schedules proved no less exasperating. Every road wanted to run fewer trains and reduce mileage, but they rarely agreed on how to do it. Back in 1914 William Sproule, president of the Southern Pacific, complimented Mohler on his road's fine service, then said in the next breath, "it does not seem to me we are justified in running so many passenger trains. . . . I have my fears we are letting our ideals run away with our dollars." Through the years the question of schedules especially bedeviled the Union Pacific because it had to coordinate with other roads at both ends of its line while competing against the Atchison's longer but scenic southern route and superior service to the coast.[18]

After the war, which deranged both schedules and service, Judge Lovett thought the *Overland Limited* should be restored "as a necessary advertising of the Union Pacific" even though it had lost money as an extra-fare train. He also emphasized that "we should strictly maintain our advantage over the Santa Fe with respect to San Francisco, due to our shorter route." Gray agreed; the *Overland Limited* was retained and its amenities were expanded. Rechristened the *San Francisco Overland Limited*, the train featured barber, manicurist, valet, and maid service. A newfangled radio piped dance music into the train by 1923, and six years later a specially-fitted dining car offered passengers the showing of a new talkie film. During the market-crazed twenties, through trains arranged to get stock reports en route.[19]

Between the wars the passenger wars got more expensive than anybody dreamed. To reduce costs, the carriers and Pullman had already replaced their ornate wood trim with steel and imitation wood. The Union Pacific cut its meal prices in 1920, and two years later launched a tray service with sandwiches and coffee at low prices for coach passengers in their seats. Longer runs with more powerful locomotives cut engine changes between Council Bluffs and Cheyenne from four to one for Ogden and none for Denver. Eight new observation cars and fifteen coaches were acquired in 1927–28 as Gray conceded that "long haul passenger business is our asset, having lost a substantial portion of the short haul business."[20]

This awareness, coupled with the onset of depression, triggered what Gray considered a foolish schedule war among the transcontinental lines in 1930. Changes in schedule were delicate affairs of diplomacy involving not only competing roads but terminal cities as well. If the time to San Francisco was shortened, Portland felt insulted if it did not receive the same advantage. Gray's rule of thumb was that a given city could stand a spread of fifteen minutes; anything more evoked howls of wounded civic pride. Attempts to mediate schedules among the competing lines stumbled over conflicting ambitions and bruised egos. It was difficult enough to make a schedule for three connecting lines, let alone coordinate it with those of competing lines and their connections.

The war commenced in April 1930 when the major roads cut an hour off eastbound and ninety minutes off westbound schedules for limited trains. Less than a month later the lines lopped off another hour, and the Denver run was shortened half an hour. To Gray's disgust, all efforts to resolve what the press called a "speed war" bogged down in the usual stew of indignation and righteousness as each road claimed the right to adjust its own schedules while loudly protesting changes imposed by others. In November the Great Northern slashed its Chicago-Northwest run by three hours eastbound and one hour westbound, forcing a reluctant Union Pacific to follow suit. "Sooner or later there will be a reaction from the California cities," Gray predicted gloomily.[21]

The schedule war persisted even though some lines were already dropping trains from unprofitable runs. In 1932 the fight escalated ominously to an "air war" when the Atchison announced plans to air-condition the diners on its premier train, the *Chief*. "It is certain that the Santa Fe will make a great advertising feature of these air cooled cars," advised Gray, "and that it will injure us considerably." The Union Pacific would have to follow suit for its *Los Angeles Limited*, and by contract it was obliged to give the *San Francisco Limited* the same service Los Angeles got. This meant a total outlay of $180,000, which Gray urgently recommended.[22]

A year later Gray was convinced the Atchison intended to air-condition the entire *Chief*. He and the other presidents would have to do likewise for the Los Angeles, San Francisco, and Portland trains, since he could not create so great a disparity in Northwest service. The Burlington was ready to air-condition its extra-fare Denver train, which would force the Union Pacific to match it. Suddenly Gray was staring at the prospect of new equipment for 44 cars, and

Pullman had 126 sleepers to outfit. Some hard bargaining among the roads limited the first round to dining, club, and observation cars for 1934, but the Atchison's persistence forced the others to tackle coaches the following year. At $8,500 to $10,000 a car, this was a major investment for roads caught in the grip of a depressed economy.[23]

All this took place before the streamliners appeared on the scene to transform train travel. In effect the sleek new trains represented one more escalation in an already bitter war, and the costliest one yet. The Union Pacific poured huge sums into its streamliner program in addition to the money spent on upgrading conventional passenger travel. Spurred again by the Atchison, which had clipped fourteen hours off the Chicago-Los Angeles run with its new streamliner, the *Super Chief*, the Union Pacific matched this time with its *City of Los Angeles*. Unveiled in May 1936, it was at eleven cars the longest streamliner in the world. A companion train, the *City of San Francisco,* made its debut the following month along with the *City of Denver*. Billed as the world's fastest train, the Denver streamliner shattered all records by making its Omaha-Denver run in seven hours and twenty-six minutes, an average speed of 75.3 miles.[24]

Encouraged by the success of these trains, the company waited only a few months before ordering two replacement models for the Pacific coast runs. The new versions were truly state of the art, with seventeen cars and six diesel engines generating a total of 5,400 horsepower. All revenue cars were wider than previous models and had nearly 50 percent more capacity. Compartment interiors were radically rearranged, and a new type of car called the roomette was put on the Los Angeles train at Averell Harriman's urging. An improved version, he stressed, "may well prove to be very popular. We ought to be the first to have it into Los Angeles." The trains also included a host of other innovations and cost an estimated $3 million.[25]

The new trains were the largest and most powerful ever built. They also offered a taste of elegance. "It was a very luxurious train," recalled a former steward. "Nice silver . . . fresh flowers on the table every day . . . in the summertime we were furnished summer tuxedos. We had a fresh white coat every night." The food was enticing: fresh trout from Colorado, whitefish from Lake Michigan, lamb and fruit from California, whatever the route offered. Pies, muffins, and rolls were baked fresh on stoves fueled with presto logs, which offered less danger of fire than oil or gas. But the company drew the line at a suggestion that it polish the floors of spare baggage cars and use them for dancing.[26]

Not all the effort went into the high-end business. Jeffers was convinced too little attention had been given to coach travelers, 60 percent of which were women and children according to one survey. Coach passengers comprised the major part of travelers and therefore of public opinion about rail travel. Harriman agreed to offer coach patrons a new deal similar to the one he had given the Pullman crowd. "Mass travel," he explained, "is what we have tried to merchandise."[27]

His solution was the *Challenger*. Like its namesake inn at Sun Valley, this train was a low-cost alternative to its more upscale cousins. The goal was

CONVERSION KIT: Not all streamliners were powered by new diesels. Here a venerable 4–6–2 Pacific passenger locomotive (A) is transformed into a sleek steam streamliner engine (B).

THE FEMININE TOUCH: Avis Lobdell, the guiding hand behind the Union Pacific women's department and corps of stewardesses.

simple: excellent service at low cost. In August 1935 the company pulled its coach and sleeping cars off the *Los Angeles Limited* and made them into a second section of the train. New low-cost meals, served from portable steam tables, enabled passengers to eat three meals for ninety cents. Free pillows were supplied, and the penny charge for drinking cups was dropped. One coach was set aside for women only, and stewardess service was provided to assist women, children, the elderly, or the infirm traveling alone.[28]

Encouraged by the results, the company sank $600,000 into creating a regular *Challenger* with its own schedule. Older cars were refitted and new ones acquired. Jeffers wanted nice, attractive sleepers; the usual Pullman tourist version, he complained, were ratty looking, dark, and smelly. But Pullman was notoriously arrogant and intransigent in its dealings, and rigid in its notion of what sleepers should be. Jeffers went to see its president, Champ Carey. When he returned, he told a passenger official, "I got you forty-eight sleepers."

"Are they any good?" asked the surprised official.

"You're darn right they're good," growled Jeffers. "I took him to lunch and told him he was a goddamn liar and a son of a bitch. And I got what I wanted."[29]

What he got were standard sleepers, all steel with no steel underfront, an older type but in good shape. The refurbished versions looked like a new model. "And boy, they were easier to keep clean," marveled an official, "and the people liked them; and half the price of standard sleepers." A new lighting

TRAVELER'S BEST FRIEND: The first generation of Union Pacific stewardesses, all of whom were registered nurses, pose in front of Omaha's Union Station.

system was rigged to dim during sleeping hours, and good meals could still be had in the "coffee shop" car for ninety cents a day. The food was ample but allowed few choices. "We made money on the *Challenger*," insisted one official. "Why? Because you didn't have to carry all this extra food."[30]

Bright new or reconditioned equipment and lower fares drew people to the *Challenger*, but what pleased them most was the new emphasis on service. To lure travelers back to the trains, Jeffers had to know what they wanted. He found out by resorting to what a later generation called market research: he hired a bright woman named Avis Lobdell to ride the entire system and interview travelers on their likes and dislikes. "Loud guffaws arose in railroad circles," noted a writer, "and rival managers declared flatly that Old Jeffers must be crazy. . . . imagine hiring a *woman* to snoop on the staff . . . what does a woman know about railroading, anyway?"[31]

Plenty, it turned out. Lobdell compiled a revealing list for Jeffers. Passengers hated the petty charge for cups and pillows; they wanted clean, bright, air-conditioned coaches with roomy toilets, porcelain wash basins, soap, and towels; they wanted cheap but tasty meals, separate smokers and washrooms for men and women in each car, dim lights at night, less annoyance from crew members taking tickets, calling stations, and talking noisily all night. They resented the indifferent, hard-boiled attitude of the crew, and the hands always out for a tip.[32]

This was a tall order, calling for not merely a new kind of train but a new type of crewman. Nevertheless, Jeffers made Lobdell's agenda his blueprint for the *Challenger*, which may have been the most aptly named train ever devised. To travelers and railroaders alike, the transformation was astonishing. Women loved the coaches reserved only for them; apart from feeling more secure traveling alone, they could move about freely without worrying who might see them. Every car had a porter, and redcaps were not allowed to take tips from coach passengers. The stewardess assigned to each train was no mere pretty face but a registered nurse reassuring to children, the elderly, and unwell people who might otherwise fear to travel alone.[33]

Women employees had always been an anomaly on railroads, that hard-bitten bastion of masculinity. They had long served as agents, especially in small-town depots. The Navigation Company had created a stir in 1915 by putting female agents in large city ticket offices "to smooth the way for women customers." Two years later women assumed a much larger role as nearly 100,000 of them went to work in a wide variety of positions on railroads during the war. After the armistice, when the Union Pacific shrank its work force, women were the first to go. Jeffers decreed in 1926 that men would replace them as vacancies occurred, and that no more would be hired except as stenographers or comptometers.[34]

The enthusiastic response given the stewardesses and the *Challenger* impressed Jeffers enough to create a Women's Travel Department and put Lobdell in charge of it. The new department was to assist women with all aspects of travel from tickets to questions about dress or luggage or meals. It began with sixty employees including the stewardesses. Privately Jeffers viewed it as an experiment, but the phones started ringing as soon as the department opened in June 1938. So popular did it become that Chicago, Denver, and Omaha got their own women's departments in 1939.[35]

The *Challenger* itself did so well that the service was extended to San Francisco and Portland in 1937. That same year a lounge car was added to the *Challenger*, and new coaches were purchased in 1938. Atop company headquarters in Omaha the largest electric sign west of Chicago beckoned travelers to ride the new train. The results seemed to herald an end to the long retreat from passenger business. During 1936 the Union Pacific led all class I railroads with a 34.5 percent jump in passenger revenue from the previous year. In 1937 the figures increased another 15 percent, and in 1938 the demand for space on the eastbound *Challenger* was so great that the train had to be split. "Union Pacific saw a greater stake in the passenger business than just the saving of a loss," observed a gratified Averell Harriman. "That stake was public opinion."[36]

Heavy expenditures for maintenance and improvements were a Harriman legacy. So was safety, which the Union Pacific continued to emphasize long after Harriman was gone. In 1912 the company formed a bureau of safety consisting of a central committee, division committees, and district shop committees that met once a month on ways to improve safety. A monthly bulletin was issued and contests held among the divisions for the best safety record, with prizes awarded the winners. To underscore its campaign, the company resorted to the novel tactic of installing an "accident map" in its ticket

WHEN THINGS GO BAD: Engine 5403 dangles above a collapsed bridge in Oregon, July 1930.

agencies to inform travelers of where accidents occurred and what progress toward safer conditions had been made over time. The map revealed graphically the effectiveness of safety devices such as block signals: in regions where they had been installed, there was but one accident in 1912 for every nine in 1903.[37]

In 1913 Mary Harriman endowed the Harriman Safety Medal program to honor each year the road, department, and employee with outstanding safety records. Although the Southern Pacific won the first medal, the Union Pacific took home more than its share over the years. The company also launched a campaign in the schools to reduce the number of children killed while playing on railroad tracks. When young Averell Harriman thought the Omaha leadership was dragging its feet on the safety campaign, he got Judge Lovett to issue a sharp reminder. His message hit home: in June 1915 the company celebrated a year with no passenger fatalities and only twenty-eight employee deaths compared to fifty-nine two years earlier.[38]

After the war Gray took up the campaign with missionary zeal. Every accident spurred him to greater efforts in getting officials to stress safety. ''The work by the men who are our real safety evangelists,'' he preached, ''will be determined by the interest which is evinced by their officers.'' Every worker received a safety book of rules; immigrants got one printed in their own

WHEN THINGS REALLY GO BAD: Fishing out a wrecked locomotive at Cayuse Station, April 1907.

language. The results began to show in 1922, when the Union Pacific boasted a lower employee casualty rate than a dozen other leading systems and a lower fatality rate than ten of them. In 1923 the Colorado division's maintenance of way department celebrated a full year without a single injury.[39]

Between 1917 and 1923 no Harriman medals were given out. When the award resumed in 1924, the Union Pacific won the first of four it captured by 1930. In 1927 it smashed all previous records by lowering its rate of employee injuries to 3.44 per million man hours. Two years later the rate dropped to 2.47. The Union Pacific won two more Harriman medals in 1933 and 1935, and led the competition in three other years.* Throughout the 1930s the drive for safety never relaxed despite the turmoil and distractions of the depression. No matter how impressive the safety record was, there were always enough accidents to furnish grisly reminders of the high price exacted by carelessness.[40]

The iron horse had undergone surprisingly little crossbreeding over the past century. It had grown larger, more powerful, and more diverse in form. The automatic air brake was introduced in 1872 and the MCB automatic coupler in

*Under the rules, no road could win the medal more than twice in a row.

1895, the same year that a new Baldwin 2–4–2 type greatly improved locomotive design. By 1902 the piston valve was firmly established, and ten years later the first mechanical stoker was perfected, freeing engines at last from the limitation imposed by the amount of coal a fireman could load by hand. An early version of the superheater emerged around 1910, and in 1913 a pneumatic power reverse gear began replacing the manual Johnson bar. These improvements enabled locomotives to grow bigger and more specialized in design.[41]

For decades gestures had been made at standardizing class detail design on power. In 1903 Harriman undertook one of the first serious attempts by settling with Baldwin Locomotive on six standard types to be used on all his systems. During World War I USRA tried to impose standard designs on the power used by all the roads under its control, but the notion fell apart after 1920. Faced with the challenge of the new competition, engine designers responded with a host of new types and some striking improvements in existing models. By 1940 the steam locomotive had been refined to the edge of its technical limitations.[42]

The Union Pacific often led the parade of roads branching out into new designs for several reasons. Efficiency demanded power suited to the particular needs of a given assignment. Competition demanded locomotives capable of hauling larger loads at higher speeds. New technology brought design improvements that required testing in new types. Any attempt to standardize the power fleet too rigidly would hamper all these objectives. Nor could the company stand pat with old equipment under modern conditions. As the superintendent of motive power observed, "Wearing out antique power is an expensive luxury."[43]

A new generation of locomotives had emerged before World War I. That faithful workhorse, the classic 4–4–0 American, went out of production around 1900, the 2–6–0 Mogul around 1910, the 2–8–0 Consolidation in 1916, and the 4–6–0 Ten-Wheeler about 1920. Even the 4–4–2 Atlantic, which had come into vogue for passenger service in 1896, lost favor after 1906 and ceased being made a decade later. In their place came a host of larger engines: the 4–6–2 Pacific, the 2–8–2 Mikado, the 2–10–2 Santa Fe, the 4–8–2 Mountain, and some Mallets for pusher service. The Union Pacific bought these types heavily before the war, and regretted not buying more as prices soared from inflation after 1917.[44]

The war left the company's power in ragged shape, prompting Gray to request a hundred new engines for 1920. Older types were redesigned to give better performance, but within a few years the engineers were impatient to speed development. Rapid advances in technology, especially metallurgy, excited them about the possibilities of creating larger yet lighter locomotives. In 1924 A. H. Fetters declared flatly that "The general practice of buying locomotives ready made should be abandoned." Within a short time he would be looking over his shoulder at the progress of the diesel; meanwhile, he worked tirelessly to promote the development of new designs in steam power.[45]

From this effort emerged in 1925 two new engines built specifically for the Union Pacific: the 4–10–2 Overland and the 4–12–2 Union Pacific or 9000, then the largest nonarticulated steam locomotive ever built. Designed to replace

THE IRON HORSE THAT STUMBLED: Judge Robert S. Lovett and Carl Gray pose in front of a giant 4–12–2 9000-class locomotive, a class that promised much but ate up its earnings in the repair shop.

HEAVY HAULER: A 4–10–2 8000-class Overland freight locomotive, first built in 1925.

SLOW BUT STEADY: A rugged 2–8–8–0 Mallet-class locomotive of a type first built in 1910 for freight service in mountain territory

the Santa Fe and the slow, inefficient Mallets doing mountain service, the 9000s performed well in extensive tests during 1926 and were hailed enthusiastically as the power of the future. But economics dictated that progress come gradually. Between 1920 and 1927 the Union Pacific retired 388 locomotives and replaced them with 318 engines. Most of the purchases were familiar types: 123 Santa Fes, 54 Mallets, 60 Mountains, 16 Mikados, and 10 Pacifics. But the most recent purchases included 10 Overlands and 15 9000s, with more to come.[46]

Gray managed to buy fifty more 9000s in 1929 and 1930 before the depression shut down orders. No more engines were acquired until 1936, when the traffic revival sparked by the debut of the streamliner spurred the company to review its overall power situation. Since 1931 the company had retired 191 locomotives without replacements, an attrition made possible in large part by the depression. In April 1936 the diesel had not shown enough to make it a clear call for transcontinental business. After long conferences with Alfred P. Sloan and the Electro-Motive people, Averell Harriman decided it was prudent to look at alternative sources of power. There were three possibilities: an engine developed at Hamilton, another by Ingersoll-Rand, and a radical turbo-electric model at General Electric.[47]

The diesel soon proved its worth, but Harriman wanted no mistakes. Anxious to keep the Union Pacific at the forefront of rail technology, especially in the passenger field, he urged Jeffers to free up good engineers from routine work so they could "devote their entire attention to this study and to other engineering problems that are developing in connection with these trains." Manufacturers could not be relied on to fulfill their needs without direct input from the railroad. "I am fearful," he added, "that we may be forced through competition into a further development of this type of the high speed service before we are ready to do so from an engineering standpoint." It was far cheaper to involve engineers directly in the design work early than to be "forced to buy in large quantities experimental units for regular service."[48]

From this reasoning emerged another stage of power development. The most daring move was the decision in 1936 to order one of General Electric's steam turbine locomotives. Hailed as the ultimate advancement of steam power, the lightweight plant used rotary engines instead of traditional pistons and driving rods. It was housed in two self-contained units each generating 2,500 horsepower and capable of being used separately or in tandem. The weight was 20 percent less than conventional steam locomotives, and speeds of 110 miles per hour could be reached with a trailing load of 1,000 tons.[49]

The steam-turbine locomotive took two years to build and another year to test. Despite some snags, the radical new engine lived up to its billing. The design was outstanding, the unit compact yet powerful. The power system was largely run by automatic controls, and electric brakes were used for the first time on a steam locomotive. An impressed authority called it "one of the most exceptional steam locomotives ever built." But by the time it emerged from test runs, the diesel had captured transcontinental passenger runs, and the Union Pacific decided to go with more conventional steam designs for freight operations.[50]

In 1936 Jeffers also managed to get fifteen more 9000s, but those engines were already showing symptoms of what ultimately proved a fatal flaw: they broke down easily and required constant maintenance. "I transferred out of Cheyenne . . . to get away from the 9000s," admitted a mechanical officer. "I watched dozens of good men . . . get fired because of the 9000-class locomotives. They were bad. . . . It was so constructed that it couldn't stand anything."[51]

Before these flaws glared, replacements were on the way. In 1936 the Union Pacific ordered yet another new type, a 4–6–6–4 articulated locomotive called the *Challenger*. Even larger than the 9000, the *Challenger* was capable of hauling 100 cars at 100 miles an hour. These performed well but were soon upstaged by a modified version of an older type, the 4–8–4 Northern. Known as the 800 class on the Union Pacific, these locomotives could haul passenger or freight trains at high speeds with ease, and their durability endeared them to the shop crews. The comparison with the 9000 class was striking: the 800s went 250,000 to 300,000 miles between overhauls, while the 9000s were lucky

FEEDING THE BEAST: A tough 4–6–6–4 Challenger-class locomotive, first built in 1936, pauses beneath a coal chute at Hanna, Wyoming.

BOLD EXPERIMENT: The Union Pacific steam turbine, hailed as the ultimate development of steam power, on a trial run in the spring of 1939.

WORKHORSE: The tough and durable 4–8–4 800- or Northern-class locomotive, first built in 1937 for both passenger and freight service.

GENERATION GAP: Four breeds of iron horse line up to celebrate the opening of the Los Angeles Union Passenger Terminal in 1939. An old 4–4–0 American belches smoke alongside an experimental coal turbine, a *City of Los Angeles* passenger diesel, and a 4–6–6–4 Challenger-class steam locomotive.

to travel 40,000 miles before an overhaul. "You could run her to death and never have any trouble," enthused a mechanical officer.[52]

The 800 class replaced Mountain and Pacific types on key runs where other roads had imposed faster schedules than the older engines could keep. Their versatility and durability were appreciated because competition kept speeding up schedules for freight as well as passenger traffic. By 1940 the power fleet looked very different from what anyone imagined possible twenty years earlier.[53]

Rolling stock showed less progress, partly because so much attention went to the passenger business. Between 1910 and 1920 the Union Pacific expanded its freight car fleet 58 percent. The first automobile cars, which were basically boxcars with doors at either end for loading, arrived in 1914. A fresh supply of steel "battleship" dump cars earned their keep carrying sugar beets as well as coal. The rush of business caused by the war in Europe sent the company scurrying for new equipment until rising steel prices slowed its ardor. Even then Calvin submitted a request for 6,700 new cars as late as June 1917.[54]

After the war Judge Lovett wondered whether it would not be cheaper for the Union Pacific to build cars rather than buy them. Gray convinced him in 1920 that it was not, and for a few years the company again bought cars heavily. In 1924 it launched a massive program to rebuild cars in hopes of squeezing another decade of life out of them. By 1930 some 14,620 cars had been rebuilt; then the depression killed off any desire to order new freight equipment. A survey by Jeffers in 1934, however, revealed some ominous facts. The average age of Union Pacific boxcars was twenty-two years; no new ones had been acquired since 1922. An estimated 13,000 cars, about 25 percent of the boxcar fleet, would have to be retired by 1938. Moreover, nearly 20 percent of the company boxcars were equipped with arch bar trucks, which would no longer be accepted for interchange after January 1, 1936.[55]

This meant heavy expenditures for new cars once business started to pick up. Gray and Jeffers urged New York to commence buying new boxcars every year until the fleet was modernized. This request came in the midst of the large outlays for streamliners and new power, but New York did not flinch. In 1936 the Union Pacific set aside $8 million for new equipment, including 300 automobile cars built in the Omaha shops. This work gave a welcome boost to employment in hard times.[56]

Like many roads, the Union Pacific had let its freight cars age past the point where replacements could match retirements. Unlike most roads, it had the funds to buy new equipment on a large scale. In 1937 the company ordered 4,088 new cars, most of them to be constructed in its own shops, at an estimated cost of $14 million. The sharp recession of 1938 slowed the work only briefly. The new equipment included fifty experimental boxcars of new lightweight design. So well did these perform that the company ordered 2,000 more in 1939.[57]

"The success of the Union Pacific," declared an officer, "has been down through the years that it was a very highly maintained property . . . we could make money with same freight rates that other people would lose money on."[58]

That tradition continued even through the dark days of the depression. Half the trick was having the money to spend and being willing to spend it; the other half was knowing what to spend it on. The Union Pacific had the money and never hesitated to spend it, but time would show that it had put too many eggs in the wrong basket. For the railroads, passenger business was not the wave of the future.

If the financial resources and competitive energy devoted to passenger service between the wars had been funneled instead into a concerted effort to improve freight operations, the postwar history of the railroads might have turned out very differently. Freight made most of the money, after all, and it desperately needed new thinking, new technology, and new techniques. But in the 1930s the threat to passenger traffic looked far more grave. Few people believed another world war was coming, and fewer still grasped what effect it would have on the national transportation system.

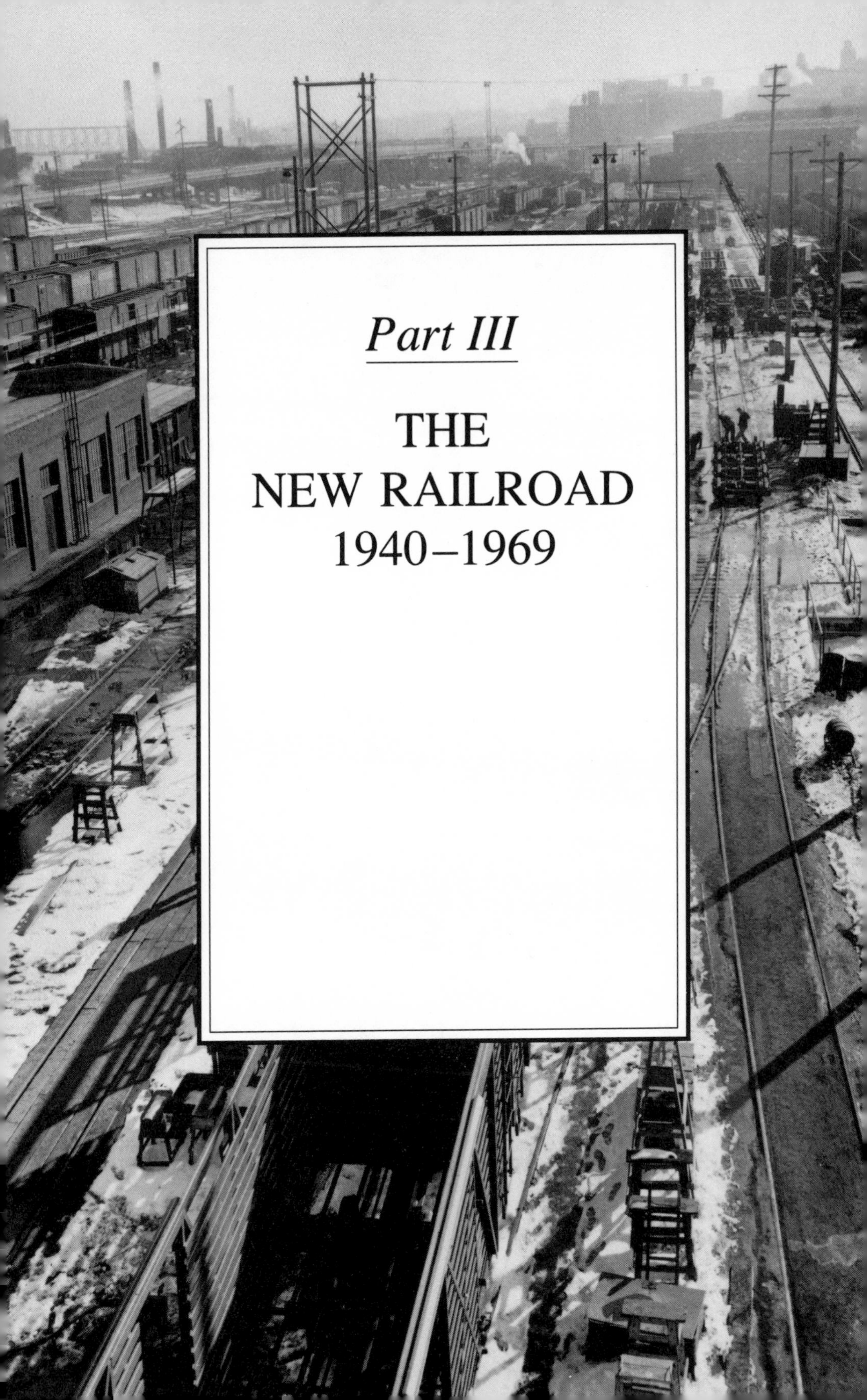

Part III

THE NEW RAILROAD 1940–1969

20

The Railroader

The world of the railroader had always been a closed one. Its members shared traditions, practices, and peculiarities that set them apart from others. They spoke their own language and endured a life-style dictated by the demands of their calling, demands that seemed inordinate if not inhuman to people who kept ordinary schedules. Like the inhabitants of any closed society, railroaders were prisoners of custom to an exceptional degree. Their behavior and values, even their vocabulary, were as rigid and unthinking as those of Newport society or the DAR.

In their own eyes "real" railroaders comprised only part of those who worked for railroads. Lawyers and accountants most certainly didn't belong, or clerks, traffic men, passenger and express agents, ticket salesmen, Pullman employees, dining car and hotel personnel, public relations people, even telegraph and telephone linemen. These were all outsiders whose attitudes derived from sources beyond the inner sanctum of the railroad. They spoke the lingo and held the values of other groups, and moved easily among people who inhabited a broader world.[1]

True railroaders were found in the operating, mechanical, and maintenance-of-way departments: enginemen, trainmen, dispatchers, telegraphers, superintendents, trainmasters, master mechanics, yardmasters, machinists, boilermakers, carmen, other shopmen, and part of the sprawling army of maintenance workers. Decades of experience had forged the pattern of their work lives, and ultimately of their social lives as well. It had honed their relationships into a pecking order that also served as an apprentice system. And it bound them together against outsiders, including other people within their own companies.

Engineers and conductors sat atop this pecking order, their prerogatives protected by union agreements that, quipped one writer, exceeded the French Civil Code in size. Firemen served as apprentice engineers and brakemen as fledgling conductors, making them together the Big Four of railway labor. Brakemen who lacked the stuff to become conductors often wound up as switchmen, or "snakes" as they were called. More than most, switchmen tended to be "boomers," roaming the country from job to job. Just below the Big Four in rank were the dispatchers, men of steel nerves who manipulated trains and equipment like chess pieces on a vast, complex board. The shopmen occupied the next rung, and below them the maintenance-of-way crews, who were the most transitory of all rail workers.[2]

In the beginning, railroading was a young man's work that required not schooling but a willingness to endure hardship and learn new skills. Once acquired, these skills bound their possessors together and set them apart from others. They became tools of a trade to be guarded as jealously as the craft of a medieval guild. For railroaders as for medieval craftsmen, job security mattered more than almost anything else. This attitude, which came early and stayed late, proved decisive in shaping the structure of labor in the industry.

Early railroaders tended to be rural or small-town boys with little education and a yen for wider horizons. They got work through family or friends or local connections, and once in place they often brought their children into the trade. The young started in modest jobs and apprenticed for better positions. Turnover was high among railroad workers, but most of it occurred in the lower ranks that relied heavily on transient workers. Those who made a career of it came to relish the work even though it was harsh, tiring, dangerous, disruptive of family life, and insecure even for those in the best positions.[3]

In this way the ranks of railroaders grew tight and largely self-selecting. A man could become an engineer or conductor only by starting at the bottom and serving his time in the ranks. The skills he learned on the way up were seldom useful in any other trade, which only drew him closer to railroading. Promotion was strictly by seniority, creating a hierarchy of age as well as of service. Intelligence, education, and imagination mattered less than loyalty and longevity, as is the case with any group that prizes security above all else. If a man earned promotion to supervisor or officer, he left the ranks of railroaders never to return except as guest. Men dreamed of rising from the bottom to become president, and those like William M. Jeffers who actually succeeded became the exceptions that proved the rule.

Loyalty and longevity were hard enough to attain in so rugged a world. Discipline on railroads, like hiring, was an intensely local and personal process. An enterprise so far flung yet requiring such precise coordination could not be run without strict discipline. This was a major problem in the early days of railroading when the men hired—mostly farmboys—were not yet accustomed to keeping schedules. The Civil War did much to impose a sense of drill and discipline on a whole generation, and most railroads evolved elaborate sets of rules to guide behavior at all levels. But how to enforce them? Of necessity managers handed the problem of enforcement over to local supervisors and held them responsible for results.

Disciplining large gangs of railroad workers was not the easiest job around. Most supervisors insisted they could do it only if they had absolute authority over their men, which was usually granted. There was little choice; how could managers in a city office do anything with crews hundreds of miles away? Thus arose a system of discipline that was local and absolute, a direct function of the personal relationship between a man and his superior officer. Here as in so many other ways the system evolved from the military model, except that supervisors could not impose as harsh punishments on the unruly. They could be mean or capricious, could penalize or fire men on a whim, but they also had to get good work out of them or their own position fell into jeopardy.

Railroading was a man's world, filled with characters who took pride in how tough they were. It took an even tougher man to exercise control over them. A man wouldn't be much good as a superintendent, said a Union Pacific lawyer with only half a smile, if he hadn't served a little time in jail back in the old days. "You ruled by fear," said another officer. "Literally. . . . It was a tradition on the railroad."[4]

This system of discipline did much to reinforce the conservative, inbred nature of railroaders. Superintendents fought any reform that curbed their absolute authority over the men; from this sprang their fear and hatred of the unions. The men in turn insisted on ever more elaborate work agreements to protect their rights from the tyranny of supervisors. In effect, the union agreement became a buffer padded with rights as numerous and meticulously formalized as the company rule book. Even so, the actual operation of the system still boiled down to the interplay between supervisors and their men. Some played the game fairly; others looked to take advantage whenever possible.

By 1940 the inner world of railroaders was still in many ways what it had been half a century earlier: inbred, isolated, scornful of outsiders, and proud of its work in a fierce, provincial way. Railroaders held college training in contempt and clung to seniority as the only basis for advancement. "College men were not looked upon favorably because they were a threat," recalled an officer. ". . . And if you *were* a college graduate . . . they tried to keep it off your personal record." Railroaders guarded every prerogative jealously as a benchmark of their status.[5]

But the larger world had changed in profound ways. Labor relations since the 1890s had been transformed by the intervention of government, two major depressions, a world war, and the New Deal. New competitors shattered the railroad's dominance of transportation and were fast reducing it to a second-class citizen. As a result, neither the industry nor its employees enjoyed the same influence or prestige they had once held. New technology was revamping the way railroaders did things in a manner that undercut the very essence of what they were and what they did.

After 1920 this most traditional of industries found itself swept along in an era of turbulent change, an old-timer in a new world that threatened it on every side. And the pace of change was growing faster. Technology menaced the ingrained habits of railroaders from opposite directions. On one side, new machines eliminated functions once performed by skilled labor, enabling companies to employ fewer and less skilled men. On the other side, some new machines required specialized knowledge or training that railroaders did not possess, forcing companies to bring in outsiders to tend them. Both were essential to cutting costs to meet the new competition.

Against these forces of change railroaders remained an obstinate and ultimately tragic barrier. Long experience dictated that their response be conservative if not reactionary. The more their prestige and position slipped, the louder grew their demands for differentials to define their status. The more technology eroded their traditional roles, the more insistent they became on preserving those roles. Graceful acceptance of change was not in the nature of men who had looked to the profession for security in the first place. That this stance was wasteful and harmful to the industry on which their survival depended, many railroaders conceded, but they could find no other course to defend their way of life.

The romance of railroading had faded like the grandeur of those temples that had once been the glory of downtown cities but were already becoming shabby. In this strange new world the once proud railroader was fast turning into an endangered species.

William Martin Jeffers was a railroader, always had been, and was proud of it. He was born into railroading in January 1876, at North Platte, Nebraska, where his father worked in the shops after a stint as section hand, and he married the daughter of a Union Pacific shopman. Like his father, Jeffers never worked for any other railroad. His lineage on the road went all the way back to the construction days. He always knew where his loyalty lay.

The fifth of nine children, Jeffers was raised in a Dutch-Irish section of North Platte the locals called "Brooklyn." It was a quick childhood. "I can't remember when I was a boy," he said later. "It seems I've always been a man, a working man." He knew how to work and how to fight. "Live every day," his father told him, "so you can look any man in the eye and tell him to go to hell." Jeffers took that advice to heart. He quit school at fourteen after a fist fight with a teacher and went to his calling on the railroad, starting out as a janitor at the local station and then advancing to call boy.[6]

As call boy his job was to round up crews for runs wherever they were, which acquainted him early with every saloon, pool hall, and whorehouse in North Platte. He knew every madam in North Platte, and they would greet him at the door and send him to the right room. Some trainmen made his work easier, like one who always left his dog outside the brothel so that all Jeffers had to do was spot the animal; others were less cooperative. On one occasion Jeffers was sent to a room and, seeing the door open, walked in to find the trainman engaged with one of the ladies. Jeffers told him he was called for a train and asked him to sign the call sheet.

STARTING OUT: William M. Jeffers, the quintessential railroader, at age 20 as a telegraph operator in Sidney, Nebraska.

"Get out of here, you little bastard!" growled the man, shoving the boy out of the room and slamming the door behind him. Jeffers went downstairs into the parlor, picked up a poker from the fireplace, went back to the room, flung the door open, and cracked the trainmen over the head with the poker. Then he closed the door, went back down the stairs, replaced the poker, and walked out, his duty done.[7]

Jeffers hung around the depot until the agents got the hint and taught him telegraphy. Within a short time he became an operator and then a dispatcher, two positions of which he would be proud all his life. In later years, boasting of his closeness to railroaders in the ranks, he would invariably flash his still active membership card in the telegrapher's union. When blistering subordinates for their ineptness, he liked to say that the dispatchers were the only ones who knew their business. After being promoted to chief dispatcher in 1900, Jeffers celebrated by marrying the daughter of a company blacksmith and indulging himself in a honeymoon. It was the only vacation he took for forty years.[8]

With impressive dedication he marched steadily through the ranks of trainmaster, assistant superintendent, division superintendent, and general superintendent, enhancing at every step his reputation for being tough and effective. Soon after taking over the Wyoming division, the roughest on the railroad to run, he asked a conductor at Rawlins where he was going.

"You may not believe it," came the insolent reply, "but I'm going to leave here on a train."

"That's what you think," replied Jeffers, smashing him in the face and leaving him out cold on the station floor.[9]

In 1914 he got into hot water by openly supporting a boyhood friend who was running for governor of Wyoming. When a Cheyenne paper accused him of intimidating railroad employees to vote for his friend, A. L. Mohler growled disapproval at the publicity heaped on the railroad. But Judge Lovett defended Jeffers's right to express his own opinion, "especially when . . . personal friendship is involved," so long as he kept the company's name out it. A few months later he was promoted to superintendent of the Nebraska division, and promptly had to defend himself from old charges of blacklisting employees and hiring gunmen to protect the road. The charges proved groundless, and in June 1916 Jeffers was made general manager, replacing a man notorious for his lack of dedication to hard work.[10]

During the next decade, as second in command to the capable but elderly E. E. Calvin, Jeffers did herculean service in operations. It was in many respects the most impressive segment of his career. His indefatigable energy did more than keep trains moving. He handled the men and the unions deftly through the labor strife of the early 1920s, spearheaded the newly launched safety movement, and looked constantly for ways to improve service. He had become the consummate railroader, and his dedication gained its reward in October 1928 when Calvin retired and Jeffers was named vice-president of operations.[11]

Drive and determination had brought Jeffers to the second highest rung in the company's management. At fifty-two he looked as much like an Irish ward politician as he did railroader. The 220 pounds spread over his 5′11″ frame still looked solid. His round, balding head with its ruddy, clean-shaven face and steely eyes beneath thick brows flashed easily from a smile that was all charm to a sneer of disgust to a bone-chilling scowl. Only a high-pitched voice marred the image he so cherished of a gruff, rugged, fighting railroader. Jeffers was a *presence*, a force that seldom went unnoticed even among strangers. Everyone considered him the classic "Irisher," but only part of the stereotype fit. He loved Irish music and grew maudlin over mothers in general and his own in particular, yet there was little of the jovial and none of the hard-drinking character in him.[12]

He rarely drank, and did not like others to drink. Jeffers enforced Rule G, the company's prohibition against drinking, with a vengeance. "He was death on this liquor," said a former secretary. Nor was he religious, though there was in him a prim, puritanical streak and an obsession with the work ethic that made him seem far more Protestant than Catholic. He was in essence a monk, with the railroad as his monastery and hard work as his devotional. Nothing else mattered to him. He had no hobbies and no other interests. The few he tried briefly, like duck hunting, never got in the way of business.[13]

His style was forceful and direct, and being an executive did not change it. Once his wife went to visit a nephew, who was a priest, in a Chicago hotel, only to have a house detective bang on the door to object to the presence of a woman in his room. Jeffers did no more business with the hotel despite a stream of apologetic letters from the manager. Then one day he appeared in the

LINE OF SUCCESSION: Carl Gray, near the end of his presidency, poses with his two top lieutenants, Frank W. Robinson (*right*) and William M. Jeffers.

lobby and asked to see the manager. Relieved that the spat seemed ended, an assistant ushered into the manager's office. Jeffers walked up to him, punched him in the nose, and left as silently as he had come.[14]

The promotion to vice-president of operations put Jeffers directly beneath Carl Gray, whose shadow would long shroud him in unfortunate ways. There was no more striking contrast than that between the courtly, dignified, genial Gray, whose saintly demeanor was enhanced by his deeply-felt religiousness, and the crude though dapper Jeffers with his tough-guy manner and macho code. Where Jeffers was respected, Gray was genuinely admired, even loved by the men in the ranks. The two made an effective management team with Gray's firm but gentle style serving as a brake for Jeffers's rough-and-tumble approach.

One small incident epitomized their difference in style. The elevator operators in the Omaha office learned quickly that when Jeffers got on, the local became an express from the twelfth floor to the first. One noontime, however, Gray got on with Jeffers. When the operator started to drop them all the way down, Gray would have none of it. ''There's other people waiting to go to lunch,'' he told the operator. ''You'll go back to the top and we'll pick them all up.''[15]

A few months after taking office, Jeffers dispatched a memo to the system officers that later acquired savage overtones of irony. ''I am intensely interested in maintaining the loyalty and efficiency of the Union Pacific personnel,'' he began. Men liked to work for officers they admired and respected, and Jeffers wanted his to show "a genuine desire to help men who are experiencing temporary difficulty." When discipline was necessary, it was to be "administered with consideration for the individual in each case." This notice was preserved by an embittered officer alongside a compilation of others from Jeffers he described as a "small fragment of the barrage of [critical] letters and telegrams supplemented by monthly diatribes in the presence of large numbers of officers in [Jeffers's] office."[16]

In a talk given in 1929, Jeffers emphasized two themes that became leitmotifs for him. Railroading was "the most exacting business that there is," and one "that a man must learn from the other fellow." There were no textbooks, no college courses, only experience and dedication. This was what appealed to him most about it, and of course what best fit his own experience. For the rest of his career he would heap contempt on college-educated railroaders and officers who relied on what he called the "swivel chair approach" to management.[17]

In 1932 Jeffers advanced to executive vice-president and suffered a rare bout of illness. He refused to admit it, but Gray thought he had stomach trouble and insisted he take some time off. Reluctantly Jeffers booked himself into the celebrated sanitarium at Battle Creek, where Woody Charske had also done time. Once recovered, he plunged back into work with the zeal of a youngster trying to make good. No one doubted his ambition, and Jeffers never disguised it. He liked to say that he would rather be president of the Union Pacific Railroad than of the United States, and his opportunity was coming. Gray turned seventy in 1937, and he was not a man to ask that the retirement rule be waived. He had built a strong organization with many good men in it, several of whom would be candidates.[18]

But Jeffers had the inside track. He was an operating man, the best they had, and no one matched his reputation for getting things done. In April 1937 the suspense ended when New York announced that Jeffers would succeed Gray in October. For the former call boy a dream had come true, but not all dreams have happy endings. Jeffers had spent forty-seven years struggling to the top, and he was sixty-one years old when he got there. He was a product of the old school in times that were changing ever faster, an old-fashioned man in a newfangled world. And he had to follow the most popular president in the company's history, an almost saintly figure. It was not an enviable position.[19]

There had been rumors that Gray might leave earlier. His name was being touted in 1933 for the new post of federal coordinator of railroads. Ultimately the job went to Joseph B. Eastman, but Gray's role as railroad diplomat expanded steadily during the 1930s. All his skills were needed as the position of the railroads collapsed under the combined weight of the new competition and the depression. Hard times also aggravated the strains among member roads in the Association of Railway Executives. Eastern roads wanted to seek a blanket 15 percent rate increase, a move Gray thought unwise and politically impractical. Most southern and western roads agreed with him, and the ICC bore out his prediction.[20]

The divisions deepened as earnings continued to plummet and more roads headed toward bankruptcy. The Reconstruction Finance Corporation, created in January 1932, provided emergency loans to many carriers, but the future looked grim—especially with an election campaign looming. Change seemed clearly on the horizon, but in what direction? ARE, standing at the crossroads of its own survival, revealed its uncertainty in two policy statements. The first, issued in June 1932, called for easing regulation so that the carriers could reduce rates and compete with other modes. Two years later the desire to compete was replaced by demands that other modes of transportation be brought under the same restrictions that bound railroads.[21]

A major reason for the change had to do with the new Democratic administration. In June 1933 Congress passed an Emergency Railroad Transportation Act creating a federal coordinator of transportation who was to study the carriers and find ways to eliminate waste, coordinate services, reorganize weak roads to cut fixed costs, and improve earnings through economy. Since heightened competition played no part in the thinking of the new act or of the man appointed to the job, Joseph Eastman, ARE promptly switched its position from more flexible rates to more rigid regulation of other modes.[22]

Amid this rapidly shifting landscape Gray occupied a crucial position. During the fall of 1932 he was instrumental in forming a new group, the Western Association of Railway Executives, which had a unique version of using a commissioner to resolve disputes. When ARE gave up the ghost two years later, Gray helped form a new rail organization, the Association of American Railroads (AAR). As early as January 1932 aspiring presidential candidate Franklin D. Roosevelt solicited Gray's advice on the railroad situation, a habit he continued during the campaign and after his election. This gave Gray some voice in the 1933 Act but did not stop him from pointing out its defects to a Senate committee.[23]

The emphasis of the New Deal was on coordination and control rather than competition, on relief and revitalization. Past policy in transportation had been a shambles and must be put right. Two approaches could be used to curb the intermodal competition that had grown so bitter: the railroads could be freed up to compete more effectively, or the other modes could be brought under regulatory restraints. The mood in Washington overwhelmingly favored the latter course, a message the railroads got early in 1934 when they had to fend off an attempt to organize them under NRA codes. Between 1935 and 1940 trucks, water carriers, and airplanes were brought under regulation, although exemptions rendered control of the first two ineffective.[24]

As federal coordinator Joseph Eastman made a vigorous and high-minded attempt to reform the railroad sector. His reports were behind the legislation that regulated both trucks and water carriers, but he found the railroads tougher going. Although he offered bold, imaginative suggestions, rail leaders greeted them with stony silence and hostility. In the words of one historian, Eastman "succeeded only in coordinating opposition to him and his office." The newly formed AAR was pivotal in coordinating this opposition despite some squabbling in the ranks.[25]

When Eastman's position lapsed in 1936, rail policy seemed as muddled as ever. Talk of government ownership to solve the problem of so many bankrupt roads still filled the air, prompting Gray to warn against such a move. Labor was trying to push a bill requiring new jobs or compensation for all workers displaced by mergers or other economies. The carriers united behind the Pettengill bill to repeal the long-short haul provision, which passed the House but got no farther. There was even talk of a bill to foist a six-hour work day on the railroads. A host of conferences and two committees appointed by President Roosevelt accomplished little. By 1938 many sick railroads seemed on the verge of expiring.[26]

Something had to be done, for by 1938 it was painfully clear that the railroads were losing their battle against the new competition despite all efforts to reverse the trend. Their share of intercity freight handled had slipped from 75.4 percent in 1926 to 64.6 percent in 1937, while trucks jumped from 3.9 to 7.7 percent, waterways from 16.8 to 19.6 percent, and pipelines from 3.7 to 8 percent. The passenger loss was even worse, dropping from 86.9 percent in 1926 to 54.5 percent in 1937 as buses soared from 9.2 to 41.7 percent. For most roads the large investment in streamliners had not paid off, a fact confirmed by the steady decline in average revenue per passenger mile from 2.936 cents in 1927 to 1.794 cents in 1936.[27]

Certain commodities underscored the loss. Where railroads had carried 89 percent of livestock and trucks only 11 percent in 1926, trucks hauled 52 percent in 1937. Since 1931 the rail share of oil had slipped from 40 to 22 percent, with the rest going by pipeline. Air traffic still posed a minor threat but was coming fast. Between 1926 and 1937 passengers carried leaped from 5,782 to 1.1 million, and during the latter year planes delivered 7.1 million pounds of express and freight. Nothing on the horizon suggested that any of these trends would be reversed.[28]

The onset of a recession left Roosevelt no less frustrated. In September 1938 he appointed a new committee of six (three from management and three from labor) to consider the transportation problem and offer recommendations for legislation. Gray served on this committee, which produced a report in December. While a later critic dismissed it as being "concerned with relieving the symptoms rather than curing the malady," the New York *Times* labeled it sweeping and comprehensive. Among other things it called for a "definite national transportation policy providing for fair, impartial regulation of all modes of transportation," repeal of the long-short haul clause, extension of ICC power over intrastate rates, and a new federal board to investigate the proper role of each mode of transportation.[29]

The report did much to shape another major transportation bill. A decade of conflict and frustration was distilled into twenty months of hearings and legislative infighting before the original omnibus bill of 1938 emerged as the Transportation Act of 1940. During the preliminaries Gray tangled with Eastman, and Jeffers with Senator Clyde Reed of Kansas, who accused the Union Pacific of being a " 'hard boiled' railroad that does many arbitrary things." Privately Jeffers doubtless relished the charge, but he was quick to reject it.[30]

Battered and bruised by compromise, the new law proved better at undoing than at doing. It buried the long-dead consolidation plan and restored the ICC's authority to decide mergers on a case-by-case basis. The bill also brought inland water carriers under the commission's authority but so riddled the proviso with exemptions that 90 percent of the barge traffic went unregulated. It also contained a proviso that hurt the railroads later. To reduce a rate, the carrier had to show the lower one was reasonable, where formerly the burden of proof had been on those protesting that the new rate was unreasonable.[31]

The Transportation Act of 1940 culminated two decades of unsuccessful grappling with the problems posed by the new competition. It embodied an approach stressing coordination and control, the orderly management of transportation by regulation. In a preamble added to the Interstate Commerce Act, it defined national transportation policy as the "fair and impartial regulation of all modes of transportation . . . to recognize and preserve the inherent advantages of each." Rail managers took a skeptical view of this promise, knowing how little their industry had got of what it wanted in the act.[32]

Gray was not there to witness the outcome of his labors. He had been active in the early rounds of testimony, pausing only long enough to join Daniel Willard of the B & O in preparing a report requested by Roosevelt on the best way to handle rail transportation in the event of war. In the spring of 1939 he was back in Washington to help the struggling transportation bill along. On the morning of May 9 he was found dead in his suite at the Mayflower Hotel, the victim of a heart attack. Like the good soldier he had always been, Gray fell on the field of battle.[33]

In December 1936, a few months before his retirement, Gray celebrated his golden wedding anniversary. The Omaha Old Timers chapter made it a grand occasion by arranging a banquet like none ever witnessed in the city. Three special trains brought the more distant of 1,400 guests, and the city auditorium was turned into a banquet hall for a gala dinner prepared by the dining car department. Amid huge stands of flowers and specially built blue and gold walls, members of the Nebraska National Guard's Company K served the sitdown dinner with military precision in thirty-eight minutes flat.

Averell Harriman and Woody Charske were there along with Samuel Bledsoe, president of the Atchison, the mayor, the governor, the president of the Mormon Church, union leaders, and 150 other dignitaries, businessmen, and old friends of Gray. Jeffers served as toastmaster. A local radio station broadcast the tributes so that all employees could hear them. Gray responded with a moving tribute to his wife. "She has been my inspiration, my helpmate, and my partner at every step of the way," he said with deep emotion. "I have grown through her guidance, her spirit and her love." This was not ordinary talk from a railroader, but Gray had never been an ordinary railroader. It was an extraordinary event that no one who was present forgot.[34]

THANKS, BOSS: The golden anniversary dinner given for Mr. and Mrs. Carl Gray by the Omaha Old Timers in December 1936.

Especially Jeffers.

The following October, when Jeffers became president, the scene was repeated on an even grander scale. This time city auditorium would not do; the Ak-Sar-Ben Coliseum was filled with special tables designed by Union Pacific engineers for 2,400 dinner guests, while another 4,500 faithful watched from the balconies. It was hailed as the largest banquet ever held in the West, and dubbed a "Loyalty Dinner" sponsored again by the Old Timers to honor the man who had risen from call boy to the top. Harriman and Gray attended along with the governor, the mayor, union chiefs, and an even more impressive roster of dignitaries: Postmaster James A. Farley, the governors of Utah and Wyoming, and a senator. A national radio hookup aired the proceedings.[35]

Huge Union Pacific seals framed in ferns loomed behind the banked rows of the speakers' table. Conductors and brakemen in uniforms acted as ushers, while uniformed stewardesses escorted distinguished guests to their seats. A hundred dining car cooks churned out plates of fried chicken served once again by guardsmen—all of them Union Pacific employees—marching in formation at the sound of a bugle. This time they pulled it off in only eighteen minutes, smashing all records for such things, and followed with rotating platoons of coffee servers. Now *that* was how to run a railroad.

"You can't slip up on something like this," Jeffers explained to a reporter.

''It can be the biggest thing of its kind put on in the country. And not for me, remember. Presidents come and go, but the railroad goes on forever.''[36]

But it was for him. The theme was not only loyalty but the Horatio Alger tale of struggling upward to success. Farley praised Jeffers's ambition as the key ingredient to success. Averell Harriman, comparing his father's career with that of Jeffers, noted that ''They had one marked similarity, of doing a job well and letting their personal success be the result of the services they rendered.'' Gray delivered some gracious remarks, and Jeffers closed with the themes dearest to his heart. ''This whole grand spectacle,'' he proclaimed, was ''a call boy's dream.'' He boasted that the Union Pacific had never had a labor dispute go to arbitration, and reminded his listeners that railroading was a profession that could not be learned at college.

And he closed with a tribute to the role of Union Pacific women, especially his own wife. ''She always helped,'' he declared, ''she has always been my most steadfast backer. She never followed, we walked step by step together, or she led the way.'' This was hardly a common theme for Jeffers at railroad functions, but Gray had done it at the earlier banquet.

It was this comparison Jeffers could never escape. Gray had been the company's only president since government control ended, and he was as widely admired in the industry as in the company. He was a railroader, but he did not look or act like a railroader. His courtly, dignified, gentle manner and

CAN YOU TOP THIS? The Loyalty Dinner given for William Jeffers by the Union Pacific Old Timers, October 1937.

devout character made him seem far more like an executive—indeed, a father figure.

Jeffers had none of those qualities and never pretended to have them. "I'm no silk stocking fellow," he liked to growl. Unable to match Gray's style, he tried to eclipse it with his own, which could not have been more different: the tough, hard-as-nails, two-fisted railroader who asked no quarter and gave none; who demanded results and rolled heads when they were not forthcoming; and who had nothing but contempt for "swivel chair" managers too squeamish to roll up their sleeves and get down into the thick of things. A financial officer once rode by a scene where crews were repairing damage from a burst dam. There, standing amid them in hip waders, was Jeffers, waving his arms, shouting orders, taking charge.[37]

But he could never escape Gray's shadow, especially in his own mind. That was part of what the banquet had been about: reassurance that whatever was done for Gray would be done for him as well. His banquet had been larger, with a huge spectator audience to boot. The roster of dignitaries was more impressive, the radio hookup carried over two national networks, the food served even faster, and the tributes equally glowing. Jeffers was unabashed in his pride over his career. At home his daughter kept voluminous scrapbooks detailing his upward climb. One of them bore the revealing title, "*Top Rung*."[38]

Yet no matter what Jeffers did as president, there was always about him a Gray eminence in the most literal sense. He took enormous pride in his closeness to the men in the ranks, and liked to boast that he knew ten thousand employees by name. Few insiders believed that. One recalled how Gray would come to Denver and walk down Seventeenth Street to the banking district and call on his friends. When Jeffers came to town, he always rode by car flanked by his omnipresent special agents. "He was scared to death," sneered the officer. "He always had this protection around him, and Gray never had any of it."[39]

One of Jeffers's former secretaries agreed, calling him a man who "presented a dictatorial atmosphere . . . had body guards around him all the time." There was bitter irony in this common image of Jeffers, the great commoner from the ranks who knew everybody by name, always with special agents at each elbow, marching in step with him and wheeling in unison like a color guard whenever he turned. "He wanted to become president so bad, you know, that he had to make sure that his competition wasn't going to get ahead of him," added the secretary. "In those days it wasn't the matter of how smart you were as . . . just how you could maintain your status with the boys."[40]

Tough guys, it seemed, made more enemies than saints did. Nevertheless, New York was confident the railroad was in good hands. Jeffers had ingratiated himself with the Harrimans through his dedication and hard work. "I thought very highly of Jeffers," Averell said later. "He was an outstanding operator, and we worked very closely together." Averell admired his dynamism and closeness to the men, a useful quality in an age of labor strife. Roland considered Jeffers an "extraordinary fellow."[41]

IRON HAT: John C. Gale, chief of the special agents, who was Jeffers's enforcer on the railroad.

Jeffers came to office at a time when a subtle change had begun to affect the New York management, which had a peculiar structure dating back to E. H. Harriman's influence. The chairman of the executive committee also acted as chief executive officer. Woody Charske, who had held this post since Seger's retirement in 1932, seemed the perfect man for an operation with finance as its primary responsibility. But he was a quiet, gentle soul content to leave the running of the railroad to the president in Omaha except when financial questions arose. The driving force in New York was Averell Harriman, who orchestrated policy as chairman of the board. But Washington had beckoned as early as 1934, when the company first "loaned" him to the NRA. His periodic absences created a vacuum of leadership in New York that grew worse as the war approached.[42]

As a result, New York made less of an imprint on Omaha than usual, which made the board even more grateful to have a man as reliable and experienced as Jeffers at the helm. The ship was Jeff's to run, and he wasted no time getting the crew in order. His two former assistants, George F. Ashby and E. J. Connors, were promoted to presidential assistants. Ashby was an accountant who had started with the Union Pacific in 1911; Connors was the labor relations whiz who was pivotal in giving the company one of the best reputations for labor harmony among the carriers. Otto Jabelmann, a tough, dour mechanical genius who had done much good work on the streamliner and was presently in charge of the steam turbine project, also became an assistant to Jeffers.[43]

In July 1938 Jeffers also elevated John C. Gale to the same position. Although Gale's promotion attracted little attention outside the company, insiders knew its importance. Known as "Iron Hat" because of his fondness for bowlers, Gale had been chief special agent for twenty years. As the police force of the railroad the special agents always took their cues from the president. Jeffers turned them into what some railroaders bitterly called his private Gestapo. Gale had been close to Jeffers for years, and became his most intimate (some said only) confidant after the death of Jeffers's closest friend in 1941.[44]

Being close to Jeffers was a huge advantage because of the emphasis he placed on loyalty. As Edd Bailey, who later became president himself, put it, "The first guy that told [Jeffers] the story would have the inside track. Particularly if Mr. Gale . . . was the guy."[45]

The contrast of working styles between Gray and Jeffers showed itself early. Where Gray handled much more work in the office, Jeffers hit the road and stayed there much of the time. He didn't like being confined to an office and never had been, regardless of his position. Still a tireless worker at sixty-one, he spent 140 nights on his business car during 1938, roaming the line to get his message across personally to employees, customers, and the public. He paid close attention to track conditions because he liked a smooth-riding road, and he spent considerable time with shippers—cattlemen, beet growers, wheat farmers, elevator people—because he felt the traffic people never worked as hard as they should.[46]

Acutely aware of his lack of polish and education, Jeffers never moved as easily among bankers, professionals, and other rail presidents as Gray had. He would never become an industry leader or diplomat. To these audiences his talks were stilted and unconvincing, but those who made him comfortable got rousing speeches and usually cheered him. Jeffers knew how to handle shippers, railroaders, business people who weren't swells. The Old Timers loved him; of course, as an officer noted pointedly, "they didn't come under the hammer." But Jeffers liked to be with people. An unabashed celebrity collector, he loved to rub elbows with politicos in Washington or the stars at Sun Valley. He enjoyed entertaining generals and senators, and took a lively interest in politics.[47]

Sometimes Jeffers was inspired enough to turn even his fun into serious railroad business. "Golden Spike Days" was a prime example. Shortly after Jeff became president, master showman Cecil B. DeMille decided to do an epic film on the building of the Union Pacific. E. E. Calvin's son Frank was hired to oversee the research, and an abandoned rail station at Iron Springs, Utah, was converted into a replica of early Cheyenne. Two old American locomotives were acquired, a historical exhibit in the company's Omaha shops provided rolling stock, and the film's track-laying scenes were performed by actual Union Pacific gangs working under a roadmaster. For once, no trick shots were needed; by the time shooting was done the crew had graded and laid rail on 2,000 feet of embankment.[48]

The premiere was set for Omaha in April 1939. As the seventieth anniversary of the Golden Spike, it offered a grand opportunity for a giant civic celebration that would also promote the film and the railroad company. "At the time it was just what this city needed," a publicist recalled, "because they had gone through the depression, terrible doldrums. And they celebrated really with a vengeance." Jeffers had his own deep emotional attachment to the railroad's past, and he harnessed the city's entire power structure to his vision. A gala four-day event was planned in which the city turned back the clock to 1869 by dressing in costume, erecting false fronts on whole blocks of buildings to recapture the old look, and staging parades, exhibits, and entertainments along with the film debut.[49]

Staging these events and dressing up Omaha cost a lot of money. When some civic groups hesitated, Jeffers took the lead. Merchants hesitated to lay in the large supply of gingham dresses, fake beaver hats, and other costume items, fearing they would be stuck with them if the idea didn't take. Jeffers anted up $40,000 for the goods, saying, "If you make money, you give me back my $40,000. If we make more than that, it goes into the kitty." Inspired by Jeffers's enthusiasm, the city plunged gleefully into the preparations for what amounted to the largest party it had ever thrown.[50]

It opened on April 26 with a historical exhibit in the city auditorium and an Indian encampment pitched on the courthouse lawn. Next morning special trains began arriving at Union Station. One from the East carried Averell Harriman, Charske, the board of directors, and other business executives. To honor the occasion, the board had agreed to hold its first meeting outside of New York since the days of the Fisk raid. That afternoon an old train with a wood-burning locomotive chugged in from the West bearing Cecil B. DeMille, Barbara Stanwyck, and other stars of the film, Heber Grant, president of the Mormon Church and a Union Pacific director, and three governors. Behind it came a passenger train powered by the new steam-turbine locomotive, making its public debut.[51]

Jeffers, dressed in costume, welcomed the guests, who were then driven to the hotel in old-style carriages with an escort of cowboys and Union Pacific employees dressed as cavalrymen. Some 200,000 people, many of them wearing period costumes, lined the parade route while others in office windows tossed out a blizzard of cardboard golden spikes. Harriman and the directors had also dressed for the occasion, as did thousands of Union Pacific employees and their wives, who marched as a unit in the parade. Jeffers oversaw the details and left nothing to chance. The movie premiere took place in three different theaters, two of them rented by the Union Pacific for its own people. There was another monster banquet, and the dedication of a giant golden spike monument in Council Bluffs. The picture did well, attracting even larger audiences overseas than at home, where it ranked among Paramount's biggest money makers for 1939.[52]

Golden Spike Days offered Jeffers a chance to mix business with pleasure. Rare was the diversion that took his thoughts far from the Union Pacific. As

HAPPY DAYS: Two master politicians, William M. Jeffers (*standing*) and Averell Harriman, work the crowd during Golden Spike Days, 1939.

one of his secretaries put it, "He was serious every minute about that railroad." Aware of his new status, he roamed the territory giving speeches on a wide range of business and rail topics. Late in 1939, however, a new theme crept into his talks. He had assumed the presidency during troubled times, and within a short time his concern for the railroad merged with his concern for world affairs. Once the war in Europe erupted, Jeffers came to the belief sooner than most that the United States had to help the Allies in every way possible. Six weeks after Hitler's invasion of Poland he called for unrestricted sale of arms and supplies to the Allies, and he delivered the message in the heart of the isolationist Midwest.[53]

Jeffers was convinced the United States might well have to fight, and if it did the railroad had to be ready. The track especially concerned Jeffers. During the 1930s improvement expenditures dropped off as most of the funds went for new equipment—especially the streamliners. But the new engines and trains took a fierce toll on the roadbed. Despite the recession of 1937–38, Jeffers persuaded New York to launch an extensive rail replacement program. The

HOLLYWOOD COMES TO OMAHA: A costumed crowd waits expectantly under the marquee for "Union Pacific" during Golden Spike Days, 1939.

Cecil B. De Mille's
UNION PACIFIC
PARAMOUNT
WORLD PREMIERE
PICTURE
OMAHA OPERA HOUSE
A·H·BLANK Prop.
Cecil B. De Mille's
UNION PACIFIC
BARBARA STANWYCK JOEL McCREA
AKIM TAMIROFF LYNNE OVERMAN ROBERT PRESTON
BRIAN DONLEVY EVELYN KEYES
WORLD PREMIERE
A PARAMOUNT PICTURE

LAST OF THE BREED: A giant 4–8–8–4 4000-class ''Big Boy,'' the largest steam locomotive ever built, dominates this scene from the Ogden, Utah, roundhouse.

company could stand the cost even though it had been making huge outlays for equipment. Since 1921 it had invested $174 million in improvements and equipment, yet its funded debt had *decreased* $31.6 million.[54]

Woody Charske continued his financial wizardry by negotiating a series of equipment trusts at low interest rates. In 1940 the company refunded $81.6 million worth of 4 and 5 percent mortgage bonds with a new issue at 3½ percent, saving about $300,000 in interest a year. It was the largest public offering of rail securities since 1928, and investors snapped the bonds up even though the industry had gone out of favor on Wall Street. Only a few roads still boasted impeccable credit in the capital market, and the Union Pacific stood high among them.[55]

Jeffers showed he could spend money faster than Charske could save it. In January 1939 he startled the industry by ordering 100,000 tons of rails and fittings, enough to do about 360 miles of track. No one had seen an order that size in years, but Jeffers was only getting started; in October the call went out for another 100,000 tons. In all the Union Pacific relaid 800 miles of main line during 1939–40, but Jeffers wanted still more. ''We should lay in 1941 a minimum of 655 miles,'' he told Charske, ''this in territory where rail was laid prior to 1925 and most of which has been in the track in excess of 20 years.'' Once again New York complied.[56]

At the same time Jeffers stepped up orders for new power and rolling stock. In 1940 he got authority for fifteen diesel switchers; the following May he acquired twenty new 4–6–6–4 Challengers. Meanwhile, a design team headed by Otto Jabelmann had come up with a new beast of a locomotive weighing 600 tons and capable of producing maximum power output continuously at seventy miles an hour. The 4–8–8–4 "Big Boy" made its debut in September 1941 and performed superbly from the start. It remained the largest steam locomotive ever built.[57]

New York did not begrudge Jeffers these outlays. On the contrary, in June 1941 Averell Harriman, who was by then on diplomatic duty in London and knew firsthand how close the war was to home, wrote Charske wistfully, "It is too bad we were not more courageous with the power and freight car situation last summer." Jeffers missed no opportunity to deliver the message. At a big company gathering in Council Bluffs, he told the faithful that the Union Pacific was going to put the road in top shape, and that he had authority for whatever was needed. The British were fighting our war, he added, and the railroad was going to bring them supplies. An accountant present that day was bemused at the sight of so fierce an Irishman ardently drumming up support for the British.[58]

Since May 1940, when the elixir of defense spending began intoxicating the economy, business had been rising slowly from the dead. The West hovered on the brink of an unprecedented expansion boom, and Jeffers wanted the railroad to be ready. But the nation was also on the brink of plunging into the war, after which neither it nor the West nor the railroads would ever be the same again.

21

The Czar

Like all czars, Jeffers was a throwback to the old school, and he made no bones about it. ''He was rough and tough,'' said his former secretary, D. O. ''Doc'' Churchill, ''and I think absolutely he ruled by intimidation.'' Controller Reg Sutton agreed: ''He was as rough and tumble as they came, and he ran a real honest-to-goodness bang-up railroad.'' While the officers came most directly under the hammer, the men in the ranks felt his wrath through their quaking superiors. ''Jeffers there, . . . he'd fire you just like that,'' said a shop man. ''It was nuthin' to him. You might have a job or you might not have a job when you went up to see him.'' Jeffers liked to boast of his popularity with the men in the ranks, but this old-timer disagreed. ''No, he wasn't liked,'' he said. ''Feared. Very much.''[1]

The czar was alternately wrathful and forgiving, passionate and tempestuous, his outbursts designed to instill fear, which he believed to be the best fuel for performance. ''Jeffers would not accept a failure, period,'' declared another shop veteran. ''Somebody paid with his scalp.'' He ruled by terror, firing men as freely as other czars imprisoned or tortured them. Officers summoned to his office never knew whether they were being fired or promoted. ''He was like my mother,'' said former secretary Stan How. ''He could love you one minute and kill you the next. . . . While he was pretty quick to fire them, he was also pretty quick to take them back.''[2]

The way Jeffers expected miracles and fired those who did not produce them tickled Roland Harriman, whose executive committee was kept busy rehiring men fired a week earlier. ''In spite of it all, he had a great character,'' noted Roland in his benign way, ''and he really made things hum.''[3]

BOTH SIDES OF THE BOSS: The two faces of William M. Jeffers that his subordinates saw.

Those on the firing line found the experience less amusing. One time Jeffers cashiered Art Stoddard, who later became president of the Union Pacific but at the time was in charge of the Wyoming division. During a terrible storm Stoddard came home after forty-eight hours on his feet, told his wife Oceain that he had been fired, and fell into bed. Jeffers tried to reach him at the office and, failing that, called his house. "Where's Art?" he growled.

"In bed asleep," answered Oceain.

"What do you mean he's in bed asleep?" the czar exploded. "Get him on the phone right away!"

"I'm not going to get him on the phone right away," countered Oceain. "He's been out there forty-eight hours, and besides, he told me when he came in that you'd fired him."

"Well, now, Oceain, you know about that," said Jeffers. "Get him on the phone. I need him."

"Nope," she said firmly. "He's fired. He's going to bed and stay till he gets rested."

"Now Oceain, you know how we do these things. Go get him out of bed and tell him I've hired him back."

But she did not. On this occasion the czar met his match.[4]

The czar wielded power through sheer force of personality, through his police force of special agents under John Gale, and through what were called "spotters" or "stool pigeons"—officers and men who spied on their fellows and filed secret reports to Omaha. Sometimes, when they had nothing to report, they manufactured charges to keep in good graces. The poison spread through the system by this reign of terror gradually undid much of the goodwill generated during Gray's time and took years to abate.[5]

While the czar's power was not absolute, he wielded it absolutely and it seemed nothing less to his subjects. Moreover, it was augmented by the weakening hold of New York on affairs in Omaha. The policy of decentralization Judge Lovett had worked so hard to implement had been a brilliant success under Gray, but now it took on a new face. Jeffers had good relations with New York, which trusted his judgment, and so long as he maintained them he was free to do what he pleased in Omaha. In that respect little had changed since the days of Oliver and Oakes Ames: the board was in New York but the railroad was in Omaha, and New York had surprisingly little grasp of what the latter really entailed.

The ranks in New York were thinning. Averell Harriman's government service escalated to full time in June 1940; a few months later he was posted to London, launching a career in politics and diplomacy that would occupy the rest of his long life. Although he remained chairman of the board until 1945 and kept abreast of company affairs, he never again assumed a major role in its management. In December 1940 Robert Lovett accepted a position as assistant to the secretary of war and went off to Washington. "I find that I am missing New York more than I expected," he reported a couple of weeks later, "because so much of the goings-on here are cockeyed." But Lovett, like Averell Harriman, soon learned his way around the corridors of power in masterful style, and was lost to the Union Pacific for most of the decade.[6]

The loss of its two brightest and most dynamic figures left the board without a dominant or even a strong leader. Death also claimed some of the most experienced directors, including Gray in 1939 and Seger and banker James H. Perkins in 1940. Robert Goelet, who had served since 1906, and Charles A. Stone, who had held a seat since 1920, both died in 1941, followed by Henry W. Clark, the general counsel, the next year. Suddenly the board took on a more parochial character than had been typical of the Union Pacific. By 1942 it included both Harrimans, Charske, Jeffers, the secretary, the controller, the general counsel, and the vice-president of traffic. Of the remaining directors only two came from outside New York: Heber J. Grant, the venerable head of the Mormon Church, and Omaha banker W. Dale Clark. Two fresh faces also gained seats: Gordon S. Rentschler of National City Bank, who replaced Perkins, and George E. Roosevelt.[7]

With Averell Harriman gone, Charske held the reins but hesitated to do much without his approval. Roland Harriman assumed Lovett's place on the executive committee. As spokesman for the family holdings he had the last word on any decision but was no more forceful a personality than Charske. By 1941, then, an ominous situation had quietly developed. Averell was abroad and confined to expressing his views by letter, while Lovett was obliged by law to sever his ties with the company. The board was inbred and obedient, eager to follow an executive committee that had little inclination to lead. The New York management, in short, had become more passive than ever before. A curious vacuum emerged in which routine was substituted for decision-making.

This vacuum left Jeffers free to run the railroad as he pleased, so long as he kept New York happy. Throughout his long career there had always been someone to harness his exuberance, first Carl Gray and then Averell Harriman. Now there was no one. At this last stop of a long and impressive career he got the freedom he had always craved, but it had come too late. The power delivered into his hands did not corrupt him absolutely, but it did corrode his virtues into self-defeating excesses.

Like all czars, Jeffers had a tendency to dwell in the past, the arena of his greatest triumphs, where he had climbed the ladder of success to the very top rung. The railroad had been his classroom, and he saw little value in any other one. He had only contempt for those who had not learned their lessons in the field. "Because . . . he had not proceeded beyond elementary school," suggested a former assistant, "anyone with a college degree he resented." Officers who did not take their cues from the men in the ranks, the true fonts of knowledge in Jeffers's view, drew withering attacks from him. He railed repeatedly against what he called "brain trusting" by his subordinates.[8]

This strain of thought deepened after he became president, moving Jeffers from merely conservative to the most reactionary of czars. "In the final analysis the last fellow you fool is the man in the service," he told the vice-president of operations (VPO) shortly after becoming president. "The rank and file will get your number quicker than anyone else." What the road needed most, he added, were "more men who understand operation, and the men who know best what to do are the men who have come up through train dispatchers." An officer would get more out of such men by learning from them instead of "having him hedged about with a lot of perfectly asinine instructions that have to do with the dignity of the Vice President's office."[9]

And he practiced what he preached, at least for a time, following up suggestions given him by employees, such as the one by a conductor who made a survey on his own of why shippers preferred trucks. Delighted at this show of initiative, Jeffers implemented the advice with faster schedules and better pickup service, and missed no opportunity to parade the incident as an example of how labor and management should cooperate to run a better railroad. He liked to tell the story of an old engineer who told him bluntly, "Dammit, Bill, don't let yourself get so busy on this new job that you haven't got time to think."[10]

This was easier said than done, especially as Jeffers allowed himself to be swallowed by his own success story. Like many self-made men, he came to believe in the infallibility of the beliefs that had carried him to the top until they became dogma he applied with an increasingly heavy hand. The transition to a legend in his own mind was hard to resist. The media doted on his image as a tough, two-fisted railroader getting things done the old-fashioned way. An age tormented by labor strife loved to read about a manager who boasted of his close touch with the common man. He even helped North Platte convert his boyhood home into a museum and shrine honoring the call boy risen to president.[11]

In this sunlight of publicity the czar blossomed. "Once he got into the swing of things," observed a public relations officer, "he understood the power of publicity, and he enjoyed being the center of attention." Sometimes his bent for the limelight ran to excess. When he was named king of Ak-Sar-Ben (an honor bestowed each year on a leading citizen for his service to Omaha and Nebraska) in 1940, Jeffers turned a discreet ceremony into a public relations blitz. Dressed in silk finery, dragging a thirty-five-pound train, a bejeweled crown atop his bald dome, he looked like a cross between the czar and Ole King Cole. To celebrate the affair, he imported a special train of railroad men along with Steve Hannagan, reporters, and cameramen to cover the party he threw. So lavish were the festivities that Ak-Sar-Ben later banned extravagant private parties.[12]

The more Jeffers basked in his new role as celebrity, the more dictatorial grew his managerial style within the company. He had always been tough, but now it was as if he felt a pressing need to live up to his image. Above all, he could not let poor performance by the railroad spoil it. Gradually Jeffers tightened his hold over operations under the guise of giving officers more responsibility. Two positions were always sore spots with him: the vice-president of operations and superintendent of the Wyoming division, the toughest division on the road to run and the one over which all the traffic passed. "I always had the feeling," confided Doc Churchill, "that he didn't want a vice-president of operations to succeed. . . . That was his old job, and I don't think he wanted anyone else to succeed in it." Churchill felt the same way about the Wyoming division, the make-or-break post that Jeffers had also once held.[13]

A pattern soon emerged. "He put somebody in a job and give 'em a pat on the back as he started," Churchill added, "and said, you take charge of this by-God operation and . . . I am all for ya; and then he would start in on 'em with the telegrams and the attacks; that this is wrong, and what the hell ya doin' about that, and how did this happen."[14]

As an old operating man, Jeffers liked being in the field. He left the office work to his assistants and stormed down the line, usually setting up shop on the Wyoming division where he could watch everything. As later president John Kenefick, then a young hand, put it, "No sparrow fell unheeded around this railroad." When Jeffers was on the road, the morning report detailing all activity on the line lay in the middle of his plate when he sat down to breakfast, and his secretary sat at his right elbow, ready to take down the stream of telegrams that soon followed. If there was trouble anywhere, Jeffers rushed to the scene and expected the officers in charge to be there. Excuses rolled feebly off his hard, grim surface. He took pride in being a slave driver, saying gruffly, "I've never asked any man to do anything I wouldn't do myself."[15]

One time a road gang was toiling in the Nevada desert despite oppressive heat until the weary foreman finally wired Jeffers that he had to rest the men

THE CZAR: William M. Jeffers as King of Ak-Sar-Ben.

because the temperature had soared above 120 degrees in the shade. Back came the reply, "What are you doing in the shade?"[16]

The officers who fared best with the czar were those tough enough to stand up to him and competent enough to be needed. "If Jeffers found some guy that he thought was going to punch him in the nose, he would put him on the staff," said a shop veteran, ". . . 'cause Jeff liked tough guys." Ashby and Connors fit his needs, and so did Otto Jabelmann, the mechanical genius whose reputation for toughness rivaled that of Jeffers. One shopman described him as "very, very bright" but "probably the meanest man that was ever in the mechanical department." A burly man with a prominent nose, Jabelmann fired people almost as fast as Jeffers when they didn't meet his exacting standards.[17]

It speaks volumes about the tenor of relationships in the company that one shopman thought Jabelmann was afraid of Jeffers while another insisted it was the reverse. The gruff Jabelmann, whose white shirt always got soaked with sweat because he was around steam, betrayed his fear: when Jeffers called him up, the sweat poured out on his face. He repaid the favor to those in the shops. "He'd come in there," said one, "and you better know what you was talkin' about. If you didn't, you was going to get your butt reamed."[18]

MECHANICAL GENIUS: Otto Jabelmann, the hard-nosed ruler of the mechanical department.

Those lower down on the ladder also felt Jeffers's wrath. He was a terror on secretaries because of his insistence that every letter or document be perfect. "A misspelled word in a letter," recalled Reg Sutton, "was practically a crime." Although most of his secretaries were male because of the constant travel, he once fired a woman in the office and sent her fleeing in tears. When Sutton asked him why, Jeffers snapped, "Well, how do you think she spelled piss ant?"[19]

One embittered woman named Olive Stephenson vented her wrath in a signed letter to the czar. "A year has passed since I got my discharge from YOU," she snarled. "I know you must have spent a very happy year since it is the firing, crushing and hurts that you pass out that goes into the making up of your sweet life. A deadening blow such as you gave to me—an employee with over 22 years of service, with a crippled 80 year old mother whom I had to look after and support. Not only the blow but the previous 6 years of persecution. It is an extra fine record for you."

The employees, she added, "do not have special agents to guard us—and to spy and stooge on others. . . . there is no honor or respect held for you. . . . Practically everyone will be relieved and happy when you retire—or expire and it doesn't make much difference which."[20]

Not all his subjects admired the czar, it seemed, and in their ranks at every level boiled intrigues of a sort rarely known in the Gray era.

Gray left behind a good organization, staffed several deep with good managers, but Jeffers wasted little time shuffling it. The vice-president of operations had been restored in January 1937 after Jeffers moved up to the post of executive vice-president. When Jeffers became president, the first VPO retired from illness after eighteen months. His successor lasted only a year, whereupon the czar appointed veteran officer W. H. Guild to the job. It took less than another year for Jeffers to decide that Guild didn't have what it took, and in July 1941 he thrust E. J. Connors into the position. The job quickly became a graveyard for ambitious officers; Connors later called it "My Waterloo with Jeffers."*[21]

In July 1936 the company had created a research bureau for equipment design and put it under Jabelmann, who was then only an assistant superintendent. This provided a base of operations for the hard-driving Jabelmann, and soon brought him into conflict with J. W. Burnett, the superintendent of motive power and machinery. For some time Jeffers had been unhappy with the quality of work done in the shops. A rash of derailments and equipment breakdowns convinced him that severe measures were needed to restore standards and discipline. When his VPO did not respond, Jeffers sent Jabelmann to inspect the shops and report on conditions.[22]

Jabelmann toured five western shops, questioned officers and men closely, and gave Jeffers an earful on his return. All the foremen and inspectors were competent, he concluded, and would do well "if the officers in charge insisted on full compliance and observance of instructions, workmanship, tests and inspection." Too many supervisors were slack or spineless in enforcing standards, and Jabelmann blasted Burnett for "not intelligently directing his organization." He did not like Burnett's attitude or his reports, "some of which are mere pettifogging and a few are of questionable veracity."[23]

Although the infight between Jabelmann and Burnett forced many shop people to take sides, it was no contest. Jeffers backed Jabelmann, promoting him in May 1939 to a new post as vice-president of research and mechanical standards. When Burnett continued to resist Jabelmann's prying into his operation, the czar extended the latter's authority to the motive departments. Hobbled by an arthritic knee, Burnett took a short leave of absence and then left the service. The position of superintendent of motive power and machinery was abolished and the operation placed under Jabelmann.[24]

Jabelmann had won, but there were casualties. One of them, Pocatello superintendent G. M. Walsh, whom Jabelmann had called spineless, protested the humiliation of being reduced to mechanic. The long fight between Jabelmann and Burnett, he added, had cost the railroad dearly. "I have seen a wonderfully efficient organization torn apart and destroyed, and inefficiency take its place," he mourned. "In my 40 years of railroad experience I have never before seen such universal disgust among employees."[25]

*The officers Jeffers fired were rarely dismissed from the company. Rather, they were demoted to other positions.

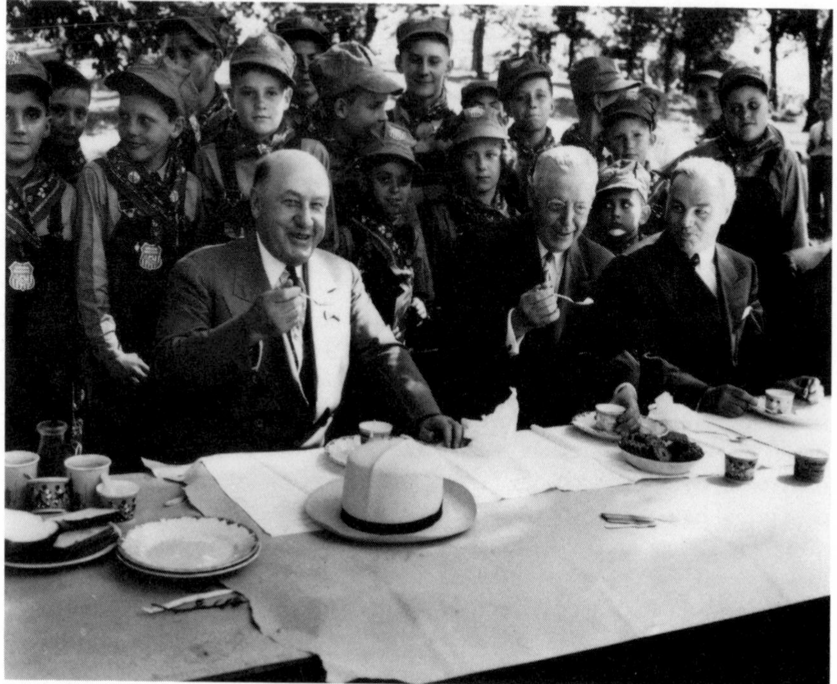

JUST DESSERTS: The Czar and two of his top officers, W. H. Guild and E. J. Connors, enjoy themselves with some young admirers at a Drum Corps picnic, June 1940.

Was this sour grapes or a legitimate complaint? While the answer is difficult to find in any individual case, the number of protests increased. This could indicate either a collapse in employee morale or a genuine attempt to improve the efficiency of officers (or both). Jeffers turned a deaf ear to this protest, telling Charske that "since Mr. Walsh was removed there has been a very decided improvement in the performance and output." One thing was certain: the amount of turmoil and grumbling in the ranks was growing and would get much worse as the infighting got more vicious.[26]

By 1941 Jeffers found himself with a peck of trouble. Business had been picking up since the spring of 1940, when defense spending first began making the economy hum. The world situation kept deteriorating, and Jeffers wanted the railroad ready in the event of war. But the money he got from New York for improvements carried a price tag in the form of admonitions from Charske to keep expenses down when business went slack. He promised Charske to keep his organization at a level lean enough to absorb any drop in traffic, yet ready to handle a rush of new business. This proved too tall an order even for the czar.[27]

Crises emerged on several fronts. In June Jabelmann suffered a heart attack, throwing the mechanical department into confusion again. Already a shortage of mechanics had developed and would get worse. The mushrooming complex of defense industries around Los Angeles piled an abnormal burden of traffic on that territory, which still operated with the skeleton staff of depression days. Problems arose on the Wyoming division and in the Northwest, and a strike threat loomed when engineers and trainmen served notice that they wanted a 30 percent hike in wages.[28]

Even without these woes, an organization pared down so severely by the depression cuts simply could not cope with the surge of business. Jeffers moved at once to overhaul the structure by making Connors the operating vice-president and sending the deposed Guild to Los Angeles as executive assistant. Connors had little more operating experience than Guild but was, in Jeffers's words, "a man of unusual intelligence, vision and initiative." Another general manager was pulled off the line to become an executive assistant and replaced by a younger, more vigorous man. To ease the crunch on Los Angeles, the Utah Division, which had been abolished during the depression, was recreated by taking territory from the Los Angeles and Idaho divisions. Several other officers were reassigned.[29]

New York gave Jeffers everything he asked for, including one other appointment: the promotion of George F. Ashby to vice-president and assistant to the president. Ashby was the man who held the office together while Jeffers roared up and down the line. He was, in the czar's words, "an important man in the organization, and it would be extremely difficult, if not impossible, to replace him." Jeffers's reliance on Ashby has always been a mystery, but there is no doubt he considered Ashby indispensable. He must have, because Ashby had the one personal problem that Jeffers loathed most: he drank.[30]

During much of 1941 Jeffers made his presence known on line. Until Jabelmann recovered, he took hold of the mechanical department while prodding the man in charge to do some original thinking. "I am not going to temporize with any half baked decisions or half baked railroading," he thundered. As he moved down the line, he complained that none of the road officers were anywhere to be found. "We are developing the type of officers who would rather hide out than be asked some embarrassing questions," he growled. In November he showed his dissatisfaction by personally taking charge of the troubled Wyoming Division for a few days.[31]

The problem in Wyoming, he explained to Charske, was a labor one. Some younger men, who were troublemakers, had influenced the older heads, but Jeffers knew the latter well and had no trouble getting them back in harness. He also found the superintendent "in such a physical and mental state that he is irresponsible." While he recovered, Jeffers handed the job to Art Stoddard, who had just taken over the new Utah Division a few months earlier. In this abrupt manner did Stoddard find himself in that other graveyard for ambitious officers. "There is nothing wrong with the Wyoming Division and there never has been except incompetent handling on the part of responsible officers," proclaimed Jeffers. It or any other division could be run by a good dispatcher and "a couple of two-fisted outside trainmasters."[32]

This was his approach to every crisis. The men were not to blame; they simply lacked two-fisted leadership. There was no shortage of power; it was just being badly handled. Dispatchers could run the road if inept officers would keep out of their way. Any problem could be solved if officers would quit "brain-trusting" and deal with it firsthand in the field. "There is nothing about railroading that requires any unusual talent," he said. "All it requires is just ordinary, common, every day horse sense and stick-to-it-iveness."[33]

An anonymous letter recorded a dissenting vote from one superintendent: "If the Godam [sic] cross-back shanty Irish at Omaha would keep there [sic] damn nose out it," he snarled, "[I] could run the railroad."[34]

One problem defied Jeffers's approach. The trainmen rejected a compromise offer and called a strike for December 5, 1941, if their demand for a 30 percent wage increase wasn't met. Worried by the prospect of higher wages and the cost of heavy flood damage caused by heavy rains in October, Jeffers overreacted. On November 6 he ordered "an immediate and drastic curtailment of expenses." Business was falling off, he added. "What I want now are reductions in all directions, and I don't want any money spent unless it is for safety." As a result the Union Pacific laid off people just when other roads were hiring madly. The timing could not have been worse, but Jeffers could not have known that Pearl Harbor lay only a month away.[35]

After some frantic bargaining, the trainmen grudgingly accepted a 10 percent hike on December 3. Four days later the world changed, and with it the role of the railroads. The company had lost so many men to the peacetime draft that it felt obliged to issue a policy protecting their job and seniority rights in April. The manpower drain grew steadily worse just as the workload soared. To older hands the switch was dizzying; in a blink they went from layoffs to constant overtime. Older engines parked in the weeds were pressed into service along with every form of rolling stock. A Jeffers edict in August had already commanded everyone along the road to horde scrap metal for the war effort.[36]

The first company casualties of war fever were the Japanese employees, many of whom had been barred from becoming citizens by the Immigration Act of 1924. Of the 193 Japanese who worked for the Union Pacific, most of them in Wyoming, eighty-one had been in company service at least twenty years and another fifty-six at least ten years—although one kitchen helper had the bad luck to start his new job on December 5. Uneasy over growing world tensions, thirty-six Japanese foremen had in June 1941 adopted a resolution pledging complete loyalty to the United States.[37]

All such efforts were drowned out by the crash of bombs at Pearl Harbor. On December 7 Connors ordered a canvas of all Japanese workers. Next day the company stopped selling tickets to Japanese travelers; on December 11 the Treasury Department stopped payment of all funds, including wages, to Japanese nationals.* Mindful of the ethnic hysteria that swept America during World War I, Attorney General Francis Biddle issued an impassioned plea for employ-

*The order applied to Japanese who were not American citizens, and limited payment to them to $100 per month for living expenses. A week later the order was modified to exclude Japanese who had been living in the continental United States since June 17, 1940.

ers not to discriminate against alien workers. "No more short-sighted, wasteful or un-American policy could possibly be adopted at this time," he declared, "than that of barring non-citizens from legitimate private employment."[38]

This plea left Jeffers unmoved. Two things worried him: a Japanese national might commit an act of sabotage, or some crackpot might commit such an act and blame it on a Japanese. Early in February 1942 an incident at Howell, Wyoming, brought matters to a head. While repairing a main-line switch, a Japanese foremen with thirty years' service had his men pull the spikes out of the switch stand as well as the rail just in advance of a troop train. Although the foreman was fired at once, the superintendent and roadmaster agreed his act was an oversight rather than sabotage. Nevertheless, the incident forced Jeffers's hand on the whole issue of the Japanese.[39]

Since Pearl Harbor the trainmen and shopmen alike had complained about keeping the Japanese employed. The Howell incident drew immediate demands from the union heads that such workers be removed. Jeffers needed little prompting. He fired all Japanese who were not American citizens, giving them five days' pay and free transportation to any point on the line. In one stroke 108 men found themselves out of work with nowhere to go. "We are handling the situation with utmost consideration for these people," Jeffers assured J. Edgar Hoover. To the press he explained it as "purely a precautionary measure" to protect the workers as well as the railroad. Two weeks later one of them, a boilermaker helper at Caliente, shot himself to death.[40]

When the Southern Pacific followed suit, Jeffers took an even harder line. He noticed that Japanese were still employed in the Portland, Seattle, and Spokane terminals. Fearful that they might pick up information on troop movements, he ordered them dismissed. "Let's clean it up so far as the Union Pacific is concerned," he barked. A banker in North Platte, who knew three of the discharged Japanese there, registered a protest at the treatment of men who had "a long, honorable record in the community." In reply Jeffers delivered a typical blast. "Make no mistake about it," he thundered, "I am unalterably opposed to the employment of Japanese on these railroads, whether they are Japanese Nationals . . . or whether they are Japanese born in this country." For that matter, he opposed employment of "enemy aliens of any nationality in railroad service."[41]

The harsh treatment of the Japanese opened an era in which nothing was quite the same on the Union Pacific except the czar's wrath when miracles were not performed. Certainly miracles were needed. Tonnage and passengers carried had each jumped 24 percent in 1941 from the previous year, but the war years dwarfed this advance. Between 1941 and 1945 tonnage increased 83 percent and passengers carried 195 percent. Most of this growth came during 1942 and 1943, when tonnage rose 53 percent and passengers carried 160 percent. Once the war came, said a shop hand, "from then on it was hop, hop, hop."[42]

The streamliner stewardesses left to do their nursing in the service. Sun Valley made it through the winter of 1942 in normal fashion, then closed in December to become a hospital for Navy convalescents. Everyone got more

WE CAN LEND A HAND: Two scenes of women working on the railroad.

overtime work than they wanted. As in the previous war, women began filling the places of men lost to the service; a few even went into the mines. "We had a big infiltration of women in the railroad," recalled one officer, "and we were glad to have anybody."[43]

By 1943 the company was losing employees as fast as it hired them, more to other industries than to the draft, which accounted for only 8 percent of the loss. In one six-month period the Union Pacific hired 20,172 new employees but increased its total force by only 2,598. Two-thirds of the new people stayed with the company an average of only sixty days. This massive turnover aggravated an even more serious problem: the lack of skilled hands. In September 1943 Jeffers complained that the company was short 500 trainmen, 545 skilled mechanics, 980 shopmen, and 1,000 other workers—figures he called "rock bottom." As possible substitutes the western roads looked at conscientious objectors, West Indians, Mexicans, prisoners, and even the "loyal Japanese" they had so rashly discharged earlier.[44]

An unstable labor force meant serious trouble. New people took time to train and often did not measure up to the work. The turnover also disrupted the traditional discipline system. Some older union hands were quick to take advantage by pulling in top wages for very little work. ''It got to where you couldn't fire a man,'' complained an officer, ''. . . because if you did, the War Production Board said, hey, you don't need people; you just fired 'em.'' Nor did the old methods work. ''You couldn't threaten people or force 'em like you had before. You . . . had to lead them and coax them.''[45]

This instability forced the road to handle the largest traffic in its history with the least experienced work force it had ever had. Troops accounted for much of the passenger increase. ''We had every kind of a passenger train we ever owned in those troop trains,'' recalled an officer. Regular service was cut back and trains were lengthened to get more work out of each engine. Since troop trains had priority in dispatching, the juggling of train movements became a nightmare. ''There's many days and nights,'' groaned an officer, ''that we had trains in almost every siding between Cheyenne and Ogden.''[46]

Some troop trains carried their own government kitchens installed in baggage cars; others were conventional passenger trains with diners or regular passenger runs with extra cars attached. Omaha's Union Station was fixed up with sleeping, lounge, reading and game rooms, showers, and plenty of coffee, doughnuts, and cigarettes for service men. In June 1942 there was no facility like it in the country.* The company also sent Tom Murray to run the station restaurant at Cheyenne, which found itself swamped with business as troop trains rolled through day and night. Since the bus depot shared the driveway, Murray also fed their passengers.[47]

The personable Murray quickly learned to apply the techniques of mass production in managing what became an early version of fast food. His crews churned out 10,000 box lunches and made 10,000 doughnuts a month along with gallons of coffee. ''We had the largest business on the railroad during the war,'' he said proudly, ''. . . and we called it the League of Nations because we had whites, blacks, Filipinos, Mexicans, everyone working. Had a crew of 25 people, and we were open 24 hours a day.'' North Platte boasted a canteen that became famous for making troops feel at home. People from miles around poured into town to greet the troops with free food and cakes for those who had birthdays.[48]

The traffic flooding over the Union Pacific was by no means confined to people. World War II triggered an economic boom in the West that transformed the region from a backward outback into a national trend-setter. California alone got 10 percent of all federal monies spent during the war. One federal agency, the Defense Plant Corporation, emerged as the largest single investor in the West. Among other things it built the world's largest magnesium plant near Boulder Dam outside Las Vegas, and two complete steel fabricating plants—one of them in Provo, Utah. Another agency, the Metal Reserves Corporation, spurred metals production in the Rocky Mountain states, and new military bases sprang up everywhere. Utah alone got ten of them, where 60,000 people were stationed and another 60,000 employed.[49]

*All the roads using Union Station collaborated on providing the service facilities there.

PREPAREDNESS: A trainload of armored trucks heads off to camp in this early version of piggyback, September 1941.

This boom, coupled with the buildup for the Pacific war, threw an unprecedented amount of traffic over the Los Angeles line. This was the weak link in the system, especially the 171-mile stretch between Las Vegas and Yermo, California. While the entire 654-mile line was single track, this portion had only 7 miles of level track, heavy curvature, and rugged grades that required a fleet of helper engines. Eastbound trains needed as many as three helpers between Kelso and Cima, the highest point on the line. Here was a classic bottleneck, the dispatcher's nightmare even in normal times.[50]

The prewar daily traffic included three passenger trains, a streamliner, and four westbound and three eastbound freight trains. By June 1942 the volume had increased 50 percent and spawned serious delays. A year later the load reached a daily average of 7.2 eastbound and 9.6 westbound freight trains, with a corresponding increase in passenger trains as well as four to six extra troop trains run twice a week. During that year the number of loaded westbound cars soared 95 percent and the number of eastbound empties 130 percent. The strain threatened to throw the entire line into gridlock.[51]

To avert disaster, the Union Pacific rushed work on what became the nation's longest existing span of centralized traffic control (CTC) over the

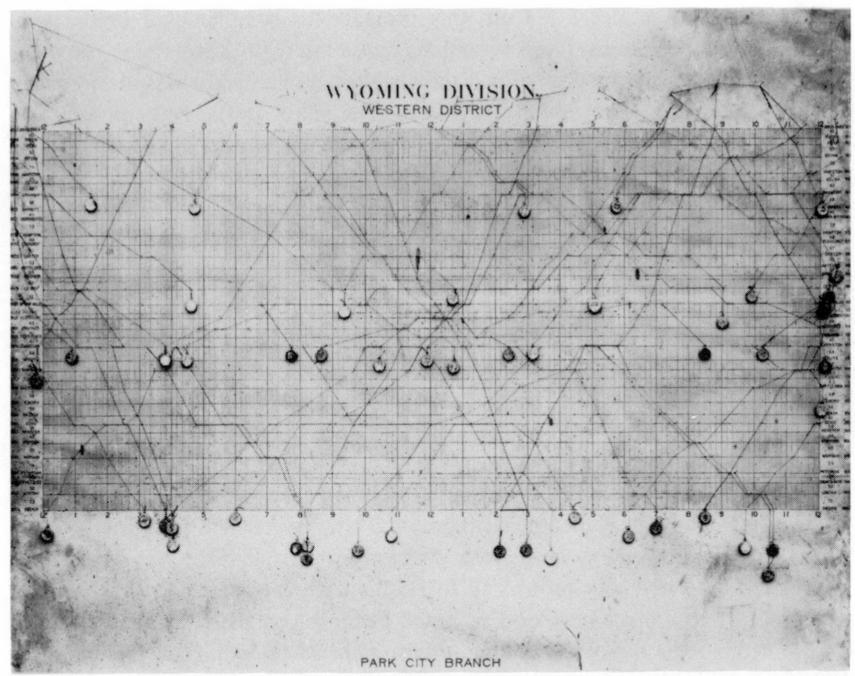

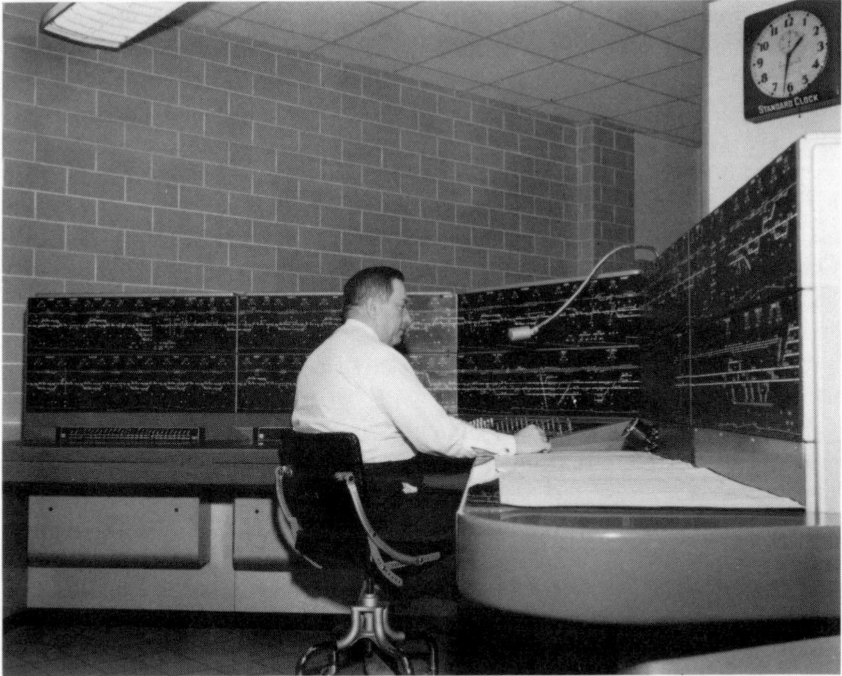

IMPROVEMENTS: Train control developed from (A) the old train chart of 1909 to (B) the sleek Centralized Traffic Control (CTC) installation at Kansas City in 1968.

entire 171-mile bottleneck.* Until that project was completed in June 1943, however, the operations force scrambled desperately to keep trains moving. Driven as always by the czar's lash, they performed heroically despite frequent tieups that brought out the worst in Jeffers. The heavy traffic and constant call for helper engines made power assignments even trickier than usual, and Jeffers's sympathies always leaned toward dispatchers in any dispute.[52]

Connors believed the division simply lacked enough power to move so huge a load; Jeffers dismissed this as the lame excuse of officers who weren't getting the job done. Privately Connors thought Jeffers was defensive about the power supply because he had not bought enough when he had the chance before the war. Now it was too late; Averell Harriman was urging Charske to "hold Jeff down" on locomotive purchases because prices had more than doubled. Unable to get more power, Jeffers insisted the division make do with what it had. When the congestion worsened in February 1943, he sent John Gale to investigate.[53]

Why Gale? In September 1942 the government had summoned Jeffers to a post in Washington. Although he monitored the railroad closely, the lack of direct touch inflamed his suspicions about every crisis. Gale was his closest confidant, the only man he trusted to be his eyes and ears. Before leaving, Jeffers had put senior vice-president Frank Robinson in charge, but as Connors later noted, "actually Gale was running the railroad in conjunction with [Paul] Rigdon," Jeffers's assistant, and N. C. Peterson, the head of maintenance. At Jeffers's behest Gale toured the line like an ambassador without portfolio, somewhat in the manner of Silas Seymour during the construction era.[54]

Gale told Jeffers exactly what he wanted to hear: there was ample power for the work if officers would quit wasting the dispatchers' time and let them do their job. Connors confirmed that in one 24-hour period officers and others spent 5½ hours on the telephone with dispatchers getting "lineups or historical data or just drivel." That was all Jeffers needed. While Gale went on to inspect the Northwest division, Jeffers blasted everyone in sight. "It is about time that Connors woke up to the fact that he has some responsibility as an operating Vice President and put a stop to this nonsense," he roared. "Unless there is an improvement in that territory I propose to put Gale on one of these jobs and see if we can't get one practical hard headed man to clean it up. . . . I am fed up on excuses."[55]

When Connors tried to ease the strain by shifting power from the Utah to the Los Angeles district, Jeffers ordered that Gale be advised of any such transfers. This was a classic Jeffers's twist: he insisted that officers exercise their responsibility, then jumped on them the moment they did something he disliked. Once Gale had "cleaned up" the Northwest, Jeffers sent him back to take charge in Los Angeles. "I have said to Gale," he told the others, "that I would give him a week or ten days to clean it up. If he doesn't I am going to fly out there and take the job over myself." From distant Washington he also

*Centralized traffic control is a system that enables a dispatcher to set all switches and trackside signals along entire stretches of track from a control panel at one central location.

My Sentiments
Wm Jeffers
"Daddy, ain't you got a uniform?"
"Yes, son, this is my uniform"
THE RAILROADS ARE THE FIRST LINE OF DEFENSE
"KEEP 'EM ROLLING"

POINTED AUTOGRAPH: Jeffers got his message across in many ways, including his autograph on this 1944 poster.

attacked "the perfectly silly notion that that territory has reached the saturation point. There is 20% slack in that operation." Yet at the same time he told Charske that traffic on the Los Angeles district "has about reached the saturation point."[56]

The congestion eased in April, but Connors thought it had more to do with diversion of traffic than anything Gale did. "Iron Hat" stroked the boss in another report and moved on to the Wyoming Division, where failure to meet freight schedules threw the czar into another rage. "We may get tight for power at certain spots," he conceded, "but that is just what we have high priced officers for—to distribute this power so we can get the work out of it." He ripped local officers for letting their subordinates do the job for them. What he wanted was "not playing at railroading, not putting on any Gilbert and Sullivan Opera buffet [sic], but just doing a bang-up job of horse-sense railroading, which we are not getting from the officers of any district on the Union Pacific."[57]

There was, of course, an edge of calculation in these outbursts. Intimidation was a tool Jeffers used to drive his people, but the strain caused him to overuse it and blunt its effectiveness. He hounded one superintendent in Wyoming, Bert Wedge, into retiring rather than having to endure more attacks by the "Big Boss" or " 'Himmler' Gale and his 'Gestapo.' " Wedge warned his friend Connors that a "very definite undercurrent of unrest and disloyalty" was rampant in the ranks, and the unions were furious over the "Gestapo" tactics then in vogue. Matters were "resting upon a keg of powder and could be set off by some unusual or improper disciplinary action."[58]

The crises mounted faster than Jeffers could muster threats to combat them. In August the Nebraska Division got snarled, and he threatened again to take it over personally. Ten engines were rushed from Wyoming to help out, only to be retrieved when the Wyoming Division backed up. When that crisis eased in September, Jeffers pointedly thanked John Gogerty, superintendent of motive power, and blasted Connors for getting in Gogerty's way. One incident revealed how much his thinking had hardened. An engine foreman devised an alternative method of braking on heavy mountain grades. Tests showed it to be successful, but Jeffers objected to any "brain trusting" that changed "long standing rules and regulations and long standing practices."[59]

The coming on line of CTC eased but did not solve the crunch at many points. As more greenhorns joined the force and more traffic poured over the road, accidents increased. Always a bear on safety, Jeffers exploded every time news of an accident reached him. But no amount of ranting could cure what was a legitimate crisis. Despite the grumbling and backbiting and some slacking, the men performed heroically under difficult conditions and enormous pressure. The czar praised their contribution in a soft voice while lashing them on loudly, as was his style. His tone was made even more sour by the bleak state of labor relations at the national level.[60]

In December 1942 the trainmen's unions renewed their demand for a 30 percent wage hike while fifteen nonoperating unions pressed for a raise of 20 cents an hour. A rate cut in the spring of 1943 threw these claims into bold relief, but the carriers again disagreed over how to meet the challenge. When an emergency board appointed by President Roosevelt awarded the operating unions a 4.5 percent increase in September 1943, the trainmen snubbed it as insulting. All twenty unions voted to strike on December 30.[61]

As the dispute raged and the deadline neared, Roosevelt intervened in typical fashion. He persuaded the nonoperating unions to stay at work and, by offering higher raises than the award, induced two of the operating unions to withdraw their strike vote. When the others held firm, he seized the railroads on December 27. Unlike 1917, the government's reign was brief. The three holdout unions accepted the raise offered the others, and the strike ended in mid-January. Although the crisis passed, labor relations remained on edge, an explosion waiting to happen once the war wound down.[62]

Not all railroaders fought the war at home. Their skills were needed overseas as well, even in theaters where American troops were not fighting. The Military Railway Service (MRS) had a distinguished history tracing back to the Civil War. Since World War I it had existed on paper, gradually adopting a battalion organization equivalent to that of a division superintendent. The headquarters unit, known as a grand division, presided over operating and shop battalions. Originally part of the Engineers Corps, MRS was moved to the newly created Transportation Corps in November 1942.[63]

Since 1916 MRS had consisted of units sponsored by or affiliated with individual railroads, which furnished all the necessary officers for the unit. During World War II the Union Pacific staffed the 702 Grand Division and the 723 Railway Operating Battalion, which was mobilized in December 1943 and saw extensive service in Europe. Another operating battalion was organized but never activated. The company also achieved the distinction of having far more men attached to the MRS headquarters unit than any of the thirty-four other railroads represented there, and the man who became director general of MRS was none other than Carl Gray, Jr.[64]

The 702 got first call to action. At the Cairo conference in the summer of 1942 the allies agreed to send MRS units to run the Iranian State Railway, a vital link in the movement of lend-lease supplies to Russia. Art Stoddard went to command the 702 with a typical blessing from Jeffers, who barked, "Put that goddamned Stoddard in charge of it!" For Stoddard the assignment could not have come at a better time. By leaving for military duty in September 1942, he avoided being fired yet again as head of the Wyoming Division; a month later he found himself in Iran, where he performed well. In September 1944 Stoddard was shifted to Europe; later he replaced Gray as general manager of First MRS.[65]

Apart from the units, which contained large numbers of Union Pacific men, individual officers went on special assignments. Harriman and Lovett were the first to depart, and Otto Jabelmann was anxious to follow. Harriman wanted him in England to help the British with their rail problems, but with his heart condition no Omaha doctor would let him go. Undaunted, Jabelmann went to New York, got a doctor there to okay the trip, and hurried to England in the fall of 1942. On January 6, 1943, he dropped dead of a heart attack, and was paid a glowing tribute by British rail men for the service he had rendered in that short time.[66]

In September 1942 Jeffers himself was tapped. A personal call from President Roosevelt summoned him to Washington, where he went immediately to the White House and was shown a report on the making of synthetic rubber.

Japanese supremacy in the Far East had cut the United States off from supplies of natural rubber. A committee chaired by Bernard Baruch noted in its brief report that the knowhow existed to make synthetic rubber, but attempts to build plants had run afoul of the priority system, which allowed other programs to grab critical components before the new plant could get them. "Of all critical and strategic materials," the report warned, "rubber is the one which presents the greatest threat to the safety of our nation and the success of the Allied cause." It urged that someone be placed in charge who could bull the program through these obstacles.[67]

Roosevelt wanted Jeffers to be that someone. Evidently he got the idea from Donald M. Nelson of Sears, who had been a Union Pacific director before heading up the War Production Board. The report called for a rubber administrator, but Jeffers demurred. The trouble with the war effort, he told Roosevelt, is that there were already too many administrators. "I'm going to be rubber director," he said flatly, "or I'm not coming." He was given the title of director and placed under Nelson, who delegated to him all authority for the rubber program. The title proved a moot point because the press promptly gave him a more fitting one: the "Rubber Czar."[68]

"The country will expect of Mr. Jeffers," said the New York *Times,* "only that he do a thorough, competent job without worrying about 'public reaction,' the elections or any political considerations." Little did the *Times* suspect how ruthlessly Jeffers would comply with these criteria.[69]

Washington was surprised at the choice, and still more surprises were soon forthcoming. When the first wave of interviewers had been handled, Jeffers flew to New York to consult Baruch and inform the Union Pacific board that he would run both the rubber program and the railroad. From there he flew to Omaha with Steve Hannagan, basked in a huge civic welcome, lined up the troops in the home office and gave them their marching orders, cleaned up some loose ends, and flew back to Washington. He had told Roosevelt he would take the job for one year; that was all the time he needed to get it done.[70]

The nation got a quick taste of the czar's style. His first act was to thank and fire everyone associated with the rubber program so that he could replace them with industry experts. When one unhappy victim hissed, "I'll ruin you," Jeffers fixed his steely glare on the man and said, "I'd be a damn poor Irishman if I let an SOB like you ruin me."[71]

Ten days after taking charge, he ordered nationwide gasoline rationing to conserve both fuel and rubber, and imposed a 35 miles-per-hour speed limit. The Baruch report had urged both moves, and Jeffers did not flinch from hitting Americans in their favorite place, the automobile. Impressed by the no-nonsense approach of the Baruch report, which one observer called "the toughest report in the history of the New Deal," Jeffers took it as gospel for the program he launched. A month after his arrival the Senate Agriculture Committee summoned Jeffers before it. The czar had upset cotton state senators with plans to expand rayon production for use in tires instead of cotton cord.[72]

Senators "Cotton Ed" Smith of South Carolina and Kenneth McKellar of Tennessee went after Jeffers in the usual Potomac style of letting newcomers know who was boss. But Jeffers dished it right back. The army wanted rayon because they thought it was better, he told them, and he was going to give the army what it wanted. Unable to budge Jeffers, Smith muttered, "Whose bread I eat, his song I sing"—implying that the rayon and other interests were influencing him. Jeffers leaped at the opening. "I resent that remark, senator," he shouted. "I don't intend to be influenced by anybody, anywhere, any time. . . . The whole damned thing has been muddled up for months and I'm going through with this or else."[73]

Smith tried to back off, but Jeffers would not relent. "We have gambled too damned long already on the rubber situation," he snapped. "I'm not going to put myself in a position where it can be said that I haven't the intelligence or guts to do a job. The trouble with this whole situation is that it has been a muddle of men who were afraid that some Congressional committee or pressure group wouldn't like their decisions. I am going to make my decisions and I'll stand by them."[74]

Any Union Pacific officer was painfully familiar with this sort of outburst, the language of which came straight out of the telegrams Jeffers dispatched to them. But neither jaded Washington nor the nation was prepared for it. The press howled gleefully, and the country had a new celebrity. "Here at last," chortled the New York *Herald-Tribune*, "is a man in high position who says in blunt words what every American has longed to hear said by those in charge of our war program in Washington." In that instant the legend of Jeffers as folk hero zoomed to national stature.[75]

And Jeffers lived up to it while he was in Washington. "He never asked a favor down there," said his secretary Doc Churchill, who was with Jeffers for most of his stay. "He was a straightforward, a straight shooter all the way. He asked no favors, he did not play politics, he did not go any place."[76]

Churchill knew this from painful experience, being compelled to share the czar's monklike regimen. Instead of cells they occupied a nice suite at the Mayflower Hotel, but it might as well have been a monastery. For nine months they ate virtually every breakfast and dinner in that suite. Only twice in that time did they go anywhere: once to a performance of *Blossom Time*, and once to a Washington Senators' baseball game. Jeffers enjoyed the game, especially when an Irish catcher got into a fight at home plate, but he never went to another one.[77]

Every day he followed the same routine. Breakfast arrived at 7:30, after which Howard Blanchard, the Union Pacific man in Washington and Carl Gray's former secretary, drove them to the office. Around 6 p.m. Blanchard picked them up and returned them to the Mayflower. Churchill got the evening papers on the way upstairs, and, depending on Jeffers's mood, they would read, visit, or work until 7 p.m., when they listened to the news from Fulton Lewis, Jr. At 7:15 Churchill switched off the radio and ordered dinner from room service. At 8 the radio went back on to hear H. V. Kaltenborn, then off again at 8:15 for another round of reading, visiting, or work. Sometime around 9 p.m. Jeffers would look at his watch and say, "Let's go for a walk, Doc."[78]

For nine months they walked the same route, turning left at the hotel door and doing a big circle around several blocks, always getting back around 9:30. On the way up Churchill got the morning papers, and they would read, visit, or work until close to midnight, when Jeffers turned in. "Anything special for breakfast?" Churchill would ask. "No, you order it," came the unvarying reply. Next morning, the routine began again. Jeffers made a few trips for the War Production Board, and an occasional one to Omaha. Otherwise, he kept to his stark schedule with the grim determination of one who had no other interests in life and allowed nothing to get in the way of what he had to do.

Just as the railroad had been his life, now for a few months it was rubber, and he gave it the same unswerving dedication. The heat exchanger bottleneck was a classic example. Under the priority system the Navy's escort vessel and the Air Force's high-octane programs vied with the rubber program for these critical parts, with each one grabbing units by waving a higher priority. Jeffers called Charlie Hardy of American Car and Foundry and asked if he could make heat exchangers.

"I don't know," answered Hardy. "What are they?"

"I don't know," said Jeffers, "but I'll put a man on a plane today to come up to Boston to explain it to you."

A day or two later Hardy called back and said, "Yeah, Bill, we can make them."

This was quintessential Jeffers. The bottleneck vanished as American Car and Foundry turned out all the heat exchangers the military needed. Jeffers demonstrated the weakness of the priority system, which was soon changed to an allocation system that did what Jeffers had done: ask everyone how many of an item were needed, and "just tell American industry you need 10,000 heat exchangers, and then get out of their way and they will make them for you."[79]

To produce synthetic rubber, Jeffers had to solve huge technical problems, wheedle enough critical materials to get the plants built, and survive the bureaucratic infighting that was the national pastime in Washington. None of it came easy. The czar fought with the oil states, who resented rationing, skeptics who doubted he knew enough to do the job, the military services who wanted their own "experts" involved, the Army Air Force, news commentator Elmer Davis, and his own boss, Donald Nelson. At one point Roosevelt had to call Nelson and Jeffers in to mediate their squabbling. As they got up to leave, Roosevelt said in his grand manner, "Well, you fellows are just going to have to get together."

Jeffers glared at him and replied, "Well, we're not going to get together on the basis of anything I heard here today." And walked out.[80]

"In Washington few die and none resign, if they can possibly avoid it," quipped a reporter who marked Jeffers as an exception. Jeffers wanted only to get his job done and go home to the railroad. He was racing against time in two ways: his pledge to hold the job only a year, and the dwindling stockpile of reserve rubber that would barely make it through 1943. If Jeffers did not have the synthetic plants on line soon, the war effort would be in deep trouble. Doggedly he pushed the work until he felt confident enough to predict in June

PUBLIC HERO: One of many political cartoons, this one from the Washington *Evening Star,* saluting Jeffers's performance as rubber czar.

1943 that production by the year's end would exceed 850,000 long tons, a higher figure than any previous import of natural rubber.[81]

Jeffers had won the race. In September it was clear that synthetic rubber production would meet all expectations by the years's end. True to his word, Jeffers resigned his post and went back to Omaha. It was an odd resignation by Washington standards: no recriminations or complaints, no undertones of ideology or political infighting, no messages sent other than "the job is done." As many commentators stressed, however, this message was itself a rarity in the capital. The press and government officials alike heaped praise on his performance, as did Bernard Baruch, who wrote Jeffers a gracious letter that called him a "champion of champions."[82]

The czar's legend had gone national, and with it his scorn for experts trying to do the work of practical men. As his speaking engagements multiplied, the theme grew as familiar as it had been on the railroad. "This is just another instance," he said of one man who had moved into the rubber program, "of the Phi Beta Kappa boys trying to get themselves into the spotlight.'' The press loved his tough, two-fisted image, and so did the country. For the rubber program Jeffers had been the right man at the right time. He had bulled it through the bureaucratic maze just as Roosevelt had hoped he would.[83]

For the railroad men in Omaha, however, the message from the czar was quite a different and more chilling one: he was coming back. The honeymoon was over.[84]

22

The Misfits

As early as 1944, E. J. Connors and the personnel staff began grappling with the question of how to handle returning veterans. The Union Pacific had 12,000 employees in the armed forces and expected to have 3,000 more by the time the war ended. Already some unions were pressing to have the returnees absorbed without discharging any of their replacements, who had swelled the union ranks. Some unions advocated a thirty-hour work week for forty hours of pay as a way to avoid postwar unemployment. The situation looked alarming. Since 1922 the proportion of wages to total operating expenses had never been less than 50 percent; by 1943 it had risen to nearly 56 percent. War had also dramatically reversed a shrinking payroll, hiking it from 32,000 in 1938 to 60,000 in 1943.[1]

A host of problems surrounded this transition. In 1944 the company still had not solved the immediate problem of constant turnover and instability in its wartime work force. The labor situation was still volatile, not only on the national scene but also in the growing number of grievances on the line. Connors managed to settle a long dispute over wage rates for section and extra gang labor, but new spats mounted faster than old ones could be resolved.[2]

The crush of war traffic did not ease, especially over the Los Angeles line and its beleagured feeder, the Wyoming Division. By 1943 the division was handling the heaviest load west of the Mississippi River; a third of *all* transcontinental traffic passed over it. Since 1941 a rash of accidents had plagued the division and marred the Union Pacific's proud safety record. To Jeffers's chagrin, most of them had resulted from rules violations by experienced railroaders. This only reinforced his suspicion that the officers were not doing their jobs, not enforcing the rules or getting out on the line enough. The men were fine; it was their superiors who were falling down. The shop force too was badly worn down and short of supervisory personnel.[3]

The czar's response to this sea of woes was predictable. "What I am going to do now," he decreed, "is build up an organization of two-fisted operating men. Naturally we need experts, but experts are not going to control this situation."[4]

Building an organization, two-fisted or otherwise, was precisely what Jeffers did not do, and the failure came back to haunt him as well as the company. In this area he fell far short of Gray, who once said that if he couldn't build an organization in three years that could run without him, he hadn't done his job. When Gray retired, he left behind an organization several men deep in key areas. In only six years Jeffers turned that strength into weakness, leaving in his wake a depleted and demoralized officer corps.[5]

Jeffers liked to talk about the importance of building an organization, but everything he did worked against that goal. The czar's way of ruling through fear and intimidation had predictable results. His tactic of praising the rank and file while pounding away mercilessly at his officers broke their spirit and drove many of them from the company. Instead of grooming potential heirs, he seemed to view ambitious officers as threats to his throne and so got rid of them. Although Jeffers captured glory enough on his own, he regarded any given to subordinates as snatched from himself and could not tolerate anyone vying with him for the spotlight.

Worst of all, the czar's use of his secret police to spy on officers created dark pools of intrigue and disloyalty within the ranks. Resentment burned fiercely everywhere in an atmosphere so paranoid that it was hard even for conscientious managers to adopt any attitude other than every man for himself. Like child abuse, this tradition of rule through intimidation transferred itself from one generation to another as newly promoted officers heaped on subordinates the same humiliation that had been inflicted on them.

This went beyond the usual rite of initiation or paying of dues. On the Union Pacific it left the management in shambles and the ranks often bereft of talent or loyalty to anything beyond personal ambitions. An older, finer tradition lay in ruins, the ironic debris of Jeffers's desire to preserve the past in his own peculiar way. The czar's reign of terror and his fear of successors ensured that the Omaha management would have more than its share of misfits.

When Jeffers left for Washington in late 1942, he placed senior vice-president Frank Robinson in nominal charge of the road. As the senior officer he seemed the logical choice, but Jeffers had more in mind. Appointing Robinson enabled him to avoid choosing between George Ashby and E. J. Connors, the most likely successors to the throne. Robinson was near retirement and neither a candidate nor likely to get in the way of those who were actually running the road on Jeffers's behalf.[6]

While Connors and Gale circled each other warily on the line, the office was handled by an odd couple who seemed anything but railroaders: George Ashby, the diminutive accountant who was shrewd and inscrutable, and Paul Rigdon, a bear of a man whose hulking figure housed a high-strung personality. Both were intelligent, sensitive men whose ambitions suffered from a fatal flaw. In Ashby's case it was alcohol; in Rigdon's, an inability to control the violent swing of his emotions or remain cool under fire. Rigdon, said a company lawyer, "couldn't take orders from *anyone*; Almighty God couldn't give him an order."[7]

Rigdon had been with Jeffers a long time, and wielded more influence as his office assistant than officers with much grander titles. "A lot of people feared Rigdon more than they feared Jeffers," said Doc Churchill. "He was tough, but he was effective; he got things done." Stan How, who had moved into the front office as Connors's assistant, thought Rigdon had missed his calling in life in not becoming an actor. He liked to recite poetry, to play the piano and sing. He also liked to intimidate people. "He had a lot of brain power," added How, ". . . but he was forceful and *rude* to people. . . . He had a lot of ability and no stability."[8]

The maneuvering over succession to the throne had long since begun. "Watching it from the sidelines was rather interesting," recalled George Proudfit, who had taken a position in the VPO's office in 1943. On his scorecard the cleverest player was Ashby, who improved his prospects by luring others into disaster. "He set up Connors as VPO," said Proudfit, "knowing he couldn't handle it." By 1944 Connors was worn down from the workload and battered into submission by the constant stream of abuse from Jeffers.[9]

But Jeffers needed Connors because of his skill at handling labor contracts. This became painfully clear after May 1944, when Connors was tapped for a post with the Office of Defense Transportation. Labor chiefs welcomed the news, and so did Connors. Jeffers handled it in his usual style. To James F. Byrnes he praised Connors as "unusually intelligent and thoroughly reliable . . . the best posted man in America on labor relations." At a farewell dinner in Omaha, however, when Connors said he had been chosen only because Washington wanted someone from the "great Union Pacific," Jeffers accused him of applauding himself.[10]

Jeffers left Connors's post vacant until November, when it became clear that Washington wanted Connors to stay on longer than expected. Then he startled everyone by appointing Rigdon as acting VPO. No one was more stunned than John Gale, Jeffers's faithful watchdog, who had been made general manager of the Eastern Division in February 1944. Soon afterward, "Iron Hat" suffered a severe heart attack; a friend assured Connors that the news of Rigdon's promotion had caused it. Whether true or not, Gale was finished. Once out of the hospital, he took his pension.[11]

The surprise over Rigdon's appointment almost obscured another promotion, that of Ashby to executive vice-president. Why Ashby was advanced was unclear; Proudfit thought Jeffers did it to give him a raise that could not be done without a change in title. Whatever the reason, the move gave Ashby a leg up in the succession derby. He encouraged Rigdon to take up his new position with zeal, and to stand up to Jeffers when he thought changes were needed. Rigdon needed little prodding. Eagerly he plunged into the work, sending a steady stream of proposed changes in personnel and organization to Jeffers and Ashby.[12]

By the spring of 1945 discontent seethed everywhere in Omaha, in the ranks as well as among the officers intriguing for advancement once the czar fell, in the offices and shops no less than on the line. A martinet named Rudolph Wipprecht had become general auditor in September 1941, and the crack of his whip drove his top assistant into early retirement. Smarting under abuse from what he called ''a German tyrant and an overrated Irish mick . . . more interested in running a slaughter house than a railroad,'' Scott Ure took a job elsewhere at less pay and swore never again to step foot inside the headquarters building. For five years he spoke to no one on the Union Pacific, breaking his silence in 1950 with a letter to Connors, who had asked after him.[13]

It bothered Ure that no one in high office seemed to know or care what was going on. He was not the only auditor who broke under the strain, and men in other areas dropped from the ranks. Most simply didn't fit the czar's mold. Ure craved a harmonious workplace; Jeffers wanted tough, hard-nosed employees like John Gogerty, who became superintendent of motive power and machinery in March 1942. A ''swashbuckling old Irishman,'' as one shopman called him, Gogerty was a likeable but volatile character who, like Jeffers, respected only those who stood up to him. He loved a good fight and once snarled at a VPO, ''I'll live to piss on your grave.''[14]

The turmoil within the company drove more people than usual to leave during the war years, when good jobs could be had elsewhere. Many crumbled under the pressure or, like Ure, grew sick of going to work every day with a knot in their stomach. Gogerty could intimidate people, but he could not solve the tangle in the shops, which were overworked and, in the view of one outsider, outmoded in several practices. Wipprecht could impose efficiency but not harmony, and no one seemed capable of slowing the corrosive spread of dissension in the ranks. ''There is no loyalty existing among the personnel and the conduct of a greater part of the officers is reprehensible,'' said a departed superintendent, ''and the sad part of the picture is that most of their activities are conducted openly so that the rank and file observe it.''[15]

To make matters worse, the czar himself was in poor shape. His wife had suffered a stroke and lost a leg to surgery; some said her mind had been affected as well. Jeffers's own health had begun to trouble him. A prostate problem sapped energy that, at age sixty-nine, he could no longer spare. Beset with woes and nearing retirement, he growled ever louder, but his bite had grown feeble. In April 1945 he notified Charske of his intention to retire when he reached the mandatory age of seventy the following January. For a man whose life had been the railroad, these were the hardest words of all to utter. They were not made public, and they did not bring peace. That summer things grew steadily worse for Jeffers.[16]

''Everything is just the same at the Union Pacific,'' a friend wrote Connors, ''they change so often that I can't tell you who runs anything.'' Several cases

TOUGH BUT SENSITIVE: The burly, quixotic Paul Rigdon, whose long friendship with Jeffers shattered after his appointment as vice-president of operations.

of drunkenness on duty led Jeffers to issue a pointed warning that anyone "from the Executive Vice President down" faced trouble if they were caught "drinking and carousing." The number of labor grievances piled up alarmingly in Connors's absence, for which Jeffers blamed Rigdon. He had long since begun his routine of heaping criticism on the newest VPO despite their long friendship. The prickly Rigdon was poorly equipped to stand this fire, and an explosion was not long in coming.[17]

On July 22 Jeffers left Omaha to attend an Old Timers' picnic in Denver. "It was one of those trips," reported Connors's longtime secretary, "on which [Jeffers] talked to every trainmaster and section foreman on the road and gathered a lot of crap." The czar promptly dumped his gatherings on Rigdon, who called on the morning of July 25 to explain what he had done about them. Jeffers refused even to listen; instead he harangued Rigdon with the old charges of too much supervision via the telephone and the business car and hung up on him.[18]

Something snapped in the volatile Rigdon. He fled Laramie on a 1 a.m. troop train, and on the way back to Omaha dictated a telegram of resignation that began, "I cannot continue to function under the storm of unfair criticism and undeserved abuse which you have dealt out to me within the past few weeks." All his good work to improve officer performance "by courteous methods and encouragement" had gone unappreciated, he complained. "I do not intend to share responsibility for breaking down their morale." A startled Jeffers got the telegram next morning and gave Rigdon twenty-four hours to change his mind. Rigdon not only stood firm but sent Charske and both Harrimans copies of his resignation.[19]

Nothing could have enraged Jeffers more than the exposure of the conflict to New York. He relieved Rigdon at once, telling him to turn in his property like a dismissed trainman. Omaha reeled in shock at the news. An officer with forty-one years' service, who had always been close to Jeffers, had at age fifty-nine thrown up his pension and quit, telling a friend he would be a nervous wreck if he stayed on the job another month. Jeffers, who had gone on to Los Angeles, tried to hurry back but fell ill and had to be hospitalized for a brief time. Charske delicately asked whether in view of Rigdon's long service he might not want to recommend a pension, but Jeffers was too livid even to discuss the matter.*[20]

The news stunned New York. "It is about time that the Board of Directors took a hand in personnel matters," an anonymous letter warned Charske. ". . . Many fine efficient men have been made to walk the plank during the past few years without just cause or reason." In distant Russia Averell Harriman got his copy of Rigdon's letter and fired off a cable letting Charske know he was disturbed by it. "Is someone on the rampage affecting morale generally?" he asked.[21]

Jeffers hastened to explain that Rigdon had done fine so long as he stayed in the office and kept in touch with the czar, "but the moment he got out on the railroad in a business car he went completely off balance." It was, he added, "the same old story of trying to make an operating officer . . . out of a routine clerk, which never has worked and just never will work." Charske in turn told Averell not to worry. "Conditions no different from always," he cabled. "Evidently Rigdon could not take criticism and was precipitate."[22]

To bewildered observers, the situation in Omaha looked near collapse. Jeffers put operations in the hands of Perry J. Lynch, who didn't want the job and wondered privately "how long his sentence will be." It soon became clear that the labor mess had been the major cause of Rigdon's downfall. There were 141 cases before the adjustment boards, and Jeffers had no confidence in any of the officers handling them. The only man he trusted on labor affairs was Connors, who was still in Washington. After leaving ODT in March 1945, he had been tapped for a special assignment by the White House. Jeffers was miffed but did not want to ask Connors to return. Now there was little choice; on August 9 he summoned Connors back to a newly created vice-presidency handling labor, reorganization, and efficiency.[23]

The return of Connors heated up the already torrid infight over succession. Connors and his friends hoped the new position meant he was the chosen heir. "If there ever existed a property that needs some one at the head who understands the results obtainable from co-ordination and co-operation it is the U. P.," confided former superintendent Bert Wedge. Another friend told Con-

*A few months later, Rigdon returned to the Union Pacific as curator of its museum, and performed the invaluable service of organizing the company's old records into the *Historical Catalogue* that proved so helpful to me in writing volume I.

nors bluntly, "I am sure that you will be the next President of Union Pacific if he will only die." Ashby's friends boasted that their man would become president and fire Connors as his first act. Jeffers heightened the mystery by running the road from Los Angeles, where he had taken an option on a house next door to Bob Hope. In October he underwent surgery for his prostate condition.[24]

In fact, Connors was never in the running. Nothing revealed more strikingly the vacuum in New York than the handling of the succession question. Two months after Jeffers made known his wish to retire, Roland Harriman held lengthy talks with Charske and Jeffers. Charske made it clear he did not want the title of president or any arrangement that required him to move to Omaha. He and Jeffers agreed that Ashby was the only alternative. "There isn't anyone else on the property who can even be considered," they told Roland, "and if Ashby doesn't make the grade we will have to look elsewhere."[25]

Why Connors was ignored is not clear, although he had been ill that summer. The lack of other candidates, however, demonstrates graphically how barren the ranks had grown during Jeffers's reign. It would have made sense to look elsewhere; after all, Judge Lovett had found Gray that way. But the Union Pacific, like most roads, was a deeply inbred company. Roland Harriman simply accepted the judgment of Charske and Jeffers on the choice, and a plan was devised. Ashby would remain executive vice-president and be told just before Jeffers retired that the presidency was his if he performed well after Jeffers left. In effect, he would be given a trail run. Charske would become president pro tem but remain in New York.[26]

Unfortunately, the plan went awry. Jeffers recovered slowly from his operation and could not do his part. Aware that something had to be done at the December board meeting, he and Charske agreed that Ashby's performance warranted his appointment as president. Jeffers reaffirmed that Ashby was "the logical man for the assignment." An uneasy Roland wanted to defer action until Averell returned, but Averell urged him not to wait because the date of his return from Russia was uncertain. Reluctantly Roland recommended to the board that Ashby be appointed.[27]

There was in this and other episodes an echo of Oliver Ames and Charles Francis Adams, Jr., fumbling about in search of the right man for a job without knowing well either the men or the job. Later Roland in his gentle way blamed Jeffers for the mistake, while Averell blamed his brother. "Roland didn't have the experience," he said. ". . . I was abroad, and I never would have appointed him, and I was very unhappy when [Roland] appointed him, because I knew him." Yet Averell approved the decision and offered no suggestions. He thought well of Connors but for some reason did not push his name forward. Perhaps he felt too far removed from events and personalities to take a strong role.[28]

Jeffers knew there was bad feeling between the two rivals. "I don't know what it is that is between you and Connors," he told Ashby shortly before news of the succession was announced, "but whatever it is must be ironed out. There are some rather ugly rumors floating about." In this half-hearted way did the czar belatedly address the internecine warfare his management style had done so much to spawn.[29]

Early in 1945 Art Stoddard in distant Europe heard that Averell Harriman planned changes after the war in which some officers "that have not been too favorably considered in the past, will be among those running the railroad." In November he received a letter from "Big Boss" in Moscow urging the Union Pacific men overseas to get home as soon as possible and hinting that he himself would soon be back on the job in New York. But "Big Boss" did not return, and many officers like Stoddard who had gone abroad came home to find themselves in jobs where they were subordinate to men they had formerly outranked.[30]

Instead of returning to the Union Pacific Averell Harriman plunged into another government job as Secretary of Commerce, which forced him to sever all ties with the railroad in October 1946. Roland had taken his place during the war, he said later, "and when I came back after the war was over, I didn't want to disturb him, so he stayed on and I didn't go back. . . . We were very close friends and partners in business, and I didn't want to interfere with his position." At the dawn of a momentous new era in railroading, the Union Pacific found itself with both a new chairman of the board and a new president.[31]

Other changes followed. Robert Lovett returned only to be lured away a year later to another government post, a pattern he would repeat for eight years. Joseph F. Mann, who succeeded the late Henry Clark as general counsel, preserved the close tie to Clark, Carr & Ellis; a protégé of George Ellis, he too belonged to the firm. Jeffers kept his seat on the board and received the same honorary post of vice-chairman given earlier to Gray. Three new directors, Artemus L. Gates, John J. McCloy, and John S. Sinclair, joined the board.[32]

Woody Charske remained the glue that held the New York office together, but at sixty-four he was slowing down. Like Ashby he was an accountant rather than a railroad man, and must have welcomed a president who spoke his language. The soft-spoken Texan, who had graduated from Texas A & M in 1901 just in time to catch the Harriman whirlwind on the Southern Pacific, still managed company finances with aplomb. A quiet, stocky figure with benevolent features beneath a thatch of white hair, Charske was more like a piece of fine furniture than a presence. He lacked the dynamism, the force of presence to lead effectively. Averell Harriman more than made up for Charske's deficiency in this area, but once Roland replaced Averell, the vacuum of leadership yawned wide.[33]

Two brothers had dominated the Union Pacific in its infancy. After the death of Judge Lovett a similar situation emerged with an eerie parallel to the reign of the Ames brothers. Fate pushed Roland into a role similar of that of Oliver Ames: the quiet, uncombative brother thrust into a leadership role he didn't want, one better suited to his more energetic and aggressive brother who could not be there because of government duty.

Their nicknames told the tale. All his life Roland was called "Bunny." Once into politics, Averell became known as "the Crocodile."

THE QUIET MAN: Woody Charske, the financial wizard who gave the New York office stability but not leadership. Taken during an interview in Los Angeles, 1937.

Bunny and the Crocodile. To other eyes they could not have been more different, yet they sprang from common roots. Both had been awkward, unathletic boys, Averell tall and lean, Roland short and plump. Both were quiet, even withdrawn, lost in the formidable shadow of their father. "You know, he's a very shy man," Roland said of his brother, "and always has been. There is nothing more difficult for him to do than to meet and speak to groups of people. But he makes himself. He made himself go into government and politics."[34]

Roland was exactly right. What separated the brothers was that Averell possessed the fierce, unquenchable drive of his father and Roland did not. Averell was brighter, more tenacious, more determined to excel, eager to make himself into something more even though the effort went against his grain. Two details illustrated vividly the difference between them. Both brothers were hard of hearing; Roland wore a hearing aid, but Averell refused to do so until very late in his long life. Part of his reluctance was vanity, part a refusal to submit to weakness.[35]

The brothers also inherited their father's passion for trotting horses. Roland learned early to drive them, and stayed with the sport all his life; indeed, he was credited with keeping it alive. He got his wife interested as well, and the hood of his Mercedes sported not its usual emblem but a bright steel trotter pulling a sulky. Averell also learned to drive trotters but had to quit when the dust aggravated his asthma. Undaunted, he took up polo and made himself into

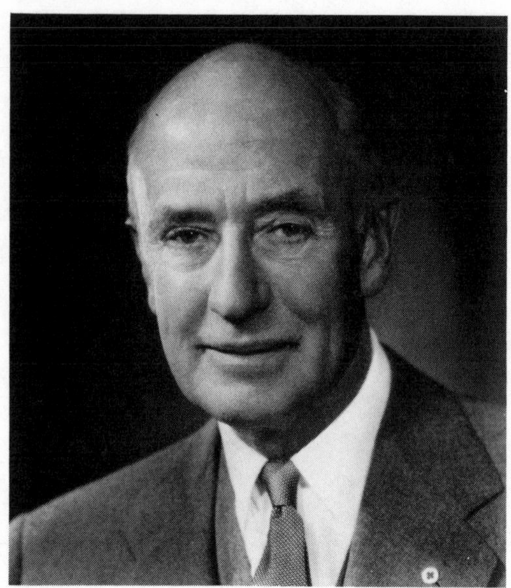

HEIR RELUCTANT: E. Roland Harriman, the youngest son of E. H. Harriman, who succeeded his brother as chairman of the Union Pacific board in 1946.

a world class player. Robert Lovett thought this a perfect image for comparing the brothers: Averell ran while Bunny trotted.[36]

Like a good English cleric, Roland was content with the ancient verities of his class and family, and never let his life or his ambitions stray beyond them. If he ever glimpsed the darker, more intense side of human complexity, he showed no sign of it. His nature had the sweetness, the simplicity of a good fellow who wore his heart on his sleeve. There was nothing prissy or self-righteous about him. To everyone, he was gracious, accommodating, and forever pleasant.

"Roland's was a more calm approach to things . . . very much more low-keyed," observed Elbridge T. Gerry of Brown Brothers Harriman, whose mother was a Harriman. "There wasn't anything high-powered about him until you crossed him." He could be argued with, added Gerry, "but once he made a decision, you didn't reopen the case." The soul of tact and discretion, he preferred management by consensus, which is why the arrangement at Brown Brothers Harriman suited him so well. "Roland Harriman," said Gerry firmly, "was never one to give an order."[37]

But sometimes orders had to be given and feathers ruffled. Unfortunately, Roland shared another quality with Oliver Ames, that early president whose good intentions paved more than one hellish road. "He didn't like controversy," said Reg Sutton. "He didn't want any. He always wanted things done quietly. If anybody was getting in trouble, just ease [him] out and don't make an issue of it."[38]

While Averell set forth to conquer new worlds, Roland stayed home to mind the family fortune and tend the things that always mattered most to him: family, friends, firm, and the railroad his father had built. Where Averell was attuned to change, Roland was the traditionalist, the conservator. They even belonged to different political parties. "It's never caused the slightest difference between us," Roland chuckled, "mostly, I suppose, because we never talk about it. Anyway, as I tell everyone, Ave is my favorite Democrat."[39]

These differences in nature and temperament were reflected in their handling of the railroad. In the 1930s Averell had responded to a major crisis in the rail industry with a bold program that overhauled not only the road's equipment but its public image as well. However one views his strategy, he did not hesitate to make sweeping changes in this stodgiest of industries, just as his father had done. In 1946 Roland found himself in a similar position, although its gravity was not immediately apparent. He took charge at a critical time when almost every basic element of the industry seemed on the verge of major change, and intermodal competition resumed in even more virulent form.

Roland's response to this tide of change was cautious but not timid. Like Judge Lovett, his instincts were those of the steward, and in this case for much the same reason. The railroad held a special place in Roland's affections because of its long family association. His father had made a spectacular success by introducing new methods that became the seedbed of tradition. Like so many stewards, Roland missed the point of his father's triumph: the key lay not merely in the new methods but in his understanding that changed conditions required new approaches.

He was the most improbable president since Charles Francis Adams, and his brief reign careened wildly between comedy and tragedy. At its abrupt end he was a ruined man whose downfall was hailed with a mixture of cheers and sighs of relief. Yet he was also a bright, far-sighted man who tried doggedly to inject fresh ideas into the cold dead hand of tradition so venerated by the czar. That he was not perceived as a "real" railroader did much to hurt his cause; that he could not control himself ultimately destroyed it.

The riddle of George F. Ashby began with his origins, which were anything but ordinary. Born in Mount Airy, North Carolina, in September 1885, he was the grandson of one of the original Siamese twins. Chang and Eng had moved to Mount Airy in 1845 and raised their families there. Ashby's mother Rosella was the ninth child of Eng, and the only one of Eng's daughters to raise a family. She was only fourteen when the twins died in 1874.[40]

No one knows what effect this bizarre lineage had on Ashby. Some of those who knew him believed these roots gave his character an Oriental twist. "[Ashby] had an Asiatic mind . . . always worked by indirection," said one officer. "Being of Oriental descent," agreed another, "[he] was very suspicious of people." Certainly he marched to a different drummer than most railroaders and so was an enigma to them. "Very peculiar sense of humor," admitted an assistant. "You weren't quite sure you knew what he was laughing at."[41]

After graduating from Mount Airy High School, Ashby landed a job as purchasing clerk with the Atlantic Coast Line in 1906. Later that same year he moved to the Seaboard Air Line, and in 1911 to the Navigation Company,

TO BE OR NOT TO BE: The enigmatic George F. Ashby in a contemplative moment.

where he spent ten years in the engineering, operating, and executive departments. His skill as a statistician impressed everyone; he was as quick with figures as he was with an acid remark. Even then, however, he had already begun grappling with the bottle. Stan How recalled that his friends in Portland used to lend Ashby drinking money. In 1921 Ashby went to the Union Pacific, and thirteen years later got the promotion to Jeffers's assistant that launched him upward.[42]

He could not have been more unlike Jeffers. A small, wiry man with squinty eyes behind wire spectacles, Ashby was sensitive about his size—a sore spot heightened, Reg Sutton thought, by a Jeffers training program that accepted only big, strapping recruits. More than one railroader believed that Ashby did not like tall men. He was overly courteous and generous, the sort who never let anyone else pick up a check, yet he could be sarcastic and withering in his criticism. There was in his nature an element of unpredictability that unsettled people, and a nasty streak that came out when he drank too much.[43]

"You never misunderstood anything Mr. Jeffers said," said Doc Churchill, who worked for both Jeffers and Ashby. "It was plain and it was direct, and it had an urgency to it. But with George Ashby you just never were sure of him, and you never could predict him either." Stan How agreed: "Sometimes he would write you a note, and he would word it in such a way that you couldn't understand it. He'd just toy you with that note."[44]

Ashby dwelled in Jeffers's giant shadow in every sense, haunted by his predecessor just as Jeffers had been haunted by Gray. Churchill, who had enlisted after Jeffers ended his year as rubber Czar, came home to work for Ashby and was told at once by others that it was death even to mention Jeffers's name. Ashby wanted nothing to do with Los Angeles because Jeffers lived there, and made his home instead in Las Vegas, which he tried to promote because it was not Los Angeles. Nor did he like giving speeches; possibly he did not want to be compared with Jeffers, who did so well at them.[45]

Once Ashby was at Sun Valley hosting a cocktail party in his room for some friends. Churchill heard the band start to play Irish music as they always did when Jeffers came to visit. He flew down the hall at once and almost crashed into manager Pat Rogers, who was hurrying down another corridor. "I know," Rogers muttered before Churchill could say anything, "God dammit, I'm gonna kill 'em." He warned the band never to play Irish music when Ashby was on the premises. "If you knew what Mr. Jeffers liked," sighed Churchill, "you knew that Mr. Ashby was not going to like it."[46]

The czar's specter affected Ashby in many ways. Fearful of being thought weak because of his size and background, he adopted his own version of the tough guy. He could not be the burly, two-fisted brawler, but he could be hard on those around him, lashing them unmercifully with his tongue instead of his fists. Where Jeffers pounded with the broadsword of abuse, Ashby used the rapier of ridicule. The photograph he liked to give friends showed him lighting a cigarette as if posing for the cover of a detective novel. This attitude led Ashby into a trap that undermined his best intentions: he tried to reform what Jeffers had done by using Jeffers's own tyrannical style.

Above all, it led Ashby, as Churchill admitted, to "prove to everybody that he was a lot better leader than Mr. Jeffers was." This was exactly what the Union Pacific needed in 1946, and Ashby possessed the equipment to do the job. Not being a railroader was actually an advantage except in his dealings with the men. Ashby saw clearly how Jeffers, shackled by traditions that had grown increasingly dear to him as he got older, had let the road fall behind in an era of turbulent change, and how wartime business had battered the physical plant. The end of the war and the change of presidents offered a chance to introduce fresh approaches at every level, to modernize a company that had been coasting on its laurels.[47]

The Union Pacific could afford to coast because it was a rich company and, like all roads, had more business than it could carry during the war. But it was not getting maximum return from the resources at its disposal. Two Harriman traditions had faded badly: high-level maintenance and large investments in innovations if they promised large future returns. Ashby saw what had to be done and was eager to do it. Churchill was not alone in calling him "very sharp mentally, very progressive in his thinking and innovative."[48]

But this clarity of vision coexisted uneasily with a tragic flaw of character. The drinking was part of it, but not the cause; those who knew him agreed there was something more. "He was his own worst enemy," mourned Churchill, "because really he could be very personable and he loved a good time. But . . . he turned everyone against him, and almost deliberately. And no one ever knew why." Reg Sutton thought he knew. "Somewhere in that man," he declared, "was . . . some sort of inferiority complex which resulted in his chief difficulty."[49]

The most revealing insight came from Ashby himself, in a remark overheard by another officer. "I don't want to be president," he told a friend, "but I don't want anybody else to be president."[50]

23

The Blizzard

Ashby wasted little time shuffling his organization. He brought W. H. Guild back from Los Angeles as vice-president and promoted A. J. Seitz to vice-president of traffic when the venerable Robinson retired in June 1946. E. J. Connors stayed on to handle the thorny labor area, and a select group of officers were given raises. The intention, Ashby assured Woody Charske, was to strengthen the organization and its outside relations. New York gave him every support. After Roland Harriman became chairman in October 1946, he scheduled a series of trips west to acquaint himself with the officers there. Ashby invited him to "spend as much time as you can in Omaha and on line with me. . . . The oftener you can come out the better I will like it."[1]

At the outset Ashby determined to shore up the operating organization, which had fallen into disarray. The old divisional structure had been eroded as general managers lost their authority over certain departments, like motive power and machinery. Morale had been shattered and the ranks depleted of promising candidates for promotion. Convinced that operations was understaffed, Ashby pushed some younger men up the ladder anyway in hopes they would show themselves ready for greater responsibility. Since the rank and file cherished the hoary tradition of promotion from within and regarded outsiders with dark suspicion, it was difficult to recruit fresh blood from other roads. The best Ashby could do was lure back an old Union Pacific man, B. F. Wells, from the Rock Island as an assistant general manager.[2]

More than the shortage of officers troubled Ashby. The railroad itself was in its worst shape since Harriman had overhauled it. Fate had dealt all the roads a one-two punch of neglect. During the depression maintenance and improve-

NEW HAND AT THE THROTTLE: George Ashby poses in the cab of a diesel while Perry Lynch and Frank Robinson watch with something less than enthusiasm.

ments had dropped sharply because business did not warrant large expenditures. Then came the war, which overwhelmed the roads with business while depriving them of the materials and manpower to get in good shape. The result was that old equipment and an undernourished physical plant were run harder than they had ever been, with little chance to upgrade or replenish them.[3]

A sharp climb in expenses led Connors to investigate what he already knew instinctively: the Union Pacific had lost its lead in maintenance and fallen behind other, less prosperous roads. For years it had boasted one of the lowest operating ratios in the industry; in August 1946 it had the fourth highest among western roads. Major expenses had soared 65 percent since 1942 on a comparable amount of net ton-miles.[4]

The source of trouble was spread across the entire operation. An aging locomotive fleet, 61 percent of which was over twenty-five years old, meant frequent and costly repairs. Worst of all, the newer engines ran up huge repair bills because of hard running. Repairs to the 4000, 3900, and 800 series totaled $32.9 million since original purchase, or 87 percent of their cost. The larger locomotives had been driven so hard since 1937 that running repairs, normally a small part of maintenance between shoppings, comprised two-thirds of total repair costs.

These figures demolished Jeffers's wartime insistence that the company had ample power if only it were used well. More important, it was the wrong power. The czar's love affair with the steam engine had lingered too long; in

1945 he had hesitated to buy diesels even for passenger service. Although a pioneer in developing the diesel engine, the Union Pacific had lagged behind other roads in converting its fleet to the new technology. The company feared a long struggle with the unions over manning the diesels, and it worried over making a heavy investment only to have some other technology, like gas turbine or atomic power, render the diesel obsolete. But other roads invested heavily in diesel power because the savings were so enormous as to surmount these risks.[5]

Rolling stock was also in sorry shape. About 35 percent of the freight cars were over thirty years old compared to an average of 19 percent on other roads. A third of the company's boxcars were thirty years old or more; the Pennsylvania had only 13 percent of its boxcars in that category. So too with passenger cars, 42 percent of which were over thirty years old. Here, as with power, an aging fleet meant high repair costs. Since it would take years to replace so many old cars, a large investment had to be made in modernizing the shops to make repairs more efficient. Moreover, the surge of transcontinental traffic meant the Union Pacific had to expand its fleet as well as overhaul it.

Deferred maintenance had also taken its toll on the roadway and structures, which lacked, in Connors's view, "the benefits of modern improvements and methods adopted by many large railroads in the past 20 years." Where other roads had reduced roadway maintenance costs by using crushed rock and processed ballast, the Union Pacific still relied on dirt and sand ballast from Sherman and other sites. This had served well until bigger, high-speed trains caused it to disintegrate at a rapid rate. Prior to 1940 only 88 of the 5,900 miles of main line had crushed rock or processed ballast; by 1946 the figure had reached 2,109 miles.[6]

Unlike other roads, the Union Pacific had invested little in off-track equipment to cut maintenance costs. It had also fallen down in another field in which it had once pioneered: signaling. The system installed between 1906 and 1917 had grown obsolete, and $7.3 million was needed to bring it up to the standard dictated by the Signal Inspection Act of 1937. The installation of CTC took care of the problem, but too many miles remained without it. The old system, with signals spaced for the traffic volume and speeds of another era, caused delays and higher expenses. This was another reason behind the nightmare snarls of the war years.

Station expenses kept climbing because there were so many small stations that needed to be closed. Yard switching costs had jumped 250 percent with only a 100 percent increase in car-miles. All the yards were inadequate and outmoded; no major improvements had been made on them in twenty years. The sharp rise in traffic volume turned yards into a tangle of congestion made worse by the lack of enough diesel switchers to do the work cheaply and efficiently.

Every yard had its own tale of woe. Ogden was a nightmare of confusion and delay. The Cheyenne yard had been rebuilt in 1927 under a plan calling for reduced switching at other points, but the plan was never carried out. At North Platte eastbound traffic had to cross the westbound main track to reach the yard and icing facilities. During the war Green River endured a volume of traffic and switching rivaling that of any yard in the nation with facilities that were outmoded, inefficient, and cursed with the harshest weather on the line.

On the line the worst bottleneck remained the single track at Aspen tunnel, which had inadequate clearances, ran high maintenance costs, and posed a safety hazard. Nothing could be done because of the badly faulted formation through which it had been built. The only solution was to construct a new, enlarged tunnel some distance away. There were also points where grade and curve needed reducing despite all that had been done in these areas over the years.

Ashby found himself facing the consequences of twenty years of unintentional neglect compounded by the legacy of Jeffers's conservatism. The improvements needed to bring the road back required huge sums, yet he saw clearly that it must be done. Part of this was vision, part a desire to show his stuff as manager by undoing the mistakes made by Jeffers. On October 23 Ashby wrote Charske a letter urging virtually the entire list of improvements recommended in Connors's report. Four days earlier he had informed Charske of the critical need to upgrade the signals system. "I feel certain," he noted, "it was a shock to you."[7]

The second letter came as much more of a shock. Ashby had the delicate task of asking for large expenditures while telling New York that past outlays, especially for power, had not been wisely spent. "If we had developed and pursued a more forward, long range policy of improvements to the property," he stressed, "we would have been just as well off currently and much better off ultimately." The most pressing need was a program of buying diesels. "I have been slow to suggest conversion of operations from steam to diesel," he admitted, "but I am now convinced that we should make a substantial start in that direction."[8]

Ashby also urged gradual replacement of the aged rolling stock fleet, more ballast, construction of a new Aspen tunnel, and enlargement of key yards. This bold wish list stunned New York. The day before Ashby wrote this letter, Charske responded to his request for upgrading signals with an admonition to "confine capital expenditures to those which will produce compensating economies or are absolutely necessary for other reasons." But Ashby's new requests fit both those conditions and could not be ignored. At the outset of his presidency, while still an apprentice in the eyes of both New York and Omaha, he assumed the thankless role of the messenger bearing unhappy news.[9]

What Ashby needed above all was breathing room to carry out the reforms he intended. Unfortunately, problems assailed him from every quarter. The smoldering labor crisis exploded in May 1946 when a threatened strike by the trainmen's unions prompted President Harry S Truman to seize the railroads. The unions struck anyway, but Truman, who a month earlier had responded to a miners' strike by taking over the mines, brought the trainmen to heel by threatening drastic legislation to curb strikes. Although the roads returned to normal operation in a few days, labor relations remained anything but normal.[10]

Even without the strike Ashby had serious internal labor problems. Jeffers had always boasted that his close ties to the men gave the Union Pacific the best labor relations in the industry. For years this had been true, but after 1940 the czar lost his touch. Since 1928 he had relied on Connors to keep the unions happy. Connors had done this job well and deserved much of the praise that went to Jeffers. His absence in Washington had overwhelmed Rigdon and triggered his break with Jeffers. "The labor job on this railroad is now and is going to continue to be a big one," Connors's secretary wrote him after Rigdon's downfall. "No one has done anything constructive with it since you left."[11]

The czar agreed. The railroads, he warned Ashby in the last month of his reign, "are confronted with the most serious situation that they have ever faced in their history. There is some doubt in my mind that the railroads can survive." Ashby saw the matter differently. "It seems to me," he told Charske, "the organizations have developed a better strategy than the railroads." The Union Pacific had already begun to reduce shop hours, close small depots, and lay off men. This jammed up the Ogden and other shops, which still had plenty of repair work to do. Superintendent of motive power and machinery John Gogerty stormed in to whip the troops into line, but there was little he could do.[12]

Nor could Ashby do much. The labor saga had entered its latest and most destructive phase. Since 1920 the number of railroaders had dwindled steadily, the casualties of changing traffic patterns and new technology. From a high of nearly two million in 1920, the rolls fell to about 572,000 by 1970. Once prized for its job security, railroading had become the most insecure of occupations. The unions used their political clout to fend off this depletion of their ranks. In the landmark Washington Agreement of 1936 railroaders became the first American workers to gain government recognition of job security as a legitimate claim.[13]

The 1936 pact, however, covered only jobs threatened by mergers. The unions were slow to grasp the effect of technology on their position until the diesel rammed the lesson home. The diesel was a classic example of "replacement technology," which changes entirely the existing way of doing something and thereby alters every aspect of its context. The elimination of water service, for instance, wiped out apprentice programs that had long furnished skilled workers, and with it a "rail union subculture." Shop craftsmen also became an endangered species, as did firemen, around whom the labor fight raged.[14]

For thirty years the rail motor cars had run without firemen because none were needed, and from 1925 to 1937 the first diesel switchers operated the same way. Once the streamliner made its debut, however, the Brotherhood of Locomotive Firemen and Enginemen saw the danger and demanded that firemen be included with the crews even though they had no function to perform. The Union Pacific and Burlington were the first roads to confront this issue, and both caved in to threats of a strike—partly because they feared that having only one man in the cab of such fast new trains might unsettle public confidence.[15]

From this agreement emerged a precedent that proved disastrous to the railroads and unions alike. It marked the beginning of a vicious cycle: the more unions pressed for higher wages and shorter hours, the more productivity dropped, driving the carriers to seek new ways of cutting the work force through technological innovation. The unions countered by demanding new rules or preserving old ones that nullified the impact of new technology. In effect they tried to protect job security at the expense of the efficiency so desperately needed if the industry was to survive in the postwar world.

This pattern sprang to life in 1937, when the union insisted on and got the assignment of firemen to all diesels, including switchers. Two years later it launched a campaign for a second fireman on each diesel. The engineers managed to hold onto the rule stipulating eight hours or a hundred miles as a day's work even though diesels were capable of making several hundred miles in much less time. As a result, when carriers began eliminating service points no longer needed for diesels, some had to be retained solely for crew changes. A great disparity emerged between trainmen who worked fast diesels and those who manned slow steam freights.[16]

The crisis of May 1946 foreshadowed a new era of rancor and strife on the labor front. Since their appeal to Woodrow Wilson in 1916 the unions had formed the habit of skirting mediation board awards by going directly to the White House for better terms. Although this tactic had worn thin, clashes over wages and work rules erupted regularly every year. In 1947 the union renewed its demand for a second fireman on diesels; the carriers managed to beat it back after a stiff fight. The nonoperating unions gained a 15½ cent-hourly raise that same year, which by Ashby's estimate added $18 million to Union Pacific payrolls.[17]

The trainmen rejected this figure and held out for more as well as for rule changes. Another imbroglio ensued in which Truman met the usual strike threat by seizing the railroads again in the spring of 1948. Negotiations dragged on until July, when the trainmen accepted the 15½-cent raise in exchange for certain concessions on rules. In March 1949, however, mediators awarded nonoperating employees a forty-hour week and 7-cent raise, which cost the Union Pacific another $33 million. The company promptly trimmed the payrolls again and closed 270 depots on Saturdays.[18]

While the trainmen retreated briefly from their tactic of confrontation, labor relations remained volatile and void of fresh, constructive thinking for dealing with the radical changes taking place in the industry. Ashby was so disgusted with the carriers' handling of labor matters that he considered going it alone. Connors thought wages had to be decided on a national level but agreed that handling other issues that way presented impossible problems. Above all, he wanted out, telling Ashby wearily, "I think I have served my time in national proceedings."[19]

Despite the labor crisis, Ashby plunged into what the *Wall Street Journal* called the "third construction era" of the Union Pacific. By the end of 1947 some 2,808 miles or nearly half the system had been redone with rock and processed ballast, 897 miles of new rail had been laid, and 177 miles of second-hand rail installed on secondary tracks. The mileage covered by CTC was extended to 638, with 324 more miles underway and another 239 miles scheduled. New, respaced signals with colored lights replaced the old semaphores on 445 miles of line. Work commenced on a new westbound Aspen tunnel, eliminating the last piece of single track on the road when it finally opened in 1949. A new retarder hump yard eased the congestion at Pocatello, and construction began on a similar facility at North Platte.[20]

The equipment fleet underwent a dramatic expansion. In January 1946 the Union Pacific had only 30 diesels in passenger, 93 diesels in yard, and none in freight service. Two years later the road boasted 70 passenger, 81 freight, and 142 yard diesels in operation with 242 more units on order. When these arrived, the main line would be dieselized from Los Angeles to Green River, Pocatello, and Rieth, Oregon. The Wyoming and Eastern divisions remained the last bastions of steam, largely because of the Wyoming coal supply and the monster "Big Boys" still on line. A total of 5,000 new freight cars went into service, with 3,950 more scheduled for 1948. Together these equaled 17 percent of the company's fleet. Ashby also ordered 180 new passenger cars, which amounted to 15 percent of the fleet.[21]

New equipment made possible service innovations such as a special new livestock train. The Union Pacific spent over $1 million to equip 800 livestock cars with Timken roller bearings and launched a new fast stock train between Montana and Los Angeles. Powered by a new diesel hauling 65 to 75 cars, the *Stock Special* cut the old schedule in half. The train was made up in Salt Lake City, where the animals were rested and watered for the last time before the nonstop run to Los Angeles. The 790-mile trip took only twenty-seven hours.[22]

It took courage for Ashby to push this program at the outset of his presidency. Expenditures for improvements and equipment had averaged $16.5 million a year during the 1920s, $4.8 million between 1931 and 1935, and $15.5 million during 1936–1940, much of the latter in streamliners. The average jumped to $20.7 million for the war years, fueled partly by inflation, but even this paled before the outlays requested by Ashby. Between 1946 and 1948 these expenditures averaged $44.7 million a year at a time when wages and other expenses rose steadily.[23]

New York shelled out the huge sums required, but not always willingly. Ashby had to persuade Roland that the diesels would not be upstaged by some version of gas turbine locomotive, the development of which the Union Pacific still followed closely. Connors too argued that the diesels were "our only salvation for economical operation and to meet competition," but New York still balked at converting the entire fleet because of a reluctance to surrender the cheap fuel Wyoming coal provided. Lovett favored wholesale conversion, but his departure in May 1947 for a government post removed him from the debate.[24]

The demand for so much so quickly did little to reassure New York about Ashby, who to their minds had two strikes against him: he had come into office without the trial period by which they had planned to take his measure, and he was not a real railroader. He had plunged vigorously into the job, but he also

A NEW LINEUP OF OLD FACES: Shortly after becoming president, George Ashby poses with his top officers. (*From left*) J. L. Haugh, E. J. Connors, William H. Guild, Ashby, Frank W. Robinson, and Perry J. Lynch.

seemed bent on changing things around, reversing what Jeffers had done. And he was quirky in a way that baffled the staid, conventional easterners. Jeffers had been a character but not a mystery to them. Lovett had the wit and acumen to understand misfits, but he was not there. How deep this vein of doubt ran in New York is not clear; nor is it known what if anything they knew of Ashby's drinking problem.

What is clear is that Ashby sensed their lack of complete faith in him, just as he felt the resentment of those men and officers who scorned him as an unworthy successor to a real railroader like Jeffers. Even in exile the czar haunted him like Banquo's ghost and aroused in him a primal wrath. No one felt it more than the faithful secretary, Doc Churchill, who tried desperately to be loyal to both his past and present bosses. "It was almost company suicide to call on Jeffers," he recalled, but on one occasion he risked visiting the old man anyway. Jeffers knew what was going on. "That's all right, Doc," he soothed, "you're handling that little son of a bitch the only way he can be handled."[25]

For one as insecure as Ashby, there is a thin line between the confidence that enables him to view critics merely as obstacles to be overcome and the paranoid belief that everyone is conspiring against him. Sometime during his first year as president, Ashby began crossing that line. "The first six months were really very pleasant," said Churchill, ". . . but after six months there was a sudden turn in his attitude.'' Friction with his major officers developed, and an unexpected clash with New York left him permanently scarred.[26]

Ashby began to withdraw and drink even more, but the problem went deeper than alcohol. ''He just felt,'' mourned Churchill, ''that there was an organized campaign to discredit him.'' The irony was that Ashby was doing a good job pushing a stubborn railroad in the right direction, but New York doubted him and the ranks resented the changes he imposed. Unable to withstand this pressure from both ends, he finally succumbed to his own fears. The well-intended Dr. Jekyll slowly dissolved into the hateful Mr. Hyde.[27]

Then and later the officers disagreed over Ashby. Everyone shared the belief that he marched to a different drummer and was difficult to deal with, yet some thought him a good president. ''I was really impressed with him,'' said Edd Bailey, who later became president himself, ''and he asked questions about things that he was very knowledgeable on.'' Stan How thought Ashby ''could be talked into things pretty readily because he didn't have the same understanding of it.'' George Proudfit emphasized that ''While he was hard to get along with, he had a lot of good ideas.''[28]

Change always brings resistance, and railroaders were notoriously intransigent. Ashby saw that he had to push his officers constantly to prod their subordinates in the direction he wanted them to go. As diesels gradually took over the district south of Salt Lake City, for example, he noticed a ''studied effort to retain and utilize every steam locomotive that it is possible to use.'' The only way to combat this tendency, he snapped, was ''to take the locomotives away from them and insist that they perform the service . . . with a smaller number.''[29]

Calling the diesel helper operation a ''racket'' on the line and annoyed by what he deemed its misuse, Ashby badgered VPO Perry Lynch to solve the problem. He wanted shop practices studied with an eye to modernizing them, questioned the method of imposing demerits for infractions, demanded a survey of passing tracks to see whether the road could do with fewer of them, and prodded a general manager to pool cabooses and eliminate ''similar archaic practices.'' Lest anyone miss his point, he added, ''I am going to have to insist that we modernize our thinking and that officers who are unable to adjust themselves thereto be replaced.''[30]

Connors received a mandate to impose force reductions. ''We have spent a lot of money for improving facilities for the purpose of effecting economy in manpower,'' Ashby growled, ''and . . . I am impatient with the results. You have my full authority to make changes in organization and operation along the lines that I have been suggesting over a period of several years without any noticeable results, and if you do not exercise them, I will take drastic action.'' He hounded Lynch to cut the number of signal maintainers, and warned Connors, ''I expect you to follow these things up or I am going *to get rid of you*.''[31]

To long-suffering lieutenants like Connors and Lynch, this stream of abuse offered little relief from what they had endured under Jeffers. But Ashby gave it a twist that baffled them. He warned top officers that raises hereafter would be selective because too many of them lacked the imagination or drive to promote change. ''I have found a reluctance and disinclination,'' he added ominously, ''which it has been rather difficult for me to overcome in the accomplishment of some of my objectives and which has delayed . . . their consummation.''[32]

A. J. Seitz hastened to assure Ashby that the traffic people favored and supported his program, but operations could do nothing to appease him. ''We have a lot of great men on this railroad who know how everything was done 25 years ago or have records to prove it,'' Ashby complained in May 1948. ''I want to get them retired as soon as possible and get somebody who doesn't know so much because they are the principal barriers that I am trying to remove to modernize railroad operations, which we are going to have to come to if we are going to avoid demanding further increases in freight rates, which are becoming so high we are about to price ourselves out of business.''[33]

There were plenty of men, he added, who could look down the track to see if the last train knocked it out of line. Ashby wanted the kind of men who would keep it from getting out of line in the first place, so the sighting could be eliminated. ''If we haven't anybody on the property who has ideas of new and more economical ways of doing things, we should start building up an organization that does.''[34]

This approach was a polar opposite from the Jeffers style of invoking the past as a golden age. Ashby understood that the railroads had entered a new age in which expenses (especially labor) continued to soar along with competition from other modes. The carriers had fallen into the habit of seeking rate hikes to offset rising wages. They gained higher rates totaling 33.6 percent between December 1946 and December 1948, but Ashby believed this pattern would only push freight into the waiting arms of rival modes. The roads had to make themselves competitive, which they could not do by simply doing things in the same old way.[35]

It must also have satisfied Ashby to depart from his predecessor's policy with a finality no knowing eye could miss. In his zeal to erase the Jeffers legacy, however, he committed a blunder that brought him serious trouble. Ashby liked to say that a smart operating man could save the company a million dollars a month without even trying. Convinced that his officers were neither smart nor trying hard enough, he decided to bring back as advisors two men whom Jeffers had fired, J. W. Burnett and A. V. James, to help him overhaul operations.[36]

Edd Bailey considered this ''one of the big mistakes he made, because they had been gone seven or eight years, and there had been a lot of things changed.'' Stan How thought Burnett was a ''progressive fellow,'' while a shop veteran denounced James as a ''little sleazy sonofabitch.'' This was largely because James stormed into the shops with what the hands considered a reign of terror disguised as an efficiency program. Burnett injected himself into the eternal squabble over assignment of power. Both men acted as ambassadors without portfolio in the Silas Seymour style, which further muddied lines of authority. When Ashby sent Burnett to check on power use around Salt Lake, Connors noted privately, "Why to Burnett? He is not on the payroll. Why not to Lynch or Gogarty [sic]?"[37]

The dissension spawned by the presence of Burnett and James grew steadily worse. "Every time [Ashby] came across the railroad," Bailey recalled, "why, of course, he would have one of them with him on the car." Their presence separated Ashby even more from officers who already had difficulty fathoming him, and aggravated the already ugly disputes over power use and other issues. Nor did Ashby endear himself to trainmen when he would pull into the Las Vegas yard and order no switching done that night because he wanted to sleep. "Well," shrugged one officer, "that almost tied the terminal up."[38]

No one on the line understood why Ashby had changed, or what Burnett and James were doing there. "I heard John Burnett say things to Ashby, and give him advice which he followed," said Doc Churchill, "which I think appalled the active operating officers." They were also worn down by Ashby's unpredictability. Like Jeffers, Ashby fired off barrages of telegrams to his officers when touring the line. One demanded that chief engineer W. C. Perkins explain why a section house had wash hanging from its train side. Because, replied a disgusted Perkins, that was where the clothes line was. Ashby summoned him at once. Perkins went expecting to be fired, only to be told what a fine job he was doing.[39]

"He was a chameleon," Churchill emphasized. In his view, however, the fatal blow to Ashby's spirits came from New York, not Omaha. There had been friction over individual policies such as Ashby's use of selective raises, which disturbed Roland Harriman. For whatever reason, New York found a suitable way to put Ashby in his place. To ensure a smooth flow of new diesels, Ashby formed the habit of ordering them fourteen months in advance, and then requesting the purchase funds from New York a couple of months before delivery. New York understood this procedure and had never objected to it. Then one time he asked for $22 million to buy diesels that were nearly ready for delivery and was turned down.[40]

This had never happened before. An embarrassed Ashby was forced to tell the manufacturers he had no authority to take the diesels. Furious and humiliated, he dictated an angry letter to Charske that never left the office thanks to Churchill. "But this cooled him toward the New York office," Doc thought. "From then on he just couldn't abide those people, and he didn't have any affection for them or anything else." Ashby began to avoid the New York people, going so far as to arrange his schedule to be elsewhere when they came out for inspection tours.[41]

Gradually Ashby sank into a trough of despondency, fueled by the suicide of an Omaha friend in March 1948 and the death of the one officer he trusted, W. H. Guild, who suffered a stroke in July and died a few hours later. These months became a horror show for Churchill, who as secretary was trapped day after day in the business car with the boss when they traveled. Ashby's already meager appetite dwindled even more, and the drinking increased—bourbon and water or gin and grapefruit juice. The business car, always cramped for space, had cases of grapefruit juice tucked in every available spot. Ashby arranged a signal with the porter: one buzz meant come, two buzzes come with a drink.[42]

On these trips Churchill at first waited for dinner until Ashby was ready; then Ashby began staying in his room without eating or letting anyone know his plans, so Churchill decided to eat on his own and sit with Ashby if he bothered to eat. Sometimes Ashby sat up all night drinking. He was a slow drinker, a sipper, and he often fell asleep in his chair, letting his cigarette drop on the carpet. The weary Churchill had no choice but to stay up and watch over him. "And boy those were torturous trips," he moaned, "and that beautiful business car bed with sheets all open and everything and [he] never got in it." When Ashby did go to his room, he drank some more; the crew told Churchill they put a fifth of bourbon in his room every night, and found it empty the next morning.[43]

The more Ashby drank, the more unreasonable he became, and nasty as well. Churchill tried feverishly to keep him in good spirits because he had to bear the brunt of anything that upset Ashby. The other officers could do little with him, especially after Burnett and James got his ear. In desperation they began using Churchill as their intermediary. "It got worse over time," he said sorrowfully, "and they would come to me and say, 'Doc, you've gotta talk to him.' "[44]

"It was tough because Doc was constantly, constantly lying [for Ashby]," added another officer sympathetically. "When Ashby was too damn drunk to talk, Doc would keep everybody away from him. He was very loyal to him . . . but it was a helluva spot."[45]

By 1948 the old pattern of bickering and intrigues had resumed in earnest. Connors had long since fallen into Ashby's disfavor, and even Guild was rebuffed before his death. Art Stoddard gained ground almost by default, rising to the vice-presidency vacated by Guild. H. E. Shumway was considered Ashby's pet and given the best chance for rapid promotion. Many thought he was being groomed to succeed Guild, but the appointment of Stoddard signaled that Shumway had fallen from grace. Ashby also rewarded others he thought had performed well, but it was painfully clear he had lost control of his organization as well as himself.[46]

The snow began falling on New Year's Day of 1949 and kept coming for three days, driven across the plains by winds that reached sixty miles an hour and piled up drifts twenty to thirty feet deep in eastern Wyoming and western Nebraska. Temperatures plummeted below zero and stayed there, bottoming out at fifty-one below and made even colder by the ferocious gale. Trains moving into the region ran smack into impenetrable walls of ice and snow. Thus began the blizzard of 1949, the worst to hit the railroad since the monster storms of the early 1870s. It was not one but two blizzards, which tied up the railroad for seven weeks.

Cuts filled up in record time, catching trains like flies on flypaper. Four of them got trapped early, while others soon followed or stacked up until the line

MAN IN THE MIDDLE: The gentle, good-natured D. O. "Doc" Churchill, who as secretary to Jeffers and then Ashby did yeoman service under difficult circumstances.

was blocked from Borie to Sidney, Nebraska. When trains got stuck and ran out of water, the rule was to knock the fire and drain the boiler. Dutifully the crews did this, thereby creating huge blocks of ice beneath their engines that imprisoned them like fossils in a glacier. Several passenger trains were caught before they could retreat, and the travelers found refuge where they could. One group of 270 stranded in Kimball, Nebraska, took turns using the eighty rooms available there.[47]

Perry Lynch and Art Stoddard alternated long shifts directing the operation from Omaha. Every available plow and hundreds of men rushed to attack the drifts that loomed high above their heads, but nothing went well. The howling winds knocked men down or turned their faces black, and cuts filled up again as fast as they were cleared. The road had some new plows that were very small-wheeled and inadequate to the huge task before them. Some crews wandered off to clear the Kearney branch instead of working the main line, saying later they had "orders." In that sideshow a double-header with a plow veered into a drift at twenty miles an hour, causing the plow to shear off a cab and killing the brakeman inside it.[48]

In all, five men lost their lives fighting the storm. The company threw 14,000 men, 15 rotary plows, 33 wedge and spreader plows, and 180 bulldozers into the fight. Dynamite was used to blast through drifts, and flame throwers were borrowed from Fort Warren to free the engines entombed in ice. So vicious was the gale that even plow trains got stuck and had to carry plows at both ends. Although the operating men worked twenty-hour shifts, the

NO WAY OUT: A rotary snowplow tries to put a dent in the fierce blizzard of 1949 in Wyoming.

numbing cold allowed crews to remain outside only a short time before seeking shelter. Some of the best work was done by a force of Indians on the Wyoming line, but everywhere the men hacked furiously at the snow until they were driven to warmth or sagged from exhaustion.[49]

Ashby was at Las Vegas when the storm hit. He started for Omaha only to be told the line was blocked. "He didn't care by this time," mourned Churchill, and the blizzard soon brought out the worst in him. "This was a disaster, a natural disaster, that had just tied this railroad up in the worst storm in a century, and he just refused to accept it." To the embittered Ashby it was simply one more conspiracy to thwart him.[50]

He rode number 28 from Ogden to Borie, Wyoming, where it joined seven other trains waiting for the line between Cheyenne and Sidney, Nebraska, to be cleared. The others had already been there eight hours; no one had thought to bring them into Cheyenne, where the passengers would be more comfortable and there was less chance of engines freezing up. Ashby ordered them there and came on himself, his disgust rising with every mile. Once in Cheyenne, he got on the phone with the officers in Omaha and vented his own peculiar brand of displeasure.[51]

Churchill, standing nearby, couldn't believe his ears: Ashby was telling them the men couldn't get anything done because they were all wearing so many clothes! "There's a car-knocker out here checking for hot boxes," he rasped. "He's got mittens on so thick he couldn't feel a hot box if it was a fire. . . .

Here's Doc, he's on his way up to the telegraph office, my God he's got on galoshes and an overcoat and a scarf and gloves and a hat.''

''Well, it's cold, Mr. Ashby,'' said Churchill meekly.

''You know,'' Ashby continued, ''this is kinda like the banana belt up here, but he's just like these other people—putting on all the by-God clothes he owns.''[52]

As Churchill hurried down the platform, he glanced up at a high overpass east of the station and noticed that the snow was piled all the way from the ground to the bottom of the overpass. A solid wall of snow, formed by the same winds that had wrapped semaphore signals around their poles. Two plows were digging into it. Ashby watched them from his car and told Omaha they were pushing at a little snow pile. ''Hell,'' he sneered, ''I could do better with a couple of teaspoons.''[53]

Churchill scurried into the depot and found Edd Bailey, who had just returned from digging out the streamliner stuck in Kimball. Bailey had gone ninety hours without sleep and had just come back in after a quick bath, shave, and breakfast. Churchill greeted him and said, ''Edd, when you go down to see the old man, don't wear an overcoat.'' Bailey gave him a quizzical look. ''This is just a dream somebody had,'' Doc shrugged. ''There's no snow . . . look at those carmen out there with so many damn clothes on they can't move.''[54]

Bailey thought this odd, but he strode briskly down the platform without a coat and jumped on the car. Ashby was at his desk. ''Edd, hello,'' he said. ''What I want to know from you is, when are you going to get me out of here?''

Just as damn soon as I can, thought Bailey to himself.[55]

Afterward the recriminations flew. Stoddard complained that the snow equipment broke down repeatedly. The reason, countered John Gogerty, was inexperienced and abusive handling. While they clawed at each other, Connors concluded privately that the whole affair had been botched. Ashby intervened only to say that he was less concerned with past mistakes than with preparations to meet the next storm.[56]

To his dismay, the test came at once. Scarcely was the line cleared when a second blizzard roared through, this time shutting down the road between Wamsutter and Walcott, Wyoming, and between Pocatello and Glenns Ferry, Idaho. Once again winds reaching sixty miles an hour piled up giant drifts and reduced visibility to zero. By February 9 some eighteen westbound and twenty-four eastbound passenger trains alone were stacked up, many of them at Rawlins, Wyoming.[57]

This storm dwarfed the first one, shifting its intensity from one locale to another and tying up the road for twelve days. Passengers stranded at Hanna, Wyoming, were moved by bus to Cheyenne and put on a relief train to Denver, but it took four days to get the westbound trains at Rawlins back to Cheyenne. The Idaho line was cleared only to be shut down again when the blizzard suddenly worsened. On February 15 Stoddard reported glumly that nothing was moving on the Wyoming Division except some rotary plows between Laramie and Bitter Creek. The wind howled a steady forty miles an hour at Cheyenne, fifty at Rawlins, with gusts hitting sixty-five, burying newly-plowed track in three hours or so.[58]

So bad was the situation that Lynch, Stoddard, and Seitz suggested diverting trains over the Rio Grande to accommodate passengers and unsnarl the line. Sending trains over another line was the last act of a desperate railroad, but the officers agreed there was no choice. Ashby would not even listen to them. This time he had been caught at Sun Valley, where one of the staff overheard him yelling over the phone to Stoddard, "I don't give a goddam how you do it, but I want you to get those trains rolling. Get a bunch of Indians to walk ahead of the trains to clear the track if you have to, but get those trains moving."[59]

At their wit's end, the officers begged Churchill to talk to Ashby about diverting the trains. One train had not only live passengers but also some corpses bound for burial in Los Angeles. Muttering that the whole thing was a plot to embarrass him, Ashby refused even to consider it. Finally, convinced that the need was critical, Churchill gave the order himself. To his relief, Ashby never said a word about it.[60]

For Ashby the whole episode was yet another exercise in humiliation. Once again he headed for Omaha, driven this time by an imperative no one knew about except himself and Doc Churchill. At Salt Lake he was told the line was blocked, and no one could get through on it. While he debated what to do, J. W. Burnett made a singular suggestion. "George," he said, "those fellows could get that railroad opened if they want to; they're just not doing it. . . . You just tell them that 'I'm coming through,' and they'll get it open."[61]

And he did. When the special was ready to depart, Churchill saw the yard men "looking up at us kind of like, I don't know what you people are doing." On they went to Wamsutter, where two trains were stuck and their engines encased in ice. Chief engineer Perkins met them there, and Ashby decided to show him it wasn't so bad by getting off the train without anything more than his sports jacket. After a few minutes he was frozen and turned to get back on the business car, but while he was talking it had been moved a distance down the line. "Come on, Perk," he said, scurrying down the platform, "let's talk in here; it's getting cold."[62]

Back they went to Salt Lake, where the yard men leered at them with smug expressions. Ashby called Bailey in Cheyenne, who assured him the line was impassable, and that the only way to reach Omaha was over the Rio Grande. In the end Ashby did just that, because he had to get to New York. This convinced some hands that he didn't belong even though his officers had pleaded with him to do the same thing. "He wasn't a true railroader," said one, "and he kind of proved that when . . . he thought he could do better going over to the D & RG, and that was undoing. He got off the property there."[63]

Many of the officers thought this episode finished Ashby. They were wrong; he was already finished. On February 8 he had received a telegram from Roland Harriman summoning him to a meeting in New York on the 16th. Normally such requests were exquisitely polite, but this one had a very different tone: "Please arrange to meet me in New York." Although the blizzard still raged, Ashby was there at the appointed hour. Earlier he had told Churchill he wanted to retire on his pension, saying "I don't want to work in this outfit anymore." This was precisely what Roland and Charske had in mind, and the meeting was short. Afterward Ashby walked down the hall to his office and told Churchill he was retiring as president March 1. Then he went out for lunch and didn't come back.[64]

While Churchill waited, Charske ambled down the hall and stopped to smoke a cigarette and visit with him. Churchill was surprised. Apart from the fact that the chairman of the executive committee rarely chatted with secretaries, Charske was a loner by nature. When Charske got up to leave, he said pointedly, "Doc, we'll be seeing *you* some more."[65]

Later most of the troops in Omaha concluded that the blizzard had done Ashby in, but there was more to it. Still rankling over the diesel incident, Ashby had continued to avoid contact with New York as much as possible, but that winter Roland Harriman had come out for a visit between storms. As usual the two business cars were coupled together at the end of the train. On his last night there, Roland invited Ashby to join him and Mrs. Harriman for dinner in their car at six-thirty. Ashby said fine. At five o'clock or so Ashby rang the porter and asked for his dinner. Knowing that he never ate at that early hour, Churchill gently reminded him of the Harrimans' invitation.

"I changed my mind," he snapped.

At six-thirty Churchill reminded him again, but Ashby would not budge or let Doc go with an apology. Finally, Roland stuck his head in the car gingerly to tell Ashby they were waiting. "Thanks, Roland, I've already had my dinner."

"Well, we thought you were going to have dinner with us."

"I changed my mind."[66]

Ever gracious, Roland left without saying anything, but Churchill was appalled. It was, he said, "almost spitting in his face." Next day the train moved on to Salt Lake, where Roland was to be honored with a luncheon at the Alta Club. Ashby was supposed to attend, and a pair of special agents waited outside his car to drive him to the club. But he was drinking and refused to go despite Churchill's pleas that it was time. The public relations man phoned and said everyone was waiting; still Ashby would not budge. Finally, well after the proceedings had started, Churchill induced him to leave.[67]

Churchill was not invited and waited anxiously in the car. He had reason to fidget. Later John Padden, the traffic manager in Salt Lake, came around to see him, his face livid with rage, and cried, "That little SOB really has torn it now." Ashby had arrived at the private dining room during dessert and sat down without eating a bite. When Roland got up to make some remarks, Ashby fell asleep and started snoring.

That evening the Harrimans started for home. When it was time for them to leave, Ashby was nowhere to be found. The frazzled Churchill offered a lame excuse for him, but Roland merely smiled and said, "That's all right, Doc, I understand." As Churchill said later, "He knew I was lying by the clock."[68]

HAPPIER TIMES: Omaha banker and Union Pacific director W. Dale Clark, Roland Harriman, and Ashby converse at a luncheon before Ashby's falling out with New York.

The telegram summoning Ashby to New York came a few days later. What role these incidents played in the decision cannot be shown, but they surely helped seal Ashby's fate. In these acts of self-immolation he came to the end of his reign. It was an inglorious climax to a well-intentioned presidency. That Ashby had disgraced himself was beyond dispute. "I've seen some things with Ashby," said a shop veteran, "that would scare you to death." Yet his vision of what the road's future required was inherently sound. The tragedy was that Ashby's personal weaknesses made it easy to discredit the ideas along with the man, and the company sorely needed the ideas.[69]

After the meeting with Roland in New York on February 16, Ashby and Churchill left that night for Chicago. Art Stoddard had been told to meet them there the next day. The blizzard still raged in Wyoming, and so badly had the fight against it gone that Stoddard feared this was his march to the scaffold. Ashby never did go to the office. Instead it was left to Churchill to meet Stoddard, who was pacing the corridor when he arrived. "What's up, Doc?" he asked anxiously. "What's up?"

"I don't think I can tell you really," replied Churchill, "but . . . let me put it this way. It's okay for you."

Stoddard brightened. "Are they going to make me exec?"

"No, they're going to make you president."[70]

The blizzard finally petered out a few days later, and the Union Pacific resumed something like normal operations on February 21 after the longest period of interruption in its history. Once the storm passed, the road also found itself under a new leader. Dale Clark, the Omaha banker who sat on the Union Pacific board, assessed the matter better than most. In his opinion Ashby had "made a real and definite contribution to the Property that was constructive in its long range effect." But, he added, "This belief does not alter the thought that it was time for a change."[71]

Doc Churchill stayed with Ashby for a month after he retired, going with him to Las Vegas to put his affairs in order before taking up a new company post in Los Angeles. It was not a pleasant month. The embittered Ashby did little more than drink and sit in stony silence. A few old-timers tried to befriend him, but he drove them away. "I don't want 'em all hanging around here, godammit!" he growled. "I don't need 'em and I don't want 'em."[72]

Ashby lived only fourteen months after leaving office. During that time he drank more and ate less until he had to be hospitalized. Doc Churchill had taken up his new job as a company lawyer in Los Angeles, had married, and was struggling to take care of a pregnant wife, his mother, and his stepfather. Yet he found himself going to Las Vegas many weekends at his own expense to visit the stricken Ashby, who had no other friends. When he walked into the hospital room, the emaciated former president looked at him with soulful eyes and murmured, "Hello, Doc. I knew you'd come."[73]

Churchill made out a will for Ashby, arranged quietly for his affairs to be placed in the hands of a guardian, and kept him company as best he could. When Ashby died in May 1950, Doc was one of only two or three Union Pacific hands at the funeral.

24

The Sleeping Giant

To Wall Street and the railroad industry alike the postwar Union Pacific was known as a sleeping giant, rich in assets and slow to maximize its use of them. Some called it the gold-plated railroad; others used a less flattering name: the fat old lady with a bag of candy. The big question was what she would do with her candy. Would someone snatch it from her?[1]

"No other railroad liked the Union Pacific," declared Jervis Langdon, a veteran railroad official who headed the Rock Island for a time. ". . . I guess it was too rich and successful, and they had all the breaks; and they had all this outside, nonrail income. They didn't have to operate their railroad very efficiently and still make a lot of money. It was a gold mine."[2]

While other roads struggled, staggered, and fell after 1945, the Union Pacific got richer. In his quiet way Woody Charske continued to work his financial magic. While other roads used their wartime profits to reduce funded debt, Charske accumulated working capital, going so far as to buy new rolling stock with equipment notes even though the company had ample cash to pay for it. This tactic not only bought money at low interest rates, it also saved the company $30,000 in excess profits tax in 1943 alone.[3]

But Charske had much larger game in mind. His real target was the $156 million of company bonds maturing in 1946 and 1947. Refunding these issues offered a golden opportunity to restructure the debt at lower rates. As a first step he moved in September 1944 to redeem $55 million of Navigation Company 4 percent bonds with new issues at 3 percent. These sold easily despite a yield of only 2.78 percent. A year later Charske redeemed $81.6 million of Union Pacific 3.5 percent refunding bonds with a new 3 percent issue. Again the bonds were snatched up by a syndicate, which sold them at a yield of 2.84 percent. Charske figured the savings on the new issue to maturity at $11 million.[4]

In December 1945 Charske dipped into his capital reserve to redeem $56 million worth of underlying system bonds. A month later he got approval to refund some other obligations with an issue of $44.5 million in thirty-year unsecured bonds at an astounding rate of 2.875 percent. Eager bankers bought them at a price that made the real interest cost 2.51 percent, or about the same as the government's Victory bonds. The yield to investors was 2.47 percent, the lowest ever recorded for a long-term railroad security.[5]

Elated by the results, Charske tried an even bolder move. In February 1946 he offered a new issue of 2½ percent bonds to take up the refunding threes sold only five months earlier. To his delight these fetched a yield of 2.453 percent, probably the lowest amount any railroad ever paid for long-term financing. By 1947 the company's debt had been sliced nearly 63 percent or $171 million from its high in 1925. Average interest rates had been cut from 4.3 percent to an incredible 2.4 percent, and annual interest charges dropped nearly $12 million. Although these low rates could not be maintained, the total debt and amount of interest paid declined steadily until 1961.[6]

The fat old lady got fatter, thanks to Charske's acumen. In 1947 the dividend returned to its predepression level of $10 a share, and the following year the stock split two for one. In 1956 it split again, this time five for one.* By then a postwar Union Pacific holder owned ten shares for every original one, had collected $65.75 in dividends per share, and had seen the stock's market value rise about 245 percent. Few if any railroads could match that record.[7]

The old Harriman formula of bolstering earnings with nonrail investments also continued to pump large sums into the company coffers. Between 1946 and 1960 these activities added an average of nearly $35 million to rail earnings each year. In 1946 nonrail income totaled about 130 percent of the amount paid out for interest; by 1950 it was nearly five times and by 1960 nine times the amount needed for interest. An analyst calculated that in 1950 the company's nonrail income alone could pay all interest plus a $2 dividend on preferred and about $5 per share on the common.[8]

Ironically, other railroads ceased being a major part of that income. As the earnings of eastern roads dropped, the Union Pacific gradually emptied its portfolio of their stocks. By 1961 it had sold off its holdings in the Pennsylvania, the New York Central, and the B & O. As early as 1955 it had disposed of its Chicago & Northwestern shares, leaving only a large interest in the Illinois Central. While income from rail stocks dwindled, oil earnings soared from $6.6 million in 1946 to $27 million in 1949. During the 1950s they averaged $28.5 million, hitting a peak of $34.3 million in 1953.[9]

While other assets contributed large sums to income, the railroad itself also did well. It still owned the longest average haul (588 miles) of any railroad,

*Put another way, the stock went from a $100 par value to a $50 par value to a $10 par value per share.

REAR WINDOW: Arthur E. Stoddard and Edd H. Bailey confer at the rear of the business car in Cheyenne, December 1954.

carried a smaller burden of passenger traffic than most, and served a region that was still growing at a phenomenal rate. The Union Pacific originated more than 60 percent of its freight tonnage, and nearly 56 percent of its freight traffic terminated on its own track. The traffic remained well diversified. How fat was the old lady? By 1951 the company's assets totaled $1.25 billion, with net working capital of $84.5 million.[10]

By all external measures the postwar Union Pacific looked to be a sound, conservative, well-managed company. In many respects it was, but prosperity was also a trap, a blind concealing needs more obvious to leaner, hungrier roads. Compared to most railroads, the Union Pacific was doing very well; compared to its own potential, it had barely scratched the surface of possibilities.

The selection of Art Stoddard as the next president reflected the problem nicely. There was nothing particularly wrong with the choice, but neither was it an inspired one. After the turmoil surrounding Ashby he represented a return to normalcy, but there was nothing normal about the era looming before him. His presence reassured the railroaders in the ranks because he was unabashedly one of them, but this hardly qualified him as the man to free the company from the shackles of traditions that impeded progress in rapidly changing times.

The insiders believed Stoddard got the job because his wartime experience had made him a favorite of Averell Harriman and Carl Gray, Jr. George

Proudfit thought Roland Harriman leaned toward traffic vice-president A. J. Seitz, but after the Ashby debacle Roland may have been more inclined to let Averell's views prevail. Both Harrimans hoped Stoddard would emerge as another Jeffers; everything they knew suggested he would.[11]

Stoddard fit the Jeffers mold in several respects. He was a Nebraskan who had come up through the ranks one rung at a time, starting at age twelve as a waterboy for his father, who did grading for the Rock Island. He had joined the Union Pacific in 1916 and was considered a "railroad man's railroad man." Tall and taciturn, he had none of Jeffers's charisma. But he had a pleasant, easy manner and a ready smile, and he liked to joke with the men. "[Stoddard was] very well liked by the employees, particularly the operating people," said Edd Bailey. "He was such a far cry from either Jeffers or Ashby." Unlike Jeffers, he did not fire people right and left or shower them with abuse.[12]

But Stoddard could be tough, and he was determined to show everyone that he was just as rugged as his predecessors. "Mr. Stoddard wanted everybody to know that he was a rough, tough old SOB railroader," said public relations man E. C. Schafer. "That was the way to get along, and that's the way his principal lieutenants got along."[13]

One story of his wartime exploits in Iran became a legend on the road. Water in the desert was scarce, and the MRS force got its supply via a long trench. Stoddard found some natives bathing in it and ordered a barbed wire fence put up with signs in different languages. This was done, but the natives tunneled beneath the fence and continued to refresh themselves in the water. The first time Stoddard's patrol dragged them out and issued a warning. The second time they were warned again. Caught a third time, Stoddard ordered them shot. After that, he said, there were no more water problems.[14]

Whether true or not, the story was widely believed. This pleased Stoddard, who had first told it to the American Legion, because it reflected both his style and his image of himself. As one who had been fired several times himself, he believed in prior warnings. When Reg Sutton was promoted to general auditor, Stoddard advised him never to get mad at anybody. When someone made a mistake, tell him about it quietly. If he erred again, remind him of the earlier warning. And if he messed up a third time, tell him he was gone. "The third time somebody flunks the test around here," he said solemnly, "we just quietly shoot him."[15]

Stoddard knew the price of war firsthand. One of his three children had been a Marine who lost his life at Iwo Jima. He ran the road in military fashion, insisting that everything go by the book and through channels. And he got along well with New York. "He was a real road man, two-fisted guy," said Elbridge Gerry, "and you couldn't print some of the language he used before the board." General counsel Frank Barnett was less delicate: "He was a bastard . . . a rough, tough guy." But that didn't bother New York; indeed, it fit the board's image of what a railroad president was or had to be.[16]

Like Jeffers, Stoddard had no hobbies or outside interests, but he lacked Jeffers's utter dedication. He kept reasonable hours and never pushed himself too hard. Proudfit considered him a man who had "coasted a lot of his life on the shoulders of subordinates,'' yet he did not delegate authority well because he was suspicious of people and unwilling to let power out of his own hands. Doc Churchill never trusted him even though Stoddard always treated him well. ''He was a fellow that never made a record of anything,'' said Stan How. ''. . . [He] wasn't going to leave any trails behind.''[17]

He was also a notorious tightwad. ''Mr. Stoddard was a man that wanted to take his money with him,'' smiled How. ''[He] got no pleasure out of spending money.'' In certain ways this attitude spilled over to the railroad. Stoddard hated waste and demanded efficiency. ''You did fine,'' stressed Edd Bailey, ''if you had black ink on the bottom line every month.'' He knew this pleased New York, and he had learned long ago that the key to holding power on the Union Pacific was to keep New York happy and chop down aspirants to the throne.[18]

It was a job Stoddard aimed to keep, if only because he was so surprised to find himself there in the first place. As one insider quipped, ''He probably pinched himself every morning to see if he's really awake and this isn't a dream that he's president of the railroad.''[19]

The operating structure commanded his attention early. Ashby had rearranged the divisions somewhat but had not tackled the larger question of whether the organization should be based on divisional rather than departmental lines. While this debate had raged for more than a century, most large roads had gone to the more decentralized divisional structure which organizes whole units by geography, as opposed to the departmental approach, which organizes by function for the entire system. The Union Pacific, however, still clung to a modified departmental structure adopted after Charles Francis Adams's brief fling with the divisional method in the 1880s.[20]

Under this mixed version three general managers took care of operations on a divisional basis while the chief engineer controlled engineering, maintenance, and signaling for the entire system. The general superintendent of motive power and machinery had charge of shop work. This arrangement meant transportation and maintenance moved along differing lines of authority. As E. J. Connors noted, ''The territorial jurisdiction of the master mechanics no longer conforms with that of the superintendents.'' But he recommended more centralization to dispense with what he called ''unnecessary supervision.''[21]

As a result, noted John Kenefick, ''There was almost no crossing of knowledge or management between the various departments, and *that* is rather unusual for a railroad of this size, particularly that the senior officers are that way.''[22]

Ashby had tinkered with operating divisions only to make them conform better to modern traffic flows. Stoddard fiddled with them for the same reason but made no basic changes in structure until 1954, when steps were taken to decentralize the Engineering Department by restoring two of the district engineers abolished in 1942. Nothing more was done until J. A. Bunjer became chief engineer in 1956. Bunjer objected to his department being so centralized because it left general managers without any authority over engineers, and it deprived the company of an adequate training ground for new engineering officers. Fresh blood was urgently needed: his own office had six positions staffed by men past sixty-five years of age.[23]

In 1957 Bunjer managed to put the district engineers under the general managers "so that work performed is actually accomplished for the benefit of the Operating Department." Here at last was an officer willing to surrender some of his own authority for the larger good, but this one change took eight years to accomplish. Stoddard favored a centralized organization for the same reasons Jeffers had: it gave the appearance of a lean, efficient structure, and it kept power firmly in the hands of the president and his top hands, who were loath to delegate authority to potential rivals.[24]

The problem went beyond an antiquated organizational structure. Since Jeffers had come to power, management of the road had become intensely personal. Job descriptions bore little relation to the realities of who did what. This was the inevitable result of Jeffers's habit of giving his favorites de facto authority on the line while stripping the officer in charge of actual power. John Kenefick, who worked on the Union Pacific in the forties, found "very little formal organization lines, really. . . . the general superintendent of transportation was not the guy who was really handling the transportation matters."[25]

The same held true in maintenance of way and other areas, which made it hard to know the players even with a scorecard. Having inherited a structure that fortified his office, Stoddard had no intention of disturbing it. He liked things to go through channels but realized the channels didn't always match the flow chart. Stoddard did not fancy himself a czar, but he kept the crucial trappings, notably the secret police, the spies, and an autocratic hierarchy staffed with favorites.

It helped that some of Stoddard's best officers were no longer threats to him. E. J. Connors's ambitions were burned out, and Perry Lynch had never been one to push himself forward. In many respects Lynch was the tragic figure of these years: a kind, considerate, scrupulously honest man who shunned office politics. "He was not susceptible to . . . brown-nosing at all," said an admiring colleague. As VPO he believed in spending money to make the road more efficient, and he was responsive to change. But he lacked a forceful personality and driving ambition. "I don't think he was a very strong guy," said Kenefick, who was originally hired by Lynch, "but in those days, good God, this was an awful place to work! I don't think I could have stood it."[26]

Stoddard watched Lynch as he did A. J. Seitz, aware that others thought one of them should have been president. Both were still young enough to be regarded as threats; Seitz was promoted to executive vice-president a few days after Stoddard took office. Seitz lasted in that position until May 1954, when Stoddard reduced him to vice-president and shipped him to the system's most remote outpost, Portland, with a big cut in salary as well. He lingered in exile eight years and never got back to Omaha. Stoddard then used Lynch's health (he had recently had a kidney operation) to move him from VPO to the president's own staff, explaining that "Mr. Lynch would be of considerable assistance to me."[27]

IT'S A TOUGH JOB, BUT . . . : A. J. Seitz, the vice-president exiled by Stoddard, confers awards on members of the Junior Drum Corps.

Lynch had once offended Stoddard simply by being in New York on official business and having Lovett ask him how many units were needed to dieselize the system. On his return Lynch dutifully reported the conversation to Stoddard, who accused him of going behind his back instead of through the proper channels. "It was a real sad thing," recalled Edd Bailey, "as far as the feeling between the two of them was concerned after that."[28]

Although his health was poor, Lynch believed he would be made senior vice-president to oversee operations and other duties. A friend warned that he was merely being lured out on a limb to be sawed off. "If I ever find myself in this position," he replied, "I'll never be spurred out."* Less than three years later, Stoddard put Lynch on the track for exile in Portland. Before he could act, however, Lynch left the company. "I'm not going to be spurred out," he repeated mournfully to the friend who had warned him. To some officers, Lynch's fall proved that nice guys did finish last.[29]

If Lynch was the tragic figure of the postwar years, the comic figure was surely Elgin Hicks, whose career embodied the Stoddard style of management.

*The "spurred out" reference meant having his career put on a spur track somewhere, as Stoddard had done with Seitz by sending him to Portland.

The two of them had been party pals coming up through the ranks. The genial, good-natured Hicks had started with the road in 1920 and worked his way up the ladder despite the usual number of firings by Jeffers. In July 1945 Jeffers had ousted him as superintendent of the Nebraska Division and replaced him with Bailey. Four months later, however, he was restored to his post when Bailey had to replace an injured superintendent on the Wyoming Division. By the time Stoddard came to office, Hicks had advanced to general superintendent of the Eastern Division.[30]

Most of the other officers had Hicks pegged. One called him "probably the most incompetent man I knew. [He was] just about the nicest man you would ever know, but he didn't know a damn thing." Another considered him "the loveliest fellow you ever saw, and he knew the least. . . . He never wrote a telegram or a letter in his life. . . . He just had been carried along by being friendly to the officers, and they just promoted him 'cause he was just a delightful guy."[31]

Stoddard liked Hicks and moved him right through the ranks, perhaps because Hicks represented no threat to him. In 1951 he was promoted to general manager ahead of Bailey, and three years later replaced Lynch as VPO. He surrendered that job to Bailey in 1957 and advanced to Seitz's old post as executive vice-president. Soon afterward he gained a seat on the board, which brought him into direct contact with New York. This proved his undoing. Usually Stoddard kept an eye on Hicks in New York, but on one occasion Hicks got away from him and showed up drunk for a board meeting, where he told the other directors that they knew nothing about railroads and didn't know enough to pour piss out of a boot. "He went to New York and made an ass of himself," said Stan How, "and they finally had to take him off the job because he didn't know."[32]

Hicks had two other major liabilities: fondness for the bottle and for the ladies. Neither was a secret to insiders at Omaha, yet Stoddard kept promoting him. As late as 1961, Hicks received a generous raise; the following year he retired early on account of ill health. "I always thought," mused one officer, "that Stoddard engineered his retirement because Hicks wasn't smart enough to do it himself." In fact, Stoddard had. Although Roland Harriman told him to get rid of Hicks, Stoddard delayed action. A few months later Hicks's son was killed in an accident, and Stoddard played on the board's sympathy to get his friend early retirement with pension. The day Hicks retired, he went on the wagon and stayed on it.[33]

Until his fall from grace, Hicks looked to be the heir apparent as Stoddard weeded out most of Ashby's old favorites. B. F. Wells, the former Union Pacific man Ashby had brought back from the Rock Island, was dispatched by abolishing his position. Eighteen months later the position was restored with a Stoddard appointee in it. Other Ashby favorites took the hint and retired early or were sent into exile like Seitz. Normalcy was in full flower.[34]

Unfortunately, normalcy for the Union Pacific meant old-fashioned. The sleeping giant, like the rail industry itself, had begun to resemble Rip van Winkle, awakening in the postwar years to find a world vastly different from that of half a century earlier. In some quarters Stoddard gained a reputation for being bold and experimental, but many of the innovations for which he got credit were either started by Ashby or pushed on Stoddard by his officers. He was slow to reform his own organization; not until 1955 did he seek to make the western general counsel and general auditor vice-presidents so they could deal with like officers of other roads and firms on an equal basis.[35]

The antediluvian flavor of the Omaha office was painfully evident to returning veterans who had held positions beyond their years during the war. "When I came back from the Air Force," recalled E. C. Schafer, "I couldn't really understand it. There were parts of the railroad we could not reach by telephone; we didn't even have telephones! But of course those are situations that grew up in tradition." Even harder to grasp was the hidebound seniority system. The war had thrust huge responsibilities on young men; Schafer had been a bomber pilot, a squadron commander. "To come back into a tradition-bound organization," he muttered, "just made you want to bust your shirt buttons."[36]

Schafer was especially appalled by the way the company disseminated information. The rule of thumb was to give out as little information as possible. General managers still set the example of standing up in front of their troops and chewing them out unmercifully. People still got fired arbitrarily even though the czar was long gone. "Those old traditions just hung on and on and on," grumbled a shop hand. "You fired a guy and then found out what happened." Reg Sutton, who became a vice-president in 1955, observed wryly, "Seems like at different times we always had somebody that we were supposed to be afraid of."[37]

Tradition dictated how officers and men alike were expected to perform. "They didn't tell you how to do your job," noted one officer ". . . But you never got away from your job. Even if you go on vacation, you might get called back. . . . You're going to wear a coat and tie and a white shirt and preferably cuff links five days a week. Now on Saturdays and Sundays you could come down in a sports coat and sports shirt." The switchboard was always open, and the operator knew where every officer was even when off duty.[38]

Despite its frequent violation, Rule G against drinking hung like a guillotine's blade above everyone. Men were fired just for being seen leaving a bar. Even wholesome forms of recreation were deemed frivolous. Stoddard frowned on golf and flatly barred the operating people from playing. Traffic men were grudgingly allowed the privilege because it got them together with customers, but no ambitious operating man dared waste his time on such distractions. Sutton was fond of enticing Bailey to sneak off to the country club, the latter hoping fervently that no one who saw them there would say something in front of Stoddard. Spies gained points by reporting a set of clubs in the car trunk of some hapless trainmaster or assistant superintendent.[39]

"Railroads run twenty-four hours a day, seven days a week," said an officer, "and there's no difference in the days." That was a tradition no amount of change had disturbed or was likely to in the near future.[40]

* * *

Nothing mirrored the way in which tradition had allowed time to pass the railroad by more than its approach to public relations and advertising. Since 1920 these fields had grown from infancy to play major roles in corporate life, yet on the Union Pacific their influence had actually regressed. During the 1930s, thanks largely to Sun Valley and the Utah Parks, the company had been a pioneer in the making of industrial motion pictures. It had a bright filmmaker in Vince Hunter and a fine still photographer in Billy Coons, both of whom did much to complement the work done by Steve Hannagan.[41]

Most of this work served the passenger trade. So did advertising, which on most railroads belonged to the passenger traffic department because it never occurred to them that they had anything else to advertise. The Union Pacific was no exception to this rule, but it had spent heavily on ads even before World War I and devised some original approaches. In 1913 it borrowed a vice-president from a New York ad agency to manage its campaign for the 1915 Panama Exposition. The company was also still innocent enough to drop a slogan, "The best dining-cars in the world," from its ads in 1914 because it could not prove that this was literally true.[42]

As early as 1915 the traffic director, who had control of advertising expenditures, urged Judge Lovett to spend more on what he called "the 'human interest' side of railroading" rather than on "a branch of service which brings us only a comparatively small part of our revenues." The idea of promoting the railroad as a whole instead of merely its passenger service was slow to catch on, however, because most railroad managers did not grasp the importance of influencing public opinion until their political woes grew acute. Even then, public relations was tied strictly to legislation. In 1916, for example, the company hired an advertising man fulltime to help with its fight against the eight-hour-day bill, then decided to keep him when he did well.[43]

Carl Gray was quick to appreciate the value of public relations. He created a department in Omaha, started the company magazine, and boosted the road with special promotions such as "Union Pacific Day" in 1923, which brought railroaders and citizens of North Platte together for a program of fun and serious events culminating in a dinner for nearly seven hundred guests. He also spent money on ad campaigns conveying facts about the railroad and boosting the Utah Parks. Traffic vice-president Frank Robinson revealed his sense of changing times in a 1930 talk to ticket agents. "Standing behind your counter or ticket window," he told them, "you sell the invisible commodity of transportation to all the world—a world mobile and astir to an extent unprecedented in history."[44]

During the depression the Union Pacific's advertising budget remained among the largest in the industry, especially as the new trains came on line. In 1935 it looked seriously into acquiring radio stations in eight major cities as both an investment and a vehicle for delivering its message. The deals did not work out, but the company soon commenced sponsoring programs. That same year Averell Harriman rescued the annual report from its traditional drab gray cover and dressed it up with a color picture of a streamliner. A year later he hired

Steve Hannagan, and Gray promoted E. C. Schmidt to be his assistant in charge of public relations.[45]

Averell, who took a close interest in public relations, thought the road's advertising still had a long way to go. "No matter who we use as an agency," he told Jeffers, "the main conception will have to come from our own organization." Jeffers responded eagerly because he liked the limelight, and his approach tended to be personal. After his successful Golden Spike extravaganza in 1939 he launched another one the following year featuring Gracie Allen and George Burns.[46]

Jeffers tended to define public relations as publicity (preferably for himself), but at least he got on well with Schmidt. They were both portly men fond of cigars. "In this business," stressed Schafer, "you have to have rapport with the boss; otherwise you just don't function well." There was none with Ashby, who was bright but shy. He loathed personal publicity and didn't get on at all with Schmidt, so the public relations effort languished despite the real innovations he was pushing that cried for good ink.[47]

Stoddard fared little better. He tolerated public relations but, like Jeffers, he tended to confuse it with publicity. He was also coy; privately he relished the attention but acted as if he did not. And, like Ashby, he was a poor speaker who shunned such appearances. "One of the shortcomings all the way through," lamented Schafer, "was the fact that we had very few people who made good spokesmen." Nor did they have anything new to say. "Some of the same speeches were made in the industry for thirty-five, thirty-six, thirty-eight years," he added in disgust. "You could just pull them out of the file and talk about socialism in transportation in recent years just as well as you did back in the thirties."[48]

Spokesmen who had nothing to say and said it badly. The problem reflected how badly public relations and advertising had slipped by the 1950s. Even Schmidt's ad campaigns never got much beyond scare tactics against the airlines. Nor had internal communications improved much. Attempts to revive the company magazine that died during the depression proved abortive. When Schmidt retired in December 1950, Stoddard waited two years before naming a replacement. Hannagan's death in 1953 left another creative vacuum no one rushed to fill. Most top officers continued to regard public relations as mere publicity rather than a useful tool for management.[49]

If the Union Pacific seemed a sleeping giant to outsiders, its New York office resembled more the Land That Time Forgot. It had changed remarkably little since the days of Judge Lovett. The company still occupied the upper floors of the Equitable Building at 120 Broadway. In 1916 the staff totaled 154, of whom only 6 were women. By 1946 the ranks had thinned to 84, including 13 women. If many of the faces looked familiar, they were: nearly a quarter of the 1946 personnel were also there in 1916.[50]

The organization had changed even less than the faces. In 1912 Judge Lovett had separated the secretary's department from the executive department, but few functions changed other than the need for a second bell because the judge had to ring for two people instead of one. The other departments included treasury, controller, transfer, law, and engineering—the latter purely advisory once the practical functions were transferred to Omaha. In 1919 Judge Lovett made Woody Charske his intermediary for all business with the accounting, treasurer's, and engineering offices, and put him in charge of all correspondence relating to financial matters.[51]

The secretary still performed the same functions Alex Millar had performed for Harriman. He handled all details surrounding executive committee and board meetings, maintained the files, took care of incoming correspondence (except financial), and kept all incoming material on subsidiary companies. Officers grappled with such weighty problems as ice for the office coolers, turning off lights at the day's end, the quality of the towel supply, switchboard hours, and Omaha's profligate use of cipher in telegrams.[52]

While wars and depression convulsed the planet, the office plodded along its well-worn path of routine. The same pallid faces hunched over the same well-thumbed files, dutifully adding new sheets to the swollen pile of yellowing documents held together by large adjustable fasteners. "It was not a live-wire office," deadpanned James P. Coughlin, who went to work there in 1949 and ultimately became office manager. When he first arrived, the top brass looked more like the "over-the-hill gang." The venerable Charske was sixty-eight and had slowed considerably. Controller L. J. Tracy was also in his sixties and not well; he required a daily nap. E. G. Smith, the secretary, was the same age and going blind.[53]

Not that the staff saw much of them. The executive committee members entered through a different door and dealt only with the officers, who themselves rarely made personal appearances in the general office. When they needed someone, they rang a buzzer. "When I first came here," recalled Coughlin, "E. G. Smith walked out of his office. The staff thought that was the second coming. Everybody leaped. Literally got up out of their desks to see what he wanted."[54]

Everything was done by hand, pretty much in the same way it had been done for half a century. "They were always great on precedent," sighed Coughlin. "If you did it the way it was done the last time, it must have been right the last time, it has to be right this time." Automation was an unknown word even in the financial offices. Each department still did its own payroll and paid people in cash, taking back receipts for every outlay. Even the directors got paid in cash.[55]

The office had no receptionist because it seldom got visitors. There was a telephone operator, but she was tucked away in her own cubbyhole. Anyone entering the office was greeted by an elderly black man named Walter Davis, who had been the chef on Judge Lovett's car and was devoted to the Lovetts and the Harrimans. In his twilight years he did odd jobs in the office, such as fielding visitors and dusting off each day the desk Roland Harriman hardly ever used. Another black employee named Ira Williams, who had started with the company in Harriman's time, was the only staff member who toted a gun. The dignified Williams carried bank deposits and securities.[56]

High above the streets, the New York office was isolated from the outside world—including Omaha. All communication with the president's office flowed through the chairman; other officers never picked up the phone to talk with their opposite number in Omaha. "There was no [direct] communication between anybody in the office and the western office," said Coughlin flatly. "It was all done either by telegram or by letter. . . . I never spoke to a person in Omaha. . . . Everything went through channels."[57]

This striking degree of insularity does much to explain why New York knew so little about what actually went on in Omaha, and why information for New York could be packaged in whatever way the president desired. The decentralized system that Judge Lovett had worked so hard to create after Harriman's death made sense in his day, but since then vast improvements had occurred in communications that made it possible to keep in close touch. The Union Pacific had done little or nothing to use them. It still relied mainly on the telegraph and the mails even for important messages between New York and Omaha.

Neither office had learned to use modern communications as a management tool. Nor had they adopted a host of other tools available to them. Railroad accounting was archaic, thanks in large part to a provision of the Hepburn Act of 1906 that prescribed uniform or what came to be known as ICC accounting for all roads. Whatever its merits, ICC accounting was too passive to serve as a management tool. It looked backward rather than forward, recorded facts instead of developing systems for financial planning.[58]

Of course, no company had to limit itself only to ICC accounting. It could have developed another system and simply kept two sets of books, as later became common. But here as elsewhere the heavy hand of regulation had a blighting effect on initiative. Like other roads, the Union Pacific fell into the habit of doing what was required rather than looking for new opportunities. As a result, the company lacked such tools as a capital budget, an income budget, or a cash-flow statement. Capital budgets consisted of an ad hoc process in which Omaha proposed and New York disposed.[59]

In his salad days Charske had kept a firm grip on this process, but as he grew older the grip loosened and New York's role grew more perfunctory. "I really don't think he did any more than the routine things to keep the shop running," said Coughlin. "The company more or less ran itself, you know. There didn't seem to be any big decisions being made here." The executive committee rubber-stamped the president's requests and confined most of its discussion to matters not on the table. As Coughlin put it, "If it wasn't going to be approved, it wasn't submitted."[60]

New York had little choice but to go along with the president. He was their only source of information about the railroad, the only voice they heard on most of the issues they had to decide. This situation was remarkable in two respects: the executive committee allowed itself to become a prisoner of the president, yet it went about appointing new presidents on an astonishingly casual basis. Why were no other management tools developed when other industries had had them well before the war? Why did New York permit this system to endure for so long? The answer has a familiar ring: tradition. Things had always been done that way.

So Omaha went its way, and New York followed. The system worked because the company was strong and prosperous enough to survive its internal weaknesses. Without reforms, however, the sleeping giant was destined to snooze on until its flaws caught up with it. "Paying attention and showing up every day on time" were the criteria for keeping a job, and people were very anxious about job security. "Nobody would ever tell you what to do," added Coughlin, because they were afraid to have someone else know how to do *their* job. The inmates of Sleepy Hollow, creaking dutifully through their rounds, knew their place and kept it—forever and ever.[61]

Change finally seeped into the New York office through that most familiar of channels, mortality. Joe Mann, the eastern general counsel, died in November 1951 and was replaced by another Clark, Carr & Ellis denizen, Frank Barnett. A brilliant tax lawyer, Barnett's driving ambition soon carried him into a pivotal role with Union Pacific. A year later Robert Lovett let Roland Harriman know he was ready to leave government for good. He had come back to the company in 1949 after serving as under secretary of state only to leave the next year to become deputy secretary of defense. In 1951 he had moved up to secretary of defense, a post he held until January 1953, when the Truman administration was packing up.[62]

Roland was delighted by the prospect of Lovett's return but had a delicate problem: there was no vacancy on the board. Someone would have to surrender his seat. The logical candidate was Jeffers, who seldom attended meetings anymore because of his health, but Roland knew the old man clutched his seat with fierce pride. Aware that it would break Jeffers's heart, Roland wrote a tactful letter in December 1952. "It has occurred to me," he said, "that you would welcome an opportunity to make a place for [Lovett] on the Board by presenting your resignation. . . . Such an action on your part would be a fitting climax to the great service that you have rendered."[63]

Roland gave the letter to Stoddard, who turned it over to the luckless Doc Churchill as the one man who might persuade Jeffers to go along. "I really felt something like a Judas," moaned Churchill, but he took the letter to the old czar and tried gently to show him what a generous act his resignation would be. Jeffers sat looking at him quietly, then said to his daughter, "Eileen, those fellas want to get rid of me."

"No, they don't want to get rid of you, Mr. Jeffers," Doc protested. "They want to get Bob Lovett back onto the board."

"Okay," said Jeffers after a pause. "Tell 'em I quit."[64]

Roland thanked him graciously, but it had little effect. Churchill was so afraid the request might kill Jeffers that he got the doctor's okay before seeing him. He may have been right. Stripped of his last tie with the road that had been his life, Jeffers died four months later.[65]

In May 1953, only two months after Jeffers's death, the venerable Charske passed away. Together he and Jeffers had given the company more than a

COMING HOME: Robert A. Lovett, the astute, urbane power broker who led the Union Pacific into a new era after his return to the company in 1953.

century of service. There was no doubt who would replace him as chairman of the executive committee. Roland had waited a long time for Lovett to return and lift some of the burden of leadership from his shoulders. Harriman and Lovett made a smooth team because they thought so much alike and yet complemented each other well. The best way to treat us, Lovett once told Reg Sutton, was "just the same as if it were one person."[66]

But no one doubted who was in charge. "Mr. Lovett was the boss," said Frank Barnett, "no question about that." Roland was a man of great common sense and shrewd insights. "But he didn't ever want to be a person who was running something," observed James H. Evans, who became a director in 1965, "so Lovett was the man who ran it." Barnett thought Lovett was a genius. Sutton called him "the finest executive that I have ever worked for. He had a way of inspiring you; he put complete faith and trust in you." He also had a high boiling point. Elbridge Gerry claimed never to have seen him angry. "When he gets mad," said Gerry, "he gets sarcastic." This remarkable self-control served him as well in Union Pacific as it had in government.[67]

It had also exacted a steep price from him. A dozen years in Washington had cost Lovett most of his stomach in a series of operations for bleeding ulcers that left him able to eat only small amounts of food several times a day. Unlike the vigorous Harrimans, he had always been something of a hypochondriac. Fate in the form of what he called his "glass insides" turned this phobia into a self-fulfilling prophecy, but Lovett bore even his physical breakdowns with typical good humor. After one intestinal operation he told Sutton cheerfully that he was through with hospitals because there was nothing left to take out. Later, when he had to get a pacemaker installed, he wrote Sutton that another corner had been turned: the doctors were starting to put stuff back in.[68]

By 1953 Lovett was a tired, unwell man who probably didn't want the chairman's job. But he was only fifty-eight and could not turn down the Harrimans' insistence that he take it. For fourteen years he stayed at the post, investing it with grace and style as well as a genius for grasping the essentials of a problem. "He was our patron saint," admitted James Evans. "Roland maybe should have been, but the guy you went to in the final clutches was Lovett, and Lovett always consulted with Roland. So there was total communication between them."[69]

"He was always a very bright guy," agreed Elbridge Gerry, "quick, and could analyze a problem like nobody's business. . . . He was the workhorse during the fifties, early sixties." However, as the staff soon learned, there was one peculiarity in Lovett's style. No matter how well something was explained to him, it didn't fully register until he saw it on paper. Once he read it, he never forgot it. Not surprisingly, the amount of paperwork in the office increased during his tenure.[70]

So did the level of work done. Lovett brought from his government experience an appreciation for the importance of staff work, a virtue sorely lacking at Union Pacific. Gerry did not exaggerate in saying that Lovett "taught them how to do staff work." At every opportunity he looked to beef up the ranks. Barnett took care of the legal end, bringing in another Clark, Carr & Ellis man, Covington Hardee, as his assistant. In 1956 Lovett brought to the board Courtney C. Brown, the dean of Columbia's graduate school of business. A year later the board was enlarged from fifteen to nineteen members, with three of the new directors coming from the West; the fourth was Elbridge Gerry from Brown Brothers Harriman.[71]

These changes were but surface indications of much deeper stirrings. Lovett did not move quickly or rashly; that was neither his nor the company's style. He needed time to diagnose the problems and find suitable remedies, which he would then have to persuade Roland to get behind. But no one else was closer to Roland or had his confidence so completely. For that reason, as well as his own bright, incisive mind, Robert Lovett was the best and perhaps the only man capable of rousing the sleeping giant with minimum uproar.

Early on, he gave the staff at least a hint that change was in the wind. After being elected chairman of the executive committee, Lovett walked through the general office and shook hands with everybody. If the staff thought *he* was the second coming, they at least had some reason for it: enough old-timers were still around who remembered the judge.[72]

25

The Awakening

In November 1958 a brokerage firm concluded its analysis of the Union Pacific by observing that "A greater separation of [its] natural resources from the railroad operations, looking towards their commercialization to a far greater degree than now exists, would be a desirable objective for Union Pacific stockholders to contemplate."[1]

Robert Lovett had already come to this same conclusion for many reasons. The most generic one had to do with the law, going back to the Hepburn Act, that forbade railroads from engaging in any other business. A tangled web of statutes, state and federal, kept the carriers from fully exploiting their assets or even using them efficiently.* "Our problem," he explained later, "was to get out of the iron maiden that we were in . . . the past construction of the law which prohibited a railroad from doing anything other than operating a railroad."[2]

Put simply, the company could not sell its coal or oil or anything else. As properties of the railroad, these outside activities had to run the gauntlet of ICC regulation. Moreover, the deepening plight of the railroads in the late 1950s spurred new demands for government ownership. If that were to happen, the government takeover would scoop up nonrail assets along with the roads. Something had to be done to preserve them for the stockholders.[3]

Apart from these industry-wide concerns, the Union Pacific had a special problem: the Omaha bottleneck. It did not take an old Washington hand like

*For example, the commodity clause of the Hepburn Act prohibited railroads from carrying any article (except timber and its manufactured products) that was mined, manufactured, or produced by it or in which it had an interest.

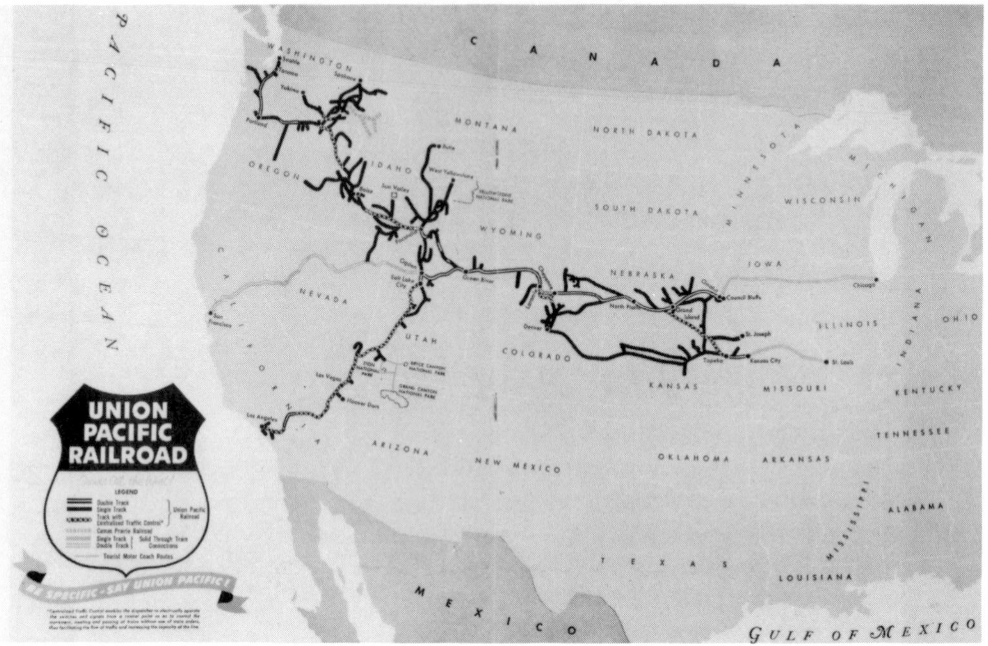

THE NEW RAILROAD: The Union Pacific system in 1955.

Lovett long to see how well Omaha had insulated itself from New York, and how ineffective New York was in dealing with the western headquarters. The nonrail assets had languished because the railroad managers had little skill and less interest in dealing with them. To their thinking a railroad was a railroad; the rest was gravy, however rich it had become. Something had to be done to restore New York's voice in the West and wrest control of these other resources from the president in Omaha.

The obvious solution was to create a holding company that spun off the nonrail assets into separate companies outside the reach of the ICC. A host of legal and structural obstacles stood in the way, however, as well as an utter lack of executive talent to run the other companies. The logical first step, then, was to devise an organizational structure that routed nonrail activities around Omaha. From this need arose the divisional plan.

It did not come quickly. Lovett had first to persuade Roland Harriman, who was wedded to tradition and slow to grasp the need for change. There were long and frequent discussions in their adjoining offices at Brown Brothers Harriman, where they were still partners. "It took a little persuading," Lovett conceded in his gracious way, "because of course everybody has a slightly different approach to things." No one else's opinion mattered; the executive committee was never involved until the final plan was presented for approval. Once Roland came around, Lovett turned to the problem of finding the right people to handle the details of restructuring the company.[4]

FROM LAWYER TO LEADER: Frank E. Barnett, who became general counsel and then chairman of the executive committee during a critical time of transition.

The obvious choice was Frank Barnett, one of the brightest corporate lawyers around. Barnett saw, as Lovett did, that the Union Pacific was a prosperous road in a failing industry. "The question was," he said later, "whether the Union Pacific would go along and be part of this failing industry, or whether we would do something else." That something else was diversification, and Barnett was eager to help bring it about. But he needed a good financial man to assist him. Controller L. J. Tracy was too old and tired to be useful. Not until Tracy retired in 1960 did Lovett find the right man to complete the team.[5]

For a time Tracy's successor remained a big secret in the office. Then, in July 1960, the position was given to Reg Sutton, the vice-president and general auditor in Omaha. An affable man with a homespun manner, Sutton was shrewd, energetic, and hard-working. His arrival brought the New York office to life. He imported several people from Omaha and also kept close tabs on things there. For a time he returned (by plane) to Omaha nearly every weekend. An office hand claimed only half in jest that Sutton wrote letters to Omaha during the week and then hurried west on the weekends to answer them.[6]

When Sutton arrived in July, he and Barnett were told they had six months to devise a plan for separating out the nonrail functions. Everyone knew Art Stoddard would, in Barnett's words, "stubbornly protect Omaha against any incursion"; in particular, he would defend his own power from erosion. Lovett took care to involve Stoddard in the plan even before Sutton came east; as an Omaha man Sutton also helped disarm Stoddard's suspicions. This was to be no surprise attack but a deft reshuffling of the lines of authority.[7]

Late in June 1960 Lovett showed Stoddard a plan creating two divisions, transportation and natural resources, each with an executive officer reporting directly to the chairman of the executive committee. Stoddard suggested a third division for land, and wanted the other executives reporting to him rather than New York. Lovett had intended to wait on the third division but agreed to go ahead with it. On the line of authority, however, he stood firm. Barnett drew up amendments to the bylaws to incorporate the new plan.[8]

In November Stoddard came to New York to discuss the proposed bylaw changes. The amendments routing authority directly to New York, he protested, disturbed many of his officers. Lovett deflected the objections gracefully. The whole point, he emphasized, was to have the New York office function like a holding company, which would "very likely be the next step before long." At the same time he granted Stoddard a major concession: the bylaws would be changed, but special letters from Lovett would instruct the land division to funnel its activities through Stoddard's office and the natural resources division to obtain Stoddard's concurrence before submitting its recommendations to New York.[9]

After Stoddard left, mollified if not consoled, Lovett briefed assistant counsel Covington Hardee on the meeting. "I infer," Hardee noted, "that he believes the new plan . . . will put the New York officers in a better position, through advance planning and otherwise, to make quick decisions based on sound analysis and judgment." The divisions would also provide top management with more flexibility and better ways to measure performance.[10]

While Lovett seemed to have negated the crucial reform, he understood the difference between a structural revision and a temporary concession. Aware that Stoddard feared losing the prestige of being in charge of everything rather than just the railroad, Lovett gave him what amounted to the status of first among equals. That same month, however, Stoddard suffered an aneurysm and underwent surgery in New York. He never fully recovered, and later had a second one. From these bouts he emerged thin and listless, a ghost of his former self who walked feebly through the last years of his presidency.[11]

The new plan went into effect January 1, 1961. Lee S. Osborne took charge of the natural resources division. A geologist who had joined the oil development department in 1949, he emerged quickly as the logical successor in 1956 to the retiring vice-president of oil development, William Reinhardt. The land division was put under A. C. Ritter, the general manager of properties. With Stoddard incapacitated, the transportation division fell into the hands of his two top subordinates, executive vice-president Elgin Hicks and VPO Edd Bailey, a longtime veteran of the road. But Hicks soon fell from grace, leaving Bailey as the heir apparent.[12]

"There was a lot of yelling and screaming from Omaha," recalled Elbridge Gerry. "It didn't do them any good. . . . When they ceased to report to Stoddard and began to report to Lovett in New York, well that's when things began to move." The nonrail activities, which Gerry thought had always been treated like orphans, were free to develop on their own.[13]

Omaha itself soon underwent some changes. In 1961 Stoddard was the highest paid rail executive in America, but his weakened condition left him little more than a figurehead. To get around this delicate problem, the board created a new post, chief executive officer of transportation, and gave it to Edd Bailey in November 1963. This enabled Bailey to run the railroad until December 1964, when Stoddard retired and he assumed the presidency. Bailey would be the last president to come up through the ranks Jeffers-style, the last inbred leader of a railroad struggling to be reborn yet again.[14]

Bailey took office January 1, 1965. On that same date some modifications of the divisions went into effect, enabling them to function as completely independent units. These changes erased the temporary concessions granted Stoddard. As Lovett and Barnett knew, however, the divisions were a halfway house. The long-range plan contemplated four steps; create the divisions; find managers for them; convert the divisions to corporations; and fold them into a holding company. As early as 1962 the way seemed clear to proceed toward step three. But the road proved a treacherous one, filled with pitfalls and detours that took years to negotiate.[15]

The oil operations, headquartered in Los Angeles, typified the old approach to doing things at Union Pacific. Little was done with the Wilmington field at first. The company bought some good lands but let others get away; Lovett once mourned that the Union Pacific blew a chance to buy most of what is now Long Beach for about $3 million. At first it drilled wells for defensive purposes, an attitude that carried over to other fields. ''It had a lot to do with self-protection,'' noted Gerry. ''. . . They just couldn't sit on them and let everybody drill around them and take the oil off their property.''[16]

In 1937 the Union Pacific had netted a modest $400,000 from its oil and gas operations; by 1946 this figure had climbed to $6.6 million. Then production mushroomed, spurred by a revived economy, the postwar automobile explosion, and rising oil prices. Between 1946 and 1960 net earnings averaged $30 million annually, with the Wilmington field alone producing an average of 10.9 million barrels a year. Analysts drooled over the boost given the company's earnings by this cash cow. ''The corporation,'' predicted one, ''may some day become a good medium-size crude oil company operating a profitable railroad on the side.'' Speculation arose as early as 1948 that the Union Pacific would create a separate company for its oil operations as the Southern Pacific had done in 1920.[17]

But nothing was done. To avoid legal, union, and other problems, Wilmington was operated through an independent contractor. The capable William Reinhardt managed the operation with a minimum staff, and in 1955 stayed on past his seventieth birthday to help Osborne take hold. Omaha knew nothing about the oil business and depended heavily on their judgment, which usually proved sound. After losing several geologists and engineers to oil companies, Reinhardt induced Omaha to pay them higher salaries. He also moved in 1950 to enhance output at Wilmington by unitizing some company wells with those

CALIFORNIA OIL RUSH: A view of the Signal Hill oil field, taken May 8, 1956.

of General Petroleum Company. When land subsidence became a serious problem in Long Beach harbor, Reinhardt used water-injection techniques to restore underground pressure.[18]

This proved a wise move. In 1958 the federal government filed suit to enjoin oil production until all operators unitized and repressured with water injections as the Union Pacific was already doing. Although the dispute got caught up in local politics, the producers agreed to join in a broad water-injection program. For its pains the Union Pacific was rewarded by a rejuvenation of the Wilmington fields, which had dwindled steadily from a peak of 13.8 million barrels in 1953. Thanks in large measure to unitization and water injection, production rose from a low of 6.6 million barrels in 1960 to 10.8 million in 1968.[19]

The success of unitization at Wilmington prompted the Union Pacific to do the same at its large Rangely field in Colorado and some smaller fields in Wyoming. Through the early 1950s the company was content to rake in record profits until problems started to pile up. A series of suits disputed the Union Pacific's ownership of mineral rights on lands owned by it. The company invited a test suit from the government on the oil beneath its right of way. When the Supreme Court ruled in favor of the government, Lovett dismissed the effects as "negligible." Some suits brought by private parties, however, challenging company ownership of mineral rights on its land grant, involved high stakes. Although the company won every round, the fight dragged on for years.[20]

After 1955 the company had to face a more immediate problem: a steady drop in production. Wilmington required more wells to produce less oil, and some of the Rocky Mountain fields disappointed in their output. By 1962 the Rangely field in Colorado, second only to Wilmington in production, had slipped 40 percent from its peak of 1955. A generous offer from Pan American Petroleum enabled the Union Pacific to sell Rangely for $62.5 million in 1963, but the sale did nothing to solve the larger problem of what to do about falling output.[21]

Concerned that some analysts might misread the disposal of Rangely, the company issued a denial that the transaction signaled a change in its mineral policy. Far from wanting out of the mineral business, the Union Pacific wanted to get much more into it. Exploration work was stepped up and new agreements were made with oil companies for joint projects. In 1960 the company invested $9.4 million in Calnev, a new pipeline project serving Las Vegas, two Air Force bases, and some California communities. The new line opened in May 1961 and began shipping 12,500 barrels a day. Traffic through the new pipe jumped 28 percent the first year.[22]

The same slow process of awakening could be seen in the company's handling of an entirely different mineral, trona. As early as 1874 Jay Gould had tried to develop the production of soda from deposits near Laramie, but that effort petered out during the 1880s. The whole episode was forgotten for decades until the appearance of a cantankerous old geologist named Robert D. Pike, who was convinced that Wyoming housed vast underground rivers, the dried-up beds of which contained enormous deposits of trona. Ashby took a liking to Pike and in the late 1930s put him on the payroll at $250 a month to search for the beds. Few in the company had any idea of what Professor Pike, as he was known, was doing.[23]

Pike turned out to be right. Near Green River he found underground beds with deposits he later estimated at 200 million tons. Here was the potential for a lucrative industry and source of traffic; the question was how best to develop it. The war intervened before anything was done. Ashby then dispatched Pike to Washington to lobby for a subsidy to mine trona and convert it to soda ash, which was needed for the production of aluminum and glass. For months Pike flailed away at an unyielding bureaucracy as well as skeptics in Union Pacific. Reinhardt protested his "very arbitrary and know-it-all attitude," but Ashby, who knew something about eccentrics, defended the geologist at every turn.[24]

The government boards showed no interest, but chemical companies did. Once again the Union Pacific, faced with a new situation and the old legal restraints on its doing anything directly, fell back on the only precedent available. It had long handled oil and gas development through leases to outside companies on the basis of royalties or shared returns. Ashby granted Westvaco and some other licensees the right to develop and process trona on this basis.[25]

As the man who had always dealt with Pike, Ashby understood the trona operation better than most. When he learned in 1948 that the Westvaco operation was both disorganized and unsafe, he told its officers bluntly to shape up or the lease would be canceled. Westvaco shaped up, but four months later Ashby was gone and Stoddard took little interest in the project. A study done in May 1951 revealed that the trona beds were even more extensive than originally thought. The geologist recommended that Union Pacific join with another operator to develop a second mining complex. Another boost came from the federal government, which issued a certificate making the project a full-fledged defense plant.[26]

After some delays a lease was granted to another chemical firm and the second mine started up. Still the operation aroused little enthusiasm; not until 1961 did the Union Pacific annual report even mention trona. A titanium find at Iron Mountain northeast of Laramie attracted far more attention. Other chemical companies nosed around Green River looking to acquire rights on both government and Union Pacific land. Then, in 1959, another large trona bed was discovered at a depth of less than a thousand feet, which meant it could be mined more cheaply than the other operations.[27]

Lovett used this opportunity to try a more forceful approach to development. A deal was struck with Stauffer Chemical to create a new subsidiary, owned 51 percent by Stauffer and 49 percent by Union Pacific, for mining and refining the trona. The operation opened in 1962 and did so well that it looked to expand at once. It was an ideal situation for Union Pacific, providing long hauls of whole trainloads on a product too bulky for trucks to touch. In the first year the company hauled 9,661 cars averaging 65 tons some 763 miles per trip. "Finally," said Reg Sutton, "there was a trainload out of Green River every night."[28]

Trona soon joined oil as a staple of the new natural resources division, but Lovett was not content to stop there. He encouraged a program of exploring for other minerals such as phosphate, fluorspar, manganese, ocher, perlite, gypsum, silica, bentonite, and uranium. As these efforts increased, Osborne felt the need to hire a general manager for mining. The company also added to its holdings in trona and other mineral lands by buying adjacent properties. It even bought a gold mine in Oregon.[29]

The oldest and once dominant of the company's minerals, coal, seemed clearly in decline. It was no longer needed as fuel thanks to dieselization, and the Union Pacific could not market it elsewhere. The war had kept the mines busy, and Senator J. C. O'Mahoney, who did much to get the trona mines classified as defense plants, tried hard in 1944 to get a pilot plant for making synthetic fuels located in Rock Springs. Missouri got the project, but efforts to interest the government in a Wyoming plant continued for years.[30]

The coal mines earned an impressive collection of safety awards; one Reliance mine went three years and 1.22 million man-hours without a lost-time injury. But they had lost their central role for the railroad and had yet to find a new one. Once the divisions were created, it made no sense to leave the coal company as an independent entity. In 1962 the Union Pacific Coal Company was dissolved and the operation folded into the natural resources division.[31]

The land operation still performed its historic role, but in a new way. Ever since J. L. Haugh had shown the importance of creating industrial parks to lure industries to sites along the railroad, the company had shifted to industrial development. Instead of selling land to attract settlers, it hoped to fill whole sites with businesses that would generate traffic for the road. To do this, it had to buy land as well as sell it; as a result the company began to acquire large parcels in every major city on the route.

Apart from Ashby's efforts on behalf of Las Vegas, this program languished until Lovett's arrival. In 1953, the year Lovett took charge, industrial development became a feature in the annual report, which had ignored it earlier. Over the next dozen years the company lured a total of 2,527 industries to locations along its lines. In 1965 the land division launched a new drive for acquisitions, spending $17 million on 3,270 acres of land in cities ranging from Omaha to Muncie, Kansas, to Walnut, California.[32]

There was a strong flavor of tradition in all these activities. Both mineral and industrial development had strong roots in the 1870s, when Jay Gould had worked hard at improving the coal operation, pushing mines, soda, even shale oil, and cultivating new industries along the route. A century later the scale and the setting had changed radically. The West was no longer virgin land or a colony of the East but rather the fastest growing area of the nation. One suspects Gould would have beamed at how far the Union Pacific and the region it served had come in a century.

One of the hardest tasks in defining the Union Pacific's future was deciding what to leave out. Tradition was an obstacle here as in so many other areas of railroading. Lovett had some strong views on this subject, many of them

MULTIDIMENSIONAL: By no coincidence a Union Pacific truck crosses an overpass above a Union Pacific freight train and the domeliner *City of Los Angeles* at Peterson, Utah.

grounded in the era between the wars when the railroads were also in deep trouble and grasping at straws. He had favored the effort to broaden the road into a diversified transportation company but urged caution because the costs were high and the legal barriers even higher.

Nothing in the postwar world changed his views. The Union Pacific had in fact retreated somewhat by selling Greyhound a large minority share of both Union Pacific Stages and Interstate Transit in 1943. Although the bus companies turned a profit after the war, the rapid growth of air and automobile travel reduced their value to the Union Pacific. In 1952 the company sold the rest of its holdings in both bus companies to Greyhound and left the business.[33]

Nor had Lovett's opinion on entering the air travel business changed. Prior to the war he had concluded that the airlines would eventually scoop long-haul passenger traffic, and there was nothing the railroads could do because the ICC would not allow them into the field. Freight was another matter. The airlines had an agreement with railway express, but both independent air companies and some railroads were itching to get into the business and had filed applications.[34]

R. V. Fletcher of the Association of American Railroads had urged the organization in 1943 to get behind legislation that would permit the carriers to engage in air and highway transport. "We are face to face," he stressed, "with one of the most important questions that has confronted the industry for a long time." Interstate Transit joined the list of those applying for a certificate, but in June 1944 Jeffers had the request withdrawn. The attempts failed, but the issue kept surfacing. In 1954 and again in 1965 Lovett reaffirmed his earlier views. "I do not believe the legislative climate has changed," he said in 1965, "and therefore do not believe it worthwhile to consider at this time entering forms of transportation in which we are not presently engaged."[35]

What Lovett wanted was not to get into new forms of travel but to get out of the business altogether. "To hell with the cheese, let's get out of the trap." That was a quip he had picked up during the banking crisis of 1929. It fit a number of crises he endured in government service, and it fit the passenger service dilemma bedeviling the railroads.[36]

Thanks to Averell Harriman, the Union Pacific had spent heavily during the depression to revive the passenger trade. It was a bold gamble to sink so much into what was the smallest part of the railroad's business, and it did not pan out. The streamliners and the *Challenger* service had captured headlines but not large profits. World War II soon wiped out whatever gains were made, deranging regular service with its enormous demands and running even the finest equipment into the ground. To revive the service in 1946 meant another large investment in a dubious enterprise with a limited future.

Unfortunately, there was little choice in the matter. The company could not get out of the business, and Roland was not about to do it in a half-hearted way. Ashby was willing to buy new equipment but had some offbeat notions about it. In 1946–47 the company ordered 180 new cars, including 50 sleepers. Ashby wanted to make the sleepers all drawing rooms, saying "Nobody wants to ride in anything but a drawing room." It took some talking to persuade him that not everyone could afford to go first class.[37]

Three years passed before the last of these new cars went on line. Meanwhile, the Union Pacific modernized some of its older cars and by 1947 was able to start daily service on all three of its main streamliner runs: Portland, San Francisco, and Los Angeles. This was an ambitious schedule; previously the California streamliners had run only three times a week and the Portland train six times a month. A coast-to-coast Pullman service was tried in cooperation with eastern roads. Schedules on other trains to the coast were cut, and in 1950 daily service between Portland and Seattle was launched. For this run the company bought an experimental train dubbed the "train of tomorrow" with observation domes on all four cars.[38]

Ashby tried hard to improve service. He dropped the old tourist cars, calling them "an antiquated, outmoded type of railroad equipment," and pushed for a survey of passengers on the value of transcoastal service even though the eastern lines showed no interest in it. But Ashby had his limits. He took a dim view of the costly new dome cars introduced by the Burlington on its *Zephyr* streamliners. Sometimes he took poor performance personally. When the *City of Portland* continually ran late, he snarled at Lynch, "This train has been treated like a stepchild just because of my interest in it, and I am not going to stand it any longer."[39]

By the time Stoddard became president, the Union Pacific was running fifty-eight passenger trains of all kinds every day. Buoyed by a survey showing that its lightweight sleepers had higher average earnings than any other major road, the company ordered another fifty coaches and fifty sleepers in 1948 and began phasing out its older type sleepers. Meanwhile, business kept declining. Passenger income had dropped 33 percent in 1946 with the loss of military traffic; by 1949 it had plummeted another 61 percent. Then the Korean War offered a temporary respite as earnings jumped nearly 22 percent between 1950 and 1952.[40]

This ripple of hope left Stoddard unimpressed. "Art Stoddard, he didn't give a damn about passenger business," snorted E. A. Klippel, the passenger traffic manager. But Perry Lynch was sympathetic and, more important, Roland Harriman wanted the level of service maintained. Just before Lovett returned, the Union Pacific took another stab at upgrading its passenger operation. It bought fifty more cars in 1951, then splurged two years later on a contingent of dome cars. Klippel even managed to get the industry's first dome diners in 1955 along with thirty redesigned sleepers known as Redwood cars, and roomier coaches.[41]

The company did more than upgrade equipment. It tried a new family fare, dropped the extra fare on the Los Angeles train to compete better with the Burlington's popular *Zephyrs,* and replaced the *Los Angeles Limited* with a reborn version of the *Challenger,* completely streamlined with a schedule under forty hours and three meals for $2.50. To improve service the Union Pacific went so far as to change partners in Chicago. In 1955 it severed the historic tie with the Northwestern to run its streamliners with the Milwaukee. The Northwestern, groaning under the cost of transcontinental service, had let its roadbed get rough and often ran behind schedule. The new arrangement also put the Union Pacific into the more convenient Union Station in Chicago.[42]

In 1956 the latest savior of the passenger business, the "Aerotrain," made its debut on the Pennsylvania amid hopes that the new lightweight train would have the same appeal and impact as the streamliners in the 1930s. The Union Pacific leased a nine-car version and used it as a high-speed shuttle between Los Angeles and Las Vegas. But it flopped and was returned to General Motors after nine months. The low-slung Aerotrain proved costly, inefficient, and more cramped for space than regular coaches. It also had to be operated as a unit; no cars could be added or removed.[43]

Undaunted, the Union Pacific bought another round of new equipment in the late 1950s, and again in the early 1960s, acquiring its last new coaches in 1966. Lovett conceded the fight was hopeless even before transcontinental jet service began capturing the last remnants of passenger traffic in the late 1950s. The dining service was a disaster, as it had always been; at one point Lovett noted wistfully that the company could save money by paying every traveler two dollars not to use it. He had fought the good fight, and all it had done was slow

A THING OF BEAUTY: The *City of Portland* domeliner curls gracefully through the Columbia River gorge.

IF LOOKS WERE ENOUGH: The highly touted General Motors Aerotrain, ballyhooed as the first American-built, complete lightweight train. Unfortunately it proved a bust in performance.

the rate of decline. Between 1953 and 1961 passenger revenues fell an average of 4 percent a year.[44]

The cheese had long since gone out of reach; the only question was how to get out of the trap. By the late 1950s Stoddard's zeal to cut the service wherever possible had gained ground. Increasingly passenger earnings were being sustained by mail and express income. In 1946 these earnings totaled only 21 percent of passenger revenues; by 1961 they had pulled even and were moving ahead. The slide in passenger income remained steady but moderate, under 3 percent a year except for a 9 percent drop in 1963.[45]

Then the bottom fell out. In 1967 and 1968 earnings plummeted 41 percent to $14.6 million in 1968 compared with $64.8 million in 1946. Even worse, the Post Office began eliminating its rail postal cars, which took away the last pillar supporting passenger travel. Mail and express income dipped from nearly $27 million in 1966 to $16 million in 1968. The passenger business was dead and only awaited a decent burial. This came with passage of the Rail Service Passenger Act in October 1970, creating a government corporation that would later be called Amtrak. For nearly all the private carriers, the long struggle over passenger service was history at last.[46]

Getting out of the passenger business also meant getting out of the resort and tour business, which had been staple of the Union Pacific since the 1920s. All the resorts lost money, but they served as a high-profile form of advertisement and drew travelers to the road. Getting into these businesses had been a daring leap of sorts; getting out proved a painful and prolonged process.

Sun Valley posed a special problem because it was a unique operation with a mood and ambience perfectly attuned to the prewar era, and because it was Averell Harriman's pet project. Right up to the war, immersed as he was in crucial diplomatic work, Averell found time to keep abreast of Sun Valley and offer detailed suggestions on every aspect of its operation. Less than a month after Pearl Harbor he telegraphed Jeffers hopefully that "Sun Valley will still have its place even in war perhaps on a changed basis."[47]

But it closed, and in 1946 the question was what to do about reopening it. The world had changed greatly in four years. Not the least of those changes was about a 50 percent rise in the costs of operating Sun Valley, which had never made money under its old setup. To restore the resort would cost a lot of money, as manager Pat Rogers itemized in a full report. Was the outlay worth it? Steve Hannagan mulled the question over and gave Averell his usual shrewd analysis.[48]

That Sun Valley had not made money Hannagan dismissed as the price for bringing "attention to the Union Pacific at a cost, cheaper than any other known means." If conceived as a money-making project, he warned, it would fail miserably. The question that had to be decided at once was whether the Union Pacific was willing to "subsidize this endeavor, as an advertising, good will and business projecting endeavor, to the extent of $350,000 to $500,000 annually." If not, he urged abandoning it.[49]

If the company chose to reopen, it had to be done with flair and enthusiasm. Hannagan thought Sun Valley could be streamlined by telescoping some services and charging for extra services like lifts and buses once given for free. He thought the place had always given too much away. At the same time it had to maintain the touch of class that set it apart from other places. Averell had long fretted over bad divorce publicity. Idaho had a six-week divorce law like Nevada's, which on occasion turned Sun Valley into a playground for celebrity divorcées. The state also permitted gambling, and neither Averell nor Hannagan wanted Sun Valley to become a casino or have to compete with one nearby.[50]

Although the decision was made to reopen on the basis Hannagan suggested, the resort never really came all the way back. Money was spent for redecorating but without the close attention to detail originally lavished on it by Marjorie Oelrichs Duchin and Marie Harriman. Averell tried to offer advice but was too far away. "Am ready [to] approve," he cabled grudgingly, "whatever is agreed upon by you all." Roland took little interest and spent far more time at the nearby Harriman "Railroad Ranch" than at Sun Valley.[51]

The celebrities flocked back after Sun Valley reopened, especially those who genuinely loved the place and the region. Actress Ann Sothern, a friend of Jeffers's, was so enchanted she finally bought a house and lived there. But it was not the same. Every year saw Averell's hand farther removed and the company less patient over deficits for a purpose that grew increasingly opaque. Pat Rogers, whose geniality held the Sun Valley style together, had grumbled for years at the abuse heaped on him by railway officers. As the deficits climbed, no one realized more than Rogers that he was the wrong man to impose economy on the operation. In 1952 he begged Stoddard to let him go back to managing the Utah Parks. Stoddard did so and replaced him at Sun Valley with Winston McCrea. A year after Rogers left, Steve Hannagan died.[52]

The next decade saw a very different tone at the resort. McCrea economized at every turn. Tom Murray was brought over to take charge of the food service. A cafeteria was installed at the Challenger Inn, and other services were reduced. The cafeteria in particular offended Averell, who had opposed the idea back in 1946, but it was more efficient and many of the guests preferred it to the long waiting lines. By the late 1950s Sun Valley was running down. At the Challenger Inn, noted Murray, "they were still sleeping on the same mattresses that they put in the building when they built it."[53]

The more passenger traffic dwindled, the less sense Sun Valley made for the Union Pacific as a national billboard or anything else. Stoddard liked Sun Valley but didn't want to spend money on it; he couldn't go there without being besieged with requests for improvements. By the early 1960s the place was, in Dorice Taylor's phrase, "patches on patches." A publicist at the resort, Taylor knew the handwriting was on the wall when she received a new map of the Union Pacific system that didn't even include Sun Valley.[54]

In 1963 the Union Pacific had the Janss Corporation, which operated several resorts, inspect Sun Valley with the idea of forming a new company in which the railroad would be a 49 percent partner in an expanded facility with a new hotel and condominium cottages. The lawyers found legal problems with this arrangement, however, and the board balked at the price tag of $6 million for the face lift. Instead, it decided to sell Janss the property outright in October 1964.[55]

The same rationale applied to the Utah Parks, even though that operation differed from Sun Valley in several respects. It was tied into an elaborate tours program run entirely by the railroad, and it involved a contract with the Department of the Interior for operating the park facilities. But it too bled cash; the El Escalante Hotel, for example, had its best year ever in 1941 and still lost $14,000. Never had the business made a profit. Despite those losses, Pat Rogers recommended that the government contract be renewed when it expired at the end of 1942.[56]

Ashby disagreed. He wanted to sell or lease the park facilities, arguing that "so far as advertising value is concerned the parks have served their purpose . . . we would get just as much benefit from them if they were operated by someone else." A deal was struck with the government to contract on a yearly basis for the war's duration. By 1945 even Rogers was eager to lease the El Escalante, but Jeffers doubted any takers could be found. Nothing was done.[57]

After the war, government dawdling over a new contract dragged on for years and so exasperated Ashby that in 1948 he announced the Union Pacific would pull out of the parks. Ashby's move sparked a political storm over rumors that the government planned to take over the concessions in all the national parks. Caught by a barrage of bad press just before the Republican convention, the Interior Department hurriedly came to terms on a new contract.[58]

New terms did nothing to solve the basic dilemma. The Utah Parks, like Sun Valley, did not pay except as a form of advertising for the railroad. But passenger traffic was dwindling; a growing proportion of the clientele came to the parks by car instead of rail. In 1952, for example, only 22 percent of the occupants at Zion, 20 percent at Bryce, and 27 percent at Grand Canyon came by rail. In effect the railroad was subsidizing the vacations of automobile travelers as part of its contribution to the Utah economy.[59]

Management and staffing problems plagued the operation as well. Pat Rogers stayed on as manager until 1957. His replacement was a disaster who inflicted more damage than an earthquake that occurred in August 1959; both he and his assistant had drinking problems. After they embarrassed the company with their behavior at a dedication ceremony in 1960, the versatile Tom Murray was brought down from Sun Valley to take charge of the parks. The change took place in a manner typical of the way the railroad did things. Murray got a call from Elgin Hicks, who said he wanted Murray to go down with him to straighten out some trouble in Utah. It was July 10, the height of the season, but Murray hopped a plane to Salt Lake, where he joined Hicks on a business car.[60]

When they got to Cedar City, Hicks told Murray to wait on the car while he went to see the manager. A few minutes later he returned and took Murray into the office. "This is Tom Murray," Hicks said curtly to the manager. "You get your hat and go home." The assistant was also fired on the spot. In this abrupt manner Murray learned he had a new job. He had been to the parks exactly once before. Hicks waltzed him through the facilities—a day or two at Zion, the same at Grand Canyon, and one at Bryce. Then back to Cedar City, where Hicks climbed on his car and was gone, leaving Murray in charge of seven hundred employees.[61]

This was probably the most decisive thing Hicks ever did, and it solved the problem. Murray did a splendid job under trying conditions, but the basic weakness remained. Sutton ran some figures in 1957 showing that the Union Pacific had swallowed a net loss of $3.5 million since the parks opened in 1923. Small wonder that Stoddard was eager to find someone to take the whole operation off the company's hands. Unlike Sun Valley, however, no willing buyer stepped forward. Not until 1967, when passenger traffic was nearly extinct, did the Union Pacific find a potential buyer in General Host.[62]

The deal was announced in January 1968, subject only to obtaining an extension of the concession for the parks from the government. But the National Park Service imposed terms for the latter that ultimately killed the deal. Other interested buyers also balked at the government demand that large sums be invested in modernizing facilities. Unable to get past this obstacle, the Union Pacific finally donated its facilities to the Park Service in 1972.[63]

By that time the company had also left the passenger business. Another casualty of that move was the guided tour operation, which had developed into one of the best in the country. Everyone in the tour department was disheartened because they were told to close up shop after their biggest season ever (1968). But the tours couldn't exist without a passenger service, and so they shut down. Some private tour companies, impressed by the operation, wanted to buy it from the railroad, but here too the old attitude prevailed. Informed of the offers, several officers scratched their heads and asked what the company had to sell.[64]

Bill Foral, the good-natured manager of tours, closed down more than his own operation. To him went the dubious honor of being the last person in the passenger department, charged with going through all the files and records with the help of a secretary to shut that venerable operation down forever. Everyone else had retired or been transferred to other departments. Two lonely figures toiling in the graveyard of what had once been the proudest and most public function of the railroad. An era had vanished forever.[65]

To old hands, the passing of these historic functions was an exercise in nostalgia. To the company, however, it was an exercise in good business. The most costly and unprofitable functions of the railroad had at last been stripped away. The awakening could proceed unencumbered by deadwood.

26

The Parts Changers

The new railroad was a creature not perceived whole for a long time. It was a whole beyond the sum of its parts, most of which were grasped through a series of painful revelations. For railroaders these revelations often came in the form of new technology, which forced everyone to do things in new ways.

Nothing rammed this point home more forcibly than the diesels. Never mind that they represented a quantum leap in efficiency and economy: few liked them at first. Older engineers eyed them like alien creatures. "They just missed the feel of the throttle," said Bill Fox, who later became VPO. "They were insecure." Those who took to them at once relished the cleaner, quieter, steadier ride, and on passenger runs abandoned their overalls for suits or sports coats.[1]

Shopmen reacted the same way. Charlie Spicka, whom Frank Acord called "the greatest steam engine man that ever walked the earth," was shop superintendent at Cheyenne. "The day they brought the diesels in," said Acord, "it was like they shot him." Spicka glared at the ugly alien beast and growled, "You're not bringing those street cars in my shop."[2]

But they did. Even for younger, more flexible men like Acord, the change went down hard. "I felt like I was a steam engine expert," he said. "I knew my business, but I get up one morning and . . . I don't know what it is. . . . I have to learn from scratch. And let me tell you, I made a lot of errors." Much of it came by trial and error. One time Acord pulled a faulty governor from a diesel, knowing that it was an expensive part but not knowing how it worked or that it required a costly test stand to inspect. "I had that governor fixed so that

THE OLD WAY: Machinist Robert W. Schlager puts a piston into an 800-class steam engine.

THE NEW WAY: Shop employees work on electric engines.

HANG-UP: Gas turbine engine no. 51 gets hoisted by the big crane in the Salt Lake City shop, where the new breed of turbines came to spend altogether too much time.

nobody else could fix it,'' he laughed. ''It was gone. . . . I went in to see why the thing wouldn't tick, and . . . I don't know yet why it didn't tick.''[3]

Many of the shopmen wouldn't touch the diesels. Acord went to Cheyenne as master mechanic and had to tell the men ''either you're gonna or you're not going to be here. . . . I was about as popular as a dose of clap.'' Men who had long regarded themselves as craftsmen found their skills no longer needed. Where the shops built everything for steam power, they merely bought parts for the diesels. ''You become a parts exchanger,'' said Acord. ''Very, very seldom do you build anything for a diesel.''[4]

Experience soon produced a new old saying in the shops: on a steam locomotive it took five minutes to find a problem and five hours to fix it; on a diesel it took five hours to find the problem and five minutes to fix it. The secret was to keep the new engines as clean as possible, and to set the timing right. The timing was done by the numbers; if you followed the book, you always got good results. Old hands found themselves looking for tough problems on diesels just to arouse their interest, and sometimes overlooked the obvious.[5]

The diesels showed their advantage early in the shops, requiring service every six or seven thousand miles compared to every hundred miles for steam locomotives. Yet the company did not rush to dieselize its fleet despite the start made by Ashby. It was reluctant to let go of the big steam power that guzzled company coal, and by 1950 Stoddard had become intrigued by a new entry. Undaunted by the failure of its steam turbine prototypes, General Electric pursued development of a gas turbine engine. In June 1949 the Union Pacific took the prototype for extended testing.[6]

The results impressed Stoddard, who liked giant power capable of hauling big payloads. "This is jet propulsion on wheels," he enthused. "It might well revolutionize American railroading." Late in 1950 the company ordered ten of the 4,500-horsepower turbines along with some diesel units. Although some railroaders called them "Messy Bessie," the turbines did well enough in service that Stoddard bought another fifteen in 1952. They showed an ability to go faster than diesels and seemed as economical at first. The treated residual fuel oil burned by the turbines caused problems, however, and in 1953 a new version that ran on propane was tested successfully.[7]

Lovett did not share Stoddard's enthusiastic conviction that the turbine represented the wave of the future. He saw clearly that, sentiment aside, the Union Pacific had to replace the rest of its steam power with modern units as rapidly as possible. Within months of his arrival in 1953 the company placed the largest diesel order in history for 205 units. In August 1954 it added another 50 to the total. By 1954 diesels or turbines hauled 80 percent of Union Pacific freight compared to only 32 percent in 1951. Gradually one city after another in Union Pacific territory shared the experience of Kansas City, which saw its last steam locomotive enter the terminal in January 1955.[8]

Lovett did not ignore the turbines entirely. In 1955 an order was placed for fifteen (later thirty) 8,500-horsepower gas turbines. These became the most powerful locomotives in the world, the "Big Boys" of the post-steam era. Experiments also continued on a coal-fueled turbine engine; as late as 1963 the Union Pacific was still testing a version. When it did not meet expectations, a coal-burning diesel engine was tried. By the late 1960s it was clear that the gas turbines had been a noble failure. Apart from the deafening noise they made, the units ran up costly repair bills and lasted only about a decade in service. The last one was phased out in December 1969.[9]

The conversion to diesels put the design people out of the locomotive business and shifted them to rolling stock, where a similar transformation was taking place. Boxcars went from forty to fifty feet, flat cars from forty to fifty, sixty, and then eighty feet to handle trailers and containers. Roller bearings, which had been applied first to passenger cars, were put on freight equipment. Many specialty cars got cushioned underframes to absorb shocks, and were also fitted with load dividers. Covered hoppers were acquired to handle grain and soda ash, and older types like rack cars for automobiles were redesigned.[10]

Reefers finally graduated to mechanical cooling. The trick was to design a unit that was both inexpensive and self-sustaining over a long trip. New forms

of insulation like fiberglass helped keep temperatures stable, but the basic problem wasn't solved until small diesel motors were installed to run compressors on each car. Early versions appeared in 1949, but Pacific Fruit Express (PFE) did not acquire its first mechanically cooled car until 1953. For a time the company built both new and old types, but within a few years it began a rapid expansion of the mechanical fleet.[11]

The new cars with mechanical refrigeration, intended chiefly for frozen foods, sparked a resurgence in PFE. Other improvements were made to the cars: forty-footers gave way to fifty-footers, and in 1961 the company jumped into the piggyback business by buying its own refrigerated trailers for Trailer-on-Flatcar (TOFC) service. Three years later it went into insulated containers for handling canned pineapple from Hawaii. After seventy years of doing things pretty much the same way, the handling of perishables was revolutionized in little over a decade.[12]

The Union Pacific needed not just better cars but more of them. It rebuilt about 1,500 old cars a year, and during the crush of Korean War traffic launched a program to redo 15,000 cars. During the 1950s the company added 24,972 new revenue cars, of which 45 percent were boxcars, 28 percent gondolas, and only 10 percent hoppers. A massive equipment program in the late 1960s helped swell the new car total between 1960 and 1968 to 31,122. Of these 61 percent were boxcars, 23 percent hoppers of all types, and only 5 percent gondolas. This shift reflected a change in the types of traffic hauled as well as the types of equipment most in need of replacement.[13]

As always, the full value of faster, larger equipment could be gained only by improving the line as well. For half a century the company had waged war on curves and grades, the twin enemies of economical train service. In this respect the new railroad was but a flatter, straighter version of the old one, and it was a work always in progress. Sherman Hill, Wyoming, remained the major bottleneck on the road. Harriman's massive line shift in the 1900s had reduced the ascending grade between Cheyenne and Dale Creek to 1.55 percent and maximum curvature to 4 degrees. These were still the highest figures between Omaha and Ogden, and at a place battered by some of the worst weather in the West.[14]

In 1951 the company decided to construct yet another new line, this one seven miles south of Sherman Hill and bypassing it entirely. The new forty-two-mile westbound track was nine miles longer than the old line, but it reduced the grade to .82 percent and maximum curvature to 2°30′. Opened in May 1953 at a cost of $16 million, the new line required 111 major fills and 114 major cuts. The result was faster trains and large savings in operating costs. A smaller

BUILDING THE FLEET: New stock cars under construction at the Omaha shops, February 1961.

ONE MORE TIME: Rebuilding the Dale Creek line yet again, 1951–53. This aerial view shows the *City of St. Louis* on the old westbound main. The new roadbed can be seen cutting in from the top right.

project near Rawlins installed ten new miles of road in place of eleven, not only to reduce grade and curvature but also to defend better against drifting snow.[15]

By the late 1950s the Union Pacific had resumed its leadership role in maintenance of way. Between 1954 and 1958 the company replaced an average of 2.1 percent of its ties every year. The figure dropped to 2.02 percent during 1959–1963 but still outranked every major western road; the closest competitor was the Northern Pacific at 1.81 percent.[16]

The company also replaced 11.3 percent of the rails on its lines between 1959 and 1963, a figure exceeded only by the Atchison (13.7 percent) and Southern Pacific (12 percent). More important, it began using an improved 133-pound rail with a deeper head and thicker upper fillet that proved much more durable than the 131-pound rail used between 1934 and 1948. New techniques used on existing rails extended their life by as much as 50 percent in some cases. One other clue showed that rails were living longer: the number of defects found by detector cars dropped 37 percent between 1959 and 1963.[17]

A host of new tools transformed the way maintenance crews did these tasks. Production tampers for ties, jack tampers for raising track, ballast regulators, track liners and undercutters, crib adze machines, multispindle bolt machines, mechanical spike pullers, rail anchor applicator machines, and the ballast plow were but some of the devices that eased the drudgery of rail maintenance. The track car gave way to the automobile, enabling fewer crews to handle larger sections in less time.[18]

At a casual glance the roadbed looked much the same, but it was tended in radically different ways. Continuously welded rail in lengths of a thousand feet or more replaced the old forty-foot rails bolted at the joints. New preservatives prolonged tie life, and the concrete tie came into use. New machines could clean or replace ballast, align and level rails, and tamp them into place, enabling the company to sharply reduce track forces. Improved signals lined the track along with networks of wire and monitor boxes. The roadway also looked more modern because of what was no longer there, notably coaling and water stations.[19]

Shops and yards also took on a more modern look. The advent of the diesel forced wholesale changes in shops that for a century had been set up to repair steam power. New shops for servicing diesels opened at Los Angeles in 1953, Salt Lake City in 1954, Council Bluffs in 1956, and Kansas City in 1958—their order of appearance matching the order in which diesels took over the districts. Large sums were spent to upgrade yards at Kansas City, Ogden, Pocatello, North Platte, and Portland. The yard at West Spokane, which had no room for expansion, was replaced by a new facility at East Spokane in 1955. A year later the first electronic humping system on the road began work at North Platte.[20]

There was a twist of irony in this impressive record as Stoddard got credit for a program of improvements that had been largely conceived by Ashby and pushed along by Lovett. But if Stoddard was not an innovator, neither was he an obstacle to innovation. He floated willingly on the ideas of subordinates who knew their business, and increasingly on the Union Pacific that business fell outside the usual bailiwick of what railroaders had always done.

One morning in 1954 Stoddard got on the elevator and spied C. Otis Jett, a bright electrical engineer who had come to the Union Pacific from the Bell System. "Mr. Jett," he asked, "what's a computer? I hear that we could use one profitably."[21]

For decades machines were used on a railroad only to run trains, fix trains, or keep the roadbed in order. Except for the typewriter and the adding machine, few devices penetrated the offices. Generations of clerks had hunched over reams of paper to produce bales of records that were dutifully gathered into enough files to overflow several warehouses. In the 1950s the twentieth-century railroad still used nineteenth-century means of communication, computation, and records management. Gradually, almost sullenly, the roads brought in outside technicians like Jett, who transformed the railroads in more ways than anyone expected.

The new technicians became the vanguard in breaking through the railroader mentality. They did not think like railroaders because they came from very different backgrounds. They performed tasks railroaders could not do because nothing in their tradition prepared them for dealing with technologies that developed elsewhere. In this way new technology transformed not only the railroad but also its work force with an infusion of fresh blood and ways of solving problems.

The period of adjustment was long and strained. As Jett observed, almost every president "somewhere along the line was a telegrapher and a dispatcher. . . . That was one of the big troubles of the communications system. It was too inbred."[22]

Two distinct problems were involved: communications and data processing. In a century communications on the railroad had progressed only from the highball* to the telegrapher using Morse code. Train orders were still done in 1950 the way they had been for decades. The conductor picked up a train order from the train order operator, who in turn got it from the dispatcher. To guard against mistakes, the dispatcher read the order, spelled out every station name, time, and number, then had the operator read it back to him. The train operator had two more men read it back to him as a precaution, and all three checked it again before giving it to the conductor.[23]

This process grew ever more cumbersome as the number of trains increased. Between 1900 and 1950 attempts to improve the flow of information moved through three stages: telegraph, telephone, and teleprinter. Ironically, the Union Pacific had been a pioneer in the development of "wireless telegraph" or telephone communications, thanks to Dr. Frederick H. Millener, who was in

*The highball method employed a pole in front of the station with a ball on a line pulled to the top. When the station operator wanted a train to stop, he lowered the ball. If the engineer saw the ball at the top, he sped on through the station.

charge of the general office building in Omaha. Since 1906 Millener had been experimenting with a device he claimed would allow moving trains to communicate with stations thirty or forty miles away. In 1914 he announced that his system was functional and commercially feasible.[24]

The company put a little money behind the work but regarded Millener as little more than an amiable crank. "The traffic people have felt that this was a good advertisement, and have used him at fairs, carnivals, etc. to good effect," A. L. Mohler explained to Judge Lovett. But Millener, he added, "is quite a genius in this work." Since 1906 the company had invested $7,179 in the work and received six patents pending. "The invention is perfectly practical," declared Mohler, who viewed the wireless system as a possible alternative when storms knocked out the telegraph system.*[25]

While Mohler tolerated the experiments, the railroad saw little value in such a system. Two more years passed before another rash of publicity about Millener's work prompted Judge Lovett to inquire again. The judge didn't want to discourage any worthwhile development, but neither did he care to squander money. "We want the Union Pacific to be in the front rank in every railroad improvement," he stressed, "but we do not wish to persist in anything foolish." Mohler liked the device but was just leaving office; E. E. Calvin took a dim view of such nonsense. A test of Millener's system arranged in July 1916 flopped badly and proved to the committee of four observing it "the uselessness of his invention."[26]

There is no doubt that the potential value of such a system escaped the committee entirely. "Even had the experiments been a success," it concluded, "the expense . . . would not warrant the Railroad Company in adopting the invention of Dr. Millener, due to the excessive cost and infrequent use." Calvin ordered the work terminated at once, and the Union Pacific lost its chance to pioneer in rail communications. Ironically, the committee's report was submitted to general manager W. M. Jeffers, who, when he became president, inherited the problem of a railroad that had outgrown its communications system.[27]

The Union Pacific got its first telephones in 1912 and its first crude printing telegraph machines six years later. Updated versions of these teleprinters were still being used in 1946, and the telephone had not advanced much farther. During the late 1920s voice repeaters were installed to let Omaha communicate directly with points as far west as Salt Lake City. As the demand for communications grew, however, serious problems arose. The poles could hold only so many wires without rebuilding the entire system.[28]

Even worse, no one in the company knew anything about modern communications. The superintendent of telegraph, P. F. Frenzer, had been a member of the committee that spurned Millener's device. Like all railroaders he equated communications with the telegraph, and he was close to Jeffers, who took great pride in having started as a dispatcher. But a brave soul in the Los Angeles office

*The Lackawanna was also experimenting with a wireless system but had rented its equipment from Marconi's firm.

IT STARTED HERE: Glenn R. Van Eaton shows Charlene Arnold how messages were sent on an old pump key and telegraph sounder of Civil War vintage.

named Charlie Sparr knew the telephone company had some three-channel carriers. In 1939 he boldly arranged on his own to have the system installed between Los Angeles and Salt Lake City. Sparr also knew Ashby and asked him to try the unit when he was in Los Angeles.[29]

Impressed by the results, Ashby got Jeffers out to Salt Lake City to try it. Afterward the czar hurried back to Omaha without a word, called up Frenzer, and demanded to know about the newfangled system. Frenzer didn't have a clue, but he knew Sparr must be involved and said so. Sparr was summoned to Omaha at once, and naturally assumed he was being fired. "How soon," Jeffers barked at him, "can you have this all over the railroad?"[30]

Always on the go, Jeffers wanted to keep tabs on everything and was constantly frustrated by his inability to get an open telephone line. He asked Frenzer if he knew about the new phone system. Frenzer admitted he did, but reminded Jeffers how proud he was of his telegraph origins and insisted the road was doing fine with the telegraph alone. Jeffers ordered his old friend to take retirement at once.

At that moment a new era in communications on the Union Pacific dawned, but it did not come easily. The three-carrier system was extended over the road just in time for the war. But how to replace Frenzer? No one else in the company knew anything except telegraphy. Someone came up with the bright idea of giving aptitude tests to the wire chiefs in hopes of uncovering a promising candidate. The winner, G. R. Van Eaton, manager of the Las Vegas telegraph office, was handed Frenzer's position and told that his job was to modernize communications on the Union Pacific Railroad.[31]

Van Eaton knew nothing about the subject, but he did know how to listen and learn. Above all, he recognized that the traditional system had failed completely in communications. There was no one to bring up through the ranks; he had to go outside for people who knew electrical engineering. The first recruit washed out. The second one was C. Otis Jett, an engineer whose diverse background included stints with the Bell System, the Forest Service, the Signal Corps, Oak Ridge Laboratory, and TVA. Van Eaton went the extra mile to get Jett. Of the six companies to which Jett applied for a job in 1945, only Van Eaton responded with a personal visit. "I won't take no for an answer," he said.[32]

The two men made a good team. Jett was a first-rate engineer whose views Van Eaton absorbed and passed along to management. It helped greatly that both Jeffers and Ashby wanted a better communications system. In hiring Jett, the personable Van Eaton initiated a crucial split between the two departments that handled communications on the road. For his operation Van Eaton went outside and hired engineers to set up circuits and do all the engineering in their own way. By contrast the Signal Department contracted their work to signal companies as they had always done. "They could get away with it," said Jett, "because the job installed twenty years ago was exactly like the job they installed ten years ago was like the job they installed today."[33]

Jett trained his own people because he didn't have any choice. "We couldn't get them anywhere," he shrugged. "We couldn't even steal them. Nobody had them." Nor could the Union Pacific rely on the telephone company to take care of a system that had to be on line every minute of every day. The operations people regarded Jett's outfit as a necessary evil and resented the money they got. Once communications began to produce, however, the signal department found itself under pressure to perform similar wonders.[34]

And perform wonders they did. As business grew and the demand for more channels increased, communications came up with newer and more economical ways to wring more use out of existing wires. A technique called "speech-plus-duplex" enabled them to double the existing teleprinter capacity. In 1955, after a review of its communications facilities, the company launched a major improvements program. Direct-distance-dial was installed throughout the system. Since the wire capacity could hold no more without a major rebuild, Jett resorted to even more advanced carrier techniques.[35]

But the company's appetite was voracious. More voice, data, and teleprinter channels were demanded faster than Jett could provide them. The pressure was intense; his operation was trying to do a decade's work in a year, every year. "It drove us even crazier," said Jett, "because we had fifteen, twenty trains each way. I know one day . . . we lost three trains. Didn't have any record of them."[36]

By 1960 the existing wire system was exhausted. Rather than rebuild the structure, Jett turned to a new technology: microwave. A microwave system offered broad-band facility with plenty of channels, required no expensive pole support system, and was immune to storms or accidents. Jett devoted a lot of time to the problem of fading, and ultimately found a workable solution. The first system was installed between Omaha and Laramie in 1960 with eighteen repeater stations, the tallest of which stood 180 feet high. Delighted by the results, management extended the system over all the lines during the 1960s.[37]

Gradually the communications revolution infiltrated operations. In 1947 the company installed two-way radios in diesel switch engines along with four experimental units in freight engines and cabooses. Engineers were leery of the devices at first, but gradually they relished having direct contact with dispatchers and conductors. ''When radio first came on,'' laughed former public relations director E. C. Schafer, ''I think they had to pay three bucks to have every engineer just use the radio in the cab. Today you can't get a crew out if their radio doesn't work.'' On a larger scale, Centralized Train Control (CTC) eventually rendered the train order operator extinct.[38]

The communications system did much more than send voices. Its ability to transmit data revolutionized the way railroads did certain things. The industry had always been buried in paper. For decades it had grappled with handling huge flows of information on everything from car movements to billing to inventories to payrolls. Keeping track of cars and consists alone was a task requiring enormous labor by whole armies of clerks merely to do a minimal job. If any area ought to have welcomed technology as a handservant it was this one. Yet here too change was greeted with suspicion and doubt.

Automation had come early to the Union Pacific. The Omaha office first used electric punch cards for freight accounting in 1909, the year E. H. Harriman died. By the end of World War II it succeeded in getting all its car movements on punch cards, a herculean task that took over a million cards a month. ''By the early 1950s,'' recalled Reg Sutton, ''we had gotten it developed to where we knew where every car was that was on our line, whose it was, where it was.'' But the labor costs and the time consumed were immense.[39]

By the 1950s the needs of several departments had converged into a swelling stream. Jett wanted faster data transmission with greater capacity. Stan How was eager to automate the yards and store supplies, Sutton the payroll. The computer was still in its infancy when the Union Pacific went looking for help. Van Eaton and Jett journeyed to Minneapolis to visit Univac. The sales people showed them around the plant, wined and dined them, and then told them somewhat sheepishly that Union Pacific was not big enough for a computer, that a railroad was no place for a computer.[40]

Disconsolate, Van Eaton and Jett returned to Omaha uncertain of their next step. A few weeks later, an IBM man called Jett and said, ''I hear you fellows are looking for a computer.'' Eagerly Van Eaton and Jett hurried to Rochester to look over IBM's equipment. A difficult task faced them: they had to learn what equipment IBM had and what it would do, and then explain all this to officers who knew nothing about such things. Top management would not commit until they could be shown there was enough work to keep such newfangled and expensive machines fully occupied.[41]

THE COMING THING: Arthur E. Stoddard (*left, holding sheet*) and Reginald M. Sutton beam approval as the first batch of paychecks roll off the new IBM 705.

Stan How and Reg Sutton had to educate both the managers above and the officers below to the advantages offered by computers. Neither group could fathom the new machines, but Stoddard supported the "experts" while they built their case. "They didn't understand too much about [it]," How said later, "but you know, they never did turn down a purchase." Although few older heads really grasped what it was all about despite some seminars, the less rigid among them went along. "Stan, you're just running wild," remarked Perry Lynch, shaking his head, "but I'm all for it because we've got to progress."[42]

How worked closely with IBM on the electronic yard system. In 1954 the first machines went into yard offices at Council Bluffs, North Platte, and Cheyenne. The yard people displayed their feelings about innovation by not showing up for work the first day the new system was to operate. Their walkout lasted only a day, however, and How proceeded to put the system into the rest of the yards and the transportation department in Omaha.[43]

Superintendents also fought it at first. One at Kansas City wrote Lynch a three-page letter about how he could eliminate thirteen jobs and manage other reforms without it. Lynch and How agreed to teach the recalcitrant a lesson by removing the machines. Next day the superintendent requested ten new people; a week later he asked sheepishly for the machines to be returned. "They became the greatest supporters of it, you know," said How with a pleased grin. "Made their life easier."[44]

Sutton had an easier time of it. He got from Stoddard twenty-three men along with the machines and training from IBM. In return he promised that within three years he would have payroll, material inventory, and interline freight accounts on the machines. "I didn't know about all my marbles either," smiled Sutton. ". . . Three years was what we figured we could do it initially. Then you had to keep them up; from then on it was just one great expansion. It wasn't too long after that we had four hundred people working."[45]

While How and Sutton pushed to automate the yard and accounting work, Jett scrambled furiously to provide enough channels for the data generated by these operations. The original system used by the Union Pacific transmitted car data on teleprinter channels and converted from card to tape and vice versa locally, but this process was slow, cumbersome, and labor intensive. In 1956 he got the company to lease two IBM Type 650 machines. A transceiver furnished by IBM eliminated the middle step of card to tape and back in 1957, but within a year even this equipment proved inadequate to the task.[46]

The breakthrough came in 1958, when IBM leased the Union Pacific a new Type 705 computer. This was no small commitment by the company. To provide the rigid temperature, humidity, and dust controls required by the machine, it built a five-story addition to the Omaha headquarters. Once the 705 went on line with its greater speed and capacity, converts flocked to the new technology. "All of a sudden," said Sutton, "they discovered what we'd been trying to tell them in the first place." Fascinated with his new toy, Stoddard prodded the technicians to find new uses for it in other departments.[47]

By 1960 the Union Pacific had embraced the new data processing and communications technology with a fervor. In 1962, only four years after the 705 went into operation, the company replaced it with a new Type 7080 computer, one of the largest commercial systems available. Not every attempt to use new devices turned out well. One program called automatic car identification (ACI) proved a fiasco. The flaw was not in the concept but in the system used; a different approach later worked fine.[48]

New technology also invaded that happy legacy of Otto Jabelmann, the research and standards laboratory. To expedite its work in alloys, fuels, and lubricants, the lab acquired an electron microscope and emission spectrograph in 1955. Until the electron microscope came along, railroads had never really known when oil had to be changed. The department also worked on a coal-burning gas turbine engine, designed a new type of rotary plow, developed reflectoscope techniques for testing axles, found ways to improve turbocharging for diesel engines, and correlated freight train schedules with locomotive performance using the 705 computer for the calculations.[49]

One sure sign of the new technology's growing importance was its presence in the annual reports, where it began as a member of the chorus and moved steadily to a starring role. By the 1960s railroads had become sensitive to their image as a stodgy, antiquated industry and were eager to show the ways they had gone with the times. New technology was to the railroads of the 1960s what the streamliners had been in the 1930s, with far more profitable results. There was another key difference as well: where the streamliners had been new trains run by old railroaders, the new technology brought to the roads an infusion of fresh blood and fresh thinking.

"When I started," said an old shop hand, "all those people I knew had a big pride in their work. . . . Later years, payday and quitting time is all they were looking for." The old-timer blamed the unions for this change. "Unions," he muttered in disgust, "were advocating to their people that they not do any more than they had to."[50]

The attitude of management, which had to deal with no less than twenty-three unions, was no secret. "We were trying to reduce the labor force to cut costs," affirmed Frank Barnett, "because the railroad industry was going out of sight. Just plain out of sight. . . . It was the simple demands of the unions which were frightful."[51]

The new railroad struggling to be born underwent the worst of labor pains. By the 1950s the long battle between management and labor resembled a barely resistible force crashing into a faintly movable object. Wages continued to rise and the ranks continued to thin, their depletion hastened by the new technology. Some areas like communications and data processing created new jobs but for outsiders, not railroaders. The dogged defense of work rules kept the parts changers from being interchangeable parts, but it could not keep them from becoming dispensable parts.

No one could find a viable alternative to the old policy of confrontation. In the long raging fight over firemen on diesels, a fact-finding board appointed by President Truman in February 1949 found the union's demand for an extra fireman could not be supported on any logical or reasonable basis, and that the work in a diesel cab was "considerably less than a full-time job" which could not be "classified as difficult or complex work." Earlier the engineers had demanded another engineer for diesel runs. The doubling of crews would more than offset savings made by diesel over steam power.[52]

Predictably, the unions rejected the finding and walked out in May 1950. The strike was brief, but a few weeks later the switchmen went out. In August the trainmen and conductors issued a strike call, prompting Truman to seize the railroads again. Unimpressed, the switchmen pulled a wildcat strike in December. This move during the Korean War effort drew biting criticism of the unions but did not dent their resolve. Not until February did Truman succeed in getting the switchmen back to work, only to face another crisis in the form of demands by nonoperating employees.[53]

This endless seesaw of long, tortuous negotiations culminating in strikes that led back to the table for more bargaining continued through the early 1950s. Apart from costing the unions credibility in the public's eye, the frequent interruptions of service added one more nail to the coffin of passenger service. Wary of a national strike after Truman's tough stand, the unions resorted to slowdowns at selected points and strikes against individual roads and places. The clerks struck Denver in 1956, for example, while the engineers singled out the Spokane, Portland & Seattle later that year.[54]

State governments complicated matters by taking very different positions on railroad labor. Some, like Washington and Oregon, passed full-crew laws compelling roads to keep firemen; eighteen others, including Nebraska, passed right-to-work laws prohibiting railroad union shop agreements only to have the Supreme Court overturn them in May 1956. That same year, however, the railroads took the offensive by notifying the enginemen and firemen of a change in work rules: in the future they would regard the use of firemen on diesel service as optional.[55]

There followed a bitter seven-year battle that culminated in 1963 with victory for the carriers. Since the original diesel agreement of 1937, four emergency and arbitration boards along with a presidential commission had studied the request for an extra fireman. Without exception they had found no need for one and were hard put to justify the need for any fireman at all. After twenty-six years of struggle the Supreme Court in March 1963 upheld the carriers' right to change work rules. It took another year of legal battles to clinch the elimination of firemen, followed by campaigns against the five states with full-crew laws.[56]

Still the firemen's union fought on, seeking reversal of the decisions and large wage hikes. A similar battle with the trainmen's union dragged on for years, as did fights with shop hands, porters, and the nonoperating unions. Attempts to repeal the obsolete full-crew laws received a stunning blow as late as November 1968, when the Supreme Court upheld the right of states to enforce such statutes. Strikes and strife over everything from wages to job protection stalked the passenger service to its grave, fueled by an edge of desperation as the end drew near.[57]

Through the 1960s railroad labor relations bore a dismal resemblance to the growing Vietnam fiasco. It was a war of attrition costly to both sides and perpetuated by a mad-hatter logic all its own. Neither side had any idea of how to get out of the old traps that had landed them there in the first place. Half a century of conflict had not produced a single piece of constructive thinking on either side for dealing with the real problems that plagued the industry and threatened the very existence of railroaders. Having floundered early into an adversarial relationship, they merely continued a ritual that made as much sense as bleeding a hemophiliac.

Meanwhile, the ranks dwindled and changed in nature. Between 1952 and 1969 the average number of employees dropped another 43 percent to 31,416. New technology and techniques created new types of work just as they rendered old types obsolete, which brought different and often younger people into the ranks. The traditional railroader still dominated operations, but even he had to learn new tricks as machines revamped the ways tasks were performed. Officers too felt the pressure as the company that once scorned college graduates as impractical, launched college recruitment, executive training, and tuition aid programs. The business of producing skilled managers had finally become a business.[58]

One tradition continued unblemished through changing times. After a rash of accidents in 1946, the Union Pacific resumed its habit of winning the Harriman

SAFETY COUNTS: Arthur E. Stoddard and Perry J. Lynch admire the Harriman Safety Award.

Safety Medal in the following year with an accident rate for employees of 1.81 killed or injured per million man-hours compared to 8.52 for all class I railroads. It marked the eighteenth time in twenty-five years the company had the lowest casualty rate among the largest roads. As always, however, accidents produced bigger headlines than safety. In November 1951 a tragic wreck in a snowstorm killed eighteen people and garnered far more ink than the Harriman award won again by the company two months earlier.[59]

Safety was always a two-edged sword for the railroads. The Harriman and other awards honored success in the area that counted most to railroaders, protection of themselves. For obvious reasons, however, passenger mishaps got more press than all other accident or safety matters. As passenger service declined, the emphasis shifted to freight accidents—particularly those with dangerous cargoes. Through this transition the Union Pacific maintained its impressive record. In 1957 it swept four major safety awards including the Harriman, the first time any railroad had done so, with the lowest casualty rate in the road's history.*[60]

Eleven years later, the company repeated this feat, capturing one prize, the Railroad Employees' National Safety Award, for the sixth straight year. Although performance improved steadily, the demand for near perfection grew faster because of sensitive cargoes. During a six-month period in 1968–69, for example, the Union Pacific handled 1,197 carloads of poison gas for the

*The rate was one casualty per 1.51 million man-hours, compared with an average of 4.44 for other railroads in the same group.

government. No accidents occurred, but the road drew criticism for suffering three derailments in that same time span even though the Union Pacific had the lowest derailment rate of fifteen major roads.[61]

Railroaders were long accustomed to coping with the ravages of nature, such as the flood that inundated Kansas City in 1951, but dangerous consists added a new wrinkle to their job. So did a host of innovations on what they hauled and how they hauled it. In 1954 the company experimented with a service of carrying truck trailers on flat cars (TOFC) between Los Angeles and Salt Lake City. Encouraged by the results, it expanded the "piggyback" program steadily despite protests from trucking firms and the Teamsters Union. The business grew so rapidly that the company had trouble providing enough flat cars. To ease the demand, it joined other roads in creating the Trailer Train Company in 1960 to own and maintain a pool of cars for piggyback service.[62]

So delicate was the train-truck issue that it took Union Pacific Motor Freight Company fourteen years to acquire full authority for its less-than-carload, pick-up and delivery, and substitute rail service, but the results were worth the wait. After victory finally came in 1961, Union Pacific Motor expanded rapidly, especially into perishable goods, where Pacific Fruit Express had also begun using trailers for supplemental hauls. A major turning point came in 1965 when "Plan I," allowing the road to handle trailers of highway common carriers, went into effect. That same year the Union Pacific also gained permission to stop handling lcl shipments, which had long since become costly and unprofitable.[63]

These innovations also relied heavily on new machines, which had the effect of eliminating more jobs. The trend was as obvious as it was inexorable. To compete, the railroad had to become more efficient. This could not happen so long as its product remained labor intensive and unions had the power to resist changes or negate their cost savings. The only recourse was to whittle down the labor force with machines that performed more work with fewer men. This strategy intensified the already desperate struggle between management and labor, driving them to still greater efforts and blinding them even more to the need for some more positive approach.

Under these gloomy circumstances it was easy for the parts changers to view themselves as victims of indifferent or vindictive managers, but they were not. Management made its share of blunders, but the fault lay in a system so encrusted with tradition that it sank beneath its own weight. The structure of management-labor relations was firmly in place when the railroads reached their zenith in the years before World War I. For half a century both sides had resisted any organic change in that structure despite the devastating impact of the new competition, two wars, a depression, and rapid changes in technology and techniques.

Small wonder that managers and parts changers alike often felt that the world had passed them by. To a large degree they had watched it go by from the sidelines.

27

The Merger Misstep

By the early 1960s two major movements had begun to emerge in the railroad industry. The first was a drive to reorganize into holding companies that separated out nonrail assets. The second was a fresh round of merger mania that threatened to redraw the nation's railroad map in startling fashion. One looked to restructure individual firms, the other the industry as a whole. Together they amounted to the most drastic overhaul of American railroads in history.

These epochal movements affected the Union Pacific in a peculiar way. The restructuring of the rail industry collided with the reorganization of the Union Pacific, causing serous delays in the latter and endless confusion in the former. A third factor complicated the situation even further: federal transportation policy showed signs of a major shift, perhaps the most dramatic since the 1920 act. But the nature and timing of the shift remained maddeningly elusive.

For two decades Washington had delivered mixed signals. In 1942 a planning board report had urged the creation of fewer regional systems through mergers, but two years later the Justice Department stunned forty-seven western roads with an antitrust suit charging conspiracy to fix rates and discourage improvements in service and equipment. Justice also accused the carriers of overcharging the government on shipments of war materials, while Congress defeated an effort to repeal the old land grant rates allowing government traffic to move at 50 percent of normal rates.[1]

After World War II policy followed the familiar course of federal control and coordination until the Transportation Act of 1958, which offered a glimmer of hope that the regulatory stranglehold might be loosened. By then the rail industry was so near the brink of collapse that a shift in federal policy seemed imperative. In April 1962 President John F. Kennedy called for far-reaching changes in what he labeled "a chaotic patchwork of inconsistent and often obsolete legislation and regulation." *Forbes* hailed his speech as a bombshell, but Congress did not rush to accommodate his wishes.[2]

Three months after Kennedy's speech, Frank Barnett sat down to review the Union Pacific's restructuring. The divisions had undergone a trial run, and separate staffs for accounting and other functions had begun to emerge. By taking the next step of turning them into separate corporations, Barnett hoped to accomplish two things. In the short run, separate companies would encourage more independent and aggressive management; in the long run, they would permit further diversification and offer some protection should the railroads come under more rigid regulation or, as some observers predicted, actual government control.[3]

The fast-growing movement toward consolidation of railroads also concerned Barnett. Apart from buying the Spokane International* in 1958, the Union Pacific had done nothing. Barnett feared the company might be weakened unless it too sought the "revenue potential and cost-savings which can be obtained through well conceived merger plans." A bridge line like the Union Pacific could not afford to sit idle with the rail map in state of flux. After careful study the company decided to reverse its most historic policy: it would go east of the Missouri River and acquire lines to Chicago and St. Louis.[4]

Although these two objectives seem unrelated at first glance, they were in fact inseparable. The formation of a holding company required a new capital structure, which would greatly complicate a tender offer for another railroad. The ICC would have final say on both a merger and the capital structure of a new company. Lovett and Barnett had long believed, for example, that the Union Pacific's preferred stock was an obstacle to spinning off nonrail properties. A merger would complicate matters by intertwining its capital structure needs with those of the holding company.

Barnett concluded that this risk had to be taken. He urged that the Union Pacific undertake to eliminate its preferred stock while simultaneously pursuing a merger. Under his complicated scheme a new holding company would own the railroad, natural resources, and land subsidiaries while the railroad would own a majority interest in the target road. Studies on which road to acquire gave each candidate a number to preserve secrecy. After much debate the choice boiled down to road number six: the Rock Island.

For years controversy has raged over two questions: Why go east of the Missouri River? And why the Rock Island, a road that had been bankrupt for seventeen of the past thirty-three years? The answers lay in changes that swept through the rail industry after the war. Schedules kept speeding up to meet air and truck competition, and roads with poor earnings found it impossible to

*The 141-mile Spokane International ran northeast from Spokane, Washington, to Eastport, Idaho, on the Canadian border, where it connected with the Canadian Pacific Railway.

keep their physical plant in condition to make these faster times. As a bridge carrier dependent on connections in both directions, the Union Pacific could not control overall service or rate-making policies no matter how efficiently it performed.[5]

The Union Pacific had always envied the Atchison's ability to control its own line from Chicago to California, allowing it to introduce new schedules without regard to what its competitors thought or whether connector roads could handle them. The more Union Pacific tried to improve its service, the more it chafed at the inability of connectors to do likewise. By 1960 three developments threatened to turn this vulnerability into a grave danger by revamping historic transcontinental relationships.[6]

In September 1960 an ICC examiner recommended that the Southern Pacific no longer be obliged to solicit a maximum amount of freight traffic for the Central Pacific-Union Pacific route. The court had imposed this requirement in 1923 as part of the deal allowing the Southern Pacific to keep the Central Pacific. Eliminating it could have a devastating effect on the flow of traffic through the Utah gateway. The commission rejected the recommendation, but the Rio Grande took the issue to court and the outcome remained uncertain.*[7]

The transcontinental division cases posed an even greater threat. In 1953 some eastern and midwestern roads asked the ICC for a larger share of the rates on transcontinental traffic. These complaints launched a fight that dragged on for fifteen years. If granted, the gains would come at the expense of western roads including the Union Pacific, which derived 57 percent of its freight revenues from such traffic that year. In December 1960 an ICC examiner recommended substantially larger divisions for the eastern and midwestern roads. With millions of dollars at stake, the Union Pacific joined other roads in fighting the case through the courts.**[8]

Together these cases, coming within months of each other late in 1960, reinforced the Union Pacific's fear of a major realignment in transcontinental relationships—especially when viewed against a third factor: the most virulent resurgence of merger fever since the 1900s. The poor showing of carriers since the war left many of them near bankruptcy after the recession of 1958, creating instability within the industry and uncertainty among stronger roads. These conditions had always been the spawning bed of mergers, but never had past movements worn such an edge of desperation.[9]

By 1960 railroads in every corner of the nation were conducting merger studies or holding exploratory talks with other lines. Between 1955 and 1966 the ICC received fifty merger applications from class I railroads. No one doubted that survival would condense the rail system into a few giants; the burning question was who would end up with whom. Once the merger quadrille began in earnest, even prosperous roads feared that longtime partners would be

*Litigation on the case dragged on until 1968, when the Supreme Court upheld an ICC order nullifying the 1923 proviso.

**These complicated cases were decided against the western lines and finally settled by a series of compromises.

snatched away, leaving them as wallflowers. The Union Pacific was no exception. Unsettled by the flurry of applications and the flood of rumors, the company decided to reexamine its historic policy of not crossing the river.[10]

Lovett approached the issue in his usual precise, unhurried manner. In December 1960 he hired Wyer, Dick, a consulting firm considered expert in western railroads, and asked Stoddard for his views on possible partners east of the Missouri. A preliminary analysis in January 1961 suggested the Rock Island as the best candidate. At the time the Rock Island was flirting with the Milwaukee. Early that winter, however, the Milwaukee's interest shifted to the Northwestern. On the other flank, the Southern Pacific and Atchison chased the Western Pacific while the northern transcontinentals revived their combination with the Burlington that had originated in the Northern Securities Company.[11]

William Wyer favored the Burlington as a partner if it could be detached from the northern merger, and wanted the Rio Grande as well. The Union Pacific had commenced a secret interchange with the Burlington to get faster schedules than other connections could provide, and it had pleased both sides. In February 1961 Lovett invited the presidents of both northern roads to Brown Brothers Harriman to discuss the possibility of sharing certain Burlington lines.* While not opposing the idea, both presidents feared that any change in the merger plan would delay ICC action. The best course, they argued, was to discuss the matter after the merger was approved in its present form. Everyone agreed to handle any action between those immediately concerned "on the highest level of courteous consideration."[12]

Aware that "in this changing climate unusual things can happen," Lovett headed west in March, stopping first in Denver to tell John Evans and Gus Aydelott of the Rio Grande that the Union Pacific had bought about 10 percent of the Rio Grande's stock for purely defensive purposes. From there he went to Los Angeles to see Donald J. Russell of the Southern Pacific. At both places the most delicate issue was the Western Pacific, which Russell wanted and Evans hoped would remain independent. If nothing else, the trip confirmed for Lovett how fluid and volatile the situation was.[13]

On May 31, traffic vice-president J. R. MacAnally produced a report analyzing the Union Pacific's traffic interchange for 1960 with all thirteen of its eastern connections. This study, which later loomed large in management's thinking about merger partners, indicated that the Union Pacific could acquire lines to Chicago and St. Louis without losing much of the business given it by other lines. Put simply, it revealed that other roads needed the Union Pacific more than the Union Pacific needed them. Only two lines, the Burlington and the Milwaukee, delivered the Union Pacific as much business as they received from it. Much of the Burlington tonnage consisted of forwarder traffic for southern California that could not make schedule on any other line except the Union Pacific. Altogether the Union Pacific originated 180,355 tons of interchange business compared with only 99,908 for all thirteen connectors combined.[14]

*Those present at the meeting were Lovett, Frank Barnett, Reg Sutton, John M. Budd of the Great Northern, and Robert S. Macfarlane of the Northern Pacific.

A vast part of the business delivered to the Union Pacific came from points for which the eastern connectors served as bridge carriers. If the Union Pacific reached Chicago, it could directly tap twenty major lines compared with eight at Council Bluffs. A similar if more complex situation existed at St. Louis, which meant that an ideal merger partner should provide lines to Chicago and from Kansas City to St. Louis. Direct interchange at these points would enable the Union Pacific to make faster, more competitive schedules.[15]

The MacAnally study launched an intensive analysis to find that right partner. By September the process singled out the Rock Island even though it stood eighth in the amount of interchange business. The Rock Island alone had lines from both Council Bluffs and Kansas City to Chicago and other Illinois gateways, and from Kansas City to St. Louis. Its capital structure promised a cheaper, less complicated takeover than most rivals, and the ICC might smile on the absorption of a weak road by a strong one.[16]

No other candidate offered this mix of advantages. The Northwestern, which interchanged more traffic with the Union Pacific than any other road, had a better line to Chicago but a circuitous one to St. Louis and none to Kansas City. It also suffered from a poor income record, low freight density, and a crippling commuter business. The Milwaukee did not reach St. Louis and groaned beneath a heavy debt load. A combination of the Illinois Central and the Gulf, Mobile & Ohio looked promising but would be expensive to acquire. In addition, the ICC would probably frown on the combination.[17]

Everyone knew the Rock Island was in poor shape. Late in 1960 the Union Pacific arrived at a ball park estimate of $147 million for improvements and $118 million for equipment to bring the road up to standard. Yet by several measures the Rock Island had outperformed even the Burlington since World War II. It seemed to be a road on the way up, while the Burlington looked to be heading the other way. Those favoring acquisition of the Burlington had to admit that the financial, legal, and regulatory obstacles were overwhelming.[18]

Early in September Lovett asked Stoddard for the views of his officers. On the two key questions MacAnally strongly favored jumping the river and going after the Rock Island. Francis Melia, the western general counsel, dodged the issue of whether the company should go east of the river; if it did, he agreed the Rock Island was the best bet. Executive vice-president Elgin Hicks showed he was out of his league by mumbling some platitudes that merely reasked the questions instead of answering them. The lone dissenter was Edd Bailey, who doubted the wisdom of crossing the river or offending other connectors by pursuing a line that handled only 6 percent of the interchange business.[19]

On September 26 Lovett summoned the Omaha officers to a conference in New York. The discussion confirmed what Barnett had already concluded: (1) that the Union Pacific must gain access to the Chicago and St. Louis gateways; (2) that the advantages of this step would outweigh any possible diversion of traffic by eastern connections; and (3) that the Rock Island best fit these needs. Instead of directly approaching the Rock Island, however, it was decided to gather as much data as possible on the road's condition under a veil of strict secrecy. Lovett imposed a November deadline for this task.[20]

The first hurdle had been surmounted. Everyone breathed easier, though realizing there was a long way to go. No one could foresee that the process thus launched would bear an uncanny resemblance to the Vietnam War. The best and brightest minds the company could assemble plunged into an earnest, intensive effort to make the right decision in the right way based on mountains of data. Despite all the expertise it could muster, however, the company found itself bogged down in a morass that outlasted even the Vietnam War and was no less filled with perils, pitfalls, and well-intended decisions that backfired.

Through this tortuous campaign the chain of command remained intact. Roland Harriman was the titular chief, Lovett the grand strategist, and Barnett the active field leader and tactician on whom Lovett depended increasingly as the fight wore on. "He had youth," said Lovett, "and he had a very good background in corporate work." Precise, methodical, and demanding, Barnett was a brilliant lawyer but not a railroad man, and his style showed it. While others talked in a meeting, his mind was busy outlining the brief. Barnett was strong but not healthy. He was a diabetic who pushed himself hard with little regard for his condition. Under stress he tended to drink too much, which he was not supposed to do at all.[21]

Barnett's mind got all it could digest that autumn as the data requested by Lovett piled up in New York. In October 1961, John D. Farrington, chairman of the Rock Island board, died, disrupting an already weak management. The road's leading stockholder, Colonel Henry Crown, one of Chicago's richest men through his supplying of building materials and later control of General Dynamics, filled the vacuum left by Farrington's death. A tough, restless bargainer, Crown soon revealed that he was willing to part with his Rock Island holdings if the price was right.[22]

By December Stoddard had second thoughts and suggested another look at the Illinois Central, which was itself eyeing the Missouri Pacific. Edd Bailey and the operating people agreed, largely because the Illinois Central was in much better shape than the Rock Island, but Charles D. Peet of Clark, Carr & Ellis presented a strong case against the Illinois Central. Stoddard wavered, then went back to supporting the Rock Island. Rumors of merger talks between the Milwaukee and the Rock Island lent fresh urgency to the decision.[23]

In February 1962 Bill Wyer submitted his analysis of MacAnally's traffic report in terms that seemed to clinch the case. Wyer refuted the old belief that the Union Pacific's prosperity had resulted from its staying west of the Missouri River gateway and argued in favor of expansion. His reasoning had an eerie echo of the defensive rationale so prevalent in the expansion wars of the 1880s. "It would appear essential," he concluded, "that the Rock Island be prevented from falling into other hands and that this road at the same time offers the best opportunity of offsetting the losses which appear likely as a result of other mergers."[24]

The decision to go after the Rock Island was made in March, but still Lovett and Barnett did not approach the road directly. Instead they ordered studies done to determine a suitable price and exchange ratio for the stocks of the two companies. This work took a new twist in June when Donald J. Russell, president of the Southern Pacific, called Lovett to inform him as a courtesy that his company had embarked on a long-range study of the Rock Island's value as a merger partner. Lovett handled the shock with his usual aplomb; Stoddard was less graceful. "Those SOBs," he growled, "are going all over the Rock Island with the idea of buying it."[25]

Lovett approached the situation gingerly. The Ogden gateway case was still pending, and President Kennedy had just appointed a committee to formulate a national policy on rail mergers. The Southern Pacific still eyed the Western Pacific and had disavowed any interest in end-to-end mergers. Knowing Crown and his friends to be "natural born traders" and fearful they would play one road off against the other, Lovett urged Russell to join him in "making haste slowly." Russell agreed but said he was already committed to doing the study.[26]

There followed a round of hard bargaining from which some common ground emerged. The Southern Pacific's interest lay in its connection with the Rock Island at Tucumcari, New Mexico, which offered a line competitive with the Atchison. Vowing not to be "cut off at Tucumcari," the Southern Pacific wanted the Rock Island lines south of Kansas City and faster service to Chicago. The Union Pacific sought lines into Chicago and St. Louis, which included the track between St. Louis and Kansas City. Meanwhile, Crown tried to peddle his stock to the Atchison and every other Chicago road, but his high price tag left the bait untouched. The Rock Island, noted an observer dryly, "behaved something like an aging spinster frantically seeking a match before the family inheritance ran out."[27]

Despite the friction, Lovett and Russell recognized that the companies had far more to lose than gain by fighting each other. Russell's interest in the Rock Island drooped when he learned how much it would cost to rehabilitate the road. By September negotiating teams headed by Barnett and Ben Biaggini of the Southern Pacific thrashed out terms to divide the Rock Island. The latter road would be merged into the Union Pacific, which would keep the northern lines and that between St. Louis and Kansas City. The Southern Pacific would buy the lines from Santa Rosa to Kansas City and all branches south of Kansas City except one.[28]

Joining forces with the Southern Pacific proved a mixed blessing. While it turned a potential enemy into an ally, it also turned some potential allies into enemies. The president of the Atchison had encouraged Stoddard to take the Rock Island and talked about going together to buy the Southern Pacific. He would not be so accommodating with the Rock Island's southern lines in the hands of a rival. Neither would the Missouri Pacific or the Rio Grande, both of which had offered Stoddard support for the acquisition. The other Iowa roads would also oppose the application both from fear and from a belief that the best merger would be one among themselves.[29]

Although the alliance had its rocky moments, it worked well for a time. The two roads agreed to make an intensive joint study of the Rock Island. Another consulting firm was hired to study the proposed division and come up with a price tag. The Union Pacific also engaged a major Chicago law firm, Sidley, Austin, Burgess & Smith, to handle its negotiations with the Rock Island and the houses of Merrill, Lynch and First Boston Corporation to assess the tough issue of a stock exchange ratio. This diligent and costly homework occupied all sides well into the winter. Not until February 1963 was the Union Pacific ready to open actual negotiations with the Rock Island, which had asked the New York firm of Glore, Forgan to serve as its financial adviser.[30]

By then the merger question had already become entangled with restructuring the Union Pacific. After studying the problem, Charles Peet concluded that "reorganization of Union Pacific corporate structure should be completed in connection with the unification with Railroad No. 6." In particular he urged that any action to eliminate the preferred stock be made an integral part of the merger proposal submitted to the ICC. This reasoning had the effect of putting the transition to a holding company in limbo until the merger was resolved, which everyone believed would take several years.[31]

At the first negotiating session on February 25 the two Pacific roads laid their offer on the table: .7 of a share of Union Pacific for one share of Rock Island. This figure had been reached through painstaking analysis and was a generous offer if one looked realistically at the Rock Island. Unfortunately, Crown had no clear notion of the road's real worth, and his financial advisers, the firm of Glore, Forgan, led him down a path that amounted to a flight of fancy. The Glore, Forgan report, based on a host of erroneous assumptions, concluded that the proper ratio should be 1.5 to 1.8 Union Pacific for each share of Rock Island. Crown snatched eagerly at this figure without having a clue as to its basis.[32]

Both Lovett and Russell dismissed the Glore, Forgan report as ludicrous, but its presence posed an obstacle that wasted precious months to remove. Crown conceded the report's flaws but clung hopefully to an inflated price for the stock. Russell discovered to his horror that Crown did not even know the Rock Island required huge outlays for improvements and equipment. "Are we behind in mechanization?" Crown asked blankly at one point. Although Crown was a shrewd trader, Russell was convinced he was genuinely ignorant of the road's needs and of railroad accounting in general.[33]

Wearily the two Pacific roads formalized their own agreement on February 28, then set about shredding the Glore, Forgan report in numbing detail. For weeks the bargaining continued, fortified by fresh battalions of data. Glore, Forgan revised its calculations but would go no lower than 1.25 Union Pacific for each Rock Island share. In April the other two major Rock Island holders, Roy C. Ingersoll and Bruce Norris, softened their position. Both were eager to get Union Pacific stock in return for their Rock Island and fearful that the deal might fall through, leaving them with a weak property requiring a massive infusion of new capital.[34]

Barnett seized this opening to make a drive at Crown. In a five-hour telephone conversation on April 30 he got Crown to accept a ratio of .718 Union Pacific per share of Rock Island. A formal plan was completed in June 1963 and submitted to both boards, where fast approval was expected. "The

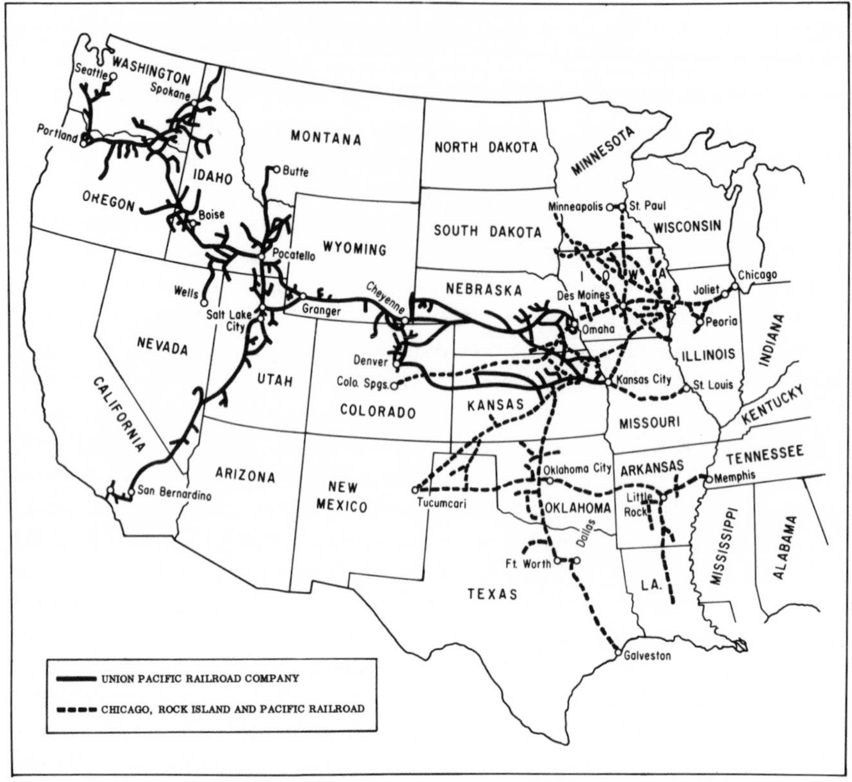

SYSTEM TO BE: The combined lines of the Union Pacific and Rock Island systems. Under the plan all Rock Island lines south and west of Kansas City would go to the Southern Pacific.

Rock Island board was so enthusiastic about a merger with the Union Pacific,'' recalled Jervis Langdon, who became the Rock Island chairman in 1965, ''that they couldn't wait to approve it.''[35]

All sides breathed a sigh of relief that the long quest was over. In fact, it had merely entered a new phase. Having consumed thirty months in reaching an agreement, the new partners now faced a long struggle to gain ICC approval and fend off the rival roads who opposed the merger. The most formidable of them stepped forward at once. Ben Heineman, the bright, quixotic lawyer who had rescued the Northwestern from bankruptcy by trampling on rail orthodoxies, was convinced the midwestern roads could survive only by merging with each other. Since 1960 he had been dickering with the Milwaukee while trying to extract reasonable terms from Crown.[36]

The prospect of seeing the powerful Union Pacific absorb the Rock Island alarmed Heineman. In May 1963 he declared that the Northwestern would vigorously oppose the merger; a month later he announced that the Northwestern would make a competing bid for the Rock Island. Lovett assured the Rock

Island directors that the Union Pacific would fight Heineman "with every resource at its command," and let them know in plain language that he expected their full support. All sides braced for a long fight, though no one in his wildest dreams imagined how prolonged it would be. The officers and staff of the Union Pacific, which had been data-producing engines for nearly three years, cranked up for yet another outpouring.[37]

Heineman's move triggered a fresh round of changing partners in the merger quadrille. The Atchison opened talks with the Missouri Pacific, which the Illinois Central still coveted, and agreed to support the Northwestern's bid in return for the Rock Island's southern lines. The Southern Pacific rebuffed a bid from the Katy after Lovett warned Russell that any such flirtation would badly complicate the Rock Island case before the ICC, and the Rio Grande asked for the Rock Island's line from Denver to Kansas City.[38]

Absorbed in the details of the fight, the Union Pacific managers were slow to grasp the merger's larger significance. In retrospect it served as a catalyst for sorting out and putting in concrete form the countless merger proposals that had been floating about for years. A major consolidation was actually going forward, and it forced every affected carrier to review its position in that light. In the great grand game of railroad musical chairs, another one had been removed, leaving every survivor to wonder where he would land. They could not help but oppose a merger that held such profound implications for their future.

Nor did the Union Pacific's leaders fully appreciate how crucial time was in their fight. All the data amassed on the Rock Island did not impress on them deeply enough the road's weaknesses and vulnerability. The Rock Island was a grain carrier with only one major industrial shipper on its lines, the Maytag Company in Newton, Iowa. It controlled no key terminal but reached them over the lines of other roads. "The Rock Island was a very highly marginal operation," admitted Langdon. ". . . [It] could disappear, and except for the grain movements that were local to it and maybe the Maytag Company . . . it wouldn't have been missed."[39]

Physically, the Rock Island was a slow, undermaintained road that had been going steadily downhill since the merger talks began. Its president, R. Ellis Johnson, was a weak, amiable figure held prisoner by a board that did not know and did not want to know how bad things really were on the road. Tough belt-tightening measures were deferred while the board paid dividends that had not been earned. Meanwhile, an already poor physical plan grew worse. Between 1960 and 1964 the serviceable car inventory dropped 18 percent, and the bad-order ratio soared from 2.7 to 10.1 percent.* During the mid-1950s the Rock Island had laid an average of only ninety miles of new rail per year; by 1964 the figure dipped below ten. Tie renewals had also been cut by 37 percent.[40]

By 1964 the road's freight capacity had actually dropped 7 percent below its 1959 level. Car shortages plagued the road, and the track was so bad the

*Bad-order cars are revenue freight cars undergoing or awaiting repairs. The ratio measures the proportion of these cars to the total revenue fleet.

company had to haul grain in boxcars because it had neither big covered hoppers nor the roadbed to sustain them. Except on the Tucumcari line, which had been kept in reasonable shape, trains could only do about forty miles an hour on the road. "All we wanted was salvation," stressed Langdon. "The Rock Island was going down; it was inevitable." The Union Pacific understood clearly that it would have to spend huge sums to upgrade the Rock Island, but it was slow to understand how much the continued delays kept pushing the price tag skyward.[41]

While Lovett tried to keep the Rock Island directors in tow, Ben Heineman of the Northwestern put together a complex package that looked on paper to outdo the Union Pacific offer. He hoped to present it at the Rock Island November stockholders' meeting called to approve the Union Pacific offer. A bitter fight for proxies wound up in a federal court when the Union Pacific charged a shadow committee of Rock Island stockholders with unethical tactics. In February 1964 Judge Julius J. Hoffman, who later gained notoriety in the trial of the Chicago Eight, upheld the Union Pacific complaint and postponed the stockholders' meeting.[42]

The decision was small consolation in a war going so badly on other fronts. In October 1963 Lovett checked into the hospital for yet another stomach operation and was lost for a time. Heineman seemed to be everywhere, wooing bankers or anyone with some Rock Island shares. By contrast the Union Pacific's leaders seemed slow and unimaginative. An officer of Hill and Knowlton, the Chicago public relations firm hired by the Union Pacific, reported bluntly that "the North Western [sic] is giving the UP and Rock Island a shellacking as far as public opinion is concerned out here." The image concocted by the press was contradictory but no less devastating: the Union Pacific as Goliath yet always on the defensive and off balance thanks to David's nimbleness.[43]

The Hoffman decision forced the Union Pacific to confront another crucial turning point. Glumly its leaders conceded that they could not count on getting the necessary two-thirds vote from Rock Island stockholders. The favorable press given Heineman and the Northwestern had boosted its stock and therefore the value of its offer. The advantage was temporary at best, but it was there. A lame attempt to buy some Rock Island stock showed the futility of that tactic, leaving the Union Pacific with three alternatives. It could go ahead with the stockholders' meeting and take its chances, abandon the fight, or sweeten its offer.[44]

In February 1964 Lovett and his top managers met with Donald Russell to consider the question. All agreed that an enlarged offer was futile without assurance that it would produce the necessary two-thirds majority vote from Rock Island stockholders. Russell went even farther, stating flatly that he opposed a new offer under any circumstances. This was the first rift between the allies, and it was soon to widen. After lunch Henry Crown and his attorney joined them. Since the votes were not there, everyone agreed the stockholders meeting should be delayed. Crown sent out feelers for a higher ratio and was rebuffed by Russell. Afterward, however, general counsel Covington Hardee let Crown know that the Union Pacific, unlike its partner, would at least consider a sweetened offer.[45]

Although a higher ratio posed serious problems—such as dealing with the inevitable question of why it wasn't offered in the first place—Lovett put First Boston and Merrill, Lynch and Wyer to work on studies while the three roads tried to round up more proxies. On April 30 the Union Pacific board authorized Lovett to "re-evaluate" the Rock Island situation. A week later Heineman called Barnett to ask whether the two companies could sit down and cut a deal to avoid a fight. Unfortunately, Barnett fell ill and was unable even to attend a pivotal meeting on May 18, during which Lovett met with top Omaha and New York officers to consider future policy.*

At that meeting the officers agreed unanimously that the Rock Island was still worth pursuing. Edd Bailey alone balked at offering a higher price; the others argued that any increase would be trifling in the long run. Lovett accepted their recommendation and turned to the question of what the new offer should be. No discussion was had of the enormous difficulties posed by this decision. The Union Pacific had declared repeatedly that it would never raise the ante. Any new offer would shred its credibility as well as alienate the Southern Pacific, its most important ally in the fight.[46]

This was the quintessential style of policy-making in the 1960s. Objectives were defined and decided apart from the problems posed by their implementation. Such obstacles were brushed aside as mere tactical problems to be dealt with once goals had been clarified. This "can do" spirit pervaded the company's entire approach to a merger that, like the Vietnam War, grew steadily more confused and complex each step of the way. Instead of pausing to take inventory of its accumulated liabilities and difficulties, management plowed bravely ahead in the confident belief that its formidable array of talent and resources could overcome any obstacles in its path.

Most leaders had yet to learn the harsh lesson that would soon puncture the hubris of modern managers in government and business alike: it was possible to do everything the right way and still have it all come out wrong. The top officers of the Union Pacific were about to discover this costly truth as their merger effort tracked its eerie parallel to the worsening conflict in Southeast Asia.

Rather than confer with its ally on the decision to expand the fight, the Union Pacific announced unilaterally that a new offer would be made and then plunged into lengthy discussions with the Southern Pacific. Two days of dickering brought no agreement. Ben Biaggini said the Southern Pacific would support the new bid provided its share of the purchase was determined at once and computed on the old ratio. Calling the Rock Island and Northwestern "two broken-down properties trying to whipsaw us into paying more than the property is worth," he named a figure of $95 million as the maximum his road was willing to pay.[47]

*Present at the meeting were Sutton, Bailey, MacAnally, Francis Melia, Hardee, and Charles Peet, who met all morning and through lunch. Lovett joined them at 2 P.M.

Sutton countered with a minimum price of $130 million. Everyone agreed the gap was too wide to be decided at once, yet the Southern Pacific refused to support any new offer until its own cost had been fixed. The conference broke up amicably but with a crucial issue and the alliance itself left dangling. Despite this impasse, the Union Pacific moved at once to finalize a new agreement with the Rock Island. This complicated plan called for Rock Island holders to deposit their shares in return for "deposit certificates." When two-thirds of the stock had been assured, the merger would be carried out on the new terms.*[48]

On September 1, 1964, the new offer was formally tendered to Rock Island holders. That same day Biaggini nudged Barnett anew on fixing a price for the Southern Pacific's share. The fact that Southern Pacific could not approve the new offer complicated matters, he added, and might jeopardize their application to the ICC. Biaggini urged that the price be settled to avoid any inconsistency in their position before the ICC. Barnett was willing to talk but gave the matter little priority. He would pay dearly for this neglect.[49]

There was also concern over how to give the Rock Island able leadership through the merger process. To help the amiable but ineffective Johnson, Lovett suggested bringing in as chairman and CEO some retired executive who would accept the limited tenure of his position. In October the Rock Island chose Jervis Langdon, Jr., a solid railroad man who had taken early retirement from the Baltimore & Ohio after that road was acquired by the Chesapeake & Ohio. Langdon was a good manager with a keen mind that often saw things in a different light than tradition-bound Union Pacific officers.[50]

While the Union Pacific was distracted by these matters, Heineman launched a series of attacks that kept his adversary constantly puzzled and off-balance. It was guerilla warfare at its best. "Ben Heineman . . . outfoxed us all," admitted James H. Evans, who joined the Union Pacific board in 1965. "I mean, he did the most brilliant piece of blockage work to keep us from getting the Rock Island."[51]

Heineman first confounded the Union Pacific in June 1964 by selling the 214,000 shares of Rock Island the Northwestern had acquired. Anyone who thought he had abandoned the fight was undeceived in September, when Heineman enjoined the new Union Pacific offer on a technicality. Barnett parried that thrust by modifying the form of the offer. Heineman then phoned Barnett to ask whether they could not find some way to avoid a costly proxy fight and litigation. Barnett agreed to talk. At their meeting Heineman suggested that both sides withdraw their proposals and let the ICC decide the case on its merits. Barnett doubted this was practical but took the idea to the Rock Island's lawyers, who agreed with him.[52]

Having rebuffed Heineman, the Union Pacific began active solicitation of proxies. By November more than half the Rock Island shares had been depos-

*Under the new plan, each share of Rock Island could be exchanged for one share of new voting preferred bearing a $1.80 dividend and convertible at the Union Pacific's option into .085 shares of Union Pacific.

ited, enough to control the road. Brushing aside a Heineman attempt to solicit proxies, the Rock Island stockholders in January 1965 approved the Union Pacific offer by an overwhelming margin. Four years after the process commenced, the way seemed clear at last to take the merger application to the ICC. Friends of the merger showered the Union Pacific's generals with congratulations. Their good wishes proved woefully premature.[53]

Once past this obstacle, the company began preparing its case for the ICC. This required the cooperation of the Southern Pacific, which meant the dispute over the latter's purchase price had to be settled. Another round of talks began in mid-February and plodded on for a month. Barnett and Biaggini came to terms on a price only to bog down over what share of the merger campaign expenses the Southern Pacific should bear. Lovett found it incredible that the two sides were at loggerheads over a sum amounting to less than one percent of the total. The Union Pacific softened its position and an agreement was finally reached in March 1965, but more time and energy had been squandered on intermural bickering.[54]

While the talks continued, other roads began lining up against the merger. The Frisco, Missouri Pacific, Milwaukee, Rio Grande, and Western Pacific joined the Northwestern in opposition, with several others waiting in the wings. From the first it was obvious that a host of carriers would intervene, yet few Union Pacific men seemed concerned. A poll of the Omaha officers in April 1965 revealed them all to be against making any deals with other lines. "We ought to fight them to the last ditch," barked MacAnally in a typical response. Bailey, who had become president, also urged a tough stand "against all opposition and their demands."[55]

This hard line alarmed Langdon, who believed that, with so many roads against the merger, some deals had to be cut. He said as much to a reporter and was promptly asked by Barnett to take it back. Langdon refused, and urged Barnett to seek some accommodations. "We're not going to compromise," Barnett replied flatly. "We're not going to talk with anybody or try to adjust these differences."

"Frank, you're never going to be able to win this case," persisted Langdon, "if you yourself don't take the lead . . . in trying to work this out."

"Oh the hell with it!" snapped Barnett. "Leave it up to the lawyers."

Years later, Langdon still recalled the exchange in disbelief. "Well, look what happened," he said with a wry smile. " . . . They left it to the lawyers, and the lawyers of course loved it. . . . Lawyers love to litigate."[56]

Barnett was not alone in his intransigence. A skilled, experienced politico like Lovett ought to have seen the urgent need for a negotiated settlement, yet he accepted Omaha's hard line without a murmur. Even Roland Harriman took the position that "If you make a deal with one intervener, you have to make one with all of them." Shunning any policy that smacked of appeasement, the Union Pacific went its lonely way against a formidable array of opposition.[57]

Langdon had some other bad news for the Union Pacific: the Rock Island was in worse shape than anyone suspected, and it was deteriorating fast. The shortage of equipment was, in his words, costing the road "literally hundreds of cars a day.'' Langdon boldly assumed the role of bearer of bad tidings and moved to correct them with draconian measures. Johnson was nudged into a ceremonial post, allowing Langdon to take direct charge. The Rock Island's top management appalled Langdon. ''They didn't have anybody who was worth a damn,'' he said. Langdon shoved most of them into retirement and brought in as VPO an able Southern Pacific man named G. W. Kelly, who in turn lured some of his former colleagues to the Rock Island.[58]

This move shocked Bailey, who harbored the traditional dark suspicions about the Southern Pacific as well as fears that the road was trying to cut some secret deal with the Northwestern. To Bailey, hiring Southern Pacific men amounted to staffing the Rock Island with fifth columnists, and he let Langdon know it. But Langdon stood his ground. Indeed, he had little choice. Kelly was competent, nearing sixty, and still eligible for Southern Pacific retirement. Few other managers would consider a job on a railroad that was about to disappear. Under his supervision the Rock Island showed solid improvement, but it desperately needed capital.[59]

While these matters distracted the Union Pacific, the nimble Heineman stung the company with one clever move after another. Already the sharp-tongued lawyer had become a darling of the press, an advantage he played to the hilt along with his role as David twitting Goliath. He made the rounds schmoozing investment bankers, parading before them the Northwestern's excellent showing during the past year. While the Union Pacific agonized over how to counter these forays, Heineman surprised them with an ingenious ploy.[60]

By September 1965 about 92 percent of the Rock Island stock had been turned in for Union Pacific certificates of deposit. Having lost the battle to prevent this exchange, Heineman got authority from the ICC to issue Northwestern certificates and offered them to Rock Island stockholders in exchange for their Union Pacific certificates. Reg Sutton dismissed the move as a ''last-ditch effort to confuse the Rock Island shareholders, the public and the markets,'' but the Union Pacific managers were thrown into confusion. Nor did their anxiety ease when market movements over the following months made the Northwestern offer steadily more attractive.[61]

Suddenly the Union Pacific found itself in several firefights at once. Heineman's bold stroke gained him a powerful ally. For months the Atchison had kept a careful neutrality, but three weeks after Heineman's announcement it agreed to buy the Rock Island's southern lines if the Northwestern succeeded in gaining control. The Rio Grande and Western Pacific were also busy pressing their demands and building cases on traffic diversion for the hearings. Their sniping was pesky but pale in comparison with the threat posed by the powerful Atchison. Ironically, some Rock Island holders even began to question the need for a merger because Langdon had done such a good job of turning the road around.[62]

By early 1966 the enemy seemed to have everything going for them while the two Pacific roads stumbled uncertainly. Lovett received a copy of some testimony drafted by Southern Pacific lawyers for its officers and couldn't believe his eyes. ''Holy Smoke!'' he scribbled in dismay. ''What is this—'tiny

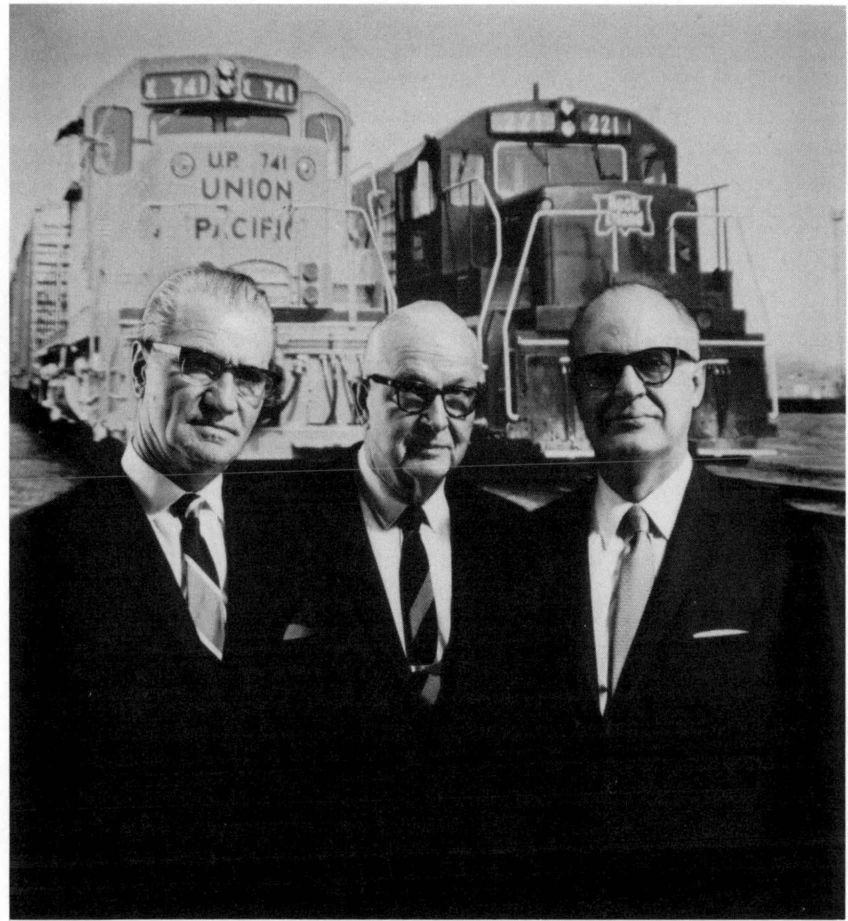

MERGER TEAM: Edd H. Bailey, Reginald M. Sutton, and Frank E. Barnett pose in front of matched diesels from the Union Pacific and Rock Island in 1966.

steps for tiny tots?' '' On that confident note the Union Pacific approached the ICC hearings, which finally opened in May 1966, or year six of the merger quest.[63]

Heineman's tactic of delay was not only brilliant but self-sustaining as nearly every western road rushed to intervene on one pretext or another, creating a jumble of conflicting demands and apprehensions that would take years to sort out. In the war of words before the hearings the Union Pacific found itself constantly on the defensive, seeking to counter Northwestern and other charges or dividing internally over the best tactic for trying to seize the offensive. The winter's war demonstrated anew that Goliath made an easy target for just about any weapon.[64]

In April 1966 the ICC flashed a negative signal by ruling against the long-pending merger of the Northern Pacific, Great Northern, and Burlington.

A month later the hearings opened in Chicago as nearly a hundred lawyers representing nineteen railroads crowded into a large room at the Conrad Hilton Hotel. Lovett led off as the first Union Pacific witness and handled it with his usual polish. Bailey, who followed him, faltered badly, however, speaking hesitantly and stumbling over the facts. ''He was just a disaster as a witness,'' said Langdon, whose opinion of Bailey and Barnett shrank steadily.[65]

Through the long summer and fall the hearings droned on, with no one expecting a decision for years. ICC examiner Paul C. Albus described the case as more complicated than even the Penn Central merger because there were ''more issues, more contradictions, and more railroads that want positive relief.'' A Rio Grande publicist mocked the lack of impact made by Union Pacific officers. ''The total absence of surprise in the testimony of its star witnesses,'' he chided, ''has amazed many who credited the big and powerful railroad's strategists with uncommon brilliance.''[66]

Two issues in particular kept the company constantly on the defensive: the raising of an offer it had insisted was fair in the first place, and the MacAnally traffic studies of 1960 and 1963 with their controversial projections of traffic diversions that would flow from the merger. Other roads also pounced on the recommended consolidations and abandonments in Wyer's report. In June 1966 the Union Pacific added another layer to an already cumbersome proceeding with a request that the Northwestern-Milwaukee merger proposal be combined with the Rock Island hearings. This fresh round of legal wrangling meant more delay and engaged fresh battalions of lawyers.[67]

Year seven opened with no end in sight and a major change in Union Pacific management. Lovett surrendered his place as chairman of the executive committee to Barnett. Although he remained on the committee, the merger quest became more than ever Barnett's quest—some said his obsession. Not everyone had confidence in him. Langdon came to believe that Barnett's outlook was too provincial. ''He was a tax lawyer,'' Langdon stressed, ''. . . and I never got the feeling that he was really on top of the situation.''[68]

In October 1967 Heineman approached Barnett with a new deal. If the Union Pacific would drop its case and support Heineman's takeover of the Rock Island, Heineman would back a Union Pacific bid to absorb the Illinois Central and Gulf, Mobile & Ohio, which were then talking merger. The talks expanded to include Biaggini but produced no workable plan that satisfied the three roads while fending off the Atchison at the same time. Heineman had attained his first goal: the Union Pacific was hopelessly mired in proceedings that still looked years away from final settlement. The policy of delay, however, was flypaper that caught his merger plans as well.[69]

Gradually the midwestern merger movement bogged down in scattered, confused firefights of litigation. The northern lines appealed their case and finally gained approval, as did the Northwestern's takeover of the Chicago Great Western, but they were the lone exceptions among the vast schemes seeking to redraw the rail map west of Chicago. All the rest dangled precariously on the outcome of the Rock Island case, which had become the longest and most hotly contested fight in rail history.

They would have a long wait. ICC examiner Paul Albus broke his ankle and was replaced by Nathan Klitenic. After Albus recovered, the two examiners sat together. Klitenic needed time to acquaint himself with testimony that by 1968 had consumed 240 hearing days and produced 43,000 pages of reading material. He also decided gradually to use the case as a springboard for merging some twenty-five midwestern roads into four strong systems, a fantasy that consumed still more years before collapsing.[70]

Through it all Barnett clung doggedly to the belief that the Union Pacific would prevail. By 1968, however, the situation was changing in significant ways. After a brief resurgence the Rock Island plunged back into the red, and its physical deterioration accelerated. Langdon rethought the whole matter and concluded that the Union Pacific could win only by offering to include the Northwestern or Milwaukee or both in the merger. ''Whether we like it or not,'' he told Barnett, ''the C&NW has made the plight of the midwestern roads the central public issue in the case.'' The ICC would not allow the Union Pacific to have the Rock Island if it meant ruining these other carriers in the bargain.[71]

Above all, Langdon wanted a decision before the Rock Island crashed into bankruptcy. ''I told the board that I didn't think this thing was going to fly,'' he recalled. If that happened, the Rock Island had to be free to make another deal to save itself. But Langdon could not budge the ICC, his own board, or Barnett, who rejected the idea of including the other roads in the merger. To Langdon's dismay, everyone decided to take their chances on the outcome.[72]

Heineman also took a fresh look at the situation. Ever a moving target dodging the ponderous thrusts of Union Pacific lawyers, he had for five years tied the Union Pacific in knots with his guerilla tactics. In 1969 he was preparing to shift his ground yet again. That July he deflected a request from Barnett for talks by saying he wanted time to rethink his whole position. This reassessment consumed the rest of the year, during which time both the Rock Island and the Milwaukee continued their slide toward bankruptcy.[73]

In 1969 the Union Pacific celebrated the centennial of its completion as the first transcontinental railroad. During that time it boasted many accomplishments of which it could be proud. The Rock Island merger was not one of them. The Union Pacific had spent a decade, 10 percent of its entire history, in the struggle with nothing to show for it. Five more years would pass before the ICC issued a decision. When the Union Pacific finally ''won'' the war, there was nothing left to win.

28

The New Railroad

The ultimate frustration of the Rock Island merger was not just that it dragged on for more than a decade without result but that it drained the energy and attention of the Union Pacific management during a crucial period. It became a meat grinder chewing up resources sorely needed elsewhere. ''Our practically total energies . . . [were] on this thing and the hearings,'' lamented Reg Sutton. Everybody got caught up in gathering data first for the case and then for rebuttal of the cases made by objecting roads. The foremost casualty of this drain was the drive to restructure the Union Pacific into a holding company.[1]

Although the divisions improved things, they had not worked as well as Lovett and Barnett hoped. In December 1964, when Edd Bailey was about to replace Art Stoddard as president, Barnett sent Lovett an updated version of his restructuring plan of July 1962. He could find no way to move ahead to the next stage of creating separate corporations while the merger proposal awaited ICC action. All he could do was make the divisions fully independent by eliminating the provision that their heads seek concurrence from the railroad president before submission to New York. This concession, which had been made to placate Stoddard, was dropped before Bailey assumed office. The company had also been buying in its preferred stock but could do little more until the merger miasma cleared.[2]

Bailey was a marked improvement over Stoddard. The last product of the old system that promoted from within, Bailey was a tall, lean westerner with a firm jaw, a ready smile, and a voracious appetite for hard work. His father had been a farmer in Hannibal, Missouri, before taking up a homestead in Colorado, where he struggled to support a family that grew to twelve children. Edd Bailey

PRESIDENT AND CABINET: Edd H. Bailey poses with his vice-presidents and two top New York officers in October 1965. (*From left*) G. L. Farr, labor relations; Francis Melia, western general counsel; Reginald M. Sutton, controller; Bailey; Frank E. Barnett, general counsel, J. R. MacAnally, traffic; D. F. Wengert, operations; and A. C. Ritter, chief of land division.

made an inauspicious debut with the Union Pacific as a scab worker during the great strike of 1922. In true Jeffers style he climbed the ladder, slipping back now and then as every officer did. He had just turned sixty when he reached the final, fabled rung of his career.[3]

When the summons to New York came, Bailey spent two days cramming frantically for whatever questions the top brass had. But none were asked. Roland Harriman merely said he was privileged to offer Bailey the presidency of the Union Pacific and would he accept. Bailey said yes indeed and bounded out into a New York rainstorm where in his joy he nearly got hit by a truck. The irony of that moment stayed with him forever: was there no end of the ways trucks brought grief to railroads and their officers?[4]

He became the most popular president since Gray, if only because he was more sensitive to those in the ranks. "People who worked for him . . . didn't fear Edd Bailey; they liked him," said Barnett. He was, agreed E. C. Schafer, one of the first to discover "that you just didn't have to be an SOB in order to be a good railroader." Aware that few employees had ever seen the president's office, Bailey made a point of bringing all of them to the top floor in groups. And he let the operating people play golf. A genial, kindly person, he was intensely proud of his high place without being pompous or overbearing. "Behind every successful man," he once quipped, "there is . . . an astounded wife."[5]

Bailey's chief flaw, thought one officer, was "his inability to detect flattery. He was sort of a sucker for it at times." And while he was a far cry from the czar, he was still a product of the old school and retained some of its flavor. He continued to use the special agents as secret police and had his informants in the ranks, and he used favors like business cars to reward favorites. He presided over a shadow organization in which an officer's title did not tell anyone what he really did, and where nothing was done without the president's approval. To New York he was a country boy with more vigor than imagination, an old dog set in his ways but at least willing and able to learn some new tricks.[6]

One new trick had to be learned early. Bailey did not like the divisions being independent of his office any more than Stoddard had. In July 1966 he tested the waters by urging that they be placed back under his direction. Lovett promptly rebuffed this overture with a reminder that the true object was a holding company, and "any backward step" was to be avoided until that goal was reached. Bailey retreated, but only to await another time.[7]

By the mid-1960s Lovett and Barnett were painfully aware that the Union Pacific had to modernize both its organization and its management techniques. But modern management required modern managers. Where were they to come from? The ranks were barren in both New York and Omaha. Lovett and Roland Harriman were nearing retirement; Barnett was relatively young but his health was questionable. The board had some capable members but their average age was in the sixties. Out west, none of the division heads impressed Lovett as being aggressive, imaginative leaders.

The company needed not only younger leaders but men from the outside who in turn could find other managers. As a first step two new directors were recruited. James H. Evans, president of the Seamen's Bank, and William D. Grant, head of a Kansas City insurance firm, became—at forty-five and forty-eight respectively—the spearhead of a youth movement. Barnett told them frankly that they were there to lower the average age of the board. Both were to become mainstays in the management.[8]

The advent of Bailey improved things somewhat in Omaha, and the head of the land division retired a year after Stoddard, allowing fresh blood to be brought in there. His successor, said Sutton wryly, "was a pretty good go-getter. He got us into quite a lot of things that later we didn't like very much." Lee Osborne of the natural resources division was capable but lacking in vision. His budget, complained Sutton while briefing Lovett for an inspection trip, had no "reach, no goals or anything." That was the guaranteed budget, Lovett laughed, "the one they guarantee they can make." But after the visit Lovett wasn't smiling. Osborne, he sighed, "didn't seem to have any comprehension of our goals and these enormous resources that . . . it was time to develop."[9]

But Osborne, like Bailey, showed some capacity for growth, and accepted New York's push to impose modern management systems as well as a new organization on the West. Lovett and Sutton pressed the division heads for real capital budgets instead of the traditional wish lists. Early in 1966 general auditor A. O. Mercer, with Sutton's blessing, launched a campaign to introduce responsibility accounting, or Management Cost Control as the Union Pacific called it. This approach allowed a road to pinpoint responsibility for expenditures, make useful projections, and perform other tasks that could not be done under the static accounting system required of all railroads by the ICC.[10]

The system, Mercer told a skeptical Bailey, was "a tool to be used to measure operating efficiency, by comparing current results with budget forecasts, and to control costs at whatever level they are originated and initially approved." Aware that the Pennsylvania and the Northwestern already used the system with excellent results, Mercer sent men to observe both operations. Significantly, they found that both systems had been introduced by men new to the railroad industry who had never been indoctrinated in ICC accounting.[11]

While Sutton prodded Mercer to establish a timetable for installing the new system, VPO Del F. Wengert urged every officer to free his mind of convention and reinvent the best type of standard report for his department. "The very things that seem impossible today," he emphasized, "may be quite ordinary a few years from now." Utilizing the new system fully required yet another overhaul of the company's computer and data-gathering system. In 1965 work began on a "complete operating information network" (COIN) linking the microwave and computer systems in a way that could transmit data from strategic points to a central office for processing and immediate retransmission.[12]

It took five years to make COIN fully operational and almost as long to install the new cost system. Not until April 1969 could Barnett decree that "establishment of objectives, plans and budgets (developed in light of our forward planning) shall be a regular part of our operations from now on." But the changes did not stop there. In 1966 Omaha created a marketing research program that included development of a computer-oriented marketing information system among its many tasks. In a more trendy vein it also explored motivational studies of rail employees.[13]

The key to improved performance lay in finding and keeping good officers. The old system of promoting from within had rewarded endurance as much as ability, and too often amounted to a process of attrition. Its value had been limited in the old days and diminished steadily as railroads grew more complicated. In 1965 the company began developing formal systems for recruiting new talent from outside and identifying officer potential within the ranks. An "Officer Potential Register" was set up to locate the best and the brightest in seven departments. Sutton asked all department heads to define their recruitment methods as a way of demonstrating to them the absence of any system.[14]

Bailey dutifully polled his fellow presidents on the subject and found that, here as elsewhere, the Union Pacific lagged well behind its neighbors. The Atchison, for example, had been sponsoring a six-week course at the University of Southern California for its managers since 1952, as well as sending promising officers to programs at Harvard, Columbia, Northwestern, and MIT. It also quietly recruited college and MBA graduates. All these activities were handled outside the personnel department, which confined itself to labor matters. The Southern Pacific, Northern Pacific, and Great Northern did similar things, while the Southern Railway worked with twenty-eight colleges in its recruitment program.[15]

Still Bailey was skeptical about sending managers to seminars. "During our busy season," he told Lovett, "the absence of Operating and Traffic officers for a protracted period of time from four to six weeks would not seem to be in the best interests of the Company." Lovett thought otherwise, and Bailey got the message. Within a year college recruitment and management training programs were well along in their development. A tuition aid program for all employees with at least two years' service went into effect in September 1967, and in April 1968 Omaha sent its first student to the Program for Management Development at the Harvard Business School.[16]

When Lovett announced at the October 1966 board meeting that he would retire at the year's end, he set in motion a chain of events that transformed the New York management. For fourteen years Lovett had been the indispensable man. No one had done more to steer the Union Pacific through the painful transition into a new era. But at seventy-one he was tired and failing, as he had been when he took office. As a favor to Roland he agreed to remain a director and a consultant.[17]

The committee of directors appointed to choose Lovett's successor found quickly that they had little choice. The logical candidate—indeed, the only candidate unless the company went outside its ranks—was Frank Barnett, who still divided his time between Union Pacific and Clark, Carr & Ellis. To succeed Lovett he had to give up the law firm, which he was reluctant to do. Finally Evans and others persuaded him to become chairman of the executive committee and devote his full attention to the job. At the same time Reg Sutton was elevated to the new position of vice-president of finance.[18]

Barnett's promotion revealed with painful clarity how empty the ranks were behind him. "Until we could get competent people . . . in there," said Elbridge T. Gerry of Brown Brothers Harriman, who had joined the Union Pacific board in 1957, "Barnett was the whole thing." For a few years Gerry had to remind Barnett that he was no longer a line officer. "Frank had to make himself into an administrator," observed Gerry, "and as the company got bigger, he began to find it more difficult to delegate, which a good CEO's got to do." Gerry also had to do some hand-holding when the scale of things made Barnett a little timid.[19]

Two different forces converged in 1967 to spur the recruitment of fresh executive talent. The first was the need for someone to back up Barnett; if anything happened to him, there simply was no one to take his place. The second was Barnett's desire to push ahead with the long-delayed holding company, which required able managers to head the new corporations. Barnett recognized that he had to solve two distinct but closely related problems: he had to devise a new organizational structure, and he had to find the right people to staff it.[20]

In both cases Barnett wasted little time seeking outside help. To help design the new organization he hired the Cambridge Research Institute (CRI) as consultants; to find new talent he enlisted the headhunting firm of Ward Howell. The Cambridge team swarmed over Omaha, asking questions and conducting interviews until Bailey and his officers began to feel a little like the last dinosaurs. "I think they are like all researchers who try to develop something spectacular," grumbled Stan How. Occasionally Bailey tried to reassert the primacy of the rail president only to have Barnett nudge him back to the concept of separate and equal companies.[21]

The dinosaurs were right to worry. Barnett wanted CRI not merely to help design the new holding company but also to redefine every department in all three divisions along with the job descriptions of its top managers. The goal went beyond restructuring to the creation of a thoroughly modern organization capable of handling diversified activities with maximum efficiency. This required not just more officers but a different breed of them, attuned to modern techniques and managerial tools, possessed of vision broader than the closed, autocratic world of the railroad itself. To Bailey and his peers the message delivered by CRI's soft-spoken academics was plain: the dinosaurs were marked for extinction.

Barnett had another reason for restructuring the company as quickly as possible. Several areas, notably the oil operations, were languishing at current levels of activity. The company had to decide whether to get out of the business or get deeper into it. Barnett had no doubts about which way to go. "It was *obvious,* at least to me," he said later, "that the railroad business was on the way down and that you damn well better be in the energy business." The CRI people also formed an "acquisitions team" to find likely companies for the Union Pacific to buy. For obvious reasons, top priority went to oil refining and chemical firms.[22]

By the spring of 1968 CRI had produced job descriptions for several new positions on the railroad. Recruiting began for an executive vice-president, vice-presidents of finance and marketing, and a director of advertising and public relations. Although CRI developed a list of six candidates for executive vice-president, Barnett knew exactly who he wanted. John C. Kenefick had started out with the Union Pacific in 1947 before moving on to the Rio Grande and the New York Central. A protégé of the New York Central's Al Perlman, he was considered one of the best operating men in the country.[23]

The Penn Central merger had just occurred when Barnett called Perlman and told him he was having lunch with Kenefick that day and was going to offer him a job if Perlman didn't object. "He went *silent* on the telephone," chuckled Barnett, "which is extraordinary for Al Perlman. He's usually yak, yak, yak." When Perlman finally regained his voice, it was to say that if he were ten years younger, he would be trying to beat Kenefick out of the job.[24]

Although Kenefick had once worked for the Union Pacific, the old guard still considered him an outsider. "It was clear that I was imposed on this group," he recalled. "I mean, Bailey didn't want any part of it for many reasons, including, I'm sure, that he immediately saw me as a threat to his own position." Instead of following the CRI plan, Kenefick was made VPO and Del

Wengert was shoved into a newly created post of executive vice-president as Bailey's assistant.[25]

Kenefick was the vanguard of a new management team that would transform the Union Pacific. His arrival roused Bailey to another defense of turf. In May 1968 Bailey warned that bringing in another outsider as vice-president of marketing would "create a pattern and result in an extremely serious morale problem affecting all departments." Instead he submitted a list of promotions to fill the new post in the traditional manner from the inside. Barnett let these go through; he had the key man he wanted in place. Warily, Bailey watched every move the CRI group made that threatened to drain power from his position.[26]

New York had an easier time of the search process, if only because there was less resistance to meet. Ward Howell surveyed the field in the fall of 1968 and told Barnett that the best candidate for a number-two man was in his own back yard. Jim Evans, who had been a director since 1965, was president of Seamen's Bank, but as a young banker in Chicago he had worked on oil production and natural gas credits as well as pipelines. This experience in the energy field fit Barnett's needs perfectly. In the new holding company he planned to oversee the railroad while his number-two man took care of the nonrail assets.[27]

Once Evans agreed to serve, he and Barnett had to convince Roland Harriman of the need to build a strong staff in New York. Roland was in some respects the last dinosaur in New York, the keeper of the grail of tradition. "I don't want a palace guard," he kept saying. "I don't want a big group in New York." The staff didn't have to be large, Barnett and Evans reassured him; it only needed "skill and talent of the highest order." Roland found this argument persuasive and yielded to it, however uneasily at times.[28]

Roland himself planned to retire once the holding company was in place, which meant a new chairman of the board would be needed. After some deliberation Barnett decided to take that position and also serve as chief executive officer of the new corporation. Evans would be president of the new holding company and vice-chairman of the board. To fill his old post as chairman of the executive committee, Barnett tapped a surprised Elbridge T. Gerry. "Absolutely the last thing I thought of," Gerry confessed, but he agreed to do it. His presence would preserve the Harriman link once Roland retired; Gerry's mother was Roland's sister.[29]

The other newcomers were hired from the outside except for William J. McDonald. Another Clark, Carr & Ellis alumnus, McDonald had walked in off the street to seek a job with the firm and in September 1968 found himself the Union Pacific's new general counsel. Two key financial figures, William S. Cook and Bruce J. Relyea, were refugees from the Penn Central debacle. Relyea became controller and Cook vice-president of finance when Sutton moved up to the new post of executive vice-president. Cook had also been at General Electric, which provided a number of the people Barnett and Evans lured to Union Pacific. "The place looked like we were a subsidiary of General Electric for awhile," said a bemused Gerry.[30]

OUTSIDER: James H. Evans, whose varied business background made him an ideal number two man in the restructured Union Pacific Corporation.

While Barnett, Evans, and Sutton all had a hand in finding new talent, it was Barnett who put the team together. A few years later, Gerry noted, Barnett was fond of indulging in a little reminiscence. "He liked to look around the room at some of these guys and say, 'all my boys.' He is pretty near right."[31]

By the fall of 1968 the Union Pacific for the first time had a management team capable of running a large, diversified enterprise. Most of it had come from outside the rail industry. In November the company announced publicly that it was considering reorganization into a holding company. In fact, its plans were so far advanced on the subject that the new Union Pacific Corporation came into being on January 30, 1969, more than eight years after the first division plan had been outlined.[32]

Early in 1970 the new company abandoned its historic offices at 120 Broadway and took over two floors of an imposing glass tower at 345 Park Avenue. The change told the tale: the Union Pacific had moved uptown in every sense.[33]

The new railroad was one that had progressively more to do with its nonrail assets. The holding company format enabled Barnett to push expansion vigorously in the lucrative energy field. As early as 1965 he had gone shopping for a major oil company to serve as the anchor of the natural resources division. The search lasted four years, pinpointing and discarding potential firms, until one summer morning in 1969 when Evans had breakfast with a friend who told him that Celanese Corporation wanted to sell their oil subsidiaries, Champlin Petroleum and Pontiac Refining.[34]

Barnett jumped at the chance and closed the deal in August, paying $240 million for the two integrated firms. ''Wall Street at that time said, 'Gee, you really paid through the nose for Champlin,' '' Barnett snorted later. ''The hell I did. Champlin Oil's cash income every year is more than I paid for the whole damn company.''[35]

Prior to the Champlin acquisition Lee Osborne had responded eagerly to Lovett's suggestion that it was necessary to spend money to make money. Osborne's natural resources division plunged aggressively into a variety of exploration programs, joining with Husky Oil in Canada, Sohio off the Louisiana shore, and a consortium working the Gulf of Alaska. It also participated in a federally-sponsored program called ''Project Gasbuggy,'' which hoped to stimulate oil and gas recovery through the use of limited underground explosions using a nuclear device. ''The prospect, when stated baldly, scares the daylights out of me,'' confessed Lovett. But the program did well enough that the Union Pacific took part in a second one called ''Rulison.''[36]

Mining activities spread in several directions. The company found uranium deposits in the Powder River basin, and scoured older mines for untapped reserves. Even the coal operation took on new life, although it had been reduced to a department in the natural resources division. Since the advent of the diesel, the chief customer for coal was no longer railroads but power companies, with whom the Union Pacific joined in a number of ventures. CRI urged the company to pursue a strategy of growth through acquisitions, pointing to Stauffer Chemical as one attractive candidate.[37]

The land division kept buying potential industrial sites wherever it could find them along the road. Its head, John W. Godfrey, was eager to expand his operation. He wanted not only to buy, develop, and sell industrial properties but also to get involved in projects not directly connected with the railroad. This was the kind of initiative Barnett hoped would flow out of the divisions, although he would not always like the results. In November 1969 Godfrey announced a new $98 million real estate development program that set a brash new tone for his operation.[38]

So diversified had the company's operations become that one analyst referred to it as ''The Union Pacific *What?*''. But the railroad was hardly neglected. Barnett was one of the few rail executives who called the railroads ''one of the great growth industries in this country today.'' The massive capital expenditure program since the 1950s had restored the road to its role of leadership in physical condition and maintenance. The giant new Bailey Yard under construction at North Platte, once completed, would make preblocked trains possible and relieve the congestion overwhelming the Kansas City yard.[39]

The traffic department had also made great strides. As early as 1964 the company became part of a line running freight to Alaska. In January 1967 it became the first American railroad to open an office in Japan. Bailey went personally to Japan to emphasize the importance of the Far East trade to the Union Pacific Railroad. A new land-bridge container program to move interna-

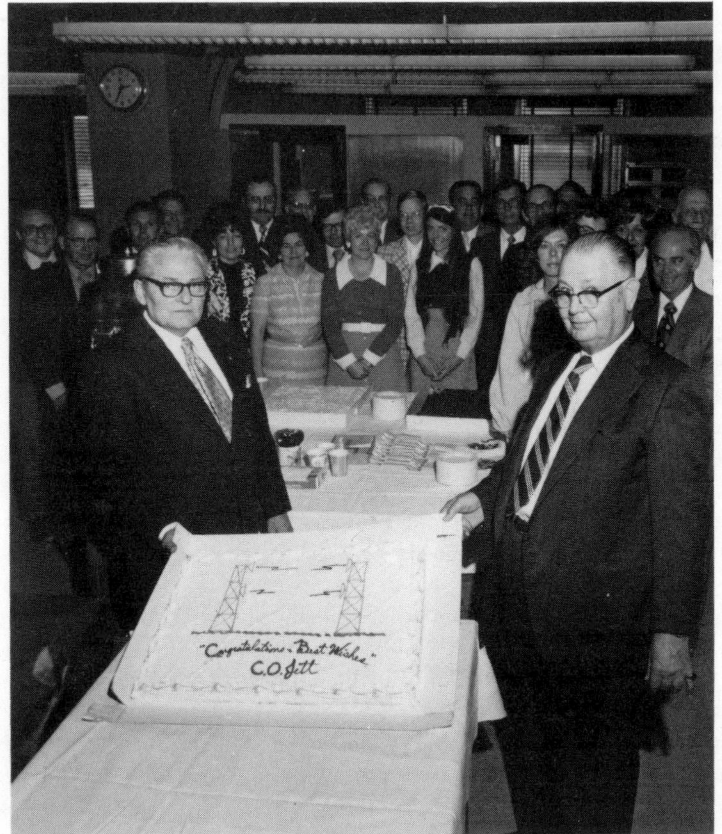

FOR A JOB WELL DONE: C. Otis Jett (*right*) accepts a cake with special microwave decorations at his retirement party, June 1973.

tional traffic between the east and west coasts was launched in 1968. The trailer-container program also expanded rapidly, generating $34.5 million worth of business in 1969. That same year the new unit trains hauled 1.1 million tons of Utah coal to the Kaiser Steel plant at Fontana, California.[40]

Early in 1969 the first phase of COIN went on line, giving the company a real-time computer-communications system. "We have stepped into the 21st century over night," enthused Bailey with good reason. The new system continuously monitored operations over the entire 9,600-mile system through a network of fifty-three IBM 1050 computers located in thirty-eight yard offices. The information it gathered could then be transmitted to any of 120 connecting sites. To administer this growing giant, the supervision of computer operations was taken away from the Accounting Department and placed under a new Department of Management Information.[41]

Otis Jett had made this system possible with the 3,194-mile microwave installation that provided 600 voice channels. Through this communications network flowed data generated by COIN, the entire direct-dial telephone system, and signals for CTC, hot-box detection, signal transmissions, and FLOCON (Flow Control), the new car-tracking division. It was at the time one of the largest private communications systems in the world, and it was still growing. The company had come a long way since the time a quarter century earlier when constant busy signals used to throw Jeffers into a rage.[42]

In 1969 the Union Pacific celebrated the hundredth anniversary of the driving of the Golden Spike. There could not have been a more appropriate year for the formation of the holding company that would launch the third era of its history. The company honored the occasion by restaging the Golden Spike ceremony at Promontory and with a new commemorative locomotive, the *Centennial*. Only one disappointment marred its otherwise glowing prospects: the interminable Rock Island merger fight.

The Rock Island story was doomed to have an unhappy ending, but for years many people doubted it would have any ending at all. True to his word, Ben Heineman rethought his position and came up with some startling conclusions. Disillusioned with the rail industry in general, he dropped his offer for the Rock Island in February 1970, sold the Northwestern to its employees two years later, and devoted his attention to the chemical firms owned by his parent company, Northwest Industries.[43]

In July 1970 ICC examiner Nathan Klitenic finally recommended approval of the merger, but not until December 1974, fourteen years after the first merger activities had begun and well over eight years after the first hearing, did the commission issue its decision. By a vote of six to four it approved the decision but with a string of unacceptable conditions attached. Thus did the longest case in ICC history grind its way to an inconclusive and unsatisfying end.[44]

The decision was much too little and far too late. Charles J. Meyer of Wyer, Dick, who had twice inspected the Rock Island during the mid-1960s, went over the road again in 1970 and was shocked at how much it had deteriorated. "It was really bad," he said ruefully. On both the Kansas City and St. Louis lines he saw evidence of derailments where the derailed cars had just been pushed out of the way. Slow orders of ten miles an hour had been imposed in numerous places because of the track's poor condition.[45]

As Jervis Langdon had warned, the Rock Island was tottering inexorably toward collapse and would require far more capital to restore than had been projected earlier. In June 1973 Bruce Relyea revised the gross cost of the Rock Island to $404 million. John Kenefick studied these figures and concluded that "the Rock Island has deteriorated both physically and financially to such an extent that we cannot afford to take them over no matter how low the price." Although Barnett conceded that the outlook was grim, he clung doggedly to a glimmer of hope until the ICC decision shattered it.[46]

By 1975 the industry looked vastly different to the Union Pacific than it had in 1960. Balking at the financial load and the conditions imposed by the ICC, it terminated the merger offer in March 1975. That same month the Rock Island went into receivership. The Milwaukee tried desperately to get included in the

THE SCEPTER PASSING: John C. Kenefick (*left*) and Edd H. Bailey share a laugh in front of a diesel.

merger, then joined the Rock Island in bankruptcy and ultimately extinction. For the Union Pacific there would be no through line to Chicago, and none to St. Louis until years later. As a system the new railroad was not much larger in 1969 than it had been in 1920, but it was an entirely different creature physically.[47]

And structurally. In September 1969 Edd Bailey turned sixty-five. The board extended his contract one year, but the next summer Barnett made his move. Ironically, his hand was forced by Langdon, who had left the Rock Island and become senior trustee of another disaster, the bankrupt Penn Central. Langdon wanted Kenefick back to take charge of the crippled giant. "You don't turn down the presidency of the biggest railroad in the world very lightly," mused Kenefick, but Barnett had him tagged as Bailey's successor. The problem was how to keep him until Bailey served out his time.[48]

LAST OF THEIR KIND: Edd H. Bailey, the last president to rise through the ranks, and Roland Harriman, pose before the memorial to E. H. Harriman at Salt Lake City, May 9, 1967.

Bailey deserved some consideration. He had been a good president who, as his public relations man stressed, "learned very quickly in management style." But he was still the last of the dinosaurs—managers who were neither evil nor incapable but merely products of another era. He represented the last stand of the old inbred management style that had dominated (some said stifled) the Union Pacific for decades, while Kenefick was regarded even outside the Union Pacific as the top operating man in the industry. To Barnett and Evans he was as much the future as Bailey was the past.[49]

Under the bylaws Barnett himself had drafted, power in the railroad flowed not to the president but to the position of chief executive officer—transportation, the same as with the other divisions. This provision became Barnett's escape hatch. He persuaded Kenefick to stay with the Union Pacific by giving him this title and with it the real power over the railroad. Bailey held the title of president until September 1971, but little else. "When we got back here that night," recalled Kenefick, "Bailey didn't have the authority to fire his secretary."[50]

Just as Bailey's departure marked the end of the old guard management in Omaha, the retirement of the two grand old men in New York marked the end of a dynasty. Two pairs of fathers and sons had ruled the Union Pacific for seventy years, an extraordinary record in modern corporate affairs. For the first time in 1969 the company would be without at least one of them in a major leadership position. Both Roland Harriman and Robert Lovett remained on the Union Pacific board until 1978. When Roland died that year, Lovett resigned because he thought it "appropriate that our memberships on the Boards should both end in the same year."[51]

Both Lovett and Averell Harriman, who had long since severed his ties with the railroad, enjoyed very long lives. But the always fragile and sickly Lovett could not compete with the more robust Averell in the longevity race. He didn't even make it to ninety-one, while Averell sailed on to the age of ninety-four.

The passing of the Harriman-Lovett dynasty and the formation of the holding company ushered in another rebirth of the Union Pacific. Unlike the birth a century earlier, there would be no mourning after this time. The second century of Union Pacific history opened with vastly more promise than the first. In 1969 the Union Pacific was no longer a pioneer but a giant of the industry.

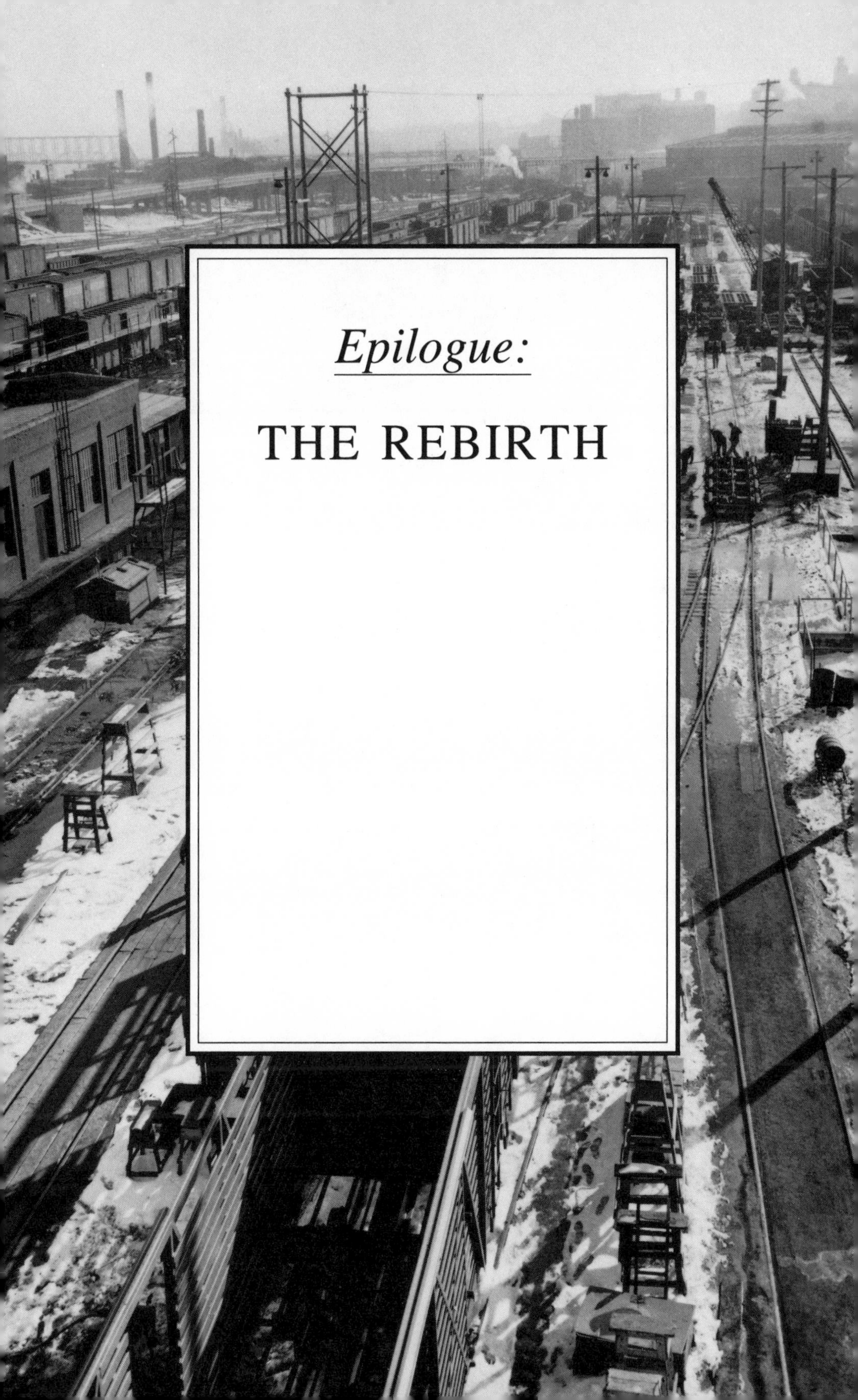

Epilogue:

THE REBIRTH

Prior to 1893 the Union Pacific was a large but unstable road struggling to stay afloat in an age when railroads ruled the transportation roost. During the twentieth century it emerged as one of the giants in an industry that lost ground steadily to competing forms of transportation. Put another way, the Union Pacific was weak when railroads were strong, and grew strong just before railroads became weak. This inversion does much to explain both its peculiar history and its promise for the future.

During its first life the Union Pacific paid the price of being the pioneer among transcontinental railways. As the earliest and most costly road, it was in poor shape to compete with newer, cheaper roads in an age of overbuilding and bitter rate wars. Receivership proved a blessing in disguise by allowing the company not only to restructure its capital obligations but also to reorganize with an eye toward a future unfettered by the shackles of the past. The company started its second life fresh in ways that not even the dreamers in its ranks could have imagined.

E. H. Harriman was the architect of this transfiguration. Under his leadership the Union Pacific again played the role of pioneer, but this time it caught the wave of the future. Harriman transformed the Union Pacific into a new railroad before most other managers grasped that such a thing existed. The empire he fashioned did not survive intact, but the Union Pacific remained one of the strongest railroads in the nation—and one of the richest.

Apart from creating a model of rail efficiency, Harriman taught the industry two crucial lessons. The first was that railroads in the new era of high-volume traffic could only make money by spending money to reduce their operating costs to the lowest possible level. The second involved the most controversial of his policies, one that other companies were slow to follow. Harriman understood the value of having diversified interests that produced investment income to supplement the railroad's earnings. Although severely criticized for this practice during his lifetime, he led the Union Pacific early into a strategy that carried it through hard times and ultimately proved the salvation of other railroads wise enough to adopt it.

While the Harriman legacy of high maintenance and emphasis on safety served the Union Pacific well in later years, the system of management he left behind fared poorly. In a sense the Union Pacific had been too "Harrimanized" for its own good. The company had always suffered from having its management divided between Omaha and New York, a duality solved only by Jay Gould and Harriman in very different ways. Where Gould exercised power through two close friends, Harriman erected a pyramid with himself at the top. Both solutions depended on the unique abilities of Gould and Harriman, and neither long survived their passing.

After Harriman's death, Judge Lovett recognized that this highly centralized management could not function effectively without Harriman at its head. His solution was to transfer considerable power back to Omaha, leaving New York to deal only with financial and major policy matters. This gradual decentralization worked well as long as it had two capable and complementary men like Judge Lovett and Carl Gray at its head. Averell Harriman might have managed to keep it intact, but his departure for government service, coupled with Gray's retirement, created a leadership vacuum that soon twisted the Harriman legacy into a grotesque caricature of itself.

Success has a way of freezing an enterprise into place, binding it to an almost mindless repetition of the policies and practices that originally enabled it to prosper. But conditions change constantly, and the very achievement of success transforms any company into a very different creature than it once was. The result is a paradox in which the same pattern that brought success becomes the surest road to decline or even disaster.

Under Jeffers's heavy hand tradition became an end in itself rather than a goal to be attained by adapting to new needs and conditions. The lack of a strong figure in New York enabled his autocratic reign to fossilize a once progressive company by draining from it the life blood of innovation. Morale declined until a corporate culture once proud of its esprit de corps dissolved into a morass of intrigue and vicious fights over turf. Ashby's attempt to reverse this trend sank beneath the weight of his own flawed character, and Stoddard was content to let mediocrity reign as long as it sustained his own position.

Prosperity helped conceal this dark night of ineptness. The Union Pacific was both a rich and a lucky company despite poor management. It owned one of the best rail routes in the country and some prime nonrail assets. When some of its outside investments slipped because of the depression, the oil bonanza filled the gap. Beneath this gilded surface, however, lay a company in turmoil. A railroad that had once been the industry standard watched other roads surpass it in almost everything except earnings until the vast changes sweeping through the industry after World War II jolted the company from its complacency and self-deception.

For nearly a century the course of the Union Pacific's history had been shaped by the flow of power between Omaha and New York. On the whole it had done best when given strong direction from the East, a force absent from 1940 until the mid-1950s. Even then the combination of Robert A. Lovett and Roland Harriman produced at best a restraining hand until the structural changes sought by Lovett were gradually implemented. The evolutionary path led first to the divisions and culminated in the new Union Pacific Corporation, a holding company that positioned the company well for the future.

These seminal changes had very distinct objectives. The most obvious was the need to create a structure that would enable the Union Pacific to realize its strategy of pursuing diversified interests. A more subtle goal was to free the nonrail assets from the control of railroad presidents who neither liked them nor understood their importance in the company's larger destiny. In short, power in this critical domain had to flow back to New York in a manner that permitted efficient management of the nonrail assets without undermining the president's running of the railroad.

Both Lovett and Barnett understood that the holding company was the most suitable vehicle for attaining these goals. Had the ill-conceived and ill-fated Rock Island merger not intervened, they would have implemented the new structure long before 1969. By that date several other roads had already reorganized into holding companies, and more would soon follow. The Union Pacific had not led the wave of the future but had at least joined it.

During the twentieth century the Union Pacific had progressed from a railroad to a transportation company to a holding company in which transportation was but a single component of a diversified operation. By the year of its centennial the company would at last be found looking forward rather than backward. The golden spike had given way to the golden mean.

SELECTIVE BIBLIOGRAPHY

Adler, Cyrus K., *Jacob H. Schiff: His Life and Letters* (New York, 1929), 2 vols.

Athearn, Robert G., *The Denver and Rio Grande Western Railroad* (Lincoln, 1977).

Bruce, Alfred W., *The Steam Locomotive in America* (New York, 1952).

Bruchey, Stuart, ed., *Memoirs of Three Railroad Pioneers* (New York, 1981).

Bryant, Keith L., Jr., *History of the Atchison, Topeka, and Santa Fe Railway* (New York, 1974).

Burr, Anna Robeson, *The Portrait of a Banker: James Stillman* (New York, 1927).

Chandler, Alfred D., Jr., *The Visible Hand: The Managerial Revolution in American Business* (Cambridge, Mass., 1977).

Cottrell, W. Frederick, *The Railroader* (Palo Alto, Calif., 1940).

———, *Technological Change and Labor in the Railroad Industry* (Lexington, Mass., 1970).

Haney, Lewis H., *A Congressional History of Railways in the United States* (Madison, Wisc., 1908).

Harriman, E. Roland, *I Reminisce* (Garden City, N.Y., 1975).

Hayes, William E., *Iron Road to Empire* (New York, 1953).

Hines, Walker D., *War History of American Railroads* (New Haven, 1928).

Hofsommer, Don L., *The Southern Pacific, 1901–1985* (College Station, Texas, 1986).

Hoogenboom, Ari and Olive, *A History of the ICC* (New York, 1976).

Isaacson, Walter, and Evan Thomas, *The Wise Men* (New York, 1986).

Keeler, Theodore E., *Railroads, Freight, and Public Policy* (Washington, 1983).

Kennan, George, *E. H. Harriman: A Biography* (Boston, 1922), 2 vols.

Kerr, K. Austin, *American Railroad Politics, 1914–1920* (Pittsburgh, 1968).

Klein, Maury, *Union Pacific: The Birth, 1862–1893* (New York, 1987).

Larson, T. A., *History of Wyoming* (Lincoln, 1965).

Martin, Albro, *Enterprise Denied: Origins of the Decline of American Railroads, 1897–1917* (New York, 1971).
———, *James J. Hill and the Opening of the Northwest* (New York, 1976).
McAuliffe, Eugene, *History of the Union Pacific Coal Mines* (Omaha, 1940).
Mercer, Lloyd J., *E. H. Harriman: Master Railroader* (Boston, 1985).
Meyer, B. H., *A History of the Northern Securities Case* (Madison, Wisc., 1906).
Morris, Ray, *Railroad Administration* (New York, 1920).
Nelson, James C., *Railroad Transportation and Public Policy* (Washington, 1959).
Olson, James C., *History of Nebraska* (Lincoln, 1955).
Overton, Richard C., *Burlington Route* (New York, 1965).
Ranks, Harold E. and William W. Kratville, *The Union Pacific Streamliners* (Omaha, 1974).
Sharfman, I. L., *The American Railroad Problem* (New York, 1921).
———, *The Interstate Commerce Commission: A Study in Administrative Law and Procedure* (New York, 1931), 5 vols.
Stover, John F., *American Railroads* (Chicago, 1961).
Stover, John F., *History of the Illinois Central Railroad* (New York, 1975).
Trottman, Nelson, *History of the Union Pacific* (New York, 1923).

SOURCE NOTES

KEY TO ABBREVIATIONS

The following abbreviations for frequently cited sources—principally archives and collections—are used throughout the notes:

AF	Material found at Arden Farms, Harriman, N.Y.
AJA	Jacob H. Schiff papers, American Jewish Archives, Cincinnati, Ohio
BA	Burlington Archives, Newberry Library, Chicago, Illinois
BB	Material obtained from Baker & Botts, Houston, Texas
DP	Grenville M. Dodge papers, Iowa State Department of Archives and History, Des Moines
DR	Dodge Record, autobiographical volumes, Iowa State Department of Archives and History, Des Moines.
DRG	Denver & Rio Grande Western Railroad Archives, Colorado State Museum, Denver
EJC	E. J. Connors papers, Union Pacific Historical Museum, Omaha, Nebraska
FAV	Frank A. Vanderlip papers, Butler Library, Columbia University, New York City
GK	George Kennan papers, Library of Congress, Washington, D.C.
HBH	Henry B. Hyde Collection, Baker Library, Harvard Graduate School of Business Administration, Boston, Massachusetts
IC	Illinois Central Archives, Newberry Library, Chicago
ICI	Records in possession of IC Industries, Chicago, Illinois
JJH	James J. Hill papers, James J. Hill Reference Library, St. Paul, Minnesota
JS	James Stillman papers, Butler Library, Columbia University, New York City
LDS	Materials in library of Church of Jesus Christ of Latter-Day Saints, Salt Lake City, Utah

MP Missouri Pacific Railroad Archives, Union Pacific System, St. Louis, Missouri
OK Otto Kahn papers, Firestone Library, Princeton University, Princeton, New Jersey
RGD R. G. Dunn & Co. collection, Baker Library, Harvard Graduate School of Business Administration, Boston, Massachusetts
SF Stuyvesant Fish papers, Butler Library, Columbia University, New York City
SMF Samuel M. Felton papers, Baker Library, Harvard Graduate School of Business Administration, Boston, Massachusetts
TR Theodore Roosevelt papers, Library of Congress, Washington, D.C.
UPL Union Pacific Railroad Company collection, Nebraska State Museum and Archives, Lincoln
UPN Union Pacific Railroad Company records, Union Pacific Corporation, New York City
UPO Union Pacific Railroad Company records, Union Pacific System, Omaha, Nebraska
UP Report Annual reports of the Union Pacif Railroad Company
WDS Willard D. Straight papers, Cornell University, Ithaca, New York
WPB Western Pacific Railroad papers, Baker Library, Harvard Graduate School of Business Administration, Boston, Massachusetts
WSJ *The Wall Street Journal*

PROLOGUE
THE FUNERAL 1916

1 Details of the funeral are drawn from the Omaha *World-Herald,* Omaha *Bee*, and Council Bluffs *Nonpareil*, Jan. 4–7, 1916.
2 Omaha *World-Herald,* Mar. 18, 1921; Omaha *Bee*, Mar. 19, 1921.
3 Stanley P. Hirshson, *Grenville M. Dodge: Soldier, Statesman, Railroad Pioneer* (Bloomington, Ind., 1967), 261–62.
4 Ibid., 227, 259–62.

CHAPTER 1
THE RECEIVERSHIP

1 David F. Burg, *Chicago's White City of 1893* (Lexington, Ky., 1976), 180.
2 Ray Ginger, *Age of Excess* (New York, 1965), 157–62.
3 Paul W. Glad, *McKinley, Bryan, and the People* (Philadelphia, 1964), 72.
4 *UP Report,* 1893, 13, 15; 1894, 34; 1896, 8.
5 Calculated from data in ibid., 1893, 84; 1894, 48. All percentages are rounded. The reports did not break down the figures for individual types of ores.
6 Ibid, 1894, 48; 1897, 20.
7 These matters are covered in detail in Maury Klein, *Union Pacific: The Birth 1862–1893 (Garden City, N.Y., 1987).*
8 *WSJ,* Apr. 10 and Aug. 20, 1894; Dodge to E. F. Atkins, June 13, 1895, UPL; *Railroad Gazette*, 27:227.
9 Orr to Millar, Nov. 24, 1893, UPL.

10 *RR Gazette,* 25:776; *Commercial and Financial Chronicle,* 57:684; *WSJ,* Oct. 31, Nov. 13, and Nov. 17, 1893; Dodge to E. F. Atkins, Nov. 3, 1893, UPL; NY *Times,* Nov. 12 and Nov. 14, 1893; NY *World,* Nov. 13, 1893.

11 The history of the Panhandle road is splendidly detailed in Richard C. Overton, *Gulf to Rockies* (Austin, Tex., 1953).

12 Dodge to Moses Hallett, Nov. 9, 1893, DP; *RR Gazette,* 25:880, 898; *WSJ,* Dec. 2–5, Dec. 12, Dec. 15, and Dec. 16, 1893; *Chronicle,* 57:980; *UP Report,* 1893, 16.

13 NY *World,* Oct. 15, 1893; *WSJ,* Oct. 18, 1893; *Chronicle,* 57:828–29.

14 Stuart Daggett, *Railroad Reorganization* (Cambridge, Mass., 1908), 237–44. For background on the Thurman Act see Klein, *Union Pacific,* 1:chaps. 19 and 27, and H. R. Meyer, "The Settlements with the Pacific Railways," *Quarterly Journal of Economics* (July 1899), 13:431–32.

15 *WSJ,* Nov. 20, Nov. 23, and Nov. 24, 1893; *Chronicle,* 57:894; NY *Times,* Nov. 29, Dec. 2, and Dec. 5, 1893.

16 *WSJ,* Dec. 13, 1893, Jan. 31, 1894; DR, 14:387; NY *Times,* Feb. 1, Feb. 10, Feb. 24, Mar. 1, Mar. 3, Mar. 6, Mar. 27, Mar. 30, Apr. 3, and Apr. 4, 1894.

17 *WSJ,* Apr. 24–28, June 12, July 9–11, 1894; NY *Times,* Apr. 27, June 7, July 8, July 12, July 21, and July 22, 1894; *Chronicle,* 58:775, 59:71, 153; *Congressional Record,* 53rd Cong., 2d Sess., 9177.

18 *WSJ,* Aug. 18 and Aug. 22, 1894; NY *Times,* Oct. 5, 1894; Nelson Trottman, *History of the Union Pacific* (New York, 1923), 256–58.

19 *WSJ,* Jan. 15–18, Jan. 29, and Jan. 31, 1895; D. B. Henderson to Dodge, Jan. 18, 1895, DR, 14:689; *RR Gazette,* 27:47, 78, 123; Gardiner M. Lane to Alexander Millar, Jan. 19, 1895, UPL. The plan is in UP Exec. Comm. Minutes, Jan. 11, 1895, 191, 193–97.

20 *WSJ,* Feb. 5, Feb. 11, Feb. 16, Feb. 21, Feb. 23, Mar. 8, and Mar. 9, 1895; NY *Times,* Feb. 5 and Mar. 9, 1895; *Chronicle,* 60:303, 437; Dodge to Trumbull, Mar. 7, 1895, DP.

21 NY *Times,* Jan. 20, Jan. 22, and Feb. 5, 1895; *WSJ,* Jan. 18, Jan. 22, Feb. 8, and Feb. 11, 1895; *RR Gazette,* 27:62; *Chronicle,* 60:178.

22 *WSJ,* May 3, June 26, and Nov. 21, 1894, Jan. 3, Jan. 5, Jan. 23, Mar. 11, Mar. 22, May 16, May 29, and June 4, 1895; NY *Times,* June 24 and June 26, 1894, June 11, 1895; *Chronicle,* 59:423, 60:523, 563, 874, 968, 1010, 1033–35, 1059; *RR Gazette,* 26:658, 27:242, 306, 398.

23 Millar to Mink, Oct. 27, 1893, UPL; George Gould to E. F. Atkins, Oct. 15, 1893, UPL.

24 *WSJ,* Nov. 1 and Nov. 10, 1893, Apr. 17, Apr. 23, July 24–26, and July 29, 1894, Jan. 8, Jan. 9, and Oct. 11, 1895, Apr. 26, 1896; Gould to Clark, Apr. 28, 1894, UPL.

25 *Chronicle,* 60:668; Daggett, *Railroad Reorganization,* 250–51.

26 *WSJ,* Sept. 18 and Oct. 8–10, 1895; NY *Times,* Oct. 9, 1895; G. W. Batson, "Final Reorganization," 3, AF. These fragments of Batson's manuscript on E. H. Harriman can be found among the papers at AF.

27 George Kennan, *E. H. Harriman: A Biography* (Boston, 1922) 1:119–21; Cyrus K. Adler, *Jacob H. Schiff: His Life and Letters* (New York, 1929), 1:50. Kennan's version is drawn from G. W. Batson's interview with Schiff, March 20, 1911, copy of which is at AF. See also Batson to Mary Harriman, March 20, 1911, AF.

28 Adler, *Schiff,* 1:92; Schiff interview, 1.

29 Adler, *Schiff,* 1:83, 93; Stephen Birmingham, *Our Crowd* (New York, 1984), 175, 183; Frieda Schiff Warburg, *Reminiscences of a Long Life* (New York, 1956). (Frieda was Schiff's daughter.)

30 *WSJ*, Oct. 11 and Oct. 14, 1895; NY *Times*, Oct. 12 and Oct. 15, 1895; Schiff interview, 2.

31 A copy of the plan is in *Chronicle*, 61:705–7. For discussions of it see Daggett, *Railroad Reorganization*, 250–54, and Trottman, *Union Pacific*, 261–67.

32 *Chronicle*, 61:683–84; *The Nation*, 61:286–87; *RR Gazette*, 27:707.

33 NY *Times*, Jan. 21, 1896; *Chronicle*, 62:187, 462, 742, 822; *WSJ*, Jan. 27, Feb. 20, Mar. 5, Mar. 23, Mar. 31, Apr. 1–4, Apr. 8, Apr. 9, and Apr. 21, 1896; *RR Gazette*, 28:84.

34 *WSJ*, Oct. 21, Oct. 31, Nov. 23, Dec. 7, Dec. 9, Dec. 15, Dec. 21, and Dec. 22, 1896; *RR Gazette*, 28:872, 890; *Chronicle*, 63:1065; NY *Times*, Dec. 13 and Dec. 15, 1896; Kennan, *Harriman*, 1:122.

35 This episode is taken from Schiff interview, 2–5. This is a brief version by Schiff himself.

36 Fish to O. O. Telerton, Dec. 28, 1896, IC; Fish to Harriman, Jan. 2, 1897, IC; Jeffery to W. H. Holcomb, Nov. 21, 1888, IC; Holcomb to Jeffery, Nov. 23 and Dec. 21, 1888, IC; Jeffery to Fish, Dec. 22, 1888, IC; J. W. Doane to Fish, Jan. 26, 1894, IC.

37 Fish to Harriman, Jan. 2 and July 2, 1897, June 28, 1898, IC; Harriman to Fish, Jan. 14, 1897, IC; Fish to J. T. Harahan, Jan. 20, 1897, Oct. 6, 1899, IC; Fish to George P. Harrison, Feb. 9, 1897, IC; John C. Coombs to Fish and Harriman, Mar. 5, 1897, IC; John F. Stover, *History of the Illinois Central Railroad* (New York, 1975), 142–43.

38 NY *Times*, Jan. 7, Jan. 9, Jan. 12, Jan. 15, Jan. 16, Jan. 21, and Jan. 22, 1897; *WSJ*, Jan. 11–15 and Jan. 19–22, 1897; *Chronicle*, 64:136.

39 *Chronicle*, 64:182, 235; NY *Times*, Jan. 23–26, 1897; *WSJ*, Jan. 25–29, 1897; *RR Gazette*, 29:88. The two classes asked to accept reductions were the Kansas Pacific consolidated mortgage and the Union Pacific sinking fund land grant eights. The actual amount owed the government was offset by about $17 million accumulated in sinking fund payments.

40 NY *Times*, Feb. 4, Apr. 9, and May 2, 1897; *WSJ*, Feb. 4, Feb. 11, Apr. 14, May 21, May 29, and June 21, 1897; *RR Gazette*, 29:106, 114, 484; *Chronicle*, 64:331, 1024–25, 1228, 65:70; H. W. Cannon to James J. Hill, undated, JJH.

41 Kennan, *Harriman*, 1:126.

42 *WSJ*, July 27, July 31, Aug. 2, Aug. 10, Aug. 12–14, Aug. 17, Aug. 24, Sept. 2–4, Sept. 10–15, Sept. 20, Sept. 24, Sept. 27–30, Oct. 5, Oct. 6, Oct. 8, Oct. 16, Oct. 18, and Oct. 21–23, 1897; *RR Gazette*, 29:548, 564, 580, 698; *Chronicle*, 65:464, 622, 758–59, 66:17; NY *Times*, Oct. 10, 1897.

43 *WSJ*, Oct. 25–30, 1897; *RR Gazette*, 29:776; NY *Times*, Oct. 26–28, 1897; *Chronicle*, 65:800–3.

44 *Chronicle*, 65:825; *WSJ*, Oct. 30, 1897.

45 NY *Times*, Oct. 31–Nov. 5, 1897; *WSJ*, Nov. 3–5, 1897.

46 *Chronicle*, 65:870, 1025, 66:52; *RR Gazette*, 29:792; Report of Government Directors, Sept. 30, 1898, in *UP Report*, 1898; *WSJ*, Nov. 18, Nov. 22, Nov. 24, Nov. 27, and Dec. 3, 1897, Jan. 10 and Jan. 12, 1898.

47 *Chronicle*, 65:928, 1090, 1127, 1222, 66:238, 339, 359, 385, 427, 70:947; *WSJ*, Dec. 7–9, 1897, Feb. 11, Feb. 14, and Mar. 15, 1898; Notice of the receivers, Jan. 28, 1898, UPL; NY *Times*, Dec. 3, Dec. 11, Dec. 15, and Dec. 19, 1897, Feb. 1, Feb. 4, Feb. 17, Feb. 18, and Feb. 20, 1898, Oct. 19 and Nov. 8, 1900; *RR Gazette*, 30:89, 268, 32:312, 368, 712.

48 *WSJ*, Apr. 9, 1896, Sept. 7, Oct. 15, and Nov. 8, 1897; C. Quarrier to Millar, May

14, 1896, UPL; NY *Times,* Nov. 9, Dec. 2, Dec. 19, and Dec. 28, 1897; *RR Gazette,* 29:877.

49 *WSJ,* Dec. 27 and Dec. 29, 1897, Jan. 6, 1898; NY *Times,* Dec. 28, 1897; *RR Gazette,* 27:830.

50 *RR Gazette,* 29:936; *Chronicle,* 66:39.

51 *RR Gazette,* 30:382.

CHAPTER 2

THE SECOND COMING

1 W. L. Park to Mary Harriman, Sept. 3, 1912, AF.

2 For a revised portrait of Gould see Maury Klein, *The Life and Legend of Jay Gould* (Baltimore, 1986) and Klein, *Union Pacific,* vol. 1.

3 Otto H. Kahn, "Edward Henry Harriman" (New York, 1911), reprinted in Stuart Bruchey, ed., *Memoirs of Three Railroad Pioneers* (New York, 1981), 5.

4 Samuel M. Felton, "The Genius of Edward H. Harriman," *The American Magazine* (April, 1925), 9; Alexander Millar to George Kennan, July 3 and July 12, 1917, AF.

5 Klein, *Jay Gould,* chaps. 13–17; Kahn, "Harriman," 14–15.

6 Edwin Lefevre, "Harriman," *The American Magazine* (June, 1907), vol. 64, no. 2, 115. It has long been believed that Harriman's personal papers were destroyed in the Equitable Building fire in 1912, but the existence of the papers seen by his biographer, George Kennan, demolishes that myth. See the discussion in Lloyd J. Mercer, *E. H. Harriman: Master Railroader* (Boston, 1985), 172–73. In fact, Judge Robert S. Lovett stated shortly after the fire that Harriman's papers had not been lost because they had been removed from the building earlier. See New York *Tribune,* January 10, 1912. (Biographer George Kennan should not be confused with diplomat George F. Kennan, a distant relative.)

7 Details on the Harriman genealogy can be found in a brief account apparently written by Orlando Jr., and a list of descendants prepared by C. C. Tegethoff, the family agent, both at AF. I am grateful to William J. Rich III for furnishing additional details.

8 Kennan, *Harriman,* 1:4–11; RGD, NY, 268:509.

9 Carl Snyder, "Harriman: 'Colossus of Roads,' " *Review of Reviews* (Jan. 1907), 35:39.

10 Francis L. Eames, *The New York Stock Exchange* (New York, 1894), 123; Kennan, *Harriman,* 1:12–14.

11 RGD, NY, 268:509, 225:133; John F. Trow, *The New York City Directory for 1863–64,* 364; Eames, *New York Stock Exchange,* 127; Rensselaer Weston to Kennan, Jan. 25, 1917, AF.

12 RGD, NY, 397:300A44, 300A116, 300A40.

13 Right Reverend J. D. Morrison, "Recollections and Impressions of the late Mr. Edward H. Harriman," 1, AF. Lovett's letter is quoted in Kennan to Mary Harriman, May 15, 1921, AF.

14 Morrison, "Recollections," 1; Lewis R. Morris, M. D., "A Successful Life, Edward Henry Harriman," 4, AF.

15 Kennan, *Harriman,* 1:60–61.

16 RGD, NY, 397:300A44, 300A116, 300A140. A copy of the dissolution notice, dated Jan. 3, 1888, is in IC.

17 RGD, NY, 397:300A140.

18 Henry V. Poor, *Manual of the Railroads of the United States for 1882* (New York, 1882), 125; H. B. LeFebore to W. W. Webb, Jan. 31, 1911, AF; J. B. Berry, "Notes of J. B. Berry's Association with Mr. E. H. Harriman," 1, AF; *Chronicle,* 30:434, 33:412.

19 *DAB,* 6:402–3; Poor, *Manual 1877–78,* 809; S. Fish, *1600–1914* (privately printed, 1942), 162–73, 191. This family volume by Fish's son contains several extracts from Fish's letters of the period.

20 Poor, *Manual 1880,* 196, *Manual 1882,* 125, 162, *Manual 1883,* 197, *Manual 1885,* 190; Berry, "Notes," 1–2; LeFebore to Webb, Jan. 31, 1911, AF.

21 John Moody and George Kibbe Turner, "Masters of Capital in America," *McClure's Magazine* (Jan. 1911), 337–38.

22 Stover, *Illinois Central,* 127–71; *Chronicle,* 34:177, 35:637, 36:298.

23 *Chronicle,* 30:218, 33:357–58, 34:144, 36:298–99, 36:310, 38:243–45.

24 IC Directors minutes, Jan. 27, Aug. 15, and Dec. 19, 1883, ICI; *Chronicle,* 38:243–45.

25 Stover, *Illinois Central,* 532; *Chronicle,* 40:716, 43:190, 44:291.

26 Stover, *Illinois Central,* 177–78; Moody and Turner, "Masters of Capital," 338–39; Kennan, *Harriman,* 1:74.

27 IC Directors minutes, Feb. 17, 1886, ICI; IC Exec. Comm. minutes, June 30 and Sept. 6, 1886, ICI; *Chronicle,* 41:585, 612, 42:306–7, 338, 43:245, 607, 671, 44:118, 291–92, 310.

28 Ibid., 42:306, 46:382; Report of Charles A. Seward to the Dubuque & Sioux City Board of Directors, Nov. 29, 1887, 3, AF. The subsidiary lines were the Iowa Falls & Sioux City and the Cedar Falls & Minnesota.

29 "Bill of Complaint," *Edward C. Woodruff v. The Dubuque and Sioux City Railroad Company et al,* Jan. 29, 1887, AF; "Answer of Anthony J. Drexel and others," *Woodruff v. Dubuque and Sioux City,* Feb. 7, 1887, AF; Fish to Harriman, undated, IC; *Chronicle,* 43:766, 44:21–2, 235, 362, 433–34, 494, 526, 539, 45:472, 509, 46:382, 384; IC Directors minutes, Apr. 6, 1887, ICI; Fish to Drexel, Morgan & Co., Oct. 4, 1887, IC; Herbert L. Satterlee, *J. Pierpont Morgan: An Intimate Portrait* (New York, 1939), 243–44.

30 Satterlee, *Morgan,* 243–44.

31 *Chronicle,* 44:653; IC Directors minutes, Mar. 16, May 18, Sept. 28, and Dec. 21, 1887, ICI.

32 *Chronicle,* 46:368; IC Exec. Comm. minutes, Apr. 5, 1888, ICI. Goelet and Luttgen joined the board in March 1884, Oliver Harriman in March 1886.

33 Fish to Harriman, May 6, 1889, IC; Fish, *1600–1914,* 238. This description of the business relationship between Fish and Harriman is drawn largely from extensive research in their correspondence in IC.

34 B. F. Ayer to Fish, Feb. 18, 1889, ICI; IC Directors minutes, Apr. 4 and Apr. 17, 1889, ICI; Jeffery to Harriman, Sept. 2, 1889, IC. For background on the ICRA see Klein, *Gould,* chap. 31.

35 IC Directors minutes, May 15, 1889, ICI; Fish to Jeffery, July 5, 1889, IC; Jeffery to Harriman, Sept. 2, 1889, IC.

36 IC Directors minutes, June 19, 1889, ICI; Harriman to H. B. Plant, July 10, 1889, IC; *RR Gazette,* 21:500–1; Harriman to Jeffery, Aug. 13, 1889, IC; Jeffery to Harriman, Aug. 15, 1889, IC; Harriman to Fish, Aug. 16, 1889, IC; Harriman memorandum, Sept. 2, 1889, ICI; Jeffery memorandum, Sept. 2, 1889, ICI.

37 Harriman to Jeffery, Sept. 2, 1889, IC; Harriman to C. A. Beck, Sept. 2, 1889, IC; Harriman to Fish, Sept. 2 and Sept. 9, 1889, IC; *RR Gazette,* 21:588, 590–91;

Harriman to Board of Directors, Sept. 9, 1889, IC; *Chronicle,* 49:316–17; Fish to Harriman, Sept. 15, 1889, IC; Fish to Jeffery, May 31, 1889, IC.

38 Harriman to Fish, Sept. 2, Sept. 9, and Sept. 24, 1889, IC; John G. Mann to Harriman, Sept. 5 and Sept. 12, 1889, IC. See chapter 7 for more detail on the department vs. division debate.

39 Harriman to Fish, Oct. 7, Nov. 11, and Nov. 27, 1889, IC.

40 IC Finance Comm. minutes, Nov. 18 and Dec. 5, 1889, ICI; IC Directors minutes, Nov. 20, Dec. 16, and Dec. 18, 1889, ICI; Harriman to Fish, Jan. 9, 1890, IC; *RR Gazette,* 22:33; Harriman to Fentress, Feb. 11, 1890, IC.

41 Fish to RRE Committee, Jan. 17 and Jan. 23, 1890, ICI; Report of Committee on Rates, Revenues and Expenditures, Jan. 24, 1890, ICI; Harriman to A. G. Hackstaff, Jan. 24, 1890, ICI.

42 Kennan, *Harriman*, 1:91–92; IC Directors minutes, Jan. 24, 1890, ICI.

43 IC Directors minutes, Feb. 19, and Mar. 19, 1890, ICI; Fish to Harriman, Feb. 28 (two items) and Mar. 1 (four items), 1890, IC.

44 Fish to Sidney Lawrence, Feb. 8, 1890, IC; Fish to William Boissevain, Mar. 25, 1890, SF.

45 Fish to William Boissevain, Mar. 25, 1890, SF.

46 IC Directors minutes, June 18 and Oct. 20, 1890, ICI; IC Exec. Comm. minutes, Oct. 15, 1890, ICI; IC Finance Comm. minutes, Nov. 17, 1890, ICI; Fish to Messrs. Boissevain Bros. and Teixeira de Mattos Bros., Oct. 23, 1890, IC; *RR Gazette,* 22:744; *Chronicle,* 51:569.

47 IC Exec. Comm. minutes, Sept. 3, 1890, ICI; Fish to Messrs. Boissevain Bros. and Teixeira Bros., Oct. 23, 1890, IC.

48 IC Finance Comm. minutes, May 19, 1890, July 13 and Aug. 19, 1891, ICI; IC Directors minutes, May 21 and July 23, 1890, Dec. 16, 1891, Oct. 26, 1892, ICI; *Chronicle,* 53:455–57, 55:528–29, 639, 56:108, 127, 57:533–34, 59:535–37, 60:1058, 61:538–39, 62:138; Harriman to Fish, Oct. 5, Nov. 29, and Dec. 8, 1892, SF.

49 Kahn, *Harriman,* 1; Kennan, *Harriman,* 1:93. Fish's remark was made at the ceremonies commemorating the company's fiftieth anniversary.

50 See the account of the Illinois Central in *Railway World,* 48:433–35.

CHAPTER 3
THE RECONSTRUCTION

1 Kahn, "Harriman," 10–11; G. W. Batson interview with James Stillman, Feb. 10, 1911, 1–2, AF.

2 Excerpts of Executive Committee minutes extracted by G. W. Batson, 1–2, AF. The Union Pacific minute books for the Harriman years were lost in the Equitable Building fire of 1912. Batson examined the books prior to the fire and compiled some notes from them. Hereafter cited as Batson minutes.

3 *RR Gazette,* 30:88, 382; Alexander Millar, "Edward H. Harriman and the Union Pacific Railroad" (New York, 1910), 5.

4 Jacob H. Schiff, "E.H. Harriman: An Appreciation," 2, AF; Kennan, *Harriman,* 1:143; *Fortune,* May 8, 1978, 202. For examples of the myth see C. M. Keys, "Harriman," *World's Work* (May 1907), 13:8791; John Kimberly Mumford, "This Land of Opportunity," *Harper's Weekly,* September 5, 1908, 12; Eckenrode and Edmunds, *Harriman,* 54–55; Frank H. Spearman, "Building Up a Great Railway

System,'' *Outlook* Feb. 27, 1909), 91:436; Jonathan Hughes, *The Vital Few* (New York, 1973), 373.

5 *WSJ,* Jan. 27, 1896. For other examples see the government directors' reports included in *UP Report,* 1895–1897; *WSJ,* Dec. 12, 1893, Nov. 22, 1895, Jan. 29, Apr. 8, Apr. 21, Sept. 2, and Nov. 16, 1896, Jan. 20, Aug. 12, Oct. 12, Nov. 18, and Dec. 29, 1897. For a description of the road's original condition see the testimony of W. L. Park, *United States of America v. Union Pacific Railroad Company et. al.,* U.S. Circuit Court for the district of Utah, docket no. 993, 9:4280–81 (hereafter cited as *USA v. UP*).

6 *WSJ,* Oct. 15, 1897, May 12, 1898; Grenville M. Dodge, ''What I Have Known of Harriman,'' in *How We Built the Union Pacific Railway and Other Papers* (Council Bluffs, Ia., n.d.), 63–64; Millar, ''Harriman,'' 4; W. H. Bancroft, ''Impressions of Mr. E. H. Harriman,'' 1, AF.

7 Details on this trip are taken from Berry, ''Notes,'' 5–11, and Mary and Cornelia Harriman, *Diary of a Trip* (privately printed, 1898), UPO. This little diary kept by the girls enables one to reconstruct where Harriman went and when. It also furnishes details not found elsewhere.

8 Quoted in Michael P. Malone, *The Battle for Butte: Mining and Politics on the Northern Frontier, 1864–1906* (Seattle, 1981), 103. Harriman lost the race but won a rematch that more than made up his first loss.

9 Bancroft, ''Impressions,'' 2–4; Berry, ''Notes,'' 5–6, 9–10.

10 Berry, ''Notes,'' 11. Stock prices are in *Chronicle,* 68:25.

11 Kahn, ''Harriman,'' 12–14.

12 Ibid.; Batson minutes, 2–3.

13 W. L. Park, ''Personal Recollections of Mr. Harriman in connection with the Union Pacific,'' 6, AF.

14 W. F. Herrin, ''Personal Impressions of Edward Henry Harriman,'' 3–6, AF; Kennan to Mary Harriman, May 15, 1921, AF. Lovett's observations are contained in the Kennan letter.

15 Clarence J. Housman, ''Recollections,'' 2, AF; Kahn, ''Harriman,'' 36.

16 Julius Kruttschnitt to G. W. Batson, Apr. 11, 1911, AF.

17 There is universal agreement among the officers who knew or worked for Harriman on these characteristics. See for example Berry, ''Notes,'' 4, 10, 12; Berry to Kennan, Apr. 10, 1917, AF; Felton, ''Genius of Harriman,'' 9–10, 184; Julius Kruttschnitt, ''Three Business Giants for Whom I Worked,'' *American Magazine* (Nov. 1921), 92:37, 137; Bancroft, ''Impressions,'' 2–4; Herrin, ''Personal Impressions,'' 4; *Fortune,* May 8, 1978, 206.

18 Berry, ''Notes,'' 8, 10; Felton, ''Genius of Harriman,'' 9; Millar, ''Harriman,'' 12; Kennan interview with F. D. Underwood, Feb. 11, 1918, 2, AF.

19 Felton, ''Genius of Harriman,'' 10–11, 184; W. V. Hill, ''Mr. Edward Henry Harriman,'' 4, AF; Millar, ''Harriman,'' 13.

20 Stillman interview, 5; Felton, ''Genius of Harriman,'' 9.

21 Berry, ''Notes,'' 2–5.

22 Park, ''Recollections,'' 2–3; *USA v. UP,* 9:4285; Kennan, *Harriman,* 1:152.

23 Batson Minutes, 2; Park, ''Recollections,'' 2–3.

24 Millar to Burt, July 22, 1898, UPO; Burt to Harriman, Apr. 3, 1899, UPL; Park, ''Recollections,'' 4.

25 Wyoming *Tribune,* Nov. 2, 1903; Kansas City *World,* Sept. 17, 1903; Berry, ''Notes,'' 7.

26 *RR Gazette,* 30:301, 333, 786; Millar to Burt, July 22, 1898, UPO; *USA v. UP,*

9:4281–83; Park, "Recollections," 3–4; Berry to Burt, May 17, 1900, UPL. The figures for work done can be followed in the *UP Reports* for 1898–1909. For background on the oxbow see Klein, *Union Pacific,* 1:chap. 4.

27 Berry to Burt, Mar. 2, 1903, UPL; Burt to Harriman, Mar. 18, 1903, UPL; *USA v. UP,* 9:4299; *UP Report,* 1905, 14; *RR Gazette,* 41:549–51.

28 Park, "Recollections," 5; *UP Report,* 1899,7; Frank H. Spearman, *The Strategy of Great Railroads* (New York, 1904), 60–62; *RR Gazette,* 30:679; *WSJ,* Dec. 27, 1899, Feb. 13, 1900, May 8, 1901. Berry approved Spearman's account of this work as correct "in a general way." See Berry to Kennan, Mar. 21, 1917, AF.

29 *RR Gazette,* 33:186–87, 36–227. These articles are useful summaries of papers given before professional associations by Berry and another engineer who worked on the Sherman project. See also ibid., 33:247.

30 Ibid., 33:226; Park, "Recollections," 6–7; *Scientific American,* 86:240; H. Bissel to Burt, Oct. 23, 1901, UPL; *WSJ,* Feb. 14 and May 8, 1901.

31 *Scientific American,* 86:240; Spearman, *Great Railroads,* 64–65; *WSJ,* Jan. 24, Apr. 4, and Apr. 18, 1899, Feb. 5, 1901; *RR Gazette,* 31:180, 272, 360, 888, 32:488, 560, 33:34, 88, 260, 35:176, 204, 450, 502, 43:190; Burt to Harriman, Oct. 4, 1899, UPL; Harriman to Burt, June 24, 1901, UPL.

32 Park, "Recollections," 12–13.

33 Ibid., 7; Harriman to Burt, Sept. 15, 1899, UPL.

34 Batson minutes, 6–10; Harriman to Burt, Sept. 9, 1902, UPL.

35 Park, "Recollections," 7–8; *RR Gazette,* 33:839; Spearman, *Great Railroads,* 65–66; Harriman to Burt, Aug. 29 and Sept. 1, 1899, UPL.

36 *RR Gazette,* 33:839; Berry to Burt, Aug. 30, 1900, UPL.

37 Berry to Burt, Aug. 30, 1900, UPL.

38 *USA v. UP,* 9:4116, 4283; H. Bissell to Burt, Oct. 23, 1901, UPL. These figures are calculated from data found in the company's annual reports for the period 1898–1909.

39 *WSJ,* Aug. 18, 1899; *RR Gazette,* 39:88–90, 319–20, 41:524–25, 42:338–39. The figures are compiled from annual reports.

40 *USA v. UP,* 9:4116, 4189–90; *WSJ,* July 24, July 25, and Nov. 24, 1899, Aug. 6, 1903, Jan. 18, 1905, Apr. 21, 1910; *RR Gazette,* 31:548, 32:264, 296, 35:400, 804, 37:47, 38:24, 42:468, 819, 43:112, 404, 45:789; NY *Times,* Nov. 23, 1899; *Chronicle,* 69:1104. See also the annual reports from 1900–1909.

41 *USA v. UP,* 9:4281–82.

42 Ibid., 9:4195, 4281, 4283.

43 Ibid., 9:4190–91, 4199, 4282–83; *UP Report,* 1905, 14, 1904, 13; John F. Stover, *American Railroads* (Chicago, 1961), 200; Harriman to Burt, Apr. 10, 1899, UPL; Berry to J. M. Gruber, Mar. 30, 1904, UPL; *RR Gazette,* 40:343, 574–77, 41:164, 308, 548–49, 575–76, 43–502, 47:113–14, 1220.

44 Omaha *Bee,* Mar. 22, 1898; Harriman to Burt, Dec. 22, 1898, Mar. 7, 1899, UPL; *RR Gazette,* 29:838–39, 32:228, 280, 42:101–102, 43:70–72, 44:75; *WSJ,* Jan. 19 and Feb. 19, 1901, June 3 and July 7, 1902, Sept. 6, 1905; NY *Times,* Nov. 15, 1901; Cheyenne *Leader,* July 24, 1902; *UP Report,* 1899, 7, 1900, 7, 1902, 12, 1903, 13, 1906, 13, 1907, 17.

45 *UP Report,* 1903, 13, 1906, 13. Details on the early history of these facilities can be found in Klein, *Union Pacific,* vol. 1.

46 *USA v. UP,* 9:4192, 4196, 4284–85. Details on these new facilities can also be found in the annual reports for 1898–1909.

47 Ibid., 9:4192, 4196, 4280, 4284.

48 Ibid., 9:4280; Park, "Recollections," 6.
49 *USA v. UP*, 9:4280, 4282.
50 Ibid, 9:4284; Park, "Recollections," 18–20.
51 Felton, "Genius of Harriman," 11.
52 Kruttschnitt to Batson, Apr. 11, 1911, 4, AF. The comparative figures are taken from W. L. Burton, "History of the Missouri Pacific," 749, manuscript copy in MP.
53 *USA v. UP*, 9:4115–16. Unless otherwise indicated, all data given here and in subsequent paragraphs are computed from company annual reports for 1898–1909.
54 The figures given here and below are for the entire Union Pacific system. After 1901 the annual reports break down progressively less data by individual member system.
55 For the steel cars see C. S. Mellen to Burt, Sept. 24, 1901, UPL; Harriman to Burt, Oct. 15 and Nov. 8, 1901, UPL; *RR Gazette*, 39:49–50, 40:203, 604, 687, 41:292, 42:229, 250–52, 822–23, 852, 916, 43:307, 530, 45:49–50; *USA v. UP*, 9:4132.
56 *WSJ*, Jan. 18, 1905.
57 Berry, "Notes," 13–14.
58 *USA v. UP*, 9:4123–25, 4286. Percentages calculated by me from data in table on p. 4125 differ slightly from those given in testimony, which appear to have been rounded off.
59 *WSJ*, Feb. 14, Mar. 12, May 26, June 1, June 6–9, June 13, June 18, June 29, Aug. 4, Aug. 8, Aug. 12, Aug. 13, Aug. 26, and Aug. 27, 1898; Omaha *Bee*, Mar. 15, 1898.
60 Berry, "Notes," 14; Batson minutes, 10; *WSJ*, Sept. 19 and Sept. 23, 1898; NY *Times*, Sept. 23, 1898; *Chronicle*, 67:635.
61 *Chronicle*, 68:25; *WSJ*, Oct. 3, Oct. 14, Oct. 20, Nov. 10, and Nov. 11, 1898.
62 Batson minutes, 4; NY *Times*, Oct. 13, 1898; *WSJ*, Dec. 2, 1898; *RR Gazette*, 30:884.

CHAPTER 4
THE SYSTEM

1 Alice Roosevelt Longworth, *Crowded Hours* (New York, 1933), 106–7.
2 *Fortune*, May 8, 1978, 197.
3 Dodge to Frank Trumbull, Apr. 25, 1895, DP; Dodge to E. A. [F] Atkins, June 4, 1895, UPL; Dodge to Clark, June 18, 1895, DP; Dodge to Morgan Jones, Jan. 25, 1896, DP; *Chronicle*, 67:957, 1112; NY *Times*, Nov. 23, 1898. A detailed account of the Gulf's receivership and relations with Union Pacific can be found in Overton, *Gulf to Rockies*, 289–376.
4 Batson minutes, 3; Harriman to Burt, July 22, 1898, UPO; *Chronicle*, 66:521, 67:128, 179, 372, 68:188; *WSJ*, Feb. 25, 1899; *RR Gazette*, 29:612, 30:190, 486, 540, 620, 640, 822; Trottman, *Union Pacific*, 274–77; *UP Report*, Nov. 1899, 3.
5 UP Exec. Comm. minutes, Apr. 26, 1897, 248–52, UPL; *RR Gazette*, 26:554, 572, 30:350, 422, 446, 504, 680; *WSJ*, June 14, 1898; Alexander G. Cochran to D. S. H. Smith, Nov. 17, 1898, MP; Draft of testimony by John Evans, Nov. 13, 1893, John Evans papers, Colorado State Museum, Denver; NY *Times*, Dec. 6, 1896; *Chronicle*, 67:736, 842; Millar to Clark, Oct. 2, 1896, UPL; Omaha *Bee*, Feb. 7, 1898. For the early history of these roads see Klein, *Union Pacific*, vol. 1.
6 *RR Gazette*, 27:16, 28:386, 836, 29:18, 178, 30:523, 539, 679, 732, 785, 804, 34:846, 35:18, 43:702; *Chronicle*, 60:43–44, 61:367, 64:472; *WSJ*, Feb. 27 and

Mar. 25,. 1897, Aug. 15, 1905; NY *Times,* Oct. 18, 1900; St. Louis *Globe-Democrat,* Oct. 23 and Oct. 24, 1902; NY *World,* Oct. 23, 1902; Raymond DuPuy to Burt, Dec. 28, 1903, UPL; UP Exec. Comm. minutes, May 29, 1906, UPL.

7 Trottman, *Union Pacific,* 277, 280.

8 The early history of this struggle is detailed in Klein, *Union Pacific,* 1:chaps. 28–30.

9 *WSJ,* June 19–21, 1895; *RR Gazette,* 27:440, 456, 508, 847, 28:202, 298, 360, 630, 782, 854, 29:53, 86, 140, 176, 194, 232; *Chronicle,* 61:69–70, 241, 420, 612, 1013, 62:503, 684, 1140, 64:611; NY *Times,* Mar. 10, 1896, Jan. 13, 1897; Mink to Millar, May 14, 1897, UPL; UP Exéc. Comm. minutes, May 19, 1897, 254–56.

10 NY *Times,* June 4, 1897; *WSJ,* June 5, June 7, and June 10, 1897; *Chronicle,* 64:1089.

11 *WSJ,* June 17, July 7, Sept. 14, Sept. 16, Sept. 22, Oct. 5, Oct. 7, Oct. 8, Oct. 13, and Oct. 19, 1897; UP Exec. Comm. minutes, July 8, 1897, 259–61, UPL; *Chronicle,* 65:572, 736.

12 *WSJ,* Nov. 23, 1897, Jan. 12, Jan. 15, Feb. 16, Mar. 5, Mar. 7, Mar. 10, May 12, and May 27, 1898; *Chronicle,* 66:135, 521, 1002; UP Exec. Comm. minutes, Mar. 22, 1898, 287–88, UPL; NY *Times,* Mar. 12 and Mar. 15, 1898; *RR Gazette,* 30:210, 316; UP Directors minutes, July 19, 1898, UPL; Harriman to Burt, Sept. 16, 1898, UPO.

13 *Chronicle,* 61:536, 62:278, 779, 64:288, 67:1131; *WSJ,* Sept. 6 and Oct. 5, 1894, June 1, July 15, and Aug. 23, 1895, Sept. 1, 1896, Feb. 4 and Sept. 6, 1897; *RR Gazette,* 27:354, 28:836; NY *Times,* Aug. 24, 1895.

14 Schiff to Hill, Feb. 9, 1897, JJH; *RR Gazette,* 29:124; Hill to Edward D. Adams, Mar. 11, 1897, JJH; *WSJ,* Mar. 11, 1897; Adams to Hill, May 11, 1897, JJH. For Mohler see *NCAB,* 33:197.

15 Mohler to Hill, Jan. 16 and Feb. 2, 1898, JJH; Hill to Mohler, Jan. 25 and May 14, 1898, JJH; *WSJ,* Jan. 17, 1898; *RR Gazette,* 30:82, 107; Hill to Adams, Mar. 28, 1898, JJH.

16 *WSJ,* Feb. 19, 1898; Hill to W. L. Bull, Apr. 4, 1898, JJH; Hill to Adams, Apr. 4, 1898, JJH.

17 Hill to Bull, July 2 and Oct. 31, 1898, JJH; Hill to D. S. Lamont, July 17, 1898, JJH; Albro Martin, *James J. Hill and the Opening of the Northwest* (New York, 1976), 458. For Mellen's early career see Klein, *Union Pacific,* 1:chap. 31.

18 *WSJ,* Oct. 10–12, Nov. 30, Dec. 1, and Dec. 8, 1898, Jan. 26, Jan. 30, Feb. 7, Feb. 14, and Mar. 30, 1899; *RR Gazette,* 30:752, 769, 803, 839, 31:461; *Chronicle,* 67:902, 1131, 1209, 68:87, 188, 381, 430, 474; UP Director's minutes, Dec. 1, 1898, Jan. 26, 1899, UPL; Omaha *Bee,* Jan. 28, 1899. Harriman abstained from voting on the $3 assessment.

19 Martin, *Hill,* 477, 482–83.

20 Ibid., 458.

21 Klein, *Union Pacific,* 1:chap. 29; W. P. Clough to Charles Francis Adams, Aug. 5, 1890, UPL; Adams to F. Gordon Dexter, Oct. 14, 1890, UPL; Gardiner M. Lane to Sidney Dillon, Dec. 15, 1890, UPL; Hill to Dillon, Dec. 15, 1890, UPL; Kilpatrick Brothers & Collins to Dillon, Dec. 20, 1890, UPL; Adams to Dillon, Mar. 21, 1891, UPL; Oliver Mink to S. H. H. Clark, Aug. 14, 1891, UPL; Dillon to Clark, Aug. 25, 1891, UPL.

22 Hill to Adams, Mar. 28, 1898, JJH; Hill to Lamont, July 17, 1898, JJH; Harriman to Burt, July 22, 1898, UPO.

23 "In the Matter of the Oregon Railroad & Navigation Company: Minutes of Conference," Oct. 3, 1898, JJH.

24 Harriman to Hill, July 6 and July 7, 1898, JJH; Hill to Harriman, July 9, 1898, JJH; Harriman to Schiff, Sept. 29, 1898, JJH; Schiff to Hill, Sept. 30, 1898, JJH; Hill to Bull, Oct. 31, 1898 (two letters), JJH.

25 *WSJ,* Nov. 16 and Dec. 14, 1898, Jan 10, Feb. 10, Feb. 25, and Mar. 15, 1899; *RR Gazette,* 30:852, 886, 904, 31:33, 73, 108, 132, 236, 305, 393; Mohler to Hill, Dec. 30, 1898, JJH.

26 Hill to J. P. Morgan & Co., Mar. 25, 1899, JJH; Hill to Coster, Apr. 15, 1899, JJH.

27 *WSJ,* July 15–18, 1899; *RR Gazette,* 31:532; *Chronicle,* 69:181.

28 Hill to Mohler, July 19 and Aug. 1, 1899, JJH; *WSJ,* July 22 and July 31, 1899.

29 Omaha *Bee,* Aug. 9, 1899; *WSJ,* Aug. 15, Aug. 28, Aug. 31–Sept. 2, and Oct. 10, 1899; *RR Gazette,* 31:620, 634, 649, 668, 702, 720; *Chronicle,* 69:492, 542, 592, 695; UP Exec. Comm. minutes, Aug. 31 and Sept. 13, 1899, UPL; OSL Exec. Comm. minutes, Sept. 12, 1899, UPL.

30 *WSJ,* Oct. 10, 1899; Hill to Bull, Aug. 18, 1899, JJH; Hill to Coster, Aug. 19, 1899, JJH; Hill to Harriman, Sept. 12, 1899, JJH.

31 Hill to Schiff, Sept. 12, 1899, JJH; Adler, *Schiff,* 1:89–90; Hill to Coster, Oct. 2, 1899, JJH; Hill to H. W. Cannon, Oct. 3, 1899, JJH.

32 L. F. Loree to Kennan, Jan. 29, 1920, AF; Mercer, *Harriman,* 126–35.

33 Quoted in Kennan, *Harriman,* 2:231. For the later controversy over Harriman's management of the road see William Z. Ripley, *Railroads: Finance & Organization* (New York, 1915), 262–67; Kennan, *Harriman,* 2:228–310; George Kennan, *The Chicago & Alton Case: A Misunderstood Transaction* and *Misrepresentation in Railroad Affairs* (Garden City, 1916); Mercer, *Harriman,* 104–25.

34 "Statement by Mr. E. H. Harriman as to the Readjustment of the Capitalization of the Chicago & Alton Railroad Company," [1907], 1–3, 9–10, AF; Felton, "Genius of Harriman," 10. Two versions of Harriman's statement on the Alton can be found at AF. I have used the earlier (though undated) draft, apparently dictated by Harriman himself. The second version, entitled "Draft" and dated July 17, 1907, is printed. Alterations to the text have been made, probably on advice of Harriman's counsel. On his copies of these documents Kennan notes that they were given him by Melville E. Stone.

35 *USA v. UP,* 9:4120–27.

36 Harriman to Fish, Apr. 19, 1899, SF.

37 Berry, "Notes," 14; *USA v. UP,* 9:4299; Felton to Burt, Jan. 29, 1902, UPL; S. Higgins to E. Dickinson, Jan. 31, 1902, UPL; Higgins to Burt, Mar. 25, 1902, UPL.

38 Spearman, "Building Up a Great Railway System," 443; Kruttschnitt to Batson, Apr. 11, 1911, AF.

39 Kruttschnitt to Batson, Apr. 11, 1911, AF; Harriman to Burt, Sept. 15, 1899, UPL. Similar examples abound in UPL and elsewhere.

40 Burt to Harriman, Sept. 16 and Oct. 2, 1901, UPL; UP Exec. Comm. minutes, Dec. 13, 1906, UPL; Spearman, "Building Up a Great Railway System," 440–44.

41 Park, "Recollections," 15–17; William A. Pinkerton to Burt, Jan. 27, 1902, UPO.

CHAPTER 5
THE EMPIRE

1 J. C. Stubbs to Burt, Sept. 2, 1899, UPL; *WSJ,* Nov. 18 and Dec. 6, 1899, Jan. 22, Jan. 24, Jan. 25, and Feb. 27, 1900; Hill to Coster, Sept. 30, 1899, JJH.
2 Harriman preferred the term "common interest." See *USA v. UP,* 2:756.
3 Anna Robeson Burr, *The Portrait of a Banker: James Stillman* (New York, 1927), 204.
4 For this earlier merger attempt see Klein, *Union Pacific,* 1:439.
5 San Francisco *Chronicle,* Apr. 9, 1899; NY *Times,* Mar. 2 and Apr. 6, 1900.
6 *USA v. UP,* 4:1666–68; Harriman to A. F. Walker, June 5, 1900, AF; *WSJ,* Dec. 5, 1899; San Francisco *Chronicle,* June 29, 1900.
7 *USA v. UP,* 10:4728–29, 4756, 11:4947–49, 5057–58; C. A. Severance to Fish, Apr. 6, 1910, SF. For earlier Union Pacific attempts to buy Huntington out see *WSJ,* Jan. 18, 1900, Feb. 2, 1901.
8 *USA v. UP,* 10:4713, 4737–38, 11:4953–57.
9 Ernest Howard, *Wall Street Fifty Years After Erie* (Boston, 1923), 18.
10 Ibid., 7–9; *USA v. UP,* 11:4954; Robert G. Athearn, *The Denver and Rio Grande Western Railroad* (Lincoln, Neb., 1977), 191.
11 UP Exec. Comm. minutes, Feb. 5, 1901, UPL; *USA v. UP,* 3:1216–22, 11:4948–52; Trottman, *Union Pacific,* 280–81; NY *Times,* Feb. 2 and Feb. 3, 1901. During January 1901, Southern Pacific sold between 40¾ and 49¼. See *Chronicle,* 74:26.
12 UP Directors Minutes, Feb. 20, 1901, UPL; *WSJ,* Feb. 9, 1901; NY *Times,* Feb. 9, Feb. 14, and Mar. 20, 1901; *RR Gazette,* 33:120, 292; *Chronicle,* 72:340, 392; Schiff to Hill, Feb. 4, 1901, JJH.
13 *RR Gazette,* 33:96; *WSJ,* Feb.11 and Feb. 12, 1901.
14 *USA v. UP,* 11:4954; *WSJ,* Feb. 8, Feb. 14, 1901; G. B. Schley to Hill, Feb. 10, 1901, JJH; NY *Times,* Feb. 14, Mar. 30, and Apr. 4, 1901; *RR Gazette,* 33:259; Paul D. Cravath, "Memorandum for Interstate Commerce Commission Giving an Outline of the History of the Relations Between Missouri Pacific Railroad Company and Its Predecessors and the Denver and Rio Grande Railroad Company and Its Predecessors," Feb. 7, 1923, 1, MP.
15 Quoted by Kennan from Batson manuscript, AF.
16 Kennan, *Harriman,* 1:241.
17 Henry Morgenthau, *All in a Lifetime* (Garden City, 1922), 73.
18 C. E. Perkins to T. S. Howland, Jan. 31, 1901, BA. For background on the early attempts see Klein, *Gould,* 433–40, 458–63.
19 J. P. Morgan et al. to President and Board of Directors of the Chicago, Burlington & Quincy System, Jan. 19, 1901, BA; Extract from Proceedings of Conference of Executive Officers of Western, Northwestern and Southwestern railroad companies, Dec. 5–7, 1900, BA.
20 W. J. Palmer to C. E. Perkins, Dec. 16 and Dec. 26, 1900, BA; Perkins to Palmer, Dec. 24 and Dec. 28, 1900, Jan. 5, 1901, BA.
21 George B. Harris to Perkins, Jan. 3, Jan. 5, Jan. 6, and Jan. 29, 1901, BA; Palmer to Perkins, Jan. 3 and Jan. 9, 1901, BA; Perkins to Harriman, Jan 6, Jan. 16, and Jan. 31, 1901, BA; Perkins to Palmer, Jan. 7, 1901, BA; Harriman to Perkins, Jan. 13 and Jan. 21, 1901, BA; Perkins to T. S. Howland, Jan. 31, 1901, BA.
22 Harriman to Mohler, Aug. 7 and Aug. 31, 1899, Jan. 16 and Oct. 2, 1900, UPO; Mohler to Harriman, Sept. 5, 1899, UPO; Memorandum of Understanding between Harriman and Mellen, Jan. 12, 1900, UPO; Hill to Coster, Oct. 20, 1899, Feb. 3,

1900, JJH; Hill to Schiff, Jan. 22, Feb. 2, and Mar. 28, 1900, JJH; Adler, *Schiff,* 1:90–91; Hill to Mellen, Feb. 19, 1900, JJH; Hill to Harriman, Mar. 28, 1900, JJH.

23 Daniel S. Lamont to Hill, July 31, 1900, JJH.

24 NY *Times,* Oct. 1 and Nov. 23, 1900; Adler, *Schiff,* 1:91–92; Harriman to Hill, Jan. 24, 1901, JJH.

25 Hill to Harriman, Jan. 29 and Feb. 6, 1901, JJH; Harriman to Hill, Feb. 6 and Feb. 7, 1901, JJH; Hill to Bacon, Feb. 7, Feb. 9, and Mar. 2, 1901, JJH.

26 *WSJ,* Apr. 18, May 17, June 2, and June 12, 1900.

27 George B. Harris to Perkins, Aug. 13, 1899, BA; Perkins to Harris, Aug. 15, 1899, BA; Richard C. Overton, *Burlington Route* (New York, 1965), 248–49. Overton's account is the fullest and most informative on this episode.

28 Overton, *Burlington Route,* 251–55.

29 Ibid., 250; Hill to Lord Mount Stephen, June 4, 1901, JJH; Schiff to Kennan, Apr. 18, 1919, AF; C. C. Tegethoff to Kennan, Jan. 30, 1919, AF; Kennan notes from syndicate documents furnished by Tegethoff, AF; James J. Pyle, *The Life of James J. Hill* (New York, 1936), 2:121; Hill to Lord Mount Stephen, Apr. 26, 1901, JJH. Tegethoff was Harriman's secretary and later the family agent.

30 Kennan notes from syndicate documents furnished by Tegethoff, AF.

31 Hill to Lord Mount Stephen, June 4, 1901, JJH; Pyle, *Hill,* 2:102–17; Martin, *Hill,* 487–88; Kennan interview with Schiff, June 12, 1919, AF.

32 Overton, *Burlington Route,* 255–61; Martin, *Hill,* 489.

33 Hill to Perkins, Feb. 18, 1901, JJH; Perkins to Hill, Feb. 19, 1901, JJH; Hill to Morgan, Feb. 20, 1901, JJH; Overton, *Burlington Route,* 256–57.

34 Bacon to Hill, Mar. 2, 1901, JJH; Hill to Perkins, Mar. 2, 1901, JJH; Perkins to Hill, Mar. 19, 1901, JJH.

35 *WSJ,* Mar. 7 and Mar. 9, 1901; Hill to Schiff, Apr. 9, 1900 [1901], JJH; Hill to J. S. Kennedy, May 16, 1901, JJH; Adler, *Schiff,* 1:102–3; Martin, *Hill,* 496–98; Kennan, *Harriman,* 1:295–96.

36 Overton, *Burlington Route,* 258; Adler, *Schiff,* 1:103–4; NY *Times,* May 13, 1901; Batson fragment, 10, AF.

37 Adler, *Schiff,* 1:104–5; St. Paul *Globe,* Dec. 22, 1901; Hill to Lord Mount Stephen, June 4, 1901, JJH.

38 Satterlee, *Morgan,* 354.

39 Schiff to Hill, Apr. 8, 1901, JJH; Hill to Schiff, Apr. 9, 1900 [1901], JJH; *WSJ,* Apr. 13 and Apr. 26, 1901; Perkins to Hill, Apr. 30, 1901, JJH; Hill to Lord Mount Stephen, Apr. 26, 1901, JJH.

CHAPTER 6
THE COMMUNITY OF INTEREST

1 Pyle, *Hill,* 2:143–44.

2 *WSJ,* Apr. 16, Apr. 19, Apr. 20, Apr. 23, Apr. 25, and Apr. 27, 1901.

3 Batson fragment, AF, quotes the correspondence on these transactions.

4 *WSJ,* Apr. 22–27, 1901; Martin, *Hill,* 498–500; Satterlee, *Morgan,* 350; G. B. Schley to Hill, Apr. 27, 1901, JJH. For an example of the myth see Kennan, *Harriman,* 1:303. Kennan evidently got his version from Batson.

5 NY *Times,* Apr. 30 and May 1, 1901; *WSJ,* Apr. 30, 1901; Mary T. Hill to Clara and Rachel Hill, Apr. 29, 1901, JJH; Burlington circular, Apr. 29, 1901, JJH; Hill to Gaspard Farrer, Apr. 30, 1901, JJH.

6 *WSJ,* Apr. 30, 1901; Perkins to Hill, Apr. 30, 1901, JJH.

7 *WSJ,* Apr. 24–May 4, 1901; *Chronicle,* 72:874, 937; NY *Times,* May 1–3, 1901. The *Times* named J. J. Mitchell, Marshall Field, and Norman B. Ream as the syndicate members.

8 *WSJ,* Apr. 27, May 3, and May 4, 1901; NY *Times,* May 4, 1901.

9 "Investigation of Chicago, Milwaukee & St. Paul Railway Company," *ICC Reports,* 131:616–17.

10 *WSJ,* May 1–4, 1901; NY *Times,* May 1–5, 1901; *Chronicle,* 72:874.

11 Adler, *Schiff,* 1:106; Martin, *Hill,* 500. Martin is the only one to put Hill in New York on April 29 instead of May 3, but he then has the meeting with Schiff take place that same Monday even though Schiff, in his letter to Morgan cited in Adler, states explicitly that he saw Hill on the morning of Friday, May 3. Since this letter was written less than two weeks after the meeting, it is doubtful Schiff confused the date. Martin does not note this discrepancy or account for it.

12 Kennan, *Harriman,* 1:303–4; Martin, *Hill,* 502; Satterlee, *Morgan,* 354.

13 Hill's versions of this interview can be found in Hill to J. S. Kennedy, May 16, 1901, JJH; Hill to Lord Mount Stephen, June 4, 1901, and July 22, 1904, JJH. Only the 1904 letter refers to Harriman's role.

14 Hill to Kennedy, May 16, 1901, JJH; Martin, *Hill,* 501.

15 Martin, *Hill,* 502.

16 Adler, *Schiff,* 1:106; Warburg, *Reminiscences of a Long Life,* 62.

17 Batson fragment, AF. Batson claimed he got this story direct from Harriman. His account is reprinted in Kennan, *Harriman,* 1:306.

18 Kennedy to Hill, May 13, 1901, JJH; Satterlee, *Morgan,* 354–55.

19 NY *Times,* May 7, 1901; *WSJ,* May 7, 1901.

20 Batson fragment, AF.

21 Ibid.; NY *Times,* May 7 and May 8, 1901; *WSJ,* May 8, 1901.

22 UP Directors Minutes, May 8, 1901, UPL; NY *Times,* May 9, 1901; *WSJ,* May 9, 1901.

23 NY *Times,* May 9–11, 1901.

24 Ibid; *WSJ,* May 9 and May 10, 1901; Batson fragment, AF.

25 Batson fragment, AF; Kennan, *Harriman,* 1:317–19; W. D. Travers to Hill, May 30, 1901, JJH.

26 UP Exec. Comm. minutes, May 10, 1901, UPL; NY *Times,* May 11, May 13, May 14, 1901; *WSJ,* May 11, May 13–15, 1901; Hill to Harriman, May 19, 1901, JJH; E. T. Nichols to Hill, May 23, 1901, JJH; Hill to Bacon, May 23, 1901, JJH.

27 Perkins to Hill, May 11, 1901, JJH; Hill to Hughitt, May 22, 1901, JJH; *WSJ,* May 22, 1901; Bacon to Hill, May 23, 1901, JJH.

28 UP Exec. Comm. minutes, May 28, 1901, UPL; *WSJ,* May 29, 1901; Memorandum of Understanding, May 31, 1901, JJH.

29 Memorandum of Understanding, May 31, 1901, JJH.

30 Harriman to Burt, June 10, 1901, UPL; Hill to Bacon, June 12, 1901, JJH; *WSJ,* June 20, 1901; *Chronicle,* 72:1239; Martin, *Hill,* 464.

31 Hill to Bacon, June 12 and July 19, 1901, JJH; Perkins to Hill, June 20, 1901, JJH; Hill to Schiff, July 19, 1901, JJH; Hill to Harriman, July 19, 1901, JJH. Soon afterward, Miller was made second vice-president of the Great Northern.

32 Schiff to Hill, July 22, 1901, JJH; *RR Gazette,* 33:535; Schiff to Harriman, July 28, 1901, Kennan notes, AF.

33 EH to Northern Pacific board, Aug. 1, 1901, AF; Hill to Lord Mount Stephen, May 25, 1901, JJH: Hill to Edward Tuck, Aug. 14, 1901, JJH; Hill to Lord Strathcona,

Aug. 13, 1901, JJH; *WSJ*, Aug. 21, 1901; Hill to Gaspard Farrer, Aug. 31, 1901, JJH; Pyle, *Hill*, 164–65; Martin, *Hill*, 508.

34 Hill to Bacon, Sept. 2, 1901, JJH; UP Directors minutes, Sept. 4 and Sept. 24, 1901, UPL; Kennedy to Hill, Sept. 6, 1901, JJH; Hill to Lefevre, London, Sept. 6, 1901, JJH; Schiff to Harriman, Sept. 11, 1901, AF.

35 Harriman to Schiff, Oct. 16, 1901, AF; Martin, *Hill*, 509; Schiff to Harriman, Sept. 11, 1901, AF.

36 *WSJ*, Nov. 4 and Nov. 15, 1901; Adler, *Schiff*, 1:110. None of the standard accounts mentions the territorial agreement, but the Schiff letter in Adler, dated Nov. 11, 1901, confirms its role in the settlement. A Batson fragment, AF, lists the territorial terms but erroneously attributes them to the Metropolitan Club agreement of May, the text of which Batson never saw.

37 E. T. Nichols to W. C. Toomey, Oct. 1, 1901, JJH; Kennedy to Hill, Oct. 10, 1901, JJH; NY *Times*, Nov. 14–16, 1901; *WSJ*, Nov. 15, 1901; *Chronicle*, 73:1062; *RR Gazette*, 33:815–16. For details on the new company see B. H. Meyer, *A History of the Northern Securities Case* (Madison, Wisc., 1906), 225–41.

38 *WSJ*, Nov. 8–11, Nov. 14, Nov. 15, Nov. 22, Nov. 23, and Dec. 2, 1901; NY *Times*, Nov. 16, 1901; Chicago *Chronicle*, Dec. 17, 1901; W. P. Clough to Hill, Dec. 26, 1901, JJH.

39 NY *Times*, Nov. 18–23, and Nov. 29, 1901; *WSJ*, Nov. 21, Nov. 26, Dec. 2, Dec. 4, and Dec. 9, 1901; *Chronicle*, 73:1112, 1264, 1314; Meyer, *Northern Securities*, 242–44.

40 W. D. Townes to Hill, Nov. 20, 1901, JJH; Darius Miller to Hill, Dec. 13, 1901, JJH; Omaha *World-Herald*, Dec. 22, 1901; Perkins to Hill, Dec. 22, 1901, JJH; Clough to Hill, Dec. 24, 1901, JJH; *WSJ*, Dec. 24, 1901; *RR Gazette*, 33:891; *Chronicle*, 73:1357; NY *Times*, Dec. 31, 1901; Hill to Greenleaf Clark, Jan. 7, 1902, JJH.

41 Burt to Harriman, Dec. 31, 1901, UPL; Harriman to Burt, Dec. 31, 1901, UPL; NY *Times*, Jan. 1 and Jan. 8, 1902; *WSJ*, Jan. 7, Jan 11, Jan. 14, 1902; Clough to Hill, Jan. 8, 1902, JJH; *RR Gazette*, 34:18.

42 *RR Gazette*, 33:809; NY *Times*, June 17, 1901; Max Lowenthal, *The Investor Pays* (New York, 1933), 11, 14; William E. Hayes, *Iron Road to Empire* (n.p., 1953), 145–48.

43 *Chronicle*, 78:1196; *WSJ*, June 6, June 15, June 17, and June 22, 1901; NY *Times*, June 17, 1901; Harriman to Roswell Miller, July 8, 1901, AF.

44 George B. Harris to Hill, Aug. 26, 1901, JJH; Chicago *Record Herald*, Oct. 26, 1901; S. C. Stickney to Burt, Nov. 22, 1901, UPL; Burt to Harriman, Nov. 11 and Dec. 16, 1901, UPL; Millar to Burt, Dec. 11, 1901, UPL; H. Roger Grant, *The Corn Belt Route: A History of the Chicago Great Western Railroad Company* (Dekalb, Ill., 1984), 63–67.

45 Hill to Bacon, July 19 and Sept. 7, 1901, JJH; Harriman to Burt, Sept. 17, 1901, UPL.

46 Stubbs to Harriman, Dec. 14, 1901, JJH; Harris to Hill, Dec. 27 and Dec. 30, 1901, JJH; Fish to Harriman, Apr. 16 and Oct. 22, 1902, IC; Fish to Burt, Aug. 9, 1902, IC; *WSJ*, Feb. 10, 1902.

47 Stubbs to Harriman, Oct. 9, 1902, IC; Harriman to Hill, Jan. 15, Jan. 20, Mar. 20, and Mar. 31, 1902, JJH; Fish to Harriman, Feb. 17 and Oct. 24, 1902, IC; Hill to Harriman, Mar. 30, 1902, JJH; Stubbs to Burt, July 22, 1902, UPL; *WSJ*, Sept. 9 and Dec. 15, 1902.

48 NY *Times*, June 8, 1887; Sharp to T. J. Potter, Sept. 23, 1887, UPL; Sharp to C. F. Adams, Sept. 30, 1887, UPL; Potter to Adams, Dec. 13, 1887, UPL.

49 Sharp to Adams, Apr. 13, 1888, UPL; LeGrand Young to Frederick L. Ames, June 14, 1888, UPL; Clarence W. Scott to L. S. Anderson, June 30, 1888, UPL; Los Angeles *Times*, Jan. 5, 1889; J. S. Cameron to Adams, Jan. 12 and Apr. 20, 1889, UPL; Adams to F. Gordon Dexter, Aug. 20, 1889, UPL.

50 Sharp to Adams, May 16, 1889, UPL; Virgil Bogue to W. H. Holcomb, Nov. 25, 1889, *DR*, 12:875–77; *Chronicle*, 51:538; R. D. Perkins (comp.), "Corporate History of San Pedro, Los Angeles & Salt Lake Railroad Company as of June 30, 1914," UPO, 28–29.

51 NY *Times*, Jan. 28, 1897; *RR Gazette*, 29:122, 775; *Chronicle*, 68:383; Perkins, "San Pedro History," 37–38; S. M. Felton, "Report on the Los Angeles Terminal Company," Apr. 29, 1899, SMF. The second company was called the Utah, Nevada & California (of Nevada).

52 W. H. Bancroft to Harriman, May 25, 1899, UPL; Harriman to Bancroft, May 25, 1899, UPL; *World's Work* (January 1906), 11:7073.

53 Bancroft to Harriman, May 25, 1899, UPL.

54 *DAB*, 4:144–46; Michael P. Malone, *The Battle for Butte: Mining and Politics on the Northern Frontier, 1864–1906* (Seattle, 1981), 12–15, 82–83, 198–99.

55 NY *Times*, Oct. 4 and Nov. 23, 1900; *WSJ*, Oct. 16, 1900; *Chronicle*, 72:184, 581; *RR Gazette*, 33:152, 230.

56 Harriman to Gates, Dec. 3, 1900, AF.

57 *USA v. UP*, 10:4790–4800; Trottman, *Union Pacific*, 318–20; *RR Gazette*, 33:286, 637, 640–41.

58 Salt Lake *Tribune*, Apr. 5 and Apr. 25, 1901; Cheyenne *Daily Leader*, Apr. 8, 1901; Denver *Evening Post*, Apr. 8, 1901; Bancroft circular, Apr. 9, 1901, UPL; *Chronicle*, 72:723; W. D. Cornish to Burt, Apr. 13, 1901, UPL; *Deseret Evening News*, Apr. 13, 1901; *Rocky Mountain News*, Apr. 24, 1901; Salt Lake *Herald*, Apr. 24 and Apr. 25, 1901.

59 *USA v. UP*, 2:606, 6:2580–88; Burt to Harriman, Apr. 16, 1901, UPL; *RR Gazette*, 33:286, 637; Salt Lake *Tribune*, Apr. 25, 1901; *WSJ*, May 15, 1901.

60 *WSJ*, June 12 and June 27, 1901; Salt Lake *Herald*, June 23, June 28, and June 30, 1901; *Deseret Evening News*, June 21, 1901; R. J. Kilpatrick to Burt, June 27, 1901, UPL; Salt Lake *Tribune*, July 4, 1901.

61 *RR Gazette*, 33:396, 640, 690; *Deseret Evening News*, July 19, July 23, July 30, and Aug. 2, 1901; Salt Lake *Tribune*, July 27, July 30, July 31, Aug. 7, Aug. 9, and Aug, 10, 1901; *Chronicle*, 73:237; Salt Lake *Herald*, Aug. 9, Sept. 17, and Sept. 18, 1901; *WSJ*, Aug. 28, 1901.

62 *USA v. UP*, 1:86–108, 2:606–13, 10:4801–4805; Burt to Harriman, Sept. 15, 1901, UPL; *WSJ*, Oct. 17, 1901, *RR Gazette*, 33:900.

63 The full agreement is reprinted in *USA v. UP*, 1:87–108.

64 Ibid., 2:644; *RR Gazette*, 37:240–41, 38:48, 114; *Chronicle*, 79:1024, 80:713, 1480, 1914.

65 *Chronicle*, 75:795, 907, 1204, 76:1193; *RR Gazette*, 34:806, 35:416; *WSJ*, Dec. 13, 1902, July 11, 1903; Perkins to Hill, Jan. 2, 1903, JJH; Hill to Perkins, Jan. 8, 1903, JJH; NY *Times*, Apr. 20, 1903.

66 *WSJ*, Mar. 26, Apr. 8, and Oct. 24, 1904.

67 Ibid., Oct. 11, Oct. 24, and Dec. 15, 1902; Omaha *Bee*, Oct. 13 and Oct. 15, 1902, Aug. 5, Aug. 11, Aug. 12, and Sept. 1, 1903; Fish to Harriman, Oct. 22, 1902, IC; Denver *Republican*, Feb. 21, 1903; Denver *Post*, Feb. 6, 1903; Harriman to Millar, Mar. 6, 1903, IC; Omaha *World Herald*, Aug. 11 and Aug. 12, 1903.

68 NY *Times,* Apr. 6, June 22, 1902; *WSJ,* May 17, May 19, May 21, May 27, and Aug. 25, 1902.
69 George Harris to Hill, Dec. 1, 1902, JJH; Denver *Post,* Feb. 6 and Feb. 11, 1903; Denver *Republican,* Nov. 13, 1902; NY *Commercial,* Nov. 13, 1902; *WSJ,* Nov. 25, Dec. 4, and Dec. 8, 1902, Mar. 7, 1903; *Chronicle,* 76:655.
70 *USA v. UP,* 3:1020, 1133–34; Bryant, *Atchison,* 184–86.
71 *USA v. UP,* 2:525, 3:1134–36.
72 Denver *Post,* Feb. 11 and July 1, 1903; Denver *Republican,* Feb. 21, 1903; Hughitt to Burt, Mar. 9, 1903, UPL; Cheyenne *Daily Leader,* Mar. 13, 1903; Burt to Harriman, Mar. 16, 1903, UPL; Kansas City *Star,* May 23, 1903; W. D. Cornish to Burt, Aug. 24, 1903, UPL; Berry to Burt, Oct. 13, 1903, UPL; *USA v. UP,* 10:4720.
73 Hill to Perkins, Jan. 8, 1903, JJH.

CHAPTER 7
THE NEW ORDER

1 Overton, *Burlington Route,* 260–61.
2 Kennan, *Harriman,* 1:278.
3 Talbot J. Taylor & Co., Analysis of the Southern Pacific Company, Aug. 1, 1901, 3–8, AF. The company did convert much of its power to oil. See *RR Gazette,* 37:387–88, 45:944; Omaha *Bee,* Aug. 17, 1903.
4 Kennan, *Harriman,* 1:241–42.
5 Don. L. Hofsommer, *The Southern Pacific, 1901–1985* (College Station, Tex., 1986), 13; Burt to Stubbs, Mar. 4, 1899, UPL; Stubbs to Burt, Mar. 7, 1899, UPL; Kruttschnitt to E. Dickinson, June 27, 1900, UPL.
6 Kennan, *Harriman,* 1:244–45.
7 Kruttschnitt to Batson, Apr. 11, 1911, AF; *USA v. UP,* 9:4099–4118.
8 *USA v. UP,* 9:4105; *WSJ,* June 28, 1902; *RR Gazette,* 37:566, 42:328–29, 44:176–77.
9 NY *Times,* Aug. 21 and Nov. 22, 1901; *RR Gazette,* 33:832, 34:750; Omaha *Bee,* Aug. 17 and Nov. 28, 1903; *USA v. UP,* 9:4106–7.
10 *WSJ,* Nov. 17, 1899, Apr. 16 and Sept. 28, 1901; San Francisco *Chronicle,* Dec. 19, 1899; Salt Lake *Herald,* June 28, 1900; *RR Gazette,* 32:472, 488, 502, 532, 764, 33:358, 644, 661, 712.
11 E. L. Lomax to Burt, Nov. 22, 1901, UPL; Kruttschnitt to Harriman, Jan. 27, 1902, UPL; NY *Times,* Jan. 28, 1902; Kruttschnitt to Burt, Feb. 1, 1902, UPL; Harriman to Burt, Feb. 3, 1902, UPL; Burt to Harriman, Feb. 14, 1902, UPL; *WSJ,* Feb. 19, 1902; Burt to Millar, Feb. 22, 1902, UPL.
12 Herbert I. Bennett, "Railroading Across Great Salt Lake," *Scientific American Supplement* (May 21, 1904), 57:23726–27; Memorandum accompanying Burt to Harriman, Feb. 14, 1902, UPL.
13 Hood to Kruttschnitt, Jan. 13, 1902, UPL; Oscar King Davis, "The Lucin Cut-off," *Century* (Jan. 1906), 71:463–64. Hood's letter contains his battle plan. Davis offers the most detailed account of the project.
14 Davis, "Lucin Cut-off," 465–66; Kansas City *Journal,* Aug. 17, 1903.
15 Davis, "Lucin Cut-off," 466–67.
16 Ibid., 468; *RR Gazette,* 35:878; San Francisco *Examiner,* Dec. 1, 1903.
17 Davis, "Lucin Cut-off," 468; *RR Gazette,* 36:54, 37:397.

18 *RR Gazette,* 42:691; Kennan, *Harriman,* 1:248.
19 Kruttschnitt to Batson, Apr. 11, 1911, AF; *USA v. UP,* 9:4087–88, 4103–18; *WSJ,* Aug. 29, 1901.
20 *USA v. UP,* 9:4182; *WSJ,* Aug. 15, 1906, Apr. 6 and July 26, 1907; NY *Times,* July 25, 1907. Details on the Keene episode are in Kennan, *Harriman,* 1:346–54.
21 All figures are taken or computed from U.S. Bureau of the Census, *Historical Statistics of the United States* (Washington, D.C., 1975), 2:740. For some background see Walter Licht, *Working for the Railroad* (Princeton, N.J., 1983), 180–201.
22 *Historical Statistics,* 2:740; Albro Martin, *Enterprise Denied: Origins of the Decline of the American Railroad, 1897–1917* (New York, 1971), 49.
23 *USA v. UP,* 9:4108–13, 4134; Kruttschnitt to Kennan, Apr. 11, 1911, AF; *RR Gazette,* 42:720.
24 E. Dickinson to Burt, July 7, 1900, UPL; Burt to Harriman, July 1, Aug. 18, Oct. 31, Dec. 18, and Dec. 19, 1901, Feb. 6, Mar. 20, and July 2, 1902, UPL; Harriman to Burt, Oct. 23, Nov. 23, Dec. 18, and Dec. 19, 1901, Feb. 6, 1902, UPL.
25 Burt to Harriman, Jan. 24, 1903, UPL; Harriman to Burt, Jan. 24, 1903, UPL; Interview with W. A. Harriman, June 23, 1981; *Fortune,* May 8, 1978, 197.
26 Park, "Recollections," 13–15.
27 *RR Gazette,* 46:984.
28 Ibid., 43:2–3, 46:985; NY *Times,* July 2, 1907; Spearman, "Railway System," 447.
29 *RR Gazette,* 45:1031–32, 1600.
30 *USA v. UP,* 9:4133; NY *Times,* Jan. 2, 1908; *RR Gazette,* 46:984–86.
31 Metropolitan Club memo, May 31, 1901, JJH; Hill to Bacon, June 12 and July 19, 1901, JJH; Martin, *Hill,* 505.
32 Batson minutes, 14, AF; Fish to Thomas Lloyd, June 28, 1901, IC; *WSJ,* June 20 and Sept. 7, 1901; *Chronicle,* 72:1239.
33 *Chronicle,* 74:96; Omaha *Daily News,* Jan. 7, 1902; *UP Report,* 1903,1, 1904,1; Spearman, "Railway System," 439–40.
34 *NCAD,* 6:488.
35 *RR Gazette,* 33:745; NY *Times,* June 16 and June 17, 1925; *American Magazine,* 92:138; *American Review of Reviews,* 73:98.
36 *Railway Age,* 78:1459–62; *American Magazine,* 92:37.
37 Schiff to Harriman, July 28, 1901, AF.
38 *WSJ,* July 10, Aug. 19, Aug. 26, and Sept. 30, 1901; San Francisco *Chronicle,* Aug. 17, 1901; Los Angeles *Times,* Aug. 18, 1901; Omaha *Bee,* Aug. 21, 1901; *RR Gazette,* 33:595; Topeka *State Journal,* Oct. 1, 1901; Schiff to Harriman, Sept. 11 and Nov. 10, 1901, AF.
39 NY *Times,* Jan. 3, 1904; *WSJ,* Jan. 6, 1904; Lefevre, "Harriman," 126; C. M. Keys, "Harriman: The Building of his Empire," *World's Work* (Feb. 1907), 13:8549; Harriman to Burt, Nov. 26, 1901, UPL; Burt to Harriman, Nov. 27, 1901, UPL.
40 Park, "Recollections," 25–27.
41 Ibid., 33; Omaha *Daily News,* July 23, 1903; Harriman to Burt, Jan. 3 and Jan. 7, 1904, UPL; Burt to Harriman, Jan. 3 and Jan 7, 1904, UPL; *Chronicle,* 78:104; *WSJ,* Jan. 6, 1904; Burt to Mahl, Jan. 16, 1904, UPL.
42 *Deseret News,* Mar. 23, 1904; *RR Gazette,* 36:71, 247, 262, 38:129; Harriman circular, Jan. 15, 1904, UPL; *Chronicle,* 78:230. Bancroft was first brought to Omaha as general manager when Burt left in January, then reassigned when Mohler was appointed.

43 "Minutes of Meeting of Superintendents," Dec. 29, 1898, UPL; Harriman to Burt, Sept. 15, 1899 (two letters), Sept. 10, 1901, UPL; *RR Gazette,* 32:289; "Coal for Locomotives," memorandum, Dec. 27, 1901, UPL; "Classification of Operating Expense and Construction Accounts," July 1, 1902, UPL; General Notice, Nov. 1, 1902, UPL.

44 Burt to Bancroft, Nov. 13, 1901, Feb. 11, 1902, UPL; S. Higgins to Burt, Nov. 18, 1902, UPL; Bancroft to Burt et al., June 15, 1902, UPL; Harriman to Bancroft, Jan. 29, 1904, UPL; Bancroft to Harriman, Jan. 28, 1904, UPL; Harriman circular, Jan. 1, 1903, UPL; Mahl circular, Jan. 1, 1903, UPL; Hofsommer, *Southern Pacific,* 28–29.

45 Millar to Burt, June 3, 1902, UPL; "Minutes of Meeting of Superintendents," Dec. 29, 1898, UPL.

46 *RR Gazette,* 43:64–66; Kruttschnitt to Batson, Apr. 11, 1911, AF.

47 Hofsommer, *Southern Pacific,* 27–29.

48 Ray Morris, *Railroad Administration* (New York, 1920), 46–89; Alfred D. Chandler, Jr., *The Visible Hand: The Managerial Revolution in American Business* (Cambridge, Mass., 1977), 176–85.

49 Quoted in Hofsommer, *Southern Pacific,* 27–30.

50 *RR Gazette,* 46:150–52, 1299–1301; Morris, *Railroad Administration,* 279–95.

51 Omaha *Bee,* Mar. 21–23, 1901; General Notice, Apr. 8, 1901, UPL; *Western Laborer,* Apr. 13, 1901; Omaha *World-Herald,* July 11, 1901; Denver *Republican,* June 14, 1902; Cheyenne *Daily Leader,* June 13, 1902; *Chronicle,* 75:1088.

52 Millar, "Harriman," 12; Kruttschnitt, "Three Business Giants," 37; Lefevre, "Harriman," 127.

53 *RR Gazette,* 47:420, 1016–18. For Adams's plans see Klein, *Union Pacific,* 1:chap. 24.

54 Burt to Harriman, Oct. 8, 1902, UPO; Burt to Hughitt, Nov. 20, 1902, UPO; Burt to Bancroft et al., Nov. 21, 1902, UPO; Omaha *Bee,* Nov. 28, 1902; General Notice, Dec. 1, 1902, UPO; NY *Times,* Dec. 6, 1902; UP Directors minutes, undated copy, UPO; *UP Report,* 1910, 23; Richard J. Sharp to Burt, Mar. 17, 1903, UPL.

55 Burt to Harriman, Apr. 25, June 18, June 23, July 1, and Oct. 29, 1902, UPL; Meeting of Committee of Boilermakers with Superintendent Motive Power S. Higgins, June 5, June 13, and June 16, 1902, UPL; "Rules and Regulations Governing Shop Employes," June 15, 1902, UPL; *WSJ,* June 30 and July 8, 1902; Burt to Stubbs, Aug. 13, 1902, UPL.

56 Dickinson to Burt, Aug. 13, Aug. 19, and Aug. 29, 1902, UPL; J. W. Lacey to W. R. Kelley, Aug. 16, 1902, UPL; Burt to Dickinson, Aug. 30, 1902, UPL; W. L. Park to Dickinson, Aug. 15, 1902, UPL; W. R. McKeen to Dickinson, Aug. 15, 1902, UPL; Burt to Harriman, Sept. 1, Sept. 3, Sept. 25, Oct. 7, Oct. 9, Oct. 29, and Oct. 30, 1902, UPL; *WSJ,* Sept. 16, 1902, Feb. 3, 1903; NY *Times,* Jan. 7 and Jan. 31, 1903.

57 Burt to McKeen, Jan. 20, 1903, UPL; Park to Burt, Mar. 18, 1903, UPL; *WSJ,* Mar. 24 and May 25, 1903; William Niland to W. S. Murrian et al, Mar. 25, 1903, UPL; Burt to J. W. Lacey, May 29, 1903, UPL; *Chronicle,* 76:1250; Cheyenne *Daily Leader,* June 10, 1903; R. J. Sutton to Burt, June 23, 1903, UPL.

58 Burt to Harriman, Sept. 5, 1903, UPL; Herbert George to Burt, Sept. 22, 1903, UPL; Cheyenne *Daily Leader,* Sept. 29, 1903, Jan. 26, 1904; Omaha *World Herald,* Oct. 20, 1903.

59 *RR Gazette,* 47:305–6, 324–26.

60 "Report of Discipline by Record, Six Months Ending June 30, 1902," UPL. The totals for these figures do not tally, and the discrepancies are in the original forms.
61 *RR Gazette,* 47:305–6.

CHAPTER 8
THE STORMS

1 *USA v. UP,* 3:1132–47, 11:4918–21; Hugh Neill to Batson, Nov. 28, 1911, AF. For background on this clash see chap. 6.
2 *USA v. UP,* 3:1025, 11:4922–24; Neill to Batson, Nov. 28, 1911, AF.
3 *USA v. UP,* 3:1104–8, 1134–38, 1164, 10:4722, 4759–62. The two "friends" were H. H. Rogers and Henry Clay Frick.
4 *WSJ,* June 29, 1904; NY *Times,* Jan. 13, 1907; *RR Gazette,* 42:96, 600. The joint California company was not organized until 1907; see *RR Gazette,* 42:861.
5 NY *Times,* Feb. 20 and Mar. 11, 1902; Meyer, *Northern Securities,* 257–58; Martin, *Hill,* 511–15. A copy of the ICC order for the investigation, dated Dec. 20, 1901, is in UPL.
6 *RR Gazette,* 35:570; NY *Times,* Mar. 19 and Apr. 10, 1903; *Chronicle,* 76:654, 811, 77:299; Meyer, *Northern Securities,* 272–78. The two earlier decisions were in the 1897 Trans-Missouri (166 U.S. 290) and 1898 Joint Traffic Association (171 U.S. 205) cases.
7 A copy of this memorandum is in D. Miller to Hill, July 30, 1902, JJH.
8 Harriman to Hill, Feb. 6, Feb. 22, April 1, April 2, April 3, and April 12, 1902, JJH; Mellen to Hill, May 8, 1902, JJH; C. W. Bunn to Hill, June 2, 1902, JJH; Louis Hill to Hill, June 16, 1902, JJH; Mellen to W. P. Clough, June 16, 1902, JJH; Clough to Hill, June 18, 1902, JJH; Hill to Mellen, June 18, 1902, JJH; *WSJ,* Jan. 16, 1902; Hill to Harriman, Mar. 31 and Apr. 9, 1902, JJH; Hill to Schiff, Mar. 31, 1902, JJH; Schiff to Hill, Apr. 2, 1902, JJH.
9 Mellen to Hill, June 9 and Sept. 29, 1902, JJH; Harriman to Hill, July 25, 1902, JJH; Hill to Harriman, July 25, July 28, and July 29, 1902, JJH; Clough to Hill, Aug. 1, Aug. 15, Aug. 29, Sept. 4, and Oct. 1, 1902, JJH.
10 George Harris to Hill, Sept. 14 and Sept. 19, 1902, JJH; Hill to Miller, Sept. 16 and Sept. 30, 1902, JJH; Hill to Mellen, Sept. 30, 1902, JJH; Clough to Hill, Sept. 30, 1902, JJH.
11 Hill to Mellen, Oct. 3 and Oct. 7, 1902, JJH; Clough to Hill, Oct. 3, 1902, JJH; Hill to Clough, Oct. 4, 1902, JJH; Hill to Miller, Oct. 5, 1902, JJH; Miller to Hill, Oct. 6, 1902, JJH.
12 Kennan notes, Nov. 19, 1902, AF; Harriman to Hill, Feb. 26 and Apr. 9, 1903, JJH; NY *Times,* Apr. 5, 1903.
13 Felton, "Genius of Harriman," 185–86; NY *Times,* May 16, May 17, and May 21, 1903; NY *Commercial,* May 16, May 20, and May 21, 1903; Chicago *Chronicle,* May 16, 1903; L. W. Hill to Hill, May 20, 1903, JJH; Harriman to Hill, May 28, 1903, JJH.
14 Hill to Harriman, May 15, May 18, May 20, and Aug. 10, 1903, JJH; Hill to Mrs. E. H. Harriman, May 19, 1903, JJH; Mellen to Hill, Jan. 20, 1903, JJH; Mellen to G. H. Earl, Jan. 26, 1903, JJH; Clough to Hill, Feb. 16, July 17, and July 24, 1903, JJH; Farrer to Hill, Aug. 20, 1903, JJH; Mount Stephen to Hill, Aug. 21, 1903, JJH; Hill to Mount Stephen, Sept. 10, 1903, JJH; Millar to Hill, Oct. 29, 1903, JJH; Clough to Hill, Jan. 21, 1903, JJH.

15 Martin, *Hill,* 518–20; *Chronicle,* 78:1138; *RR Gazette,* 36:212.

16 Kennan, *Harriman,* 1:387–89; Mercer, *Harriman,* 96.

17 *WSJ,* Mar. 21–28, Apr. 5–9, Apr. 12–14, Apr. 20–23, Apr. 28–30, May 21–24, and June 14, 1904; Hill to Harris, Mar. 21, 1904, JJH; Hill to Perkins, Mar. 21, 1904, JJH; Hill to Harriman, Mar. 24, 1904, JJH; *RR Gazette,* 36:248, 274, 307; *Chronicle,* 78:1223–24, 1392–93, 1447, 1497–98; Hill to Bacon, Mar. 26, 1904, JJH; "Petition for Leave to Intervene," *USA v. Northern Securities Company et al.,* UPL; Denver *Republican,* Apr. 9, 1904; NY *Commercial,* Apr. 5, 1904; Lovett to Harriman, Apr. 19, 1904, UPL; Schiff to Mount Stephen, May 8, 1904, JJH; Felton to Harriman, June 10, June 15, and June 16, 1904, SMF; Hill to Mount Stephen, June 15, 1904, JJH.

18 Mount Stephen to Harriman, July 1 and July 15, 1904, JJH; Farrer to Hill, July 11, Aug. 9, and Aug. 25, 1904, JJH; Hill to Farrer, July 22 and July 24, 1904, JJH; George F. Baker to Hill, July 26, 1904, JJH; E. T. Nichols to Hill, Aug. 5, 1904, JJH; Mount Stephen to Hill, Aug. 10, 1904, JJH; Hill to Mount Stephen, July 22, 1904, JJH.

19 Meyer, *Northern Securities,* 298–304; NY *Times,* Jan. 4, Jan. 31, Mar. 7, Apr. 4, and Apr. 18, 1905; *WSJ,* Jan. 4, 1905; *RR Gazette,* 38:38, 93, 197; *Chronicle,* 80:118, 600, 1059, 1363; Hill to Schiff, Mar. 10, 1905, JJH; Martin, *Hill,* 651, note 49.

20 Farrer to Hill, Dec. 24, 1904, JJH; Mount Stephen to Hill, Dec. 30, 1904, JJH; *Chronicle,* 80:1940; *WSJ,* May 25, Oct. 25, Oct. 28, Oct. 31, and Nov. 3, 1905; NY *Times,* May 25, Oct. 28, and Nov. 5, 1905; Hill to Louis Hill, July 20, 1905, JJH; *RR Gazette,* 43:406.

21 *WSJ,* Sept. 22, Nov. 30, and Dec. 2, 1905; Lowenthal, *The Investor Pays,* 15–19; Moffat to Hill, Apr. 1 and May 2, 1904, JJH; Athearn, *Rio Grande Western,* 201–5.

22 "Denver & Rio Grande Investigation," 113 ICC 85–90; Denver *Post,* Feb. 6, 1903; *Chronicle,* 76:655; "The Western Pacific Railway," 1–3, WPB.

23 *WSJ,* Mar. 7, 1903, Feb. 8 and Sept. 21, 1904; *Chronicle,* 76:655, 1194, 77:38, 252, 1875, 78:584, 822, 1168, 79:1024, 1267; Denver *Post,* July 2, 1903; NY *Times,* Feb. 6, Sept. 10, and Sept. 19, 1904.

24 *WSJ,* Sept. 29 and Oct. 13, 1904, Jan. 18 and Apr. 25, 1905; *Chronicle,* 79:2749, 80:1425, 1480; NY *Times,* Mar. 20, Apr. 21, Apr. 23, and Apr. 28, 1905; *USA v. UP,* 1:208–9.

25 *WSJ,* May 15, 1905, Feb. 12, 1906; NY *Times,* June 8, 1905, Jan. 12, 1906; *Chronicle,* 81:845–46, 1494; "Denver & Rio Grande Investigation," 92–93; Athearn, *Rio Grande Western,* 207–210.

26 Thomas Warner Mitchell, "The Growth of the Union Pacific and Its Financial Operations," *Quarterly Journal of Economics* (Aug. 1907), 21:608; *WSJ,* Feb. 7, 1906; *Chronicle,* 81:232.

27 *Chronicle,* 68:25, 81:232, 266, 82:356, 84:30; *WSJ,* June 1, June 29, July 1, July 21, July 27, and Dec. 22, 1905, Jan. 6, Jan 20, Jan. 26, 1906; *RR Gazette,* 39:32, 40:56; Farrer to Harriman, Mar. 8, 1906, AF; Harriman to Farrer, Mar. 30, 1906, AF.

28 *USA v. UP,* 1:223–24, 251–52, 2:789.

29 Ibid., 1:223–25, 2:789–90.

30 *WSJ,* Aug. 4, Aug. 17, and Aug. 18, 1906; NY *Times,* Aug. 18, 1906.

31 NY *Times,* Aug. 18–20, 1906; *WSJ,* Aug. 18, Aug. 22, and Sept. 14, 1906; *Nation,* Aug. 23, 1906, 157–58; *RR Gazette,* 41:151–52; *Chronicle,* 83:407–9; *Forum,* 38:194; Mitchell, "Growth of the Union Pacific," 609–610. The *Journal* thought Harriman made $25 million on the deal.

32 Report of E. E. Calvin to Harriman, June 18, 1906, 1–1a, AF; Calvin to Kennan, Apr. 10, 1921, AF; Kennan, *Harriman,* 2:66–67.
33 Calvin report, June 18, 1906, 1–1a, AF.
34 W. V. Hill, ''Mr. Edward Henry Harriman,'' 2, AF.
35 Ibid.; Calvin report, June 18, 1906, 2.
36 Calvin report, June 18, 1906, 3–6.
37 Ibid., 8–12.
38 Ibid., 12–14.
39 Calvin to Kennan, Apr. 10, 1921, AF; *WSJ,* Apr. 23–26, May 4, and May 10, 1906; E. H. Harriman, ''San Francisco's Experience,'' *Sunset* (May 1906), 37–41.
40 *WSJ,* Apr. 23, Apr. 25, and May 2, 1906; NY *Times,* May 13, 1906; *RR Gazette,* 40:499; W. F. Herrin to Mary Harriman, May 8, 1906, AF.
41 Hill, ''Harriman,'' 3–4; NY *Times,* May 9, 1906; Kahn, *Harriman,* 38; Millar, ''Harriman,'' 3.
42 Except where otherwise noted, this account is drawn from the following sources: ''Southern Pacific Imperial Valley Claim: Evidence, Statement, and Argument before the Committee on Claims,'' House Bill 13997, 60 Cong., 1st Sess. (1908), AF; F. H. Newell, ''The Salton Sea,'' *Annual Report of the Board of Regents of the Smithsonian Institution,* 1907 (Washington, 1908), 331–45; *RR Gazette,* 41:144, 420, 42:489–92; Kennan, *Harriman,* 2:88–173.
43 Randolph to Kennan, Nov. 16 and Dec. 2, 1916, AF. Randolph affirmed that these were Harriman's exact words.
44 Ibid., Nov. 16, 1916, AF; ''Imperial Valley Claim,'' 8.
45 Kennan, *Harriman,* 2:148–51; Roosevelt to Harriman, Dec. 15 and Dec. 20, 1906, Theodore Roosevelt papers, Library of Congress.
46 Millar to Kennan, June 15, 1917, AF; Hill, ''Harriman,'' 5; NY *Times,* Jan. 3 and Jan. 6, 1907; *WSJ,* Jan. 30, 1907; Harriman to Roosevelt, Dec. 20, 1906, Roosevelt papers; Randolph to Kennan, Nov. 16, 1916, AF; *RR Gazette,* 41:180.
47 Randolph to Mary Harriman, Nov. 20, 1911, AF; Maxwell Evarts statement, AF; Kahn, *Harriman,* 34–35; Randolph to Kennan, Nov. 16, 1916, AF. For the controversy over reimbursement see ''Imperial Valley Claim''; NY *Times,* Mar. 12, 1908, Jan. 18, Jan. 24, Feb. 21, and Nov. 14, 1909.

CHAPTER 9
THE RECKONING

1 *WSJ,* May 30 and July 18, 1901; *Chronicle,* 72:1035, 75:136; Trottman, *Union Pacific,* 312–13; *USA v. UP,* 1:265.
2 Schiff to Harriman, Sept. 11, 1901, AF.
3 William Rockefeller to Harriman, Sept. 26, 1902, AF; *WSJ,* June 5 and Nov. 1, 1902, July 16, Aug. 20, Aug. 24, Sept. 10, and Sept. 16, 1904, Jan. 5, 1905; ''Agreement to form syndicate for $50,000,000 to buy Union Pacific preferred stock,'' Nov. 11, 1902, AF; Schiff to Kennan, May 3, 1920, AF. The new pool included Harriman ($10 million), Kuhn, Loeb ($10 million), Stillman ($10 million), William Rockefeller ($5 million), H. H. Rogers ($5 million), W. K. Vanderbilt ($5 million), James Hazen Hyde ($2 million), Henry Clay Frick ($1.25 million), and P. A. Valentine ($1.25 million). The other $500,000 is not accounted for in Kennan's copy of the pact.

4 *Chronicle,* 80:1060, 1364; *WSJ,* Mar. 14, Apr. 6, 1905; *RR Gazette,* 38:104, 112, 160; NY *Times,* Apr. 5, 1905.

5 *WSJ,* May 29, June 1, June 29, July 21, Nov. 28, and Dec. 22, 1905; *Chronicle,* 81:232; Stillman to Harriman, Apr. 16, 1906, AF.

6 *RR Gazette,* 40:30, 124, 138, 168; *WSJ,* May 1–4, 1906; *Chronicle,* 82:1041, 1270, 83:97, 156, 493; *UP Report,* 1906, 10, 1907, 14; *USA v. UP,* 1:264–65. The new Short Line issue was forced by the court action over Northern Securities. For a succinct explanation see Mercer, *Harriman,* 97–98.

7 *USA v. UP,* 1:256–57; *UP Report,* 1907, 12–13; *WSJ,* Dec. 21, 1906; Trottman, *Union Pacific,* 308–10; Mercer, *Harriman,* 98–99. There are minor errors in the figures of both Trottman and Mercer.

8 *UP Report,* 1910, 13; Snyder, "Harriman," 48. The figures given here differ from other sources and reflect the amounts actually received for the securities sold. Both Trottman and Mercer apparently relied on the calculations in Mitchell, "Growth of Union Pacific," 600–1. Since Mitchell was writing in 1907, his calculations included the figures of stock sold by that date and paper profits on stock still held, using current market prices. For some reason, neither Trottman nor Mercer used the actual receipts of sales given in the company's 1910 report.

9 *UP Report,* 1907, 13; 12 *ICC Rep.,* 292–95; *WSJ,* Jan. 19, 1907; Trottman, *Union Pacific,* 310–11.

10 *UP Report,* 1906, 8, 1907, 13, and 1909, 9; *USA v. UP,* 2:748–49.

11 Kahn, "Harriman," 39.

12 *WSJ,* May 10 and May 15, 1907, June 11 and July 30, 1908; NY *Times,* July 27, 1908; *Chronicle,* 72:27, 87:1507–9; Adler, *Schiff,* 1:113–16.

13 *WSJ,* Aug. 31, 1906.

14 Ibid., Nov. 30 and Dec. 2, 1905, July 28, 1906, Jan. 4, 1907; *RR Gazette,* 39:550–52; Stillman to Harriman, Mar. 2, 1906, AF; NY *Times,* Aug. 26 and Dec. 2, 1907.

15 "The Western Pacific Railway," 3–8, WPB; *Chronicle,* 84:932.

16 *Western Pacific Mileposts,* Spring–Fall 1978, H-6–23, March 1983, 13–23; 113 *ICC* 103–5.

17 NY *Times,* Oct. 1, 1905. For the collapse of Gould's empire see Howard, *Wall Street Fifty Years After Erie,* 32–162; Athearn, *Rio Grande Western,* 210–38; 113 *ICC* 101–60.

18 NY *Times,* May 20, 1908; *WSJ,* July 19, 1908.

19 Hill to Lewis Hill, July 20, 1905, JJH; Hill to W. H. Taft, May 13, 1907, JJH; *WSJ,* Oct. 28, 1905, Mar. 12, 1906; NY *Times,* Oct. 28 and Nov. 5, 1905.

20 Hill to Lewis Hill, July 20, 1905, JJH; *WSJ,* Jan. 10 and Apr. 10, 1906, Mar. 12, 1907; *RR Gazette,* 41:291; NY *Times,* Oct. 11, 1906; "The Hill Invasion of Harriman Territory," 1–4, AF; Martin, *Hill,* 563–66. The north bank road was originally chartered as the Portland & Seattle in 1905 to build from Pasco, Washington, to Portland. It was renamed in 1908 and authorized to build from Spokane to Portland.

21 *RR Gazette,* 38:199, 39:40, 123, 193, 40:72, 137, 189; 41:31, 42:30, 61, 727, 879, 43:404, 638, 44:73, 45:555, 1121, 1374, 46:139, 1008, 1145, 1329; Short Line Exec. Comm. minutes, Aug. 31, 1905, UPL; *WSJ,* Feb. 19 and May 1, 1906; *Chronicle,* 82:871.

22 Hill to Steele, May 26, 1911, JJH; *RR Gazette,* 41:291, 42:321, 43:83, 605, 45:981, 1460, 46:524, 656, 1144; NY *Times,* Jan. 22, Mar. 23, July 16, and Oct. 11, 1906, Mar. 5 and Mar. 23, 1907, Sept. 7, 1908, Mar. 30, and May 27, 1909; *WSJ,* Jan.

27, Apr. 10, and June 13, 1906, Mar. 12, Oct. 28, and Oct. 30, 1907, Mar. 19, May 20, and June 9, 1909.

23 Hill to Steele, May 26 and June 8, 1911, JJH; *RR Gazette,* 47:905–6.

24 *RR Gazette,* 47:215, 298, 340, 943; NY *Times,* Aug. 10, 1909; Hill to John F. Stevens, Aug. 14, Aug. 23, and Sept. 4, 1909, Feb. 7, 1910, JJH; *WSJ,* Sept. 9, 1909; Hill to R. S. Lovett, Feb. 11 and March 14, 1910, JJH.

25 This episode is treated at length in Kennan, *Harriman,* 2:174–274. Most of the sources used and cited by Kennan are at AF.

26 Ibid.; Roosevelt to Sherman, Oct. 8, 1906, TR.

27 12 *ICC Rep.* 277; NY *Times,* Nov. 10, Dec. 7, and Dec. 30, 1906; *Chronicle,* 83:1412.

28 NY *Times,* Feb. 26, Feb. 27, and Mar. 3, 1907; *WSJ,* Feb. 26, 1907.

29 Harriman testimony extracts, TR; Vanderlip to Stillman, Mar. 15, 1907, FAV; Adler, *Schiff,* 1:44–50; Evarts statement, undated, AF. The latter is reprinted in Kennan, *Harriman,* 2:223–26.

30 Evarts statement, AF; NY *Times,* Mar. 9 and Mar. 12, 1907.

31 NY *Times,* Mar. 7–12, Mar. 16, Mar. 20, and Mar. 30, 1907; *WSJ,* Mar. 30, 1907.

32 NY *Times,* Mar. 22 and Mar. 23, 1907; *World's Work,* 13:8713–14.

33 NY *Times,* Apr. 2–5 and Apr. 14, 1907; NY *World,* Apr. 2, 1907; Kennan, *Harriman,* 2:203–9.

34 NY *Times,* Apr. 3–5, Apr. 8, 1907.

35 E. M. to Straight, c. Mar. 19, 1907, WDS; Evarts statement, 10, AF; Kahn, *Harriman,* 38.

36 NY *Times,* June 8, July 14, and Aug. 8–10, 1907; *WSJ,* July 15–17, 1907; *Nation,* 85:49–50.

37 NY *Times,* Aug. 13, Nov. 13, and Nov. 14, 1907, Jan. 2, Jan. 17, Jan. 26, Jan. 27, Feb. 2, and Feb. 15, 1908; *WSJ,* Aug. 15 and Nov. 14, 1907, Dec. 15, 1908; *Chronicle,* 86:170, 257; 22 *ICC Rep.*, 17–20; *RR Gazette,* 1581:82.

38 NY *Times,* Jan. 27, 1908; *Nation,* 86:96–97; *Chronicle,* 86:255–57.

39 *RR Gazette,* 44:141; Church Journal, Feb. 28, 1908, LDS.

40 Batson interview with Stillman, 3, AF.

41 Ibid.; NY *Times,* May 27, 1905; Burr, *Stillman,* 249.

42 *WSJ,* Nov. 15, Nov. 17, and Dec. 1, 1906, Feb. 26, Apr. 30, Oct. 26, Oct. 30, Oct. 31, Nov. 2, Nov. 6, and Dec. 3, 1907, Dec. 9, 1908, Aug. 21, 1909; NY *Times,* Dec. 3, 1906, Oct. 31, 1907, Oct. 21, 1908, Aug. 13 and Aug. 26, 1909; *Chronicle,* 84:1053, 85:1083, 1144; *RR Gazette,* 43:542; Stillman to Prince A. Poniatowski, Oct. 30, 1907, JS.

43 *WSJ,* Apr. 11, 1906, Mar. 16, and Sept. 11, 1907; NY *Times,* Apr. 11, Apr. 12, Apr. 17, May 3, and Oct. 9, 1907, Jan. 26 and Jan 27, 1908; Church Journal, Nov. 8, 1907, LDS; Stillman to Harriman, Jan. 10, 1908, JS.

44 NY *Times,* Feb. 26, 1907; Schiff to Harriman, Feb. 2, 1908, AF.

45 Schiff to Harriman, Feb. 2, 1908, AF; NY *Times,* Feb. 23, 1908. The Far Eastern episode is treated in Kennan, *Harriman,* 2:1–29; George Kennan, *E. H. Harriman's Far Eastern Plans* (Garden City, N. Y., 1917), and Michael H. Hunt, *The Making of a Special Relationship* (New York, 1983).

46 *WSJ,* Mar. 29, 1909.

47 NY *Times,* Jan. 3, Jan. 6, Jan. 8, and Sept. 27, 1907, Apr. 9, Apr. 10, and Apr. 13, 1908; *WSJ,* Jan. 30, 1907, Apr. 9, Apr. 10, Apr. 14, Sept. 30, 1908; Kennan, *Harriman,* 2:311–25 gives more detail on the Erie episode.

48 Harriman to Schiff, May 23, 1908, AF.

49 NY *Times,* Sept. 8, Sept. 9, Sept. 11, Dec. 5, and Dec. 22, 1908, Jan. 17, Jan. 27, Mar. 10, Mar. 16, Mar. 19, and Apr. 1, 1909; *WSJ,* Sept. 16, 1908, Jan. 28, 1909; NY *Times,* Dec. 22, 1908; Burr, *Stillman,* 260–61; Stillman to Vanderlip, Dec. 21, 1908, FAV; Vanderlip to Stillman, Jan. 8, Jan. 12, and Feb. 4, 1909, FAV; Vanderlip to Lord Revelstoke, Feb. 4, 1909, FAV.

50 Vanderlip to Stillman, Feb. 12, 1909, FAV.

51 Ibid., Stillman to Vanderlip, Mar. 12, 1909, FAV.

52 Vanderlip to Stillman, Feb. 18 and Feb. 22, 1909, FAV; NY *Times,* Mar. 19, 1909;

53 Stillman to Vanderlip, Apr. 8 and Apr. 22, 1909, FAV; Stillman to Vanderlip, Feb. 19, 1909, FAV.

54 Vanderlip to Stillman, May 28 and June 3, 1909, FAV; Stillman to Vanderlip, June 8, 1909, FAV; *WSJ,* June 8 and June 14, 1909; Kennan, *Harriman,* 2:345.

55 Burr, *Stillman,* 268–69; Batson interview with Stillman, 4, AF; Oakland *Tribune,* Sept. 10, 1909; San Francisco *Bulletin,* Sept. 10, 1909; Kennan, *Harriman,* 2:346. Harriman's most trusted secretary, C. C. Tegethoff, confirmed that Harriman had cancer, yet Kennan persisted in ascribing his death to "gastric ulceration." (Tegethoff to Kennan, May 12, 1921, AF).

56 Harriman to Willard Straight, Aug. 18, 1909, WDS.

57 NY *Evening World,* Aug. 25, 1909. All the New York newspapers for this date carry an account of Harriman's return, many of them with photographs.

58 *WSJ,* Aug. 26 and Aug. 31, 1909; NY *Times,* Aug. 26, 1909; Adler, *Schiff,* 1:117; Stillman to Prince Poniatowski, Sept. 10, 1909, JS.

59 San Francisco *Bulletin,* Sept. 10, 1909; *WSJ,* Sept. 11, 1909; Adler, *Schiff,* 1:117; Stillman to Prince Poniatowski, Sept. 10, 1909, JS.

CHAPTER 10
THE STEWARDSHIP

1 Salt Lake City *Herald-Republican,* Sept. 14, 1909.

2 Seattle *Times,* Sept. 10, 1909; Adler, *Schiff,* 1:117; NY *Times,* Jan. 14, 1910; Vanderlip to Stillman, Jan. 14, 1910, FAV; *Chronicle,* 90:169; *Railway Age Gazette,* 48:165.

3 Frank A. Vanderlip, *From Farm Boy to Financier* (New York, 1935), 202; San Francisco *Chronicle,* Sept. 13, 1909.

4 Interview with Robert A. Lovett (Judge Lovett's son), Sept. 8, 1981.

5 Statement of Ed Peavy re R. S. Lovett, undated, BB; Walne to Wharton, Mar. 14, 1936, BB; Salt Lake City *Telegram,* Sept. 17, 1909; Salt Lake City *Herald-Republican,* Sept. 19, 1909; NY *Times,* June 20, 1932. I am indebted to Kenneth Lipartito for making this material from Baker & Botts available to me.

6 Ibid.; Baker, Botts, Andrews & Parish Office Review, Dec. 29, 1949, 30:192–93, BB.

7 Lovett interview, Sept. 8, 1981.

8 F. C. Nicodemus, Jr. to R. A. Lovett, Sept. 1, 1938, BB; *Chronicle,* 88:565; Salt Lake City *Tribune,* Sept. 14, 1909.

9 *American Magazine* 69:331–34; *Current Literature,* 47:499–500.

10 Ibid.; *World's Work,* 18:12089–90.

11 Lovett to A. L. Mohler, Nov. 16, 1914, UPN; Mohler to Lovett, Nov. 23, 1914, UPN.

12 NY *Times*, Sept. 14 and Oct. 22, 1909; *WSJ*, Sept. 14, Sept. 15, and Oct. 22, 1909, Mar. 15, 1910; *Chronicle*, 89:722, 995, 1069, 1142.

13 Adler, *Schiff*, 1:117; *WSJ*, Aug. 21, 1911.

14 Vanderlip to Stillman, Dec. 24, 1910, FAV.

15 Dividend summary 1906–1917, undated, UPN; *WSJ*, Jan. 28, Feb. 3, Feb. 15, Apr. 7, Aug. 11, Aug. 13, and Oct. 29, 1910, Jan. 7, Feb. 13, June 6, Nov. 17, and Dec. 6, 1911; William Mahl to Kahn, Dec. 10, 1910, OK; *Chronicle*, 93:1356–58; NY *Times*, Nov. 19, 1911; *Railway Age Gazette*, 51:1086–89.

16 Vanderlip to Stillman, Oct. 22, 1909, May 13, 1910, Apr. 15, 1911, FAV.

17 *Railway Age Gazette*, 51:629.

18 *WSJ*, Aug. 21, Sept. 26, Sept. 29, and Dec. 29, 1911, Jan. 10 and Jan. 11, 1912; NY *Times*, Sept. 29 and Nov. 28, 1911, Jan. 23, 1912; *Chronicle*, 93:797, 872–73, 1022, 1106; *Railway Age Gazette*, 51:629–33, 52:63; UP Exec. Comm. minutes, Jan. 9, 1912, UPN; NY *Tribune*, Jan. 10–12, 1912; Lovett to Sproule, Jan 10, 1912, UPN; Thorne to Lovett, Apr. 1, 1912, UPN. Losses from the fire included the minute books and all files of the chairman, secretary, and controller. The traffic, legal, and operating departments had already moved to the new building.

19 Lovett to Mohler, May 5, 1913, Nov. 12, 1914, UPN.

20 Ibid., July 16, 1912, Apr. 4, 1913, UPN; Mohler to Lovett, Aug. 29, 1912, UPN; Lovett to C. W. Barron, Aug. 20, 1912, UPN; Lovett to Sproule, Nov. 15, 1912, UPN.

21 Vanderlip to Stillman, Nov. 29, 1910, FAV; Stillman to Vanderlip, Dec. 9, 1910, FAV; *Railway Age Gazette*, 48:329, 335, 850, 1115, 50:258, 526, 1085, 51:816; NY *Times*, Feb. 1, 1911; *WSJ*, Feb. 1–3, Mar. 10, Apr. 6, 1911; *Chronicle*, 92:324. The best account of the clash between the carriers and the government is Martin, *Enterprise Denied*—for the Mann-Elkins Act and rate hearings of 1910 see especially chapters 6 and 7.

22 NY *Times*, Feb. 1, 1911; *Chronicle*, 92:285–86; *WSJ*, Feb. 2, 1911.

23 Lovett to Charles W. Reeder, Feb. 14, 1916, UPN; Lovett to Mohler, Feb. 25, 1916, UPN.

24 Lovett to Mohler, June 11 and Dec. 26, 1913, Apr. 29, 1915, Feb. 25, 1916, UPN.

25 *WSJ*, Sept. 22, 1909; NY *Times*, Sept. 26, 1909; *Railway Age Gazette*, 47:599–600, 895, 48:213, 919, 49:600, 887–88, 51:65, 105, 304, 1149–50, 1259, 52:701, 1140, 1589, 53:229, 492, 1163. All figures compiled from UP annual reports, 1910–1916.

26 Vanderlip to Stillman, Jan. 14, Feb. 3, and Feb. 11, 1910, FAV; NY *Times*, Jan. 11–13, Jan. 29, Feb. 16–19, Feb. 24– 26, Mar. 1–5, Mar. 8, Mar. 30, Apr. 6, Apr. 9, and Apr. 26, 1910; *WSJ*, Jan. 21, Feb. 16–19, Feb. 22, Feb. 24–26, Mar. 8, Mar. 30, Apr. 6, Oct. 11, Oct. 14, Oct. 15, Oct. 20, and Dec. 24, 1910; *Railway Age Gazette*, 48:371, 423, 539–40, 707–8, 754–55; *Chronicle*, 91:718.

27 188 *Federal Reporter* 105–9. The main points of both cases are conveniently summarized in *WSJ*, Oct. 15, 1910.

28 See chapter 5 for more detail on these points.

29 For the defense argument on these points see the brief by N. H. Loomis, *USA v. UP*, 1–124.

30 Ibid.; 188 *Federal Reporter* 116; Trottman, *Union Pacific*, 334–43.

31 188 *Federal Reporter* 109–120.

32 NY *Times*, July 3, 1911; *Harper's Weekly*, 55:22; *Railway Age Gazette*, 50:1678.

33 NY *Times*, June 25, June 26, July 30, and Sept. 10, 1911, Mar. 13 and Mar. 27, 1912; *WSJ*, June 26 and July 8, 1911; *Chronicle*, 93:7–9; Evarts to Lovett, Apr. 23, 1912, UPN.

34 The decision was unanimous except for new justice Willis Van Devanter, who did not participate because he had been one of the circuit justices in the original decision. Obviously he would not have gone with the other justices had he voted.

35 226 *U.S.* 85–89. The text of the decision can also be found in *Railway Age Gazette,* 53:1081–85 and NY *Times,* Dec. 3, 1912.

36 Ibid., 88; *Journal of Political Economy,* 21:72.

37 226 *U.S.* 70, 89–90.

38 *Railway Age Gazette,* 53:1075–76. See also *Chronicle,* 95:1502–4.

39 *Railway Age Gazette,* 1075.

40 226 *U.S.* 96–98; *WSJ,* Dec. 3, 1912.

41 Kahn to Lovett, Dec. 3, 1912, UPN; Lovett to C. A. Severance, Dec. 2, 1912, UPN.

42 Vanderlip to Stillman, Sept. 9, 1910, with enclosed memorandum of proceedings dated Sept. 7, 1910, FAV.

43 Ibid.

44 *Lippincott's Magazine,* 30:653.

45 "Withdrawal from Joint Agencies," memorandum, Dec. 12, 1912, UPN; Traffic Department notice, undated but 1913, UPN; L. J. Spence to Lovett, Jan. 31, 1913, UPN; Lovett to Evarts, Jan. 9, 1913, UPN; NY *Times,* Jan. 14 and Feb. 7, 1913; *Chronicle,* 96:203, 420.

46 Wickersham to Lovett, Dec. 17, 1912, UPN; Lovett to James C. McReynolds, May 24, 1913, UPN; NY *Times,* Dec. 12 and Dec. 19, 1912, Jan. 5, Jan. 7, Jan. 9–12, 1913; *WSJ,* Dec. 19, 1912, Jan. 13 and Jan. 15, 1913; *Chronicle,* 95:1685, 96:113.

47 Lovett to McReynolds, May 24, 1913, UPN. This letter is a full and useful summary of the negotiations through May 1913.

48 S. F. Booth to Mohler, Jan. 15, 1913, UPN; Wickersham to Lovett, Jan. 17, 1913, UPN; Lovett to Wickersham, Jan. 18, 1913, UPN; NY *Times,* Jan. 18, Jan. 22, Jan. 23, Jan. 31, Feb. 4–10, Feb. 16, Feb. 20, Feb. 23, and Feb. 25, 1913; *WSJ,* Jan. 20, Feb. 1, Feb. 4, Feb. 7–9, Feb. 11, and Feb. 20, 1913; Kruttschnitt to Lovett, Jan. 24, 1913, UPN; Kuhn, Loeb to M. M. Warburg, Jan. 25, Jan. 27, Jan. 28, 1913, UPN; Kuhn, Loeb to Kahn, Mar. 26, 1913, UPN; *Chronicle,* 96:361–62, 420; *Church Journal,* Feb. 7, 1913, LDS; Kuhn, Loeb to A. Spitzer & Co., Feb. 7, 1913, UPN; Lovett to Vanderlip, Feb. 8, 1913, UPN; *Railway Age Gazette,* 54:276–77, 300–1; C. B. Seger to F. G. Athearn, Feb. 6, 1913, UPN; Gerrit Fort to Lovett, Feb. 12, 1913, UPN; E. O. McCormick to William Sproule, Feb. 12, 1913, UPN.

49 *Chronicle,* 96:655; *WSJ,* Mar. 5 and Mar. 7, 1913; *Railway Age Gazette,* 54:405, 454.

50 "California Ruling on the U.P.–S.P. Unmerging," *Public Service Regulation* (March 1913), 2:123; *WSJ,* Mar. 5, 1913.

51 *Railway World,* 57:181; *Railway Age Gazette,* 54:405; NY *Times,* Mar. 14 and Mar. 16, 1913; Lovett to McReynolds, May 24, 1913, UPN.

52 Lovett to McReynolds, May 24, 1913, UPN; NY *Times,* Mar. 14–16, Mar. 18, Mar. 22, Mar. 26, Mar. 27, and Apr. 3, 1913; W. W. Cotton and Guy V. Shoup to Lovett, Mar. 14, 1913, UPN; *Chronicle,* 96:791, 864; *WSJ,* Mar. 15, Mar. 17, and Mar. 18, 1913; *Harper's Weekly,* 57:22.

53 Loomis to Lovett, Apr. 8, 1913, UPN; Lovett to Loomis, Apr. 8, 1913, UPN; NY *Times,* Apr. 10, Apr. 17–19, Apr. 22–25, Apr. 27, May 6, May 9, May 16, May 23, and May 25, 1913; *Railway Age Gazette,* 54:864, 965, 1014, 1054; *WSJ,* Apr. 11, Apr. 19, Apr. 22–24, Apr. 30, May 1, May 8, May 9, and May 19– 21, 1913;

Chronicle, 96:1158, 1230, 1366; Lovett to McReynolds, May 24, 1913, UPN.

54 NY *Times,* May 27–30, June 1, June 7, and June 10, 1913; *Chronicle,* 96:1558; *WSJ,* June 7, 1913; *Railway World,* 57:447–48.

55 Mortimer L. Schiff to Lovett, Apr. 21, 1913, UPN; UP Exec. Comm. minutes, June 10, 1913, UPN; NY *Times,* June 13, June 15, June 22, June 25, June 28–30, 1913; *WSJ,* June 13, June 18, June 24, 1913; Lovett to Truesdale, June 14, 1913, UPN; *Railway Age Gazette,* 54:1532; *Chronicle,* 96:1841.

56 NY *Times,* July 1, July 8, and July 17, 1913; *WSJ,* July 1, 1913; *Railway Age Gazette,* 55:12–13, 38; *Chronicle,* 97:50–51; *Railway World,* 57:630–32.

57 *Literary Digest,* 47:41–42; *WSJ,* July 2, 1913; NY *Times,* July 1, 1913.

58 NY *Times,* Sept. 14, 1913, May 1, 1914.

59 *WSJ,* Aug. 7, Aug. 12, Aug. 14, Sept. 8, Sept. 11–13, and Sept. 15, 1913; *Chronicle,* 97:366–67, 445–46, 667, 730; NY *Times,* Aug. 13–16, Sept. 3, Sept. 7, and Sept. 11–13, 1913; *Literary Digest,* 47:497.

60 *WSJ,* Sept. 16, Sept. 18, Sept. 24, Sept. 30, Oct. 1, and Oct. 16, 1913, Jan. 7–9, 1914; NY *Times,* Sept. 19, 1913, Jan. 7–9, 1914; *Literary Digest,* 47:548, 656–58, 48:122, 124; *Chronicle,* 97:1025, 98:92, 156–57; *Railway Age Gazette,* 55:728, 56:103; *Harper's Weekly,* 58:32; Extra Dividend Notice, Jan. 8, 1914, UPN. A suit by some holders of preferred stock delayed payment of the dividend until July 1914.

61 *WSJ,* Apr. 14 and June 10, 1914; Lovett to Charles S. Thomas, Apr. 18, 1914, UPN; Loomis to Lovett, Apr. 19, 1914, UPN; *Congressional Record,* Apr. 22, 1914, 7600–4; Reed Smoot to Lovett, Apr. 29, 1914, UPN; W. S. McCarthy, May 2, 1914, UPN; Lovett to Smoot, May 7, 1914, UPN; Calvin to Lovett, June 3, 1914, UPN; McCarthy to Calvin, June 5, 1914, DP; NY *Times,* June 11, 1914.

62 Millar to Dodge, June 12, 1914, DP; H. W. Clark to Miles Poindexter, Feb. 29, Mar. 7, and Apr. 11, 1916, UPN; Poindexter to Clark, Mar. 2 and Apr. 7, 1916, UPN.

CHAPTER 11
THE TURNING POINT

1 Memoranda by H. W. Clark, Nov. 23, 1916, Jan. 2, 1917, UPN; Lovett to Clark, Nov. 22, 1916, UPN.

2 Martin, *Enterprise Denied,* 194–230; Vanderlip to Stillman, Feb. 11 and June 3, 1910, FAV. Vanderlip noted that Lovett and George F. Baer were the two railroad men most opposed to the Mann-Elkins Act.

3 NY *Times,* Aug. 11, 1900; Teller & Dorsey to W. R. Kelly, Mar. 14, 1901, UPL; Kelly to Burt, Mar. 19, 1901, UPL; Trumbull to Burt, Mar. 23, 1901, UPL; Kelly to Willard Teller, Mar. 25, 1901, UPL; Burt to DeForest Richards, Aug. 15, 1902, UPL; Burt to Loomis, Jan. 15, Feb. 6, and Feb. 25, 1903, UPL; C. C. Dorsey to Burt, Jan. 22, 1903, UPL; John W. Lacey to Burt, Feb. 23, 1903, UPL; LeGrand Young to Burt, Mar. 3, 1903, UPL.

4 Loomis to Burt, Mar. 12, 1903, UPL; Loomis to Kelly, Mar. 12, 1903, UPL.

5 Lacey to Burt, Mar. 3, 1903, UPL; Bancroft to Burt and Mohler, Mar. 30, 1903, UPL; John N. Baldwin to Burt, Apr. 4 and Aug. 31, 1903, UPL; Mohler to Lovett, Jan. 30, Jan. 31, Feb. 19, Mar. 15, and Apr. 22, 1913, UPN; R. W. Blair to Loomis, Jan 30, 1913, UPN; Lovett to Mohler, Mar. 24, 1913, UPN; Loomis to Mohler, May 5, 1913, UPN.

6 Remarks by Robert Mather at the National Conference on Trusts and Corporations, Oct. 23, 1907, UPN.

7 Martin, *Enterprise Denied,* 235; NY *American,* June 7, 1912; Baltimore *Sun,* Feb. 16, 1912.

8 R. C. Duff to Lovett, Jan. 30 and Apr. 17, 1912, UPN; Lovett to Duff, Apr. 24, 1912, UPN; Lovett to James A. Baker, May 6, 1912, UPN; F. S. Hastings to S. M. Swenson & Sons, May 16, 1912, UPN; *Financial America,* May 24, 1912.

9 Martin, *Enterprise Denied,* 256–57.

10 Vanderlip to Stillman, Feb. 3, 1910, FAV; Trumbull et al. to President Woodrow Wilson, Feb. 17, 1914, UPN.

11 *Chronicle,* 95:751, 1474; I. L. Sharfman, *The Interstate Commerce Commission: A Study in Administrative Law and Procedure* (New York, 1931), 1:104–11.

12 Martin, *Enterprise Denied,* 249–50.

13 NY *Times,* Mar. 31, 1912; San Francisco *Chronicle,* May 10, 1913; Martin, *Enterprise Denied,* 177; Ari and Olive Hoogenboom, *A History of the ICC: From Panacea to Palliative* (New York, 1976), 68–69; Sharfman, *Interstate Commerce Commission,* 1:117–32.

14 NY *Times*, Mar. 31, 1912; San Francisco *Chronicle*, May 10, 1913; Martin, *Enterprise Denied*, 177; Ari and Olive Hoogenboom, *ICC*, 68–69; Sharfman, *Interstate Commerce Commission*, 1:117–32.

15 M. E. Ailes to Lovett, Dec. 1, 1913, UPN; Trumbull to C. H. Markham, Feb. 14, 1914, UPN. Markham was president of the Illinois Central, which owned the road that had offended Adamson.

16 Alfred P. Thom to Lovett, June 20, 1914, UPN; NY *Times,* May 12, 1914; Paul D. Cravath to Lovett, July 24, 1914, UPN.

17 Stover, *American Railroads,* 136; Walker D. Hines to Thom, June 29, 1914, UPN; Trumbull et al. to Wilson, Feb. 17, 1914, UPN; NY *Times,* June 4, 1914; Lovett to Trumbull, Dec. 15, 1915, UPN.

18 Sharfman, *Interstate Commerce Commission,* 1:100–101; Martin, *Enterprise Denied,* 126–28; Hoogenbooms, *ICC,* 59.

19 Seth Low to Lovett, June 12, 1913, UPN; W. C. Brown to W. J. Jackson, July 7, 1913, UPN; Sharfman, *Interstate Commerce Commission,* 1:100–101.

20 C. D. Bates to Lovett et al., July 19, 1913, UPN; Martin, *Enterprise Denied,* 228; *WSJ,* Aug. 25, 1911.

21 "Shopmen's Strike," undated, UPN; *Chronicle,* 93:560–61, 591.

22 *WSJ,* Aug. 8, Aug. 22, Aug. 26, Sept. 28, and Sept. 30, 1911; NY *Times,* Aug. 8, Aug. 23, Aug. 25–28, Aug. 31, Sept. 1–3, Sept. 6, Sept. 11, Sept. 12, Sept. 16, and Sept. 29, 1911; *Chronicle,* 93:528; Lovett to Kahn and M. Schiff, Sept. 20, 1911, OK.

23 "Shopmen's Strike," undated, UPN; *WSJ,* Oct. 2, 1911, Mar. 6, 1912; Lovett to Kahn and M. Schiff, Oct. 5, 1911, OK; *Chronicle,* 93:941; NY *Times,* Oct. 11, 1911; Millar to C. C. Whinery, Dec. 6, 1912, UPN; Lovett to Mohler, Apr. 15, 1913, UPN; Lovett to Markham, Apr. 15, 1913, UPN.

24 *Chronicle,* 93:499–500.

25 Martin, *Enterprise Denied,* 320; Mohler to Lovett, Mar. 3 and Sept. 29, 1913, UPN.

26 H. G. S. Noble, *The New York Stock Exchange in the Crisis of 1914* (Garden City, N.Y., 1915), 3–13, 85.

27 Mohler to Lovett, July 28, 1914, UPN; Martin, *Enterprise Denied,* 271.

28 Lovett to Mohler, July 30, 1914, UPN.

29 Mohler to Lovett, July 30, 1914, UPN; Hugh Neill to Kruttschnitt, Aug. 3, 1914, UPN; NY *Times,* Aug. 4, 1914; Chicago *Herald,* Aug. 4, 1914.

30 ''The Railroads' Appeal to the President of the United States,'' Sept. 9, 1914, UPN; Wilson to Trumbull et al., September 10, 1914, UPN; Lovett to Kahn, Dec. 15, 1914, OK; Lovett to A. H. Harris and A. P. Thom, Dec. 19, 1914, UPN; Kahn to Lovett, Dec. 28, 1914, OK; Thom to Lovett, Apr. 27 and May 13, 1915, UPN.

31 Lovett to Harris and Thom, Dec. 19, 1914, UPN; Lovett to W. J. Moroney, Dec. 22, 1915, UPN.

32 M. E. Ailes to Lovett, Mar. 26, 1915, UPN.

33 Telephone message for Lovett, Jan. 4, 1915, UPN.

34 Martin, *Enterprise Denied,* 306–9; NY *Sun,* Dec. 1 and Dec. 8, 1915; NY *Tribune,* Dec. 6, 1915; NY *Times,* Dec. 8, 1915; NY *Press,* Dec. 8, 1915.

35 Quoted in Martin, *Enterprise Denied,* 311.

36 Ibid., 320–22; NY *Times,* Jan. 7 and Jan. 28, 1916.

37 Mohler to Lovett, Feb. 25, Mar. 8, Mar. 30 (two items), May 5, and May 17, 1916, UPN; W. S. Stone to A. L. Konold, Mar. 24, 1916, UPN; W. J. Jeffers to D. W. Smith et al., Mar. 30, 1916, UPN; Konold to Stone, May 5, 1916, UPN.

38 Lovett to Mohler, Mar. 14, 1916, UPN; Mohler to Lovett, May 17, 1916, UPN; Farrell to Lovett, June 14, 1916, UPN; Calvin to Lovett, June 14, 1916, UPN; NY *World,* June 3, 1916; NY *Times,* June 3 and June 16, 1916; Arthur S. Link, *Wilson: Campaigns for Progressivism and Peace, 1916–1917* (Princeton, 1965), 83.

39 Martin, *Enterprise Denied,* 323–24.

40 NY *Times,* Aug. 7–14, 1916.

41 W. G. Bierd to Lovett, Aug. 4, 1916, UPN; Calvin to Lovett, Aug. 7, 1916, UPN; Mohler to Lovett, May 18 and May 22, 1916, UPN.

42 NY *Times,* Aug. 15, 1916; Link, *Wilson,* 84.

43 NY *Times,* Aug. 16 and Aug. 17, 1916; Link, *Wilson,* 85; Martin, *Enterprise Denied,* 325–26.

44 Wilson to Calvin, Aug. 17, 1916, UPN; NY *Times,* Aug. 18 and Aug. 19, 1917; Link, *Wilson,* 85–86; Martin, *Enterprise Denied,* 326–27.

45 NY *Times,* Aug. 19 and Aug. 20, 1916; Link, *Wilson,* 86; Winthrop M. Daniels, *American Railroads: Four Phases of Their History* (Princeton, 1932), 84–85.

46 Daniels, *American Railroads,* 85–86.

47 NY *Times,* Aug. 20–22, 1916; Link, *Wilson,* 86–87.

48 NY *Times,* Aug. 23–28, 1916; Martin, *Enterprise Denied,* 328–29.

49 Lovett to Calvin, Aug. 26, 1916, UPN; NY *Times,* Aug. 29 and Aug. 30, 1916; Link, *Wilson,* 87–89; Martin, *Enterprise Denied,* 329–30.

50 Link, *Wilson,* 89–90.

51 NY *Times,* Sept. 1, 1916; *Literary Digest,* 53:591–92. A printed copy of Lovett's testimony is in UPN. The hearings are in Sen. Doc. 549, 64 Cong., 1st Sess.

52 NY *Times,* Sept. 1, 1916.

53 Link, *Wilson,* 90–91.

54 Chicago *Journal,* Sept. 13, 1916; Lovett to Clark, Sept. 1, 1916, UPN.

55 Link, *Wilson,* 91.

CHAPTER 12
THE TAKEOVER

1 T. M. Orr to Lovett, Jan. 23, 1916, UPN; NY *Times,* Jan. 24, 1916; Howard Bruner to ?, Jan. ?, 1916, UPN; Louis Hill to Mohler, Feb. 17, 1916, UPN; Mohler to George Kennan, Mar. 2, 1916, AF.
2 Lovett to Mohler, May 16, 1916, UPN; Mohler to Lovett, May 18 and June 20, 1916, UPN; *Chronicle,* 102:1898, 2078; NY *Times,* June 11, 1916, Mar. 18, 1938; *Church Journal,* Mar. 17, 1938, LDS.
3 Calvin to Lovett, Nov. 14, 1916 (two items), UPN.
4 *UP Report,* 1916, 8, 16. The company issued two reports in 1916, changing its fiscal year from June 30 to December 31, to conform with an ICC order. The report cited here is the one dated December 31.
5 B. L. Winchell to Lovett, Apr. 10 and July 27, 1916, UPN; Calvin to Lovett, Aug. 30, 1916, UPN; Farrell to Lovett, Aug. 30, 1916, UPN; Lovett to Calvin, Aug. 30, 1916, UPN; Calvin to Jeffers, Nov. 1, 1916, UPN; Jeffers to Calvin, Nov. 2, 1916, UPN.
6 Calvin to Lovett, Nov. 21, 1916, UPN; Lovett to Winchell, Dec. 16, 1916, UPN; *Church Journal,* Dec. 27, 1916, LDS; A. W. Stone to Lovett, Dec. 23, 1916, Jan. 8, 1917, UPN.
7 *Church Journal,* Jan. 28, Feb. 3, and Feb. 4, 1917, LDS; Cheyenne *State Leader,* Feb. 1, 1917; Calvin to Lovett, Feb. 7, 1917, UPN; Jeffers to Calvin, Apr. 25, 1917, UPN; C. B. Irwin to C. C. Stillman, Feb. 7, 1917, UPN.
8 Calvin to Lovett, Jan. 19, Apr. 20, Apr. 21, and Apr. 23, 1917, UPN; Farrell to Lovett, Jan. 18, 1917, UPN; Calvin to Farrell, Jan. 19, 1917, UPN.
9 Calvin to Winchell and Lovett, Jan. 24, 1917, UPN; Winchell to Calvin, Jan. 25, 1917, UPN; Calvin to Lovett, Jan. 25, 1917, UPN; Winchell to Lovett, Mar. 10, 1917, UPN; Lovett to Calvin and Winchell, Mar. 13, 1917, UPN; Farrell to Lovett, Mar. 21, 1917, UPN.
10 Calvin to Lovett, Apr. 14 and Apr. 27, 1917, UPN; Jeffers to Calvin, Apr. 25, 1917, UPN.
11 Martin, *Enterprise Denied,* 335–37.
12 Winchell to Fairfax Harrison, Apr. 19, 1917, UPN; Lovett to Winchell, May 3 and May 28, 1917, UPN; Winchell to Lovett, May 19 and May 25, 1917, UPN; NY *Times,* Apr. 12, 1917. Details on the War Board and its organization are in Walker D. Hines, *War History of American Railroads* (New Haven, 1928), 242–44.
13 Martin, *Enterprise Denied,* 332–35; Lovett to H. W. Clark, Oct. 31, 1916, UPN; NY *Times,* Nov. 11, 1916, Mar. 20 and Mar. 21, 1917; Lovett to J. M. Dickinson et al., Nov. 23, 1916, UPN; *Railway Age Gazette,* 61:863; Calvin to Lovett, Mar. 15, 1917, UPN.
14 Martin, *Enterprise Denied,* 337–40.
15 Blewett Lee to Lovett, May 9, 1917, UPN; "Railway Regulation and Control," Mar. 19, Mar. 21–24, and Mar. 27, 1917, UPN. These were a series of bulletins on the hearings put out each day by the Railway Executives' Advisory Committee.
16 Lovett to Mohler et al., Aug. 3, 1914, UPN; Lovett to Mohler and Calvin, Sept. 18, 1914, UPN; C. B. Seger to Lovett, Mar. 2, 1915, UPN; Lovett to Calvin, Dec. 1, 1916, UPN.
17 Martin, *Enterprise Denied,* 343–44.
18 Ibid., 345, 351.

19 Ibid., 348–49; Sharfman, *Interstate Commerce Commission,* 3B:83–95; K. Austin Kerr, *American Railroad Politics, 1914–1920* (Pittsburgh, 1968), 49–54; Winchell to Lovett, Mar. 22, 1917, UPN; NY *Times,* May 12 and May 25, 1917; *The New Republic,* 11:257.

20 NY *Times,* July 29, Aug. 21, Aug. 25, and Oct. 28, 1917, Jan. 5, 1918; Hines, *War History,* 13–14; Kerr, *Railroad Politics,* 56.

21 *WSJ,* Dec. 22, 1917; Calvin to Lovett, Apr. 27 and Sept. 25, 1917, UPN; Lovett to Calvin, Apr. 30 and Oct. 1, 1917, UPN; Farrell to Winchell, May 29, 1917, UPN; UP Exec. Comm. minutes, June 5 and Aug. 28, 1917, UPN.

22 Sharfman, *Interstate Commerce Commission,* 3B:139–53; Kerr, *Railroad Politics,* 65–71.

23 Sharfman, *Interstate Commerce Commission,* 3B:150–53; UP Exec. Comm. minutes, Dec. 31, 1917, UPN. Wilson's entire message is in Hines, *War History,* 245–49.

24 Sharfman, *Interstate Commerce Commission,* 3B:151–52; Martin, *Enterprise Denied,* 353–54.

25 *WSJ,* Dec. 17, 1917.

26 Mohler to Lovett, Aug. 14, 1915, UPN; Lovett to Mohler et al., June 28, 1916, UPN; Calvin to Lovett, July 20 and Nov. 7, 1917, UPN; *Railway Age Gazette,* 63:441, 450–51; Bond Circular, Oct. 9, 1917, UPN.

27 Organizational details are on Hines, *War History,* 23–27, 249–55.

28 Ibid., 27–29, 256–64; Kerr, *Railroad Politics,* 72–81.

29 Hines, *War History,* 25–26; Kerr, *Railroad Politics,* 81.

30 Lovett to UP Board of Directors, Mar. 4, 1918, UPN; Seger biographical sketch, UPN; Thomas Price to Calvin et al., Mar. 19, 1918, UPN; UP Directors minutes, Mar. 19, 1918, UPN; *Chronicle,* 106:1231–32, 2758, 107:83, 182; NY *Times,* Mar. 5 and July 12, 1918; Farrell to Seger, June 19, 1918, UPN; Seger to Farrell, July 20, 1918, UPN; Seger to Calvin, July 11, 1918, UPN.

31 H. A. Scandrett to Seger, July 2, 1918, UPN; J. P. O'Brien to Seger, July 2, 1918, UPN; Seger to Lovett, June 7, 1918, UPN; F. W. Sercombe to Seger, July 10, 1918, UPN; Kerr, *Railroad Politics,* 70.

32 Sharfman, *Interstate Commerce Commission,* 1:153–67; Hoogenbooms, *ICC,* 84–89; Hines, *War History,* 32–41; Kerr, *Railroad Politics,* 81–82.

33 Hines, *War History,* 193–94; NY *Times,* Jan. 10, 1918.

34 Hines, *War History,* 30–38.

35 Farrell to Lovett, Jan. 2 and Jan. 5, 1918, UPN; Sproule to Winchell, Jan. 2, 1918, UPN; Winchell to Lovett, Jan. 9, Jan. 19, and Jan. 28, 1918, UPN; Winchell to Calvin, Jan. 10, 1918, UPN; Calvin to Winchell, Jan. 10, 1918, UPN; George B. Agnew to McAdoo, Jan. 17, 1918, UPN; Lovett to Winchell, Jan. 23 and Jan. 25, 1918, UPN.

36 Seger to G. E. Bissonnet, June 20, 1918, UPN; Lovett to Seger, Oct. 18, 1918, UPN; Hines, *War History,* 42.

37 Gray speech, "Proceedings of the St. Louis Railway Club," May 9, 1919, UPN; Hines, *War History,* 40.

38 *Railway Age,* 65:1015–16; *Chronicle,* 107:2189; H. W. Clark to Kahn, Dec. 13, 1918, OK; Price to C. M. Secrist, Feb. 24, 1919, UPN. Seger remained on the board and the executive committee.

39 Hines, *War History,* 42–45.

40 Sharfman, *Interstate Commerce Commission,* 1:170–76; I. L. Sharfman, *The Ameri-*

can Railroad Problem (New York, 1921), 357–74; NY *Times,* Oct. 19, 1919; Daniel Willard to Vanderlip, Dec. 4, 1918, FAV; Thomas Price to Vanderlip, Dec. 17, 1918, FAV; Paul M. Warburg to Vanderlip, Jan. 7, 1919, FAV.

41 Lovett to McAdoo, undated but Nov. or Dec. 1918, UPN; Lovett, "Governmental Railroad Policy," Jan. 1, 1919, UPN. The italics are all in the original.

42 Howard Elliott to Lovett, Dec. 14, 1918, UPN; Robert P. Binkerd to Seger, Jan. 8, 1919, UPN; "Principles which should be incorporated in a plan providing for government regulation of carriers engaged in interstate commerce," Jan. 5, 1919, UPN. This document was the final draft of the Philadelphia plan.

43 Trumbull to T. D. Cuyler, Jan. 2, 1919, FAV; Trumbull to Vanderlip, Jan. 6, 1919, FAV; Trumbull to Lovett, Jan. 20, 1919, UPN.

44 Kerr, *Railroad Politics,* 141–42; NY *Times,* Jan. 26, 1919.

45 Albert B. Cummins, "What Shall We Do with the Railroads?", *Review of Reviews,* 60:61–66; Kerr, *Railroad Politics,* 149–56; "Proposed Solutions of the Railroad Problem," Mar. 1919, UPN. This latter document was a flyer distributed by Equitable Trust Company comparing the position of seven plans on nine major questions.

46 Kerr, *Railroad Politics,* 160–92; Sharfman, *Interstate Commerce Commission,* 1:171.

47 Lovett to R. C. Duff, Aug. 14, 1919, UPN; Lovett to Alfred P. Thom, Aug. 15, 1919, UPN. The Warfield plan is described in the Equitable flyer mentioned above and in Kerr, *Railroad Politics,* 156–59.

48 Lovett to Alfred P. Thom, Aug. 15, 1919, UPN; Chicago *Tribune,* Aug. 13, 1919. For the Red Scare see Robert K. Murray, *Red Scare: A Study in National Hysteria, 1919–1920* (Minneapolis, 1955).

49 Lovett to Thom, May 12, 1919, UPN; Schiff to Lovett, June 25 and June 30, 1919, UPN, July 15, 1919, AJA; UP Exec. Comm. minutes, July 1, 1919, UPN; Lovett to Kahn, June 30, 1919, UPN; NY *Times,* July 13–15, 1919; *WSJ,* July 14, 1919; Lovett to Trumbull, July 15, 1919, UPN; Burnett Walker to Lovett, July 15, 1919, UPN; John J. Esch to Lovett, July 16, 1919, UPN; Kerr, *Railroad Politics,* 164–74. The pamphlet is reprinted in *Railway Age,* 67:173–75, 197–202; a list of its distribution is in UPN.

50 *Railway Age,* 67:173–75, 197–202, 415–17. The latter pages excerpt Lovett's testimony before the House committee.

51 Ibid., 67:202; Lovett to L. W. Hill, Aug. 30, 1919, UPN; Mortimer Schiff to S. Davies Warfield, Sept. 2, 1919, UPN; Lovett to Thom et al., Sept. 4, 1919, UPN; Warfield to M. Schiff, Sept. 6, 1919, UPN; Warfield to Cummins, Sept. 8, 1919, UPN; Lovett to M. Schiff, Sept. 10, 1919, UPN; Warfield circular, Sept. 12, 1919, UPN; Carl Gray to Lovett, Sept. 18, 1919, UPN.

52 *Railway Age,* 67:201–2; NY *Sun,* July 28, 1919.

53 Trumbull to Lovett, Sept. 16, 1919, UPN.

54 Kerr, *Railroad Politics,* 206–7; NY *Times,* Oct. 24 and Nov. 9, 1919.

55 Thom to Charles Hayden, Oct. 2, 1919, UPN; NY *Times,* Sept. 3, Sept. 10, Sept. 11, Sept. 14, Sept. 24, and Nov. 9, 1919.

56 Hines, *War History,* 48–56.

57 Ibid., 170–210

58 Lovett to Trumbull, Nov. 28, 1919, UPN; Los Angeles *Times,* Dec. 11, 1919; *WSJ,* Dec. 11, 1919; NY *Times,* Dec. 11, 1919.

59 NY *Times,* Nov. 10–18, Nov. 24, Dec. 1–20, 1919; *WSJ,* Nov. 13, 1919; Los Angeles *Times,* Dec. 11, 1919; Fresno *Republican,* Dec. 11, 1919; *Journal of Commerce,* Dec. 11, 1919; Kerr, *Railroad Politics,* 207–11. For more detail on the bills see Sharfman, *Railroad Problem,* 382–90.

60 UP Exec. Comm. minutes, Jan. 6, 1920, UPN; McAdoo to Lovett, Dec. 15, 1919, UPN; Lovett to New York World Editor, Dec. 19, 1919, UPN; NY *World,* Dec. 22 and Dec. 24, 1919; NY *Times,* Dec. 21, 1919.

61 Sharfman, *Railroad Problem,* 390–92.

62 Ibid., 392–97.

63 Kerr, *Railroad Politics,* 213–17; Thom to Lovett, Feb. 9, 1920, UPN; NY *Times,* Dec. 27–30, 1919, Jan. 8–10, Jan. 21–23, and Jan. 26–30, 1920; *Railway Age,* 68:4–6, 184, 291–92; *WSJ,* Jan. 8, Jan. 13, Jan. 15, Jan. 19, and Jan. 21, 1920.

64 *Railway Age,* 68:357, 435–38, 490, 518–19, 619–27; NY *Times,* Feb. 4–6, Feb. 13, Feb. 16–25, Feb. 28, Feb. 29, and March 1–4, 1920; *WSJ,* Feb. 7, Feb. 12, and Feb. 18–20, 1920. This discussion of the 1920 Act is drawn from Sharfman, *Railroad Problem,* 397–431; Sharfman, *Interstate Commerce Commission,* 1:177–244; Kerr, *Railroad Politics,* 217–27; Hoogenbooms, *ICC,* 94–97.

65 NY *Times,* Feb. 24, 1920; Alfred P. Thom, "Report on The Railroad Bill as Agreed upon in Conference," Feb. 21, 1920, 20, UPN. This lengthy analysis is a useful comparison of what the ARE wanted and what the bill provided.

66 Kerr, *Railroad Politics,* 225; Sharfman, *Railroad Problem,* 383.

67 Lovett to A. B. Johnson, Feb. 23, 1920, UPN; NY *Times,* Mar. 9, Apr. 28, and July 15, 1920; draft of Lovett statement on the new act, undated, UPN.

CHAPTER 13
THE FRESH START

1 Thomas D. Cuyler to Lovett, June 1, 1920, UPN; Thom to Lovett, June 1, 1920, UPN; Lovett to Thom, June 4, 1920, UPN; John Barton Payne to Lovett, June 5, 1920, UPN; Lovett to Payne, June 10, 1920, UPN.

2 Hines to R. H. Aishton et al., May 27, 1919, UPN; H. W. Clark memorandum, June 18, 1919, UPN; F. W. Charske memorandum, June 18, 1919, UPN; W. T. Tyler to Lovett, June 18, 1919, UPN; Lovett to Tyler, June 23, 1919, UPN; C. R. Gray to Lovett, Jan. 24, 1920, UPN; Hines, *War History,* 108–20.

3 Lovett to Gray, July 26 and Dec. 1, 1920, UPN; Gray to Lovett, Oct. 2 and Dec. 3, 1920, UPN; C. E. Mitchell to Lovett, June 28, 1921, UPN; Gray to Lovett, June 29, 1921, UPN; Lovett to Gray, June 30, 1921, UPN.

4 James C. Davis to Lovett, Oct. 10, 1921, UPN; Lovett to Davis, Oct. 11, 1921, UPN; Hines, *War History,* 115.

5 Julius Kruttschnitt, "Railroad Efficiency: Past and Present," *Atlantic Monthly,* 129:106–9.

6 Ibid., 115.

7 W. S. V. Thorne to Lovett, Feb. 4, Feb. 13, and Feb. 19, 1913, UPN; Lovett to Thorne, Feb. 14, 1913, UPN.

8 Lovett memorandum, Apr. 11, 1914, UPN; Lovett to Mohler and Farrell, Apr. 29, 1914, UPN; Lovett to Thorne, May 5, 1914, UPN; W. A. Harriman to C. C. Stillman, May 21, 1914, UPN.

9 Lovett memorandum, May 29, 1914, UPN; NY *Times,* June 24, 1914; *Chronicle,* 98:1995; C. P. Parker to W. A. Harriman, Aug. 11, 1915, UPN; Harriman to Lovett, Aug. 24, 1915, UPN; Lovett to Mohler, Dec. 23, 1915, UPN; Mohler to Lovett, Apr. 7, 1916, UPN; Lovett to Gray, Jan. 2, 1920, UPN.

10 Lovett to Bancroft, Jan. 15, 1914, UPN; Mohler to Bancroft, Jan. 21, 1914, UPN;

Bancroft to Lovett, Jan. 24, 1914, UPN; Hughitt to Seger, Mar. 25, 1918, UPN; Seger to Lovett, Mar. 26, 1918, UPN; UP Directors minutes, Apr. 11, 1918, UPN; *Chronicle,* 106:1462, 1578, 111:2326; Seger to Marvin Hughitt, Jr., May 13, 1918, UPN; UP Exec. Comm. minutes, Sept. 9, 1919, UPN; NY *Times,* Dec. 10, 1920.

11 Seger to Farrell, Dec. 20, 1918, UPN; Lovett to F. W. Sercombe, Aug. 7, 1919, UPN.

12 NY *Times,* July 12, 1918; *Chronicle,* 107:182; interview with George J. Proudfit, Sept. 5, 1982.

13 *DAB,* supp. 2, 22:260–61; *NCAB,* 36:20–21; Hines, *War History,* 179; "Proceedings of the St. Louis Railway Club," May 9, 1919, 30, UPN.

14 *DAB,* supp. 2, 22:260–61; *American Magazine,* 99:171; *Railway Age Gazette,* 52:1058; *Railway Age,* 106:827–28.

15 Hines, *War History,* 163; Eugene McAuliffe, *Some Memories of Mr. Carl R. Gray* (privately printed, 1939).

16 Terese White to W. M. Jeffers, Oct. 25, 1933, UPO; Gray to W. F. Truelsen, Nov. 1, 1933, UPO.

17 Seger to Charske, July 16, 1918, UPN; Seger to Calvin, July 18, 1918, UPN; Charske to Seger, July 18, 1918, UPN; UP Exec. Comm. minutes, Sept. 9, 1919, UPN; *Chronicle,* 109:1081, 2264, 110:972; Lovett to Calvin, Dec. 6, 1919, UPN; NY *Times,* Nov. 20, 1919; *Railway Age,* 68:751; *UP Report,* 1920, 3–4.

18 *UP Report,* 1911, 8, 1921, 15; *Chronicle,* 91:1447, 1513, 1768–69, 112:2307, 113:417; *WSJ,* Nov. 26, 1910; *Railway Age Gazette,* 50:63; Lovett to H. A. Scandrett, May 23, 1921, UPO; *Church Journal,* May 24, 1921, LDS; Lovett to Gray, May 25 and July 11, 1921, UPO; Gray to Lovett, July 16, 1921, UPO; NY *Times,* May 26 and July 18, 1921; *WSJ,* May 26 and May 27, 1921; *Railway Age,* 70:1249, 1297; *Chronicle,* 112:2307.

19 259 U.S. 907–22; *Railway Age,* 73:891–92.

20 76 ICC 510–11; Hofsommer, *Southern Pacific,* 84.

21 A. S. Halsted to Gray, June 6, 1922, UPO; *Railway Age,* 73:1154; Hofsommer, *Southern Pacific,* 82–88.

22 Gray to Lovett, June 27, July 2, and Oct. 4, 1922, UPO.

23 Conference memorandum, Sept. 30, 1922, UPO; Gray to Lovett, Oct. 13, 1922, UPO; Lovett to Gray, June 9 and Oct. 30, 1922, UPO; NY *Times,* June 12, 1922; Lovett to L. W. Meyer, Oct. 30, 1922, UPO; *Railway Age,* 73:1153–55. Hofsommer, *Southern Pacific,* 82–83, claims that Gray "strained credulity" in asking only for independence, and that his "veracity returned" when he stated that the Union Pacific would be willing to take the Central Pacific. The evidence is solid that Lovett and Gray were sincere in this desire.

24 *WSJ,* Oct. 19 and Nov. 23, 1922; NY *Times,* Oct. 28 and Nov. 23, 1922; *Railway Age,* 73:797–98, 891–92, 960, 987–90; Gray to Lovett, Nov. 22, 1922, UPO.

25 NY *Times,* Dec. 9, 1922; *WSJ,* Dec. 9, 1922; *Railway Age,* 73:1151–54.

26 Lovett to Gray, Dec. 16, 1922, UPO.

27 H. W. Clark to Gray, Dec. 27, 1922, UPO; *Railway Age,* 73:1151; Gray to Lovett, Jan. 3, 1923, UPO; Lovett to Hale Holden, Jan. 27, 1923, UPN.

28 Gray to Lovett, Jan. 3, 1923, UPO; Lovett to Gray, Jan. 6 and Jan. 10, 1923, UPO.

29 Lovett to Gray, Jan. 10 and Jan. 11, 1923, UPO; Lovett to H. W. Clark, Jan. 4, 1923, UPO; Paul Rigdon to Gray, Jan. 6, 1923, UPO; Clark to Lovett, Jan. 20, 1923, UPO.

30 *WSJ,* Jan. 15, 1923; Omaha *Bee,* Jan. 17, 1923; *Railway Age,* 74:234, 279–80,

427–30, 471–72, 1382–84, 1490; *Chronicle,* 116:685–87; Gray to Lovett, Jan. 24, 1923, UPO. For details on the decision see 76 ICC 508–31.

31 Sharfman, *Interstate Commerce Commission,* 4:53–54, 70–86; Hoogenbooms, *ICC,* 81–82, 98–99.

32 NY *Sun,* July 28, 1919; Sharfman, *Interstate Commerce Commission,* 4:65–69, 292–96; Hoogenbooms, *ICC,* 99.

33 Sharfman, *Interstate Commerce Commission,* 3B:99–102.

34 Ibid., 3B:102–13.

35 Ibid., 3B:113–34; Hoogenbooms, *ICC,* 101–2; *UP Report,* 1920, 15, 1921, 6; Alfred P. Thom to Executives and General Counsel of Member Roads, Nov. 17, 1921, UPN.

36 Sharfman, *Interstate Commerce Commission,* 3B:130–31; NY *Times,* Nov. 4, 1921, Dec. 25, 1922; *UP Report,* 1921, 6, 1922, 8–9.

37 Sharfman, *Interstate Commerce Commission,* 3B:132, 134–61; Hoogenbooms, *ICC,* 102–3; *Railway Age,* 80:1480–81.

38 Lovett to Ivy L. Lee, Jan. 25, 1933, UPN.

39 Gray to Homer Hoch, Nov. 3, 1926, UPN; Sharfman, *Interstate Commerce Commission,* 3B:221–55; Hoogenbooms, *ICC,* 104–5.

40 Hoogenbooms, *ICC,* 105; Sharfman, *Interstate Commerce Commission,* 3A:430–74.

41 63 ICC 455–64; *World's Work,* 42:335–40; *WSJ,* July 29, 1921.

42 *WSJ,* Jan. 23, 1923; *Railway Age,* 74:269–72; M. Schiff to Kahn, Feb. 20, 1923, OK; M. Schiff to Lovett, Feb. 19, 1923, OK; Overton, *Burlington Route,* 324–29.

43 159 ICC 522–89; Sharfman, *Interstate Commerce Commission,* 3A:475–501; Hoogenbooms, *ICC,* 106–8; Gray to Lovett, Feb. 24, 1927, UPO; *WSJ,* Dec. 23, 1929; *Railway Age,* 87:1469–76.

44 Overton, *Burlington Route,* 329–36.

45 Sharfman, *Interstate Commerce Commission,* 3A:127.

46 Ibid., 3A:121–37; 169 U.S. 466.

47 Sharfman, *Interstate Commerce Commission,* 3A:127–28; *WSJ,* Dec. 5, 1919. For the depreciation fight see Charske memorandum, Nov. 14, 1923, UPN; Lovett to Scandrett, Nov. 16, 1923, Apr. 10, 1924, Feb. 26, 1927, UPN; NY *Commercial,* Nov. 30, 1923; Lovett to W. G. Brantley, Mar. 10, 1927, UPN; Memorandum, Apr. 4, 1927, UPN; Lovett to F. W. Charske, Jan. 13, 1928, UPN; Charske to Leslie Craven, Dec. 18, 1929, UPN; *WSJ,* Dec. 23, 1929.

48 Scandrett to Lovett, Mar. 15, 1920, UPN; Clark to Lovett, Mar. 20, 1920, UPN; Sharfman, *Interstate Commerce Commission,* 3A:246–47. The ICC issued its first "single-sum" value report in 1922 but in summary form. The Los Angeles & Salt Lake was the first road given a figure or single-sum value with a full report.

49 Lovett to Scandrett, May 23, 1921, UPO; *Chronicle,* 113:1360; NY *Times,* Sept. 13, 1923; Scandrett to Lovett, Sept. 15, 1923, UPO; *Railway Age,* 75:489–94, 508, 797–99.

50 *UP Report,* 1926, 8; NY *Times,* Dec. 28, 1923, Feb. 19, July 24, and Dec. 15, 1925, Nov. 19 and Dec. 23, 1926, Jan. 5, 1927; *Chronicle,* 121:583, 2873, 123:204, 124:1216; *Railway Age,* 80:998–99, 81:1220–21, 82:189–91, 580–82; Lovett to Gray, Feb. 28, 1927, UPO.

51 Gray to Lovett, Mar. 1, 1927, UPO; *Railway Age,* 82:638.

52 *Railway Age,* 68:1089, 1677.

53 Gray to Lovett, Jan. 30, 1923, UPN.

54 Lovett to Gray, Feb. 3, 1923, UPN; Lovett to T. H. Price, Feb. 21, 1923, UPN; Price to Lovett, Mar. 5, 1923, UPN; Ivy Lee to Lovett, Jan. 30, 1923, UPN.

55 *Chronicle,* 114:12–13; *Railway Age,* 72:1339–40; Lovett to Gray, Feb. 3, 1923, UPN.

56 NY *Times,* May 10–13, 1921; *Weekly Review,* 4:553–54; Lovett to Alfred P. Thom, June 24, 1925, UPN.

57 Lovett to Thom, June 24, 1925, UPN; Markham to Lovett, Apr. 27, 1923, UPN.

58 Lovett to A. H. Smith, Apr. 6, 1922, UPN; Charske memorandum, Mar. 10, 1921, UPO.

59 Markham to Lovett, Apr. 13 and Oct. 16, 1922, UPN; W. R. Cole to Lovett, Apr. 22, 1922, UPN; Lovett to Cole, Apr. 24, 1922; UPN; Thom to Lovett, May 4, 1922, UPN; Lovett to Cuyler, Aug. 4, 1922, UPN; Lovett to Markham, Oct. 19 and Oct. 20, 1922, UPN; Felton to Lovett, Oct. 26, 1922, UPN; Lovett to Felton, Oct. 30, 1922, UPN.

60 Lovett to Mrs. T. DeWitt Cuyler, Nov. 2, 1923, UPN; NY *Tribune,* Nov. 5, 1922; ''In Memoriam Thomas DeWitt Cuyler,'' Nov. 9, 1922, UPO; *Railway Age,* 74:856–58; undated resolutions redefining ARE, 1922, UPO.

CHAPTER 14
THE NEW COMPETITION

1 C. Pustau to Lovett, July 29, 1919, UPN.

2 Lovett to Pustau, July 30, 1919, UPN.

3 Gray to Seger, May 9, 1931, UPN.

4 Charles F. Kettering and Allen Orth, *The New Necessity* (Baltimore, 1932), 25, 28.

5 *WSJ,* Mar. 18 and Oct. 26, 1912; Mohler to Lovett, June 18 and Dec. 30, 1914, UPN; B. L. Winchell to Lovett, Nov. 12, 1914, UPN; Hughitt to Lovett, Sept. 17, 1914, UPN.

6 W. W. Cotton to J. D. Farrell, Dec. 13, 1913, Jan. 2, 1914, UPN; NY *Times,* Feb. 18 and Mar. 4, 1914, Feb. 14, 1915, May 12, 1921; R. B. Miller to Winchell, July 28, 1914, UPN; Winchell to Lovett, Nov. 12, 1914, UPN; *Chronicle,* 100:1673; Miller to Farrell, Sept. 18, 1915, UPN.

7 Lovett to Gray, Sept. 29, 1921, with enclosed report, UPN.

8 Ibid.

9 Ibid.; Association of Railway Executives, ''Declaration of Policy Deemed Necessary to the Continuance of Adequate Transportation Service to the Public,'' Nov. 20, 1930, 2–3, UPN; *Historical Statistics,* 2:764.

10 *Historical Statistics,* 2:722; ''Railroads and Pipe Lines,'' undated but probably 1931, 11–14, UPO.

11 ''Railroads and Pipe Lines,'' 18–19; ''Declaration of Policy,'' 3.

12 James J. Flink, *The Car Culture* (Cambridge,. Mass., 1975), 141; *Historical Statistics,* 716; John B. Rae, *The Road and the Car in American Life* (Cambridge, Mass., 1971), 50; Robert S. Lynd and Helen Merrell Lynd, *Middletown* (New York, 1929), 253.

13 Rae, *Road and Car,* 44–48; Flink, *Car Culture,* 141–42.

14 Lynds, *Middletown,* 119, 253, 255; Flink, *Car Culture,* 145.

15 *Historical Statistics,* 2:729; Rae, *Road and Car,* 88–94.

16 Rae, *Road and Car,* 97.

17 William R. Childs, *Trucking and the Public Interest: The Emergence of Federal Regulation 1914–1940* (Knoxville, 1985), 7–8.
18 Ibid., 8–24; Rae, *Road and Car,* 114.
19 Childs, *Trucking and the Public Interest,* 19–20; *Historical Statistics,* 2:716; Rae, *Road and Car,* 114.
20 *Historical Statistics,* 2:711; Rae, *Road and Car,* 65–68; Childs, *Trucking and the Public Interest,* 14.
21 UP Exec. Comm. minutes, May 20, 1919, UPN; UP Finance Comm. minutes, Nov. 15, 1927, UPN; Clark to F. W. Charske, undated memoradum, UPN; Gray to Charske, Nov. 11, 1927, UPN; Thomas Price to Gray, Nov. 17, 1927, UPN.
22 *Historical Statistics,* 2:711; Flink, *Car Culture,* 149–50.
23 "Declaration of Policy," 3–4, 7–9.
24 Ibid., 4–6; *Historical Statistics,* 2:729–35.
25 *UP Report,* 1929, 12: *Railway Age,* 80:888, 81:839, 82:627–29, 91:297.
26 *Railway Age,* 80:509, 918–19, 81:839–40; NY *Times,* Oct. 26, 1926.
27 *Railway Age,* 82:325, 336, 83:171, 176, 84:506, 1007–11, 1489, 85:397–98, 1067, 86:1002, 1263, 1542.
28 Interview with Francis J. Melia, Nov. 16, 1981, 44–46.
29 Ibid., 46; *Railway Age,* 90:464.
30 Melia interview, 46–47; *Railway Age,* 87:125, 317, 90:461, 464; NY *Times,* July 14, 1929.
31 NY *Times,* Aug. 16, 1929; *Railway Age,* 87:520, 799–800, 1031–32, 1261, 1532, 90:464, 91:296–97; *UP Report,* 1919, 12.
32 *Deseret News,* July 31, 1929; *Railway Age,* 87:322, 1534, 88:534, 1298, 1544, 89:212, 421, 91:296–98; *WSJ,* Mar. 22 and May 8, 1930; UP Exec. Comm. minutes, July 8, 1930. UPN.
33 *Railway Age,* 87:1035, 88:174, 276, 301–3, 89:422, 92:375.
34 Ibid., 88:1539, 90:464; NY *Times,* July 14, 1929.
35 *Railway Age,* 90:778, 1214, 97:833–35; NY *Times,* May 31, 1931; *Chronicle,* 137:2271.
36 "Competitive Conditions as Related to the Express Rate Situation," Sept. 24, 1929, 1–3, UPN.
37 *Railway Age,* 88:277; E. G. Buckland to Elisha Lee, May 24, 1932, UPO.
38 *WSJ,* Sept. 22, 1909; NY *Times,* Sept. 26, 1909; *Railway Age Gazette,* 47:599, 895, 48:210, 213, 919, 49:600, 887–88, 51:65, 105, 304, 1149–50, 1259, 52:701, 1140, 1589, 53:229, 492, 1163, 55:170, H. J. Stirling to Seger, July 27, 1912, UPO.
39 *UP Report,* 1924, 13, 1927, 12; *Railway Age,* 69:418, 951, 70:261, 75:1085, 80:1416, 81:530, 83:232, 84:260–61; *Chronicle,* 111:2230, 116:78, 118:909, 122:346, 1307, 2945, 123:1995, 126:712, 127:1804; *Union Pacific Magazine,* Jan. 1922, 27; Gray to Lovett, Nov. 24, 1923, Feb. 19, 1924, UPN; *WSJ,* July 11, 1925, Nov. 29, 1926, NY *Times,* Aug. 18, 1927, Jan. 28, 1928.
40 *UP Report,* 1923, 15, 1929, 12, 1930, 12; *Chronicle,* 114:2116, 117:88, 325, 440, 118:432; *Railway Age,* 75:135, 180, 320, 76:1392, 88:178; NY *Times,* May 8, 1924, Apr. 12, 1929; *WSJ,* Oct. 27, 1925.
41 Portland *Journal,* Oct. 26, 1923; *Railway Age,* 83:628.
42 *Railway Age,* 87:1411–12. For the depot case see ibid., 70:1140.
43 *Railway Age,* 88:1392–93, 89:768, 90:162, 208, 90:338–39, 1159, 92:927, 94:44–45; *Chronicle,* 130:4602, 132:846, 1027, 136:199, 325; NY *Times,* Jan. 30, 1931.
44 Gray to Lovett, July 16, 1921, UPO; NY *Times,* July 18, 1921; *Railway Age,* 71:185, 646, 739.

45 *Railway Age,* 73:1213, 74:167, 75:497, 803–6, 81:886–88.

46 Los Angeles *Herald,* Aug. 5, 1924; Los Angeles *Examiner,* Mar. 22, 1925; Gray memorandum, Oct. 19, 1925, UPO; A. S. Halsted to Gray, Feb. 19, 1932, UPO; Gray to R. H. Aishton, Apr. 21, 1932, UPO; NY *Times,* Apr. 22, 1932; *Railway Age,* 92:750; *UP Report,* 1932, 12.

47 *Chronicle,* 115:308, 1942; *Railway Age,* 73:134, 401, 821, 74:299; *Union Pacific Magazine,* May 1922, 14–15.

48 NY *Times,* Jan. 1, 1929; *Railway Age,* 89:302–3; *Chronicle,* 131:932, 1418, 132:4755; *UP Report,* 1930, 12.

49 *Railway Age,* 82:437, 86:849–50, 868, 90:187, 256; *Chronicle,* 132:653.

50 *Railway Age,* 89:1241, 1048, 1050, 91:610; NY *Times,* Sept. 17, 1933.

51 Los Angeles *Times,* Sept. 12, 1933; *Railway Age,* 95:480, 576, 97:184, 106:768–78, 786; *UP Report,* 1939, 20.

52 NY *Times,* Mar. 7 and May 7, 1912; *Chronicle,* 94:700; Mohler to Lovett, May 3, 1913, UPN.

53 J. E. Gorman to Gray, Aug. 27 and Sept. 9, 1921, UPO; Gray to Gorman, Aug. 31, 1921, UPO.

54 Lovett memorandum, May 1, 1923, UPN; Gray to H. M. Adams, May 15, 1923, UPN.

55 Ogden *Examiner,* Jan. 5, 1914; W. H. Bancroft to Mohler, Jan. 7, 1914, UPN; Calvin to Mohler, May 25, 1914, UPN; Bancroft to W. A. Clark, June 26, 1914, UPN; Calvin to Lovett and Mohler, Jan. 30, 1915, UPN; Mohler to Lovett, Feb. 2, 1915, UPN; Calvin to Lovett, May 4, 1916, UPN; Gray memorandum, Jan. 18, 1927, UPN.

56 Stover, *American Railroads,* 221–22; Gray to Lovett, July 23, 1929, UPN.

57 Gray to Lovett, Mar. 30, 1928, UPO, July 23, 1929, UPN; Lovett to Gray, Feb. 10, 1931, UPO; Bryant, *Atchison,* 254–58.

58 Seger to Lovett, Aug. 1 and Sep. 11, 1930, UPN; Dow, Jones bulletin, Aug. 6, 1930, UPN; Paul Shoup to Seger, Aug. 12, 1930, UPN; Lovett to Seger, Sept. 9, 1930, UPN; UP Exec. Comm. minutes, Sept. 23, 1930, UPN; Gray to Lovett, May 21 and June 4, 1931, UPN; H. W. Clark to Lovett, Feb. 2, 1932, UPN; Hofsommer, *Southern Pacific,* 187–88.

59 Gray to Lovett, Jan. 30, 1930, Jan. 25 and Feb. 28, 1931, UPO; Lovett to Gray, Jan. 24, 1930, Feb. 10, 1931, UPO; F. W. Robinson to Gray, Dec. 9, 1933, UPO; Gray to Robinson, Dec. 16, 1933, UPO; Hunter L. Gary to Gray, Dec. 28, 1929, UPO.

60 *WSJ,* Sept. 10, 1925; Athearn, *Rio Grande Western,* 160–61, 174–75, 201; M. F. Leech to E. Dickinson, June 19, 1902, UPL; NY *Times,* June 22, 1902.

61 Ibid., 201, 214; George B. Harris to J. J. Hill, Dec. 1, 1902, JJH; Denver *Post,* Feb. 13, 1903; Lovett to C. C. Dorsey, Feb. 27, 1919, UPN.

62 Athearn, *Rio Grande Western,* 204–5; Perkins to Hill, Jan. 10, 1903, JJH; Moffat to Hill, Apr. 1, 1904, JJH; Moffat to George F. Baker, Apr. 1, 1904, JJH; Harris to Hill, May 2, 1904, JJH.

63 Lovett to Gray, Oct. 21, 1920, UPO; W. D. Cornish to Burt, Nov. 5, 1903, UPL.

64 Mohler to Kruttschnitt, June 26, 1911, UPO; C. C. Dorsey to Mohler, June 28, 1911, UPO.

65 Lovett to Gray, Oct. 21, 1920, UPO; Lovett to Kahn, Oct. 12, 1911, OK.

66 Athearn, *Rio Grande Western,* 257–73.

67 Ibid., 274–75; Lovett to Dorsey, Feb. 27, 1919, UPN; Lovett to Gray, Oct. 21, 1920, UPO; Gray to Lovett, Nov. 3, 1920, UPN; Loomis to Gray, Feb 6, 1922, UPO; Gray to L. J. Spence, Jan. 26, 1925, UPO.

68 *WSJ*, Sept. 10, 1925; Gray to Blodgett & Co., July 23, 1925, UPO.
69 Gray to Lovett, Feb. 10, 1927, UPN; Lovett to Gray, Feb. 12, 1927, UPN; NY *World*, Mar. 12, 1927.
70 Gray to Lovett, Mar. 14, 1927, Nov. 1, 1928, UPN; Lovett to Gray, Mar. 18, 1927, UPO; *WSJ*, May 7, 1927.
71 Charske memorandum, Aug. 2, 1928; UPN; Gray to Lovett, Nov. 1, 1928, UPN, Jan. 3 and Feb. 19, 1930, UPO; W. H. Paul to Gray, Feb. 19, 1930, UPO. Details on the legal fight are in Athearn, *Rio Grande Western*, 276–92.
72 Athearn, *Rio Grande Western*, 292–310.

CHAPTER 15
THE COUNTERATTACK

1 *Barron's*, July 7, 1924.
2 *UP Report*, 1923, 15–16; UP Board minutes, Oct. 11, 1923, UPN; Press statement, Oct. 11, 1923, UPN; Lovett to Vanderlip, Feb. 12, 1923, FAV; NY *Evening Post*, Oct. 11, 1923.
3 Lovett to Board of Directors, Oct. 11, 1923, UPN; NY *Times*, Oct. 12, 1923; *WSJ*, Oct. 12, 1923; NY *Herald*, Oct. 12, 1923; NY *World*, Oct. 12, 1923; NY *Tribune*, Oct. 12, 1923; *Chronicle*, 117:1665; *Railway Age*, 75:716.
4 NY *Times*, Jan. 4 and Aug. 20, 1924; UP Finance Comm. minutes, Aug. 12, 1924, UPN; *Wall Street News*, Aug. 22, 1924; *Railway Age*, 77:351; *Chronicle*, 119:943; Seger profile, UPN. Seger remained president and chairman of U. S. Rubber until January 1929.
5 Lovett to Vanderlip, Jan. 14, 1921, FAV; NY *Times*, Dec. 2, 1921, Apr. 13, 1922; *Railway Age*, 71:1176, 72:946; Morti Schiff to Lovett, Mar. 3, 1922, UPN; *Chronicle*, 114:1653, 116:1651; Peabody to Vanderlip, Apr. 8, 1924, FAV; UP Finance Comm. minutes, Apr. 8, 1924, UPN; Kahn to Morti Schiff, Aug. 21, 1924, OK.
6 NY *Times*, Apr. 12, 1923; Price to Lovett, Apr. 6, 1926, UPN; *Chronicle*, 122:2188; *WSJ*, Oct. 12, 1923.
7 Lovett to Gray, Apr. 12, 1924, UPO; Lovett to Clark, Apr. 22, 1924, UPO; Lovett memorandum, Apr. 23, 1924, UPO.
8 Gray to Lovett, May 9, 1924, UPO.
9 Lovett memorandum, Apr. 23, 1924, UPO; 207 ICC 543; NY *Times*, Mar. 1, 1932.
10 Gray to Seger, Dec. 21, 1929, UPN.
11 *WSJ*, Nov. 24 and Dec. 11, 1919, Jan. 16, Apr. 28, July 26, Aug. 18, and Oct. 8, 1920; NY *Times*, Apr. 28, 1920.
12 *WSJ*, June 27, 1921. Stock prices are taken from January issues of *Chronicle* for each year.
13 Ibid., Mar. 5, 1921, June 14, Sept. 7, and Sept. 8, 1923; *Chronicle*, 117:1018, 1130; NY *Times*, Sept. 7, 1923. The comparative figures are computed from data taken from company annual reports and *Historical Statistics*, 2:736.
14 NY *Times*, Mar. 27, 1927. Operating ratio averages are computed from data taken from annual reports and *Historical Statistics*, 2:736.
15 *WSJ*, Aug. 25, 1911.
16 Ibid., Aug. 2, 1910, Aug. 19 and Nov. 23, 1911, Jan. 9, 1918, Jan. 19, 1919; NY *Times*, Nov. 25, 1911; Seger to Lovett, Mar. 2, 1915, UPN; UP Exec. Comm.

minutes, May 4 and Oct. 26, 1920, Nov. 9, 1921, UPN; *Railway Age,* 65:569, 71:150–51.

17 *Railway Age,* 71:150, 76:991–93; *WSJ,* June 21 and Dec. 18, 1923, Aug. 5 and Aug. 19, 1924, May 2, 1925, June 2, 1926, Aug. 12, 1927; *Magazine of Wall Street,* 40:1118–19, 1158–61; *Chronicle,* 3:28–29 (1930). The investment income is computed from company annual reports.

18 *Railway Age,* 71:151; UP Exec. Comm. minutes, Nov. 28, 1922, Mar. 13, 1923, UPN; UP Finance Comm. minutes, May 12, 1925, UPN; *Barron's,* May 15, 1933, 7.

19 *Historical Statistics,* 2:732; *Chronicle,* 136:1011.

20 *Barron's,* May 5, 1930, Apr. 27, 1931, Jan. 18, 1932, May 15, 1933; NY *Times,* Apr. 29, 1931; *Magazine of Wall Street,* 49:598–99, 628, 630, 58:767–69, 800. The comparative figures are computed from data in company annual reports and *Historical Statistics,* 2:736.

21 NY *Times,* May 12, 1932; *WSJ,* May 13, 1932; *Magazine of Wall Street,* 53:559. Figures computed from data in company annual reports and *Historical Statistics,* 2:736.

22 For some details on maintenance policy see the statement by E. J. Connors, Apr. 10, 1932, EJC.

23 *Railway Age,* 106:827.

24 Seger to Charske, Sept. 18, 1928, UPN; *UP Report,* 1929, 8, 1931, 8; *Chronicle,* 132:3711, 135:4559; UP Exec. Comm. minutes, Oct. 27, 1931, Aug. 16, 1932, May 11, 1933, UPN; NY *Times,* Dec. 29, 1932; UP Directors minutes, Apr. 12, 1934, UPN.

25 NY *Times,* Nov. 19, 1928, June 20, 1932; UP Exec. Comm. minutes, July 1, 1930, UPN.

26 Seger to Charske, Sept. 18, 1928, UPN; UP Finance Comm. minutes, Oct. 16, 1928, UPN; *Chronicle,* 132:3711.

27 E. Roland Harriman, *I Reminisce* (New York, 1975), 73–87.

28 UP Finance Comm. minutes, May 3, 1927, UPN; W. A. Harriman–R. A. Lovett cable exchange, Aug. 20–22, 1932, UPN; Charske to Kuhn, Loeb, Aug. 23, 1932, UPN; Kuhn, Loeb to Charske, Aug. 23, 1932, UPN; W. A. Harriman to R. A. Lovett, Aug. 23, 1932, UPN.

29 Charske to W. A. Harriman, Aug. 24, 1932, UPN.

30 Connors report, Nov. 11, 1931, May 13, 1933, EJC; *Historical Statistics,* 2:740.

31 Connors report, March 15 and May 13, 1933, June 19, 1935, May 29, 1936, EJC; Connors to Jeffers, Apr. 29, 1932, EJC.

32 NY *Times,* Mar. 1, 1932, Feb. 1 and Feb. 2, 1933; *Church Journal,* May 6 and May 22, 1932, LDS; *Railway Age,* 92:891, 93:134–35, 94:199, 313; *WSJ,* July 21 and Sept. 20, 1932, Feb. 1, 1933; *Chronicle,* 135:2171, 136:839–40, 1198; 189 ICC 357–68. Technically the ICC had to approve the leases by which the merger was to be accomplished.

33 *UP Report,* 1936, 6; *Railway Age,* 94:463, 523, 98:836, 99:169, 802, 829, 101:262; *Chronicle,* 136:2065, 141:1608, 3705, 4027, 143:932; NY *Times,* Mar. 29, May 10, and May 11, 1933, May 18 and Dec. 18, 1935, Jan. 2, 1936; UP Exec. Comm. minutes, Dec. 11, 1934, UPN; 207 ICC 543–45; *WSJ,* Dec. 18, 1935. The two roads in question were the 111-mile Laramie, North Park & Western (Coalmont, Colorado, to Laramie, Wyoming) and the 90-mile Pacific & Idaho Northern (Weiser to New Meadows, Idaho).

34 *UP Report,* 1936, 6; NY *Times,* Aug. 4, 1935.

35 NY *Times,* Aug. 12, 1932; *Chronicle,* 135:1161; UP Exec. Comm. minutes, Jan. 2, 1934, UPN; Tribune Publishing Co. to Harriman, Aug. 2, 1933, UPN; Harriman to Tribune Publishing Co., Aug. 2, 1933, UPN.

36 NY *Times,* Apr. 8 and Apr. 10, 1936.

37 Ibid., Aug. 19, Sept. 18, Sept. 27, 1936; NY *Evening Journal,* Apr. 11, 1936; *Chronicle,* 142:2520, 143:1895, 2229, 2540; *Railway Age,* 100:742, 101:575; *WSJ,* Sept. 17 and Sept. 18, 1936.

38 Figures computed from data in company reports.

39 *Railway Age,* 60:703, 61:1205, 1208, 62:95–97, 124, 658, 63:329–34, 1157, 1159–60, 64:1552–56, 69:41; NY *Times,* Nov. 10, 1916, Aug. 24, 1926; Lovett to Calvin, Dec. 1, 1916, UPN; *Scientific American,* 116:637.

40 Figures computed from data in *Historical Statistics,* 2:728. For details on abandonments see Charles R. Cherington, *The Regulation of Railroad Abandonments* (Cambridge, Mass., 1948), especially chapter 5.

41 Gray memorandum, ''Study of Obsolescent Branch Lines,'' Dec. 14, 1932, UPN.

42 Ibid.; *UP Reports,* 1931–1939; *Chronicle,* 135:4213, 139:2532, 140:3567; *Railway Age,* 93:995, 95:139, 97:489, 104:930, 988; Jeffers to Charske, Jan. 21, 1933, UPN; *WSJ,* Oct. 17, 1934, Jan. 14 and Jan. 15, 1935.

43 David Halberstam, *The Best and the Brightest* (New York, 1972), 95; *Fortune,* Jan. 1939, 64.

44 Harriman to Arthur Brisbane, June 2, 1933, UPN.

45 Harriman to E. H. Harriman, Nov. 16, 1904, AF; Interview with W. A. Harriman, June 23, 1981, 5.

46 Harriman interview, 22; Harriman to Gray, July 19, 1932, UPN.

47 Harriman interview, 19; UP Exec. Comm. minutes, July 30, 1918, UPN.

48 *WSJ,* Aug. 8, 1917; *Literary Digest,* 66:20–21.

49 *WSJ,* Oct. 15, 1924, July 10, 1928.

50 Harriman to Lovett, Mar. 23, 1931, UPN; Lovett to Harriman, Mar. 26, 1931, UPN; Stover, *Illinois Central,* 314–41, 365, 540; Harriman interview, 61.

51 NY *Journal,* July 14 and July 15, 1932; NY *Herald-Tribune,* July 15, 1932; *Railway Age,* 93:135.

52 *WSJ,* Mar. 26, 1925, July 11, 1927; *Barron's,* Nov. 16, 1931, Feb. 8, 1937.

53 *Union Pacific Magazine,* Aug. 1922, 12, Apr. 1923, 7; *Railway Age,* 84:1165; Harriman to Kenneth D. Dawson, Oct. 10, 1933, UPN; W. S. Basinger to F. W. Robinson, Nov. 28, 1936, UPN; Jeffers to Gray, Dec. 7, 1936, UPN.

54 Harriman to Jeffers, Oct. 29, 1937, UPN: Jeffers to Harriman, Nov. 1, 1937, UPN; J. P. Warburg to Robert E. Gross, Dec. 7, 1939, UPN; Gross to Warburg, Dec. 12, 1939, UPN; A. J. Seitz to Robinson, Sept. 24, 1940, UPN; E. G. Smith memoranda for Charske, Sept. 13 and Sept. 23, 1940, UPN; Charske to R. A. Lovett, July 31, 1940, UPN.

55 *UP Report,* 1933, 8.

56 Interview with Edgar A. Klippel, Jr., Apr. 11, 1982, 94–95; Edgar A. Klippel, Jr., ''My Tour Over the Line from Milepost One,'' unpublished ms., 7–8.

CHAPTER 16
THE PROJECTS

1 *Fortune,* May 8, 1978, 220.
2 *WSJ,* Apr. 6 and May 6, 1905; *RR Gazette,* 40:653.
3 *RR Gazette,* 40:609, 652–53.
4 Ibid., 40:652–53, 41:437–38; NY *Times,* May 27, 1906.
5 *WSJ,* Nov. 21, 1906, Feb. 7, 1927; *RR Gazette,* 42:761–62, 43:199–200, 242, 49:287; E. E. Adams to Lovett, Apr. 21, 1914, UPN; W. V. S. Thorne to Lovett, May 7, 1914, UPN; Charles Ware to Mohler, May 20, 1914, UPN; Mohler to Lovett, June 27, 1914, UPN; *Railway Age Gazette,* 58:1485; UP Exec. Comm. minutes, Dec. 23, 1919, Apr. 20 and July 20, 1920, Mar. 23, 1926, UPN; P. R. to Gray, Mar. 2, 1920, UPO; Charske memoranda, Mar. 9 and Aug. 5, 1920, UPO; Loomis to Gray, Apr. 16, 1920, UPO; Thomas Price to Gray, Aug. 13, 1920, UPO; Omaha *World-Herald,* Sept. 1, 1920; *Railway Age,* 86:149–50.
6 *Railway Age,* 98:363–64; *Sphere,* Dec. 1934, 31.
7 *Railway Age,* 87:95–96, 98:364.
8 *RR Gazette,* 40:652.
9 Gray to Seger, Jan. 20, 1927, UPN.
10 A. H. Fetters, "The Diesel Locomotive," December 1926, 1–2, UPN.
11 Ibid., 3–6.
12 Ibid., 6; *Railway Age,* 87:95–98, 94:761. For more detail on the engine see Harold E. Ranks and William W. Kratville, *The Union Pacific Streamliners* (Omaha, 1974), 61–63. This book also contains a wonderful selection of photographs on every aspect of the streamliner's history.
13 *Railway Age,* 98:364; Ranks and Kratville, *Streamliners,* 11–14; E. C. Schmidt, "High Speed, Light Weight, Stream Lined Passenger Train: Tomorrow's Train Today," Jan. 2, 1934, 3, UPO. This packet of information put together for newsmen is a convenient source of details on the first streamliner.
14 "Union Pacific—Proposed 100 M.P.H. Diesel-Electric Streamlined 3-Car Articulated Passenger Train," undated but probably February 1933, 1–4, UPO; Schmidt, "Tomorrow's Train Today," 1; NY *Times,* May 20, May 24, 1933; *WSJ,* May 24, 1933; *Railway Age,* 94:761–62, 96:184–97.
15 Description of the M-10000 is drawn from Schmidt, "Tomorrow's Train Today," 3–20 and *Railway Age,* 96:184–97.
16 NY *Sun,* Feb. 13, 1934; NY *Times,* Feb. 13, 1934; NY *Tribune,* Feb. 13, 1934; *Railway Age,* 96:268–70; *UP Report,* 1933, 8.
17 *Railway Age,* 99:701–2; Overton, *Burlington Route,* 379–80, 393–98. The *Zephyr* was also the first to go into revenue service, two months ahead of the M-10000. It is curious that Overton, normally the most generous of historians, does not even acknowledge the existence of the Union Pacific train in his account of the *Zephyr*.
18 NY *Times,* Feb. 7 and Feb. 16, 1934; NY *Sun,* Feb. 13, 1934; Gray memorandum for Charske, Feb. 20, 1934, UPN; Ranks and Kratville, *Streamliners,* 31–39.
19 Gray memorandum, Feb. 20, 1934, UPN; Gray to Charske, Mar. 9, 1934, UPN; *Railway Age,* 96:359; Paul Rigdon to Gray, Mar. 12, 1934, UPN; Harriman to Charske, Apr. 18, 1934, UPN; JVL to Mr. Downs, July 31, 1934, UPN; Overton, *Burlington Route,* 396–98.
20 NY *Sun,* Feb. 21, 1934.

21 *Railway Age,* 97:427–30, 453; *Newsweek,* Nov. 3, 1934, 30; Charske to E. E. Adams, June 13, 1933, UPN; "Outstanding Dates on Streamliners," undated, UPO.
22 NY *Times,* Oct. 14, Oct. 20, and Oct. 22–25, 1934; *Railway Age,* 97:486, 512.
23 NY *Times,* Oct. 25, Oct. 26, and Oct. 30, 1934; *Chronicle,* 139:2693; *Railway Age,* 97:512; *Newsweek,* Nov. 3, 1934, 30–31.
24 "Outstanding Dates on Streamliners," UPO; "Historical record of streamline train locomotives," undated, UPO; *Railway Age,* 99:701–2.
25 NY *Times,* Oct. 27, Oct. 29, Oct. 30, and Dec. 31, 1934, Feb. 21, May 25, June 9, and Dec. 13, 1935; UP Exec. Comm. minutes, Nov. 27, 1934, UPN; *Railway Age,* 98:57, 279, 363–64, 473, 703, 751, 829, 875–79, 99:500–2, 701–7, 796, 828, 102:16–20; *WSJ,* May 6, 1935; Jeffers to Gray, Aug. 25, 1935, UPN.
26 "Union Pacific—Proposed . . . Train," 4–6.
27 Ibid., 6–8.
28 Harriman interview, 28–29; *Fortune,* Jan. 1939, 84.
29 Gray to Harriman, Sept. 25, 1935, UPN; Harriman to Gray, Oct. 2, 1935, UPN.
30 Harriman interview, 29; Doug Oppenheimer and Jim Poore, *Sun Valley: A Biography* (Boise, Idaho, 1976), 22.
31 Oppenheimer and Poore, *Sun Valley,* 22–24.
32 Ibid., 25–28.
33 Schaffgotsch to Harriman, Jan. 18, Jan. 21, and Jan. 28, 1936, UPN.
34 Harriman interview, 29; Oppenheimer and Poore, *Sun Valley,* 19, 31, 50; Harriman to E. M. Sawyer, Feb. 20, 1936, UPN; Sawyer to Harriman, Feb. 21, 1936, UPN; Gray to Harriman, Mar. 17, 1936, UPN.
35 Harriman interview, 30; Harriman to H. C. Mann, Apr. 13, 1936, UPN. A member of the firm Gilbert, Stanley, Underwood & Co, Underwood had earlier designed the hotel for the company's North Rim facility.
36 Jeffers to Harriman, Apr. 11, 1936, UPN; *Fortune,* Jan. 1939, 84. The poster is reproduced in Oppenheimer and Poore, *Sun Valley,* 54.
37 *Fortune,* Jan. 1939, 84.
38 UP Exec. Comm. minutes, May 5, 1936, UPN; Harriman to Mann, Apr. 16, 1936, UPN; Morgan to Harriman, with memorandum, May 29, 1936, UPN; Poore and Oppenheimer, *Sun Valley,* 57.
39 Harriman interview, 30–31; Oppenheimer and Poore, *Sun Valley,* 57–60.
40 *Railway Age,* 102:180–82; Oppenheimer and Poore, *Sun Valley,* 60–64.
41 Oppenheimer and Poore, *Sun Valley,* 64; *Railway Age,* 101:352, 388, 102:179–80; *Fortune,* Jan. 1939, 84; K. M. Singer memorandum for Charske, Sept. 23, 1936, UPN. The Singer memo, dealing with the beauty and barber shop concession, is a good example of the detail work involved in starting up the resort.
42 Oppenheimer and Poore, *Sun Valley,* 81–83; Harriman to Mann, Oct. 9, 1936, UPN; John Morgan to E. C. Smith, Oct. 19 and Oct. 28, 1936, UPN; Mann to Harriman, Oct. 27, 1936, UPN.
43 Harriman to Gray, Sept. 29 and Oct. 30, 1936, UPN; *Railway Age,* 102:179; H. A. Toland to E. C. Webster, Jan. 8, 1937, UPO.
44 Oppenheimer and Poore, *Sun Valley,* 85; Harriman to Schaffgotsch, Nov. 13, 1936, UPN; Harriman to Gray, Nov. 14, 1936, UPN. Selznick's telegram is quoted in full in the telegram to Gray. Randolph/Robb's column appeared in the New York *Daily News.*
45 Harriman to Gray, Sept. 21, Nov. 14, and Dec. 1, 1936, UPN; John Ward to Morgan, Nov. 14, 1936, UPN; Gray to Harriman, Nov. 30, 1936, UPN; Selznick to Harriman, Dec. 2, 1936, UPN; Harriman to Selznick, Dec. 7, 1936, UPN.

46 Hannagan to Raymond Stevens and E. C. Schmidt, Dec. 5, 1936, UPN; Schmidt to Hannagan and Morgan, Dec. 6, 1936, UPN; HJP to Jeffers, Dec. 18, 1936, UPO; *Fortune,* Jan. 1939, 86; NY *Daily News,* Jan. 9, 1937; Harriman interview, 32.
47 Harriman to Schaffgotsch, Dec. 3 and Dec. 29, 1936, UPN; WTW to Mann, Dec. 4, 1936, UPO; Harry C. Bates to Harriman, Dec. 9, 1936, UPO; Harriman to Bates, Dec. 14, 1936, UPO; Mann to ECW, Dec. 15 and Dec. 16, 1936, UPO; Gray to Jeffers, Dec. 16, 1936, UPO; Mann to Jeffers, Dec. 23, 1936, UPO; Gray to Bates, Dec. 26, 1936, UPO.
48 *Fortune,* Jan. 1939, 86; Oppenheimer and Poore, *Sun Valley,* 86–94.
49 Harriman to Morgan, Schaffgotsch, and Raymond Stevens, Dec. 29, 1936, UPN; Morgan and Schaffgotsch to Harriman, Dec. 29, 1936, UPN; NY *Daily News,* Jan. 9, 1937; W. P. Rogers to Harriman, July 29, 1939, UPN.
50 *Railway Age,* 102:177.
51 Ibid., 102:733; Harriman to Mann, Mar. 22 and May 4, 1937, UPO; Mann to B. H. Prater, Mar. 24, 1937, UPO; W. S. Basinger to Mann, May 8, 1937, UPO; "Notes on Landscaping of Sun Valley Development," May 3, 1937, UPO.
52 UP Exec. Comm. minutes, Apr. 6 and May 25, 1937, UPN.
53 *Railway Age,* 104:182–85; Harriman to H. L. Hamilton, Dec. 9, 1937, UPN; Chicago *Journal of Commerce,* Dec. 15, 1937; NY *Times,* Dec. 18 and Dec. 20, 1937; *The Valley Sun,* Dec. 21, 1937, Jan. 11, 1938, UPO; R. P. Meiklejohn to E. C. Schmidt, Jan. 28, 1938, UPN.
54 *The Valley Sun,* Jan. 11, 1938, UPO; NY *Daily Mirror,* Sept. 6, 1941; *Fortune,* Jan. 1939, 84; "Sun Valley Special," flyer, 1938, UPO.
55 Harriman to L. G. McNeil, May 15, 1937, UPO; W. T. Wellman to Harriman, Sept. 23, 1937, UPO; R. P. Meiklejohn to Ned Moss, Oct. 5, 1937, UPN; Wellman to B. H. Prater, Dec. 24, 1937, UPO; Prater to Mann, Jan. 15, 1938, UPO; Harriman to K. M. Singer, Jan. 17 and Aug. 3, 1938, UPN; Harriman to Hannagan and Schmidt, Mar. 11, 1938, UPN; Jeffers to Mann, Apr. 8, 1938, UPO; Conference memorandum, Mar. 30, 1938, UPN; Meiklejohn to Singer, Apr. 2, 1938, UPN; Jeffers to Harriman, May 3, 1938, UPN; Harriman to Schaffgotsch, June 9, June 26, and July 1, 1938, UPN; Harriman to Schmidt, June 28, 1938, UPN; Prater to G. J. Adamson et al., Nov. 23, 1938, UPO.
56 Interview with D. O. Churchill, Nov. 8, 1982, 85–87; Oppenheimer and Poore, *Sun Valley,* 164.
57 Harriman to Rogers, June 8, 1939, UPN; Oppenheimer and Poore, *Sun Valley,* 135.

CHAPTER 17
THE TRIMMINGS

1 For the early history of these activities see Klein, *Union Pacific,* 1:chaps. 16 and 26.
2 *UP Report,* 1936, 9, 1937, 7, 1938, 6, 1939, 8, 1940, 8; *Railway Age,* 101:196, 102:348, 852, 888, 103:216–17, 465, 105:380, 108:753; NY *Times,* July 24, 1937.
3 *WSJ,* Mar. 2, 1940; Haugh to Jeffers, Mar. 12, 1940, UPN.
4 Childs, *Trucking and the Public Interest,* 25–34.
5 Ibid., 35–82.

6 *Railway Age,* 97:833–35; 108:215–19, 1120–25; 109:153–55, 445–47, 595–97, 801–2, 803, 988–90.
7 Ibid., 100:844; UP Exec. Comm. minutes, Dec. 31, 1935, UPN; NY *Times,* Apr. 8, 1936.
8 *Railway Age,* 101:41, 126, 698, 806, 105:526–27; NY *Times,* Sept. 30, 1938.
9 Lehman Brothers to Seger, Mar. 4, 1929, UPN; John B. Rae, *Climb to Greatness* (Cambridge, Mass., 1968), 45.
10 Interviews with Robert A. Lovett, Sept. 8, 1981, June 13, 1982; *CAB,* 4:15–16; R. S. Lovett to Kahn, Aug. 1, 1916, OK; R. S. Lovett to Schiff, Aug. 30, 1917, AJA.
11 Lovett interview, Sept. 8, 1981; *CAB,* 4:16.
12 Gray to Harriman, June 22, 1929, UPN; Rae, *Climb to Greatness,* 40–42.
13 Warburg to Charske, Sept. 13, 1932, UPN; Cyril Chappellet to Charske, Feb. 23, 1933, UPN.
14 Rae, *Climb to Greatness,* 52–54.
15 Haugh to Gray, Aug. 21, 1935, UPN. This thirteen-page report offers an excellent insight into the state of commercial aviation in 1935.
16 Ibid.
17 UP Exec. Comm. minutes, Nov. 19 and Dec. 31, 1935, UPN; Haugh to Gray, Feb. 24, 1936, UPN.
18 Gordon D. Brown to Harriman, June 8, 1938, UPN; Jeffers to Charske, June 27, 1938, UPN.
19 *Railway Age,* 108:466, 540, 788, 1027, 1031, 1196.
20 "Airlines," memorandum, May 23, 1940, UPN; memorandum for Charske, May 23, 1940, UPN.
21 Jeffers to F. N. J. Gindorff, July 18, 1940, UPN; Warburg to Charske, July 24, 1940, UPN.
22 Harriman to Charske, July 26, 1940, UPN; Harriman to Warburg, July 26, 1940, UPN.
23 Lovett to Charske, Aug. 28, 1940, with attached memorandum, UPN.
24 Ibid.; "Memorandum Concerning Air Express and Air Freight Operations in the United States," Sept. 18, 1940, UPN; Lester N. Selig to L. O. Head, July 9, 1940, UPN; Head to Selig, July 13, 1940, UPN; Head to Charske, Aug. 22, 1940, UPN.
25 *WSJ,* May 8, 1986.
26 Klein, *Union Pacific,* 1:522–24.
27 Oregon Short Line Exec. Comm. minutes, Aug. 31, 1905, UPL; *Railroad Gazette,* 39:104, 42:30, 879; *Railroad Age Gazette,* 45:555; *WSJ,* Aug. 13, 1910; Gerrit Fort to Mohler, Sept. 7, 1912, UPN.
28 Fort to Mohler, Sept. 7 and Oct. 21, 1912, UPN; Mohler to W. A. Gardner, Apr. 10, 1913, UPN; Lovett to B. L. Winchell, Jan. 19, Jan. 22, and July 3, 1914, UPN; Mohler to Calvin, May 9, 1914, UPN; "Memorandum re Loans to Yellowstone Park Companies," July 26, 1935, UPO.
29 UP Exec. Comm. minutes, June 12, 1917, UPN; G. A. Ellis memorandum, Mar. 12, 1919, UPN; H. M. Adams to Gray, Aug. 20, 1920, UPN; Clark to Gray, Feb. 9, 1920, UPN; Gray to Lovett, Sept. 7 and Sept. 22, 1920, UPN.
30 *Union Pacific Magazine,* Feb. 1922, 16–17; interview with William J. Foral, Nov. 17, 1981, 30–31; Gray to Lovett, Sept. 7, 1920, UPN.
31 *Union Pacific Magazine,* Jan. 1922, 31, 34, Nov. 1922, 15; *Deseret News,* Oct. 16, 1922.
32 Salt Lake *Telegram,* Mar. 15, 1923; Utah Parks Co. minutes, Mar. 26, 1923, UPO; Agreement between Utah Parks Co. and E. C. Finney, June 9, 1923, UPO; Traffic

Dept. circular on Lund to Cedar City branch, June 15, 1923, UPO; Salt Lake *Tribune,* Oct. 11, 1923.

33 George H. Smith memoranda, Nov. 26 and Dec. 19, 1923, UPO; Robert L. Judd to Smith, Jan. 7, 1924, UPO; Smith to H. M. Adams, Jan. 8, 1924, UPO; Gray to Adams and Calvin, Apr. 21, 1924, UPO; *Railway Age,* 77:769, 80:456, 82:1981, 85:19–20; Salt Lake *Tribune,* Dec. 17, 1926, June 7, 1927; Adams to Gray, Jan. 8, 1927, UPO; Gray to Seger, Jan. 10, 1927, UPO; Press release, Feb. 17, 1927, UPO; Smith to Gray, Feb. 16, 1927, UPO; Gray to Smith, Feb. 23 and May 21, 1927, UPO.

34 George A. Croft, ''Establishment of North Rim Facilities,'' 3–5, UPO.

35 Ibid., 4–6; Smith to H. C. Mann, Nov. 5, 1928, UPO.

36 *WSJ,* Sept. 3, 1932; *Railway Age,* 93:374, 100:259, 101:161, 104:386; NY *Times,* Feb. 23, 1936; Smith memorandum, July 21, 1937, UPO; W. J. Larsen to Smith, Sept. 30, 1941, UPO; Smith to Larsen, Oct. 4, 1941, UPO.

37 *RR Gazette,* 30:317, 31:111; UP Directors minutes, June 28, 1899, UPL; *Chronicle,* 67:1162, 68:525; NY *Times,* Mar. 6, Mar. 7, and Dec. 16, 1899; Omaha *World Herald,* Mar. 7, 1899, Aug. 5, 1903; *WSJ,* Oct. 22 and Dec. 18, 1899, Apr. 7 and July 11, 1900, Feb. 7, 1901; Omaha *Daily News,* Aug, 9, 1901; B. A. McAllaster to Burt, Dec. 5, 1901, UPL.

38 McAllaster to W. D. Cornish, Oct. 30, 1901, UPL; *WSJ,* Aug. 5, 1902; *Harper's Weekly,* 52:24–25, 28; H. J. Shumhof memorandum, Oct. 23, 1916, UPO; Calvin to F. A. Manley, Feb. 14, 1917, UPO.

39 Kansas City *Star,* June 12 and Dec. 21, 1923; promotional brochure, June 25, 1923, UPO; Kansas City *Journal,* June 30, 1923; *Engineering and Contracting,* 64:651–54. For some later developments see *Railway Age,* 92:576, 106:626, 109:157.

40 For the early history of the mines see Klein, *Union Pacific,* 1:328–34, 482–88, 515–19. More detail can be found in [Eugene McAuliffe], *History of the Union Pacific Coal Mines 1868 to 1940* (Omaha, Neb., 1940).

41 UP Coal Co. Exec. Order No. 1, Mar. 10, 1898, UPL; ''Nationality of Mine Employees,'' Dec. 1896, UPO; D. O. Clark to Burt, Mar. 11, 1898, UPL; George L. Black to Clark, Mar. 14, 1898, UPL; McAuliffe, *UP Coal Mines,* 15; Black to Burt, Dec. 4, 1898, UPL.

42 Clark to Burt, June 6, Sept. 5, and Dec. 13, 1898, UPL.

43 Ibid., Jan. 20, Feb. 15, and Apr. 26, 1899, UPL; Omaha *World-Herald,* Jan. 13, 1899; Black to Burt, July 1 and Sept. 3, 1899, UPL.

44 Clark to Burt, Nov. 22, 1899, Jan. 15, July 24, Aug. 10, and Dec. 13, 1900, UPL.

45 Ibid., Aug. 10 and Oct. 3, 1900, UPL.

46 Ibid., Sept. 6, 1902, UPL; Burt to Harriman, Nov. 7, 1902, UPL.

47 Harriman to Burt, Nov. 11 and Nov. 13, 1902, Feb. 5, 1903, UPL; Burt to Harriman, Nov. 28, 1902, Feb. 6, 1903, UPL; Clark to Burt, Nov. 28, 1902, UPL; Cornish to Burt, May 4, 1903, UPL; McAuliffe, *UP Coal Mines,* 117.

48 Burt to Cornish, Oct. 19, 1903, Nov. 9, Nov. 10, Nov. 11, and Nov. 16, UPL; Cornish to Burt, Nov. 6, 1903, UPL; Burt to Harriman, Nov. 6 and Nov. 9, 1903, UPL; Clark to Burt, Nov. 6, 1903, UPL.

49 McAuliffe, *UP Coal Mines,* 118, 138–45; *Chronicle,* 82:335, 90:687; NY *Times,* Feb. 13, 1906, May 7 and Aug. 22, 1907, Mar. 29 and Dec. 4, 1908, Mar. 9, 1909; *RR Gazette,* 40:61, 42:157, 688; *Outlook,* 91:610.

50 Mohler to R. S. Lovett, June 8, 1914, UPN; ''Correspondence between the President of the United States and the Colorado Coal Mine Operators relative to the strike

in that state,'' Sept. 1914, UPN; UP Coal Co. circular, Feb. 1, 1917, UPO; Charske memorandum, Oct. 7, 1919, UPN; McAuliffe, *UP Coal Mines,* 150–53.

51 Lovett to J. D. Farrell, Oct. 17, 1919, UPN; Lovett to Walker D. Hines, Oct. 27, 1919, UPN; A. Mitchell Palmer to Lovett, Nov. 1, 1919, UPN; Farrell to Lovett, Nov. 13/14, Nov. 21, and Dec. 2, 1919, UPN.

52 McAuliffe, *UP Coal Mines,* 188–89, lx. The reason for Brooks's short tenure is unclear. He was sixty-five in 1923, when he stepped down, and possibly in poor health; he died a year later. See Gray to Lovett, Mar. 18, 1924, UPN.

53 McAuliffe, *UP Coal Mines,* 189–91; *Coal Age,* 23:422.

54 Eugene McAuliffe, ''The Union Pacific Coal Company,'' *Mining Congress Journal* (Feb. 1930), 16:93–96.

55 Ibid.

56 McAuliffe, *UP Coal Mines,* 164–73.

57 Ibid., 174–78, 191–92; McAuliffe, ''Union Pacific Coal Company,'' 94; Gray to Seger, Dec. 30, 1925, UPN.

58 McAuliffe, ''Union Pacific Coal Company,'' 94–95; McAuliffe, *UP Coal Mines,* 176–78, 258–59, xli–xliii; Gray to Charske, May 18, 1926, Dec. 4, 1928, UPN, Feb. 2, 1935, UPO.

59 Gray to Charske, Sept. 24 and Oct. 2, 1935, UPN; *WSJ,* Sept. 28, 1935, Dec. 10, 1936; W. M. Jeffers to W. A. Harriman and Charske, Apr. 3, 1939, UPN; Jeffers to Charske, Apr. 7, Apr. 20, May 6, and May 8, 1939, UPN; McAuliffe to Jeffers, Apr. 15, 1939, UPN. The snag in contract negotiations had to do with Lewis's insistence on a closed shop provision to shut out the rival AFL-backed Progressive Miners' Union.

60 McAuliffe, *UP Coal Mines,* 126–30; A. Briggs to D. O. Clark, Mar. 9, Mar. 10, Mar. 16, Mar. 19, 1903, UPL; Briggs to George L. Black, Apr. 19, 1903, UPL.

61 Omaha *Bee,* Aug. 27, 1901.

62 *WSJ,* Apr. 4, 1899; B. A. McAllaster to Burt, Aug. 10, 1901, UPL; C. A. Black to McAllaster, Dec. 13, 1902, UPL; Loomis to Farrell, Dec. 11, 1918, UPN; Gray to Lovett, Oct. 23, 1922, UPN.

63 *WSJ,* Feb. 6 and July 21, 1924; NY *Times,* Mar. 28, 1924; Gray to Lovett, Mar. 18, 1925, UPN; UP Exec. Comm. minutes, Sept. 22, 1934, UPN; *UP Report,* 1936, 9–10.

64 *UP Report,* 1936, 9–10, 1937, 7; NY *Times,* Apr. 11, 1937; *WSJ,* May 17, 1937.

65 *UP Report,* 1937, 7; UP Exec. Comm. minutes, Mar. 15, 1937, UPN; *WSJ,* Aug. 30, 1937.

66 Jeffers to Charske, Aug. 24, 1937, UPO; J. M. Hughes to W. H. Hulsizer, Sept. 21, 1937, UPO; William Reinhardt to G. F. Ashby, Oct. 25, 1937, UPO; A. C. Spencer to Ashby, Dec. 3, 1937, UPO; Hulsizer to Charles Adams et al., Dec. 6, 1937, UPO.

CHAPTER 18
THE FAMILY

1 For Adams's plan see Klein, *Union Pacific,* 1:493–95.

2 NY *Times,* Feb. 5, 1898; *WSJ,* Feb. 7, 1898; J. C. McConnell to E. Dickinson, May 23, 1899, UPL; M. K. Barnum to McConnell, May 20, 1899, UPL.

3 Details on the 1902–1903 strike are in chapter 7 of this volume; for the 1911–1912 strike see chapter 11.

4 Hines, *War History,* 152–70.

5 Ibid., 169–70, 180.
6 Ibid., 170–79; Hines to Woodrow Wilson, July 30, 1919, UPN.
7 Hines, *War History,* 181–91; WSJ, Mar. 18, 1920. See also chapter 12.
8 Lovett to Loomis, Nov. 26, 1919, UPN; Calvin to Lovett, Dec. 2, 1919, UPN; J. Ross Clark to W. A. Clark, Apr. 8, 1920, UPN; Gray to Lovett, Apr. 10, Apr. 12, 1920, UPN; C. B. Irwin to Jeffers, Apr. 14, 1920, UPN.
9 B. M. Jewell to E. T. Whiter, Mar. 24, 1920, UPN; Gray to Lovett, Apr. 10, 1920, UPN.
10 Gray to Lovett, Sept. 4, 1920, UPN.
11 Ibid., Apr. 14, 1920, UPN.
12 Ibid., Apr. 16, Apr. 19, Apr. 20, and Apr. 21, 1920, UPN; Lovett to Gray, Apr. 19, 1920, UPN; C. B. Irwin to Lovett, Apr. 22, 1920, UPN.
13 Hines, *War History,* 160–68; Gray to McAdoo, June 3, 1920, attached to Gray to Lovett, June 3, 1920, UPN.
14 Gray to McAdoo, June 3, 1920, UPN.
15 Ibid; *Railway Age,* 70:297–99.
16 *Railway Age,* 70:298.
17 NY *Times,* Feb. 27, Mar. 11, Mar. 12, Mar. 20, and Aug. 21, 1921; H. E. Byram to Gray, Mar. 28, 1921, UPO; Omaha *World Herald,* May 18, 1921; G. E. Bissonnet to Calvin, June 1, 1921, UPO; P. R. to Gray, June 2, 1921, UPO; Lovett to Fairfax Harrison, Sept. 1, 1921, UPN.
18 Lovett to Gray, Oct. 20, 1921, UPN; Gray to Lovett, Oct. 25, 1921, UPN.
19 Gray to Lovett, Oct. 27 and Oct. 31, 1921, UPN.
20 Ibid., Jan. 18, 1922, UPN; NY *Times,* Jan. 11, 1922; Omaha *Bee,* Mar. 10, 1922.
21 Omaha *Bee,* June 17, 1922; *Brotherhood of Maintenance of Way Employees and Railway Shop Laborers vs. Union Pacific Railroad Company et al.,* [July 1922], UPO; Gray to Lovett, July 11, July 24, July 27, Aug. 1, Aug. 5, and Aug. 10, UPN; *Church Journal,* July 16, 1922, LDS.
22 NY *Herald,* July 29, 1922.
23 Clark memorandum for Lovett, July 31, 1922, UPN; NY *Herald,* Aug. 2, 1922; NY *World,* Aug. 2, 1922; NY *Times,* Aug. 2, 1922; Gray to Lovett, Aug. 8 (two items) and Aug. 9, 1922, UPN; Lovett to Gray, Aug. 8, Aug. 9, and Aug. 18, 1922, UPN.
24 Lovett to Gray, Aug. 18, 1922, UPN; Gray to Lovett, Aug. 10, 1922, UPN.
25 Lovett to Gray, Aug. 10 (three items), Aug. 11, and Aug. 18, 1922, UPN; Gray to Lovett, Aug. 18 and Sept. 7, 1922, UPN; *Church Journal,* Aug. 21, 1922, LDS; NY *Times,* Aug. 23 and Aug. 31, 1922; "Announcement," Sept. 7, 1922, UPO.
26 NY *Times,* Sept. 20 and Dec. 8, 1922; Gray to Lovett, Sept. 29, 1922, UPN; *Railway Age,* 73:603–4, 75:765; T. B. McGovern et al. to Mrs. E. H. Harriman, Nov. 15, 1922, UPN; *Church Journal,* Dec. 7, 1922, LDS.
27 Gray to Lovett, Dec. 12, 1923, Mar. 31, 1924, UPN; Lovett to Gray, Jan. 19, 1924, UPN; NY *Times,* Mar. 29, 1924; *Railway Age,* 81:691.
28 Gray to Charske, Dec. 1, 1924, Dec. 7, 1927, UPN; *Railway Age,* 81:1057, 82:537, 673, 83:852, 1227, 85:39, 86:550; NY *Times,* Nov. 27, 1926, Dec. 11, 1927, Feb. 26, 1929; Jeffers to Gray, Apr. 7, 1930, UPN.
29 Calvin to Lovett, Dec. 9 and Dec. 10, 1914, UPN; Mohler to Lovett, Dec. 9, 1914, UPN; C. H. Markham to Lovett, Aug. 30, 1915, UPN; Lovett to Farrell and Mohler, Sept. 23, 1915, UPN; Farrell to Lovett, Nov. 3, 1915, UPN; Lovett to Markham, Nov. 19, 1915, UPN; Calvin to H. C. Nutt, Nov. 23, 1915, UPN; Mohler to Calvin and Farrell, Nov. 24, 1915, UPN; Markham to Lovett, Dec. 4, 1915, UPN.

30 Gray to Lovett, June 14, 1920, Oct. 11 and Nov. 15, 1923, UPN, Oct. 14, 1920, UPO; Lovett to Gray, June 22, 1920, June 7, 1922, Oct. 22 and Nov. 19, 1923, UPN, Aug. 10, 1920, UPO; Thomas Price to Gray, June 25, 1920 and Sept. 28, 1921, UPN; Price to Dr. Russell S. Fowler, Feb. 2, 1921, UPN; *Union Pacific Magazine,* Nov. 1922, 22; Calvin to Gray, Oct. 25, 1927, Sept. 25, 1928, UPO.

31 Gray to Charske, Mar. 22, 1929, UPO; Jeffers to Gray, Apr. 27, 1933, May 30, 1935, UPO; Dr. John R. Nilsson, "Instructions Pertaining to Application of Hospital Department Regulations," Feb. 10, 1937, UPO.

32 All figures taken from pension data compiled by controller L. J. Tracy, Feb. 8, 1932, UPN.

33 H. J. Stirling to Calvin, Oct. 24, 1916, UPO; Gray to Lovett, July 6, 1920, UPO; Jeffers notice, Sept. 1, 1920, UPO; *Railway Age,* 69:495; L. J. Tracy pension data, Feb. 8, 1932, UPN.

34 Lovett memorandum, Dec. 17, 1919, UPN.

35 Tracy data, Feb. 8, 1932, UPN; Charske memorandum, Feb. 18, 1932, UPN; Gray to Seger, Mar. 31, 1932, UPN; UP Directors minutes, Aug. 11, 1932, UPN.

36 Jeffers to Gray, July 23, 1934, UPO; L. M. Eddy summary of Railroad Retirement Act. Aug. 1, 1934, UPO; NY *Times,* Oct. 25, 1934, May 8 and May 18, 1935; NY *Herald-Tribune,* May 7 and May 8, 1935; *Railway Age,* 98:761–62; UP Exec. Comm. minutes, Nov. 25, 1936, Mar. 5 and May 4, 1937, UPN; Gray notice, May 4, 1937, UPO.

37 Erastus Young to Mohler, July 26, 1901, UPL; NY *Times,* Dec. 22, 1916.

38 E. P. Ripley to Lovett, Nov. 27 and Dec. 28, 1916, UPN; NY *Times,* Dec. 31, 1916; Calvin to Lovett, Sept. 14, 1916, UPN. Details on the plan are in *Railway Age Gazette,* 61:1209; a copy of its rules and regulations is in UPO.

39 Lovett to John B. Andrews, Jan. 11, 1917, UPN; S. R. Barr to Millar, Feb. 7, 1917, UPN; E. J. Engel to C. C. Stillman, Feb. 12, 1917, UPN; *Outlook,* 115:333–34; George Ziegler to Millar, Mar. 24, 1917, UPN; Millar to J. F. Sears, May 25, 1917, UPN. The full list of claims paid in March 1920 is in UPN.

40 Gray to Lovett, July 6, 1920, UPN, Sept. 8, 1921, UPO; Lovett to Gray, July 12, 1920, UPN, Sept. 14, 1921, UPO.

41 Lovett to Gray, Oct. 20, 1921, UPN; H. M. Adams to Gray, Nov. 23, 1922, UPO; Gray notice, Dec. 15, 1922, UPO; Paul Rigdon to Gray, Dec. 16, 1922, UPO; Gray to W. A. Day, Dec. 26, 1922, UPO.

42 *Railway Age,* 92:1044; Lovett to Calvin, Aug. 16, 1916, UPN; G. C. Warner to Lovett, Sept. 7, 1916, UPN; Lovett to John H. Patterson, Mar. 9, 1920, UPN; Gray to Lovett, Sept. 7 and Nov. 16, 1920, UPN; Lovett to Gray, Sept. 15, 1920, UPN; Gray circular, Dec. 25, 1920, UPN; NY *Times,* Dec. 25, 1920; *Chronicle,* 112:63; *Church Journal,* July 28, 1921, LDS; Gray to Charske, Nov. 14, 1932, UPN.

43 Details on the bureau, its courses and methods, are in *Railway Age Gazette,* 46:1158–60, 47:420, 1016–18, 48:1419–22, 49:1118, 50:1424–26, 1415.

44 *Railway Age Gazette,* 50:1430–31.

45 Ibid., 55:63.

46 Ibid., 52:1017, 1351, 56:755; Mohler to Lovett, Feb. 14, 1913, UPN; *Union Pacific Magazine,* Sept. 1922, 19–20; Gray to Charske, July 26, 1926, UPN.

47 *Railway Age Gazette,* 50:1425.

48 *Monthly Labor Review,* 27:99–101.

49 Francis Lynde to Lovett, July 23, 1919, UPN.

50 *Union Pacific Magazine,* Jan. 1922, 48, Feb. 1922, 45; "Report of the Thirteenth Annual Meeting of the Union Pacific Retired Employees Association," June 3,

1926, UPN. Family League activities can be followed in the magazine. The Retired Employees Association was originally called the Pensioners Association.

51 *Union Pacific Magazine,* Feb. 1925, 6.

52 Ibid., 7–9; *Railway Age,* 77:168; E. J. Connors, "Memorandum of Discussion with President Fowler and General Secretary-Treasurer Sims . . . ," n.d., EJC.

53 *Church Journal,* Mar. 31, 1929, LDS; *Union Pacific Magazine,* Feb. 1925, 6.

54 Lovett to George Kennan, May 9, 1922, GK; *Union Pacific Magazine,* Jan. 1922, 9, Feb. 1922, 21–22, Apr. 1922, 30, Aug. 1927, 10, Dec. 1928, 18–19.

55 *Union Pacific Magazine,* Jan. 1922, 51; *Railway Age,* 77:518.

56 *Union Pacific Magazine,* Apr. 1922, 56; *Railway Age,* 88:1325–28.

57 *Railway Age,* 85:470, 88:1325; *Church Journal,* Aug. 15, 1930, LDS.

58 *The Diamond,* Apr. 22 and June 21, 1929, UPO; *Railway Age,* 89:1198, 90:1264, 91:219, 93:96; Boosters memorandum, Feb. 1939, UPN; Ralph Foral to E. J. Connors, Aug. 11, 1939, UPO; Omaha *World-Herald,* Sept. 9 and Sept. 10, 1939.

59 McAuliffe, *UP Coal Mines,* 94–97.

60 Ibid.; Sing Yee to Pryde, Sept. 27, 1929, UPO; Ah Sandy to Pryde, Sept. 29, 1929, UPO; You Kwong to Pryde, Sept. 30, 1929, UPO; Ah Fan to Pryde, Oct. 1, 1929, UPO; Joe Bow to Pryde, Oct. 1, 1929, UPO; Pryde to Frank Tallmire, Nov. 13, 1929, UPO; McAuliffe to Pryde, Dec. 19, 1929, UPO; Pryde to McAuliffe, Dec. 23, 1929, Jan. 10, 1930, UPO; Ah How to Pryde, Apr. 21, 1930, UPO; Leo Chee to Pryde, May 19, June 3, June 10, July 25, and July 28, 1930, July 8 and Aug. 16, 1931, UPO; Leo Chee to Tallmire, Oct. 29, 1931, UPO; Tallmire to Pryde, Dec. 4, 1931, UPO. The file in UPO includes photographs of the miners who returned to China.

CHAPTER 19
THE OPERATION

1 Adams to Lovett, Apr. 21, 1919, UPN; E. W. Englebright memorandum, Oct. 8, 1919, UPN; Lovett to Gray, Oct. 30, 1919, UPN; Adams memorandum, Nov. 24, 1919, UPN; Gray to Lovett, Feb. 1, 1920, July 29, 1924, UPN; Gray to Kahn, Apr. 5, 1928, OK.

2 Lovett to Gray, Jan. 10, 1922, UPN.

3 *WSJ,* July 26 and Aug. 25, 1923; *Railway Age,* 75:999–1003, 77:671, 701–2, 85:121; NY *Times,* Aug. 28, 1924.

4 "History and Functions of Pacific Fruit Express Company," July 1, 1967, 1–2, UPO; NY *Times,* Dec. 8, 1906; UP Exec. Comm. minutes, Dec. 13, 1906, UPL; *Chronicle,* 83:1595.

5 "Pacific Fruit Express," 2–3; *RR Gazette,* 41:231, 43:374–75, 50:1404; NY *Times,* Sept. 7, 1907.

6 Interview with E. L. Prouty, Feb. 16, 1982, 53.

7 *Railway Age,* 68:1066, 69:726, 1145–48, 70:532, 72:533–34, 1312, 77:1004, 1100, 83:1054; NY *Times,* May 11, 1920, Nov. 14, 1923; *Chronicle,* 114:530, 115:425, 2591, 116:1658, 117:2332, 118:675, 122:761.

8 NY *Times,* Jan. 11, 1933, Apr. 7, 1934; *Chronicle,* 136:338, 137:4370, 138:2586; *WSJ,* Jan. 23, 1934, Feb. 6, 1936; UP Exec. Comm. minutes, May 12, 1936, UPN; *Railway Age,* 101:846, 107:200; *Business Week,* Dec. 9, 1939, 39; "Pacific Fruit Express," 3–5, UPO.

9 E. J. Connors, "Permanency of Operating Economies," n.d., 1, EJC; NY *Times,* Dec. 25, 1932; *Railway Age,* 96:1181–84.

10 *Railway Age,* 90:1181–84.

11 Ibid., 69:111–12, 557–62, 687–90, 78:1146–50, 1205–9, 1332–36.

12 "Permanency of Operating Economies," 1, EJC; "Memorandum of Reductions," n.d., 2–4, EJC; *Railway Age Gazette,* 52:18–19; *Union Pacific Magazine,* May 1928, 14.

13 "Permanency of Operating Economies," 2–6, EJC; "Memorandum of Reductions," 4, EJC; *Railway Age,* 92:1013.

14 "Permanency of Operating Economies," 5, EJC; interview with Earl O. Joest, Sept. 4, 1982, 5–6, 60.

15 Jeffers to Gray, May 13, 1933, EJC; NY *Herald-Tribune,* Feb. 24, 1936; NY *Times,* Feb. 24, 1936, Mar. 8, 1937; interview with Frank Acord, Nov. 8, 1984, 8.

16 *WSJ,* Mar. 17, 1931; UP Exec. Comm. minutes, Mar. 20, 1934, UPN; *Railway Age,* 90:697, 95:645, 98:549, 99:95; NY *Times,* Dec. 6, 1935, Nov. 17, 1936, Jan. 11 and Sept. 22, 1939.

17 W. A. W. memorandum, Nov. 11, 1912, UPN; John W. Blodgett to L. J. Spence, Nov. 14, 1912, UPN; Lovett to Mohler, Dec. 19, 1912, UPN; Charles Ware to Mohler, Dec. 30, 1912, UPN; Mohler to Lovett, Jan. 4, 1913, UPN; F. A. Wann to B. L. Winchell, Oct. 12, 1914, UPN; Lovett to Mohler and Farrell, Sept. 18, 1915, UPN; Seger to Lovett, Feb. 9, 1916, UPN.

18 Lovett to Kahn and Mortimer L. Schiff, Feb. 10, 1911, OK; Winchell to Lovett, Dec. 30 and Dec. 31, 1913, UPN; Lovett to Winchell, Dec. 30, 1913, Aug. 12, 1914, May 3, 1915, UPN; Sproule to Mohler, Mar. 18, 1914, UPN; Mohler to Winchell, Aug. 29, 1914, UPN; Farrell to Winchell, Sept. 19, 1916, UPN.

19 Lovett to Gray, Jan. 20, 1920, UPN; *Union Pacific Magazine,* Jan. 1923, 15, Apr. 1923, 9; *Railway Age,* 87:1119; NY *Times,* Apr. 9, 1926. The history of the *Overland Limited* is lovingly if not always accurately recounted in Lucius Beebe, *The Overland Limited* (San Diego, 1963).

20 E. E. Adams to Lovett, Apr. 20, 1915, UPN; *Railway Age,* 58:1475–76, 61:202, 74:1605, 83:933–35, 85:765–67; NY *Times,* Mar. 18, 1920; *Union Pacific Magazine,* Feb. 1922, 9; Gray to Charske, July 12, 1958, UPO. For details on discontinued passenger runs see "Changes in Passenger Train Service," Apr. 16, 1933, and "Passenger Car Runs Discontinued or Added," May 1, 1933, EJC.

21 *Railway Age,* 88:842, 939, 1089, 1259, 89:1057; Gray to Seger, Apr. 26 and May 3, 1930, UPN; NY *Times,* Apr. 28, 1930; Gray to Charske, Oct. 25 and Nov. 6, 1930, UPN.

22 *Railway Age,* 90:925, 92:904, 1092, 96:704, 97:451; NY *Times,* May 7 and Oct. 11, 1934; Gray to Charske, Jan. 13, 1932, UPN.

23 Gray to Charske, Oct. 7 and Dec. 29, 1933, Feb. 20 and Oct. 9, 1934, Jan. 2, 1935, UPN; *Railway Age,* 98:316, 585–86.

24 NY *Times,* Oct. 19, 1935, Apr. 23 and June 28, 1936; Gray memorandum, Mar. 14, 1936, UPN; *Journal of Commerce,* Apr. 10, 1936; *Railway Age,* 100:705, 864–75, 928, 1069, 101:4–11; NY *Herald-Tribune,* Apr. 18, 1936; E. G. Smith to Gray, May 27, 1936, UPN; Gray to Smith, May 27, 1936, UPN.

25 NY *Times,* Dec. 2, 1936; *Railway Age,* 102:291–94, 639–40, 103:698–99, 868–70; Harriman to Jeffers, Mar. 21, 1937, UPN.

26 Interview with T. E. Murray, Aug. 29, 1982, 41–42, 45–48; interview with E. A. Klippel, Apr. 11, 1982, 61; H. A. Lawrence to E. G. Smith, Aug. 13, 1935, UPN.

27 *Railway Age,* 104:224–31; *American Business,* 8:18–19, 50.

28 *Railway Age,* 99:54, 261, 376, 100:719.
29 Klippel interview, 82–83.
30 *Railway Age,* 100:719–20; Klippel interview, 21, 36, 83–84.
31 *Collier's,* Aug. 1, 1936, 30.
32 Ibid.
33 Ibid., 30, 32; *Railway Age,* 100:719–20, 103:129–32, 142.
34 P. J. Nichols circular, May 1, 1896, UPL; George L. Black to Frank A. Manley, Aug. 4, 1911, UPO; *Railway Age Gazette,* 59:263; *Railway Age,* 65:1016–18, 81:300; NY *Times,* Aug. 7, 1926; *Church Journal,* Aug. 10, 1926, LDS.
35 Los Angeles *Evening Herald-Express,* June 17, 1938; Los Angeles *Daily News,* June 17, 1938; Jeffers to Charske, June 17, 1938, UPN; Los Angeles *Times,* June 20, 1938; Charske to Jeffers, June 28, 1938, UPN; A. V. Kipp to W. S. Basinger, July 1, 1938, UPN; *Railway Age,* 105:414–15, 106:239; Denver *Post,* June 3, 1939; *UP Report,* 1937, 6, 1938, 5, 1939, 7.
36 *UP Report,* 1935, 9, 1936, 8; *Railway Age,* 101:695, 103:129–32, 42, 104:838–42; Jeffers to Charske, Apr. 14, 1938, UPN; *American Business,* 8:50.
37 *Railway Age Gazette,* 53:261–62, 357, 54:29–30, 336; *Financial America,* Jan. 29, 1913; NY *Times,* Feb. 2, 1913; *Union Pacific Magazine,* Dec. 1930, 5–6.
38 *Railway Age Gazette,* 54:400, 55:708, 1197; NY *Times,* Nov. 9, 1913, Jan. 25 and Mar. 15, 1914; Lovett to Farrell, July 20, 1914, UPN; W. A. Harriman to Lovett, Aug. 12, 1914, UPN; Lovett to Mohler, Aug. 20, 1914, Nov. 22, 1915, UPN. The awards were administered by the American Museum of Safety.
39 *Railway Age,* 71:608, 1217, 72:1031, 74:384, 961, 1696, 76:457–58, 801, 77:27–29, 313, 648; Gray to Lovett, Dec. 3 and Dec. 9, 1921, May 15, 1923, UPN.
40 NY *Times,* Nov. 16, 1925, Jan. 7 and Dec. 8, 1926, Jan. 14, Dec. 5, and Dec. 29, 1927, Dec. 13, 1928, Dec. 2 and Dec. 6, 1929, June 20, 1931, and June 11, 1936; *Safety Engineering,* Jan. 1926, 41–44; *Railway Age,* 81:1177, 1184, 1195–96, 82:312, 1342, 84:516; *Railway Review,* Dec. 11, 1926, 865; *Railroad Trainmen,* Aug. 1930, 582–84; *National Safety News,* 30:48.
41 Details on these improvements are in Alfred W. Bruce, *The Steam Locomotive in America* (New York, 1952), 34–39, 76–84, 121–275.
42 Ibid., 77, 82–120; *American Engineer,* Jan. 1913, 5. The six types were a 4–4–0, a 4–6–2, one heavy and one light 2–8–0, a 2–6–0, and a 0–6–0.
43 *Railway Age,* 81:621.
44 Bruce, *Steam Locomotive,* 282–301; *Railway Age Gazette,* 50:167, 58:781, 64:1573–74; NY *Times,* Apr. 16, 1914; E. E. Adams to Lovett, Aug. 15, 1916, Feb. 3, Feb. 17, and Feb. 20, 1917, UPN; Lovett to W. A. Harriman, Feb. 11 and Nov. 20, 1917, UPN; Lovett to Calvin, May 3 and June 28, 1917, UPN; Calvin to Lovett, Feb. 1, 1919, UPN.
45 "Proposed 100 Locomotives for 1920," Feb. 12, 1920, UPN; *Railway Age,* 72:1325–29, 73:687–89, 76:193–95, 77:222; NY *Times,* Aug. 22, 1922; Gray to Lovett, Dec. 11, 1922, UPN.
46 *Railway Age,* 80:850–51, 1295–1300, 81:621–22, 1265–67, 82:49–53; Jeffers to Calvin, Apr. 23, 1926, EJC; Jeffers to Calvin et al., May 15, 1926, EJC; E. E. Adams to Gray, May 17, 1926, EJC; Gray to Charske, May 17, 1926, EJC; NY *Times,* Jan. 13 and Feb. 18, 1928; Charske memorandum, Feb. 9, 1929, UPN; Charske to Seger, Feb. 11, 1929, UPN.
47 Seger to Charske, Feb. 27, 1930, UPN; L. J. Tracy memorandum, Apr. 4, 1933, UPN; Averell Harriman to Alfred P. Sloan, Jr., Apr. 17, 1936, UPN; Harriman to Jeffers, Apr. 17, 1936, UPN.

48 Harriman to Jeffers, Apr. 17, 1936, UPN.

49 NY *Times,* July 29, 1936; *WSJ,* July 29, 1936; *Railway Age,* 101:178.

50 *Railway Age,* 102:468–72, 104:311, 105:916–18; NY *Times,* Nov. 6, 1937, Jan. 3, 1938, May 7 and May 16, 1939; Bruce, *Steam Locomotive,* 337–38.

51 Jeffers to Harriman, Feb. 9, 1936, UPN; UP Exec. Comm. minutes, Feb. 18, 1936; NY *Times,* Feb. 18, 1936; Acord interview, 65.

52 NY *Times,* Sept. 5, Oct. 11, and Nov. 10, 1936, Jan. 20, Jan. 26, 1937, Mar. 12, 1939; *WSJ,* Oct. 31, 1936, Jan. 26, 1937; *Railway Age,* 101:900–3, 106:417–18, 420, 107:515–18; Bruce, *Steam Locomotive,* 308–9, 327–28; Acord interview, 16, 64.

53 Jeffers memorandum, Oct. 10, 1936, UPN; Jeffers to Charske, Feb. 23, 1939, UPN; Charske to Averell Harriman, Feb. 23, 1939, UPN.

54 *Railway Age Gazette,* 51:1172, 58:225–26, 61:707; *WSJ,* May 2, 1912; NY *Times,* Jan. 28 and May 17, 1914; Averell Harriman to Millar, Feb. 9, 1915, UPN; Calvin to Lovett, Feb. 8, 1916, June 12, 1917, UPN; Averell Harriman to Calvin, Feb. 9, 1916, UPN; Mohler to Lovett, Feb. 19, 1916, UPN; Lovett to Averell Harriman, Oct. 30, 1916, UPN; Farrell to Lovett, Nov. 23, 1916, UPN.

55 Lovett to Gray, Nov. 28, 1919, UPN; Gray to Lovett, Dec. 4, 1919, Apr. 24, 1920, UPN; E. E. Adams to Gray, Apr. 24, 1920, UPN; NY *Times,* Jan. 8 and Jan. 10, 1922, Feb. 10, 1924; Gray to Charske, June 6, 1934, UPN.

56 Jeffers to Gray, Feb. 27, 1936, UPN; Gray to Harriman, Mar. 14, 1936, UPN; L. J. Tracy memorandum, May 1, 1936, UPN; Gray to Charske, May 27, 1936, UPN; *WSJ,* Nov. 5, 1936.

57 Gray to Charske and Harriman, Apr. 19, 1937, UPN; Gray to Charske, Apr. 21, 1937, UPN; NY *Times,* May 16, 1937, Feb. 17, 1938, Sept. 18, 1939; *WSJ,* May 22, 1937, Feb. 24, Mar. 25, and Apr. 3, 1939; *Railway Age,* 104:355, 883–84.

58 Interview with Reginald M. Sutton, Feb. 15, 1982, 13–14.

CHAPTER 20
THE RAILROADER

1 For more detail on this distinction see W. Frederick Cottrell, *The Railroader* (Palo Alto, Calif., 1940), 4–35.

2 Ibid., 17–33.

3 For a portrait of nineteenth-century railroaders see Licht, *Working for the Railroad.*

4 Interview with C. Otis Jett, Mar. 12, 1982, 29; interview with E. C. Schafer, Aug. 29, 1982, 40.

5 Interview with Stanley J. How, Feb. 17, 1982, 6–7.

6 *Life,* Feb. 22, 1943, 92; *Who's Who in Nebraska* (Lincoln, Neb., 1940), 344; interview with D. O. Churchill, Nov. 8, 1982, 168–69.

7 Churchill interview, 171.

8 Ibid., 172–73; *Life,* Feb. 22, 1943, 92.

9 *Life,* Feb. 22, 1943, 90–91.

10 Wyoming *Tribune,* Nov. 2, 1914; Cheyenne *State Leader,* Nov. 3, Nov. 5, and Nov. 8, 1914; John W. Lacey to N. H. Loomis, Nov. 5, 1914, UPN; Mohler to Lovett, Nov. 10, 1914, UPN; Jeffers to Charles Ware, Nov. 12, 1914, UPN; Lovett to Mohler, Nov. 16, 1914; Millar to Mohler, Mar. 23, 1915, UPN; Jeffers to

Loomis, Apr. 15, 1915 (two letters), UPN; Calvin to Lovett, June 5, 1916, UPN; UP Exec. Comm. minutes, June 6, 1916, UPN.

11 Gray to Charske, Oct. 11, 1928, UPN; UP Finance Comm. minutes, Oct. 16, 1928; *Union Pacific Magazine,* Nov. 1928, 1, 8, 29.

12 Churchill interview, 37, 49, 85–86; How interview, 18–19; *Current Biography,* 1942, 415.

13 Churchill interview, 157, 162; How interview, 21, 85.

14 *Life,* Feb. 22, 1943, 90.

15 Interview with George Proudfit, Sept. 5, 1982, 7–8; Churchill interview, 36.

16 Jeffers to N. A. Williams et al., Dec. 8, 1928, EJC; notebook title, EJC.

17 *Railway Age,* 87:101.

18 Gray notice, Aug. 11, 1932, UPN; UP Directors minutes, Aug. 11, 1932, UPN; *Union Pacific Magazine,* Sept. 1932, 5; Gray to Charske, Sept. 15, 1932, UPN; Charske to Gray, Sept. 20, 1932, UPN; NY *Times,* Apr. 25, 1937; *Church Journal,* Dec. 11, 1937, LDS.

19 NY *Times,* Apr. 13, Apr. 25 and Sept. 24, 1937; *Railway Age,* 103:445–47; *WSJ,* Apr. 13, 1937; *Newsweek,* Apr. 24, 1937, 38.

20 NY *Times,* Mar. 26 and Apr. 5, 1933; Gray to Seger, May 9 and June 1, 1931, UPN; Sharfman, *Interstate Commerce Commission,* 3B:161–79, 191.

21 R. H. Aishton to Gray, June 24, 1932, with attached policy statement, UPO; "The Railroads: A Statement as to Policies," June 21, 1934, UPN; HWC [Clark] to W. A. Harriman and Charske, Oct. 28, 1932, UPN.

22 Emory R. Johnson, *Government Regulation of Transportation* (New York, 1938), 240–42. The act also repealed the recapture clause of the 1920 act, which had proved wholly ineffective. For more detail on the act and developments under it see Earl Latham, *The Politics of Railroad Coordination, 1933–1936* (Cambridge, Mass., 1959).

23 *DAB,* supp. 2, 22:260; NY *Times,* Jan. 23, Nov. 30, and Dec. 11, 1932, Nov. 4, 1934; *Chronicle,* 136:3212; UP Exec. Comm. minutes, Sept. 25, 1934, UPN.

24 R. V. Fletcher to Hugh S. Johnson, Feb. 24 and Mar. 13, 1934, UPN; *WSJ,* Mar. 1, 1934; NY *Herald-Tribune,* Mar. 16, 1934.

25 Hoogenbooms, *ICC,* 125–30; Gray to W. A. Harriman, June 2, 1934, UPO; Latham, *Politics of Coordination,* 140–243.

26 NY *Times,* Nov. 21, 1935, Apr. 2, 1936, Apr. 15 and Apr. 19, 1937; NY *Herald-Tribune,* May 15, May 20, and Dec. 17, 1936; *WSJ,* Oct. 17, 1936; Hoogenbooms, *ICC,* 133–35.

27 All figures are taken from *Report of Committee . . . to Submit Recommendations Upon the General Transportation Situation,* Dec. 23, 1938, UPN.

28 Ibid., 47, 72, 74, 75; *Railway Age,* 104:492–94.

29 Hoogenbooms, *ICC,* 135; *Report of Committee,* 4–5; NY *Herald-Tribune,* Dec. 24, 1938; NY *Times,* Dec. 24, 1938.

30 *WSJ,* Jan. 20 and Feb. 2, 1939, Mar. 6, 1940; NY *Herald-Tribune,* Feb. 2, 1939; Clark to Charske, May 25, 1939, UPN; *Railway Age,* 108:126–29, 180, 289–91, 370–71, 487–88, 501, 583, 714–15, 743–44, 777–81, 787, 818–20, 851–54, 864–69, 1043–45, 109:118, 220–21, 257–58, 271–74, 313–14, 335–36, 371–73, 399–403; Clyde M. Reed to Jeffers, Feb. 20, 1940, EJC; Jeffers to Reed, Feb. 20 and Feb. 29, 1940, EJC; Reed to Walter Wilson, Feb. 20, 1940, EJC.

31 Theodore E. Keeler, *Railroads, Freight, and Public Policy* (Washington, 1983), 27.

32 Hoogenbooms, *ICC,* 136; *Railway Age,* 109:273, 503.

33 NY *Times,* Feb. 1, Feb. 8, and May 10, 1939.

34 Omaha *Bee-News,* Dec. 6, 1936; *Railway Age,* 101:874, 880.
35 *Railway Age,* 103:488–89; NY *Times,* Oct. 3, 1937; undated account (probably press release), EJC; *Newsweek,* Oct. 11, 1937, 33. Unless otherwise indicated, all details about the dinner that follow are from these sources.
36 *Life,* Feb. 22, 1943, 95.
37 How interview, 9; interview with Reginald M. Sutton, Feb. 15, 1982, 44.
38 *Life,* Feb. 22, 1943, 94.
39 Proudfit interview, 36; interview with John C. Kenefick, Aug. 13, 1985, 11.
40 How interview, 16.
41 Averell Harriman interview, 41–42; Roland Harriman, *I Reminisce,* 124.
42 Interview with Elbridge T. Gerry, Oct. 20, 1981; UP Directors minutes, Oct. 11, 1934, UPN; UP Exec. Comm. minutes, Jan. 22, 1935, UPN.
43 Jeffers to Gray, Jan. 6, 1934, UPN; Gray to Charske, Jan. 9, 1934, UPN; Jeffers to Charske, Oct. 8, 1937, UPN; *Railway Age,* 103:445–47; NY *Times,* Oct. 17 and Nov. 13, 1937.
44 NY *Times,* July 26, 1938; *Life,* Feb. 22, 1943, 95; Klippel interview, 98; interview with Edd H. Bailey, Feb. 15, 1982, 30.
45 Bailey interview, 40.
46 How interview, 68–69, 74–78; Proudfit interview, 15.
47 How interview, 69, 75–78.
48 *Railway Age,* 106:785; Cecil B. DeMille to J. P. Carey, June 2, 1938, UPO; Salt Lake *Tribune,* Nov. 20, 1938.
49 Schafer interview, 26.
50 Ibid.
51 *Railway Age,* 106:765–67, 785; Omaha *World-Herald,* Apr. 30, 1939. Unless otherwise indicated, the account of the festivities that follows is drawn from these sources.
52 H. A. Milotz et al., to Union Pacific employees, Feb. 28, 1939, UPO; ''Golden Spike Days'' general outline, Mar. 5, 1939, UPO; NY *Times,* Mar. 6 and Mar. 23, 1939; *Railway Age,* 106:443, 579, 674–75, 708: Jeffers to department heads, Apr. 12 and Apr. 18, 1939, UPO; Connors to D. A. Smith, May 3, 1939, UPO; E. C. Schmidt to Jeffers, July 20, 1939, UPO; Schafer interview, 27.
53 Churchill interview, 46; NY *Times,* Oct. 15, 1937, Oct. 15, 1939, May 23 and May 30, 1940; Los Angeles *Examiner,* June 17, 1938; *Reader's Digest,* 35:56–58; *Business Week,* Oct. 14, 1939; *American Magazine,* 130:9; *Time,* July 30, 1945, 80.
54 Jeffers to Charske, June 16, 1939, UPN; *UP Report,* 1939, 6.
55 *Barron's,* Nov. 29, 1937; *Chronicle,* 144:4027, 4364; NY *Times,* June 24, 1937, Apr. 30, May 23, and Dec. 24, 1940, Jan. 9 and Sept. 28, 1941; E. G. S. memorandum to Charske, Mar. 1, 1939, UPN; E. G. Smith memorandum, Oct. 3, 1939, UPN; *WSJ,* Feb. 23, Apr. 30, and May 1, 1940; NY *Herald-Tribune,* Apr. 30 and May 1, 1940; *Railway Age,* 108:801, 994, 109:1001, 110:161, 234.
56 NY *Times,* Jan. 11, Jan. 27, Sept. 22, and Oct. 16, 1939, Apr. 22, 1941; *WSJ,* Jan. 12, Feb. 9, and July 21, 1939, Apr. 21, 1941; Jeffers to Charske, June 16, 1939, Dec. 28, 1940, UPN: UP Exec. Comm. minutes, Aug. 27, 1940, UPN.
57 UP Exec. Comm. minutes, Apr. 2 and July 2, 1940, UPN; NY *Times,* Dec. 10, 1940, May 29, Aug. 30, and Nov. 30, 1941; Jeffers to Charske, Sept. 7, 1941, UPN; Jabelmann memorandum, Sept. 9, 1941, UPN; Charske to Harriman, Sept. 16, 1941, UPN; *Railway Age,* 111:519–26; Bruce, *Steam Locomotive,* 328–30.
58 Harriman to Charske, June 4, 1941, UPN; Sutton interview, 31–32.

CHAPTER 21

THE CZAR

1 Churchill interview, 50; Sutton interview, 40; interview with Earl O. Joest, Sept. 4, 1982, 55–56.
2 Acord interview, 66; How interview, 18–19.
3 Roland Harriman, *I Reminisce,* 124–25.
4 Sutton interview, 41–42.
5 Interview with Edd H. Bailey, Sept. 11, 1982, 2–3; Klippel interview, 98; Proudfit interview, 30.
6 UP Exec. Directors minutes, June 20, 1940, Feb. 20, 1941, UPN; Lovett to Charske, Dec. 19, 1940, UPN; UP Exec. Comm. minutes, Dec. 26, 1940, UPN; Lovett to E. G. Smith, Jan. 4, 1941, UPN.
7 *UP Report,* 1940, 2, 10, 1941, 2, 9, 1942, 2, 8; NY *Times,* Sept. 27, 1940, Mar. 18 and Mar. 21, 1941, May 13, 1942.
8 Proudfit interview, 30.
9 Jeffers to H. C. Mann, Dec. 7, 1937, EJC.
10 *Reader's Digest,* 35:56–58; *Business Week,* Oct. 14, 1939, 28; Jeffers to Charske, Feb. 20, 1939, UPN; Salt Lake City *Tribune,* Feb. 27, 1939; *American Magazine,* Oct. 1940, 9.
11 *Railway Age,* 107:49.
12 Schafer interview, 6, 24; *Life,* Feb. 22, 1943, 95.
13 Churchill interview, 52–54; Melia interview, 66.
14 Churchill interview, 52–53.
15 Ibid., 166; Proudfit interview, 15; Kenefick interview, 7; *Life,* Feb. 22, 1943, 94.
16 Roland Harriman, *I Reminisce,* 125.
17 Acord interview, 98, 100; Joest interview, 55.
18 Acord interview, 101; Joest interview, 54–55.
19 Sutton interview, 42–43. For another story of a fired secretary see Churchill interview, 173–80.
20 Olive M. Stephenson to Jeffers, July 29, 1940, EJC.
21 UP Exec. Comm. minutes, Dec. 1, 1936, May 31, 1939, June 11, 1940, UPN; Jeffers to Charske, May 29, 1939, UPN; NY *Times,* June 16, 1940; Connors scrapbook, EJC; Jeffers to Charske, July 22, 1941, UPN; Omaha *World-Herald,* July 27, 1941.
22 NY *Times,* July 10, 1936; *Railway Age,* 101:85; Jabelmann to H. C. Mann, July 9, 1938, UPO; Jeffers to Mann et al., July 10 and Nov. 9, 1938, UPO; Mann to Jeffers, Nov. 9, 1938, UPO; Jeffers to Jabelmann, Nov. 29 and Dec. 5, 1938, UPO.
23 Jabelmann to Jeffers, Dec. 18 and Dec. 19, 1938, UPO; Jabelmann report, Dec. 18, 1938, UPO.
24 Jabelmann to N. A. Williams, July 7, 1939, UPO; Burnett to H. C. Mann, May 16, 1939, UPO; "Consolidated Organization Plan . . . ," June 14, 1939, UPO; Jeffers to Williams, Nov. 23, 1939, UPO; Jeffers to Charske, May 24 and July 11, 1940, UPO; Burnett to Jabelmann, May 24, 1940, UPO; Connors to H. A. Toland, July 9, 1940, UPO.
25 G. M. Walsh to E. H. Harriman, Sept. 28, 1940, UPN. It is intriguing to wonder why Walsh made the error of addressing his appeal to E. H. Harriman.
26 Jeffers to Charske, Oct. 15, 1940, UPN.
27 Charske memorandum, Oct. 18, 1939, UPN.

28 Jeffers to W. A. Harriman, Apr. 4, 1941, UPN; Charske to W. A. Harriman, May 23 and July 18, 1941, UPN; Jeffers to Guild et al., June 16, 1941, UPO; Jeffers to Charske, June 3 and July 22, 1941, UPN; Connors to F. G. Gurley, May 23 and May 29, 1941, EJC; Gurley to Connors, May 26, 1941, EJC.

29 Connors to Jeffers, July 21, 1941, UPO; Jeffers to Charske, July 22, 1941, UPN.

30 Jeffers to Charske, July 22, 1941, UPN; UP Exec. Comm. minutes, July 24, 1941, UPN; NY *Times,* July 27, 1941; Omaha *World-Herald,* July 27, 1941.

31 Jeffers to Guild et al., June 16, 1941, UPO; Jabelmann to S. C. Smith, Sept. 17, 1941, EJC; Jeffers to Charske, Nov. [30], 1941, UPN.

32 Jeffers to Charske, Nov. [30], 1941 (two items), UPN; Jeffers to F. C. Paulsen, Dec. 2, 1941, EJC.

33 Jeffers to Paulsen, Dec. 2, 1941, EJC.

34 "An employee" to Jeffers and Connors, Jan. 12, 1942, EJC.

35 Chicago *Herald-American,* Oct. 14, 1941; *WSJ,* Oct. 15, 1941; NY *Times,* Nov. 8, 1941; Jeffers to Charske, Oct. 30, 1941, UPN; Jeffers to Connors et al., Nov. 6, 1941, EJC; Jeffers to Ashby and Connors, Nov. 7, 1941, UPO.

36 NY *Herald-Tribune,* Dec. 3, 1941; NY *Times,* Dec. 3, 1941; L. J. T. memorandum, Apr. 24, 1941, UPN; *Railway Age,* 109:260; Acord interview, 9–10; Jeffers to Connors and Robinson, Aug. 8, 1941, EJC.

37 "Japanese Employed by Union Pacific Railroad," Dec. 8, 1941, UPO; "Japanese Employees," Feb. 11, 1942, UPO; NY *Times,* June 22, 1941.

38 Connors to GJM et al., Dec. 7, Dec. 11, and Dec. 12, 1941, UPO; R. J. O'Connor notice, Dec. 8, 1941, UPO; Biddle statement, Dec. 28, 1941, UPO.

39 Jeffers to Charske, Feb. 14, 1941, UPN.

40 Ibid.; E. J. Connors notice, Feb. 11, 1942, UPO; J. S. Little to F. M. Perrine, Apr. 5, 1942, UPO; Jeffers to Hoover, Feb. 13, 1942, UPO; Omaha *World-Herald,* Feb. 14, 1942, UPO; Hoover to Jeffers, Feb. 28, 1942, UPO.

41 Jeffers to Connors et al., Feb. 20, 1942, UPO; H. D. Wiese to Jeffers, Feb. 27, 1942, UPO; Jeffers to Wiese, Feb. 28, 1942, UPO.

42 Acord interview, 9. All figures are computed from data in company annual reports, 1941–45.

43 Jeffers to station agents, Jan. 8, 1942, EJC; *Railway Age,* 112:177, 622, 1252–53; W. H. Olin to Jeffers, July 24, 1942, UPN; NY *Times,* Oct. 14, 1942; Schafer to Hannagan, Dec. 8, 1942, UPN; Dorice Taylor, *Sun Valley* (Sun Valley, 1980), 121–32; How interview, 83–84; Prouty interview, 9.

44 F. E. Baukhages to F. W. Robinson, with attached report, Aug. 18, 1943, EJC; Baukhages to Connors, Aug. 24, 1943, Jan. 12, 1944, EJC; Jeffers to Ashby, Sept. 14, 1943, EJC; extract from AAR report. Nov. 16, 1943, UPO.

45 Acord interview, 11–12.

46 How interview, 85; Klippel interview, 31; interview with E. L. Prouty, Feb. 16, 1982, 10–11.

47 *Railway Age,* 112:1212; interview with Thomas E. Murray, Aug. 29, 1982, 6.

48 Murray interview, 7–8, 27, 30.

49 Gerald D. Nash, *The American West Transformed* (Bloomington, Ind., 1985), vii, 3–36.

50 *Railway Age,* 115:371–72; S. Kip Farrington, Jr., *Railroads at War* (New York, 1944), 9–11.

51 Ibid.

52 Ibid. The CTC system is described in both sources.

53 "Jeffers-criticisms in office conference diatribes-fragmentary," EJC; Jeffers to F. W. Robinson, May 20, 1943, EJC; Averell Harriman to Charske, Mar. 23, 1942, UPN. Jeffers's sensitivity on the power question is obvious from the sources, though the reason for it cannot be proven.
54 "Jeffers-criticisms in office," EJC.
55 J. C. Gale to Jeffers, Feb. 8, 1943, EJC; Connors to R. E. Titus et al., Feb. 9, 1943, EJC; Robinson to Connors et al., Feb. 12, 1943, EJC. Jeffers's telegram is quoted in the Robinson telegram.
56 J. Gogerty to Connors, Feb. 11, 1943, EJC; Connors to Titus et al., Feb. 22, 1943, EJC; Robinson to Connors et al., Feb. 24, 1943, EJC; Jeffers to Robinson et al., Mar. 4, 1943 (two items), EJC; Robinson to Jeffers, Mar. 5, 1943, EJC; Jeffers to Charske, Mar. 9, 1943, UPN.
57 "Jeffers-criticisms in office," EJC; Gale to Jeffers, Apr. 19 and May 24, 1943, EJC; Gale to R. E. Titus, Apr. 19, 1943, EJC; Jeffers to Robinson, May 20 and May 28, 1943, EJC.
58 Jeffers to Connors, July 27, 1943, EJC; B. O. Wedge to Connors, Sept. 1, 1943, EJC.
59 Jeffers to F. C. Paulsen, Aug. 6, 1943, EJC; Jeffers to Connors, Aug. 8 (two items), Aug. 12, Aug. 18, Sept. 15, and Dec. 10 (five items), 1943, EJC; Jeffers to Robinson, Sept. 2, 1943, EJC; Jeffers to John Gogerty, Sept. 21, 1943, EJC; O. H. Swan to Connors, Oct. 5, 1942, EJC.
60 Jeffers to Union Pacific Employees, Sept. 14, 1943, EJC; Jeffers to Connors, Dec. 11, 1943, EJC; Jeffers to Titus, Dec. 18, 1943, EJC; Jeffers to Gogerty, Dec. 23, 1943, EJC.
61 Jeffers to Charske, Dec. 7, 1941, UPN; F. G. Gurley to C. E. Johnston, Dec. 16, 1941, EJC; "Stevens Report," Dec. 16, 1941, EJC; NY *Times*, Dec. 10, 1942, Feb. 3, 1943; *WSJ*, May 27, 1943; NY *Herald-Tribune*, Sept. 29, Nov. 9, Nov. 13, and Dec. 17, 1943; Washington *Times-Herald*, Nov. 13, 1943.
62 NY *Times*, Dec. 18, 1943; NY *Herald-Tribune*, Dec. 28–30, 1943, Jan. 18, 1944; *WSJ*, Jan. 15, 1944.
63 For details on the history and organization of MRS see Carl R. Gray, Jr., *Railroading in Eighteen Countries* (New York, 1955), 1–23.
64 Ibid., 24–40, 135, 185.
65 Ibid., 36, 256–68; Bailey interview, 61–62; Churchill interview, 65.
66 Joest interview, 53–54; *Railway Age*, 114:1240–41.
67 Churchill interview, 179–83; *Life*, Feb. 22, 1943, 88; NY *Times*, Jan. 3, 1943.
68 Ibid., 184; *Time*, Sept. 28, 1942, 71; NY *Journal-American*, Sept. 16, 1942; NY *Herald-Tribune*, Sept. 16, 1942; NY *Times*, Sept. 16, 1942; *WSJ*, Sept. 17, 1942.
69 NY *Times*, Sept. 17, 1942.
70 Churchill interview, 185–86. Nearly all the press accounts refer to the appointment as a surprise.
71 Ibid., 186–88, 190.
72 NY *Daily News*, Sept. 26, 1942; *Business Week*, Sept. 26, 1942, 18; *Time*, Sept. 28, 1942, 71; NY *Times Magazine*, Oct. 11, 1942, 8.
73 Churchill interview, 188–90; *Time*, Oct. 19, 1942, 17; NY *Times*, Oct. 13, 1942; Charske to Averell Harriman, Oct. 23, 1942, UPN.
74 *Time*, Oct. 19, 1942, 17.
75 NY *Herald-Tribune*, Oct. 13, 1942; *Barron's*, Oct. 19, 1942; *Collier's*, Nov. 21 and Dec. 12, 1942, 106; *Christian Science Monitor*, Dec. 5, 1942.
76 Churchill interview, 191.

77 Ibid., 191–92.

78 Ibid., 192–94.

79 Ibid., 196–98.

80 Ibid., 199; *WSJ*, Nov. 21, Nov. 25, and Nov. 28, 1942, Jan. 22, Jan. 26, Jan. 30, and Apr. 20–24, 1943; NY *Times*, Dec. 21, 1942, Jan. 3, and Apr. 29, 1943; NY *Herald-Tribune*, Jan. 28 and May 3, 1943; *Time*, Feb. 8, 1943, 15.

81 *Time*, Apr. 26, 1943, 17; *WSJ*, Mar. 17, Apr. 7, May 4, May 18, and June 12, 1943; NY *Times*, Apr. 4 and May 23, 1943. Details on the operation and technical problems are in William M. Jeffers, "Progress Report No. 2," Feb. 18, 1943, UPN.

82 Bernard Baruch to Jeffers, June 9, 1943, EJC; *American Mercury*, 57:153–57; NY *Herald-Tribune*, Sept. 6, 1943; Jeffers to Charske, Sept. 9, 1943, UPN; *Railway Age*, 115:417, 424; *Newsweek*, Sept. 13, 1943; *Chronicle*, 158.1:1114. The *Chronicle* reprints Jeffers's letter of resignation and Roosevelt's reply.

83 Denver *Post*, Oct. 4, 1943; Jeffers to editor, Philadelphia *Record*, Oct. 4, 1943, EJC; Philadelphia *Record*, Oct. 6, 1943; NY *Times*, Jan. 19, 1944.

84 Acord interview, 60.

CHAPTER 22
THE MISFITS

1 F. E. Baukhages to Connors, Apr. 10, 1944, EJC.

2 Ibid., May 3, 1944, EJC; Arthur A. Murphy to Jeffers, June 17, 1944, UPN; Baukhages to Jeffers, June 23, 1944, EJC; Connors to Jeffers, May 21, 1944, UPN; Jeffers to Charske, June 10, 1944, UPN.

3 John W. Barriger III to R. C. Morse, Mar. 6, 1944, EJC; "List of Rear End Collisions January 1927 to Date [Nov. 1941], EJC; "Statement Showing Derailments and Collisions November 1st to December 9th, 1943, inclusive," EJC; NY *Times*, May 2, 1941, Aug. 21, 1942, June 29, 1944; Jeffers to All Employes [sic], Nov. 26, 1941, EJC; Jeffers to Employes of the Wyoming Division, Nov. 26 and Nov. 27, 1941, EJC; *Railway Age*, 113:651; *Church Journal*, May 8, 1943, LDS; Robinson to Connors, Sept. 9, 1943, EJC; Connors to Ashby, Jan. 15, 1945, EJC.

4 Jeffers to Gale et al., July 12, 1944, UPO.

5 Proudfit interview, 7, and notes taken afterward.

6 UP Directors minutes, Sept. 24, 1942, UPN; Sutton interview, 46.

7 Churchill interview, 74; Melia interview, 66.

8 Churchill interview, 21; How interview, 64–66; Proudfit interview, 16–17; *Railway Age*, 111:599.

9 Proudfit interview, 16; Averell Harriman to Connors, Sept. 11, 1941, EJC; Jeffers to Connors, Sept. 18, 1941, EJC.

10 Clippings in EJC; UP Exec. Comm. minutes, May 9, 1944, UPN; Connors to Jeffers, May 17, 1944, EJC; Jeffers to Byrnes, May 19, 1944, EJC; "Jeffers-criticisms in office," EJC.

11 Jeffers to Connors, Nov. 22 and Nov. 27, 1944, EJC; UP Exec. Comm. minutes, Nov. 28, 1944, UPN; NY *Times*, Nov. 25, 1944; [Rigdon] to Jeffers, Jan. 16, 1945, EJC; B. F. Danbaum to Connors, Feb. 23, 1945, EJC.

12 Jeffers to Charske, Nov. 3, 1944, UPN; NY *Times*, Nov. 25, 1944; UP Exec. Comm. minutes, Nov. 28, 1944, UPN; Proudfit interview, 17, 22; Rigdon to

Jeffers, Dec. 19, 1944, UPO; Rigdon to Ashby, Jan. 15, 1945 (three items), EJC; Rigdon to M. C. Williams, Jan. 17, 1945, EJC.

13 Charske to Averell Harriman, Sept. 9, 1941, UPN; NY *Times,* Sept. 10, 1941; Scott Ure to Connors, Apr. 5, 1950, EJC.

14 NY *Times,* Sept. 19, 1941, Jan. 2, 1943; Jeffers to Charske, Feb. 9, 1942, UPO; UP Exec. Comm. minutes, Feb. 17, 1942, UPN; Acord interview, 23.

15 M. C. Williams to Robinson, Apr. 16, 1943, UPO; Connors to Robinson, May 29, 1943, EJC; Gale to Jeffers, June 5, 1943, UPO; NY *Times,* Nov. 15, 1943, Feb. 2 and Apr. 21, 1944; H. A. Hansen to Rigdon, Jan. 10, 1945, UPO; B. F. Danbaum to Connors, Feb. 23, 1945, EJC; Connors to Ashby, Jan. 15, 1945, EJC; P. J. Norton to Connor[s], June 3, 1942, EJC; B. O. Wedge to Connors, June 30, 1945, EJC.

16 How interview, 79, 87, 94; Melia interview, 71–72; Jeffers to Charske, June 10, 1945, UPN.

17 Danbaum to Connors, Feb. 23, 1945, EJC; Jeffers to Rigdon, May 6, 1945, EJC, June 16, 1945, UPO; Connors to Bert O. Wedge, July 3, 1945, EJC.

18 MLH to Connors, July 30, 1945, EJC. MLH or "May" was Connors's secretary who, although now working for Rigdon, was still loyal to Connors.

19 Ibid.; Rigdon to Jeffers, July 26 and July 27, 1945, EJC; Jeffers to Rigdon, July 26 and July 27, 1945, EJC; Rigdon to Charske, July 27, 1945, EJC; Rigdon to Roland Harriman, July 27, 1945, EJC.

20 May [MLH] to Connors, July 30, 1945, EJC; Omaha *World-Herald,* Aug. 1, 1945; Charske to Averell Harriman, Sept. 7, 1945, UPN; *WSJ,* Aug. 6, 1945.

21 "A small stockholder" to Charske, Aug. 2, 1945, UPN; Averell Harriman to Charske, [Sept. 1, 1945], UPN.

22 Jeffers to Charske, Aug. 10, 1945, UPN; Charske to Averell Harriman, Sept. 4, 1945, UPN.

23 MLH to Connors, Aug. 2 and Aug. 7, 1945, EJC; Danbaum to Connors, Feb. 23, 1945, EJC; Jeffers to Connors, Aug. 9, 1945, EJC; Connors to Wedge, Aug. 22, 1945, EJC; NY *Times,* Sept. 1, 1945.

24 Wedge to Connors, June 30, 1945, EJC; Connors to Wedge, July 13, 1945, EJC; Danbaum to Connors, Sept. 26, 1945, EJC; Charske to Averell Harriman, Oct. 2, 1945, UPN; Steve Hannagan to Jeffers, Oct. 25, 1945, UPN; Jeffers to Charske, Oct. 30, 1945, UPN; *Time,* July 30, 1945, 82.

25 Roland Harriman to Averell Harriman, June 12, 1945, UPN.

26 Ibid. Connors had been in poor health, but he did not retire from the company until 1959.

27 Jeffers to Charske, Nov. 9, 1945, UPN; Roland Harriman to Averell Harriman, Nov. 30, 1945, UPN; Averell Harriman to Roland Harriman, undated but probably Dec. 1, 1945, UPN; Charske to Averell Harriman, Dec. 10, 1945, UPN; UP Directors' minutes, Dec. 20, 1945, UPN; NY *Times,* Dec. 21, 1945.

28 Roland Harriman, *I Reminisce,* 125; Averell Harriman interview, 43–44.

29 Jeffers to Ashby, Dec. 8, 1945.

30 Stoddard to Connors, Jan. 31 and Nov. 16, 1945, EJC.

31 Averell Harriman interview, 40–41; NY *Times,* Oct. 16, 1946; *Chronicle,* 164.2:2060.

32 UP Exec. Comm. minutes, Aug. 4 and Aug. 10, 1942, UPN; Charske to Ashby, Feb. 25, 1946, UPN; NY *Times,* Mar. 22, Oct. 30, and Nov. 22, 1946; Jeffers to Roland Harriman, Mar. 22, 1946, UPN; Mann to Charske, June 14, 1946, UPN; George W. Ellis to Roland Harriman, Nov. 18, 1951, UPN.

33 Steve Hannagan press release, Apr. 5, 1951, UPN.

34 Robert Creamer, "Harriman of Goshen," *Sports Illustrated,* July 9, 1962, 35. See also the portrait of Averell in Walter Isaacson and Evan Thomas, *The Wise Men* (New York, 1986).
35 Interview with James H. Evans, Oct. 20, 1987, 20.
36 Creamer, "Harriman of Goshen," 32–35, 37; Lovett interview, 2.
37 Interview with Elbridge T. Gerry, Oct. 20, 1981, 49–52; Evans interview, 18, 21.
38 Sutton interview, 72.
39 Creamer, "Harriman of Goshen," 35.
40 Irving and Amy Wallace, *The Two* (New York, 1978), 185, 331. Chang had nine children, Eng eleven.
41 How interview, 24–25, 28; Proudfit interview, 24.
42 *Who Was Who in America, 1951–60,* 3:34; Churchill interview, 88–89; How interview, 26.
43 How interview, 27–28; Churchill interview, 80, 110; Sutton interview, 51–52; interview with William J. Fox, Sept. 6, 1982, 56.
44 Churchill interview, 82–83; How interview, 26.
45 Churchill interview, 83, 86; Sutton interview, 52.
46 Churchill interview, 85–87.
47 Ibid., 84.
48 Ibid., 77; Sutton interview, 46.
49 Churchill interview, 102–3; Sutton interview, 52–53.
50 Proudfit interview, notes taken afterward.

CHAPTER 23
THE BLIZZARD

1 NY *Times,* Jan. 25 and June 21, 1946; Ashby to Charske, Jan. 31 and July 20, 1946, UPO; UP Exec. Comm. minutes, July 25, 1946, UPN; Roland Harriman to Ashby, Oct. 31, 1946, UPN; Ashby to Roland Harriman, Nov. 3, 1946, UPN.
2 Connors notes, EJC.
3 Jeffers to Charske, Feb. 12, 1942, UPN.
4 Unless otherwise indicated, all data in the section on maintenance and physical plant are taken from E. J. Connors, "Transportation Expenses: August 1946 compared with August 1945," Oct. 19, 1946, EJC.
5 Jeffers to Charske, Apr. 6, 1945, UPN.
6 Bailey interview, 56.
7 Ashby to Charske, Oct. 23, 1946, EJC.
8 Ibid.
9 Charske to Ashby, Oct. 22, 1946, UPO; Bailey interview, Sept. 11, 1982.
10 Connors to Jeffers, Jan. 10, 1946, UPN; Charske to Ashby, Jan. 30, 1946, UPN; Ashby to Charske, Feb. 5, 1946, UPN; Connors to Ashby, Mar. 8, 1946, UPN; NY *Herald-Tribune,* Apr. 27, 1946; C. J. Collins to C. E. Peterson, May 16, 1946, UPL; NY *Times,* May 18, 1946; HWS to Collins, May 18, 1946, UPL; "Federal Manager's Notice and Order No. 1," May 18, 1946, UPL; NY *Times,* May 17–25, 1946; HBB to Ashby, May 27, 1946, UPL. Telegrams detailing the effect of the strike can be found in UPL.
11 MLH to Connors, Aug. 2 and Aug. 7, 1945, EJC. For Jeffers's reputation in labor relations see *Survey Graphic,* December 1937, 26:692–94, 726, 728–30.

12 Jeffers to Ashby, Dec. 8, 1945, EJC; Salt Lake *Tribune,* Jan. 5, 1946; Ashby to Charske, Feb. 5, 1946, UPN; Connors to Ashby, Feb. 7, 1946, EJC; *WSJ,* Nov. 26, 1946; Acord interview, 22.

13 Cottrell, *Technological Change and Labor,* 124–27, 144–47.

14 Ibid., 128–29.

15 "Background of Diesel Dispute," n.d., UPL; James C. Nelson, *Railroad Transportation and Public Policy* (Washington, D. C., 1959), 273–74; Overton, *Burlington Route,* 435–36.

16 "Background of Diesel Dispute," UPL; Cottrell, *Technological Change and Labor,* 130–31.

17 Connors to Ashby, June 26, 1947, UPN; UP Exec. Comm. minutes, Sept. 16, 1947, UPN; NY *Herald-Tribune,* Nov. 15, 1947; *WSJ,* Nov. 17, 1947.

18 *WSJ,* Mar. 11, 1948, Mar. 28 and Aug. 17, 1949; Connors to Ashby, Apr. 10, 1948, UPN; Ashby to Charske, Apr. 28, 1948, UPN; NY *Times,* Apr. 29 and May 7–12, 1948; Chicago *Tribune,* May 6, 1948; C. Peterson to C. J. Collins, May 7, 1948, UPL; Denver *Post,* May 7, 1948; NY *Herald-Tribune,* May 7–11, May 20, June 3, and July 9, 1948, Mar. 22, 1949; W. T. Burns and C. J. Collins to W. Conrey, May 10, 1948, UPL; E. A. Klippel memorandum, May 8, 1948, UPL; Chicago *Journal of Commerce,* May 8, 1948; AAR, "Current Comment on the Threatened Railroad Strike," May 10, 1948, UPN; Connors phone message, June 8, 1948, UPN; Connors to Roland Harriman, Mar. 2, 1949, UPN; NY *Daily News,* Mar. 15, 1949.

19 Ashby to Connors, May 24, 1948, EJC; Connors to Ashby, May 24, 1948, Jan. 20, 1949, EJC.

20 Ashby to Charske, Nov. 19, 1947, EJC, Nov. 6 and Nov. 20, 1947, UPO; NY *Times,* July 17, 1946, Oct. 24, 1947; *WSJ,* Feb. 27 and Oct. 20, 1947; *UP Report,* 1949, 6. For details on this work see S. Kip Farrington, Jr., *Railroads of Today* (New York, 1949), 61–77.

21 Ashby to Charske, Nov. 19, 1947, EJC, Jan. 15 and Mar. 30, 1948, UPO; *UP Report,* 1946, 7–8, 1947, 6–7, 1948, 6–7, 1949, 6; *WSJ,* Aug. 3 and Dec. 20, 1946, Nov. 17 and Nov. 19, 1947; NY *Times,* Nov. 19, 1945, July 13, Aug. 3, Dec. 16, and Dec. 20, 1946, Aug. 12, Aug. 13, and Nov. 18, 1947.

22 Churchill interview, 89–90; NY *Times,* Mar. 18 and Oct. 13, 1947; Farrington, *Railroads of Today,* 234–35.

23 All figures are calculated from data in annual reports.

24 Ashby to Roland Harriman, June 1, 1947, UPO; Connors to Kip Farrington, Jan. 9, 1947, EJC; Lovett to Roland Harriman, May 29, 1947, UPN; UP Exec. Comm. minutes, June 3, 1947, UPN.

25 Churchill interview, 55.

26 Ibid., 84–85.

27 Ibid., 103.

28 Bailey interview, 44–45; How interview, 91; Proudfit interview, 24.

29 Ashby to Lynch, Nov. 3, 1947, EJC, Nov. 12, 1947, UPO.

30 Ashby to Lynch, July 8 and July 13, 1947, EJC; Lynch to Ashby, July 9, 1947, EJC; Ashby to Connors, Nov. 3 and Nov. 4, 1947, EJC; Ashby to H. E. Shumway, Dec. 29, 1947, EJC; Shumway and W. R. Rouse to Ashby, Dec. 30, 1947, EJC; Ashby to W. C. Perkins, Mar. 31, 1948, EJC; V. W. Smith to Ashby, Apr. 7, 1948, EJC; Perkins to Lynch, Apr. 7, 1948, EJC; *Trainman News,* May 22, 1948.

31 Ashby to Connors, Nov. 4 and Nov. 23, 1947, EJC; Ashby to Lynch, Nov. 22 and Nov. 23, 1947, EJC.

32 Ashby to Lynch and A. J. Seitz, Nov. 12, 1947, UPO. Connors and Guild received copies of this letter.
33 Seitz to Ashby, Nov. 22, 1947, UPO; Ashby to Lynch et al., May 10, 1948, EJC.
34 Ashby to Lynch et al., May 10, 1948, EJC.
35 Lewiston, Idaho, *Morning Tribune,* June 11, 1946; NY *Herald-Tribune,* Dec. 7, 1946; NY *Times,* Oct. 8, 1947, Dec. 31, 1948.
36 Churchill interview, 78, 91–92.
37 Ibid., 92; Bailey interview, 45–46, 53–55; How interview, 30–31; Acord interview, 68–71; Connors notes, Feb. 22, 1948, EJC.
38 Bailey interview, 57; interview with William J. Fox, Sept. 6, 1982, 13–14.
39 Churchill interview, 92, 106–7.
40 Ibid., 107, 116–18; Ashby to Charske, Dec. 12, 1947, UPN; Roland Harriman to Ashby, Dec. 16, 1947, UPN.
41 Churchill interview, 117–19; Ashby to Charske, June 14, 1948, UPN; Charske to Ashby, June 18, 1948, UPN.
42 Telephone interview with G. J. Proudfit, Oct. 22, 1988; Ashby to Roland Harriman, Mar. 6, 1948, UPO; Bailey second interview, Sept. 11, 1982, 1; Proudfit interview, 25; *Union Pacific Bulletin,* Aug. 1948, 1; *Chronicle,* 168.1:589; Churchill interview, 108–9.
43 Churchill interview, 108–12, 164.
44 Ibid., 111–14.
45 Proudfit interview, 47.
46 Connors notes, EJC; Ashby to Charske, Aug. 12, 1948, UPN; Lynch notice, Sept. 1, 1948, UPO; Ashby to Roland Harriman, Oct. 31, 1948, UPO.
47 "January 1949 Snowstorm," EJC; Bailey interview, 23–24; Ashby to Charske, Jan. 4 and Jan. 6, 1949, UPN; Charske to Ashby, Jan. 6, 1949, UPN; NY *Herald-Tribune,* Jan. 6, 1949.
48 "January 1949 Snowstorm," EJC; Churchill interview, 93.
49 Blizzard brochure, Mar. 1, 1949, UPN; Churchill interview, 94–95, 98, 101; Ashby to Charske, Jan. 7, 1949, UPN.
50 Churchill interview, 100–1.
51 "January 1949 Snowstorm," EJC.
52 Churchill interview, 96–97; Proudfit interview, 25–26.
53 Churchill interview, 97–98.
54 Bailey interview, 50–51.
55 Ibid., 52.
56 "January 1949 Snowstorm," EJC.
57 Ibid.; NY *Times,* Feb. 7, 1949; Ashby to Charske, Feb. 7 and Feb. 9, 1949, UPN.
58 Ashby to Charske, Feb. 10, Feb. 11, Feb. 12, Feb. 13, Feb. 15, and Feb. 16, 1949, UPN; Churchill to Ashby, Feb. 15, 1949, UPN; D. H. Voltz to Connors, Feb. 16, 1949, EJC.
59 Taylor, *Sun Valley,* 206.
60 "January 1949 Snowstorm," EJC; Churchill interview, 98–100; *Journal of Commerce,* Feb. 16, 1949.
61 Churchill interview, 93; Bailey interview, 47.
62 Churchill interview, 95.
63 Bailey interview, 48–49; Prouty interview, 13.
64 Churchill interview, 128–29, 138; Roland Harriman to Ashby, Feb. 8, 1949, UPN; Ashby to Roland Harriman, Feb. 9, 1949, UPN; Roland Harriman to Artemus L. Gates, Feb. 18, 1949, UPN.

65 Churchill interview, 130–31.
66 Ibid., 119–21.
67 Ibid., 122–25.
68 Ibid., 125–27.
69 Acord interview, 85.
70 Churchill interview, 130–33.
71 Clark to Roland Harriman, Mar. 16, 1949, UPN.
72 Churchill interview, 135–36; "GFA" to Charske, Feb. 17, 1949, UPN; ? to EBF, Feb. 17, 1949, EJC; Stoddard to Charske, Feb. 21, 1949, UPN. The Feb. 17 telegram cited here bore Ashby's initials but was not sent by him. He was in Chicago that day, and a copy of the telegram was sent to him there.
73 Churchill interview, 140–44.

CHAPTER 24
THE SLEEPING GIANT

1 See for example *Barron's,* May 29, 1944, which called Union Pacific "probably the wealthiest railroad in the world."
2 Interview with Jervis Langdon, Jr., Mar. 15, 1988, 17–18.
3 *Railway Age,* 113:905, 1016, 114:303; NY *Times,* Jan. 3, 1943, July 27, 1944; *Chronicle,* 157.1:479, 160.1:771; *WSJ,* Aug. 11, 1944; *Magazine of Wall Street,* 75:195.
4 NY *Times,* Aug. 1, Sept. 1, Sept. 19, and Sept. 28, 1944, Sept. 27, 1945; *Chronicle,* 160.1:988, 1190, 1298–99, 160.2:1530, 1636, 2407, 161.1:1099, 162.1:78, 1441, 162.2:1557; *Barron's,* Sept. 11, 1944; *WSJ,* Feb. 27 and Sept. 27, 1945; Charske to Averell Harriman, Sept. 26, 1945, UPN.
5 NY *Times,* Dec. 6, 1945, Jan. 23, Feb. 7, and Feb. 14, 1946; *WSJ,* Dec. 6, 1945, Jan. 23, 1946; *Chronicle,* 162.2:2862; 163.1:696.
6 NY *Times,* Feb. 26, Feb. 27, and Mar. 14, 1946, Dec. 10, 1947, Apr. 29, 1953; *Chronicle,* 163.1:1292, 1483–84, 165.2:2715, 166.2:2605; UP Exec. Comm. minutes, Jan. 1, 1947, UPN; *UP Report,* 1961, 10.
7 E. G. Smith to Stockholders, Nov. 20, 1947, UPO; NY *Times,* Nov. 21, 1947, May 12, 1948; *WSJ,* Nov. 21, 1947, Feb. 2, 1956; *Chronicle,* 166.2:2216, 167.1:158, 182.2:2362; A. C. Sherwood to Stockholders, Nov. 23, 1955, UPO; *UP Report,* 1956, 17, 1957, 18.
8 *Barron's,* Jan. 14, 1952. All other figures calculated from data in company reports.
9 UP Exec. Comm. minutes, Nov. 29, 1949, Sept. 4, 1952, July 12 and Sept. 13, 1955, Dec. 4 and Dec. 18, 1956, Jan. 13 and Dec. 15, 1959, Jan. 13, 1960, UPN; *WSJ,* Mar. 11, 1954, Oct. 5, 1955; Mar. 24, 1960; *Business Week,* Mar. 20, 1954; NY *Times,* Oct. 5, 1955; *Chronicle,* 188.2:1361, 189.1:140; Stoddard to L. J. Tracy, Jan. 15, 1959, UPN.
10 *Barron's,* Jan. 14, 1952.
11 Bailey interview, 63; Proudfit interview, 12–13.
12 Bailey interview, 66; How interview, 43–44; Prouty interview, 15; *Railway Age,* 126:497.
13 Schafer interview, 39–40.
14 Barnett interview, 18–19; Sutton interview, 63–65.
15 Sutton interview, 65–66; *Collier's,* Nov. 11, 1955, 106.

16 *Business Week,* Mar. 12, 1949, 6; Bailey interview, 72–73; Barnett interview, 18–19, 45; Gerry interview, 65; How interview, 34, 43–44, 89.
17 Barnett interview, 45; Churchill interview, 65; Proudfit interview, 12, 43; How interview, 42–43, 89–90.
18 How interview, 89; Bailey interview, 89.
19 Kenefick interview, 31.
20 For background information see Chandler, *Visible Hand,* 98–109, 175–87.
21 Connors to Ashby, Nov. 13, Dec. 10, and Dec. 12, 1947, EJC; Connors to Lynch, Dec. 13, 1947, EJC; Lynch notice, Dec. 23, 1947, June 18, 1948, EJC; NY *Times,* Dec. 27, 1947; Connors to Stoddard, Jan. 30, 1949, EJC.
22 Kenefick interview, 21.
23 Lynch notice, July 15, 1949, EJC; E. J. Hicks to Stoddard, Nov. 24, 1954, UPO; Stoddard to Lovett, Nov. 9, 1954, UPO; E. H. Bailey to Stoddard, July 7, 1957, UPO.
24 Bailey to Stoddard, July 7, 1957, UPO.
25 Kenefick interview, 19.
26 Proudfit interview, 5, 29; Acord interview, 56; How interview, 35, 92; Kenefick interview, 14.
27 Stoddard to Charske, Mar. 4, 1949, UPN; Stoddard to Lovett, May 17, 1954, UPN; salary list, June 1, 1954, UPN; Proudfit telephone interview, Oct. 22, 1988.
28 Bailey interview, 72–74; Acord interview, 58.
29 Source withheld by request; How interview, 35; Proudfit telephone interview, Oct. 22, 1988.
30 Proudfit telephone interview, Oct. 22, 1988; Jeffers to Charske, July 3 and Nov. 26, 1945, UPN; Connors to Bert O. Wedge, July 13, 1945, EJC.
31 Acord interview, 76, 79; How interview, 36–37.
32 Stoddard to Charske, Mar. 4, 1949, Dec. 16, 1951, Jan. 2, 1952, UPN; Omaha *World-Herald,* Jan. 2, 1952; Stoddard to Lovett, May 17, 1954, Mar. 12, 1957, UPN; NY *Times,* Mar. 30, 1957; Proudfit telephone interview, Oct. 22, 1988; How interview, 36.
33 Exec. Comm. minutes, Jan. 26, 1961, Oct. 25, 1962, UPN; Hicks to Roland Harriman, July 2, 1962, UPN; Acord interview, 77; Proudfit interview, 51–53; Proudfit telephone interview, Oct. 22, 1988.
34 Stoddard to Lynch, Apr. 27, 1949, UPO; Wells to Stoddard, Apr. 29, 1949, UPO; Stoddard to Charske, Oct. 2, 1950, Dec. 16, 1951, UPN; F. M. P. to Stoddard, July 23, 1954, UPO; Stoddard to Roland Harriman, Aug. 2, 1954, UPO. The position was somewhat changed: Wells was assistant general manager, and the restored post was general superintendent.
35 *Collier's,* Nov. 11, 1955, 106–9; Stoddard to Lovett, Apr. 5, 1955, UPN; *WSJ,* May 2, 1955.
36 Schafer interview, 49–53.
37 Ibid., 54–55; Acord interview, 81; Sutton interview, 56.
38 Jett interview, 63–64; Churchill interview, 70.
39 Schafer interview, 55; Bailey interview, 117–19.
40 Jett interview, 63.
41 Schafer interview, 2–3.
42 *Printers' Ink,* 68:24, 85:28, 87:27; Judge Lovett to L. J. Spence, June 7, 1912, UPN; *Railway Age,* 56:1598.
43 Judge Lovett to Mohler et al., June 18, 1915, UPN; B. J. Winchell to Judge Lovett,

July 7, 1915, UPN; Schafer interview, 61; Mohler to Judge Lovett, May 18 and May 22, 1916, UPN; Calvin to Judge Lovett, Sept. 27, 1917, UPN.

44 *Railway Age,* 74:1351, 1365–66, 75:599, 603, 84:427; *WSJ,* Feb. 28, 1924; *Church Journal,* Nov. 23, 1924, LDS; Salt Lake *Tribune,* Nov. 25, 1924; *Union Pacific Magazine,* Sept. 1930, 5.

45 Gray to Charske, July 26 and Oct. 5, 1935, Mar. 17, 1937, UPN; *Time,* May 11, 1936, 75–76; Charske to Gray, June 5, 1936, UPN; *Chronicle,* 142:3873; *Railway Age,* 102:301.

46 Averell Harriman to Jeffers, June 29, 1937, UPN; Schafer interview, 27; *Railway Age,* 106:115, 108:792, 115:915; "Tentative Program," Mar. 19, 1940, UPO; Jeffers notice, May 14, 1940, UPO; NY *Times,* Jan. 8, 1944; E. C. Schmidt to Jeffers, Aug. 24, 1945, UPN.

47 Schafer interview, 27, 30, 32–36.

48 Ibid., 28–29, 36, 39–40, 61.

49 Ibid., 42, 47, 54; Stoddard to Charske, Dec. 5, 1950, UPO; NY *Times,* Dec. 27, 1950, Feb. 6, 1953; Charske to Roland Harriman, Feb. 5, 1953, UPN; Stoddard to Lovett, Apr. 3, 1955, UPN.

50 Office rosters, Feb. 5, 1916, Jan. 28, 1946, UPN. Twenty names are found on both lists. The company left the Equitable Building after the 1912 fire and returned in 1919.

51 Judge Lovett memoranda, Jan. 10, 1912 and Feb. 17, 1919, UPN; C. C. Stillman to W. V. Thorne, June 24, 1912, UPN.

52 Thorne to departments, July 3 and Sept. 5, 1913, UPN; Stillman to Seger et al., Sept. 26, 1913, UPN; Charske to Clark et al., June 14, 1920, UPN; Averell Harriman to Crescent Towel Supply Co., Oct. 1, 1915, UPN; Seger notice, Oct. 28, 1915, UPN; A. V. Howell to Stillman, Nov. 15, 1915, UPN; Howell to Thomas Price, Jan. 14, 1916, UPN.

53 Interview with James P. Coughlin, Aug. 22, 1985, 5–7.

54 Ibid., 43, 48.

55 Ibid., 19, 38, 48–50.

56 Ibid., 29–30.

57 Ibid., 11–12, 27.

58 See the fine discussion in Stephen Salsbury, *No Way to Run a Railroad: The Untold Story of the Penn Central Crisis* (New York, 1982), 50–55.

59 Coughlin interview, 56.

60 Ibid., 9, 40–41.

61 Ibid., 61

62 Charske to Lovett, Feb. 24, 1949, UPN; Lovett to Charske, Feb. 25, 1949, UPN; Mann to Charske, Oct. 2, 1951, UPN; NY *Herald-Tribune,* Sept. 18 and Nov. 6, 1951; Charske to Barnett, Dec. 27, 1951, UPN.

63 Roland Harriman to Jeffers, Dec. 22, 1952, UPN.

64 Churchill interview, 56–62.

65 Ibid., 59–60; Jeffers to Roland Harriman, Dec. 29, 1952, UPN; Roland Harriman to Jeffers, Dec. 30, 1952, UPN; NY *Times,* Mar. 7, 1953.

66 NY *Times,* May 5 and May 9, 1953; *WSJ,* May 9, 1953; Sutton interview, 69.

67 Barnett interview, 6, 12; Evans interview, 18; Sutton interview, 67; Gerry interview, 54.

68 Evans interview, 19; Sutton interview, 67–68. A fine portrait of Lovett and his health concerns can be found in Isaacson and Thomas, *The Wise Men,* which also includes a portrait of Averell Harriman.

69 Evans interview, 19.
70 Gerry interview, 44–46.
71 Ibid., 45; Barnett to Lovett, July 27, 1954, UPN; *WSJ,* Aug. 31, 1956, Jan. 25, 1957.
72 Coughlin interview, 42.

CHAPTER 25
THE AWAKENING

1 Dick & Merle-Smith analysis, Nov. 20, 1958, UPO.
2 Lovett interview, Sept. 8, 1981; telephone interview with Robert A. Lovett, June 13, 1982; Sutton interview, 21; 34 *Stat.* 584 c.3591. For another example see the conflict over the Kansas City produce terminal in *Railway Age,* 106:300, 108:421, 109:959, 966, 110:1016, 1026.
3 Lovett telephone interview, June 13, 1982; Gerry interview, 10–11; Sutton interview, 10.
4 Lovett interview, Sept. 8, 1981; Lovett telephone interview, June 13, 1982.
5 Lovett interview, June 13, 1982; Barnett interview, 9.
6 Coughlin interview, 16, 22–23.
7 Barnett interview, 17; Sutton interview, 14.
8 Organizational chart, June 30, 1960, UPN; Lee S. Osborne to Stoddard, July 15, 1960, UPO; Stoddard to Lovett, July 23, 1960 (two letters), UPN; Lovett to Stoddard, Aug. 8, 1960, UPN.
9 Hardee to Barnett, Nov. 9, 1960, UPN; Hardee to Gerald A. Simon, Oct. 25, 1967, UPN.
10 Hardee to Barnett, Nov. 9, 1960, UPN; Barnett to Lovett, July 19, 1962, UPN.
11 Bailey interview, 87, 95–96; Evans interview, 9; How interview, 48, 88–89, 94; Sutton memorandum, Nov. 22, 1960, UPN; Stoddard to Roland Harriman, Mar. 3, 1961, UPN.
12 UP Directors minutes, Nov. 29, 1960, UPN; news release, Dec. 14, 1960, UPN; *WSJ,* Dec. 14, 1960; *UP Report,* 1960, 4.
13 Gerry interview, 6–7, 12–16, 65.
14 *WSJ,* Sept. 19, 1962; Stoddard to Lovett, Nov. 5, 1963, UPN; Roland Harriman and Lovett to Bailey, Dec. 12, 1963, UPN; NY *Times,* Dec. 23, 1964; Roland Harriman to Stoddard, Nov. 17, 1964, UPN; UP Directors minutes, Dec. 22, 1964, UPN; Bailey interview, 81–83.
15 Sutton interview, 10–11.
16 Lovett interview, Sept. 8, 1981; Gerry interview, 14.
17 *Barron's,* May 24, 1948, Jan. 10, 1949; *Chronicle,* 168.1:16. All figures calculated from data in annual reports. The Southern Pacific actually spun off its oil assets. See Hofsommer, *Southern Pacific,* 114.
18 Reinhardt to Stoddard, Apr. 5, 1949, Dec. 11, 1953, Mar. 9, 1955, UPO, Oct. 13, 1950, July 15, 1953, UPN; Stoddard to Charske, Sept. 16, 1949, UPO; Stoddard to Lovett, July 21 and Aug. 29, 1954, UPN, Jan. 5 and Sept. 7, 1955, UPO.
19 LJB to Stoddard, Mar. 6, 1958, UPO; *WSJ,* May 6, 1957, June 6, 1958; George W. Trammell to E. C. Renwick, Sept. 4, 1958, UPO; W. R. Rouse to Stoddard, Sept. 11, 1958, UPO; Stoddard to Lovett, Aug. 5, 1959, UPO; Renwick to F. J. Melia, Aug. 12, 1959, UPO; *Oil and Gas Journal,* Aug. 31, 1959, 55–60; Barnett to

Lovett, Sept. 30, 1959, UPN; Stoddard to L. J. Tracy, Nov. 7, 1959, UPN; Lovett to James L. Sheehan, Nov. 23, 1959, UPN; Bert Goss to Stoddard, May 20, 1960, UPO; *UP Report,* 1958, 14, 1959, 14, 1960, 10–11, 1961, 18.

20 Reinhardt to Stoddard, July 14 and Aug. 28, 1953, UPO; Barnett to W. R. Rouse, Oct. 30, 1953, UPO; Wyoming *Eagle,* Apr. 18, 1954; Omaha *World-Herald,* Sept. 1, 1954; Denver *Post,* Dec. 31, 1954; *Business Week,* Jan. 22, 1955, 76, Jan. 14, 1956, 28; Barnett to Lovett, Aug. 25, 1955, UPN; *Oil and Gas Journal,* Feb. 20, 1956, 91, Feb. 27, 1956, 88–89, Mar. 5, 1956, 69; *WSJ,* Apr. 9 and Aug. 22, 1957, Oct. 29, 1958; Lovett to R. Guy Wilson, June 18, 1957, UPN; Stoddard to Lovett, June 27, 1958, UPN; *UP Report,* 1955, 14–15, 1956, 14–15, 1957, 15.

21 MMW report on interview with Osborne, May 24, 1963, UPN; Osborne to Lovett, June 20, 1963, UPO; Sutton memorandum on Rangely, June 25, 1963, UPO; Jack Snyder to Osborne, July 26, 1963, UPO; NY *Times,* Oct. 24, 1963.

22 Lovett to Osborne, Aug. 6, 1963, UPO; Osborne to Stoddard, Feb. 14, 1958, UPO; *Wyoming Eagle,* Apr. 28, 1960; C. M. Collins to Calnev Pipe Line Co., Dec. 5, 1959, UPN; Lovett to Stoddard, Apr. 27, 1960, UPN; F. J. Melia to Stoddard, May 5, 1960, UPN; UP Exec. Comm. minutes, May 17, 1960, UPN; Osborne to Lovett, May 17, 1961, UPN; Gerry interview, 8–9; *UP Report,* 1961, 21, 1962, 19.

23 Sutton interview, 23–24. For the earlier efforts see Klein, *Union Pacific,* 1:335, 519–21.

24 Reinhardt to Ashby, Mar. 4, 1942, UPO; Ashby to Reinhardt, Mar. 5, 1942, UPO; Pike to Ashby, May 30, July 5, July 8, July 10, and July 13, 1942, May 29, 1944, UPO; Ashby to Pike, July 8 and July 19, 1942, UPO; F. Eberstadt to Pike, July 1, 1942, UPO; Denver *Post,* July 14, 1942; Pike to Howard B. Blanchard, July 18, 1942, UPO; Pike memorandum, Sept. 20, 1942, UPO.

25 M. Y. Seaton to Westvaco Co. Exec. Comm., May 15, 1944, UPO; Pike to George W. McMath, Aug. 1, 1944, UPO; H. C. Van Schaack to Jeffers, Sept. 26, 1945, UPO; Pike to Reinhardt, May 15, 1946, UPO; Ashby to Charske, July 5, 1946, UPO; *UP Report,* 1961, 20.

26 J. A. Marsh to Reinhardt, Oct. 13, 1948, May 31, 1951, UPO; Marsh memorandum, Oct. 13, 1948, UPO; I. N. Bayless to Ashby, Oct. 20 and Oct. 23, 1948, UPO; Reinhardt to Ashby, Oct. 21, 1948, UPO; Rock Springs *Rocket,* May 23, 1951; Reinhardt to Stoddard, June 13 and Sept. 10, 1951, UPO; Stoddard to Reinhardt, Sept. 28, 1951, UPO; *Wyoming Eagle,* Nov. 7, 1951. The defense status gave the project important tax benefits.

27 Reinhardt to Stoddard, Nov. 5, 1952, UPO; *WSJ,* Feb. 1, 1954; Stoddard to Jean E. D. Galloway, June 30, 1954, UPO; Stoddard to Osborne, Oct. 7, 1957, UPO; Osborne to Stoddard, Oct. 19, 1957, Aug. 6, 1959, UPO; Stoddard to J. R. Simplot, Dec. 10, 1959, UPO; Osborne to Ritter, Dec. 13, 1959, UPO.

28 C. W. Rossworn to Stoddard, Aug. 27, 1960, UPO; Lovett to Stoddard, Sept. 14, 1960, UPO; Sutton report, Oct. 21, 1960, UPO; Sutton memorandum, Sept. 26, 1961, UPN; I. N. Bayless to Stoddard, May 10, 1963, UPO; *UP Report,* 1961, 20, 1962, 18, 1963, 20, 1964, 20, 1965, 20; *WSJ,* Nov. 19, 1965; Sutton interview, 25.

29 *UP Report,* 1963, 21, 1964, 20–21; Osborne to Lovett, June 22, 1965, Aug. 31, 1966, UPN; Barnett memorandum, Aug. 23, 1965, UPN; *WSJ,* Sept. 23, 1965.

30 Eugene McAuliffe to Ashby, Nov. 15, 1945, UPO; I. N. Bayless to Ashby, Apr. 1 and Sept. 16, 1948, UPO; Bayless to Ashby, et al., report copy, Dec. 1948, UPO; Joseph Q. Berta to Bayless, June 1, 1949, UPO; news release, June 6, 1949, UPO; Bayless to A. J. Seitz, Nov. 7, 1949, UPO; Stoddard to Charske, Feb. 8, 1950, UPO; Bayless to J. C. O'Mahoney, May 11, 1951, UPO; *Wyoming Eagle,* June 5,

1951; O'Mahoney to Bayless, June 14, 1951, UPO; Bayless to Stoddard, July 30, 1951, UPO.

31 NY *Times,* Apr. 5 and Apr. 6, 1947; *Explosives Engineer,* Sept.–Oct. 1951, 138–40, 156–57; UP Exec. Comm. minutes, Jan. 9 and Nov. 8, 1962, UPN; Osborne to Lovett, Nov. 19, 1962, UPN; Stoddard to Lovett, Feb. 23, 1963, UPN; Lovett to Stoddard, Mar. 1, 1963, UPN.

32 *WSJ,* Nov. 7, 1955, Feb. 26, 1957, Jan. 30, 1961, Sept. 4, 1966; J. W. Godfrey to E. H. Bailey, Sept. 13, 1966, UPO; press release, Apr. 7, 1967, UPO; *UP Report,* 1953, 26, 1954, 26, 1955, 30, 1956, 29, 1957, 30, 1958, 31, 1959, 28, 1960, 28, 1961, 22, 1962, 20–21, 1963, 22–23, 1964, 22–23, 1965, 22–23.

33 NY *Times,* Nov. 30, 1943; *Business Week,* Dec. 25, 1943, 108–9; UP Exec. Comm. minutes, Mar. 11, 1952, UPN; *WSJ,* Apr. 2, 1952.

34 *WSJ,* Jan. 27, 1941; L. O. Head to J. J. Pelley, July 6, 1942, UPN; Head to Fitzgerald Hall, Aug. 18, 1942, UPN.

35 Fletcher to J. J. Pelley, July 6, 1943, UPN; UP Exec. Comm. minutes, June 22, 1944, UPN; Lovett to Connors, Sept. 1, 1954, EJC; Lovett to E. H. Bailey, July 12, 1965, UPN.

36 NY *Herald-Tribune,* Jan. 3, 1951.

37 *UP Report,* 1949, 6; Klippel interview, 81–82.

38 *UP Report,* 1947, 6, 1948, 6, 1950, 6; Klippel, "My Tour Over the Line from Milepost One," 11–12; Ashby to Charske, Mar. 17, Mar. 19, and Mar. 20, 1946, UPN; NY *Times,* Mar. 20, Apr. 28, May 16, May 18, May 21, Sept. 1, and Sept. 29, 1946; *WSJ,* Apr. 1, 1946.

39 NY *Times,* Mar. 28, 1947; Ashby to Lynch, Aug. 28, 1947, EJC; Ashby to Board of Directors, Mar. 21, 1948, UPN; Seitz to Ashby, June 2, 1948, UPN; Roland Harriman to Ashby, July 2, 1948, UPN; Ashby to Roland Harriman, July 25, 1948, UPN.

40 Klippel, "My Turn Over the Line," 11–12; NY *Times,* Feb. 28, 1948. Figures calculated from data in annual reports.

41 Klippel interview, 41–42, 45, 51–52; Klippel, "My Turn Over the Line," 12; Stoddard to Charske, Apr. 9, 1953, UPN; *UP Report,* 1952, 13, 1953, 19, 1954, 19, 1955, 20, 1956, 20.

42 *WSJ,* Aug. 17, 1953, Jan. 29, 1954, Sept. 21, 1955; Stoddard to Lovett, Oct. 2, 1953, UPN; *Challenger* flyer, UPN; Stoddard to P. E. Feucht, Sept. 14, 1955, UPN; Barnett memorandum, Sept. 20, 1955, UPN; NY *Times,* Sept. 21, 1955; *Business Week,* Sept. 24, 1955, 32; Klippel interview, 27.

43 *WSJ,* Jan. 6 and Nov. 20, 1956; UP press release, Nov. 19, 1956, UPO; DAS to Stoddard, Nov. 1, 1957, UPO; *Railway Age,* Dec. 2, 1957, 521–23.

44 *UP Report,* 1958, 20, 1959, 19, 1960, 16, 1961, 13, 1964, 15, 1965, 16, 1966, 16; Lovett interview, Sept. 8, 1981.

45 Klippel interview, 53. Figures calculated from data in annual reports.

46 *UP Report,* 1967, 7, 14, 1968, 14, 1969, 6, 1970, 6.

47 Averell Harriman to Jeffers, Jan. 2, 1939, June 7, 1940, UPO; Mar. 7, May 16, May 21, and May 22, 1940, Jan. 2, 1942, UPN; Averell Harriman to Rogers, June 8, Aug. 10, and Nov. 10, 1939, Aug. 16 and Sept. 8, 1940, Jan. 4, 1941, UPN; Jeffers to Averell Harriman, Aug. 13, 1939, May 15, 1940, July 14, 1941, UPN; *Railway Age,* 107:500; Meeting memorandum, Sept. 14, 1940, UPN.

48 Jeffers to Charske, Dec. 1, 1945, UPN; Rogers report, Nov. 23, 1945, UPN; Hannagan to Averell Harriman, Apr. 2, 1946, UPN.

49 Hannagan to Averell Harriman, Apr. 2, 1946, UPN.

50 Ibid.; Averell Harriman to Hannagan, Nov. 10, 1939, Mar. 12, 1940, UPN; NY *World-Herald,* Dec. 3, 1939; Hannagan to Averell Harriman, Jan. 22, 1947, UPN.

51 Taylor, *Sun Valley,* 149; Averell Harriman to Charske, July 24, 1946, UPN.

52 Taylor, *Sun Valley,* 149–92; Oppenheimer and Poore, *Sun Valley,* 168–73; Jeffers to Charske, Dec. 1, 1945, UPN; Ashby to Charske, Jan. 3, 1946, UPO; Rogers to Stoddard, Mar. 1 and Apr. 1, 1952, UPO; Stoddard to Rogers, Mar. 28, 1952, UPO; Stoddard to McCrea et al., Mar. 28, 1952, UPO.

53 Taylor, *Sun Valley,* 229; Averell Harriman to Charske, July 24, 1946, UPN; Murray interview, 9, 34.

54 Taylor, *Sun Valley,* 243–45.

55 Ibid., 243–45; Victor H. Palmieri to Stoddard, Dec. 27, 1963, UPO; F. J. Melia to Stoddard, Jan. 6, 1964, UPO; Roland Harriman to Averell Harriman, Aug. 6, 1964, UPN; Salt Lake *Tribune,* Oct. 7, 1964; *WSJ,* Oct. 7, 1964.

56 Rogers to Jeffers, Oct. 8, 1942, UPO; Rogers to Ashby, Nov. 12, 1942, UPO.

57 Ashby to Newton B. Drury, Dec. 3, 1942, UPO; Drury to Ashby, Dec. 17, 1942, UPO; Jeffers to Harold L. Ickes, Dec. 26, 1942, UPO; Ashby to Jeffers, Apr. 15, 1943, UPO; Rogers to Ashby, May 18, 1943, UPO; Ashby to Rogers, May 21, 1943, UPO; Salt Lake *Tribune,* Sept. 30, 1945; Rogers to Jeffers, Nov. 19, 1945, UPO; Jeffers to Ashby, Nov. 27, 1945, UPO; Omaha *World-Herald,* Jan. 14, 1946.

58 Ashby, to J. A. Krug, May 21, 1948, UPN; Krug to Ashby, May 26, 1948, UPN; Salt Lake *Tribune,* May 26, 1948; Charske to Ashby, May 27 and June 29, 1948, UPN; Ashby to Charske, May 27 and May 28, 1948, UPN; Daggett Harvey to Ashby et al., June 15, 1948, UPN; Rogers to Ashby, June 21, 1948, UPN; Salt Lake *Telegram,* July 7, 1948; E. G. Smith to Ashby, Oct. 26, 1948, UPN.

59 Rogers to Stoddard, Oct. 22, 192, UPO.

60 Stoddard notice, May 1, 1957, UPO; OMN to L. J. Tracy, Aug. 18, 1959, UPN; Stoddard to Lovett, Aug. 19, 1959, UPN; Tracy memorandum, Aug. 26, 1959, UPN; Murray interview, 9–12.

61 Murray interview, 9–15; G. R. Shideler to F. M. Perrine, July 8, 1960, UPO; R. A. Fimmel to Perrine, July 11, 1960, UPO; Stoddard notice, July 11, 1960, UPO; Rulon Iverson to Stoddard, July 16, 1960, UPO; Hicks to Stoddard, July 18, 1960, UPO; Murray to Stoddard, July 18, 1960, UPO; Conrad L. Wirth, Aug. 29, 1960, UPO.

62 Sutton to Stoddard, Jan. 20, 1957, UPO; James J. Murray to William J. McDonald, Jan. 15, 1968, UPO.

63 Press release, Jan. 26, 1968, UPO; Omaha *World-Herald,* Jan. 30, 1968; E. H. Bailey to George B. Hartog, Jr., Mar. 15, 1968, UPO; How to Bailey, Apr. 21, 1968, UPO; Murray to Bailey, Apr. 22, 1968, UPO; Bailey to Barnett, Apr. 26, 1968, UPO; Bailey to James J. Murray, May 3, 1968, UPO; Idaho *State Journal,* May 28, 1969; Sutton memorandum, Sept. 23, 1969, UPN; Harlan L. Bill to Bailey, Oct. 24, 1969, UPN; AOM to Bailey, May 19, 1970, UPO; J. P. Deasey to John C. Kenefick, Mar. 10, 1971, UPO; Kenefick to James H. Evans, Mar. 11, 1971, UPO; Kenefick to George C. Fleharty, Mar. 11, 1971, UPO; W. S. Cook to Barnett, Sept. 17, 1971, UPO; Ogden *Standard-Examiner,* Mar. 15, 1972; *WSJ,* Mar. 20, 1972.

64 Foral interview, Nov. 17, 1981, 11–61; Murray interview, 36–37. The Foral interview gives a detailed account of the tours and how they worked.

65 Foral interview, 19–22.

CHAPTER 26

THE PARTS CHANGERS

1 Fox interview, 15, 33–34.

2 Acord interview, 40; Fox interview, 48.

3 Acord interview, 29–31.

4 Ibid., 41–42.

5 Ibid., 33, 42.

6 *Reader's Digest,* 56:121–23; Thomas R. Lee, *Turbines Westward* (Manhattan, Kan., 1975), 7–14. Lee's loving volume contains full detail on both versions of the turbine locomotives along with superb photographs.

7 *Reader's Digest,* 56:121–23; NY *Times,* Jan. 28 and May 2, 1951; *WSJ,* May 2, 1951, Dec. 6, 1952, June 6, 1953; *UP Report,* 1950, 6, 1951, 12, 1952, 13; Lee, *Turbines Westward,* 18–25; *Time,* Dec. 29, 1952, 62.

8 Barnett interview, 5–6; Harriman interview, 39; Lovett interview, Sept. 8, 1981; *WSJ,* Dec. 12, 1953, Aug. 6, 1954; *Chronicle,* 179.1:49; *Business Week,* Jan. 15, 1955, 162; *Newsweek,* Jan. 24, 1955, 76; *Up Report,* 1954, 20.

9 *WSJ,* Dec. 1, 1956, Feb. 19, 1957, Feb. 24, 1959, May 24, 1960; Chicago *Tribune,* Dec. 1, 1955; LJB to Stoddard, Mar. 15, 1957, UPO; Stoddard to Lovett, Feb. 24, 1958, UPO; D. S. Neuhart to Bailey, June 20, 1958, May 7 and June 30, 1963, UPO; Report by Harold Rees, July 1963, UPO; Lee S. Osborne to Bailey, June 6, 1966, UPO; Fox interview, 33; Lee, *Turbines Westward,* 25–45, 150–53. Lee's book has a complete roster of Union Pacific turbines.

10 Joest interview, 14, 20–23, 34–38; *UP Report,* 1958, 21; Bailey interview, Sept. 11, 1982.

11 "History and Functions of Pacific Fruit Express," 10–11, UPO; *WSJ,* July 14, 1954, Feb. 28 and Dec. 8, 1955, Sept. 16, 1957, Aug. 5, 1959; *UP Report,* 1953, 19, 1954, 19, 1955, 21.

12 "History and Functions," 12–26; *WSJ,* June 27, 1961, Feb. 15, 1962, Jan. 19, 1967; memorandum, Sept. 1, 1967, UPO; news release, Oct. 30, 1968, UPO.

13 Joest interview, 16; *WSJ,* Jan. 17, Jan. 22, 1951, June 23 and Nov. 23, 1955, Oct. 6, 1958, June 16, 1961; NY *Times,* Aug. 10, 1954; Bailey to Lovett, May 24, 1965, UPN; press release, Nov. 28, 1967, UPO. Figures calculated from data in annual reports.

14 *UP Report,* 1951, 13, 1953, 20.

15 Ibid. 1951, 13, 1952, 14, 1953, 20, 22; *WSJ,* Jan. 18, 1952, Jan. 15, 1953; Portland *Oregonian,* Jan. 18, 1952; Denver *Post,* June 4, 1952, May 10, 1953.

16 Report of J. A. Bunjer, Oct. 1964, UPO.

17 Ibid. The 133-pound rail did much better at preventing head and web separations common in the 131-pound rail.

18 *UP Report,* 1961, 16.

19 Cottrell, *Technological Change and Labor,* 15.

20 *UP Report,* 1951, 13, 1952, 14, 1953, 22, 1954, 22–23, 1955, 22, 1956, 21–22; *WSJ,* Dec. 2, 1952, June 29, July 14, and Dec. 20, 1955, May 6, 1957.

21 Interview with C. Otis Jett and Ralph Judson, Mar. 12, 1982, 6–7.

22 Jett interview, 67–68.

23 Ibid., 2.

24 NY *Times,* Feb. 18, 1911, Sept. 10, 1914; Mohler to Judge Lovett, Sept. 15, 1914, UPN. The Navigation Company also experimented with telephone dispatching. See *Railway Age Gazette,* 50:1701.

25 Mohler to Judge Lovett, Sept. 15 and Sept. 18, 1914, UPN.

26 Mohler to Judge Lovett, Apr. 22, 1916, UPN; Lovett to Calvin, July 7, 1916, UPN; *Railway Age Gazette,* 61:53; E. C. Manson et al. to Jeffers, July 31, 1916, UPN.

27 Manson et al. to Jeffers, July 31, 1916, UPN; Calvin to Judge Lovett, Aug. 1, 1916, UPN.

28 C. O. Jett, "Wire-Line and Carrier Communications on the Union Pacific Railroad," *Electrical Engineering* (Nov. 1960), 894.

29 Jett interview, 69–70.

30 Ibid., 71–72.

31 Ibid., 73–75; Jett, "Wire-Line and Carrier Communications," 894.

32 Jett interview, 26.

33 Ibid., 77–78, 82–85.

34 Ibid., 19, 81–82, 89–90.

35 Ibid., 9–10; Jett, "Wire-Line and Carrier Communications," 894–96; *UP Report,* 1957, 22.

36 Jett interview, 40–41, 61.

37 Ibid., 44–49; *UP Report,* 1960, 17, 1961, 14, 1962, 15, 1963, 16, 1964, 16, 1965, 17, 1966, 17; *Chronicle,* 191.1:550; press release, June 23, 1966, UPL. There were actually two pole lines. Communications used one; the Signal Department used the other for signals and CTC operation in some areas.

38 NY *Times,* Sept. 27, 1947; Jett interview, 34–35; Prouty interview, 46; Schafer interview, 58.

39 Sutton interview, 26, 76; *UP Report,* 1957, 21.

40 Jett interview, 8.

41 Ibid., 8–9, 52.

42 How interview, 54.

43 Ibid., 51–56.

44 Ibid., 55–56.

45 Sutton interview, 72–75.

46 Jett interview, 8–9; Jett, "Wire-Line and Carrier Communications," 896–97; *UP Report,* 1957, 21–22.

47 *UP Report,* 1957, 21–22, 1958, 22; Sutton interview, 28.

48 *UP Report,* 1962, 13; Jett interview, 54–55.

49 *UP Report,* 1955, 22, 1957, 28, 1958, 29, 1959,27, 1960, 27. I am indebted to Dr. Morton Maser of the Electron Microscopy Society of America for this information on electron microscopes.

50 Acord interview, 93–94.

51 Barnett interview, 30.

52 "Background of Diesel Dispute," UPL.

53 NY *Herald-Tribune,* Apr. 25, May 12, Aug. 25, Aug. 27–30, Dec. 15, and Dec. 22, 1950, Jan. 9 and Feb. 7–9, 1951; C. J. Collins to CHS et al., May 13 and May 16, 1950, UPL; Collins to J. C. Cumming, May 18, 1950, UPL; NY *Times,* June 8, June 26, and Dec. 15, 1950, Feb. 9, 1951; Harry S Truman, "Executive Order," Aug. 25, 1950, UPN; JCP to CJC, Jan. 30, 1951, UPL; PJL to JEM et al., Feb. 1, 1951, UPL.

54 NY *Times,* Mar. 1, 1951; NY *Herald-Tribune,* Apr. 26, 1951; Stoddard to Charske, Apr. 1, 1952, UPN; E. A. Klippel to W. T. Burns, Aug. 29, 1956, UPL; Portland *Oregonian,* Dec. 3, 1956; C. W. Rexroads to Klippel, Dec. 5, 1956, UPL. Details on individual strikes, actions, and settlements are in the passenger department files, UPL.

55 *WSJ,* Feb. 8, 1954, May 22, 1956; NY *Times,* July 2 and Dec. 6, 1955, May 13, May 22, May 23, and May 27, 1956; NY *World-Telegram,* Apr. 30, 1956; Nelson, *Railroad Transportation and Public Policy,* 274–75.

56 *UP Report,* 1963, 15, 1964, 14, 1965, 15. Details on the long firemen's battle are in "Transcript of Proceedings of the National Labor Arbitration Board No. 282," Sept.–Oct. 1963, OHS.

57 *UP Report,* 1965, 15, 1966, 15, 1967, 14, 1968, 14; G. W. Bohannon to Stoddard, Dec. 4, 1963, Mar. 22, 1965, UPL; *WSJ,* Dec. 19, 1963, Feb. 7, 1968; TFS to Stoddard, Apr. 8, 1964, UPL; J. E. Wolfe to A. D. Hanson, Mar. 26, 1965, UPL; Hanson to DFW et al., Mar. 27, 1965, UPL; CWJ memorandum, Apr. 5, 1966, UPL; Omaha *World-Herald,* Sept. 28, 1966, July 17 and July 18, 1967; F. J. Melia to E. H. Bailey, Nov. 30, 1966, UPO; D. F. Wengert and G. L. Farr to Bailey, Nov. 6, 1967, UPO; Farr to Bailey, Aug. 22, 1968, UPO; *Journal of Commerce,* Nov. 19, 1968.

58 *UP Report,* 1967, 14. All figures are calculated from data in annual reports.

59 NY *Times,* Jan. 21 and Sept. 27, 1946, Nov. 14, 1951; Ashby to Charske, June 11, Aug. 22, and Aug. 26, 1946, UPN; B. F. Wells to Ashby, Nov. 12, 1946, EJC; press release, May 18, 1947, UPN; WGM to Joe Copps, Sept. 20, 1951, UPN; Stoddard to Charske, Nov. 12, 1951, UPN.

60 *UP Report,* 1957, 26.

61 Ibid., 1968, 17; Omaha *World-Herald,* May 15, 1968; Bailey to Barnett, Mar. 12, 1969, UPN.

62 Stoddard to Charske, July 15 and Aug. 7, 1951, UPN; NY *Times,* July 18, 1951; *WSJ,* June 15, 1954, May 2, 1958, July 3, 1962; *UP Report,* 1960, 20.

63 *UP Report,* 1961, 17, 1962, 16, 1963, 18, 1964, 18, 1965, 14, 1966, 18, 1968, 18.

CHAPTER 27
THE MERGER MISSTEP

1 NY *Times,* Nov. 6, 1942, Aug. 24 and Aug. 25, 1944; *WSJ,* Oct. 27, 1941, Feb. 21 and Nov. 6, 1942, Mar. 20, 1943, Apr. 18 and Oct. 30, 1945; AAR press release, Sept. 4, 1947, UPN; "Railroad Land Grants," Jan. 26, 1944, UPO.

2 *WSJ,* July 12, 1949, May 2, 1962; NY *Times,* Apr. 6, 1962; Melia to Stoddard, Apr. 9, 1962, UPO; *Forbes,* Apr. 15, 1962, 15.

3 Barnett to Lovett, July 19, 1962, UPN.

4 Ibid.; *WSJ,* Dec. 30, 1955, Aug. 14 and Dec. 27, 1956, Jan. 24, Feb. 27, and July 11, 1957, Jan. 21, Aug. 29, and Oct. 7, 1958; UP Exec. Comm. minutes, Jan. 26 and Jan. 29, 1956, UPN; Lovett to Stoddard, Oct. 6, 1958, UPN; *UP Report,* 1955, 27, 1958, 24.

5 "Memorandum Dealing with Union Pacific–Rock Island Merger," Nov. 5, 1965, 8, UPN.

6 Ibid., 8–9; A. J. Seitz to Jeffers, May 2, 1945, UPN.

7 "Memorandum . . . ," Nov. 5, 1965, 11–12; *UP Report,* 1954, 29, 1955, 28–29, 1968, 26.

8 "Memorandum . . . ," Nov. 5, 1965, 12–14; *UP Report,* 1954, 28, 1955, 29, 1956, 27–28, 1957, 28, 1959, 26, 1960, 21, 1961, 26, 1962, 22, 1963, 26, 1964, 26, 1965, 26, 1966, 26, 1967, 26. The documentation of the court process in UPN is abundant and too full to be cited here.

9 Nelson, *Railroad Transportation and Public Policy,* 3–8, 182–83, 315–16; U.S. Senate Committee on Commerce, *National Transportation Policy,* Sen. Report No. 445, 87 Cong. 1st Sess. (Washington, 1961), 58–80, 229–42 (hereafter cited as Doyle Report).

10 Lou Dombrowski, "Merger Madness," *Modern Cities via Transportation,* July/August 1966, 38–39.

11 J. R. MacAnally to Stoddard, Oct. 12, 1960, UPN; William Wyer, to Barnett Dec. 5, 1960, UPN; Lovett to Stoddard, Dec. 22, 1960, UPN; Stoddard to Lovett, Jan. 10, Jan. 14, and Jan. 31, 1961, UPN.

12 Wyer to Barnett, Feb. 1, 1961, UPN; Prouty interview, 38–39; memorandum of discussion, Feb. 17, 1961, UPN.

13 Hardee memoranda for Barnett, Feb. 21, Mar. 3, Mar. 7, and Mar. 9, 1961, UPN; C. W. Rossworn to L. H. Oehlert, Apr. 6, 1961, UPN.

14 J. R. MacAnally, "Analysis of Traffic Interchanged with Eastern Connections, Year 1960," May 31, 1961, UPN; MacAnally to Stoddard, June 1, 1961, UPO; Stoddard to Lovett, June 3, June 17, and June 20, 1961, UPN; "Memorandum . . . ," Nov. 5, 1965, 45A–47A; "Report on Competitive Situation—Eastern Connections," Sept. 2, 1961, 1–16. It was the MacAnally study that first identified each line by number.

15 "Report on Competitive Situation," Sept. 2, 1961, 26–48.

16 Ibid.

17 Ibid.

18 "Memorandum . . . ," Nov. 5, 1965, 49; "Supplemental Report on Competitive Situation—Eastern Connections," Sept. 3, 1961, UPN.

19 Barnett to Lovett, Sept. 6, 1961, UPN; Lovett to Stoddard, Sept. 7, 1961, UPN; Bailey to Stoddard, Sept. 16 and Sept. 23, 1961, UPN; MacAnally to Stoddard, Sept. 21, 1961, UPN; Francis Melia to Stoddard, Sept. 21, 1961, UPN; Hicks to Stoddard, Sept. 27, 1961, UPN.

20 Barnett to Lovett, Sept. 6, 1961, UPN; memorandum of meeting, Sept. 26, 1961, UPN; Lovett to Stoddard, Sept. 28, 1961, UPN.

21 Lovett interview, June 13, 1982; Evans interview, 23; Gerry interview, 39–40; interview with Jervis Langdon, Jr., March 15, 1988, 23.

22 Sutton to Hicks, Oct. 7, 1961, UPN; Stoddard to Lovett, Oct. 30, Nov. 10, Nov. 16, and Nov. 28, 1961, UPN; Lovett to Stoddard, Nov. 22, 1961, UPN; Melia memorandum, Nov. 1, 1961, UPN; Bailey to Stoddard, Nov. 8, 1961, UPN; MacAnally to Stoddard, Nov. 8, 1961, UPN; Melia to Stoddard, Nov. 9, 1961, UPN; Charles D. Peet memorandum, Nov. 10, 1961, UPN; Dan Cordtz, "The Fight for the Rock Island," *Fortune,* June 1966, 141. The Cordtz article is the best contemporary account, a judicious, balanced survey of a complex event.

23 Stoddard to Lovett, Dec. 5, 1961, Jan. 31 and Feb. 21, 1962, UPN; W. A. Johnston to Roland Harriman and Lovett, Dec. 8, 1961, UPN; Barnett memorandum, Dec. 14, 1961, UPN; Peet memorandum, Jan 12, 1962, UPN; Bailey to Stoddard, Jan. 16 and Feb. 1, 1962, UPN.

24 Charles D. Peet to Wyer, Feb. 9, 1962, UPN; Wyer to Barnett, Feb. 16 and Feb. 26, 1962, UPN.

25 Barnett to Lovett, Mar. 1, 1962, UPN; Lovett to Stoddard, Apr. 9, 1962, UPN; memorandum of meeting, Apr. 30, 1962, UPN; Lovett to D. J. Russell, June 7, 1962, UPN; Hofsommer, *Southern Pacific,* 265.

26 Lovett to Russell, June 7, 1962, UPN; Russell to Lovett, June 9, 1962, UPN.

27 Barnett memoranda, June 12 and June 15, 1962, UPN; "Random observations,"

June 18, 1962, UPN; *Business Week,* June 23, 1962, 33; Hardee memoranda, June 27 and June 29, 1962, UPN; Lovett memorandum, July 2, 1962, UPN; Cordtz, "Fight for the Rock Island," 142.

28 Sutton to Lovett, July 9, 1962, UPN; memoranda, July 16, Aug. 27, Aug. 29, Sept. 1, and Sept. 6, 1962, UPN; Barnett memorandum, Aug. 10, 1962, UPN; meeting minutes, Aug. 23 and Sept. 13, 1962, UPN; Stoddard to Lovett, Aug. 25, 1962, UPN; Peet memorandum, Sept. 7, 1962, UPN; Barnett notes, Sept. 11 and Sept. 12, 1962, UPN; *WSJ,* Sept. 18, 1962.

29 Stoddard to Lovett, July 20 and July 28, 1962, UPN; Lovett to Stoddard, Nov. 21, 1962, UPN.

30 Sutton and Biaggini to Coverdale & Colpitts, Sept. 24, 1962, UPN; Lovett to Stoddard, Sept. 28, 1962, UPN; EMK to Sutton, Oct. 1, 1962, UPN; meeting minutes, Oct. 2, 1962, UPN; H. J. Bearss memorandum, Oct. 3, 1962, UPN; Barnett to Biaggini, Oct. 3, 1962, UPN; Barnett to Douglas F. Smith, Oct. 6, 1962, Feb. 7, 1963, UPN; Russell to Lovett, Dec. 17, 1962, UPN; John C. Gardiner to Barnett and Biaggini, Jan. 4, 1963, UPN; Barnett memorandum, Jan. 10 and Feb. 6, 1963, UPN; Barnett and Sutton memorandum, Jan. 21 and Jan. 24, 1963, UPN.

31 Peet memorandum, Feb. 8, 1963, UPN.

32 Barnett memorandum, Feb. 27, 1963, UPN; Russell memorandum of telephone conversation with Crown, Feb. 27, 1963, UPN.

33 Ibid.; Hardee memorandum, Mar. 1, 1963, UPN.

34 Lovett to Stoddard, Feb. 28, Mar. 11, 1963, UPN; Union Pacific–Southern Pacific agreement, Feb. 28, 1963, UPN; Barnett memoranda, Mar. 5, Mar. 11, Mar. 21, Mar. 25, and Apr. 24, 1963, UPN; JAC–TET memorandum, Mar. 15, 1963, UPN; MacAnally and W. G. Peoples to Stoddard and Russell, Mar. 15, 1963, UPN; Bailey–E. M. Kerrigan memorandum, Mar. 16, 1963, UPN; Melia memorandum, Mar. 14, 1963, UPN; memoranda 1 and 2, Mar. 16, 1963, UPN; Stoddard to Lovett, Apr. 7, 1963, UPN; Wyer to Barnett, Apr. 9, 1963, UPN; Sutton memorandum, Apr. 17, 1963, UPN; Peet memorandum, Apr. 17, 1963, UPN; Ingersoll to Lovett, Apr. 17, 1963, UPN; Wyer to Sutton, Apr. 22, 1963, UPN; Stoddard to Sutton, Apr. 23, 1963, UPN.

35 Barnett interview, 23–24; "Chronology of Developments UP–CRIP Merger," 69–70, UPN; Barnett to Crown, May 3, 1963, UPN; *WSJ,* May 8, May 14, and June 28, 1963; Ingersoll to Barnett, May 10, 1963, UPN; UP Directors minutes, May 16 and June 27, 1963, UPN; UP Exec. Comm. minutes, June 11, 1963, UPN; Langdon interview, 2.

36 Keith L. Bryant, ed., *Railroads in the Age of Regulation, 1900–1980* (New York, 1988), 193–97. This is a volume in the *Encyclopedia of American Business History and Biography* series.

37 *WSJ,* May 22, June 25, and June 28, 1963; NY *Times,* May 22, 1963; Hardee memorandum, July 3, 1963, UPN; memorandum, July 8, 1963, UPN; Lovett to Ingersoll et al., July 9, 1963, UPN; Ingersoll to Lovett, July 10, 1963, UPN. Ingersoll was chairman of the Rock Island executive committee, Crown of its finance committee.

38 Barnett memorandum, May 22, 1963, UPN; E. S. Marsh to W. A. Johnston, June 6, 1963, UPN; *WSJ,* June 6, 1963; Johnston to Board of Directors, June 7, 1963, UPN; Stoddard to Lovett, July 30, 1963, UPN; *Modern Cities via Transportation,* July/August 1966, 35.

39 Langdon interview, 3–5.

40 Cordtz, "Fight for the Rock Island," 200.

41 Langdon interview, 3–4, 8.

42 Alan C. Furth to Barnett, July 18, 1963, UPN; Hill and Knowlton to Union Pacific, July 22, 1963, UPN; Avery McBee to Barnett, July 26, 1963, UPN; Chicago *Sun-Times,* July 26, Sept. 14, and Nov. 20, 1963; Stoddard to Lovett, July 30, 1963, UPN; Chicago *Tribune,* Aug. 2, 1963; WCB memorandum, Aug. 13, 1963, UPN; Wyer, Dick analysis, Sept. 19, 1963, UPN; *WSJ,* Sept. 23–27, Oct. 1, Oct. 25, Nov. 18, Nov. 25, and Nov. 29, 1963, Feb. 19, 1964; W. J. McDonald to David Ferber, Oct. 31, 1963, UPN; *Business Week,* Nov. 2, 1963, 119–24; "memorandum for Douglas F. Smith," Sept. 26, 1963, UPN; memorandum, Oct. 14, 1963, UPN; Hayden, Stone & Co. report, Oct. 16, 1963, UPN; NY *Times,* Oct. 24, 1963; "Memorandum of Decision . . . ," *Union Pacific Railroad Company et al. v. Chicago and North Western Railway Company et al.*, Feb. 18, 1964, UPN.

43 Lovett to Crown, Oct. 11, 1963, UPN; Crown to Lovett, Oct. 14, 1963, UPN; Russell to Roland Harriman, Oct. 17, 1963, UPN; J. W. Seder to Sutton, Nov. 4, 1963, UPN; JRM memorandum, Nov. 12, 1963, UPN; *WSJ,* Dec. 3, 1963; Avery McBee to Richard E. Cheney, Sept. 13, 1963, UPN.

44 UP Exec. Comm. minutes, Nov. 27, 1963, UPN; *WSJ,* Dec. 2 and Dec. 3, 1963, Feb. 19, 1964; Chicago *American,* Dec. 4, 1963; Barnett memorandum, Jan. 30, 1964, UPN; "Memorandum . . . ," Nov. 5, 1965, 62, UPN.

45 Hardee memoranda, Feb. 26, 1964, UPN.

46 Hardee memorandum, May 18, 1964, UPN; Lovett to Stoddard, May 18, 1964, UPN.

47 Hardee memorandum, May 29, 1964, UPN; *WSJ,* May 25 and May 27, 1964; "Memorandum of Agreement," May 26, 1964, UPN; UP Directors minutes, May 28, 1964, UPN.

48 Hardee memorandum, May 29, 1964, UPN; memorandum, June 24, 1964, UPN; *Chronicle,* 199.2:2175; Johnson circular, June 17, 1964, UPN.

49 Exchange offer circular, Sept. 1, 1964, UPN; Biaggini to Barnett, Sept. 1, 1964, UPN; Hardee to Biaggini, Sept. 3, 1964, UPN.

50 Sutton memorandum, July 30, 1964, UPN; memorandum, Aug. 3, 1964, UPN; *WSJ,* Oct. 9, 1964; NY *Times,* Oct. 9, 1964; Langdon interview, 1–2.

51 Evans interview, 28.

52 Chicago *Daily News,* June 19, 1964; *WSJ,* Sept. 22, Sept. 24, and Sept. 29, 1964; J. L. Markham to Barnett, Sept. 24, 1964, UPN; Barnett memorandum, Oct. 8, 1964, UPN.

53 Langdon circular, Nov. 2, 1964, UPN; *WSJ,* Oct. 9, Dec. 3, Dec. 11, and Dec. 29, 1964, Jan. 7 and Jan. 11, 1965; press release, Nov. 11, 1964, Jan. 10, 1965, UPN; Chicago *Tribune,* Nov. 12, 1964; NY *Herald-Tribune,* Dec. 29, 1964; Markham to Barnett, Jan. 18, 1965, UPN.

54 A. C. Furth to Barnett, Jan. 12, 1965, UPN; Barnett memoranda, Feb. 15 and Feb. 26, 1965, UPN; Barnett to Furth, Mar. 3, 1965, UPN; Hardee memorandum, Mar. 17, 1965, UPN; memorandum of meeting of counsel, Mar. 12, 1965, UPN; Hardee to Furth, Mar. 16 and Mar. 17, 1965, UPN; Biaggini to Sutton, Mar. 19, 1965, UPN; UP Directors minutes, Mar. 25, 1965, UPN; *WSJ,* Mar. 26, 1965. By February 1965 expenses already totaled $2.5 million.

55 *WSJ,* Dec. 12, 1964; Chicago *Daily News,* Jan. 11, 1965; [Western Pacific], "Rock Island Case," Nov. 29, 1965, UPN; Melia memorandum, Apr. 9, 1965, UPN; MacAnally memorandum, Apr. 9, 1965, UPN; Bailey to Lovett, Apr. 19, 1965, UPN.

56 Langdon interview, 13–14.

57 Cordtz, "Fight for the Rock Island," 142.

58 Chicago *Sun-Times,* Mar. 29, 1965; Langdon to Bailey, Apr. 23 and Apr. 27, 1965, UPN; Langdon to Barnett, Apr. 26, 1965, UPN; Barnett memorandum, May 12, 1965, UPN; Barnett and Sutton memorandum, July 16, 1965, UPN; Markham to Barnett, Aug. 10, 1965, UPN; Langdon interview, 9.

59 Bailey to Lovett, Mar. 29, 1965, UPN; Langdon to Bailey, Apr. 27, 1965, UPN; Langdon interview, 9–10; Cordtz, "Fight for the Rock Island," 142.

60 NY *Daily News,* Mar. 23, 1965; NY *Times,* Mar. 4, 1965; *Forbes,* Sept. 1, 1964, 20–24; Chicago *American,* Sept. 25, 1964; *Harper's,* Jan. 1966, 65–68, 73–75; Edward R. Busch to Mrs. Warner, Sept. 30, 1965, UPN; P. V. W. memorandum, Oct. 1, 1965, UPN.

61 *WSJ,* Oct. 8 and Dec. 29, 1965; merger report no. 79, Oct. 1965, UPN; Richard E. Cheney to William McDonald, Oct. 8, 1965, UPN; NY *Herald-Tribune,* Oct. 8, 1965.

62 Peet memorandum, Sept. 15, 1965, UPN; *WSJ,* Aug. 12, and Oct. 27, 1965; Denver *Post,* Oct. 3, 1965; Lovett to Bailey, Oct. 26, 1965, UPN; Bailey to Lovett, Nov. 15, 1965, UPN; M. M. Christy to Santa Clara City Council, Dec. 3, 1965, UPN; Barnett to G. B. Aydelott, Dec. 10, 1965, UPN; Chicago *Tribune,* Dec. 9, 1965; Cheney to Barnett and Sutton, Dec. 10, 1965, UPN; Melia to Bailey, Dec. 21, 1965, UPN; Aydelott to Barnett, Dec. 29, 1965, UPN.

63 Lovett note attached to Furth to Barnett, Dec. 15, 1965, UPN.

64 Melia to Bailey, Jan. 12, Jan. 21, Jan. 24, and Feb. 11, 1966, UPN; Bailey to Lovett, Jan. 14, Feb. 21, and Mar. 13, 1966, UPN; Cheney to Barnett, Feb. 9, 1966, UPN; *Business Week,* Mar. 19, 1966, 131, 135, 140–42; Barnett to J. W. Bush, Mar. 31, 1966, UPN; *WSJ,* Apr. 6, 1966; Heineman circular, Apr. 8, 1966, UPN.

65 *Business Week,* May 14, 1966, 135; Langdon interview, 10.

66 *Business Week,* May 14, 1966, 136; Rio Grande Facts–Letter No. 7, June 10, 1966, 1, UPN.

67 Press releases, June 9–30, 1966, UPN; Barnett memorandum, June 7, 1966, UPN; *WSJ,* June 30, July 22, and Nov. 1, 1966; Sutton memorandum, July 21, 1966, UPN.

68 UP Directors minutes, Dec. 29, 1966, UPN; Langdon interview, 23.

69 Hardee memoranda, Oct. 10, Oct. 16, and Oct. 18, 1967, UPN.

70 Draft of Barnett testimony, May 9, 1968, UPN; interview with Charles J. Meyer, July 29, 1988; Hoogenbooms, *ICC,* 176–77.

71 Langdon to Barnett, May 29, 1968, UPN.

72 Ibid., July 2, 1968, UPN; Langdon interview, 14–17; Barnett memorandum, June 20, 1968, UPN.

73 Barnett memoranda, July 9 and July 10, 1969, UPN; Langdon circular, Oct. 8, 1969, UPN.

CHAPTER 28
THE NEW RAILROAD

1 Sutton interview, 12–13.

2 Barnett to Lovett, Dec. 8, 1964, UPN; NY *Times,* Dec. 23, 1964; UP Exec. Comm. minutes, Feb. 9, 1965, UPN.

3 Bailey interview, 5–12; *Midlands Business Journal,* Oct. 30, 1981.
4 Bailey interview, 81–84.
5 Barnett interview, 43–44; Schafer interview, 46; Bailey interview, 117–18, 123.
6 Acord interview, 27; Proudfit interview, 45–46; Kenefick interview, 6–8, 18–21.
7 Bailey to Lovett and Roland Harriman, July 13, 1966, UPN; Lovett to Bailey, July 19, 1966, UPN.
8 NY *Times,* Dec. 29, 1965; Evans interview, 1.
9 Sutton interview, 17–18; Lovett to A. C. Ritter, July 13, 1965, UPN.
10 Sutton to Lovett, July 5, 1966, UPN; Lovett to Bailey, July 6, 1966, UPN; Bailey to Lovett, July 7, 1966, UPN; Mercer to Sutton, Jan. 3, 1966, with attached report, UPN. For background see Salsbury, *No Way to Run a Railroad,* 50–55.
11 Bailey to Mercer, Jan. 16, 1966, UPN; Mercer to Bailey, Feb. 5, 1966, UPN; memorandum of meeting, Feb. 24, 196[6], UPN; AJK and JLJ memorandum, May 25, 1966, UPN.
12 Sutton to Mercer, Sept. 28, 1966, UPN; minutes of meeting, Oct. 13, 1966, UPN; *UP Report,* 1965, 17, 1966, 17, 1967, 17, 1968, 17.
13 Barnett to Bailey et al., Apr. 10, 1969, UPN; *UP Report,* 1966, 14, 1970, 7; R. C. Pretti memorandum, Sept. 28, 1966, UPN; Albert F. Hammer to John W. Godfrey, Nov. 7, 1966, with attached report, UPO.
14 G. L. Farr to Mercer, July 23, 1965, UPN; Mercer to Sutton, Aug. 20, 1965, UPN.
15 A. Z. Gray memorandum, Oct. 20, 1965, UPN; Louis W. Menk to Bailey, Dec. 1, 1965, UPN; J. M. Budd to Bailey, Dec. 2, 1965, UPO; E. S. Marsh to Bailey, Dec. 3, 1965, UPN; Ben Biaggini to Bailey, Dec. 2, 1965, UPN; Robert S. Macfarlane to Bailey, Dec. 8, 1965, UPN; D. W. Brosnan to Bailey, Dec. 16, 1965, UPN.
16 Bailey to Lovett, Nov. 23, 1965, Mar. 9, June 16, and June 27, 1966, UPN; G. L. Farr to Arthur Z. Gray, Jan. 28, 1966, UPN; Farr and Gray memorandum, Apr. 19 and Nov. 22, 1966, UPN; Mercer to Sutton, May 6, 1966, UPN; Gray memorandum, June 28, 1966, UPN; J. W. Godfrey to Bailey, July 20, 1966, UPO; Lovett to Bailey, Dec. 20, 1966, UPO; Farr memorandum, Aug. 26, 1967, UPO; Thomas W. Dunn to Bailey, Apr. 26, 1968, UPN; Bailey to Dunn, Apr. 30, 1968, UPN.
17 Roland Harriman to JWG, Nov. 23, 1966, UPN; UP Directors minutes, Nov. 23, 1966, UPN; NY *Times,* Nov. 24 and Dec. 4, 1966; UP Exec. Comm. minutes, Jan. 10, 1967.
18 Harriman to JWG, Nov. 23, 1966, UPN; NY *Times,* Nov. 24 and Dec. 4, 1966; Evans interview, 1–3. Barnett had been vice-president and general counsel.
19 Gerry interview, 33–41.
20 Evans interview, 22–23.
21 How to Bailey, Aug. 1, 1967, UPO; PVW memorandum, Aug. 15, 1967, UPN; Barnett to Bailey, Sept. 6, 1967, UPN; Bailey to Barnett, Sept. 16, 1967, UPN; N. B. Marvin to Bailey, Sept. 20, 1967, UPO; Gerald A. Simon to Barnett, Oct. 14, 1967, UPN.
22 Barnett interview, 20–23; Frederick V. Fortmiller to Barnett, June 14, 1968, UPN.
23 Simon draft, Dec. 13, 1967, Apr. 4 and Apr. 9, 1968, UPN; Simon to Barnett, Jan. 3, 1968, UPN; Simon to Bailey, Apr. 8, 1968, UPN; Kenefick interview, 11–15.
24 Barnett interview, 33–34; Gerry interview, 37–38.
25 Bailey to Barnett, Apr. 15, 1968, UPN; press release, Apr. 19, 1968, UPO; Kenefick interview, 24.
26 Bailey to Barnett, May 3 and May 31, 1968, UPN; Simon to Bailey, May 9, 1968, UPN; Bailey to Simon, June 20, 1968, UPO.
27 M. J. Hoover, Jr., to Barnett, Oct. 22, 1968, UPN; Evans interview, 3–6; Barnett interview, 35–36.

28 Evans interview, 13; Roland Harriman, *I Reminisce,* 143–45.

29 Gerry interview, 1, 35; Barnett interview, 37–38; *UP Report,* 1968, 6.

30 Gerry interview, 35–37; Barnett interview, 35–36; Evans to Dean Courtney C. Brown et al., Sept. 27, 1968, UPN; NY *Times,* May 20, 1969; Barnett circulars, June 1 and Oct. 8, 1969, UPO; Salsbury, *No Way to Run a Railroad,* 148.

31 Gerry interview, 39.

32 Simon to Richard E. Cheney, Oct. 23, 1968, UPN; *WSJ,* Nov. 22, 1968, Jan. 31, 1969; NY *Times,* Jan. 31, 1969; Barnett to Langdon, Jan. 17, 1969, UPN; press release, Jan. 30, 1969, UPN.

33 NY *Times,* Sept. 28, 1969; *UP Report,* 1969, 2.

34 Lovett to Osborne, Apr. 22, 1965, UPN; R. B. Resnik to Bailey, June 4, 1965, UPN; John M. Kelly to Frederick V. Fortmiller, Feb. 2, 1968; Fortmiller to Barnett, Mar. 19, 1968, UPN; Evans interview, 14–15.

35 Barnett interview, 12–13; *WSJ,* Aug. 29, 1969; UP Directors minutes, Sept. 30, 1969, UPN. The Union Pacific formally took title to Champlin and Pontiac on Jan. 1, 1970.

36 Oscar T. Lawler to Lovett, Mar. 12, 1965, UPN; Lovett to Lawler, Mar. 19, 1965, UPN; Osborne to Lovett, Apr. 8, 1965, June 7, July 26, Sept. 1, and Dec. 1, 1966, UPN; Lovett to Osborne, June 24, 1965, UPN; Osborne to Barnett, June 13, 1967, Jan. 4, Jan. 26, July 10, and Dec. 16, 1968, Feb. 20 and Oct. 29, 1969, UPN; *Railway Age,* Aug. 14, 1967; Barnett to John M. Kelly, Nov. 10, 1967, UPN; "Project Gasbuggy General Information," Nov. 7, 1967; Fortmiller to Gene E. Roark, Apr. 30, 1968, UPN; UP Exec. Comm. minutes, June 11, 1968, Jan. 21, 1969, Feb. 17, 1970, UPN; *WSJ,* Sept. 4, 1968, Mar. 20, Sept. 11, and Oct. 2, 1969; NY *Times,* Feb. 16, 1969.

37 UP Exec. Comm. minutes, July 27, 1967, UPN; Fortmiller to Barnett, Jan. 4, Apr. 3, and June 10, 1968, UPN; *WSJ,* Jan. 29, 1969; Osborne to Barnett, Jan. 6 and Nov. 3, 1969, UPN; Ken Holum to Osborne, Aug. 6, 1969, UPN.

38 Press releases, Apr. 6, 1967, Oct. 10, 1969, UPO; Sutton memorandum, Nov. 8, 1967, UPN; Godfrey to Barnett, Feb. 14, 1969, UPN; Barnett memorandum, Apr. 30, 1969, UPN.

39 *Forbes,* Nov. 1, 1969, 32; *Railway Age,* 167:15–16; *UP Report,* 1969, 7.

40 MacAnally to Bailey, Mar. 7, 1966, UPO; *Railway Age,* Mar. 30, 1964; How to Lovett, Sept. 24, 1966, UPO; *WSJ,* Nov. 18, 1966, June 17, 1968; *Shipping and Trade News,* Jan. 16, 1967; press release, June 12, 1968, UPO; *UP Report,* 1969, 6.

41 Press release, Feb. 3, 1969, UPO; J. L. Jorgenson to Bailey, Oct. 22, 1969, UPO.

42 Press release, Feb. 3, 1969, UPO; Los Angeles *Herald-Examiner,* Nov. 2, 1969; *UP Report,* 1969, 7.

43 Chicago *Tribune,* Feb. 26 and Mar. 10, 1970; Bryant (ed.), *Railroads in the Age of Régulation,* 176–77.

44 Kansas City *Times,* July 9, 1970; Chicago *Tribune,* July 10, 1970; Hoogenbooms, *ICC,* 176–77.

45 Meyer interview, July 28, 1988.

46 JEH memorandum, Oct. 16, 1970, UPN; Relyea memorandum, June 13, 1973, UPN; Kenefick to Barnett, June 14, 1973, UPN; Barnett to Kenefick, July 9, 1973, UPN.

47 C. E. Crippen to Bailey, Dec. 16, 1970, Mar. 1, 1971, UPN; JEH memorandum, Dec. 31, 1970, UPN; Bailey to Crippen, Mar. 18, 1971, UPN; Meyer memorandum, Nov. 29, 1971, UPN; Charles J. Meyer to William J. McDonald, Mar. 12, 1973, UPN; Kenefick to Barnett, Feb. 23, 1975, UPN; press release, Mar. 18, 1975, UPN; Barnett to Rock Island board, Mar. 31, 1975, UPN.

48 Bailey to Merle Waterman, Feb. 5, 1969, UPO; Barnett memorandum, Aug. 25, 1970, UPN; Kenefick interview, 1–3.
49 Schafer interview, 44–45; Barnett interview, 34; Evans interview, 10.
50 Barnett memorandum, Aug. 25, 1970, UPN; Kenefick interview, 1–6.
51 Lovett to Evans, Mar. 7, 1978, UPN.

INDEX

Note: References to illustrations, including maps, are italicized.

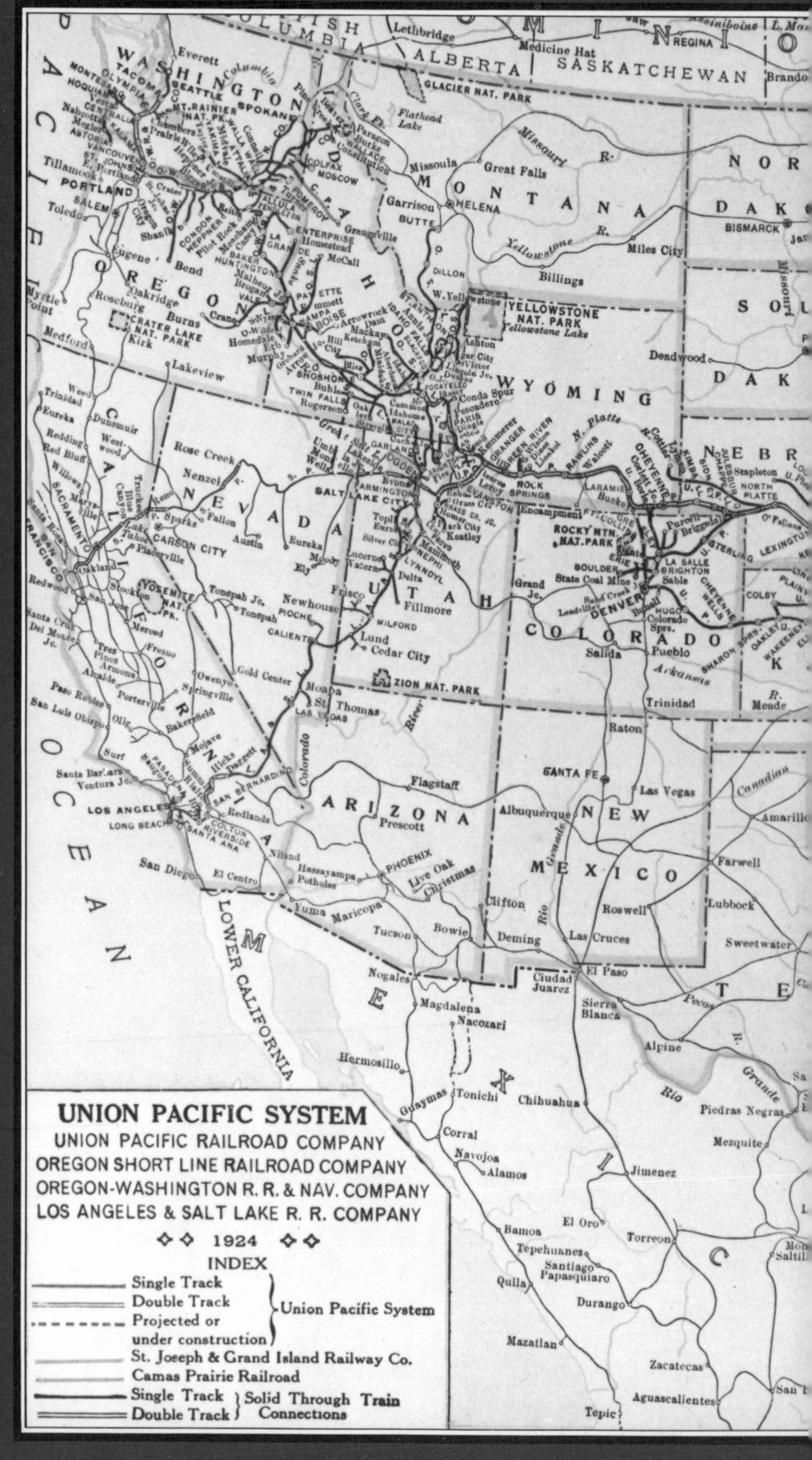
UNION PACIFIC SYSTEM
UNION PACIFIC RAILROAD COMPANY
OREGON SHORT LINE RAILROAD COMPANY
OREGON-WASHINGTON R. R. & NAV. COMPANY
LOS ANGELES & SALT LAKE R. R. COMPANY
1924
INDEX
Single Track
Double Track
Projected or
under construction
Union Pacific System
St. Joeeph & Grand Island Railway Co.
Camas Prairie Railroad
Single Track
Double Track
Solid Through Train
Connections